AKIRA

KATSUHIRO OTOMO

**BOOK
ONE**

DARK HORSE COMICS®

translation and english-language adaptation
YOKO UMEZAWA, LINDA M. YORK,
and **JO DUFFY**

graphics adaptation and sound effects lettering
DAVID SCHMIT *for* **DIGIBOX**
and **ÉDITIONS GLÉNAT**

digital lettering and additional graphics adaptation
DIGITAL CHAMELEON
and **DARK HORSE COMICS**

publisher
MIKE RICHARDSON

original series editor
KOICHI YURI

editor
CHRIS WARNER

consulting editor
TOREN SMITH *for* **STUDIO PROTEUS**

collection designer
LIA RIBACCHI

art director
MARK COX

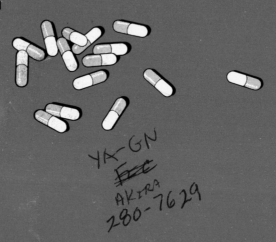

YA-GN
AKIRA
280-7629

AKIRA BOOK ONE

© 2000 MASH • ROOM Co. Ltd. Translation and English-language adaptation © 1988, 2000 MASH • ROOM Co. Ltd. and Kodansha Ltd., Tokyo. Graphics adaptation © 1999 Éditions Glénat. All other material © 2000 Dark Horse Comics, Inc. All rights reserved. Publication rights arranged through Kodansha Ltd., Tokyo. Originally published in Japan in 1982 and 1983 in Young Magazine by Kodansha Ltd., Tokyo. No portion of this publication may be reproduced, in any form or by any means, without the express written permission of the copyright holders. Names, characters, places, and incidents featured in this publication are either the product of the author's imagination or are used fictitiously. Any resemblance to actual persons (living or dead), events, institutions, or locales, without satiric intent, is coincidental. Dark Horse Comics® and the Dark Horse logo are trademarks of Dark Horse Comics, Inc., registered in various categories and countries. All rights reserved.

The artwork of this volume has been produced as a mirror-image of the original Japanese edition to conform to English-language standards.

Published by Dark Horse Comics, Inc., 10956 S.E. Main Street, Milwaukie, OR 97222 • www.darkhorse.com

To find a comics shop in your area, call the Comic Shop Locator Service toll-free at 1-888-266-4226

First edition: December 2000 • ISBN: 1-56971-498-3

Printed in Canada • 10 9 8 7 6 5 4 3 2

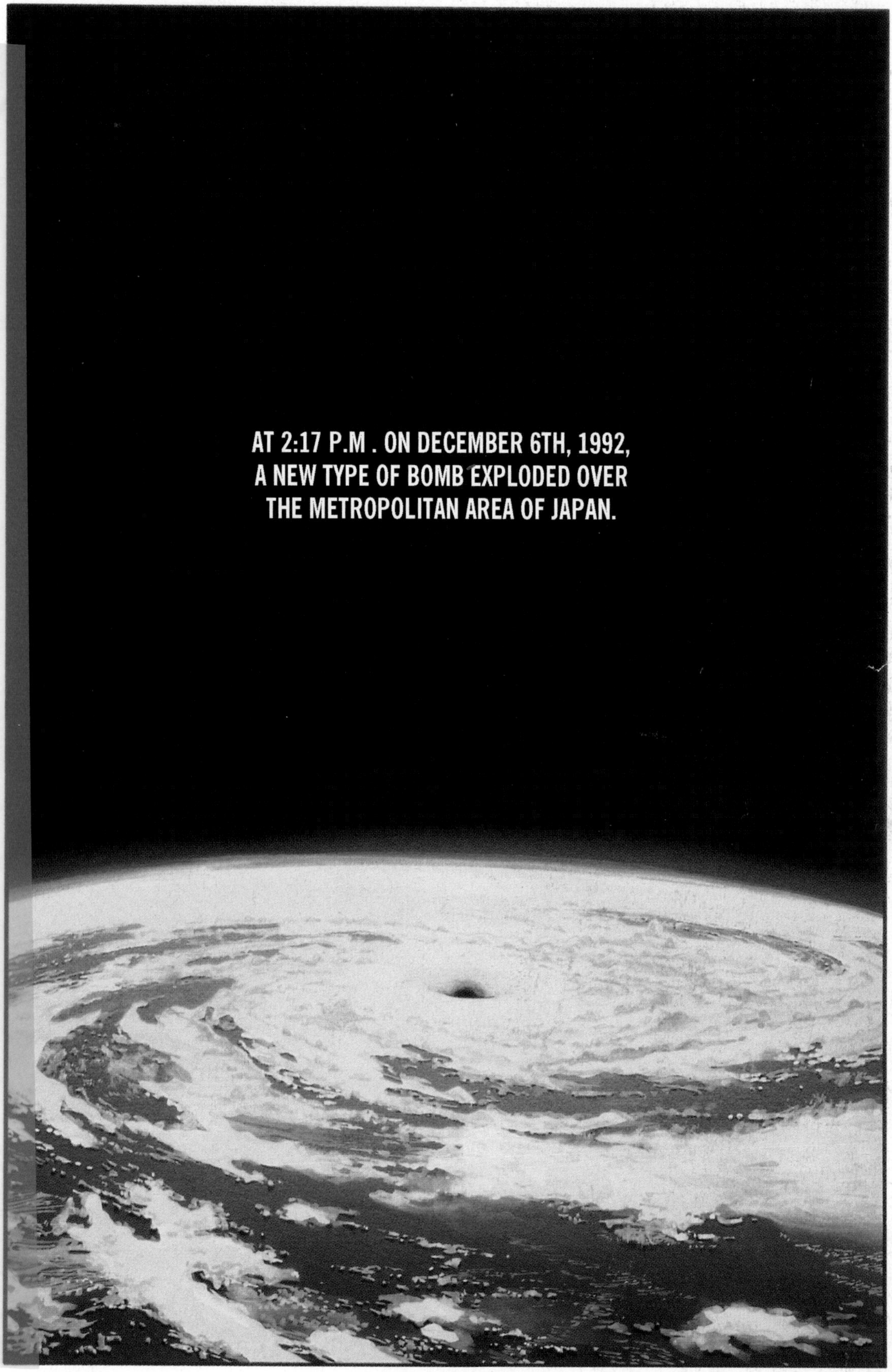
AT 2:17 P.M . ON DECEMBER 6TH, 1992,
A NEW TYPE OF BOMB EXPLODED OVER
THE METROPOLITAN AREA OF JAPAN.

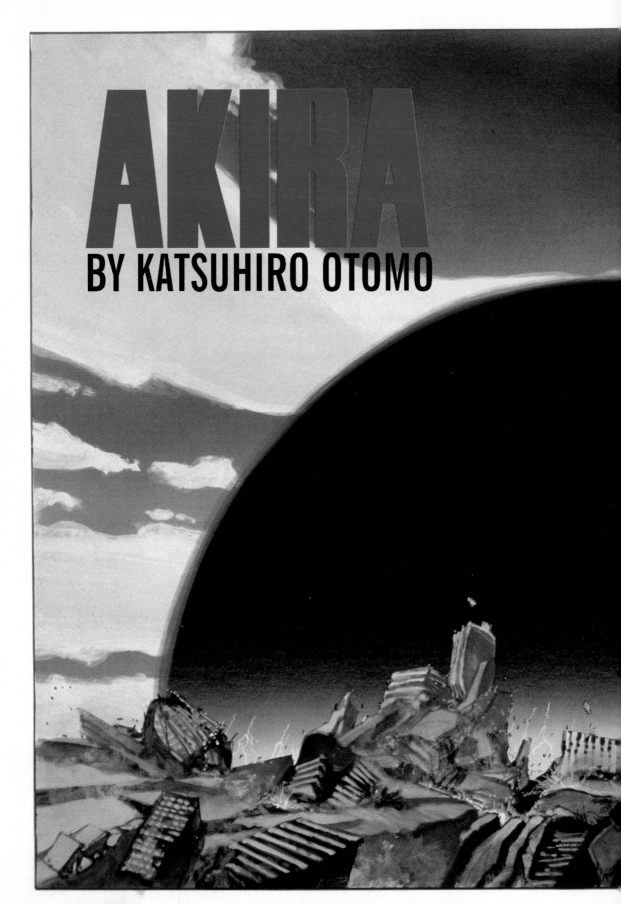

AKIRA

BY KATSUHIRO OTOMO

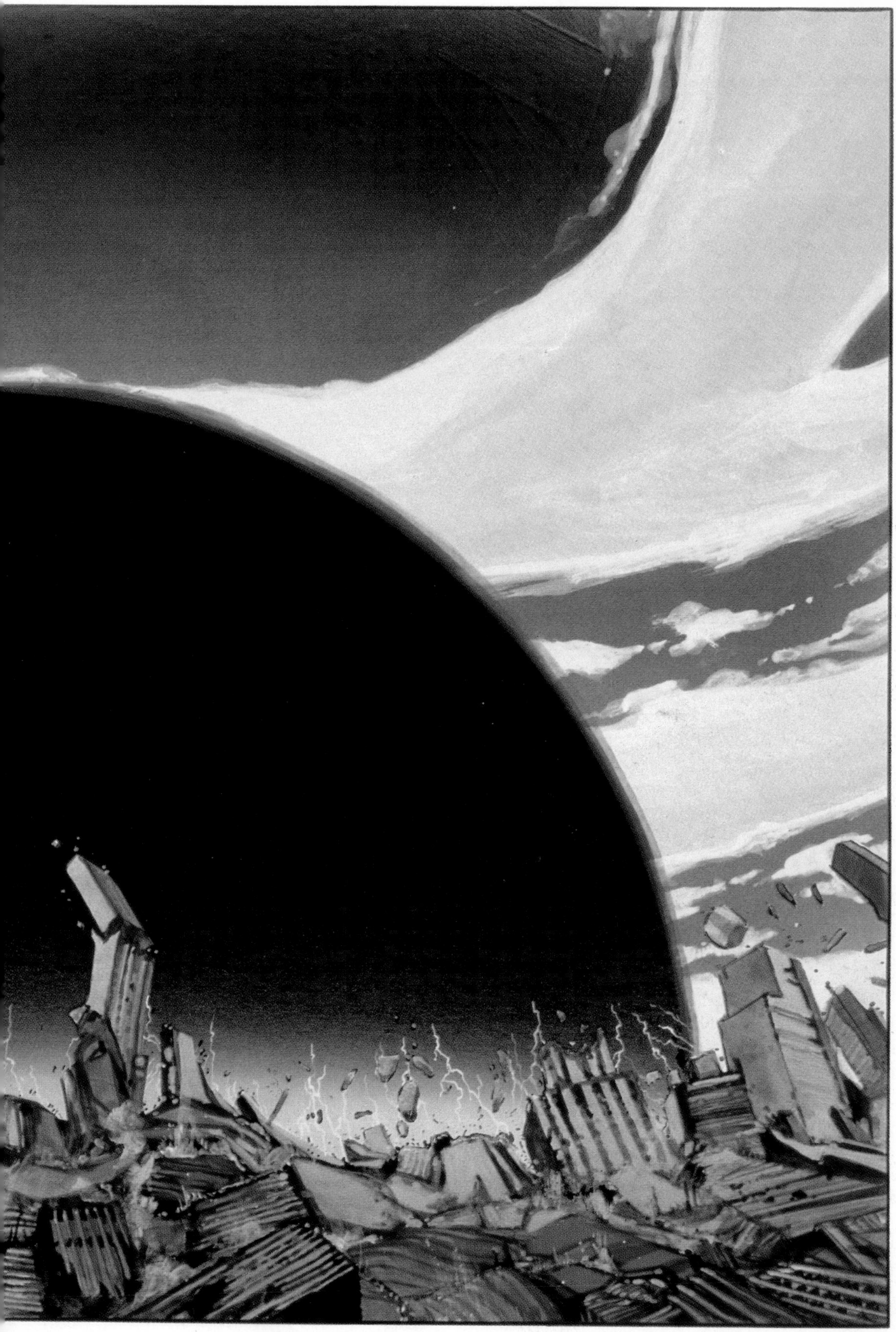

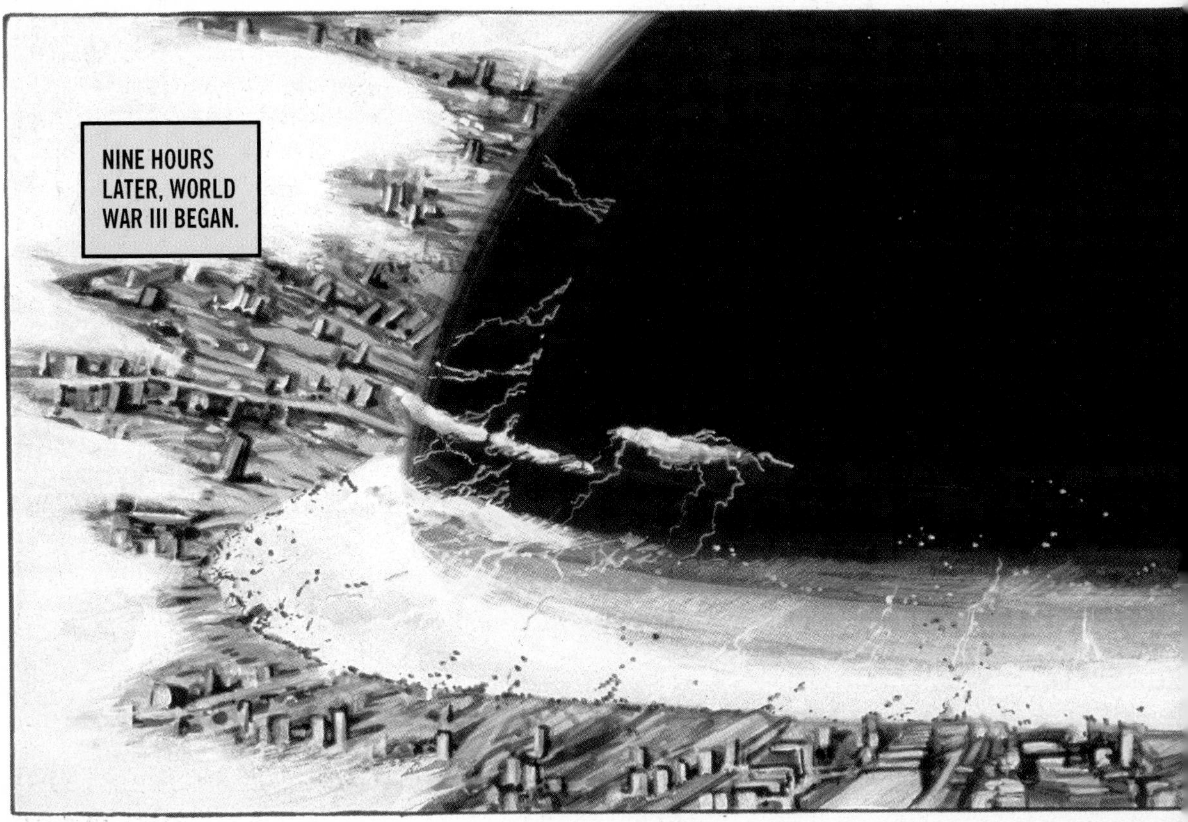
NINE HOURS
LATER, WORLD
WAR III BEGAN.
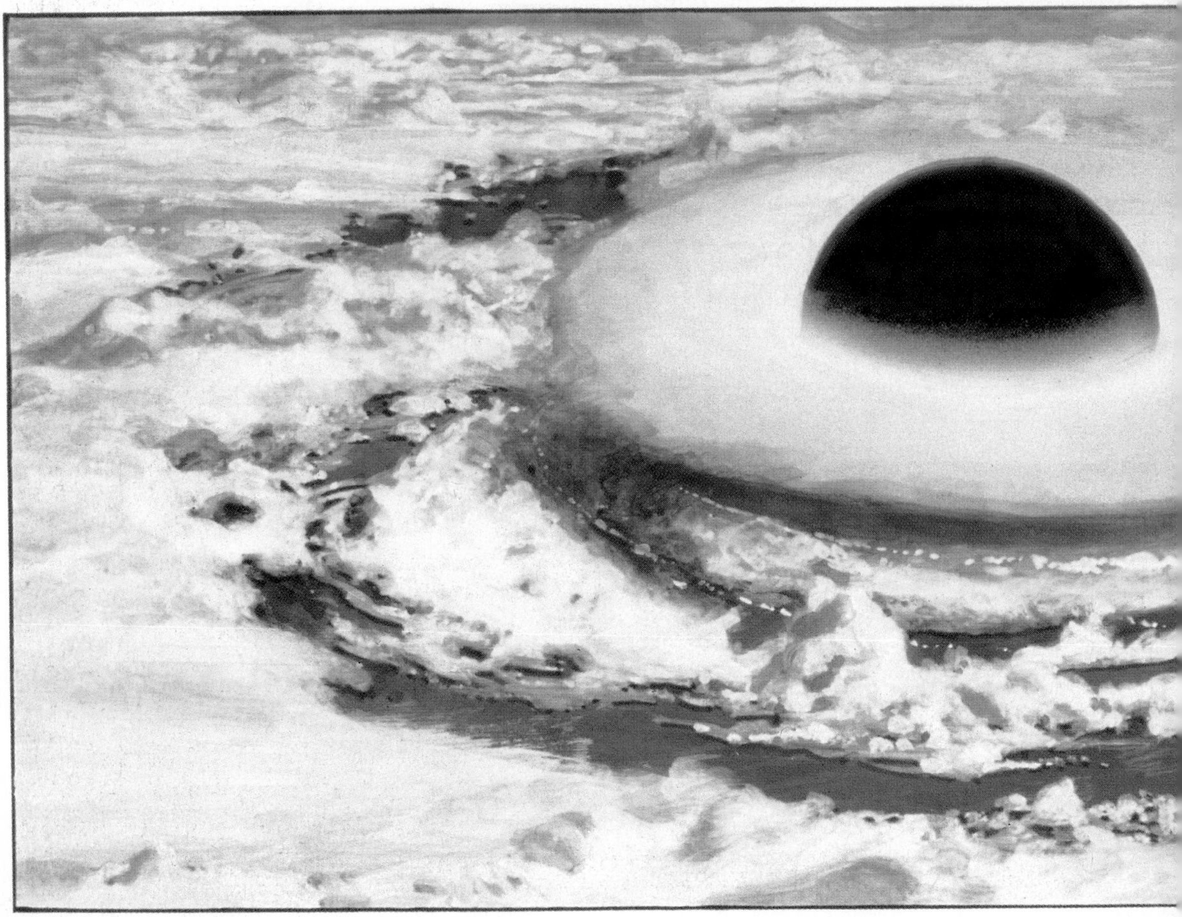

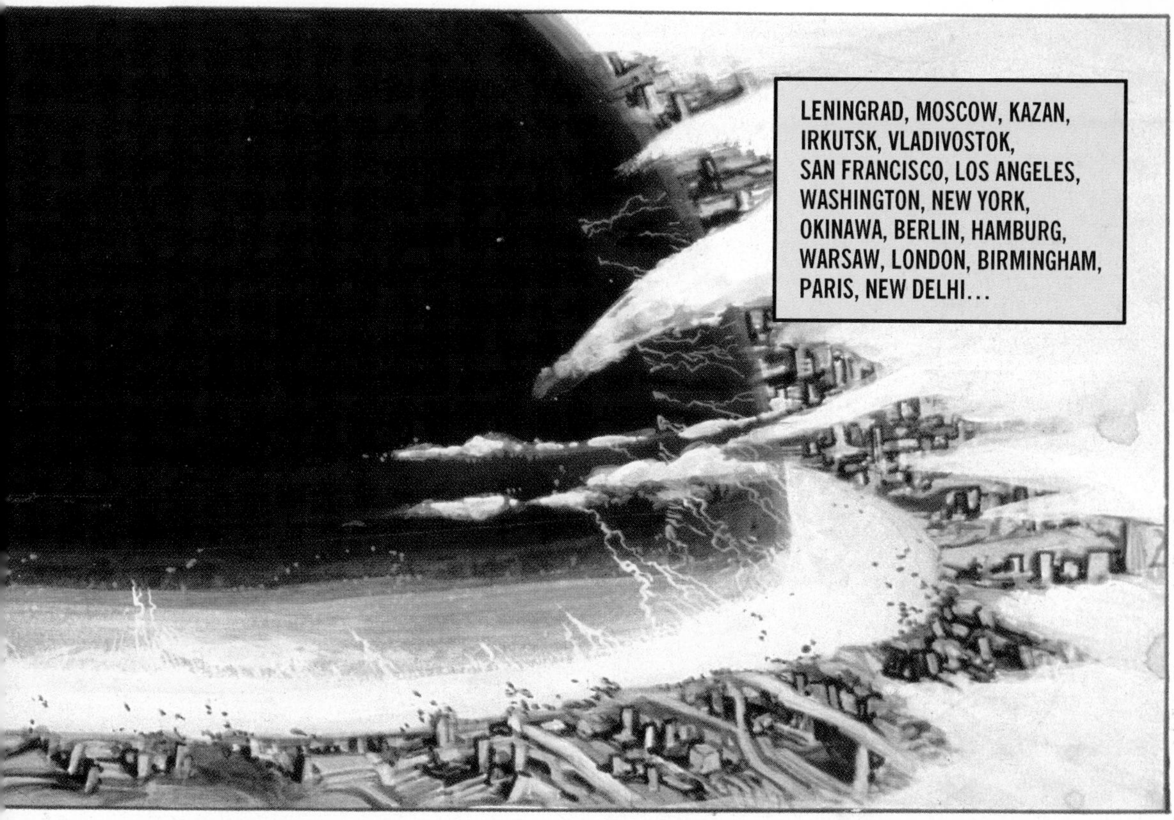
LENINGRAD, MOSCOW, KAZAN, IRKUTSK, VLADIVOSTOK, SAN FRANCISCO, LOS ANGELES, WASHINGTON, NEW YORK, OKINAWA, BERLIN, HAMBURG, WARSAW, LONDON, BIRMINGHAM, PARIS, NEW DELHI...

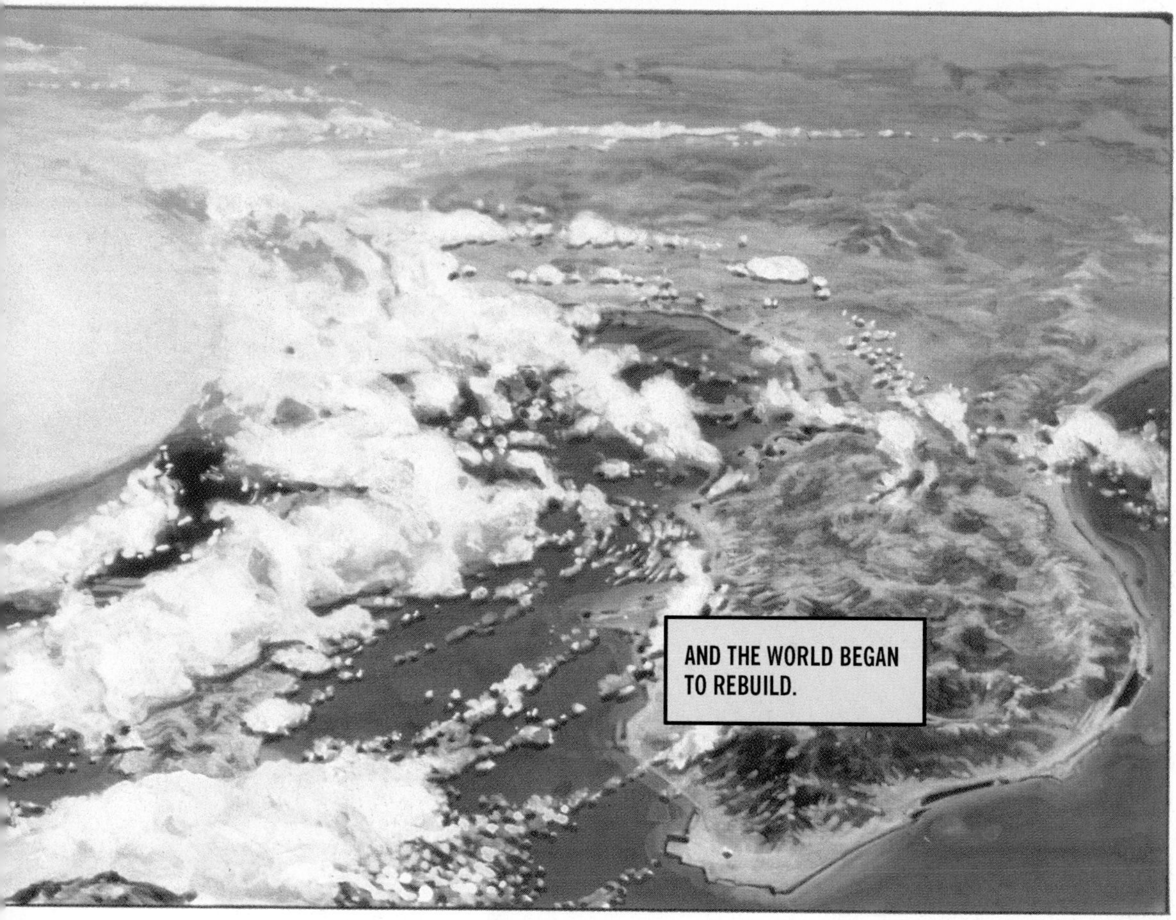
AND THE WORLD BEGAN TO REBUILD.

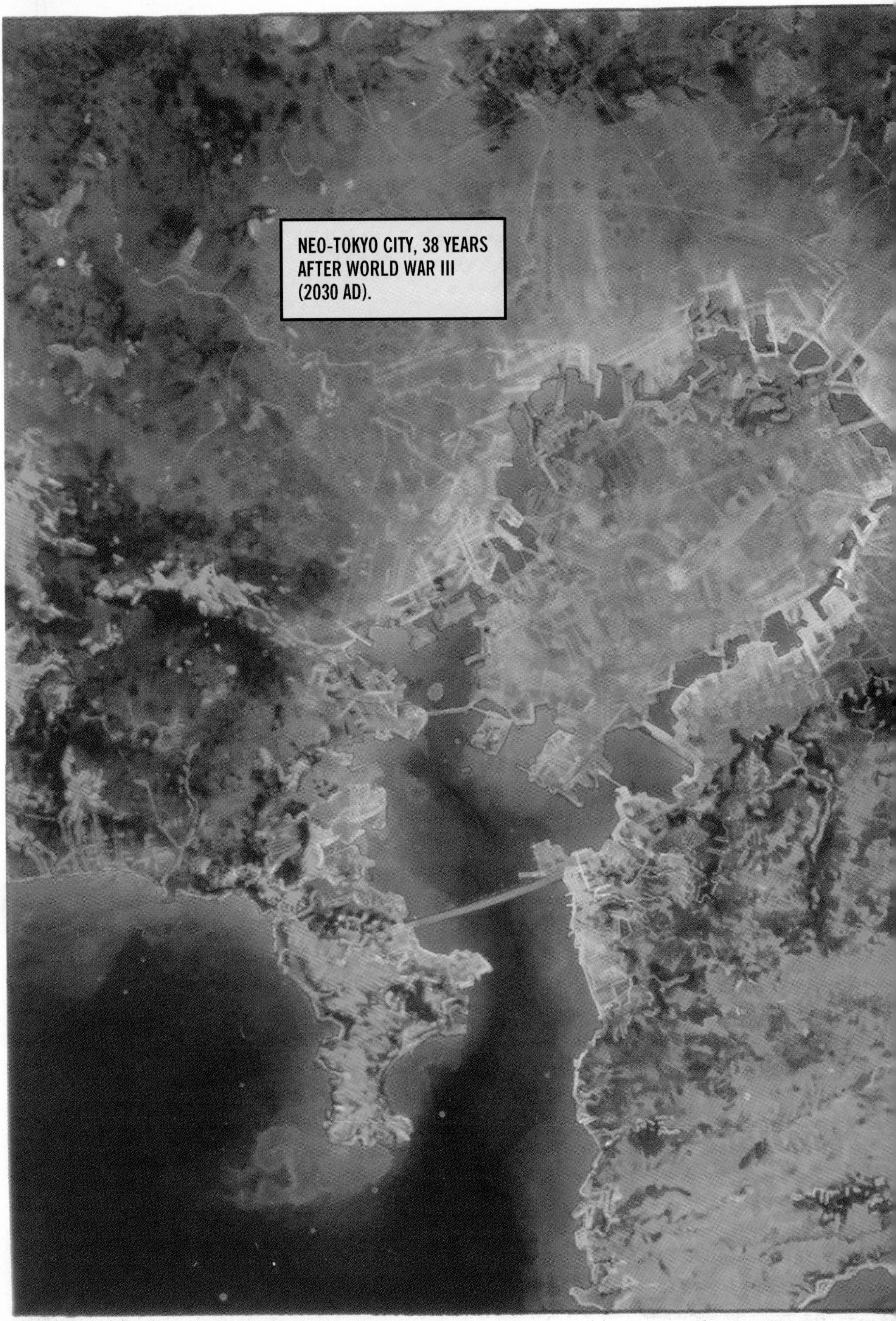
NEO-TOKYO CITY, 38 YEARS AFTER WORLD WAR III (2030 AD).

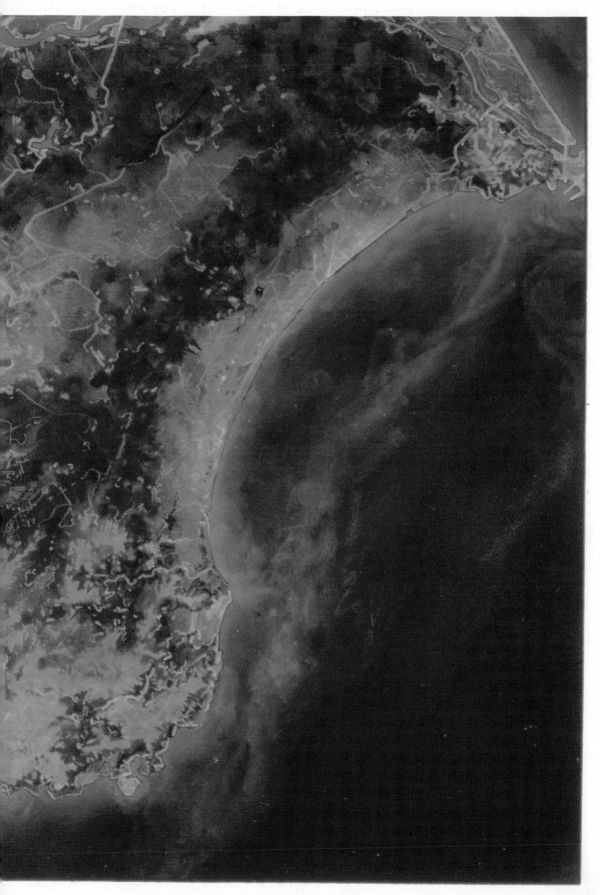

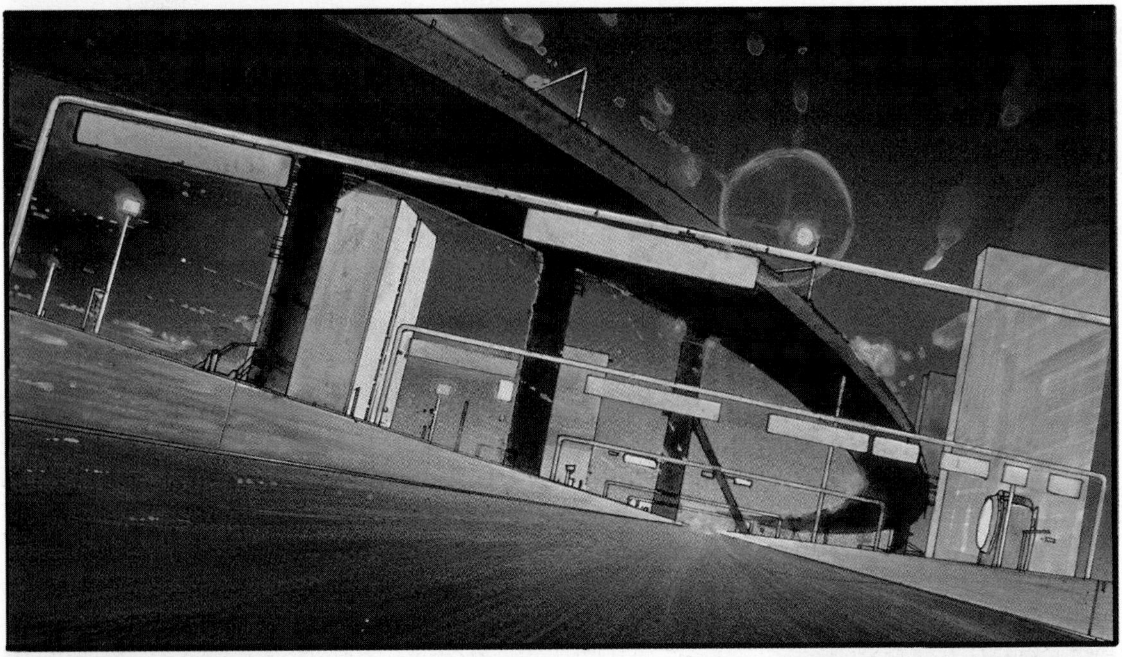

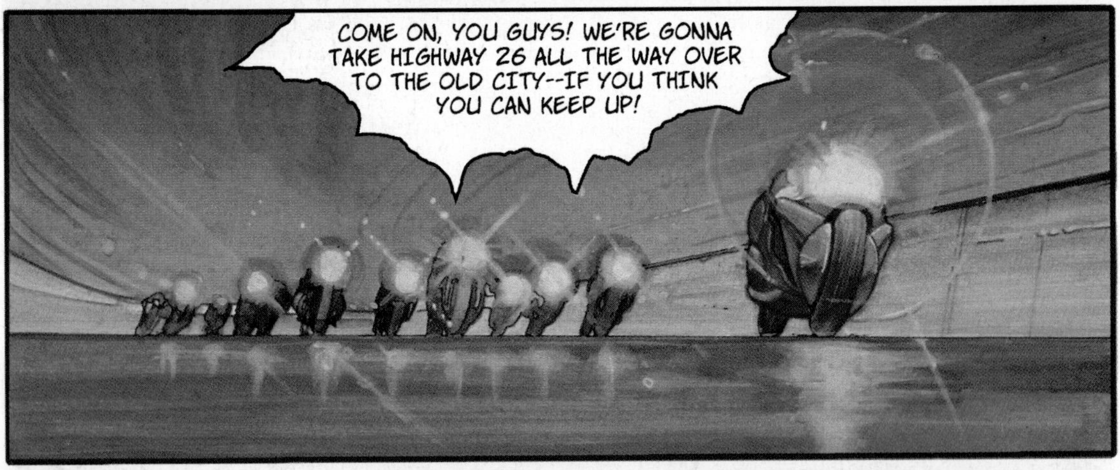
COME ON, YOU GUYS! WE'RE GONNA TAKE HIGHWAY 26 ALL THE WAY OVER TO THE OLD CITY--IF YOU THINK YOU CAN KEEP UP!

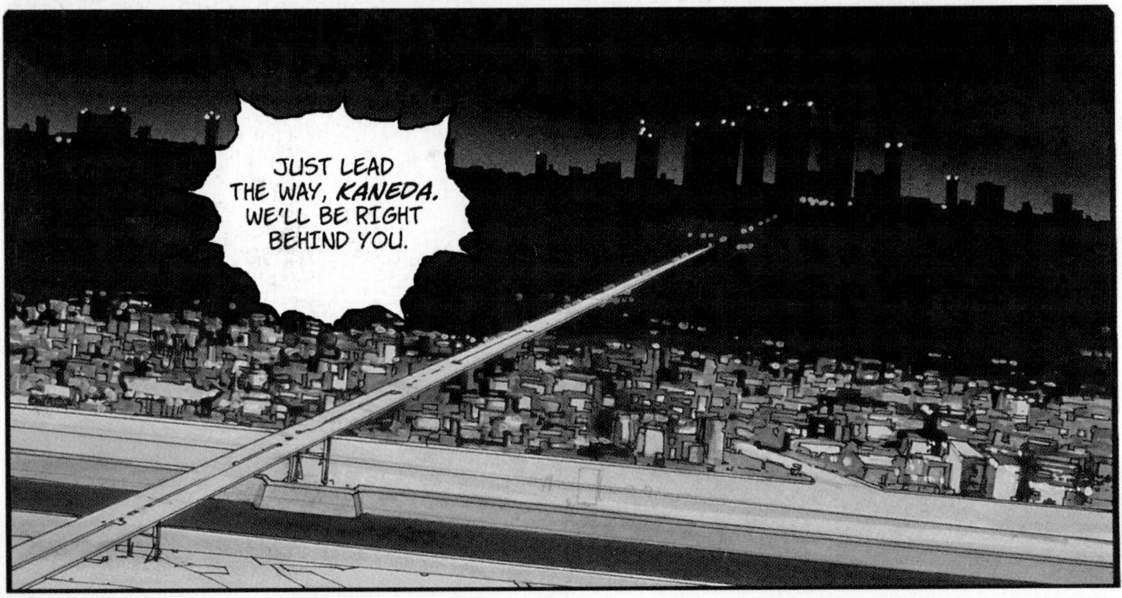
JUST LEAD THE WAY, ***KANEDA.*** WE'LL BE RIGHT BEHIND YOU.

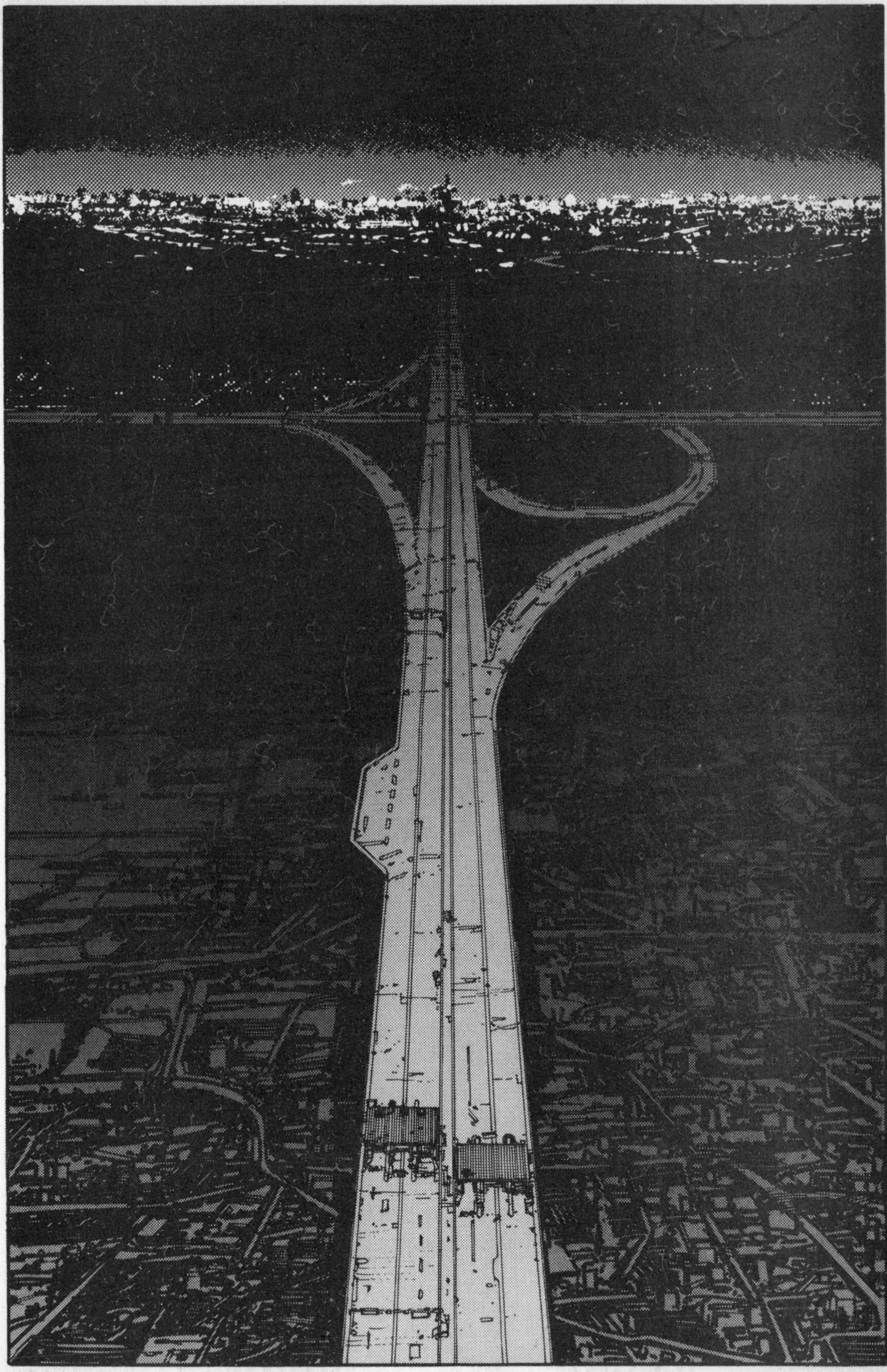

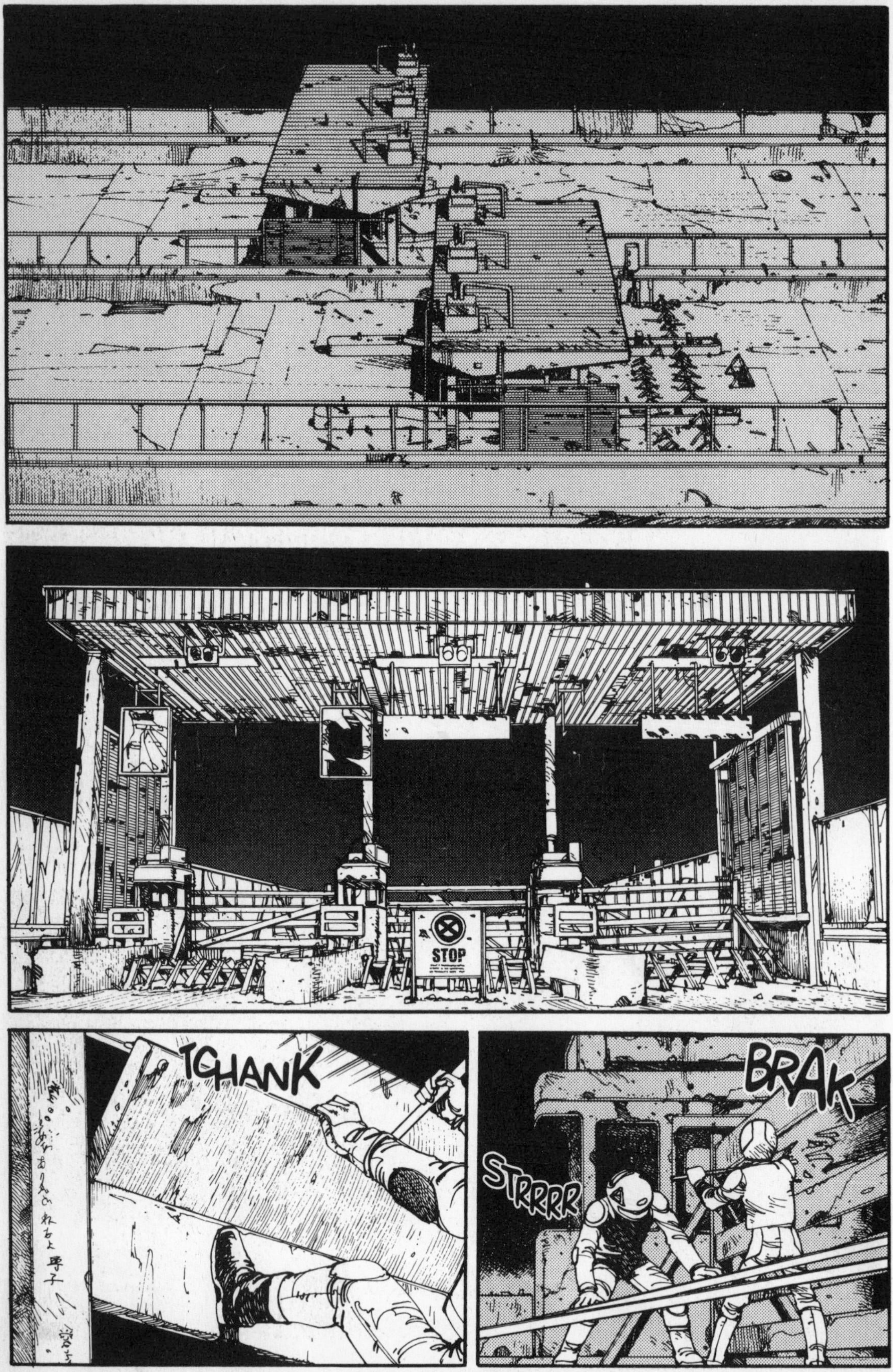
STOP
TCHANK
BRAK
STRRRR

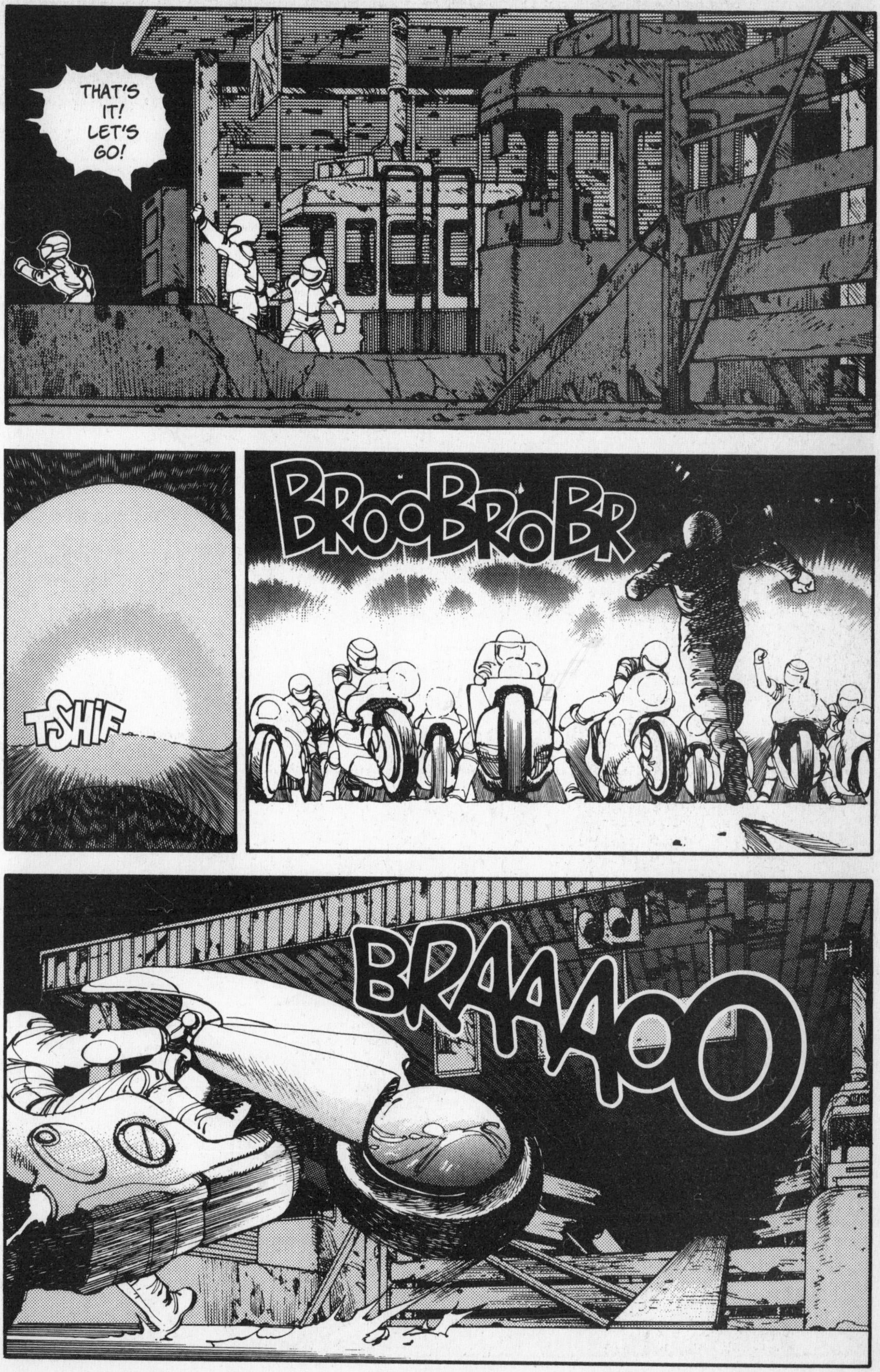

THAT'S IT! LET'S GO!
TSHIF
BROOBROBR
BRAAAOO

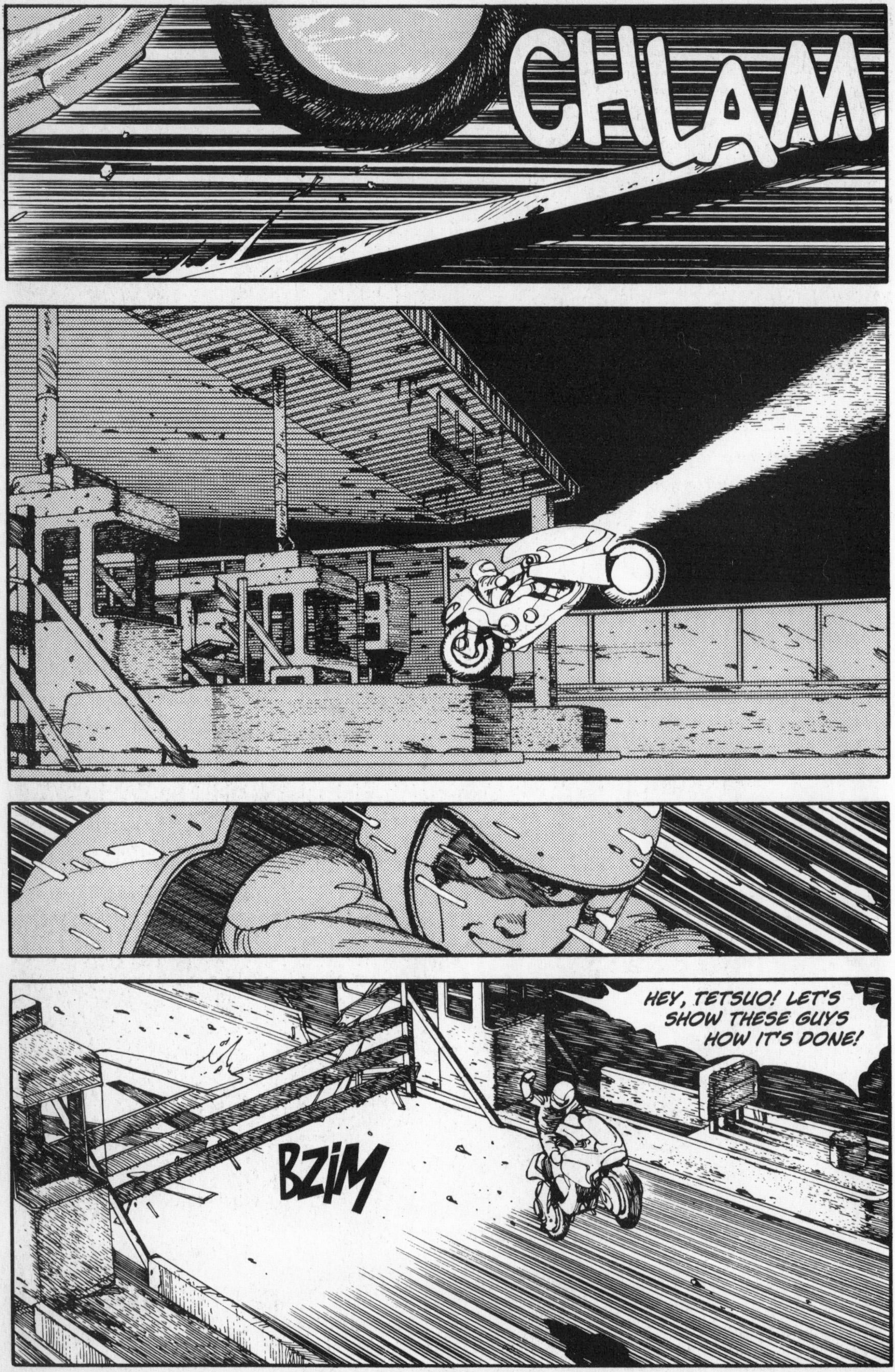
CHLAM
HEY, TETSUO! LET'S SHOW THESE GUYS HOW IT'S DONE!
BZIM

CHLAM

ZBAM

VRAOOOM

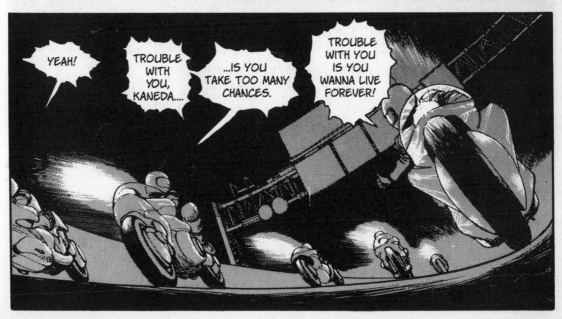

YEAH!

TROUBLE WITH YOU, KANEDA....

...IS YOU TAKE TOO MANY CHANCES.

TROUBLE WITH YOU IS YOU WANNA LIVE FOREVER!

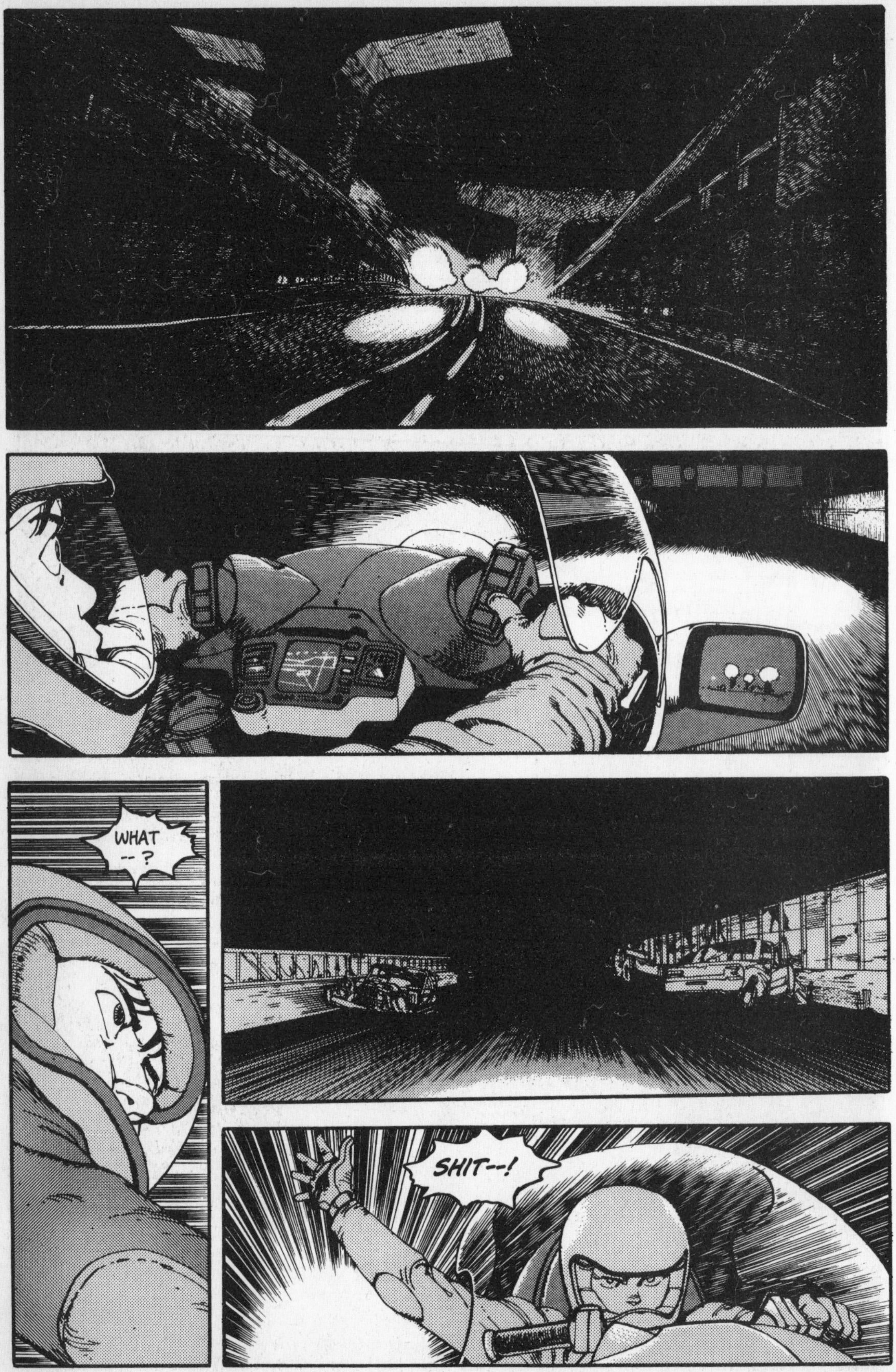
WHAT --?
SHIT--!

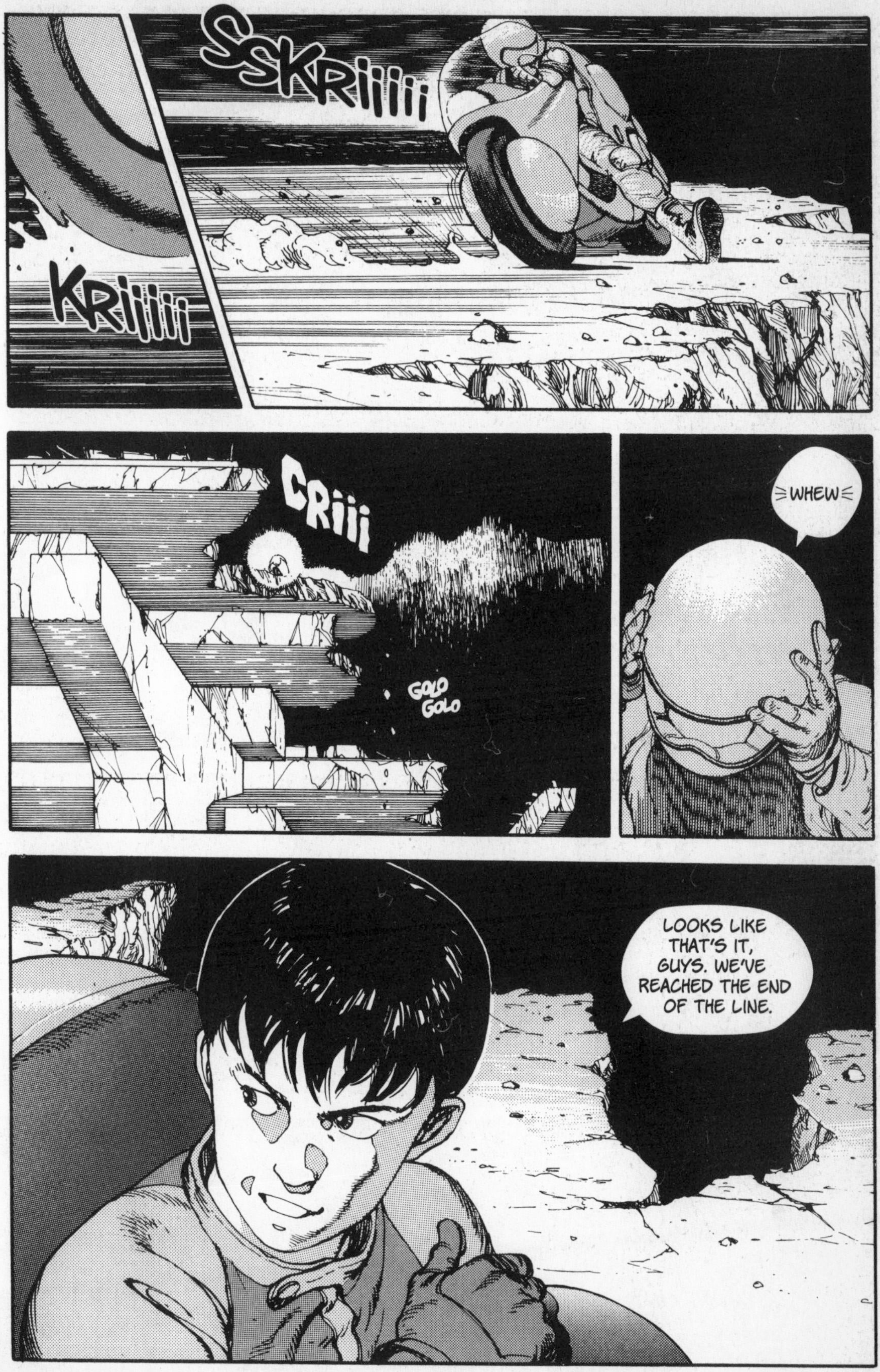
SSKRIIIII
KRIIIII
CRIII
GOLO GOLO
WHEW
LOOKS LIKE THAT'S IT, GUYS. WE'VE REACHED THE END OF THE LINE.

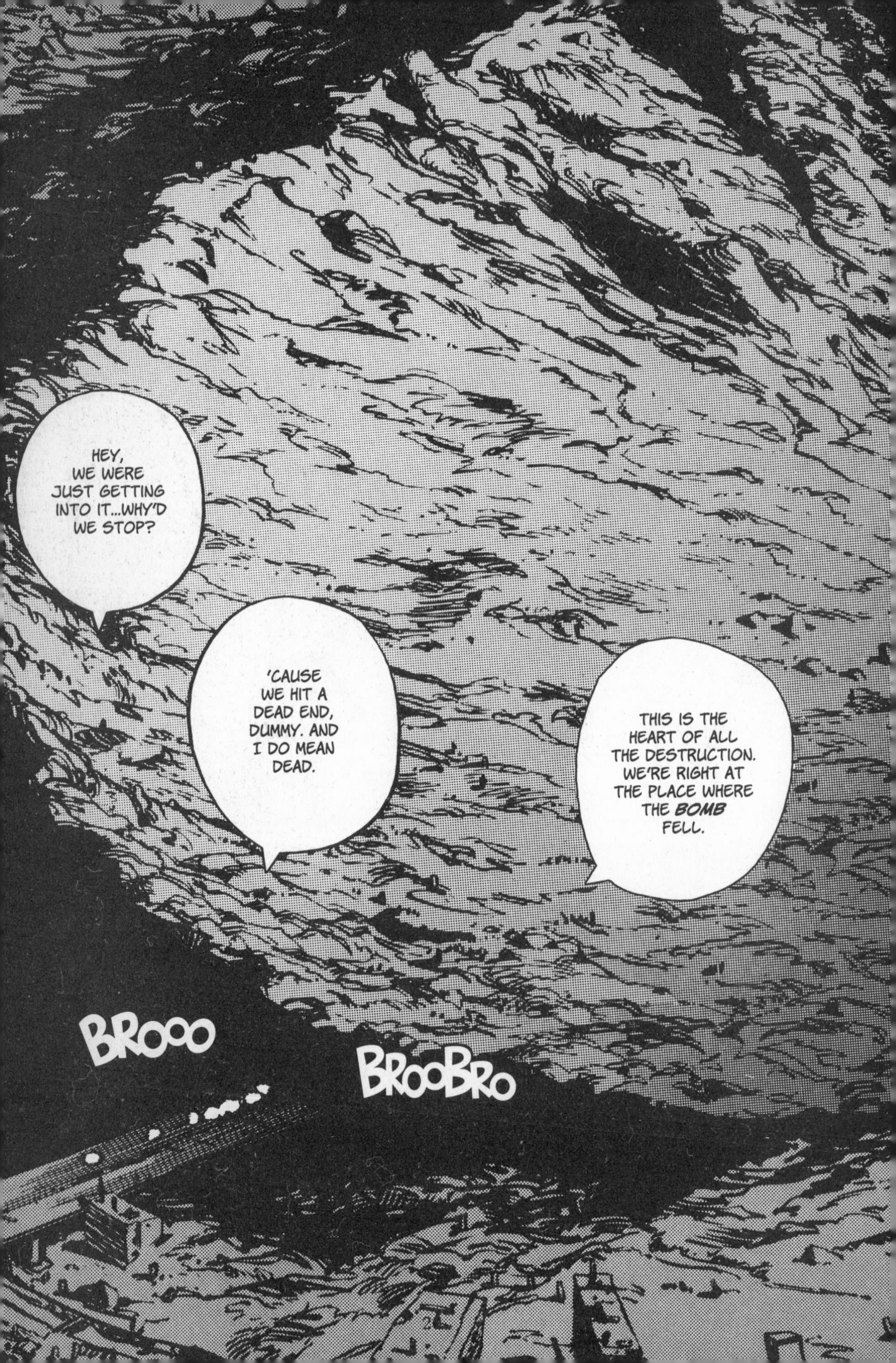
HEY, WE WERE JUST GETTING INTO IT...WHY'D WE STOP?
'CAUSE WE HIT A DEAD END, DUMMY. AND I DO MEAN DEAD.
THIS IS THE HEART OF ALL THE DESTRUCTION. WE'RE RIGHT AT THE PLACE WHERE THE *BOMB* FELL.
BROOO
BROOBRO

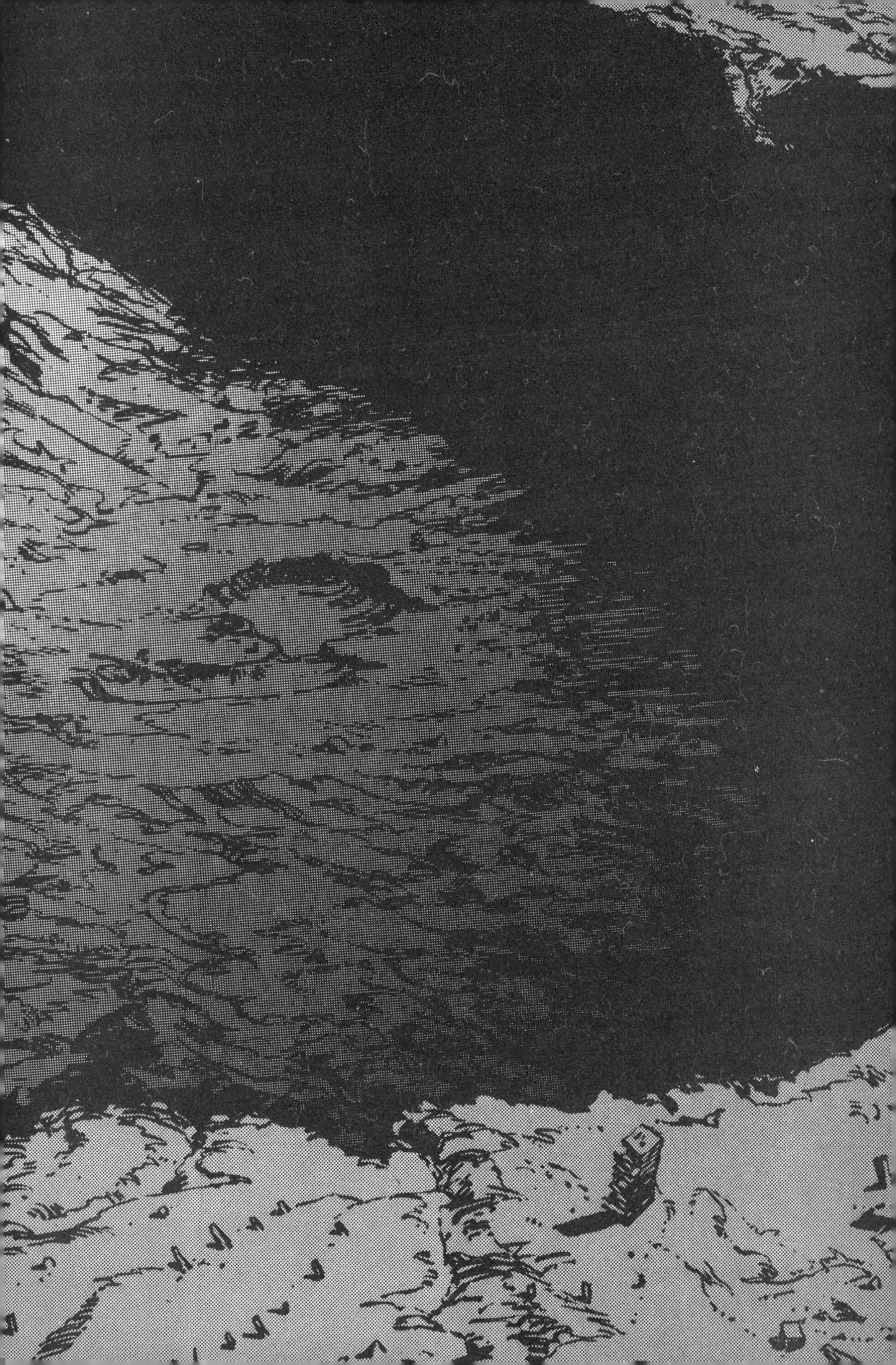

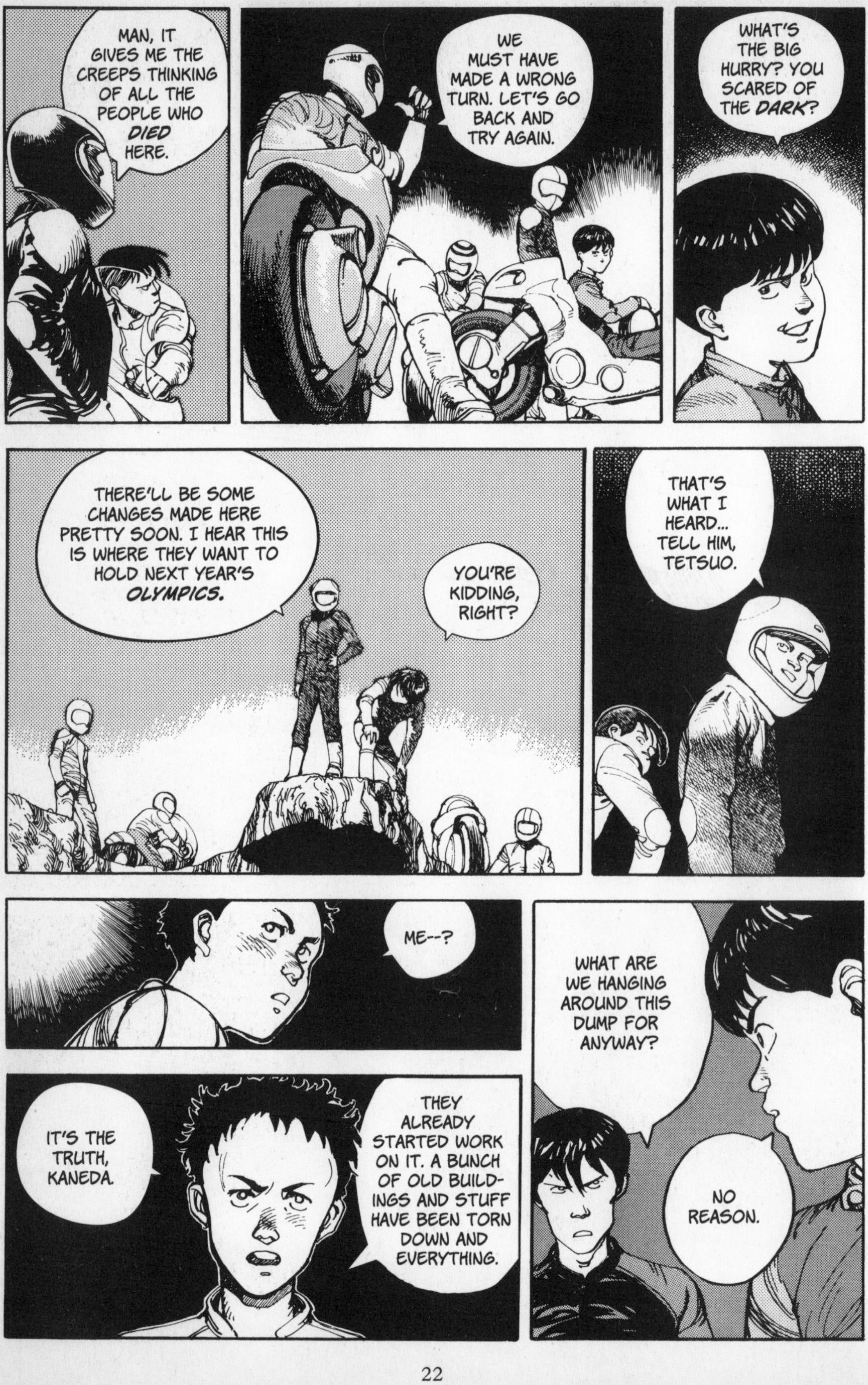
MAN, IT GIVES ME THE CREEPS THINKING OF ALL THE PEOPLE WHO *DIED* HERE.
WE MUST HAVE MADE A WRONG TURN. LET'S GO BACK AND TRY AGAIN.
WHAT'S THE BIG HURRY? YOU SCARED OF THE *DARK*?
THERE'LL BE SOME CHANGES MADE HERE PRETTY SOON. I HEAR THIS IS WHERE THEY WANT TO HOLD NEXT YEAR'S *OLYMPICS.*
YOU'RE KIDDING, RIGHT?
THAT'S WHAT I HEARD... TELL HIM, TETSUO.
ME--?
IT'S THE TRUTH, KANEDA.
THEY ALREADY STARTED WORK ON IT. A BUNCH OF OLD BUILD-INGS AND STUFF HAVE BEEN TORN DOWN AND EVERYTHING.
WHAT ARE WE HANGING AROUND THIS DUMP FOR ANYWAY?
NO REASON.

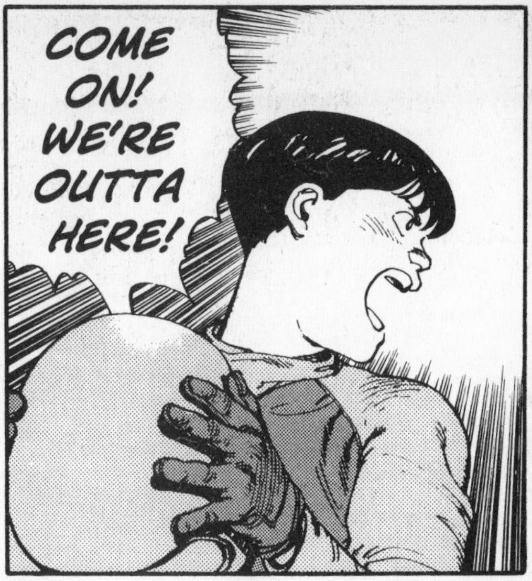
COME ON! WE'RE OUTTA HERE!
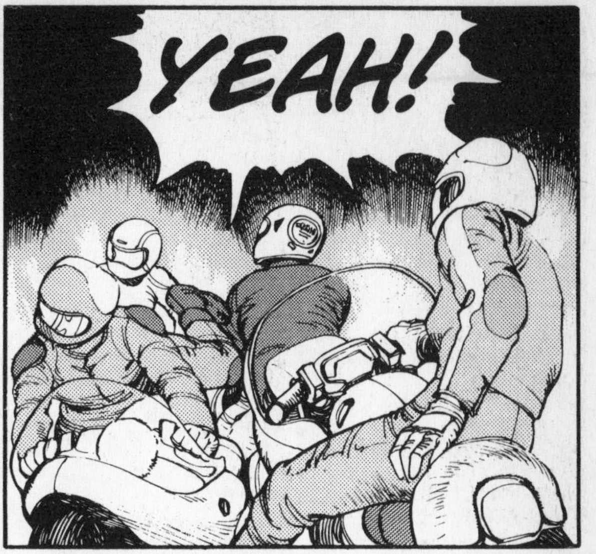
YEAH!
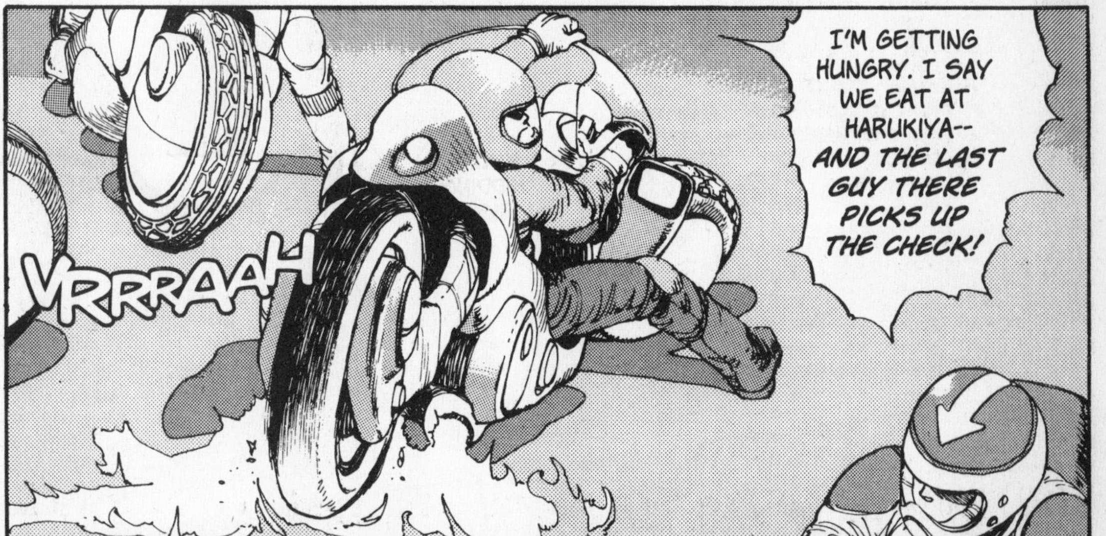
VRRRAAH
I'M GETTING HUNGRY. I SAY WE EAT AT HARUKIYA-- AND THE LAST GUY THERE PICKS UP THE CHECK!
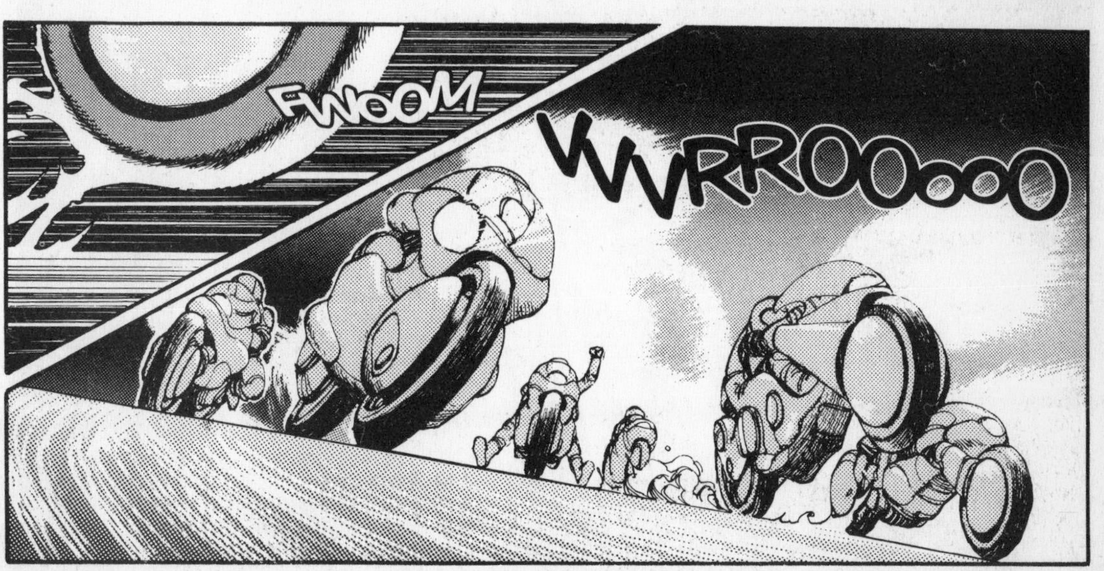
FWOOM
VVVRROO...O

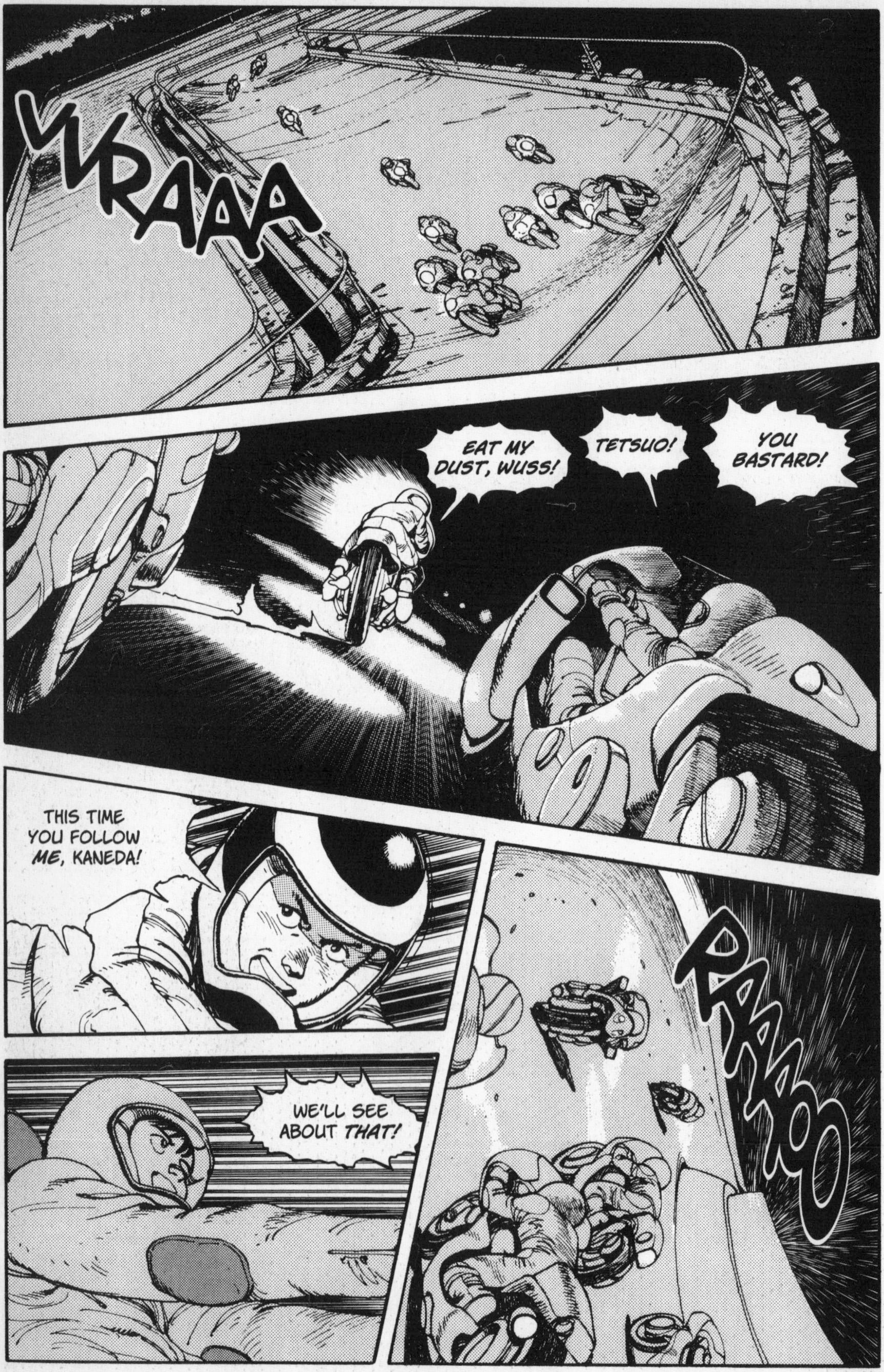
VVRAAA
EAT MY DUST, WUSS!
TETSUO!
YOU BASTARD!
THIS TIME YOU FOLLOW *ME*, KANEDA!
WE'LL SEE ABOUT *THAT*!
RAAAOO

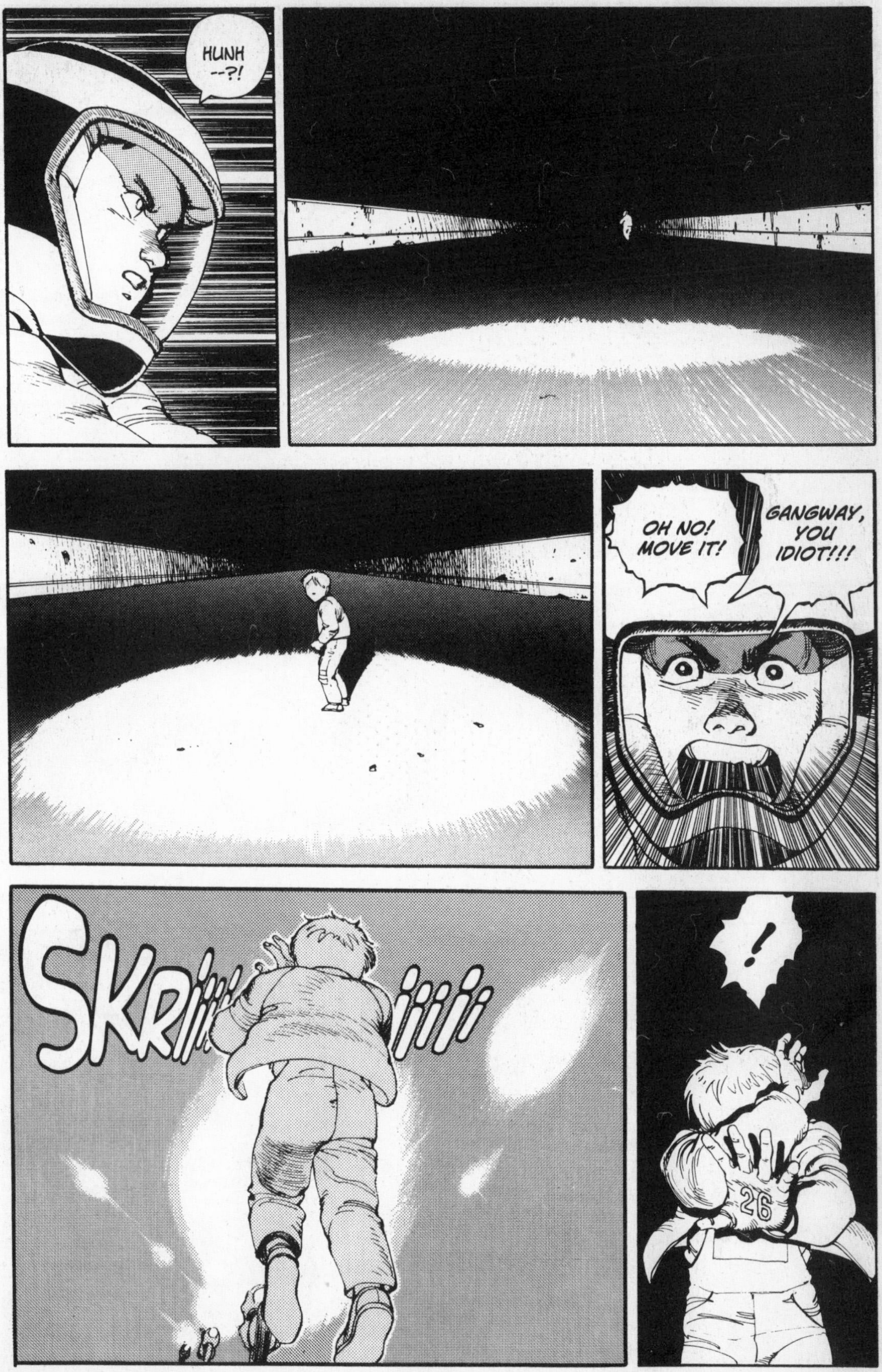
HUNH --?!
OH NO! MOVE IT!
GANGWAY, YOU IDIOT!!!
SKRiiiiiiiii
!
26

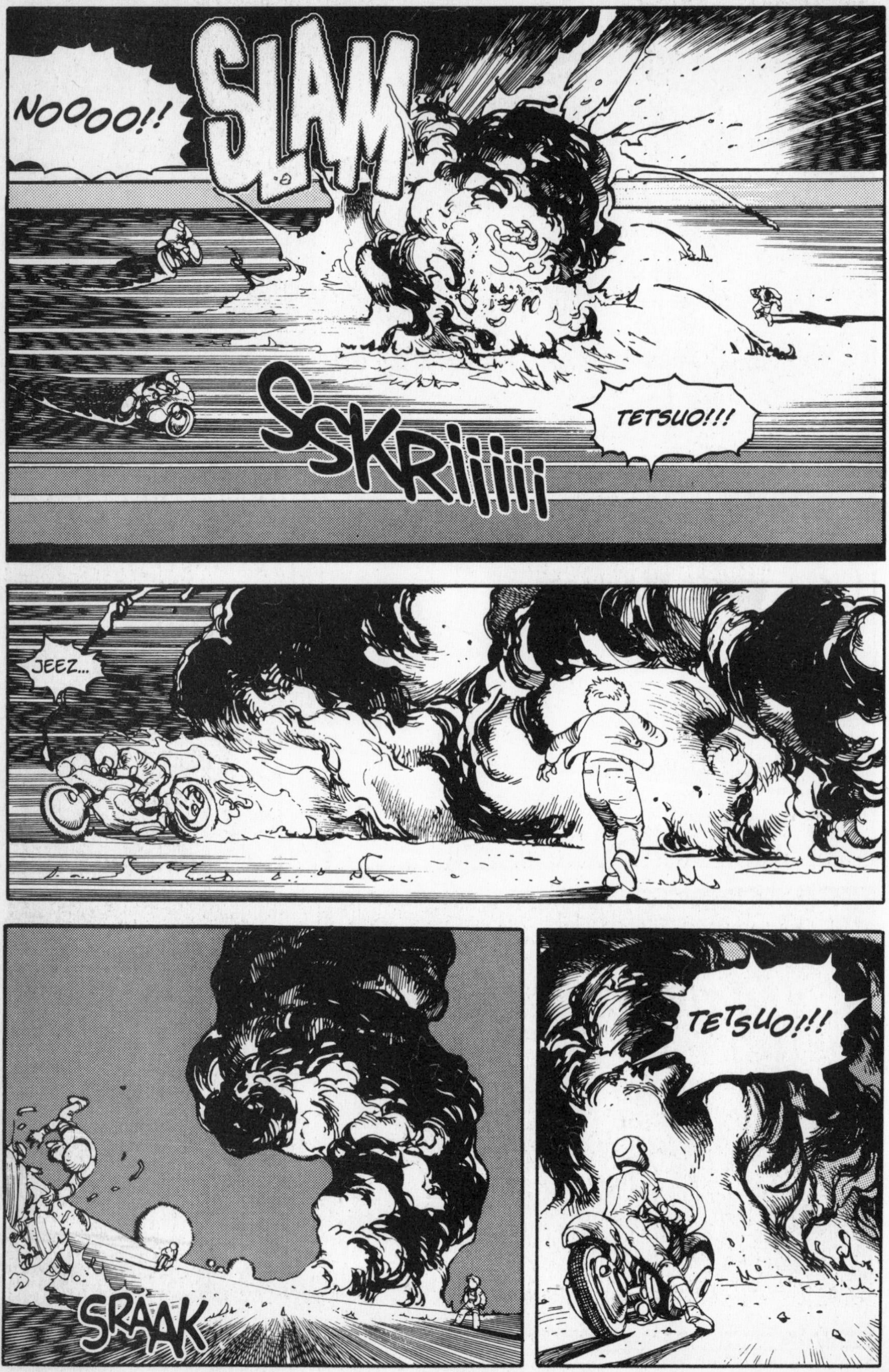
NOOOO!!
SLAM
SSKRiiiiii
TETSUO!!!
JEEZ...
SRAAK
TETSUO!!!

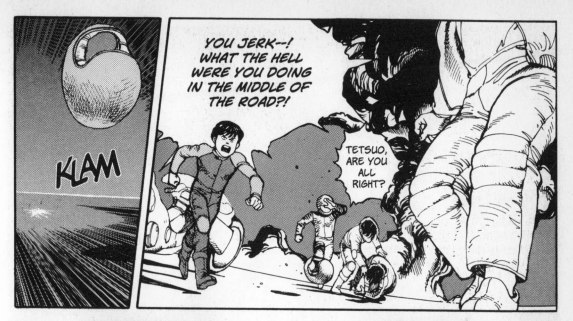

KLAM

YOU JERK--! WHAT THE HELL WERE YOU DOING IN THE MIDDLE OF THE ROAD?!

TETSUO, ARE YOU ALL RIGHT?

!

...

SAY SOME-THING!

PLEASE, TETSUO!

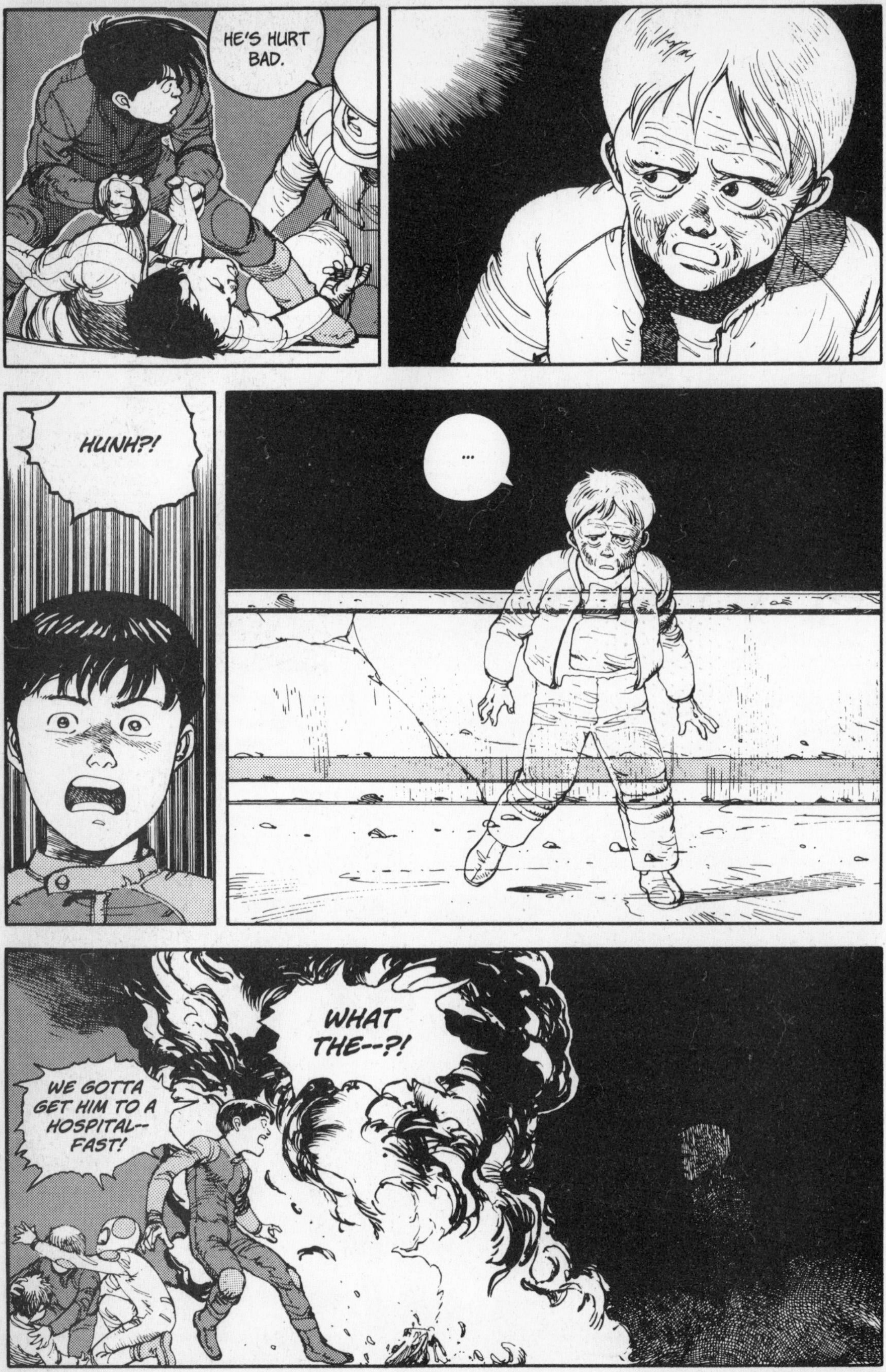
HE'S HURT BAD.
HUNH?!
...
WE GOTTA GET HIM TO A HOSPITAL-- FAST!
WHAT THE--?!

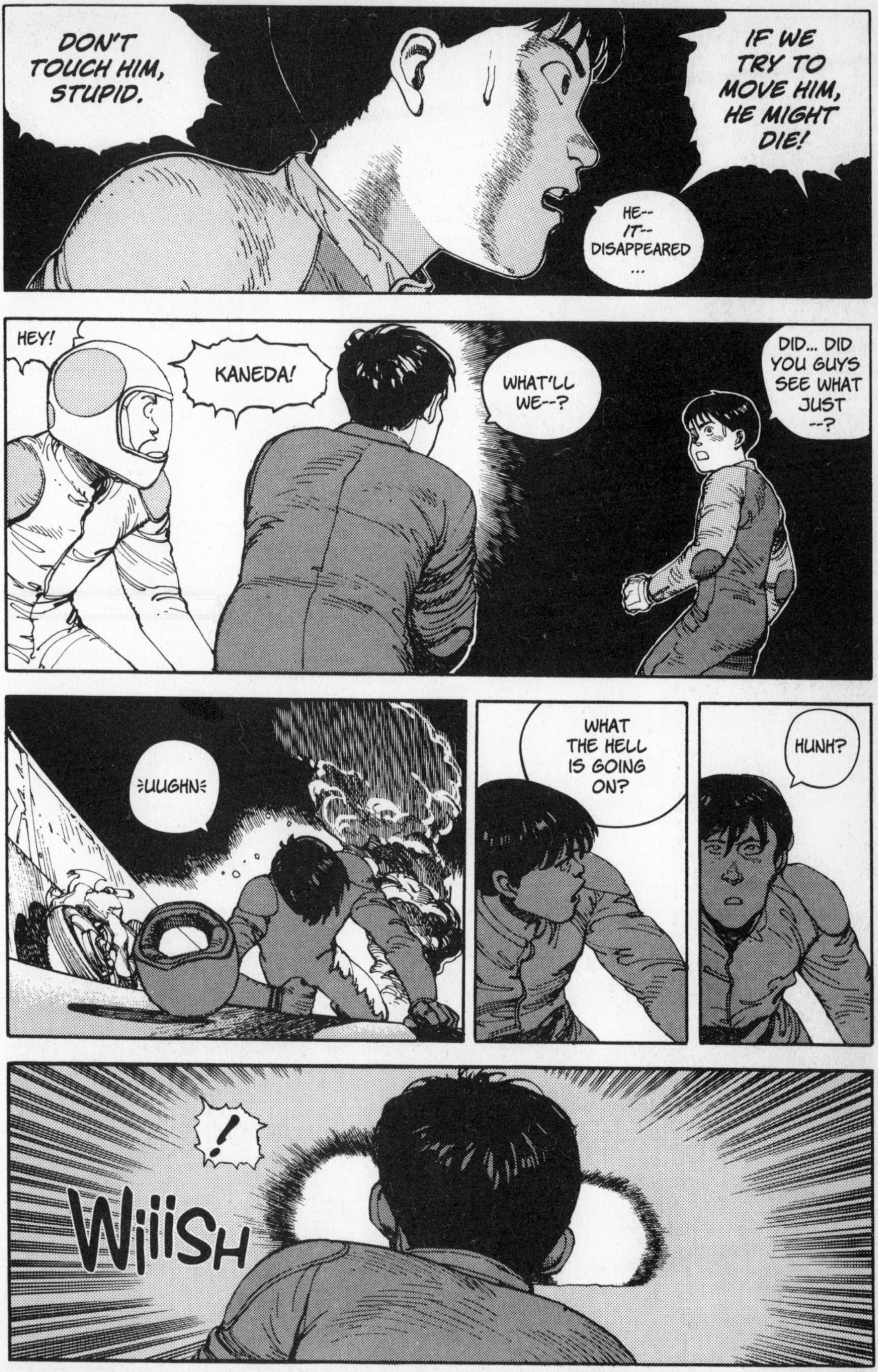

DON'T TOUCH HIM, STUPID.
IF WE TRY TO MOVE HIM, HE MIGHT DIE!
HE-- IT-- DISAPPEARED ...
HEY!
KANEDA!
WHAT'LL WE--?
DID... DID YOU GUYS SEE WHAT JUST --?
UUGHN
WHAT THE HELL IS GOING ON?
HUNH?
!
WIIISH

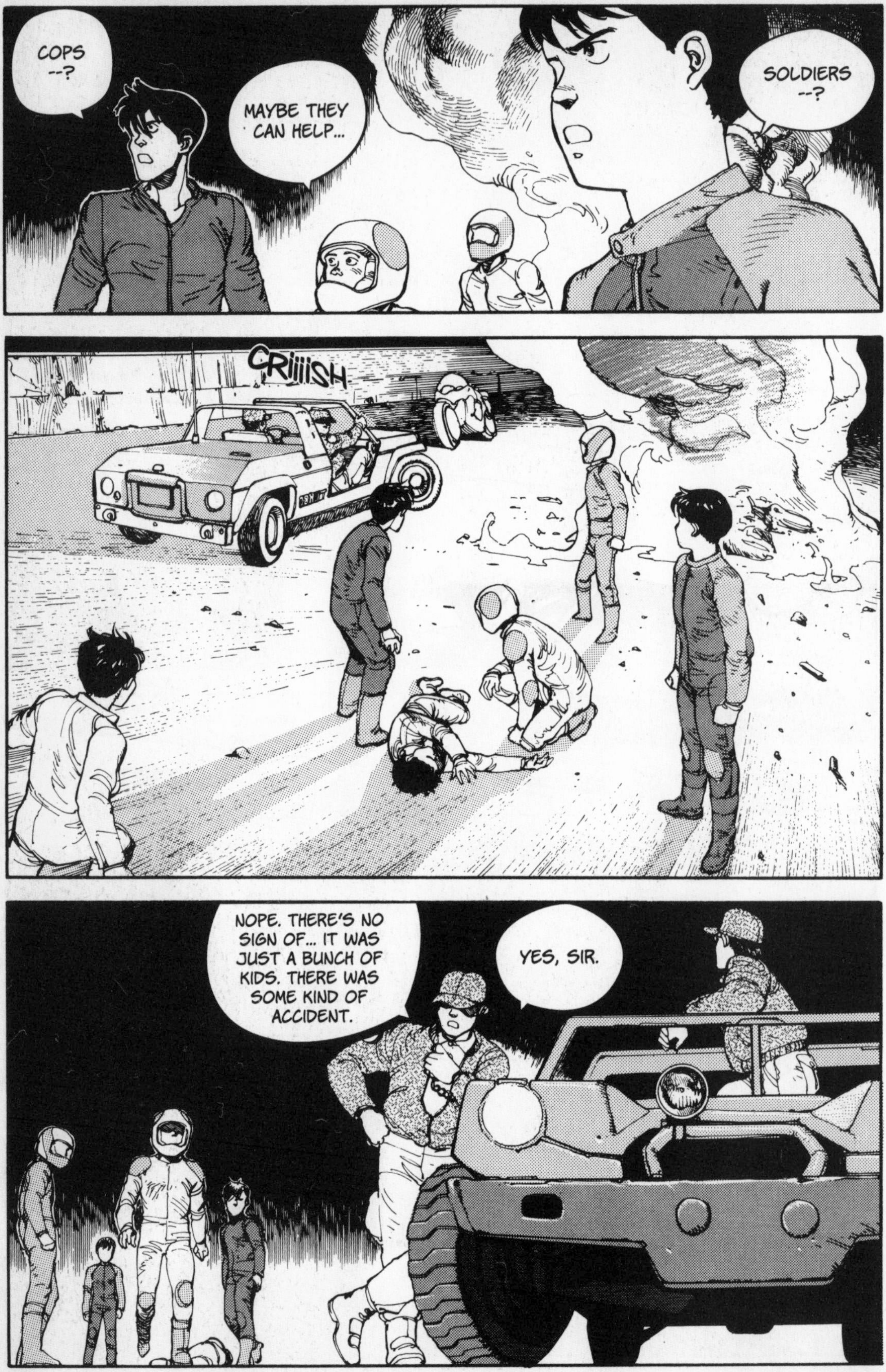
COPS --?
MAYBE THEY CAN HELP...
SOLDIERS --?
CRIIIISH
NOPE. THERE'S NO SIGN OF... IT WAS JUST A BUNCH OF KIDS. THERE WAS SOME KIND OF ACCIDENT.
YES, SIR.

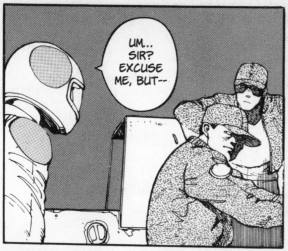

UM.. SIR? EXCUSE ME, BUT--

YOU SHOULDN'T HAVE COME HERE. THIS IS A RESTRICTED AREA.

UH... UH... YEAH, BUT...

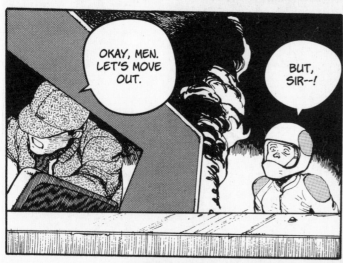

OKAY, MEN. LET'S MOVE OUT.

BUT, SIR--!

AN AMBULANCE IS ON ITS WAY. JUST SIT TIGHT.

WHEN THE POLICE GET HERE, TELL THEM HOW IT HAPPENED.

BUT... BUT AREN'T *YOU* THE POLICE?

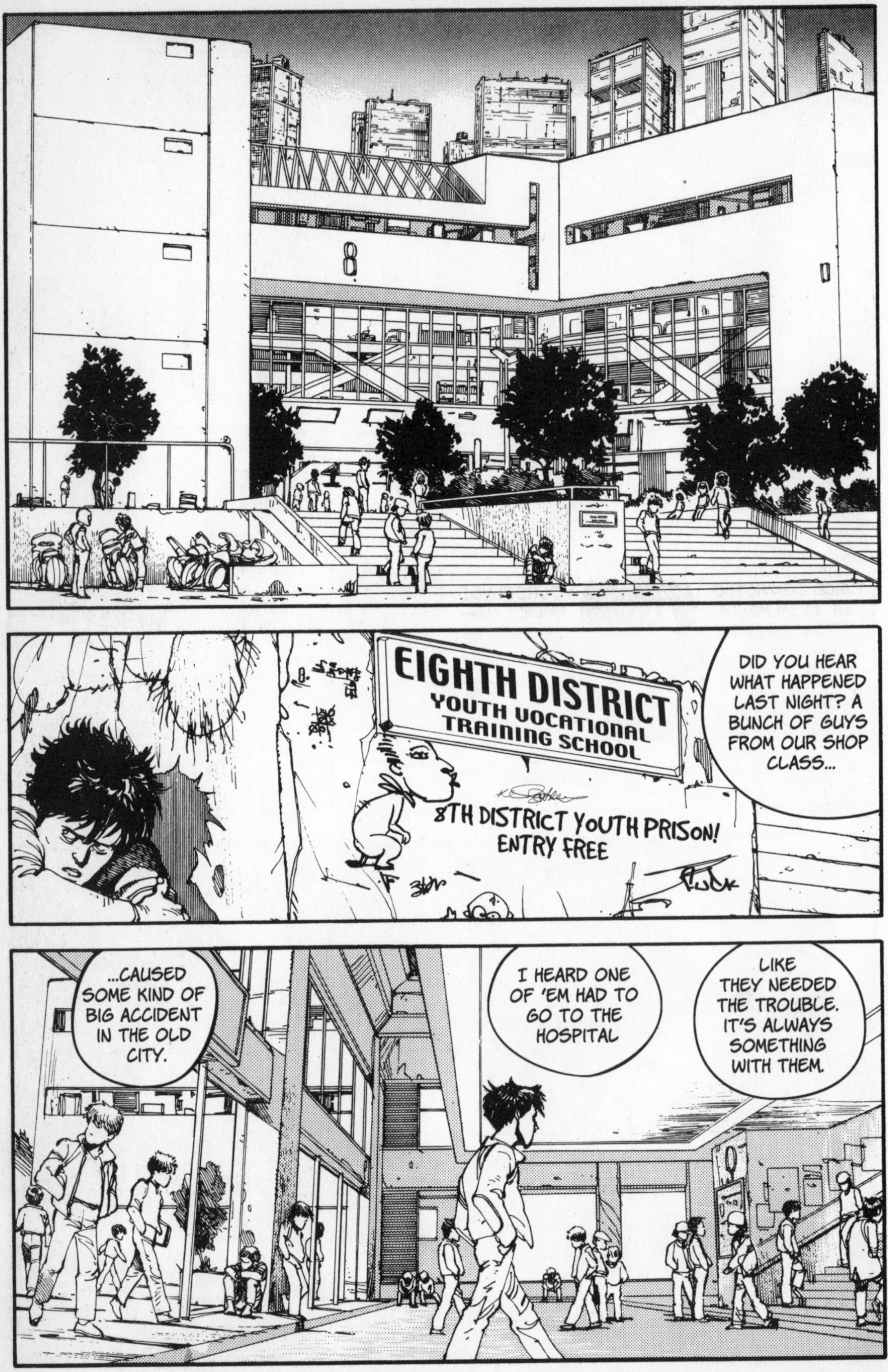
EIGHTH DISTRICT
YOUTH VOCATIONAL TRAINING SCHOOL
8TH DISTRICT YOUTH PRISON! ENTRY FREE
DID YOU HEAR WHAT HAPPENED LAST NIGHT? A BUNCH OF GUYS FROM OUR SHOP CLASS...
...CAUSED SOME KIND OF BIG ACCIDENT IN THE OLD CITY.
I HEARD ONE OF 'EM HAD TO GO TO THE HOSPITAL
LIKE THEY NEEDED THE TROUBLE. IT'S ALWAYS SOMETHING WITH THEM.

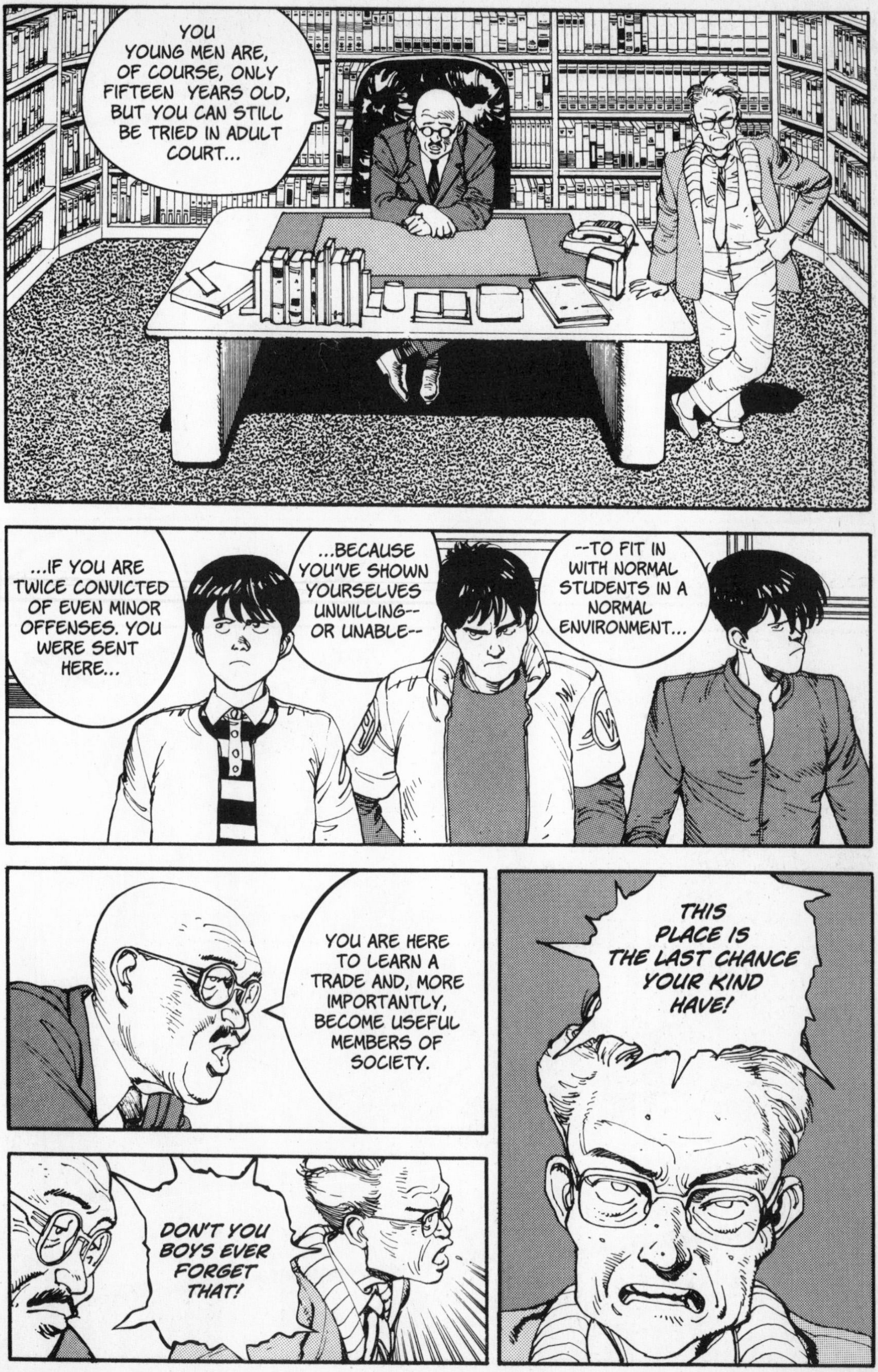
YOU YOUNG MEN ARE, OF COURSE, ONLY FIFTEEN YEARS OLD, BUT YOU CAN STILL BE TRIED IN ADULT COURT...
...IF YOU ARE TWICE CONVICTED OF EVEN MINOR OFFENSES. YOU WERE SENT HERE...
...BECAUSE YOU'VE SHOWN YOURSELVES UNWILLING-- OR UNABLE--
--TO FIT IN WITH NORMAL STUDENTS IN A NORMAL ENVIRONMENT...
YOU ARE HERE TO LEARN A TRADE AND, MORE IMPORTANTLY, BECOME USEFUL MEMBERS OF SOCIETY.
DON'T YOU BOYS EVER FORGET THAT!
THIS PLACE IS THE LAST CHANCE YOUR KIND HAVE!

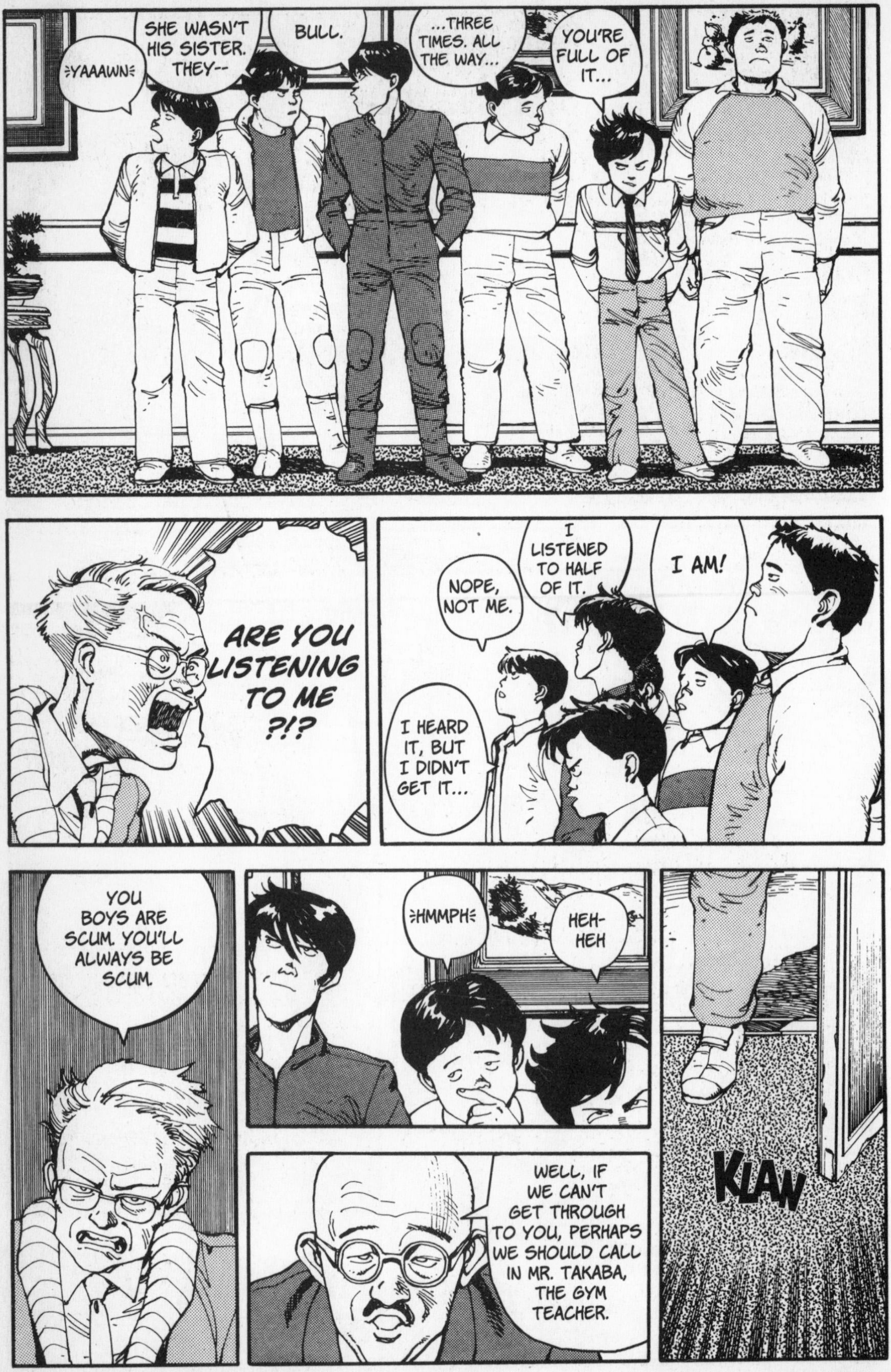

≥YAAAWN≤
SHE WASN'T HIS SISTER. THEY--
BULL.
...THREE TIMES. ALL THE WAY...
YOU'RE FULL OF IT...
ARE YOU LISTENING TO ME ?!?
NOPE, NOT ME.
I LISTENED TO HALF OF IT.
I AM!
I HEARD IT, BUT I DIDN'T GET IT...
YOU BOYS ARE SCUM. YOU'LL ALWAYS BE SCUM.
≥HMMPH≤
HEH-HEH
WELL, IF WE CAN'T GET THROUGH TO YOU, PERHAPS WE SHOULD CALL IN MR. TAKABA, THE GYM TEACHER.
KLAN

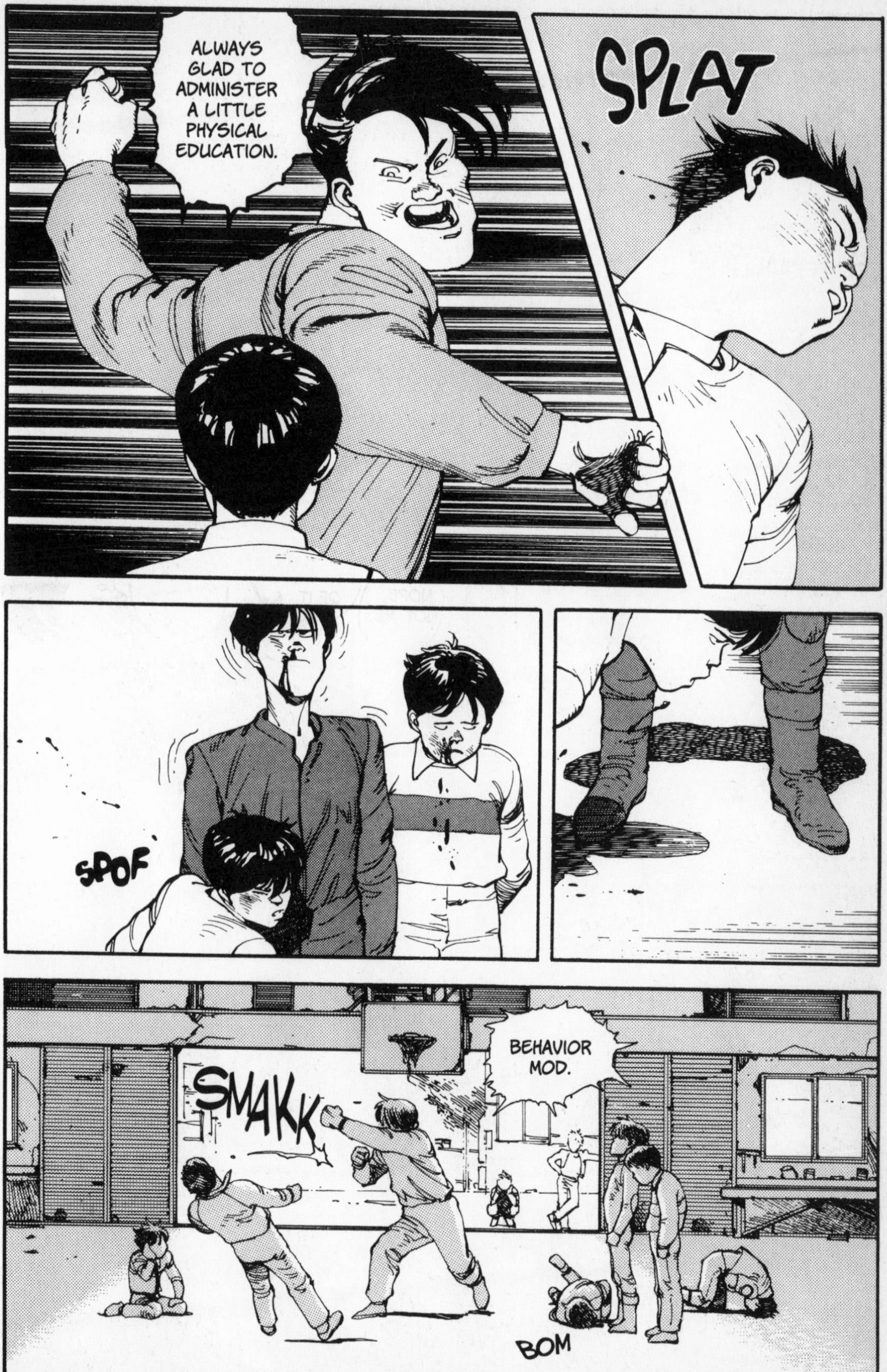

ALWAYS GLAD TO ADMINISTER A LITTLE PHYSICAL EDUCATION.
SPLAT
SPOF
SMAKK
BEHAVIOR MOD.
BOM

OKAY, FALL IN!

YOU OKAY?

=WHUFF=

THAT'S IT FOR TODAY.

GOT ANYTHING TO SAY?

THANK YOU VERY MUCH, SIR!

THANK YOU, SIR.

ANY TIME YOU WANT A LITTLE MORE, I'M ALWAYS AVAILABLE.

SLOP

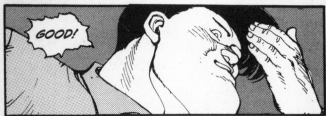

GOOD!

HEY, MISTER JAW! BITE ME!

WE WON'T FORGET THIS!

SCUMBAG!

GO TO HELL!

WATCH YOUR BUTT, JAWHEAD!

YOU'RE GONNA GET YOURS!

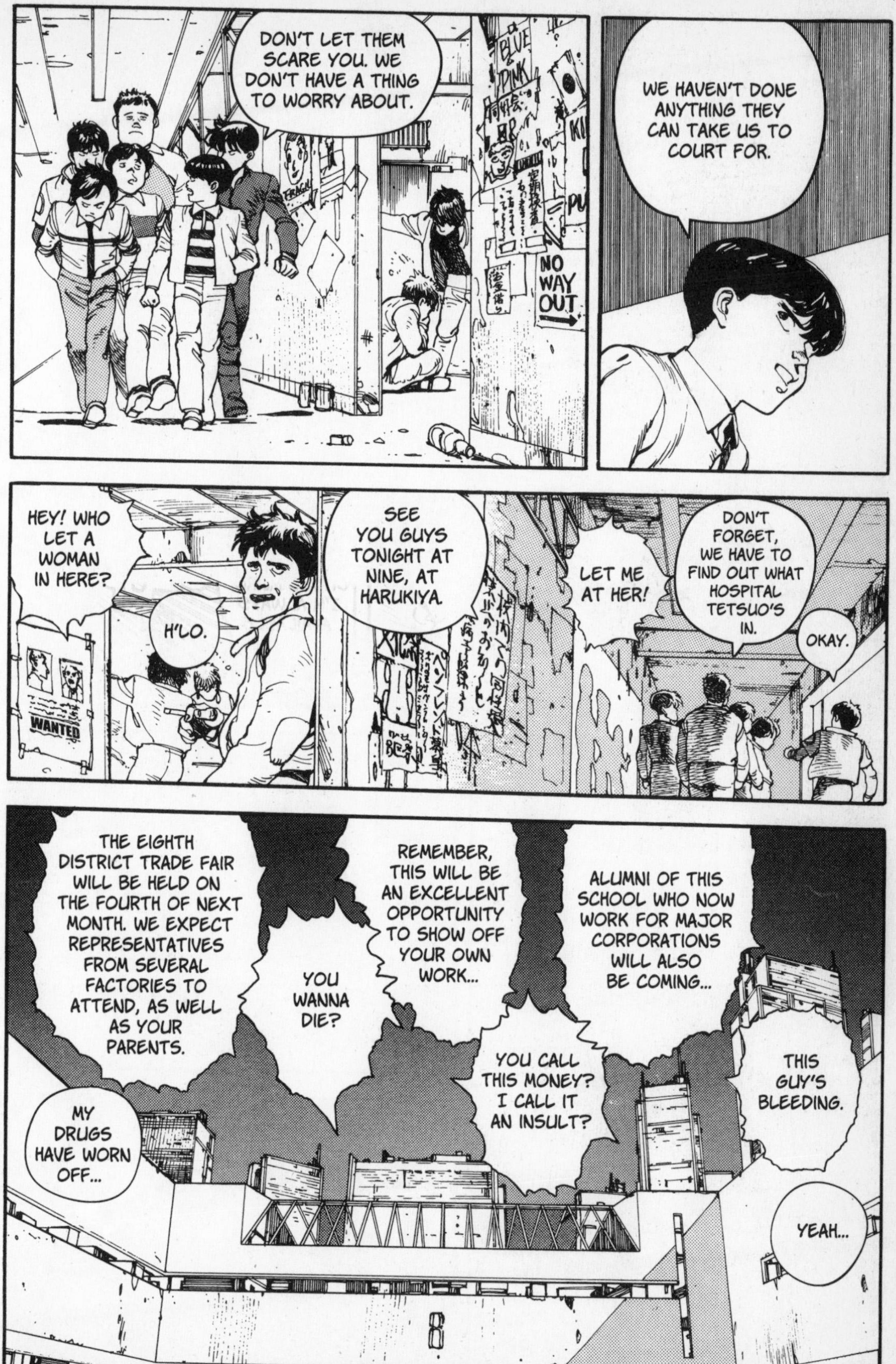
DON'T LET THEM SCARE YOU. WE DON'T HAVE A THING TO WORRY ABOUT.
BLUE PINK
NO WAY OUT
WE HAVEN'T DONE ANYTHING THEY CAN TAKE US TO COURT FOR.
HEY! WHO LET A WOMAN IN HERE?
WANTED
H'LO.
SEE YOU GUYS TONIGHT AT NINE, AT HARUKIYA.
LET ME AT HER!
DON'T FORGET, WE HAVE TO FIND OUT WHAT HOSPITAL TETSUO'S IN.
OKAY.
THE EIGHTH DISTRICT TRADE FAIR WILL BE HELD ON THE FOURTH OF NEXT MONTH. WE EXPECT REPRESENTATIVES FROM SEVERAL FACTORIES TO ATTEND, AS WELL AS YOUR PARENTS.
YOU WANNA DIE?
REMEMBER, THIS WILL BE AN EXCELLENT OPPORTUNITY TO SHOW OFF YOUR OWN WORK...
ALUMNI OF THIS SCHOOL WHO NOW WORK FOR MAJOR CORPORATIONS WILL ALSO BE COMING...
MY DRUGS HAVE WORN OFF...
YOU CALL THIS MONEY? I CALL IT AN INSULT?
THIS GUY'S BLEEDING.
YEAH...
8

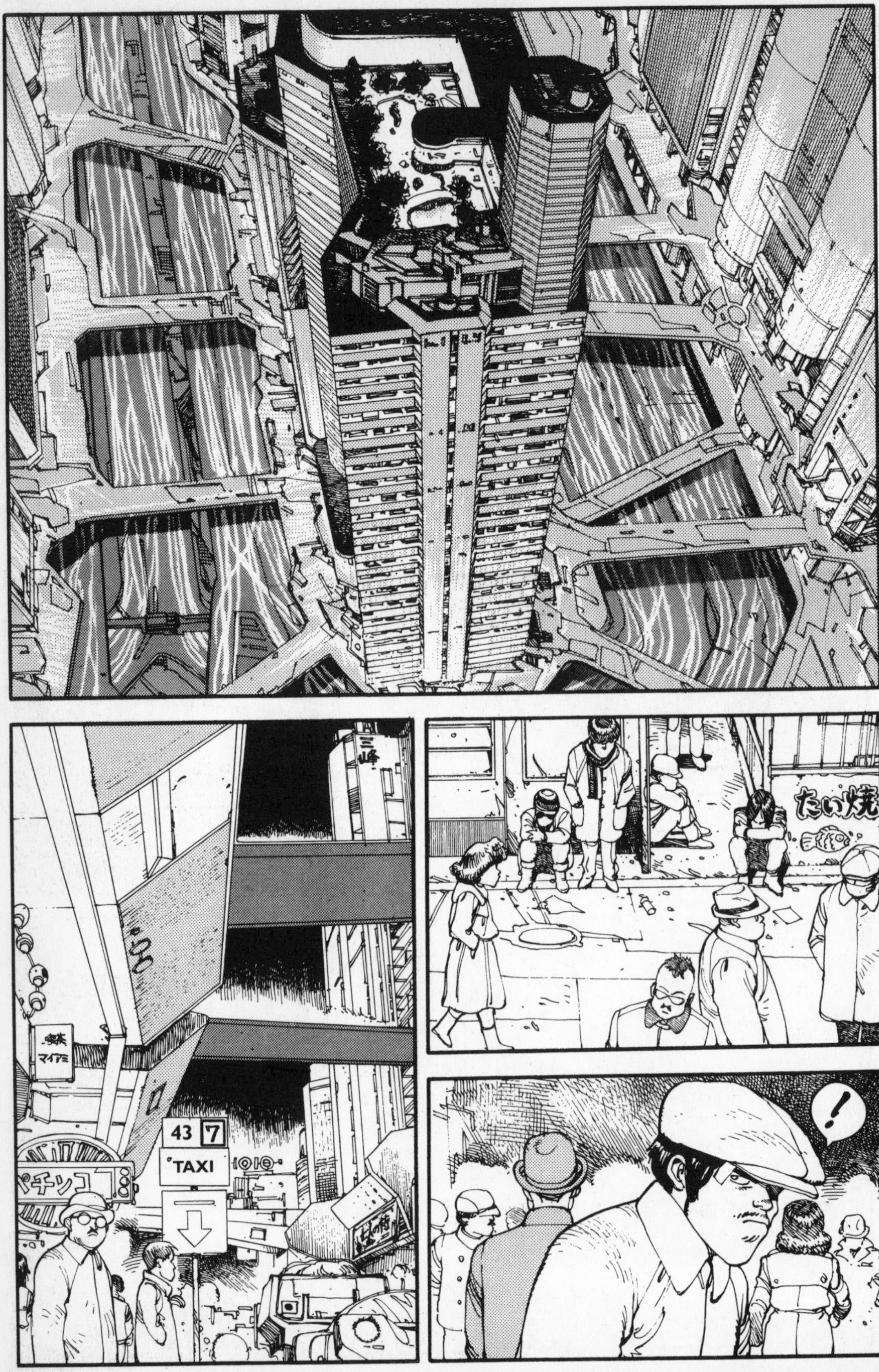
43
7
TAXI
パチンコ
たい焼
!

HOW?

SHHH...

WHERE ARE YOU MEETING RYU?

TONIGHT AT NINE, AT HARUKIYA. IT'S OFF THE EASTERN EXPRESS HIGHWAY IN THE SEVENTEENTH DISTRICT.

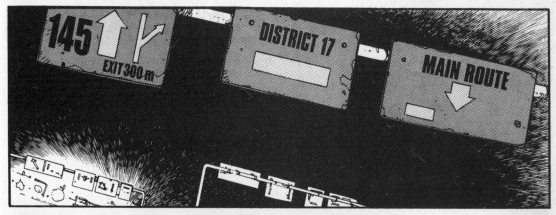

145 ↑ Y
EXIT 300 m

DISTRICT 17

MAIN ROUTE
↓

3F
ビリヤード
2F
卓球

BRRRR

春木屋
HARUKIYA
BAR
↓

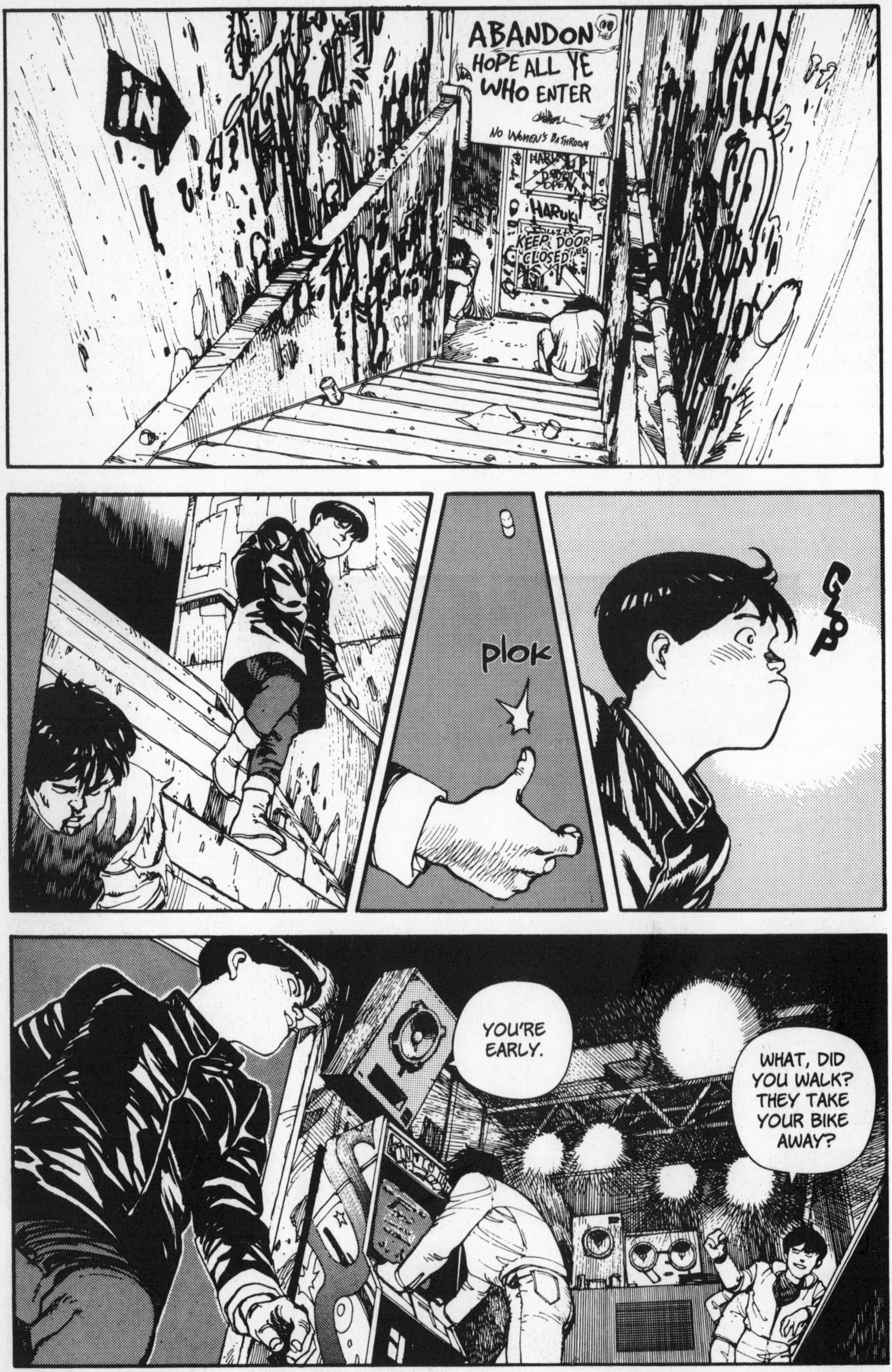
IN
ABANDON
HOPE ALL YE
WHO ENTER
NO WOMEN'S BATHROOM
HARUKI
KEEP DOOR CLOSED!
plok
GLOP
YOU'RE EARLY.
WHAT, DID YOU WALK? THEY TAKE YOUR BIKE AWAY?

YOU BRING ANY, KANEDA?

SURE DID.

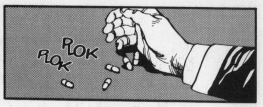

PLOK PLOK

BRING ME A COKE.

BY THE WAY, YAMAGATA, YOU FIND OUT WHERE TETSUO IS?

I TRIED, BUT...

ME, TOO. NO LUCK.

I THINK SOMETHING WEIRD'S GOING ON.

I ASKED THE POLICE AND TETSUO'S MOTHER.

...NOTHING.

Y'KNOW, I THOUGHT IT WAS PRETTY STRANGE YESTERDAY. THE POLICE LET US GO AWFULLY FAST.

YEAH. NO ONE KNOWS WHERE THEY TOOK HIM.

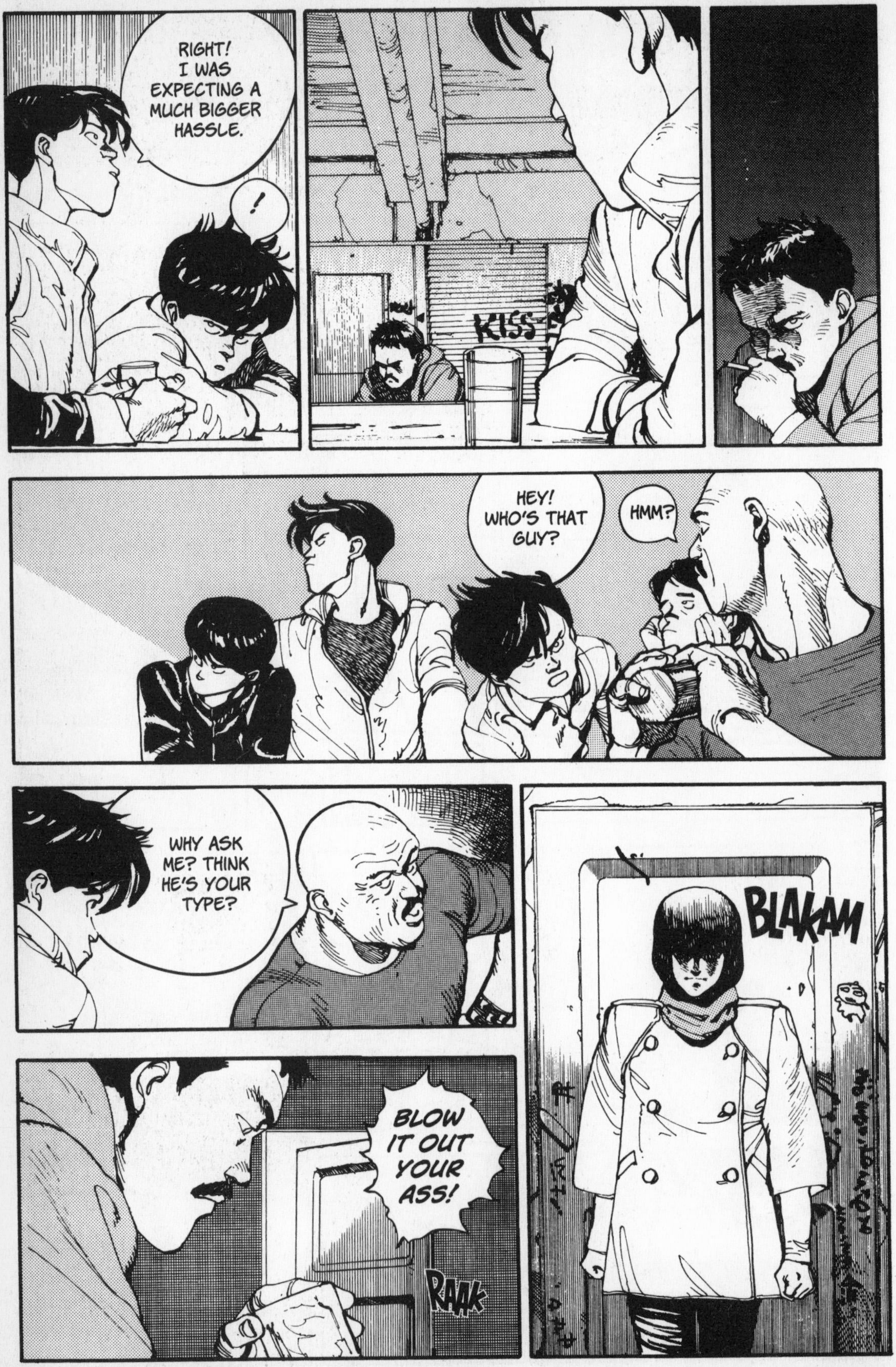
RIGHT! I WAS EXPECTING A MUCH BIGGER HASSLE.
!
KISS
HEY! WHO'S THAT GUY?
HMM?
WHY ASK ME? THINK HE'S YOUR TYPE?
BLAKAM
BLOW IT OUT YOUR ASS!
RAAK

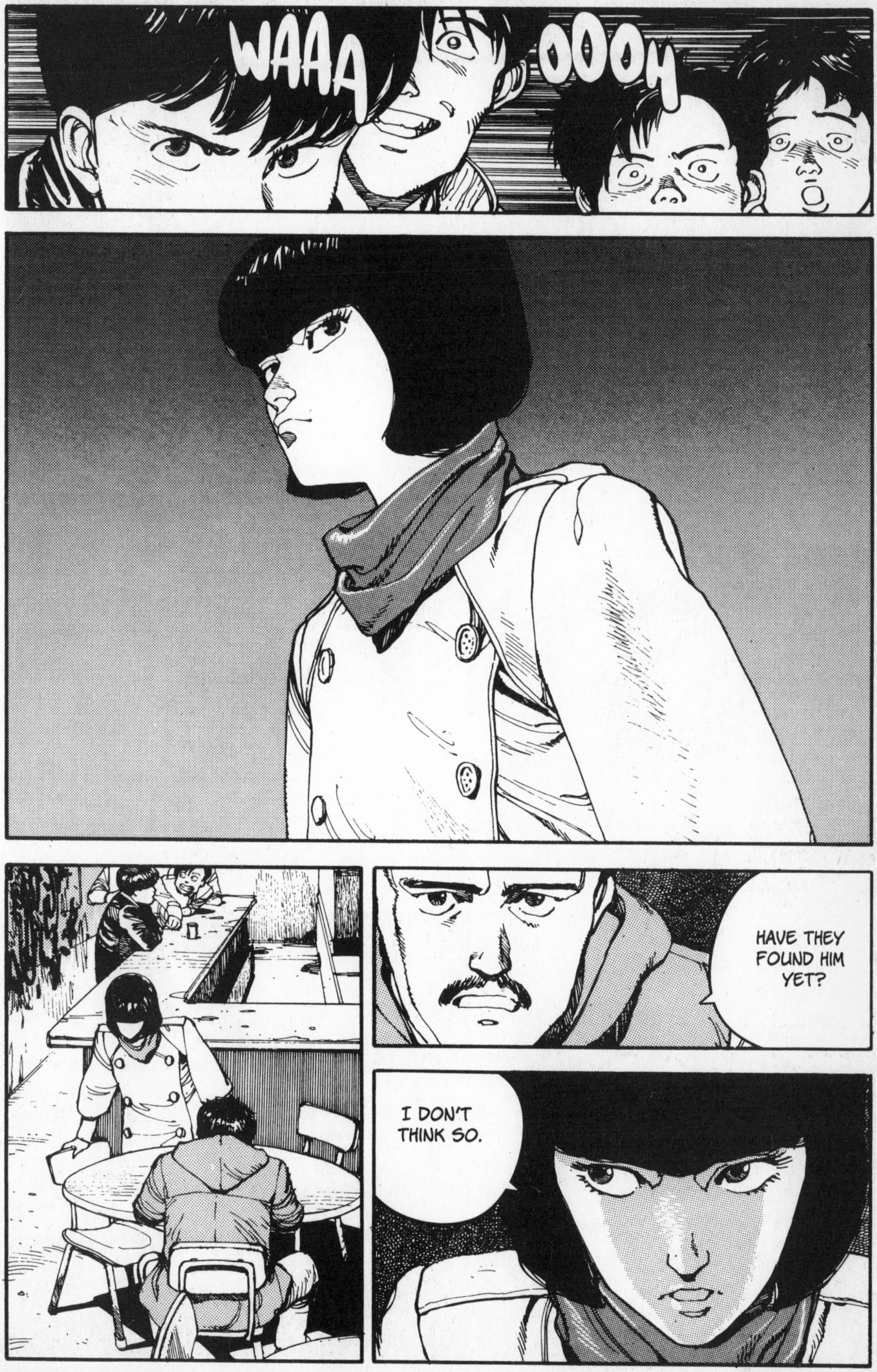
WAAA
OOOH
HAVE THEY FOUND HIM YET?
I DON'T THINK SO.

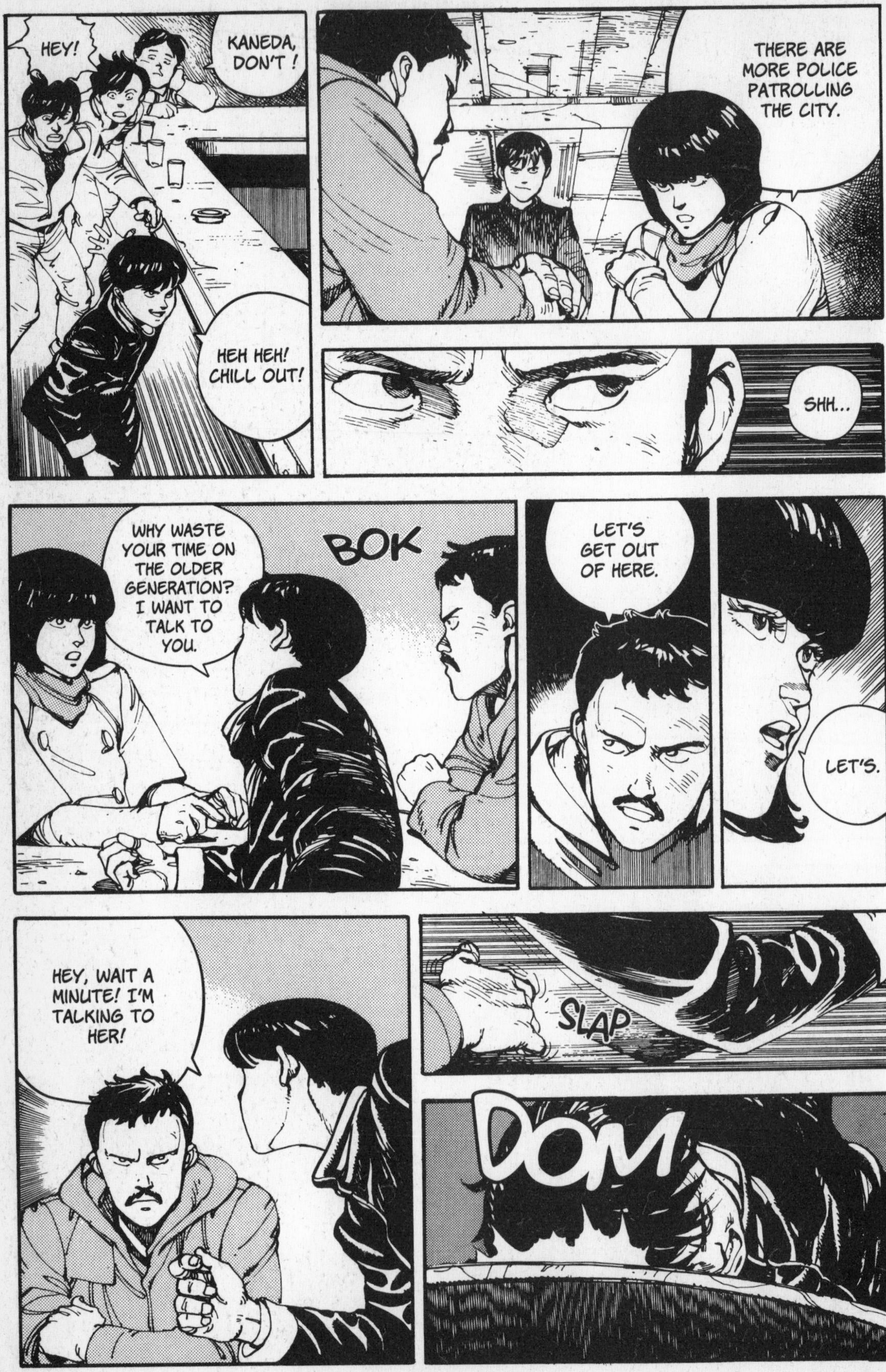
HEY!
KANEDA, DON'T !
HEH HEH! CHILL OUT!
THERE ARE MORE POLICE PATROLLING THE CITY.
SHH...
WHY WASTE YOUR TIME ON THE OLDER GENERATION? I WANT TO TALK TO YOU.
BOK
LET'S GET OUT OF HERE.
LET'S.
HEY, WAIT A MINUTE! I'M TALKING TO HER!
SLAP
DOM

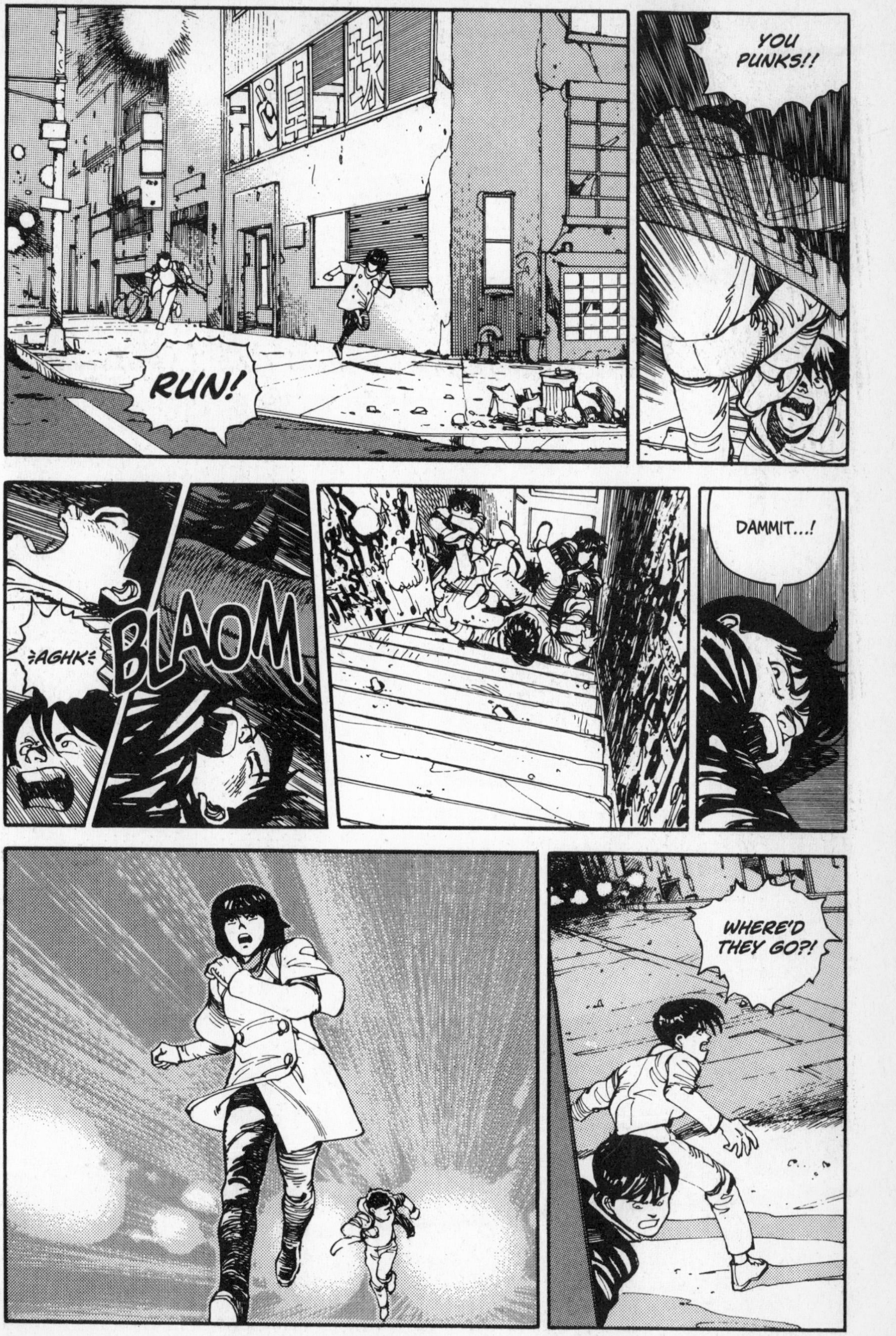
RUN!
YOU PUNKS!!
AGHK
BLAOM
DAMMIT...!
WHERE'D THEY GO?!

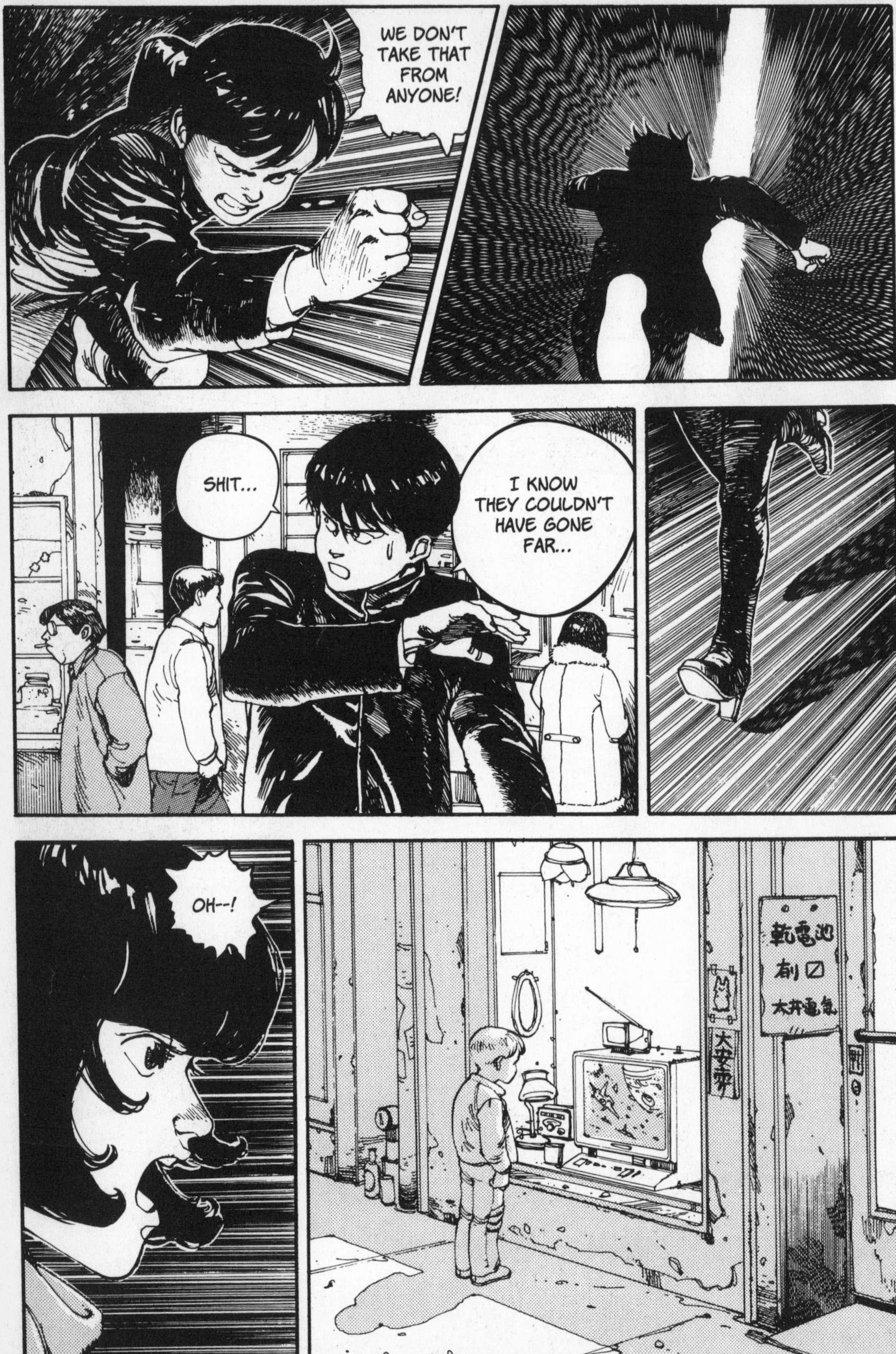
WE DON'T TAKE THAT FROM ANYONE!
SHIT...
I KNOW THEY COULDN'T HAVE GONE FAR...
OH--!

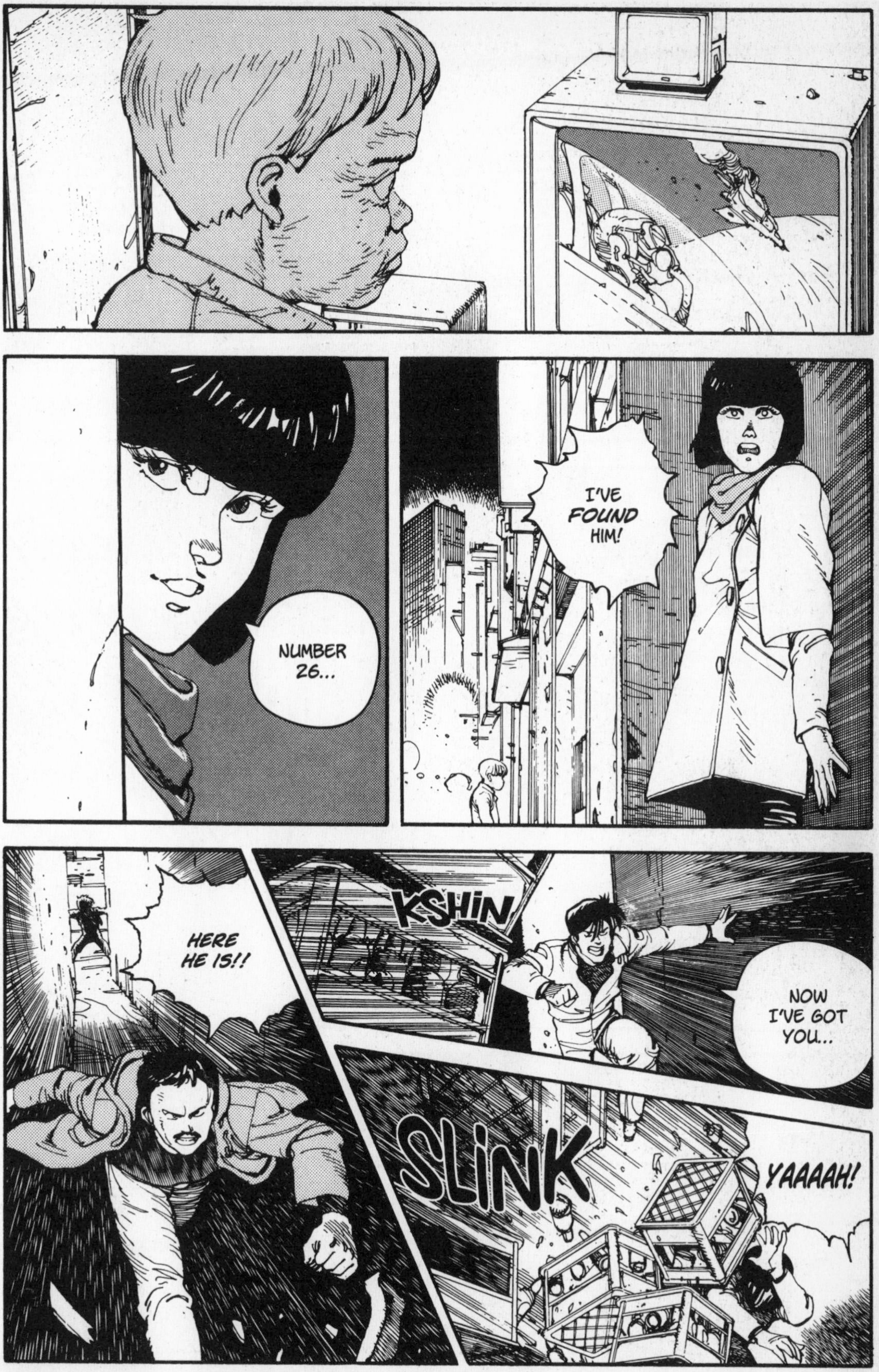
NUMBER 26...
I'VE FOUND HIM!
HERE HE IS!!
KSHIN
NOW I'VE GOT YOU...
SLINK
YAAAAH!

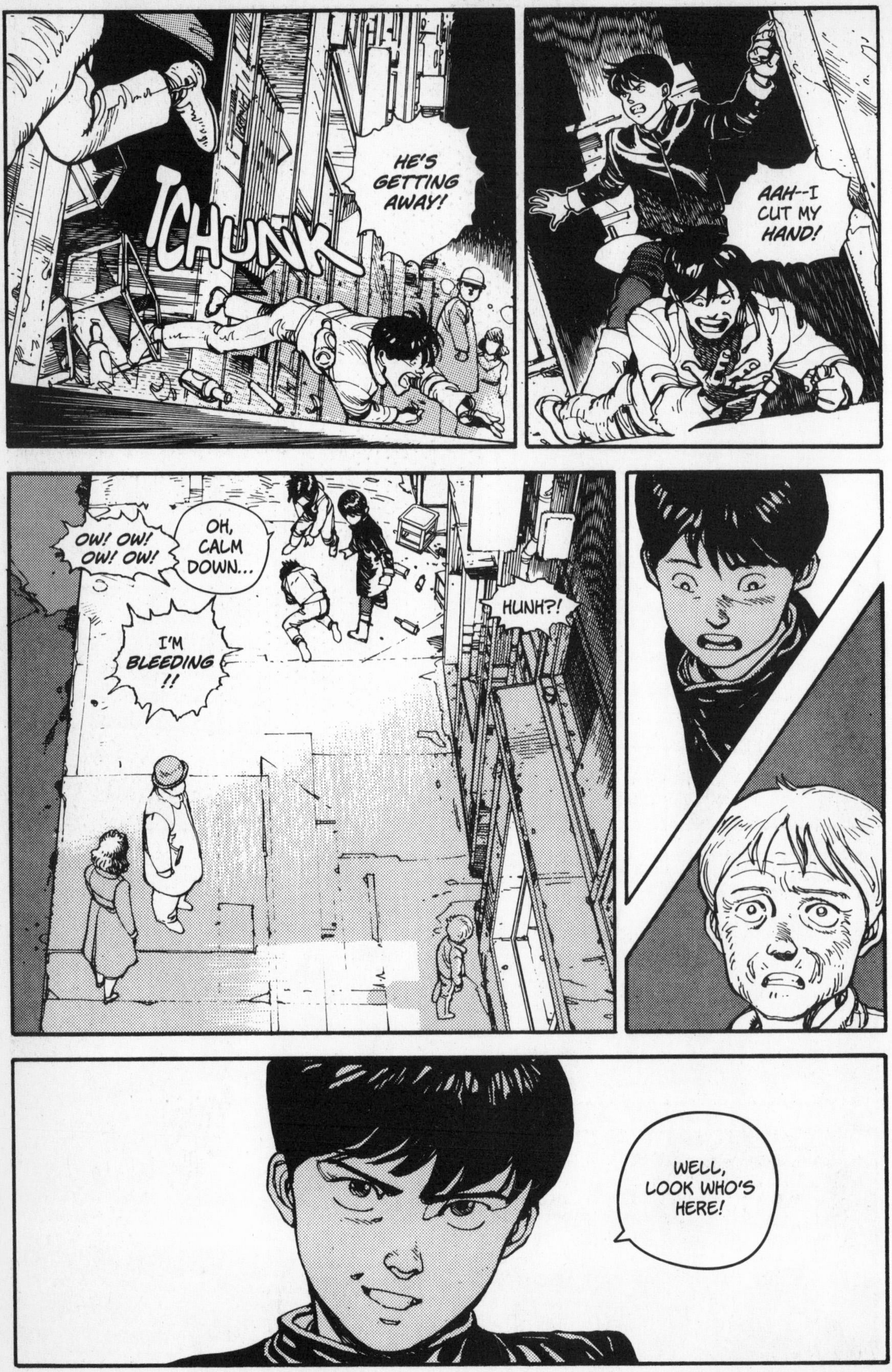
TCHUNK
HE'S GETTING AWAY!
AAH--I CUT MY HAND!
OW! OW! OW! OW!
OH, CALM DOWN...
I'M BLEEDING !!
HUNH?!
WELL, LOOK WHO'S HERE!

KANEDA...?

YOU PROBABLY DON'T KNOW WHO HE IS--HE'S ONE OF OUR BEST RIDERS...

BECAUSE OF YOU, TETSUO IS...

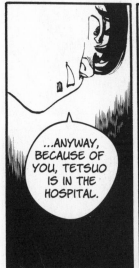

...ANYWAY, BECAUSE OF YOU, TETSUO IS IN THE HOSPITAL.

HE'S MY FRIEND, SO I OWE YOU FOR WHAT YOU DID TO HIM. AND I'M GONNA PAY YOU BACK, RIGHT NOW.

WHAT ARE YOU TALKING ABOUT, KANEDA? YOU *KNOW* HIM?

SINCE LAST NIGHT.

LAST NIGHT?

THIS CREEP WAS IN THE MIDDLE OF THE ROAD. TETSUO GOT HURT TRYING TO AVOID HIM.

WHAT--?! ARE YOU *SERIOUS?*

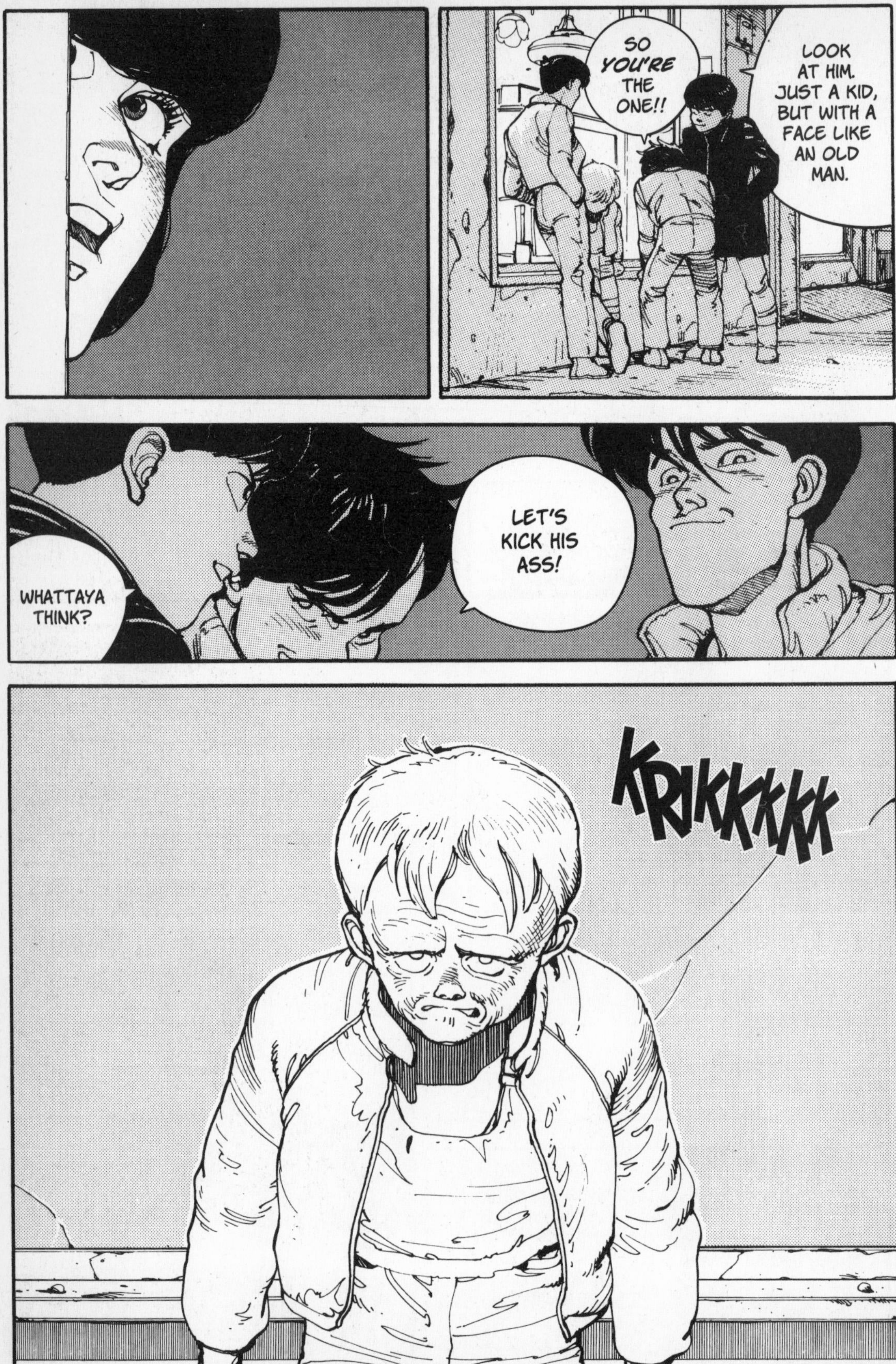
SO YOU'RE THE ONE!!
LOOK AT HIM. JUST A KID, BUT WITH A FACE LIKE AN OLD MAN.
WHATTAYA THINK?
LET'S KICK HIS ASS!
KRIKKKKK

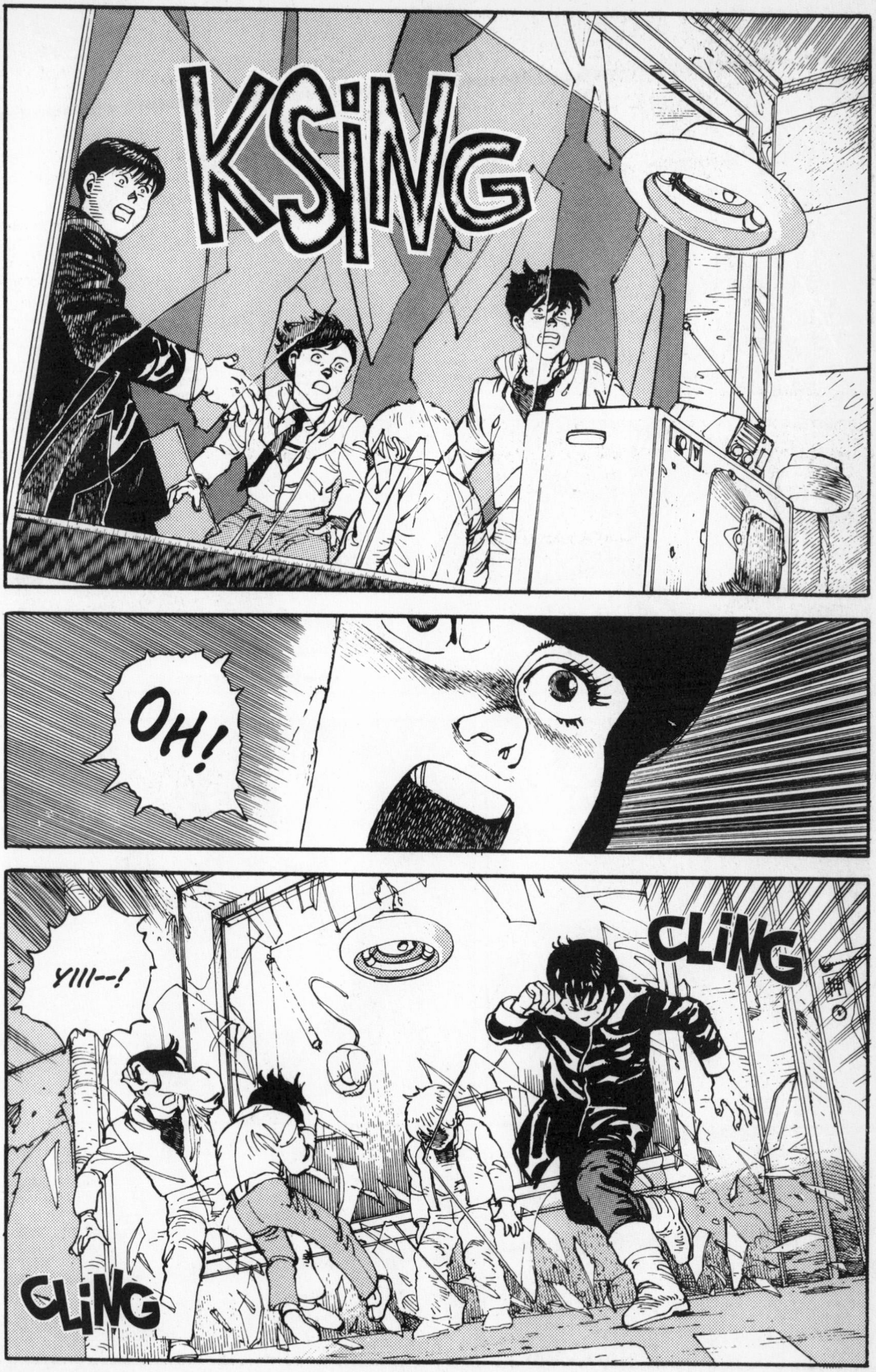
KSING
OH!
YIII--!
CLING
CLING

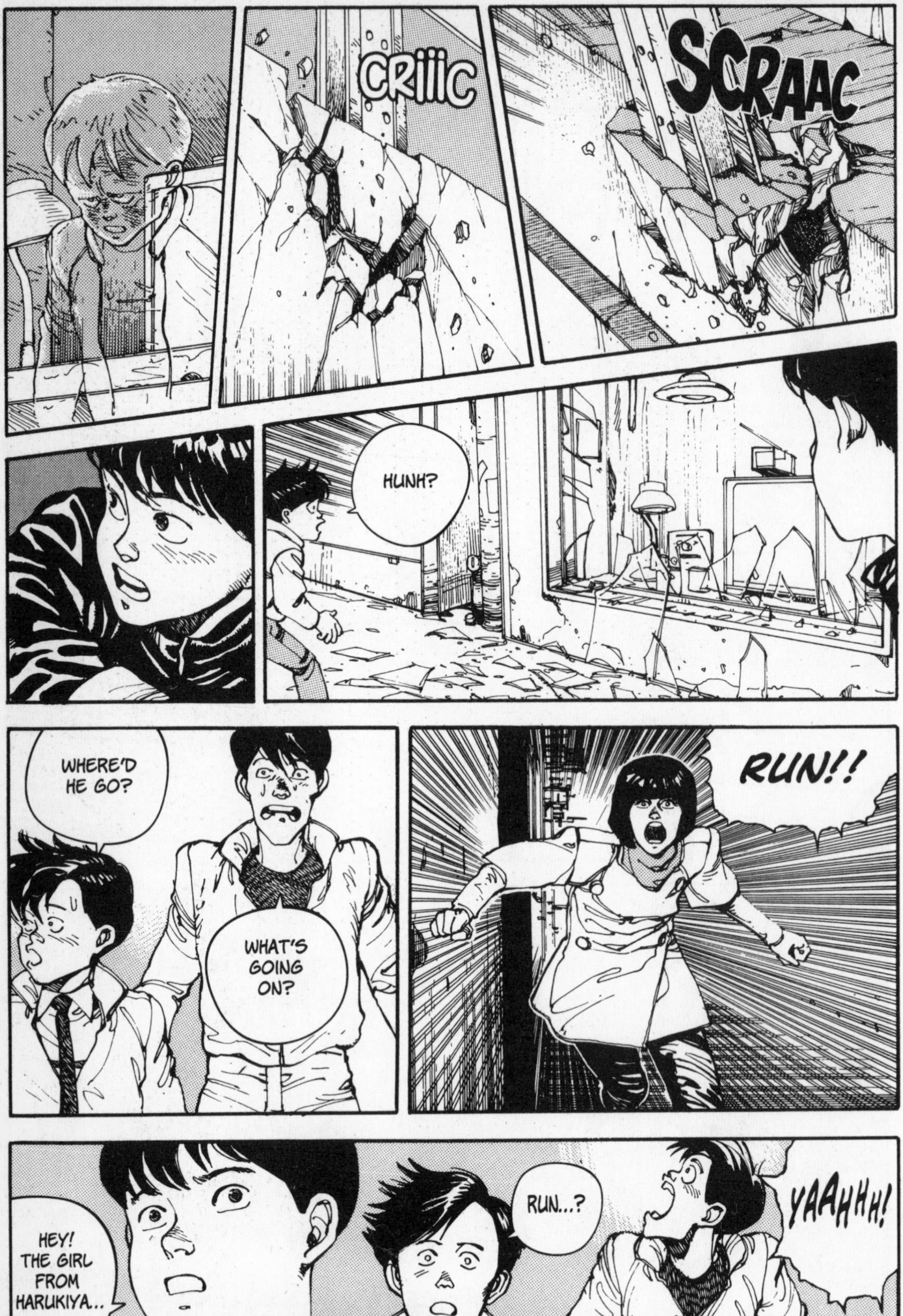
CRIIIC
SCRAAC
HUNH?
WHERE'D HE GO?
WHAT'S GOING ON?
RUN!!
HEY! THE GIRL FROM HARUKIYA...
RUN...?
YAAHHH!

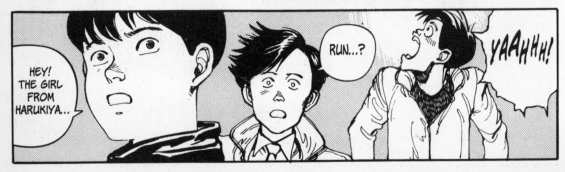

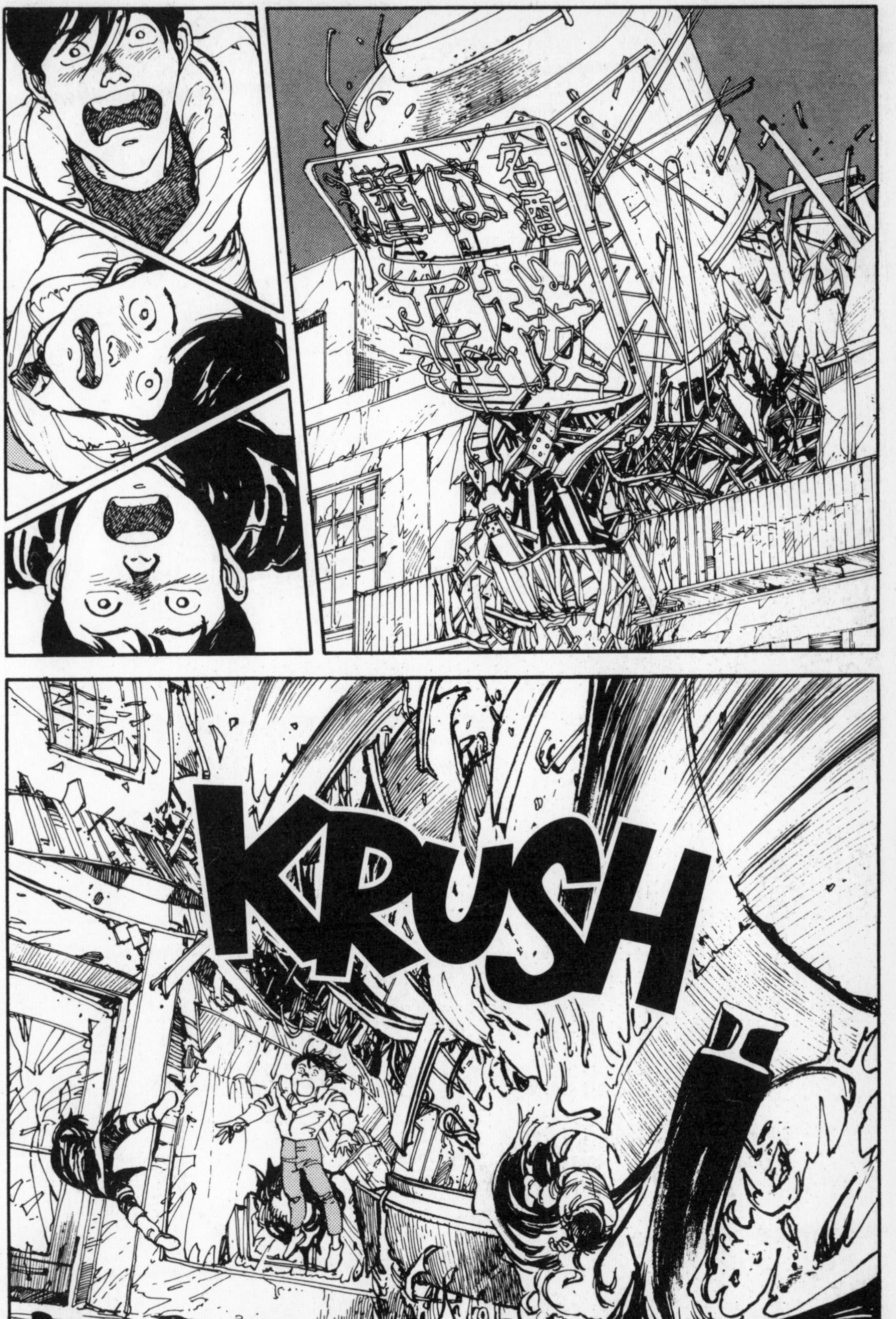
KRUSH

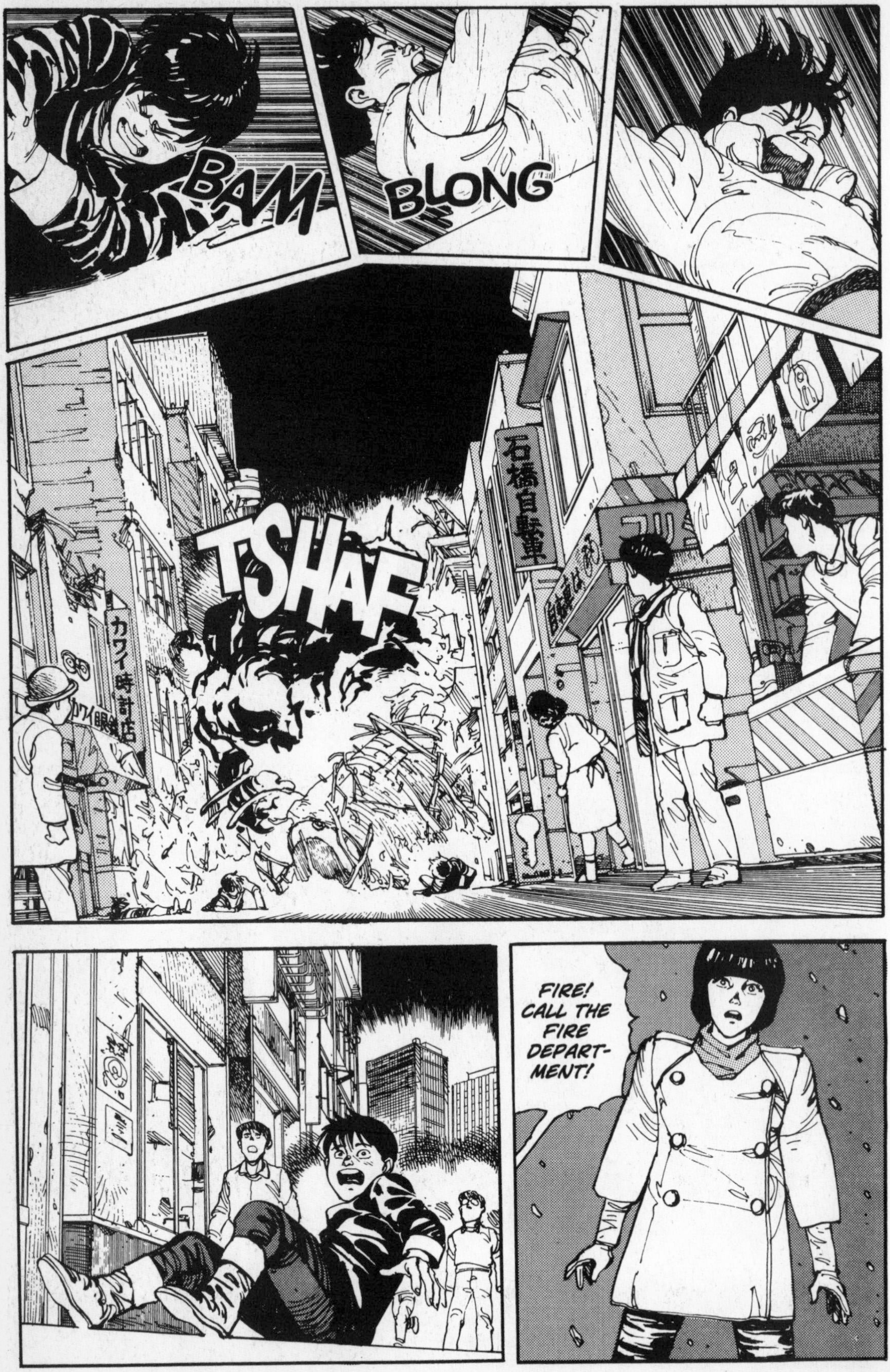
BAM
BLONG
TSHAF
カワイ時計店
カワイ眼鏡店
FIRE! CALL THE FIRE DEPART-MENT!

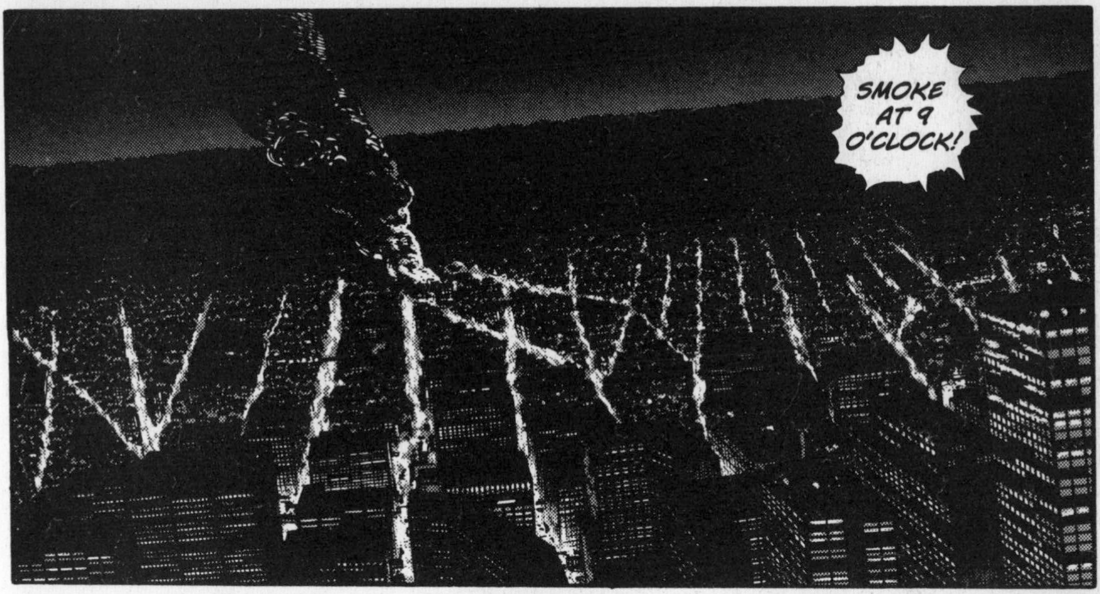
SMOKE AT 9 O'CLOCK!

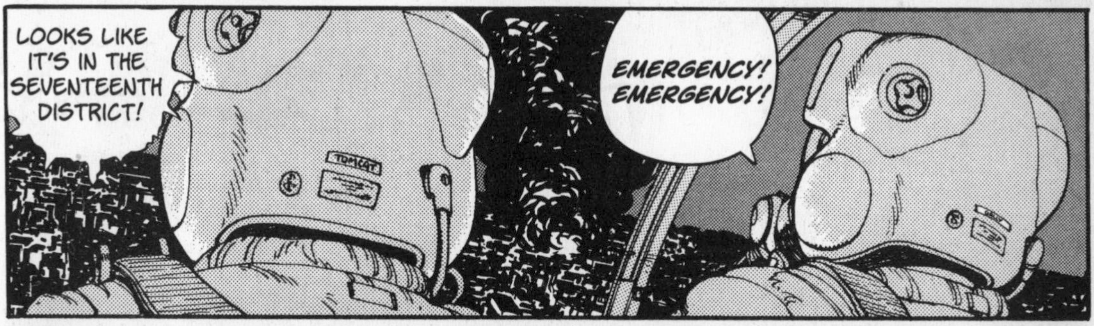
LOOKS LIKE IT'S IN THE SEVENTEENTH DISTRICT!
EMERGENCY! EMERGENCY!
TOMCAT

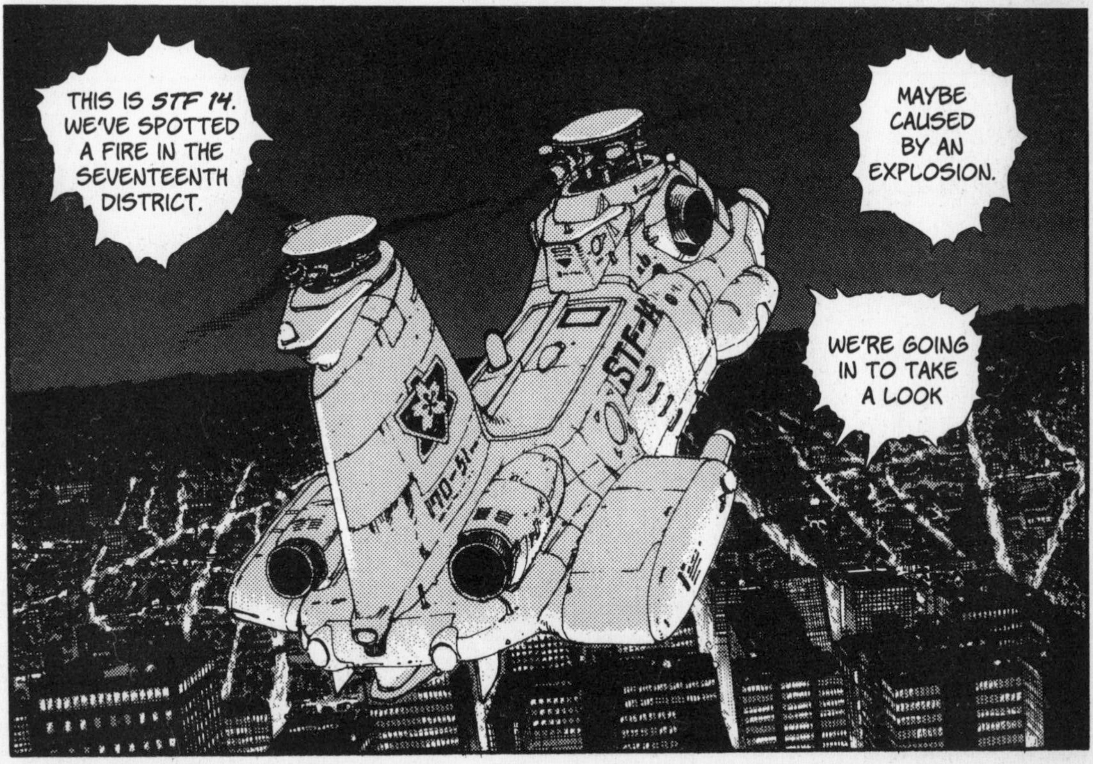
THIS IS STF 14. WE'VE SPOTTED A FIRE IN THE SEVENTEENTH DISTRICT.
MAYBE CAUSED BY AN EXPLOSION.
WE'RE GOING IN TO TAKE A LOOK
STF-14

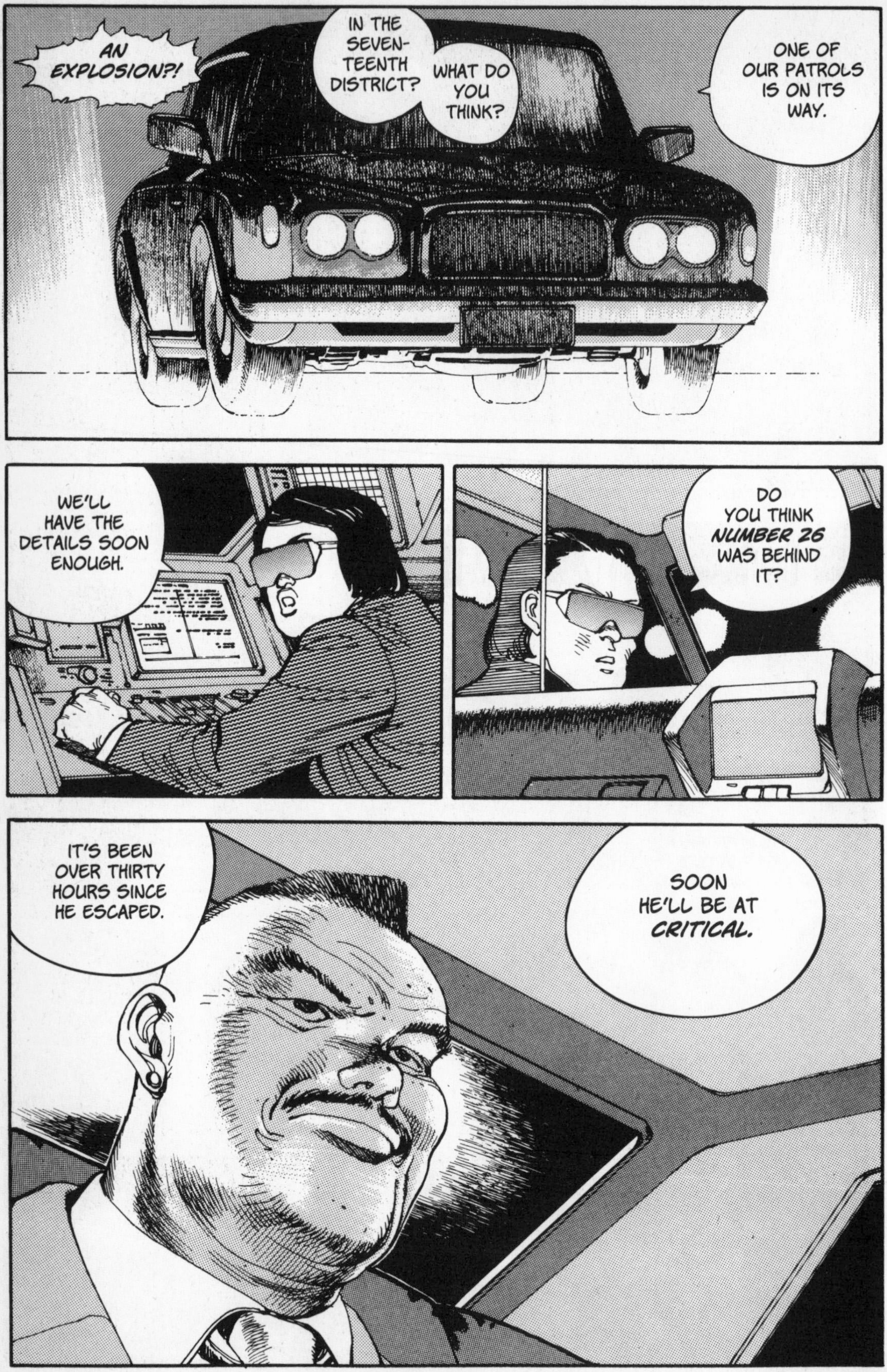
AN EXPLOSION?!
IN THE SEVEN-TEENTH DISTRICT?
WHAT DO YOU THINK?
ONE OF OUR PATROLS IS ON ITS WAY.
WE'LL HAVE THE DETAILS SOON ENOUGH.
DO YOU THINK *NUMBER 26* WAS BEHIND IT?
IT'S BEEN OVER THIRTY HOURS SINCE HE ESCAPED.
SOON HE'LL BE AT *CRITICAL.*

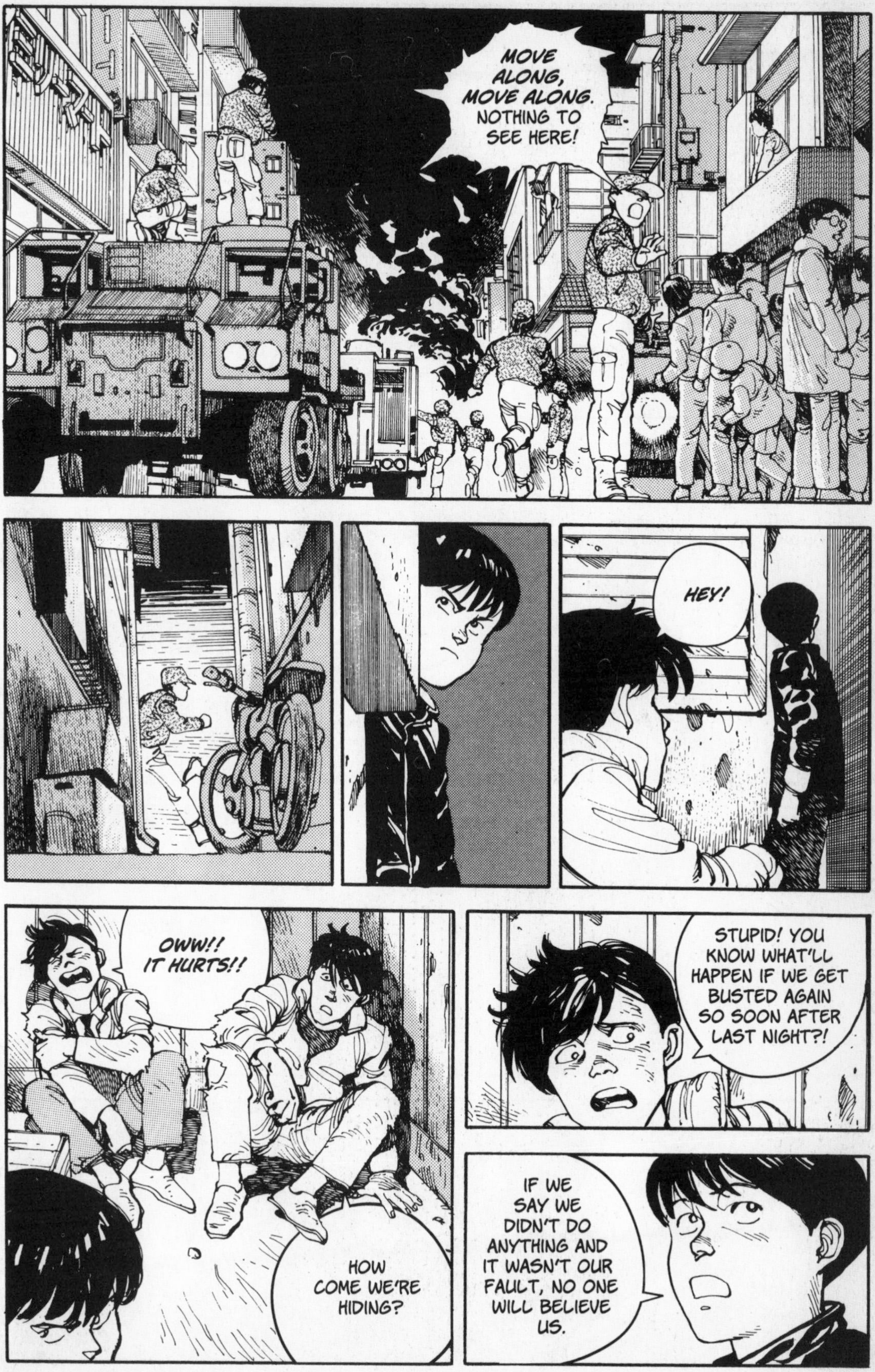
MOVE ALONG, MOVE ALONG. NOTHING TO SEE HERE!
HEY!
OWW!! IT HURTS!!
HOW COME WE'RE HIDING?
STUPID! YOU KNOW WHAT'LL HAPPEN IF WE GET BUSTED AGAIN SO SOON AFTER LAST NIGHT?!
IF WE SAY WE DIDN'T DO ANYTHING AND IT WASN'T OUR FAULT, NO ONE WILL BELIEVE US.

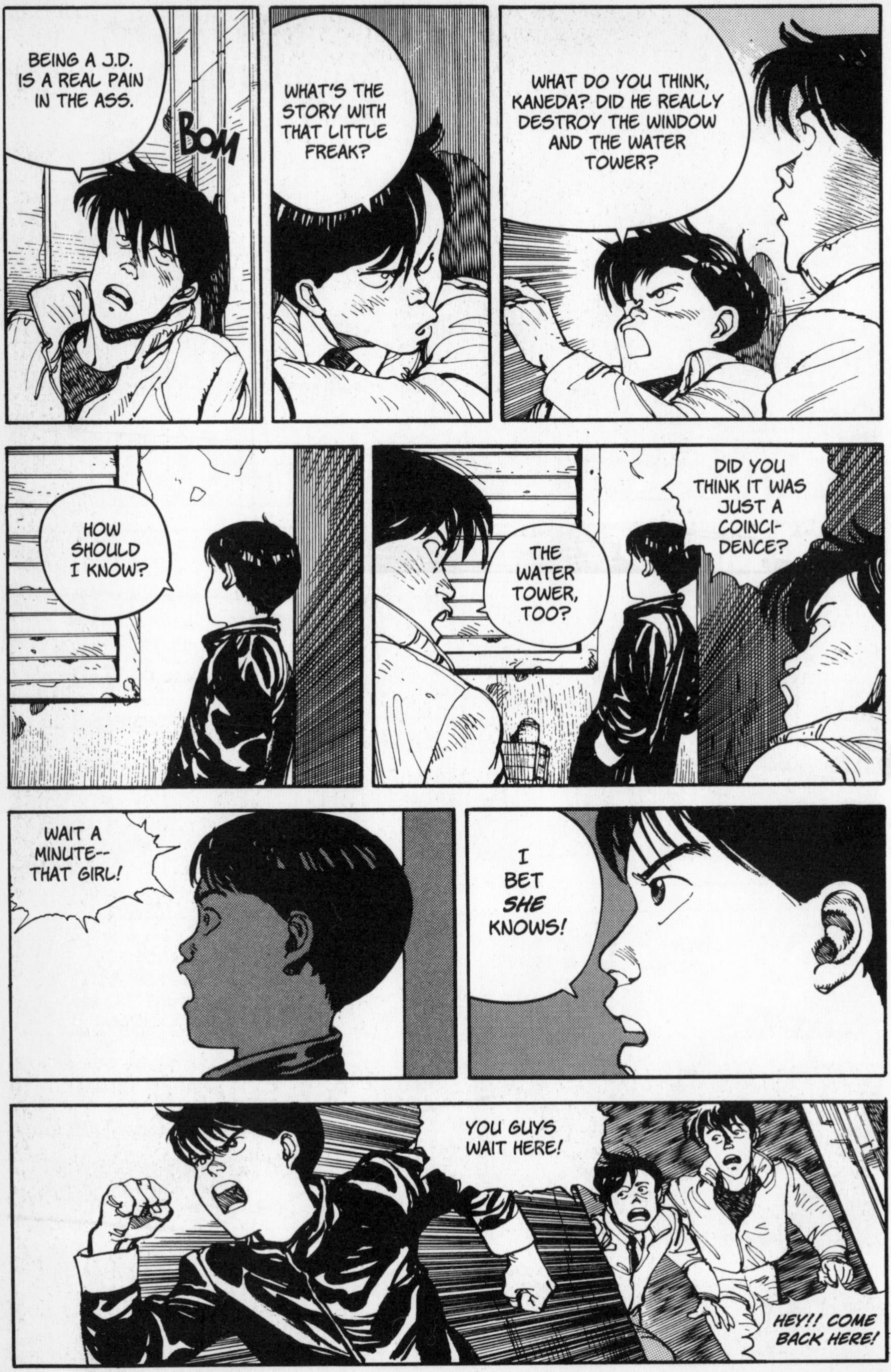
BEING A J.D. IS A REAL PAIN IN THE ASS.
BOM
WHAT'S THE STORY WITH THAT LITTLE FREAK?
WHAT DO YOU THINK, KANEDA? DID HE REALLY DESTROY THE WINDOW AND THE WATER TOWER?
HOW SHOULD I KNOW?
THE WATER TOWER, TOO?
DID YOU THINK IT WAS JUST A COINCI-DENCE?
WAIT A MINUTE-- THAT GIRL!
I BET *SHE* KNOWS!
YOU GUYS WAIT HERE!
HEY!! COME BACK HERE!

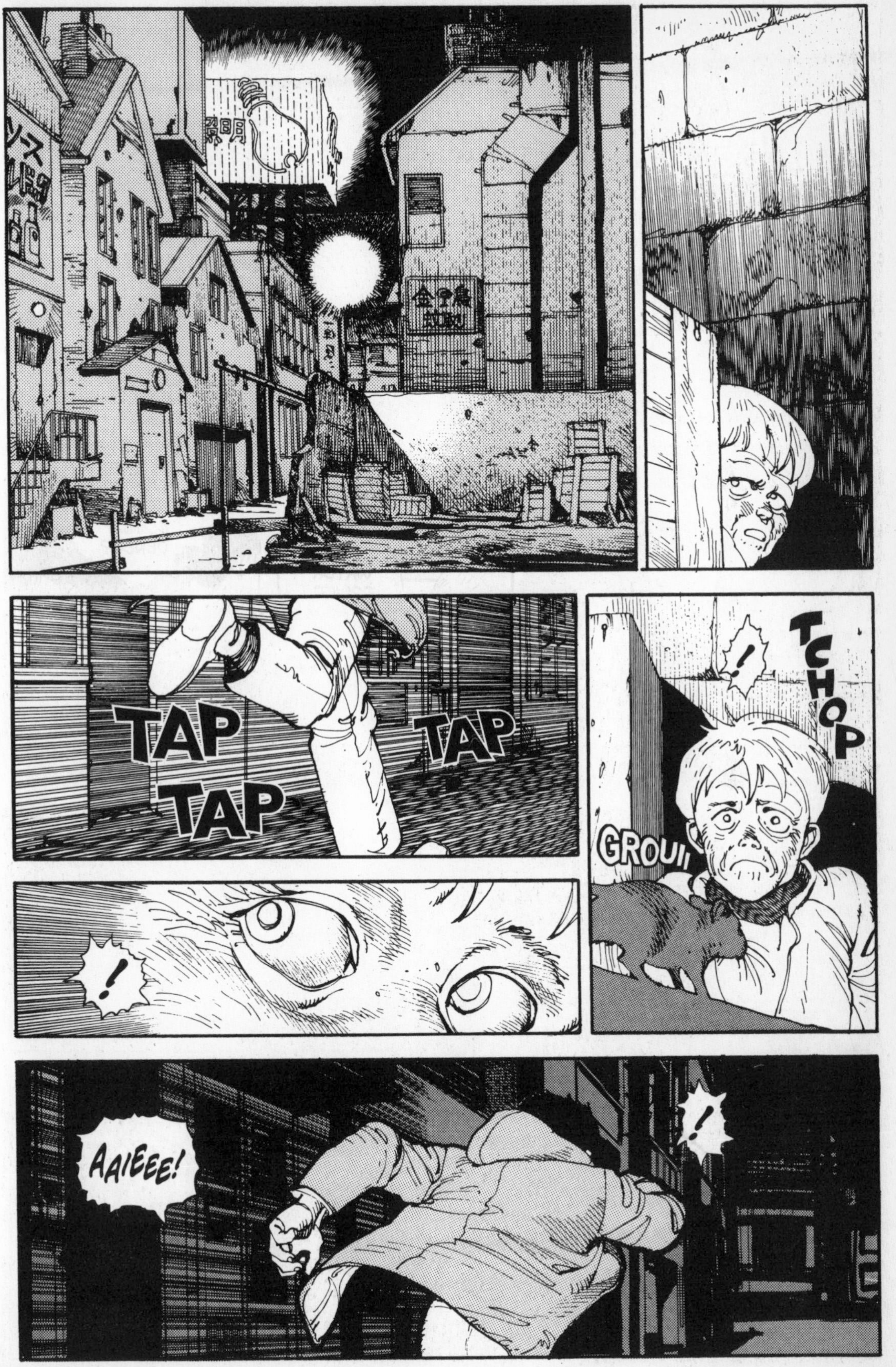
TAP
TAP
TAP
!
!
TCHOP
GROUII
AAIEEE!
!

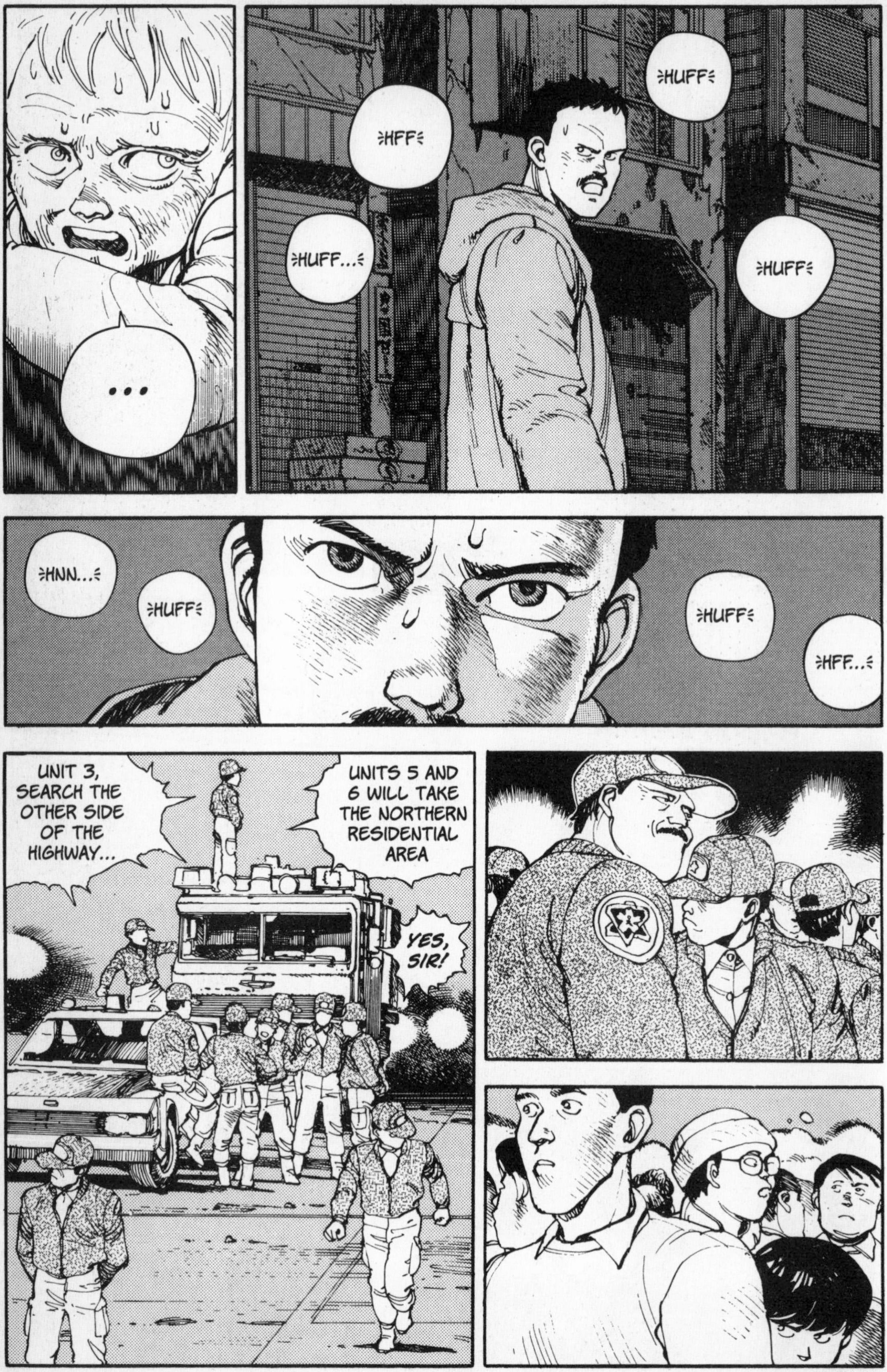
...
⋛HFF⋚
⋛HUFF...⋚
⋛HUFF⋚
⋛HUFF⋚
⋛HNN...⋚
⋛HUFF⋚
⋛HUFF⋚
⋛HFF...⋚
UNIT 3, SEARCH THE OTHER SIDE OF THE HIGHWAY...
UNITS 5 AND 6 WILL TAKE THE NORTHERN RESIDENTIAL AREA
YES, SIR!

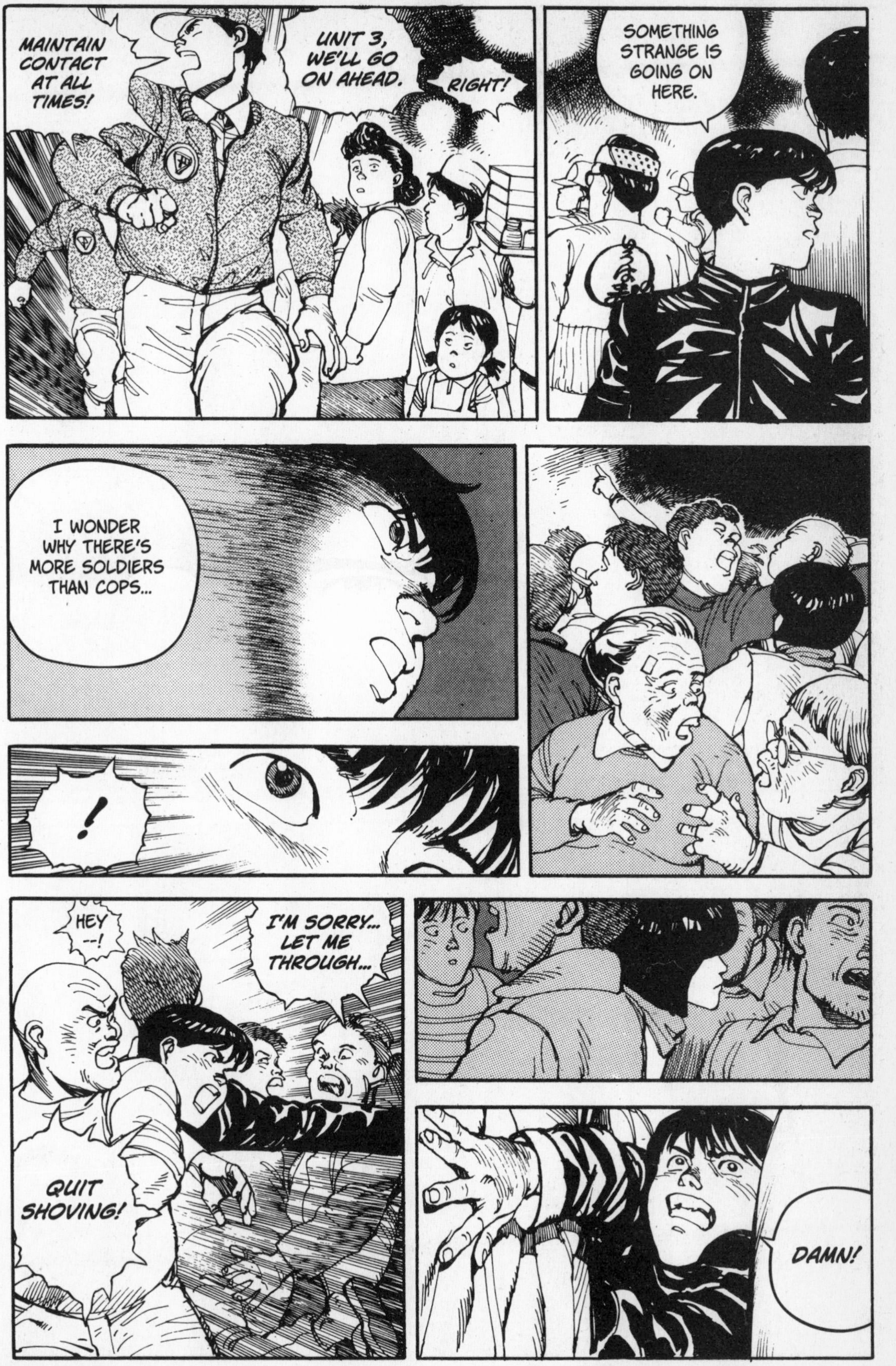
MAINTAIN CONTACT AT ALL TIMES!
UNIT 3, WE'LL GO ON AHEAD.
RIGHT!
SOMETHING STRANGE IS GOING ON HERE.
I WONDER WHY THERE'S MORE SOLDIERS THAN COPS...
!
HEY --!
I'M SORRY... LET ME THROUGH...
QUIT SHOVING!
DAMN!

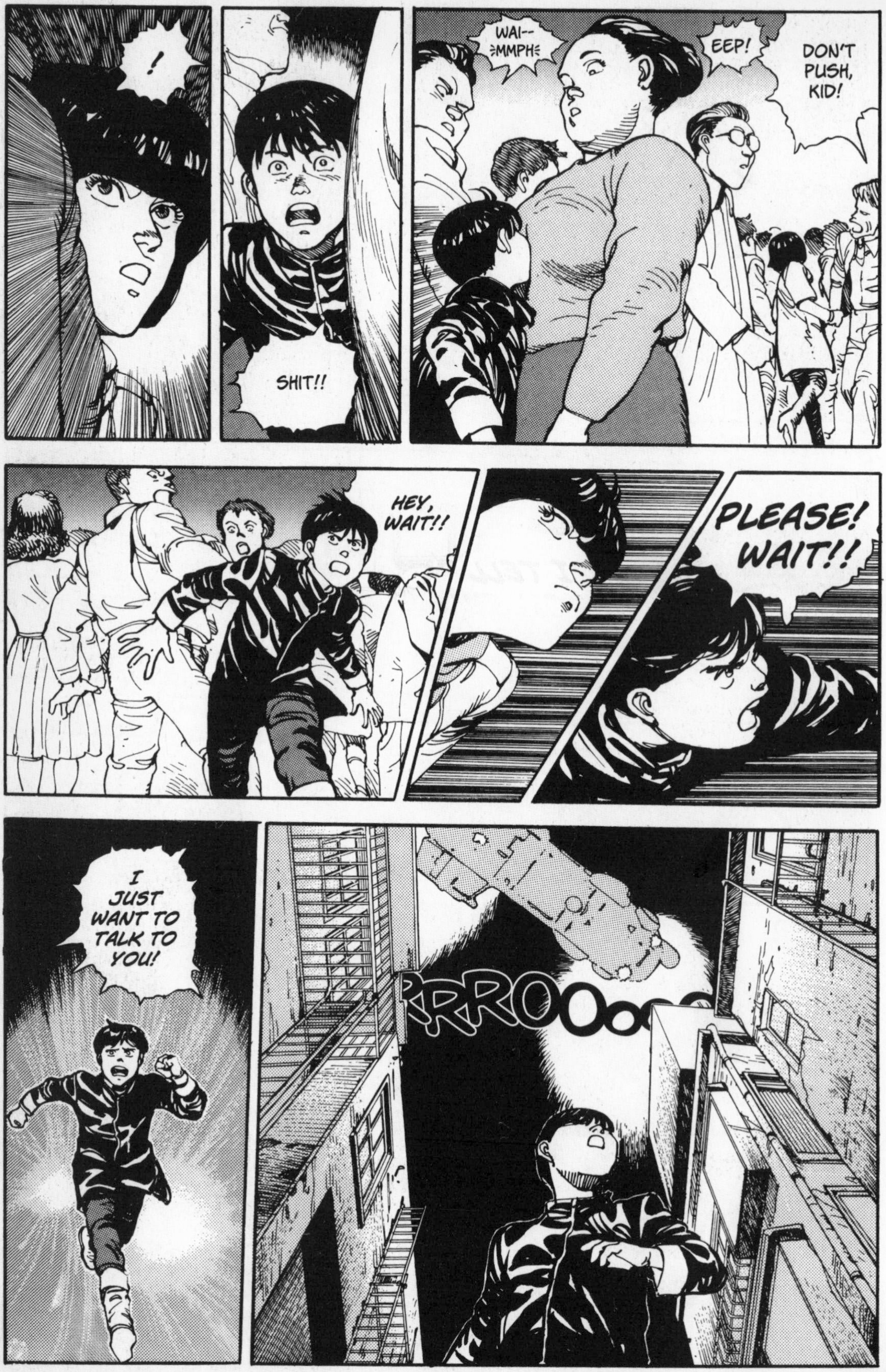
!
SHIT!!
WAI-- MMPH
EEP!
DON'T PUSH, KID!
HEY, WAIT!!
PLEASE! WAIT!!
I JUST WANT TO TALK TO YOU!
RRROO...

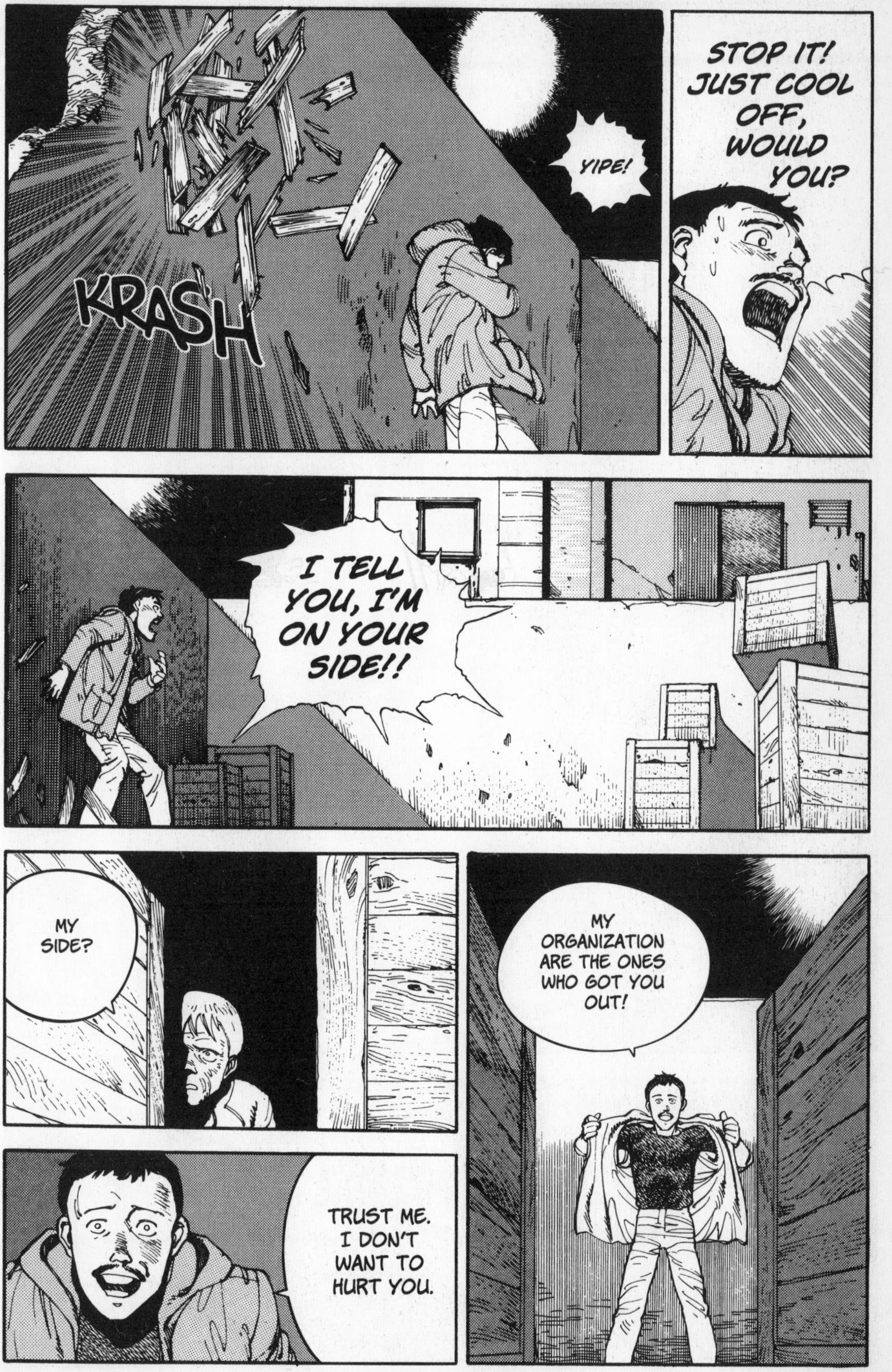
KRASH
YIPE!
STOP IT! JUST COOL OFF, WOULD YOU?
I TELL YOU, I'M ON YOUR SIDE!!
MY SIDE?
MY ORGANIZATION ARE THE ONES WHO GOT YOU OUT!
TRUST ME. I DON'T WANT TO HURT YOU.

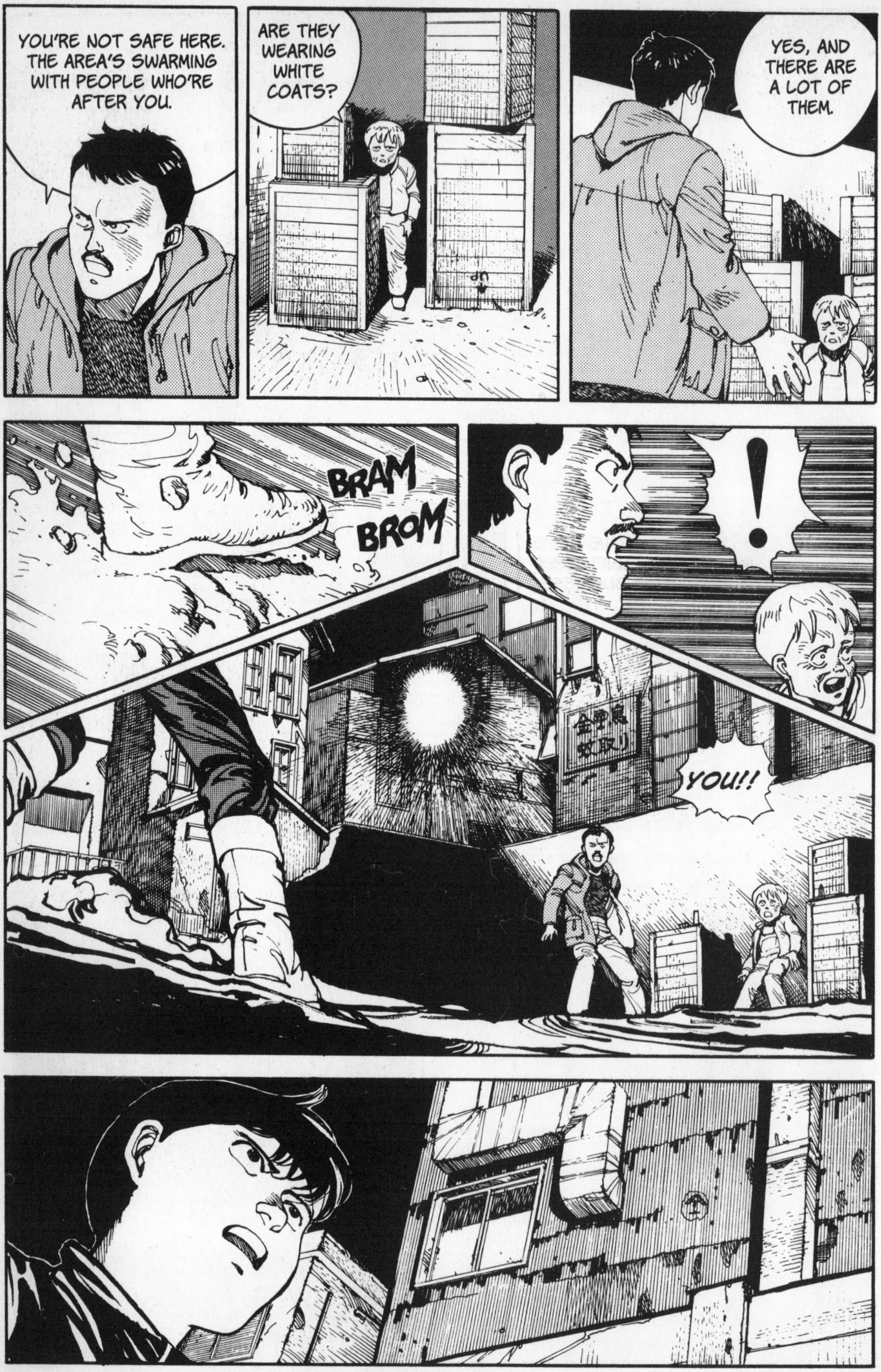
YOU'RE NOT SAFE HERE. THE AREA'S SWARMING WITH PEOPLE WHO'RE AFTER YOU.
ARE THEY WEARING WHITE COATS?
YES, AND THERE ARE A LOT OF THEM.
BRAM
BROM
!
YOU!!

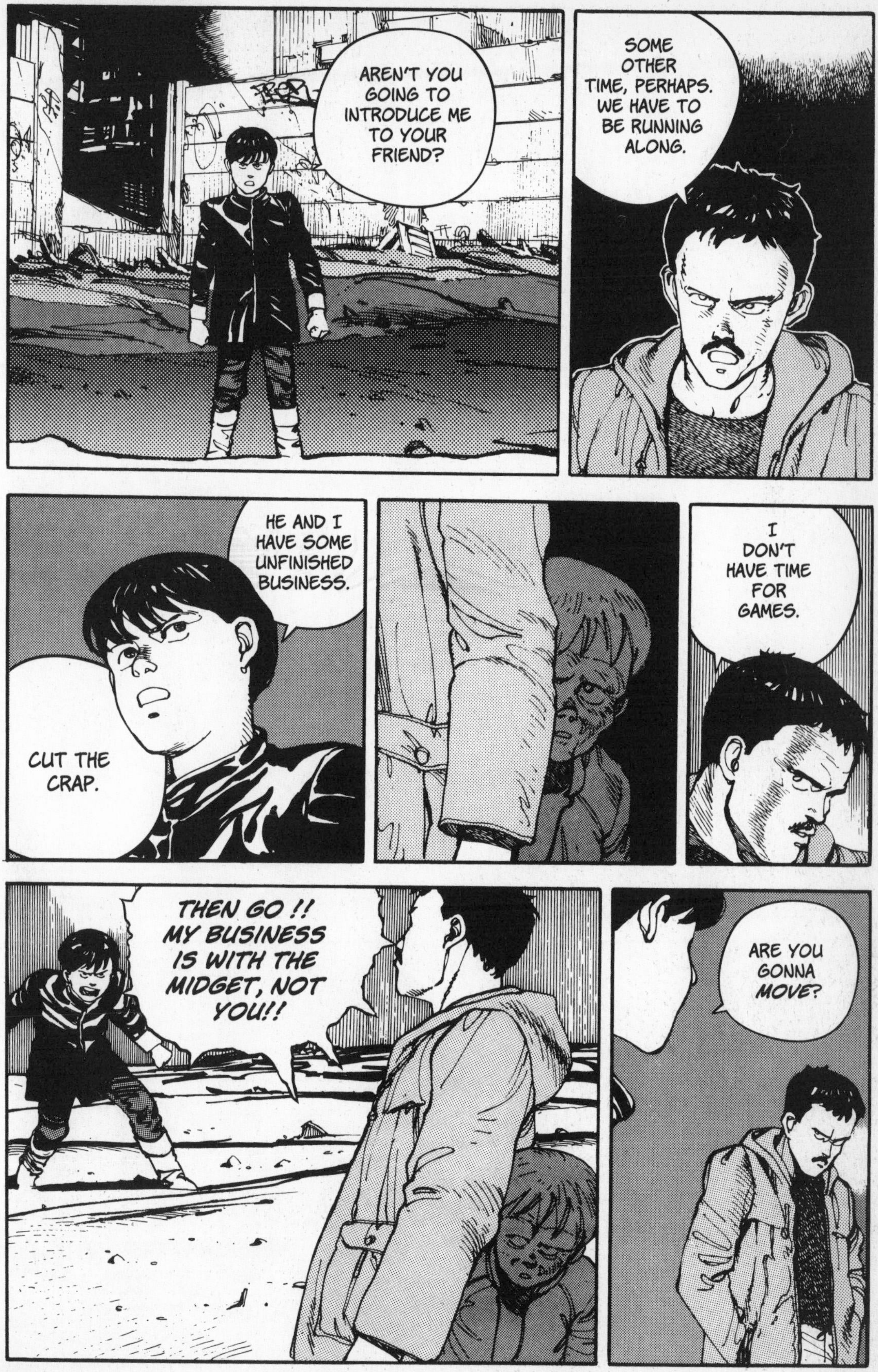
AREN'T YOU GOING TO INTRODUCE ME TO YOUR FRIEND?
SOME OTHER TIME, PERHAPS. WE HAVE TO BE RUNNING ALONG.
HE AND I HAVE SOME UNFINISHED BUSINESS.
CUT THE CRAP.
I DON'T HAVE TIME FOR GAMES.
THEN GO !! MY BUSINESS IS WITH THE MIDGET, NOT YOU!!
ARE YOU GONNA MOVE?

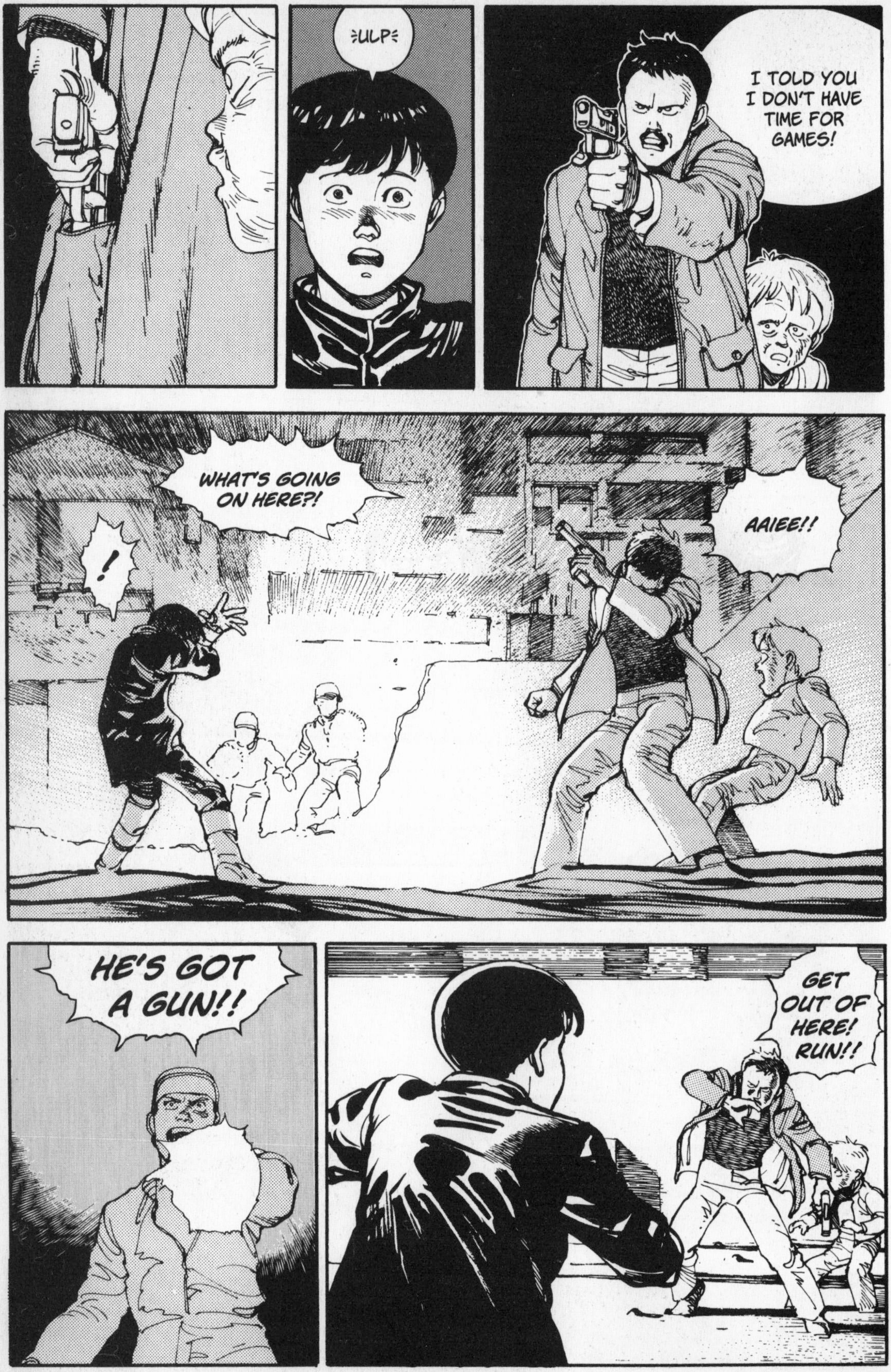

ULP
I TOLD YOU I DON'T HAVE TIME FOR GAMES!
WHAT'S GOING ON HERE?!
!
AAIEE!!
HE'S GOT A GUN!!
GET OUT OF HERE! RUN!!

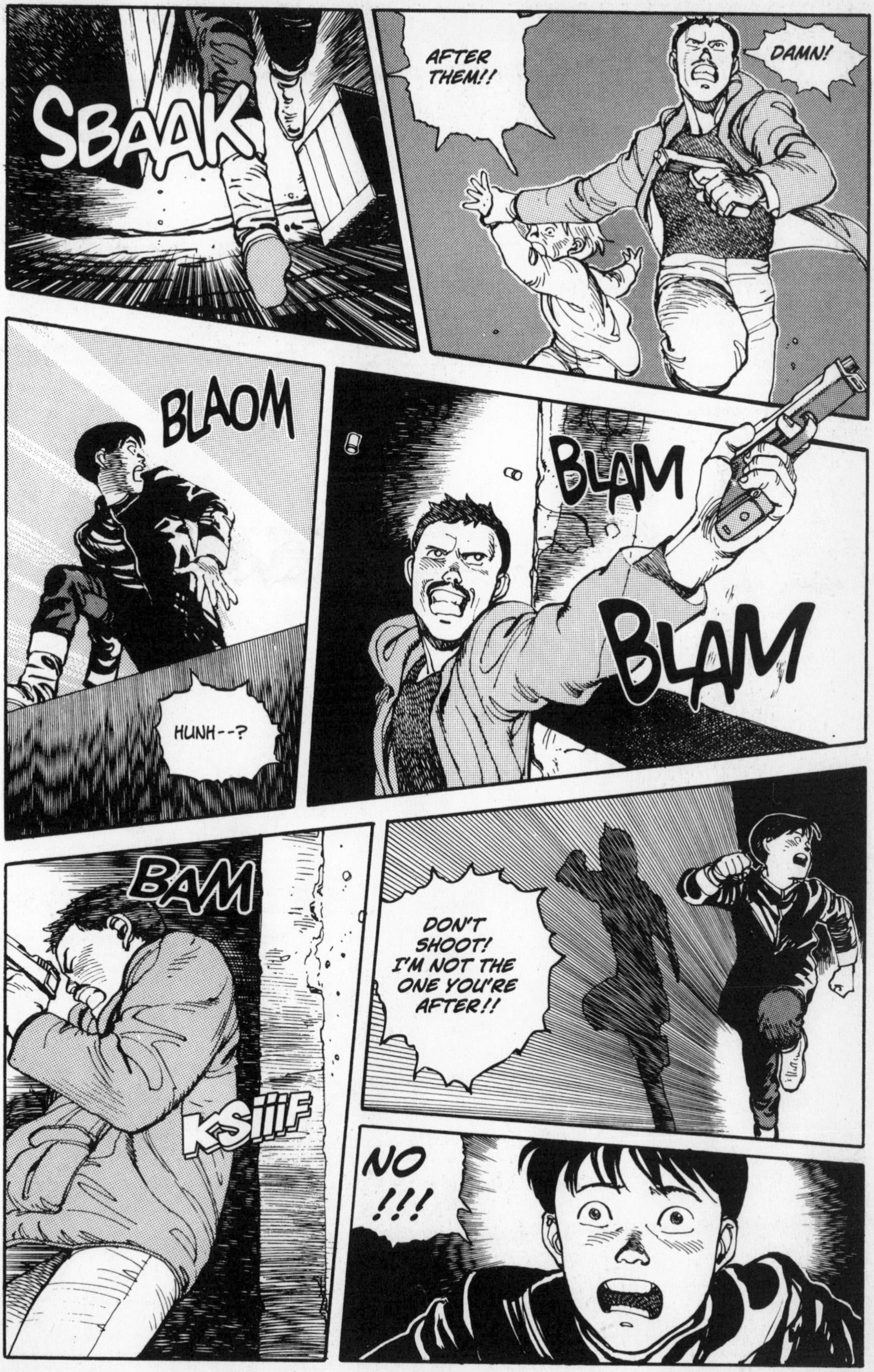
SBAAK
AFTER THEM!!
DAMN!
BLAOM
HUNH--?
BLAM
BLAM
BAM
KSiiiF
DON'T SHOOT! I'M NOT THE ONE YOU'RE AFTER!!
NO !!!

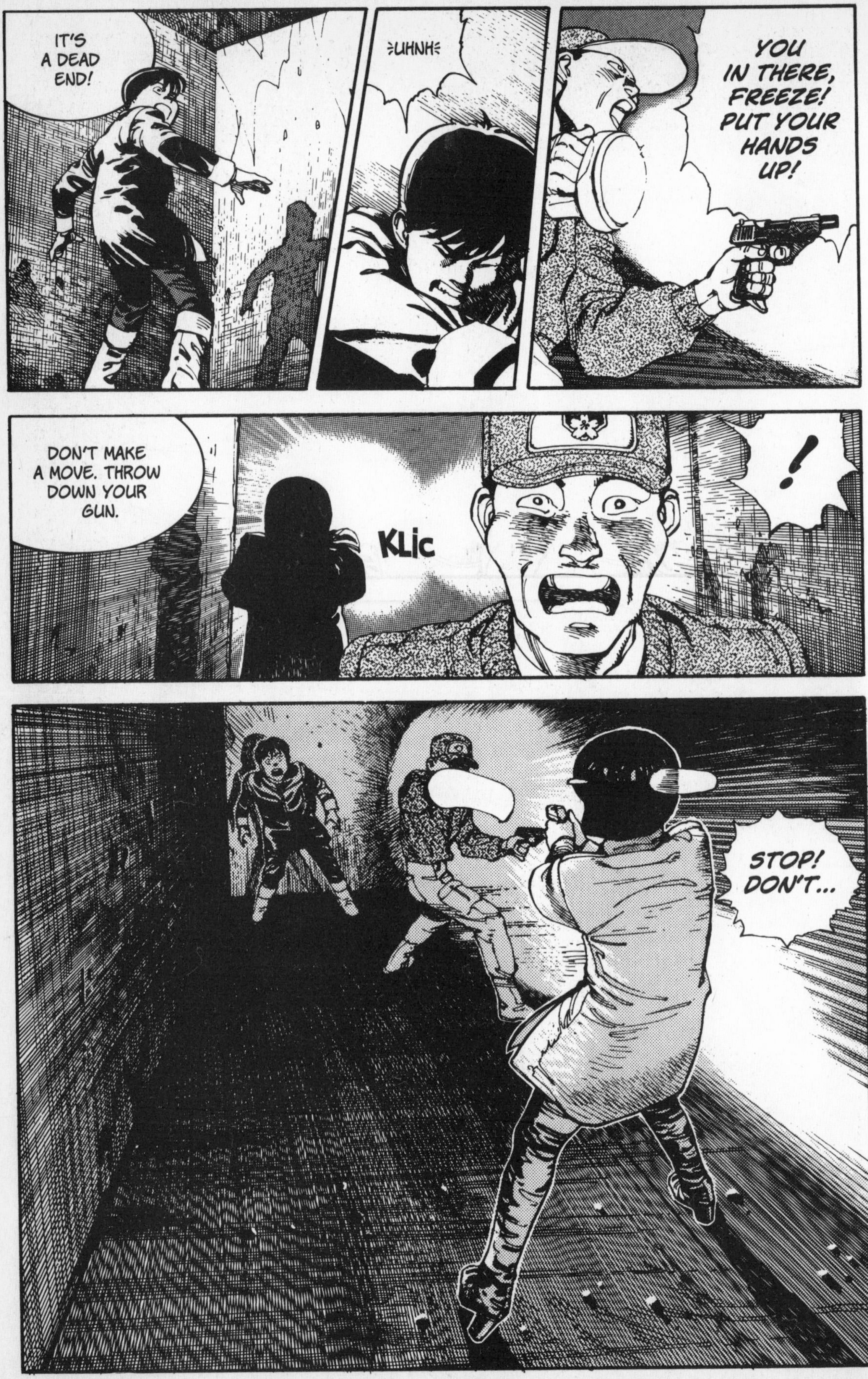
IT'S A DEAD END!
≑UHNH≑
YOU IN THERE, FREEZE! PUT YOUR HANDS UP!
DON'T MAKE A MOVE. THROW DOWN YOUR GUN.
KLIC
!
STOP! DON'T...

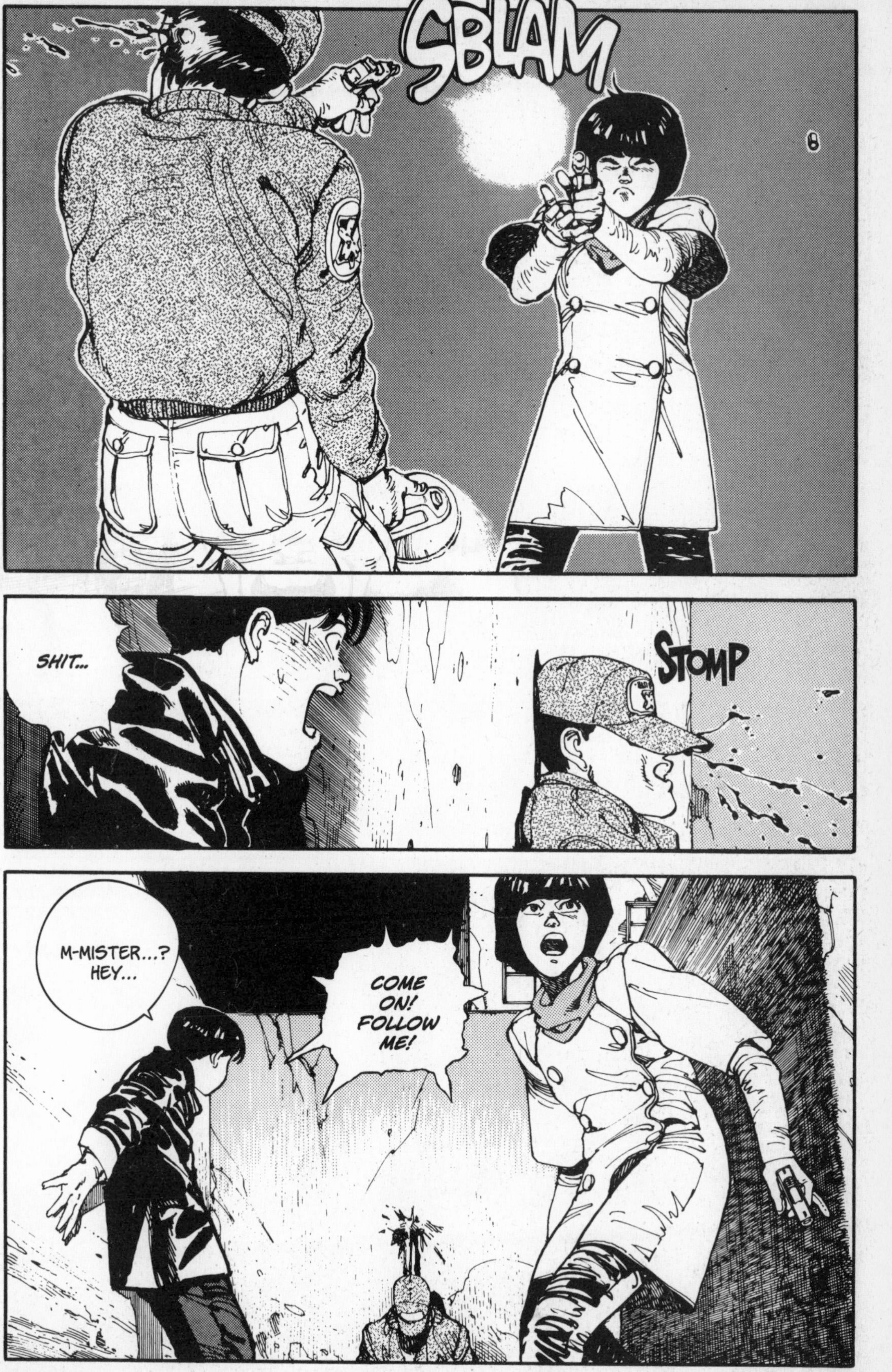

SBLAM
SHIT...
STOMP
M-MISTER...? HEY...
COME ON! FOLLOW ME!

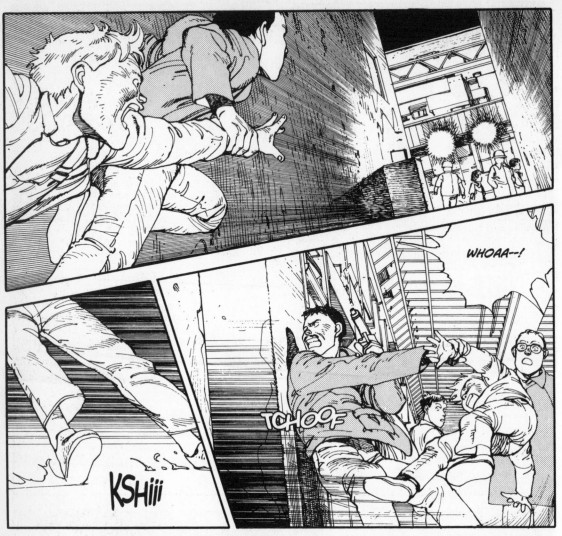

WHOAA--!

KSHiii

TCHOOF

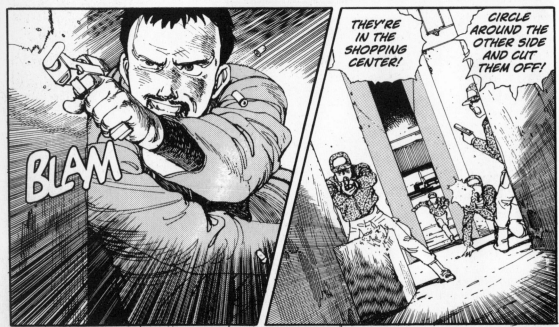

BLAM

THEY'RE IN THE SHOPPING CENTER!

CIRCLE AROUND THE OTHER SIDE AND CUT THEM OFF!

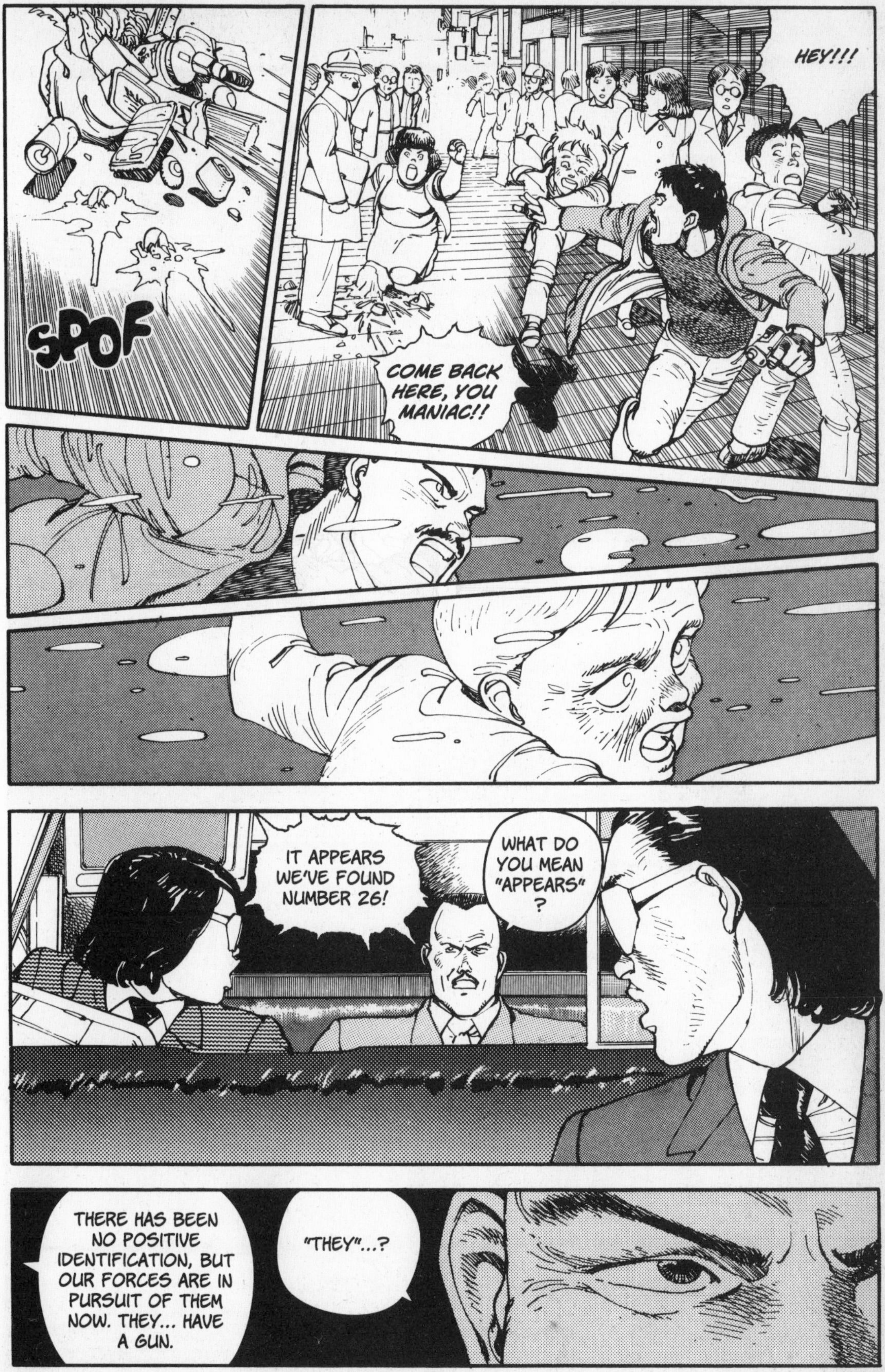
SPOF
HEY!!!
COME BACK HERE, YOU MANIAC!!
IT APPEARS WE'VE FOUND NUMBER 26!
WHAT DO YOU MEAN "APPEARS" ?
THERE HAS BEEN NO POSITIVE IDENTIFICATION, BUT OUR FORCES ARE IN PURSUIT OF THEM NOW. THEY... HAVE A GUN.
"THEY"...?

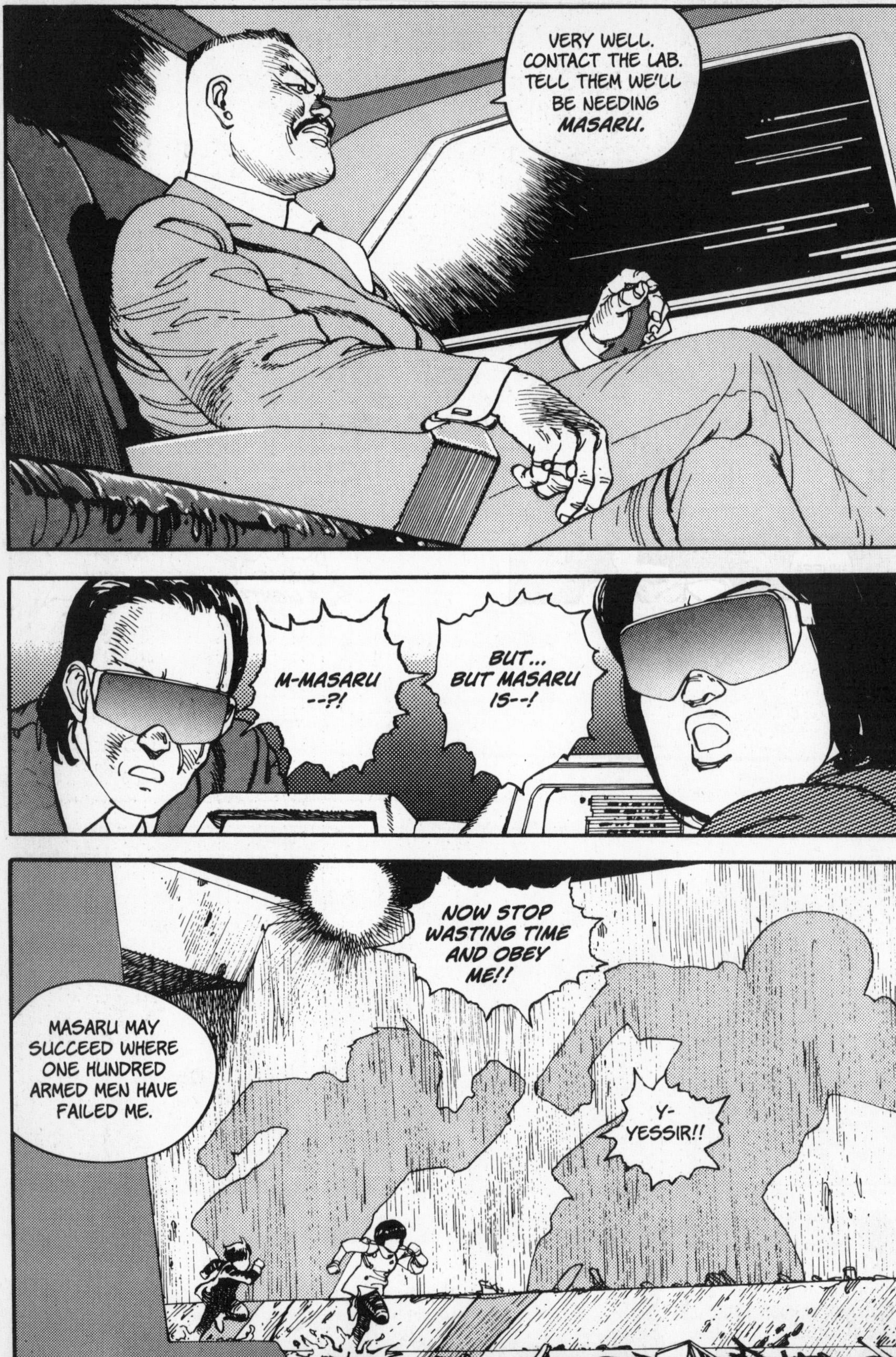
VERY WELL. CONTACT THE LAB. TELL THEM WE'LL BE NEEDING MASARU.
M-MASARU --?!
BUT... BUT MASARU IS--!
MASARU MAY SUCCEED WHERE ONE HUNDRED ARMED MEN HAVE FAILED ME.
NOW STOP WASTING TIME AND OBEY ME!!
Y-YESSIR!!

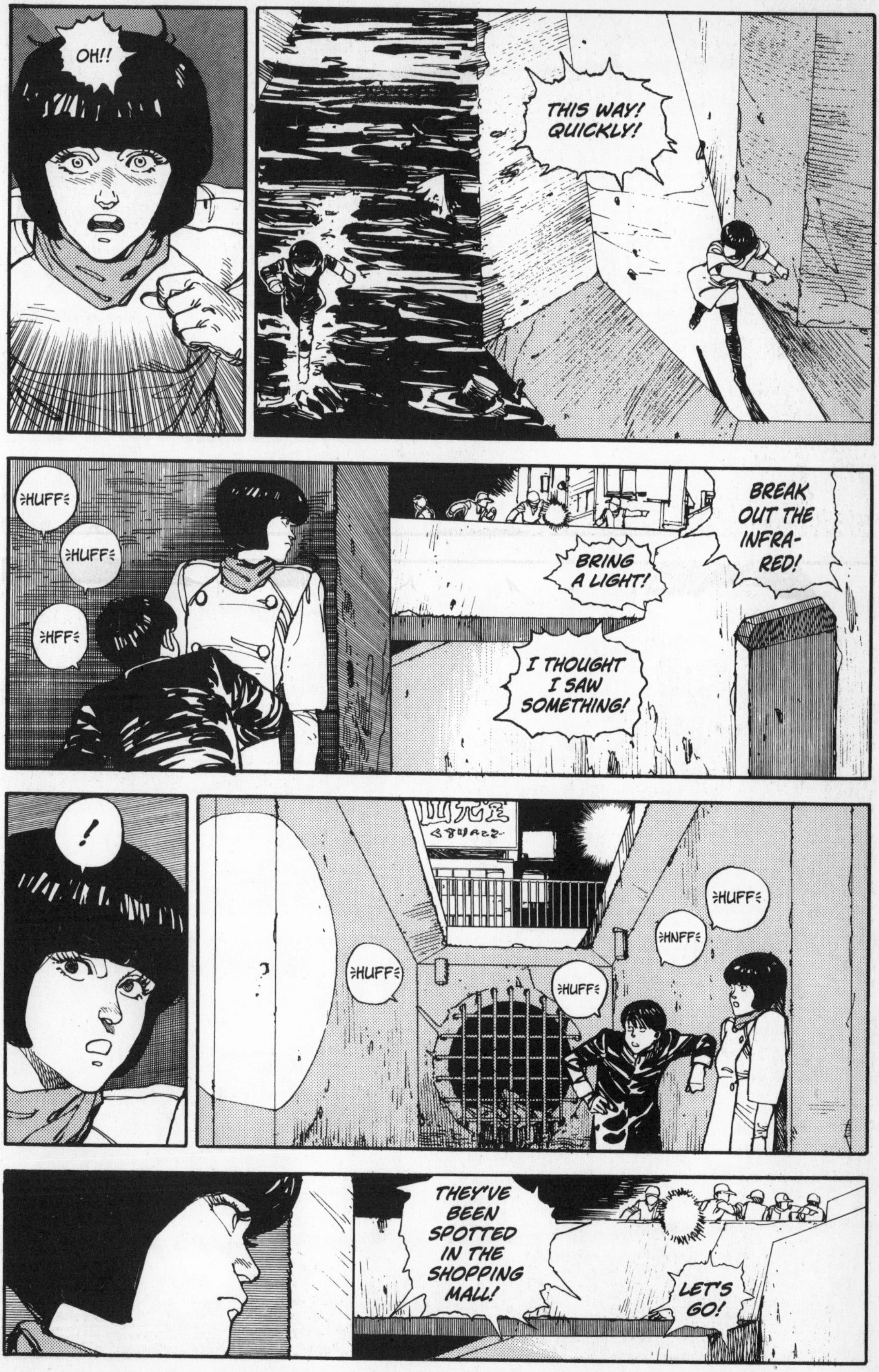
OH!!
THIS WAY! QUICKLY!
HUFF
HUFF
HFF
BREAK OUT THE INFRA-RED!
BRING A LIGHT!
I THOUGHT I SAW SOMETHING!
!
HUFF
HNFF
HUFF
HUFF
THEY'VE BEEN SPOTTED IN THE SHOPPING MALL!
LET'S GO!

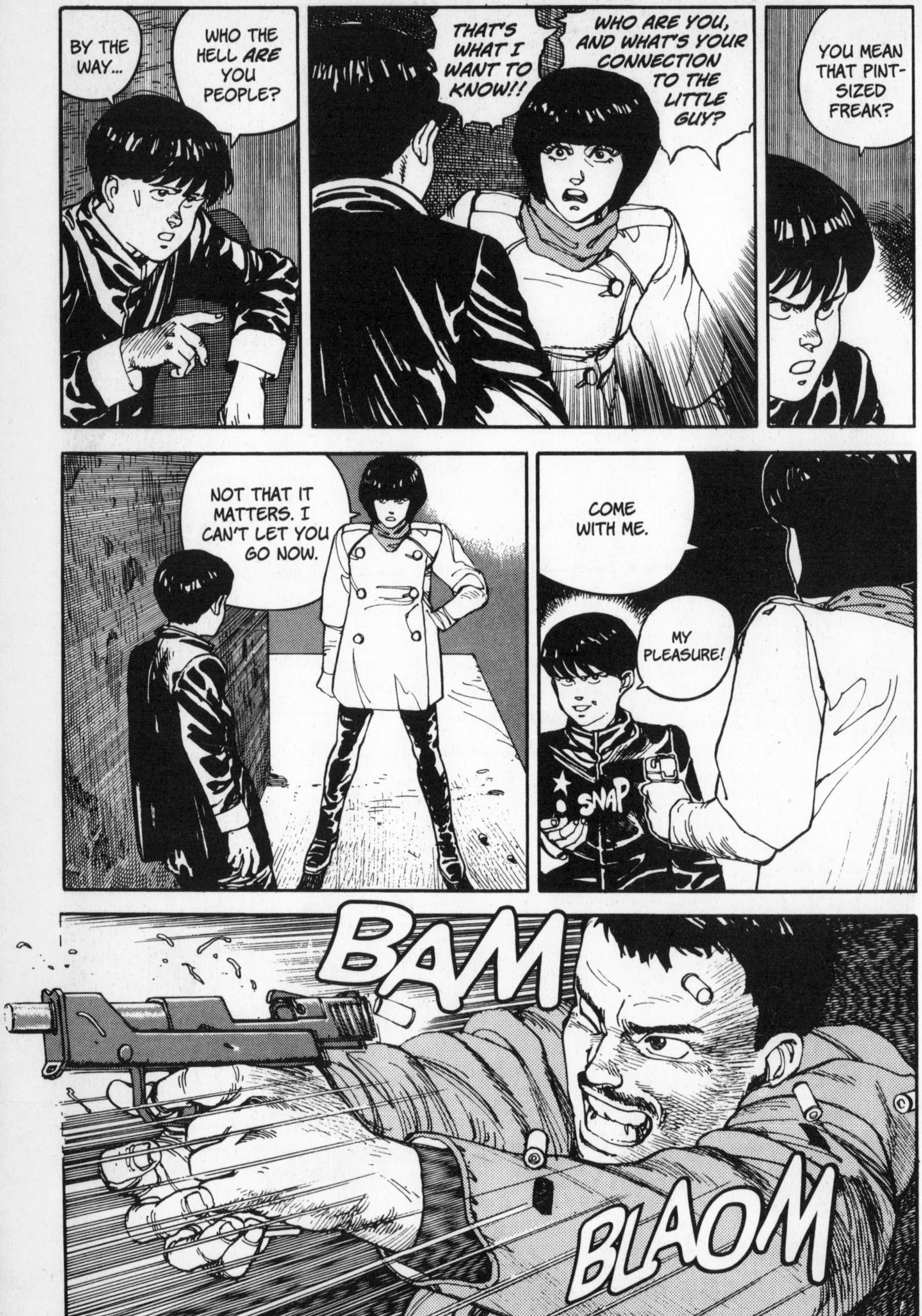
BY THE WAY...
WHO THE HELL ARE YOU PEOPLE?
THAT'S WHAT I WANT TO KNOW!!
WHO ARE YOU, AND WHAT'S YOUR CONNECTION TO THE LITTLE GUY?
YOU MEAN THAT PINT-SIZED FREAK?
NOT THAT IT MATTERS. I CAN'T LET YOU GO NOW.
COME WITH ME.
MY PLEASURE!
SNAP
BAM
BLAOM

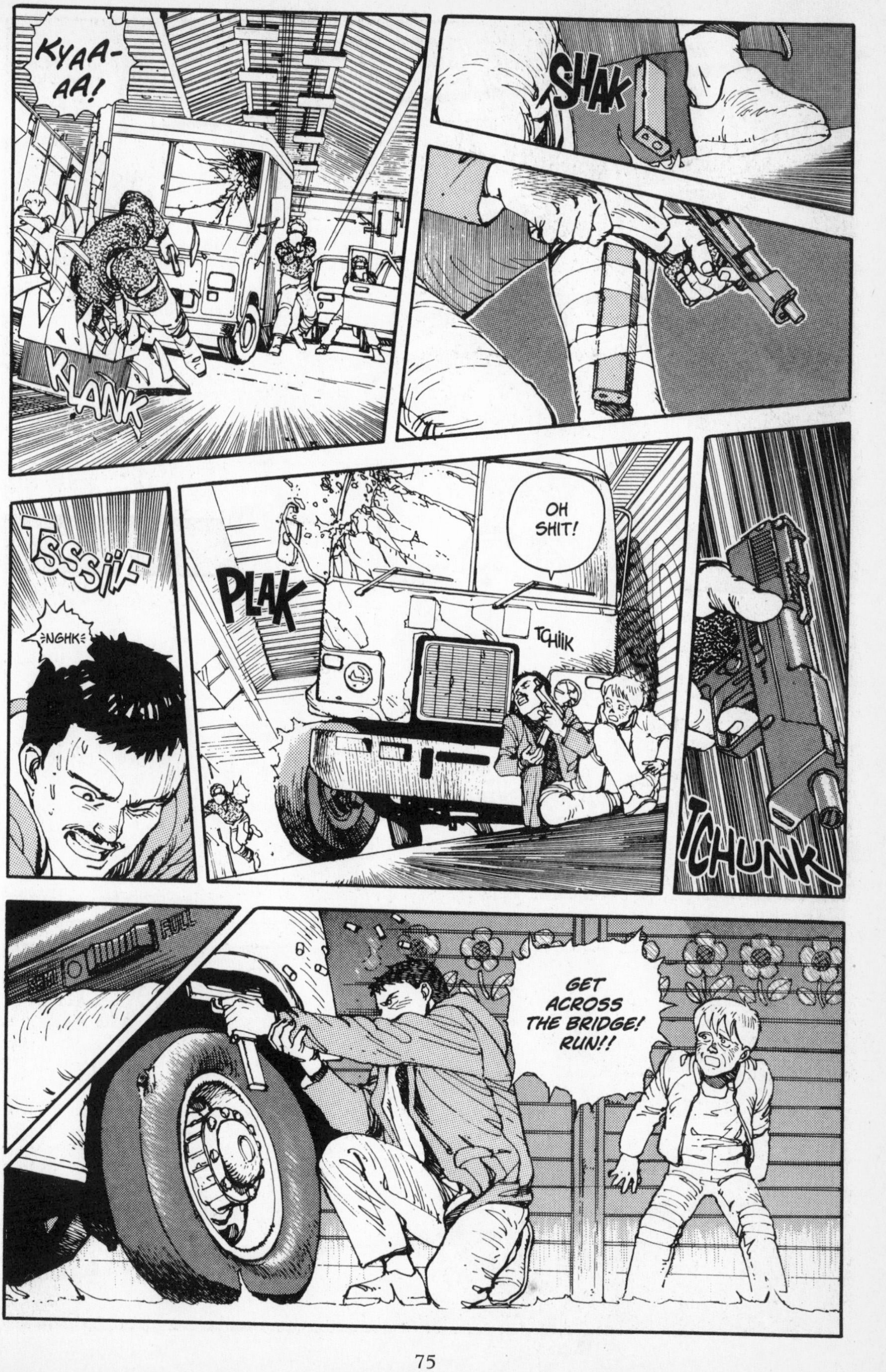
KYAAA-AA!
KLANK
SHAK
TSSSIIF
NGHK
PLAK
OH SHIT!
TCHIIK
TCHUNK
SEMI
FULL
GET ACROSS THE BRIDGE! RUN!!

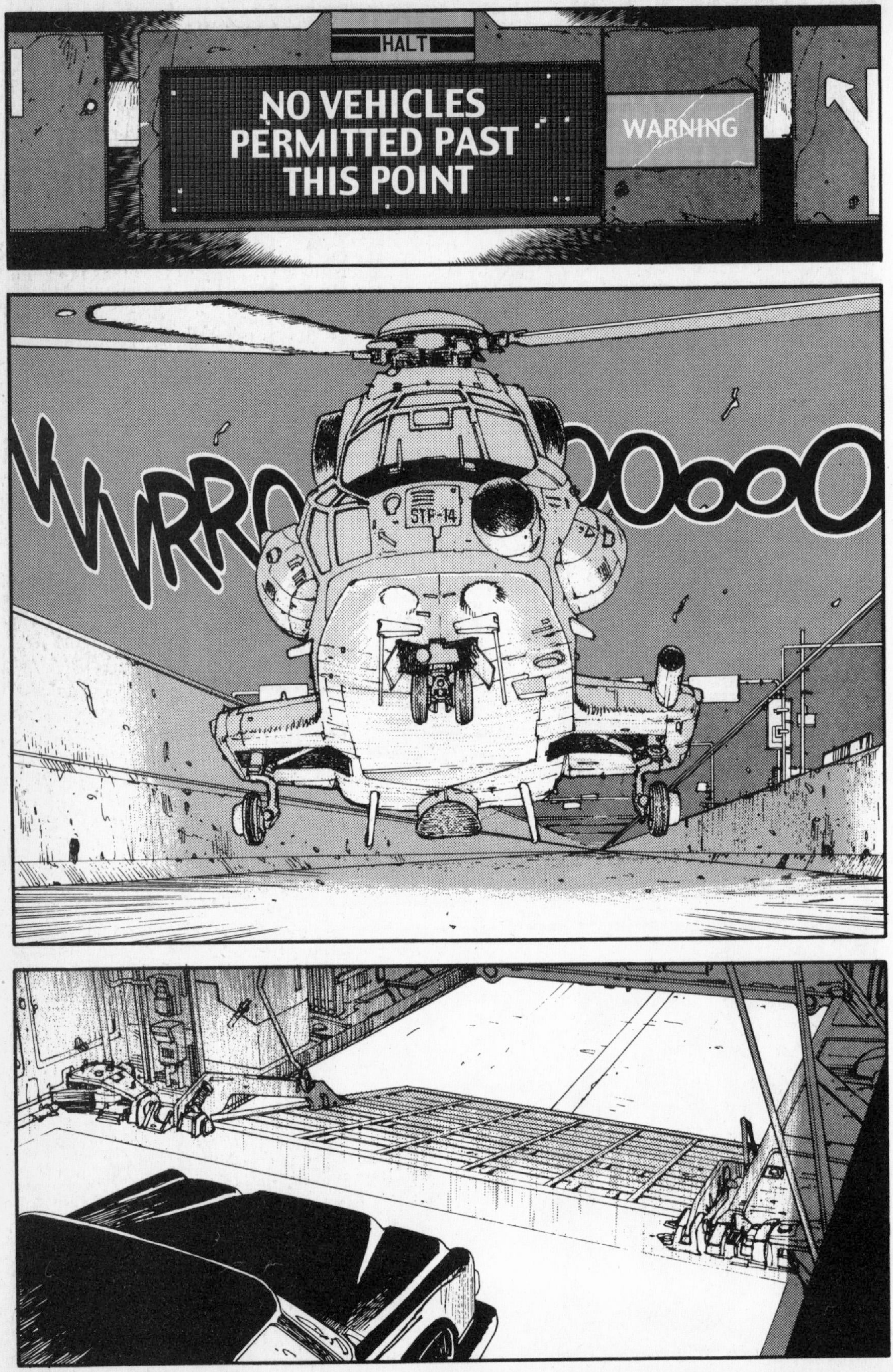
HALT
NO VEHICLES PERMITTED PAST THIS POINT
WARNING
VVVRROOOO0oooO
STP-14

WE'VE RECEIVED WORD HE'S PINNED DOWN BY THE CANAL IN THE EIGHTEENTH DISTRICT, SIR.

WHEN IS MASARU EXPECTED?

HIS *ETA* IS TWENTY MINUTES.

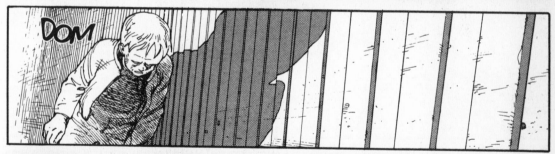

DOM

WHAT ARE YOU WAITING FOR?! GO!!

≥UHN≤

≥UHN≤

≥UHN≤

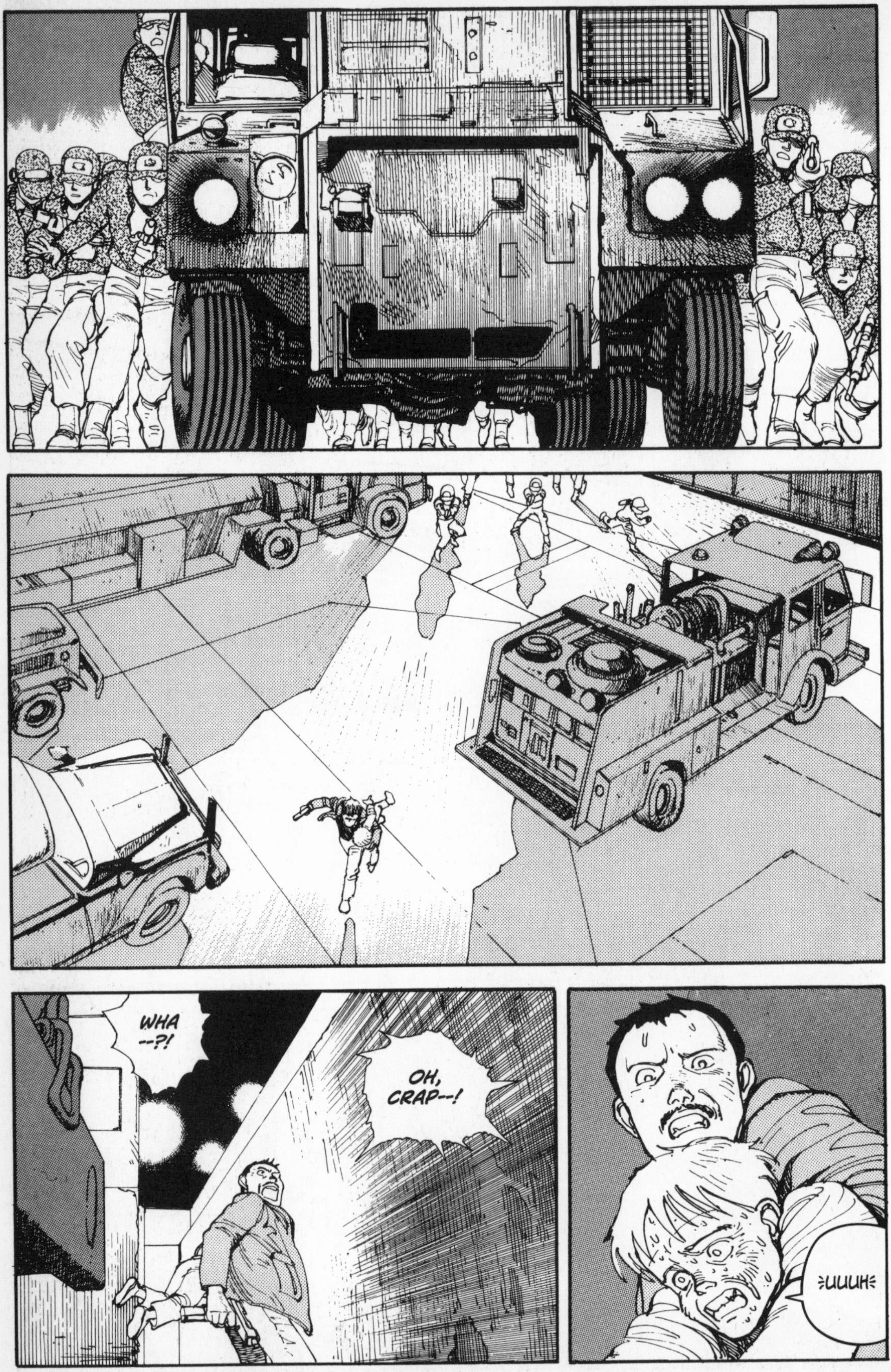
WHA --?!
OH, CRAP--!
≷UUUH≶

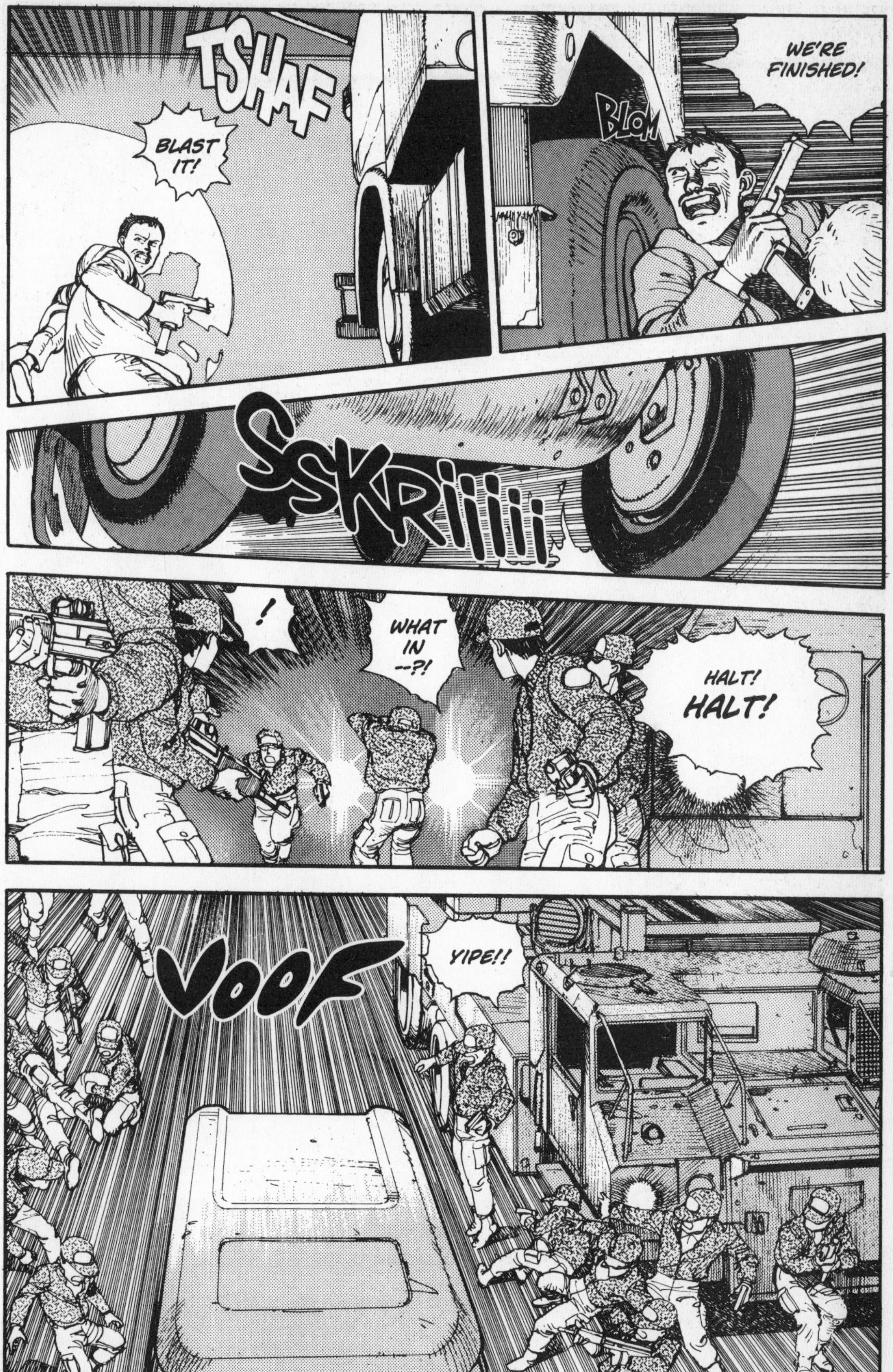
TSHAF
BLAST IT!
WE'RE FINISHED!
BLOM
SSKRiiiiii
!
WHAT IN --?!
HALT! HALT!
VOOF
YIPE!!

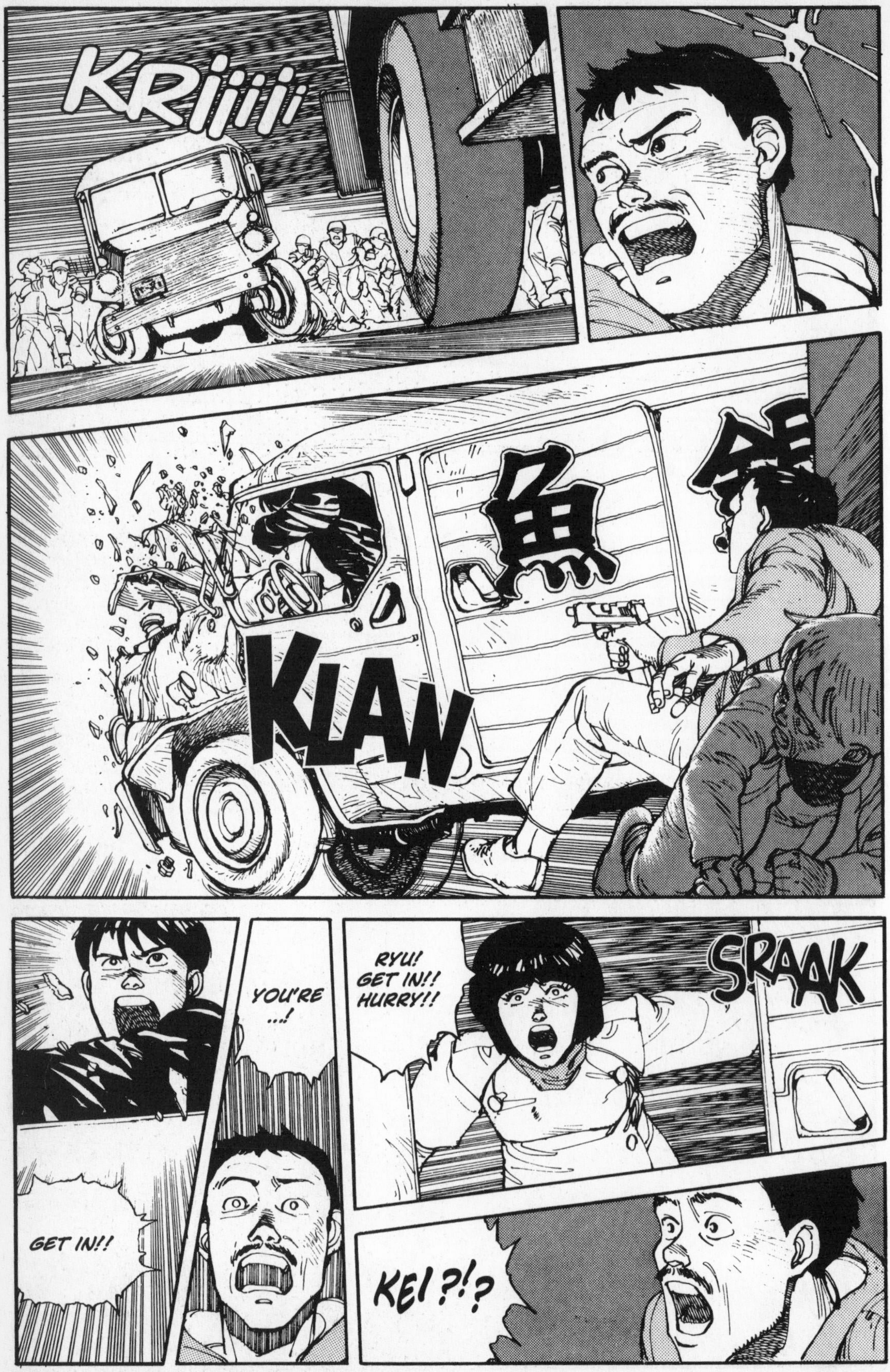
KRiiiii
魚
KLAN
YOU'RE ...!
RYU! GET IN!! HURRY!!
SRAAK
GET IN!!
KEI ?!?

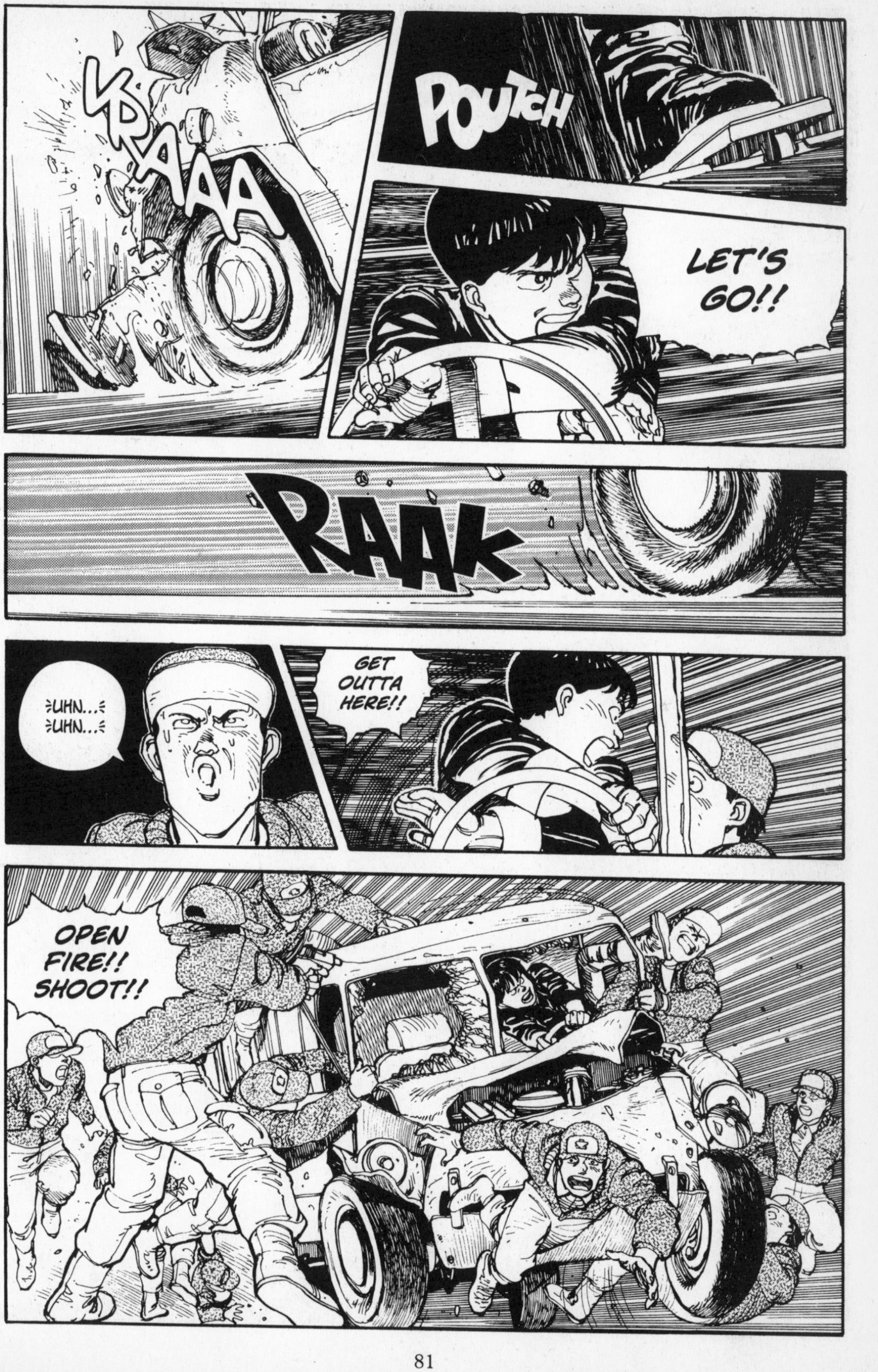
KRAAAA
POUTCH
LET'S GO!!
RAAK
UHN... UHN...
GET OUTTA HERE!!
OPEN FIRE!! SHOOT!!

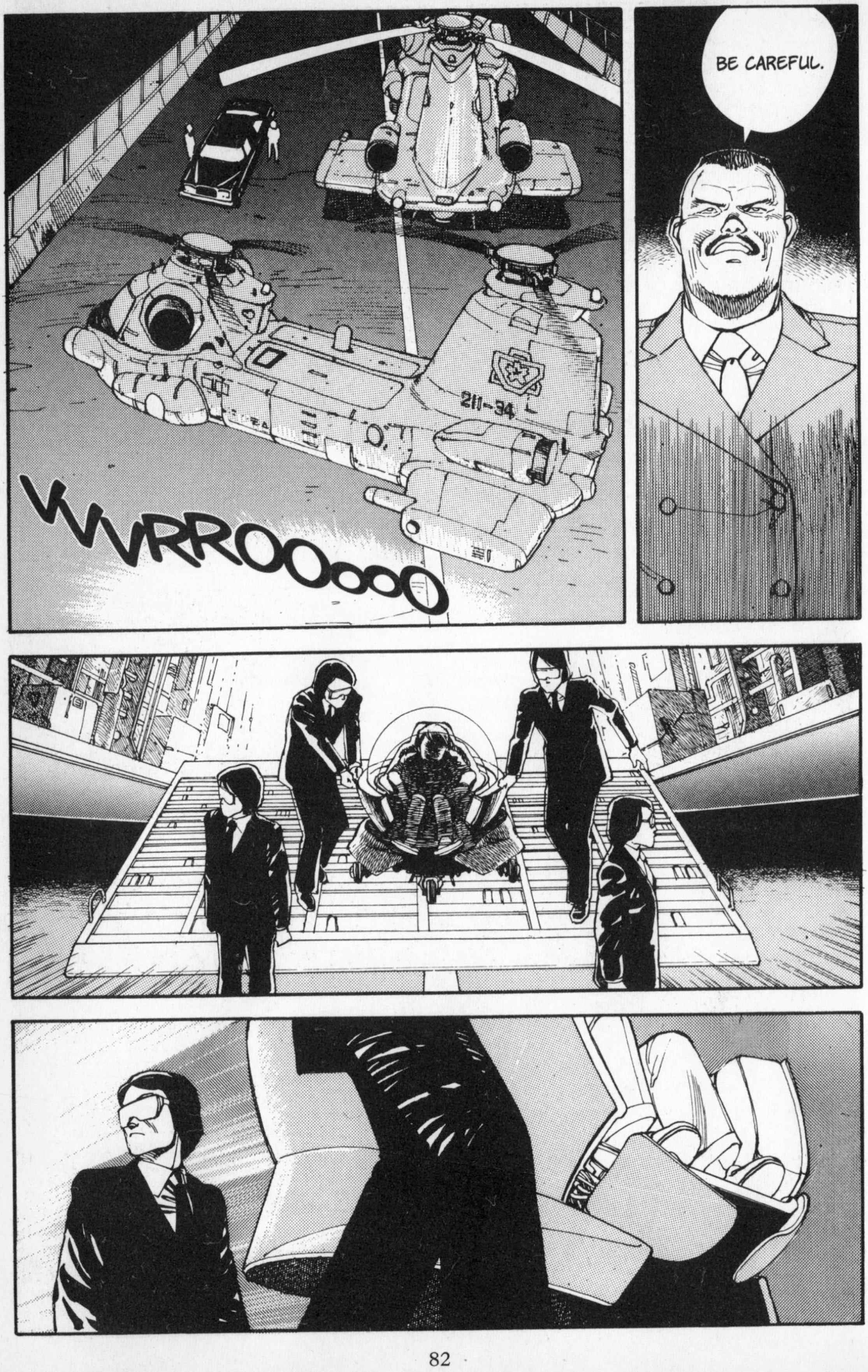
211-34
VVVRROOoooO
BE CAREFUL.

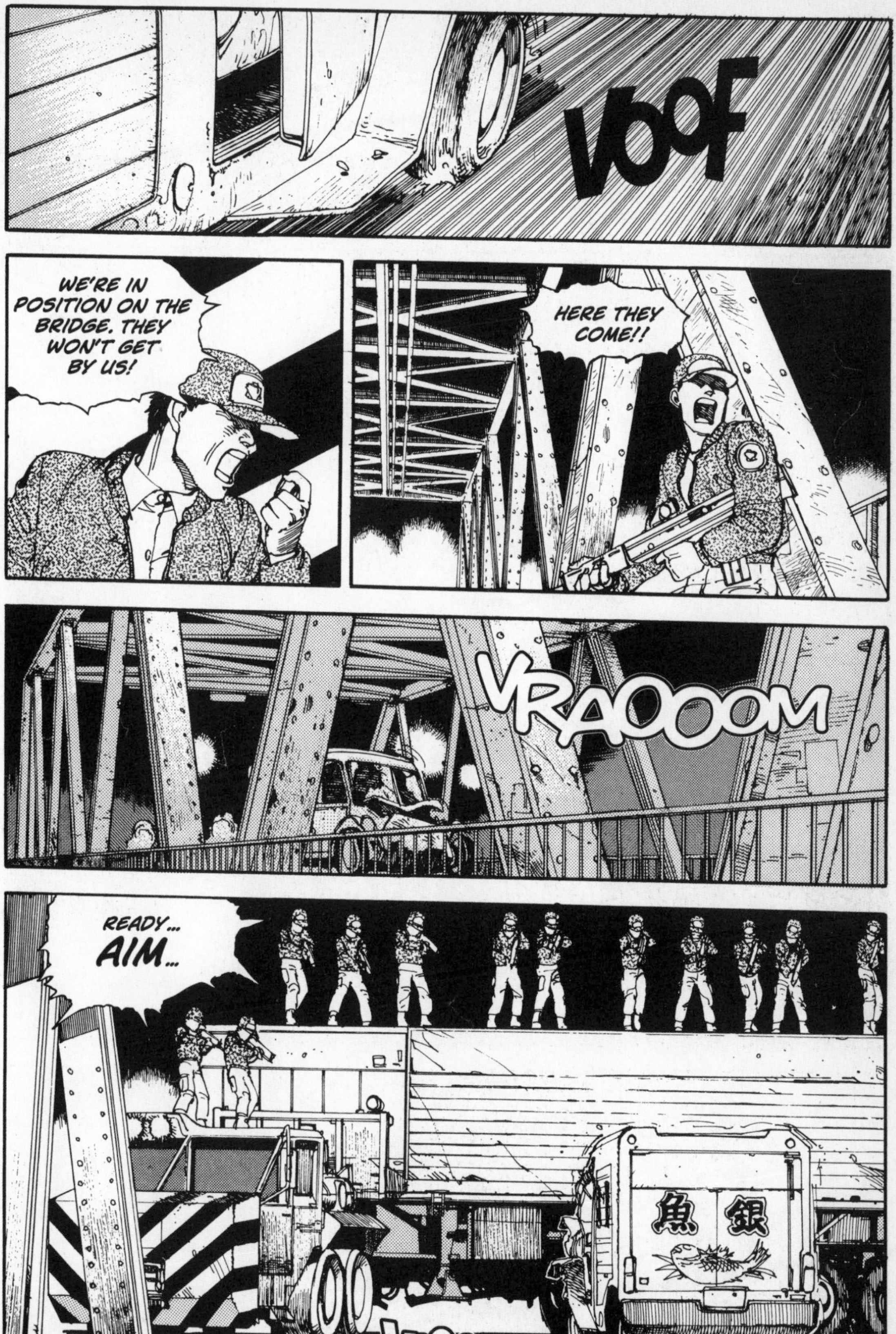
VOOF
WE'RE IN POSITION ON THE BRIDGE. THEY WON'T GET BY US!
HERE THEY COME!!
VRAOOOM
READY... AIM...
魚銀
VOOOOOO

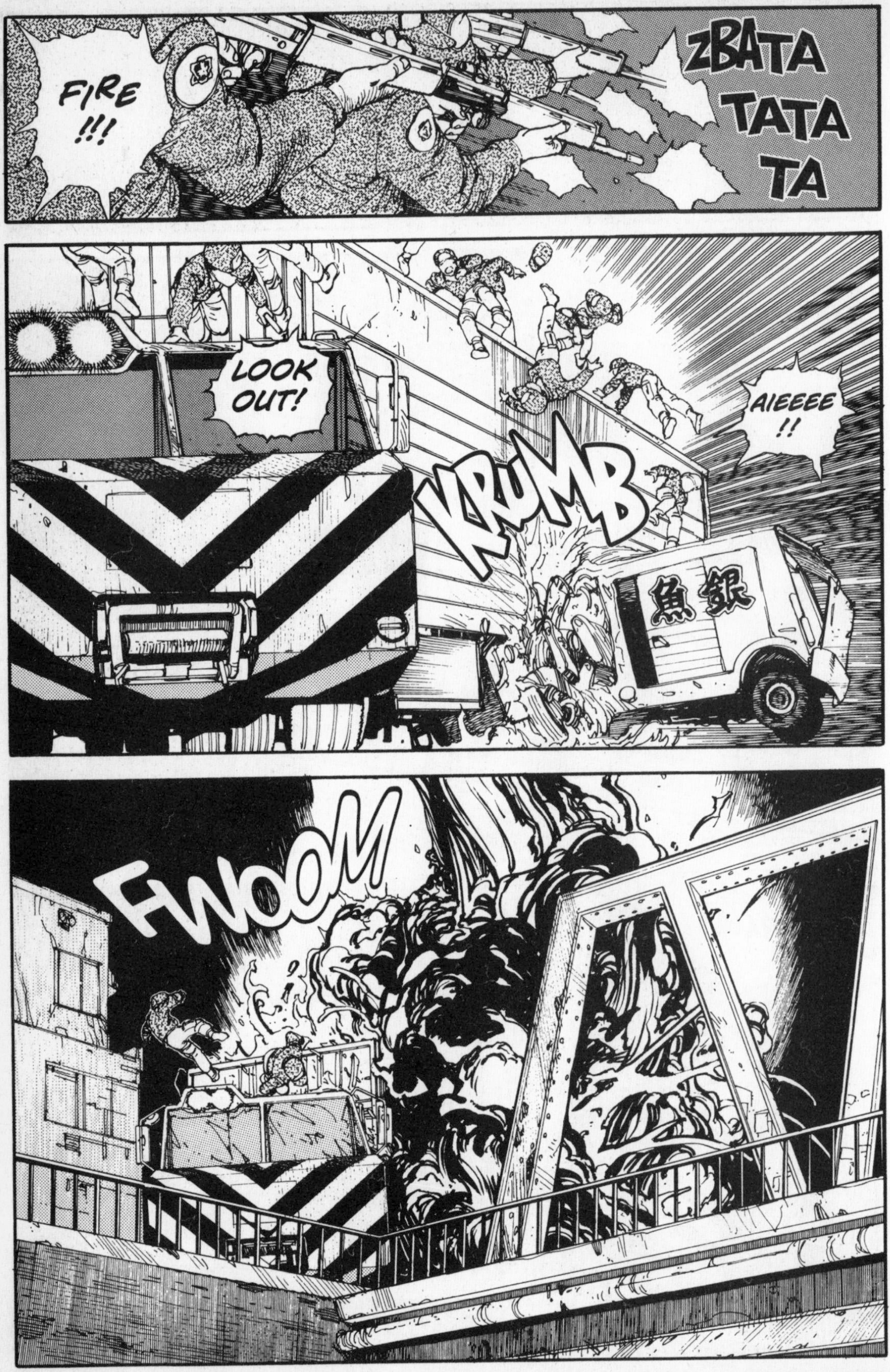
FIRE !!!
ZBATA TATA TA
LOOK OUT!
AIEEEE !!
KRUMB
魚銀
FWOOM

I SUPPOSE I OUGHT TO THANK YOU.

KEEP YOUR THANKS, MISTER. JUST REMEMBER YOU OWE ME ONE.

RIGHT. LET'S GET OUT OF HERE.

RYU, WAIT A MINUTE! THERE'S SOMETHING WRONG WITH HIM!

WHAT?

HE'S SWEATING AND SHAKING LIKE A LEAF.

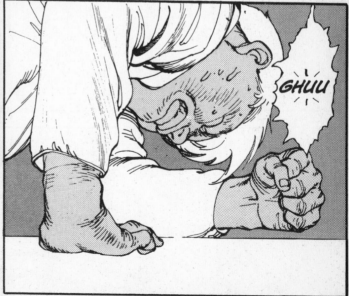
GHUU

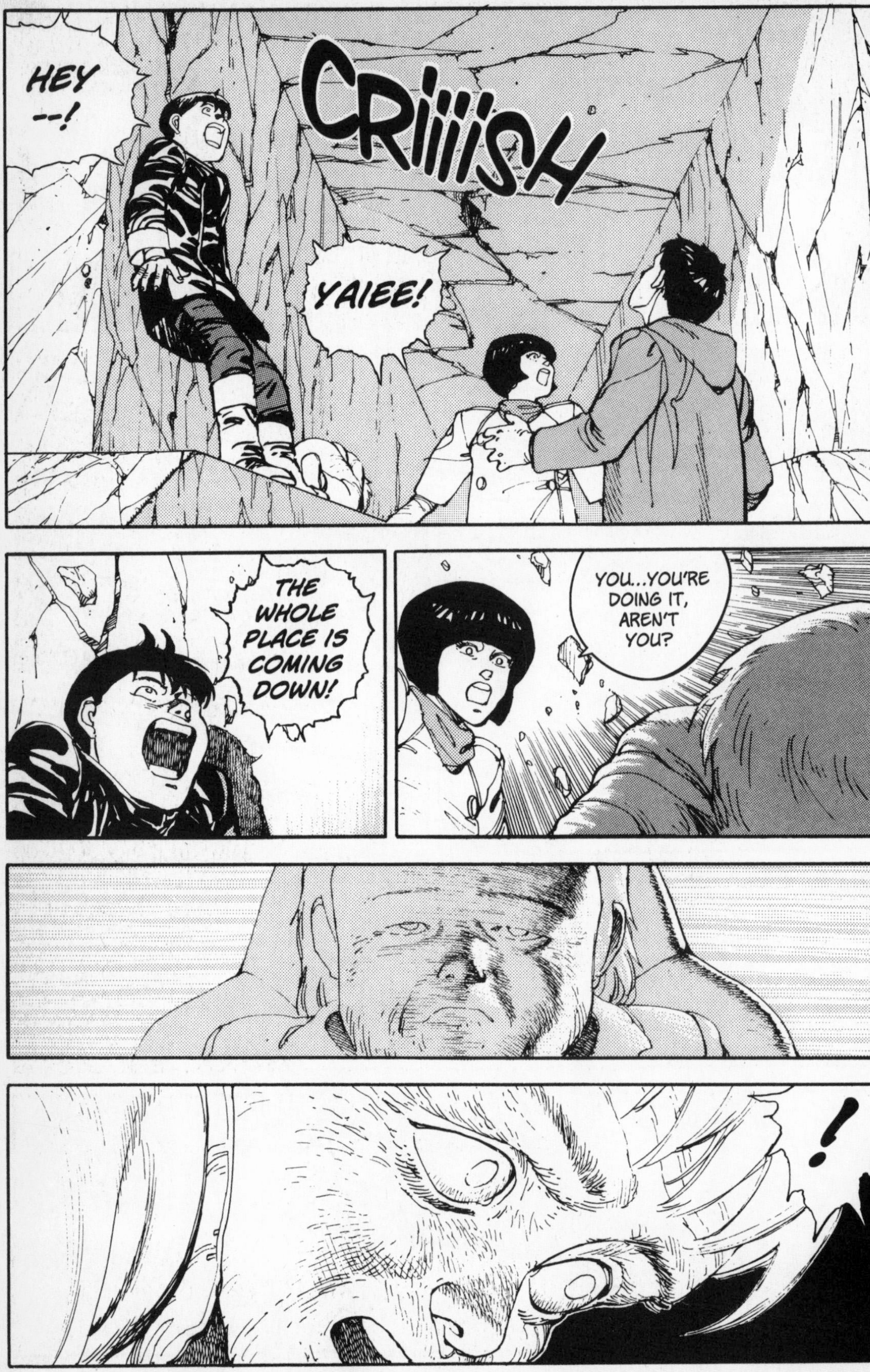
HEY --!
CRIIIISH
YAIEE!
THE WHOLE PLACE IS COMING DOWN!
YOU...YOU'RE DOING IT, AREN'T YOU?
!

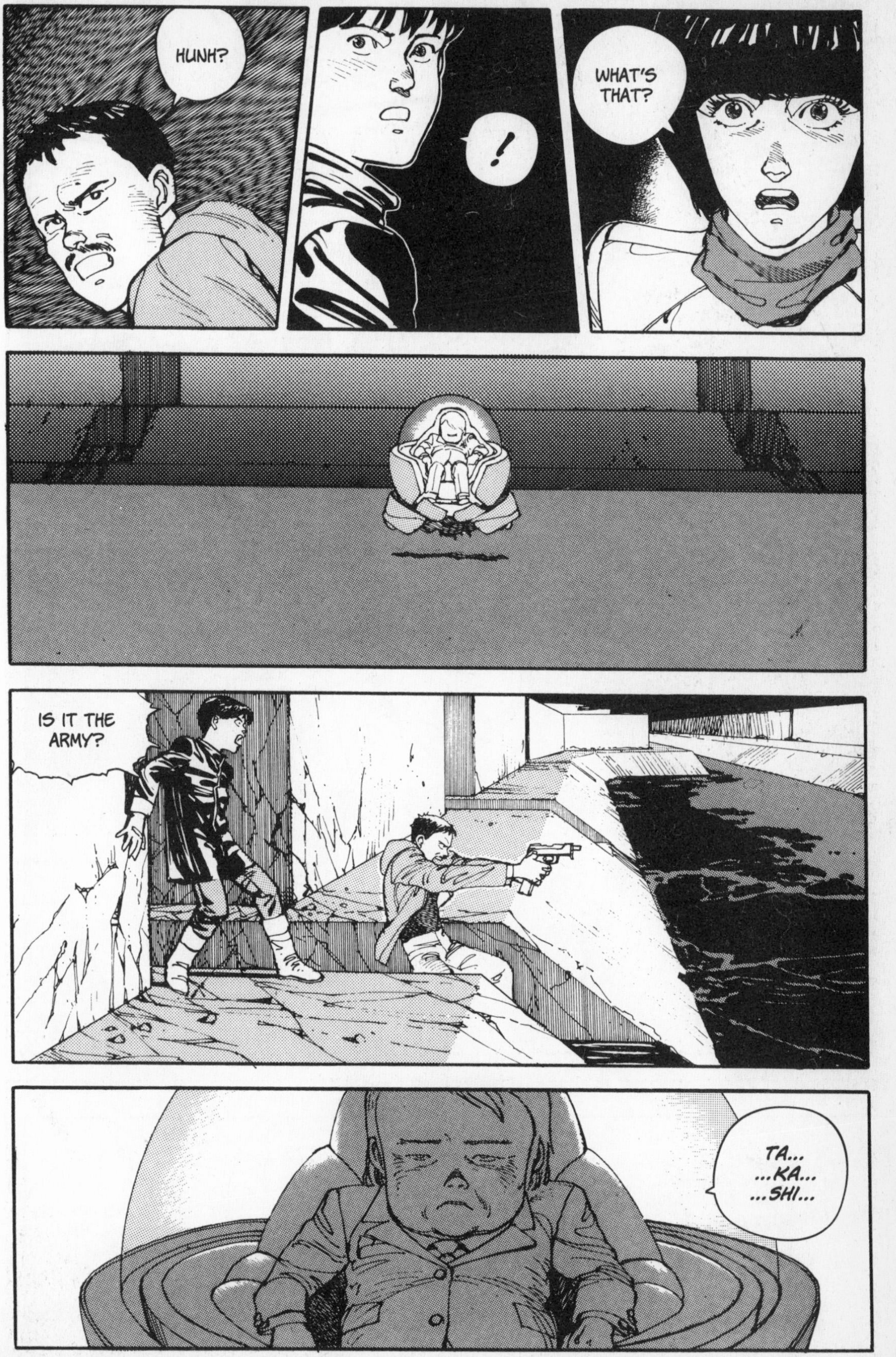
HUNH?
!
WHAT'S THAT?
IS IT THE ARMY?
TA... ...KA... ...SHI...

!

TAKASHI
--?!

IS
THAT
YOUR
NAME?!

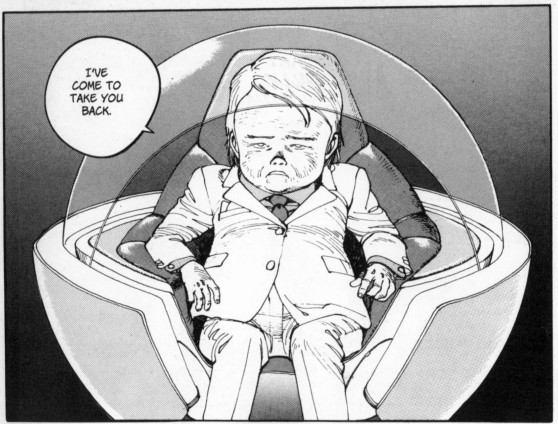

I'VE
COME TO
TAKE YOU
BACK.

WE'RE NOT LIKE
THE OTHERS...
WE CAN'T LIVE
OUTSIDE.

COME WITH
ME...COME
HOME...

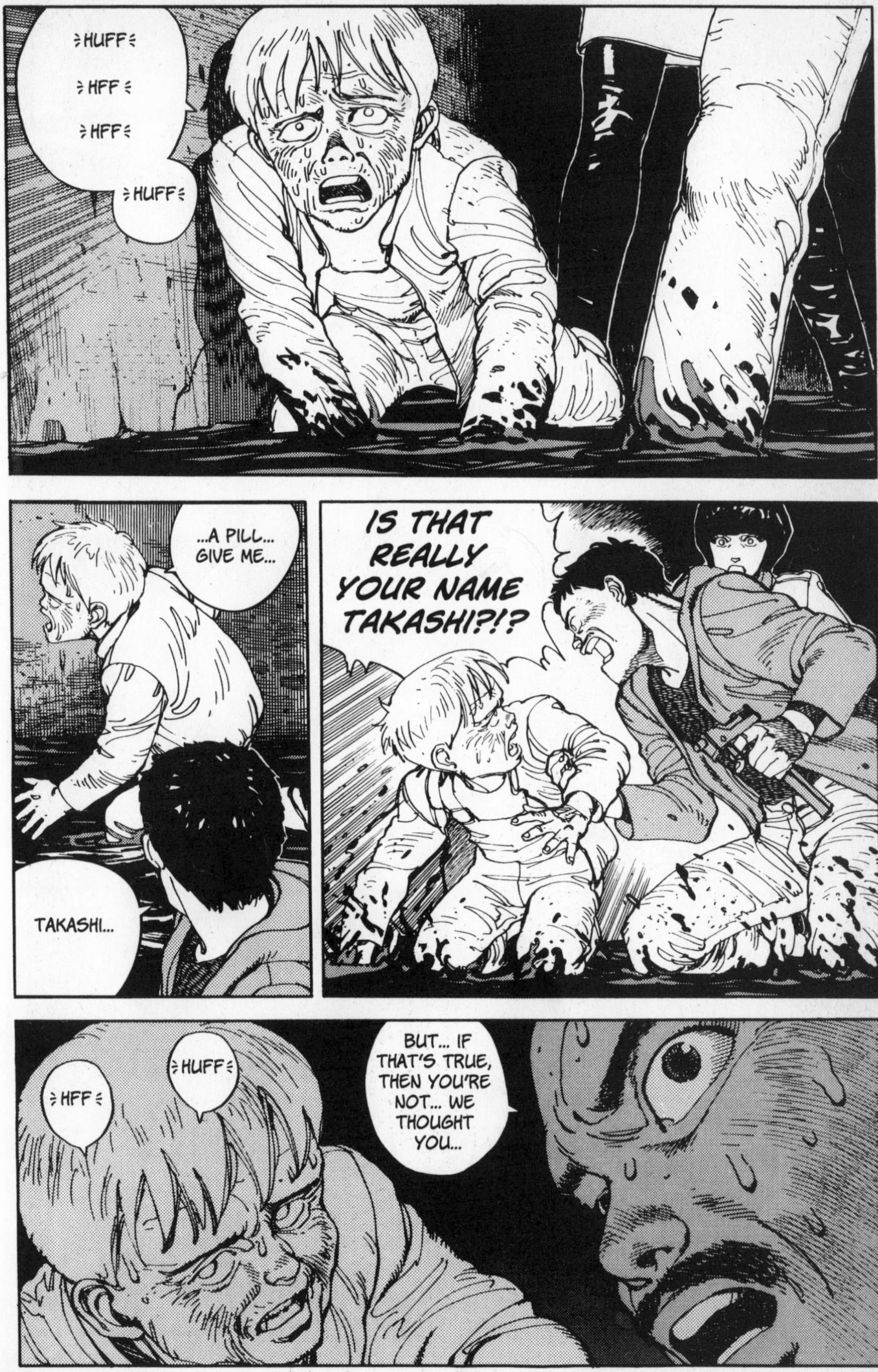
HUFF
HFF
HFF
HUFF
...A PILL... GIVE ME...
TAKASHI...
IS THAT REALLY YOUR NAME TAKASHI?!?
HFF
HUFF
BUT... IF THAT'S TRUE, THEN YOU'RE NOT... WE THOUGHT YOU...

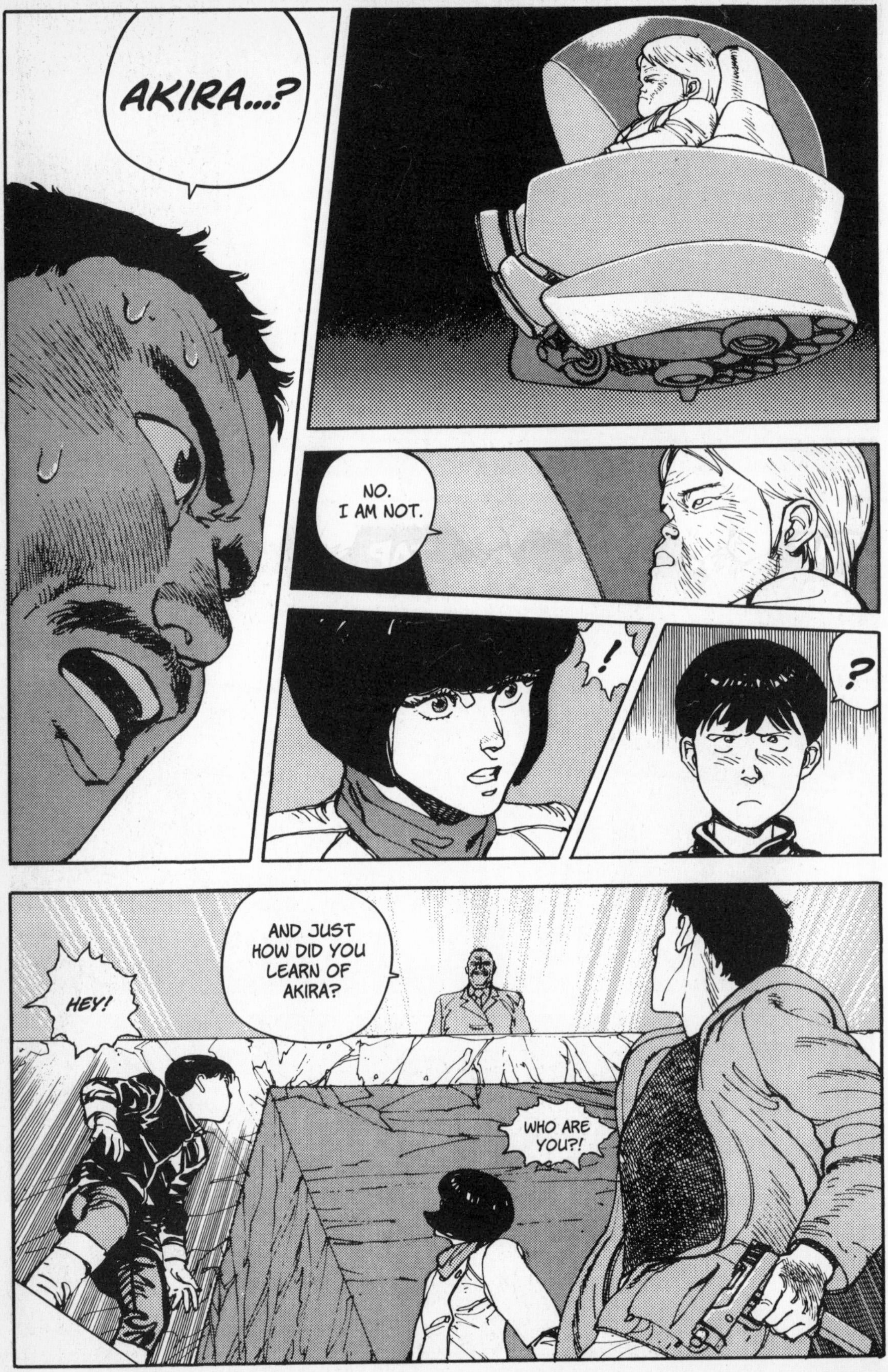
AKIRA...?
NO. I AM NOT.
!
?
HEY!
AND JUST HOW DID YOU LEARN OF AKIRA?
WHO ARE YOU?!

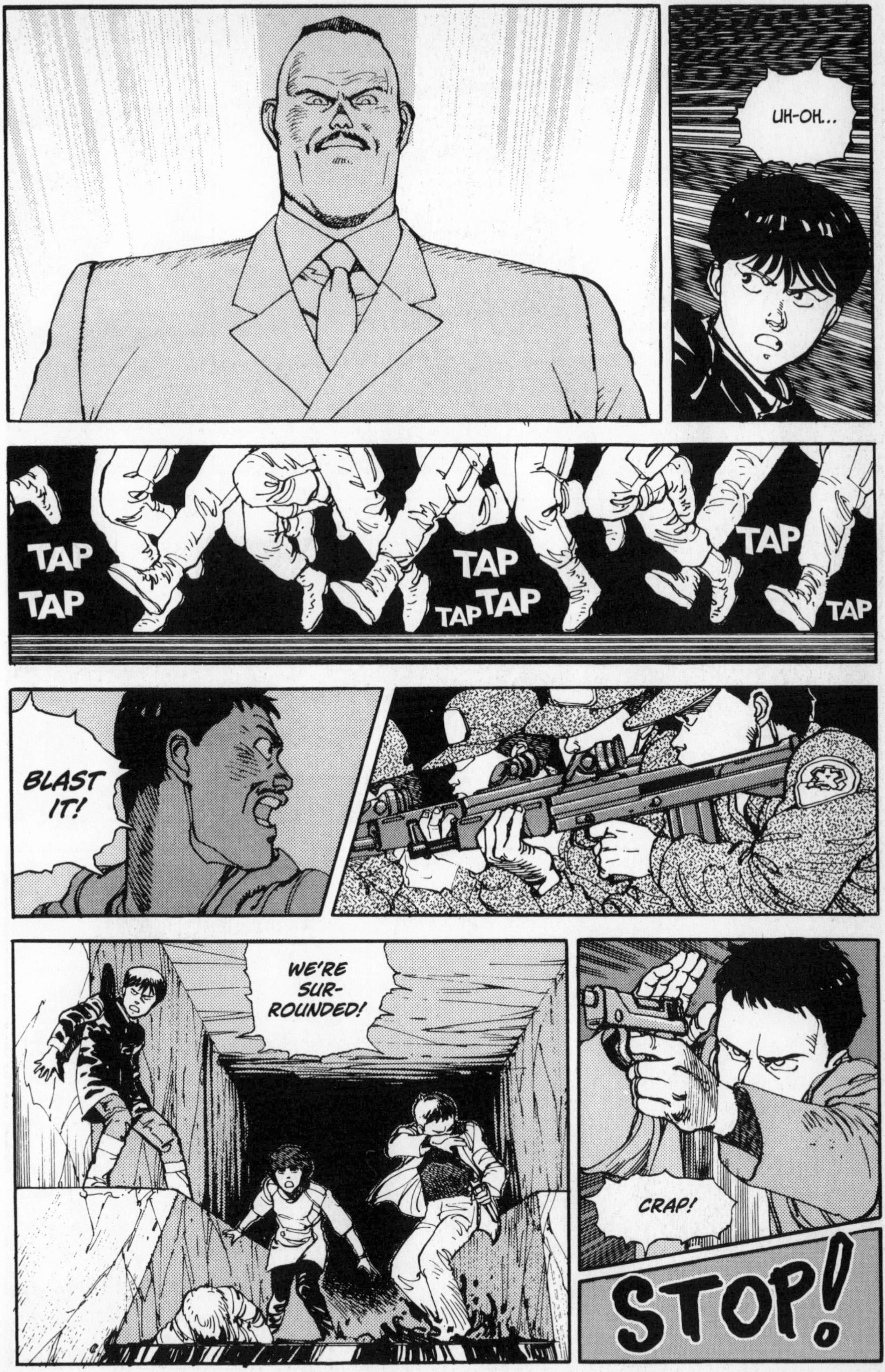
UH-OH...
TAP
TAP
TAP
TAP TAP
TAP
TAP
BLAST IT!
WE'RE SUR-ROUNDED!
CRAP!
STOP!

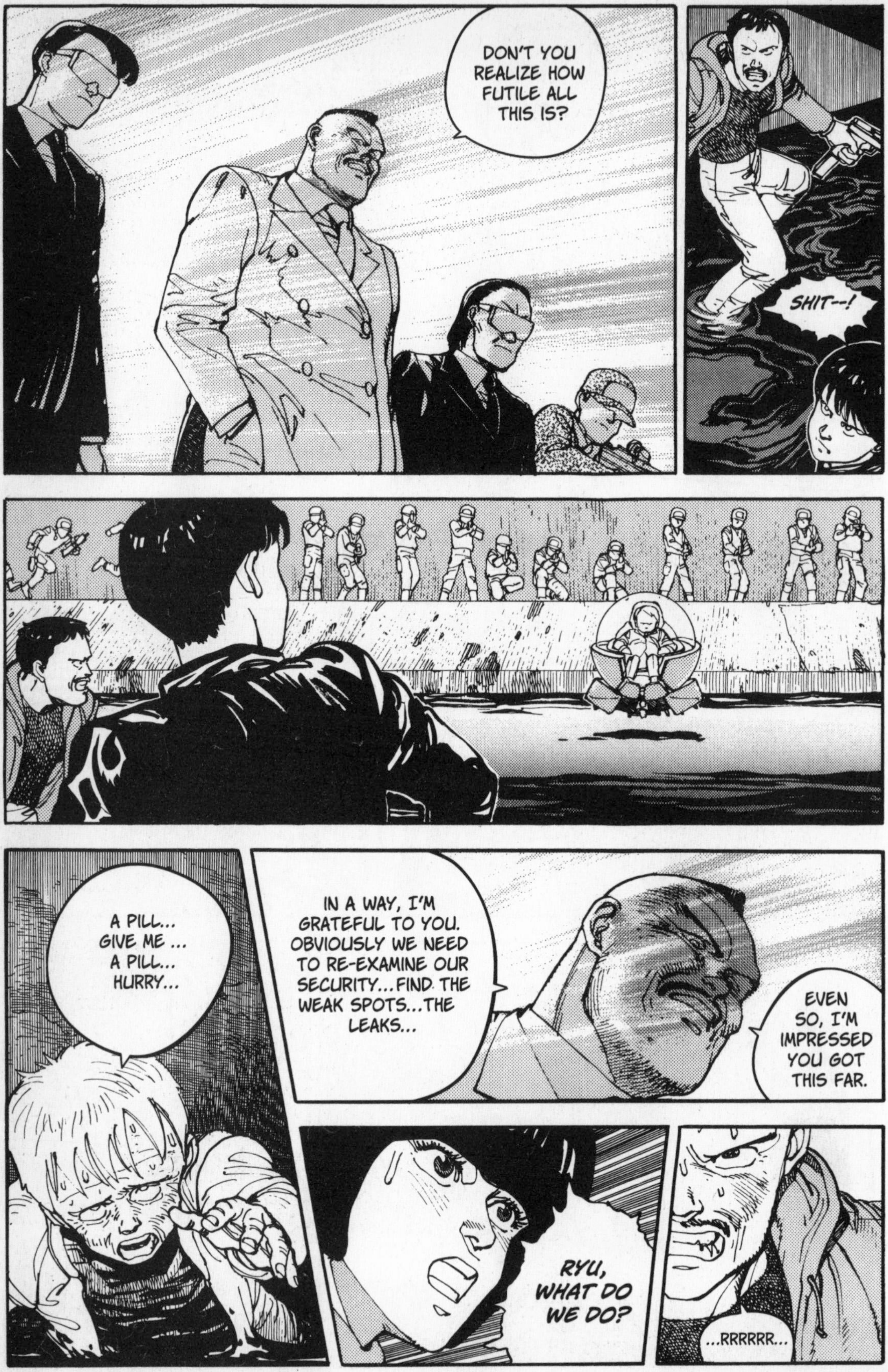
DON'T YOU REALIZE HOW FUTILE ALL THIS IS?
SHIT--!
A PILL... GIVE ME ... A PILL... HURRY...
IN A WAY, I'M GRATEFUL TO YOU. OBVIOUSLY WE NEED TO RE-EXAMINE OUR SECURITY...FIND THE WEAK SPOTS...THE LEAKS...
EVEN SO, I'M IMPRESSED YOU GOT THIS FAR.
RYU, WHAT DO WE DO?
...RRRRRR...

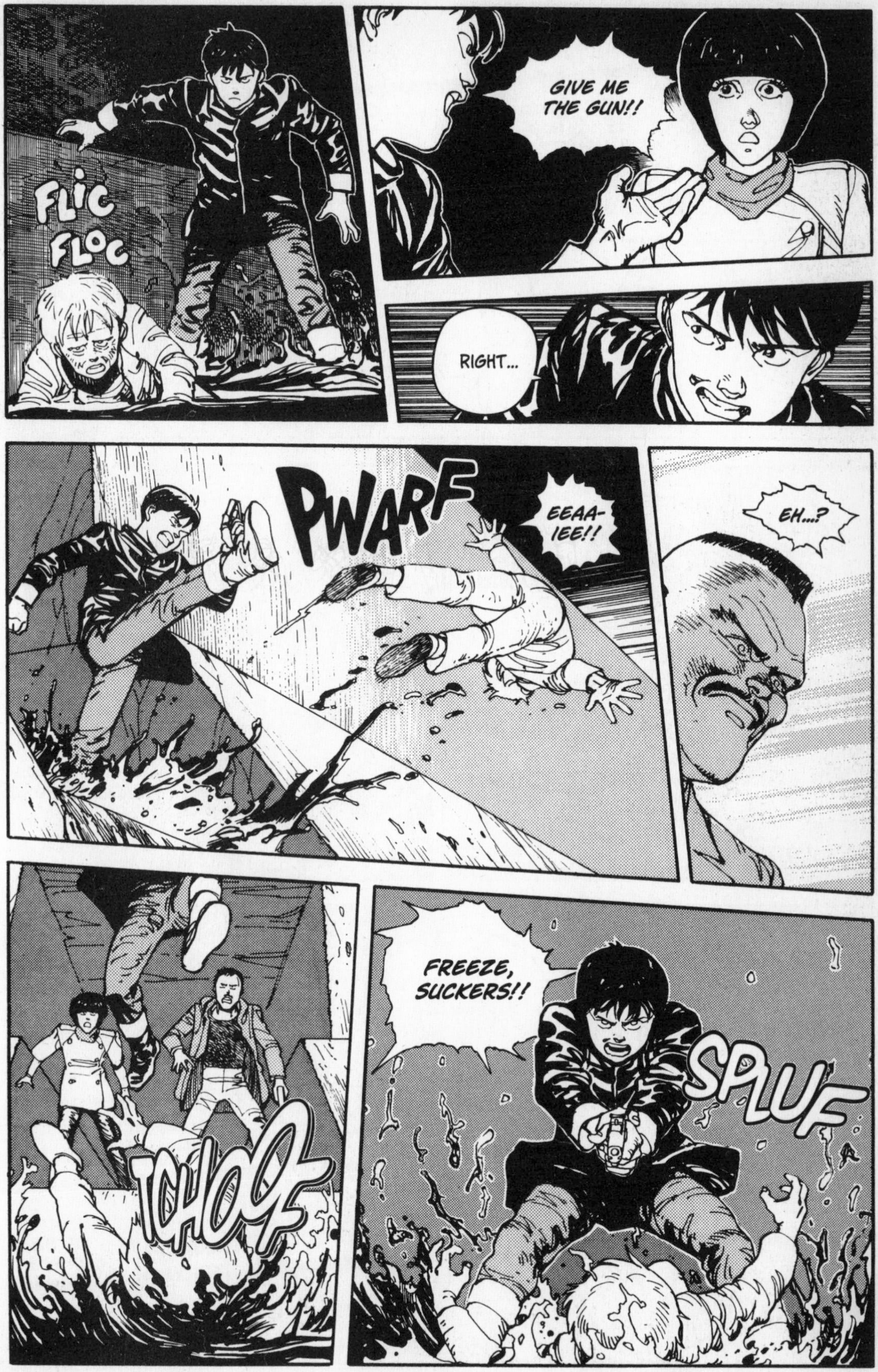
FLIC
FLOC
GIVE ME THE GUN!!
RIGHT...
PWARF
EEAA-IEE!!
EH...?
TCHOF
FREEZE, SUCKERS!!
SPLUF

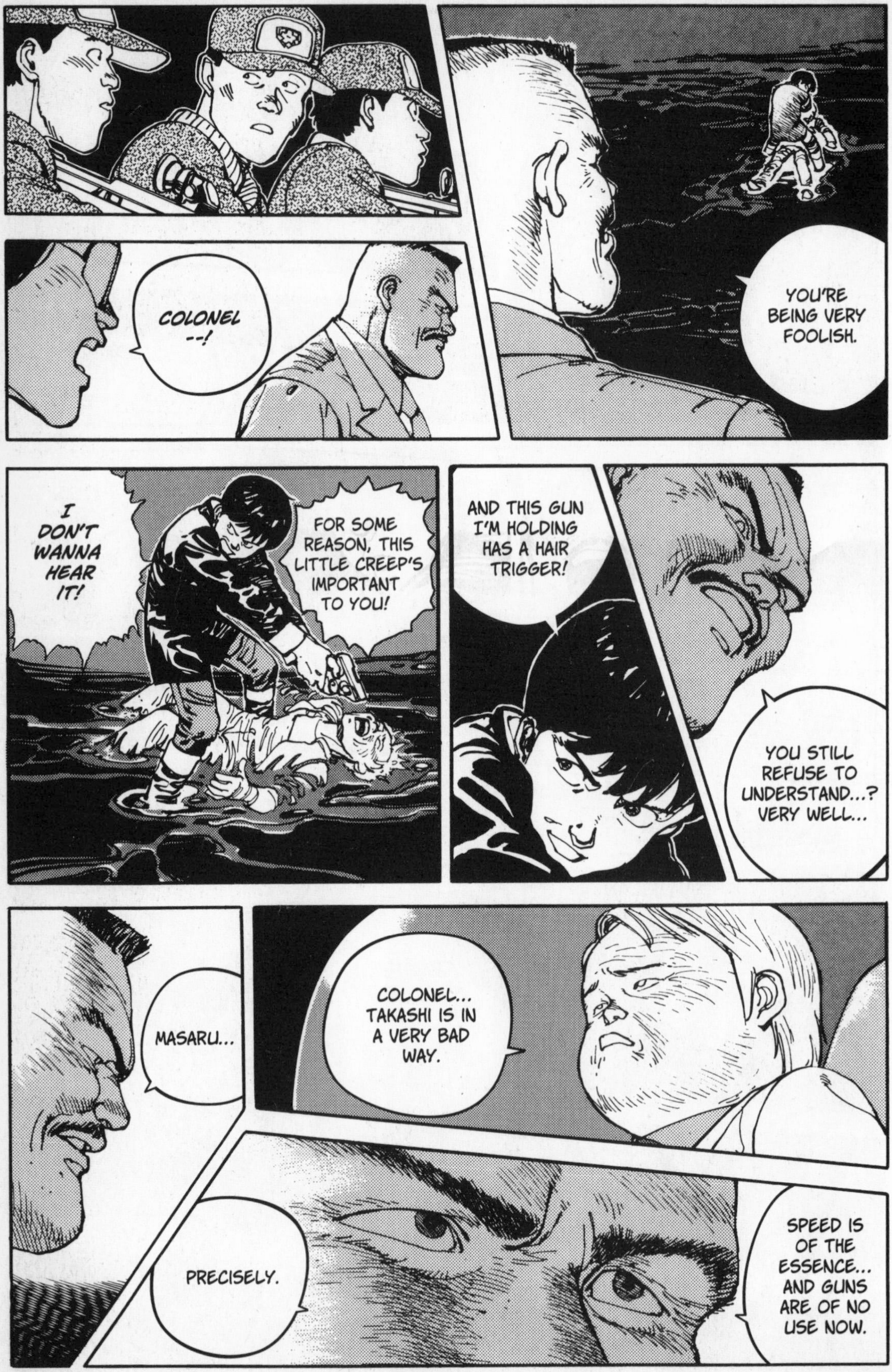
COLONEL --!
YOU'RE BEING VERY FOOLISH.
I DON'T WANNA HEAR IT!
FOR SOME REASON, THIS LITTLE CREEP'S IMPORTANT TO YOU!
AND THIS GUN I'M HOLDING HAS A HAIR TRIGGER!
YOU STILL REFUSE TO UNDERSTAND...? VERY WELL...
MASARU...
COLONEL... TAKASHI IS IN A VERY BAD WAY.
PRECISELY.
SPEED IS OF THE ESSENCE... AND GUNS ARE OF NO USE NOW.

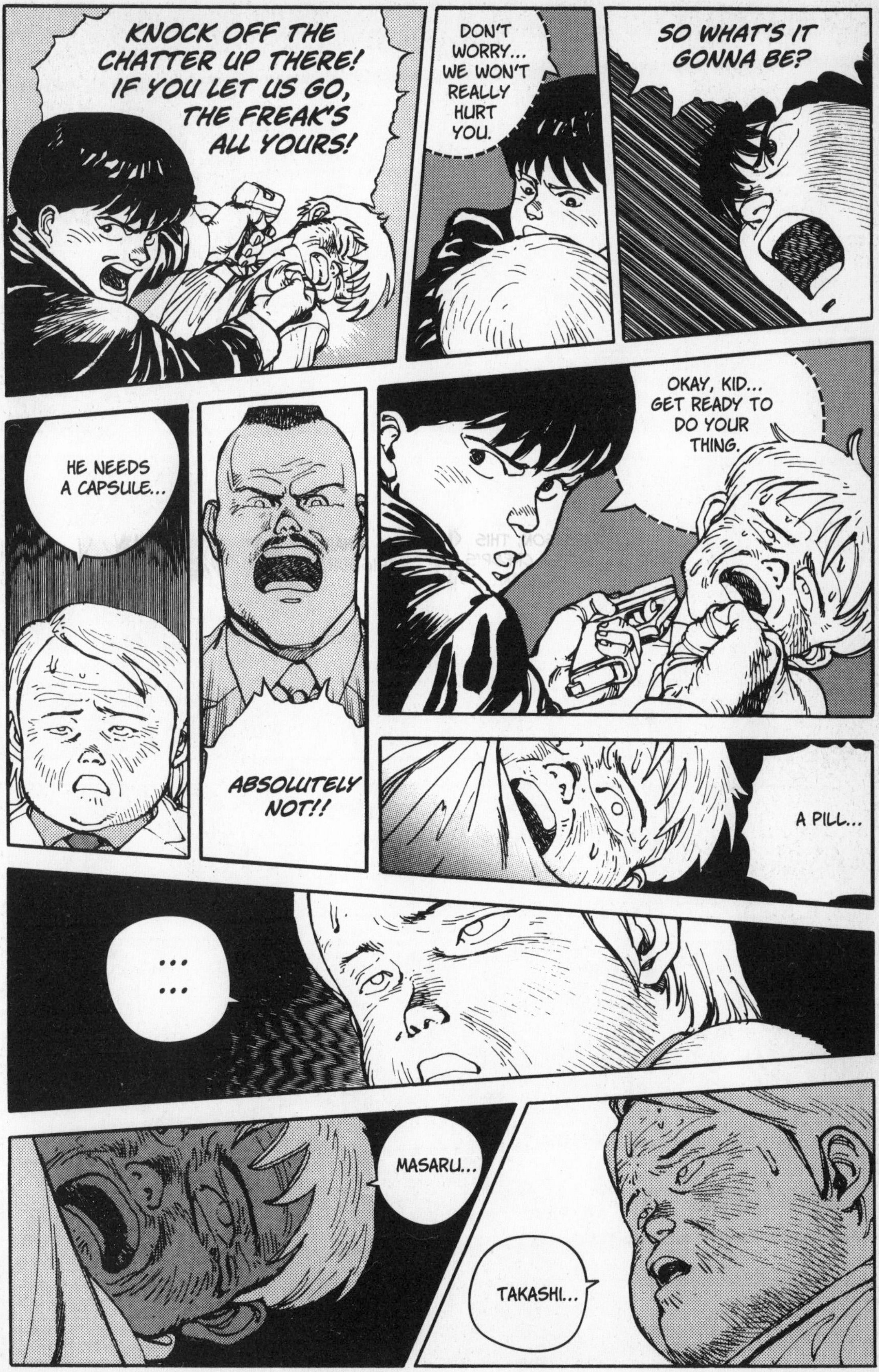

KNOCK OFF THE CHATTER UP THERE! IF YOU LET US GO, THE FREAK'S ALL YOURS!
DON'T WORRY... WE WON'T REALLY HURT YOU.
SO WHAT'S IT GONNA BE?
HE NEEDS A CAPSULE...
ABSOLUTELY NOT!!
OKAY, KID... GET READY TO DO YOUR THING.
A PILL...
...
...
MASARU...
TAKASHI...

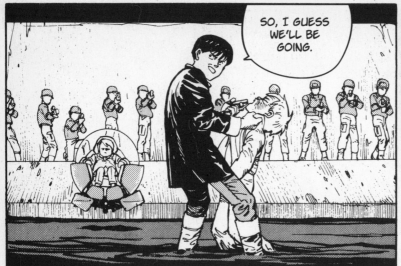

SO, I GUESS WE'LL BE GOING.

MASARU!

HEY, MASARU, OR WHATEVER YOUR NAME IS... WHAT'S YOUR PROBLEM? BUTT OUT--

--IF YOU CARE ABOUT YOUR FRIEND.

?!

DZZiiiiiii

!

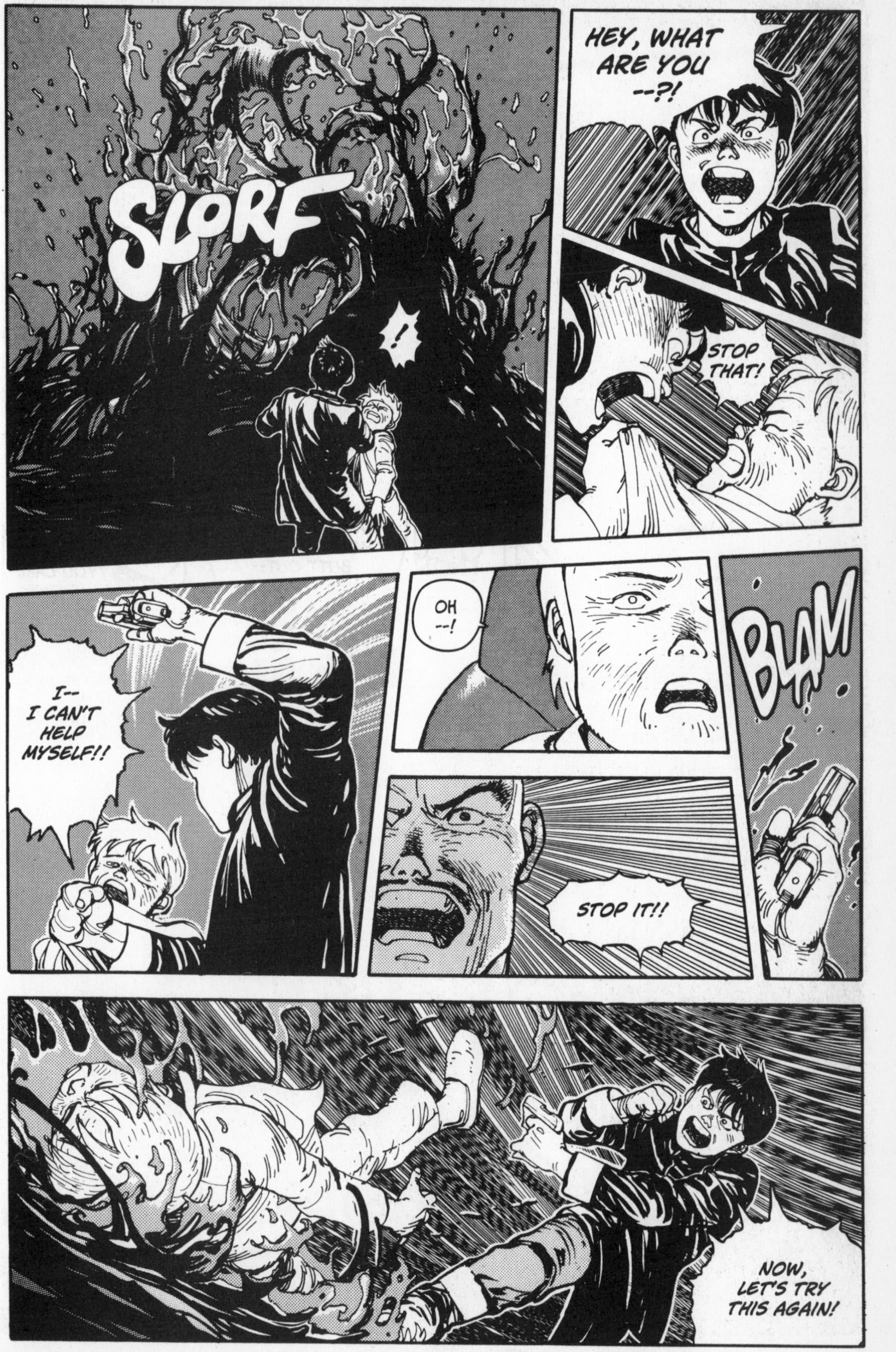
SLORF
!
HEY, WHAT ARE YOU --?!
STOP THAT!
I-- I CAN'T HELP MYSELF!!
OH --!
BLAM
STOP IT!!
NOW, LET'S TRY THIS AGAIN!

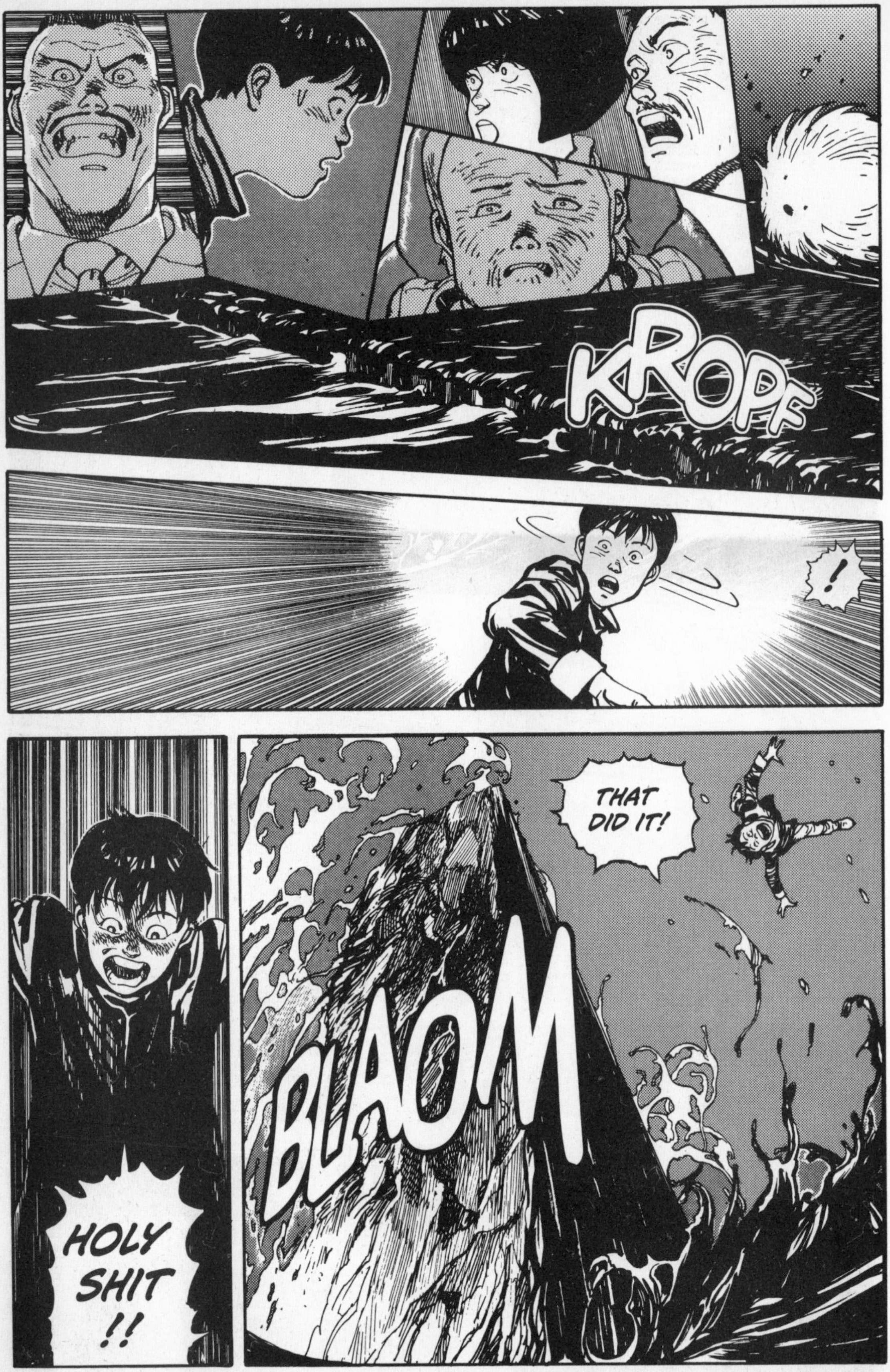
KROPF
!
HOLY SHIT !!
THAT DID IT!
BLAOM

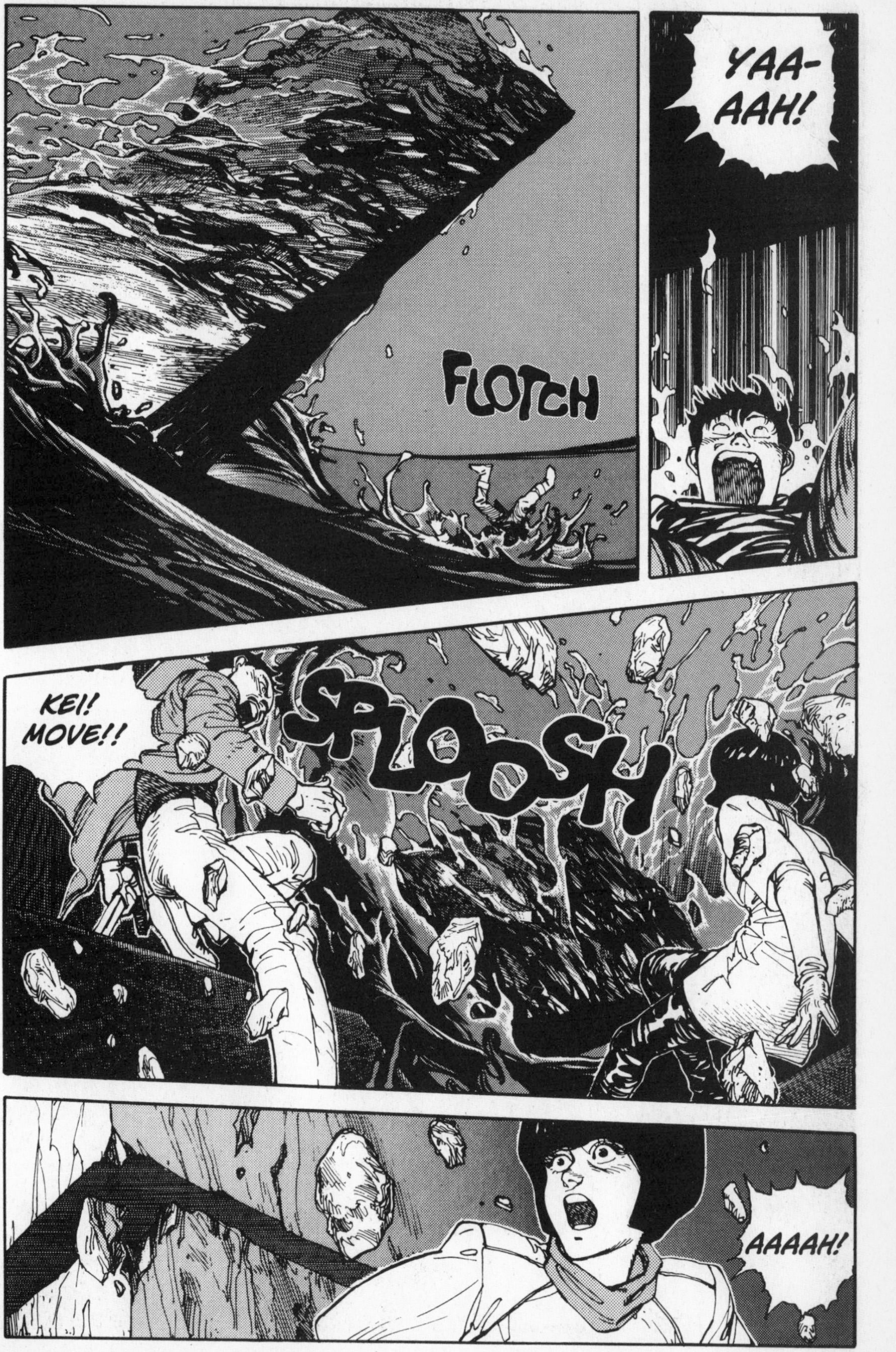
FLOTCH
YAA-
AAH!
KEI!
MOVE!!
SPLOOSH
AAAAH!

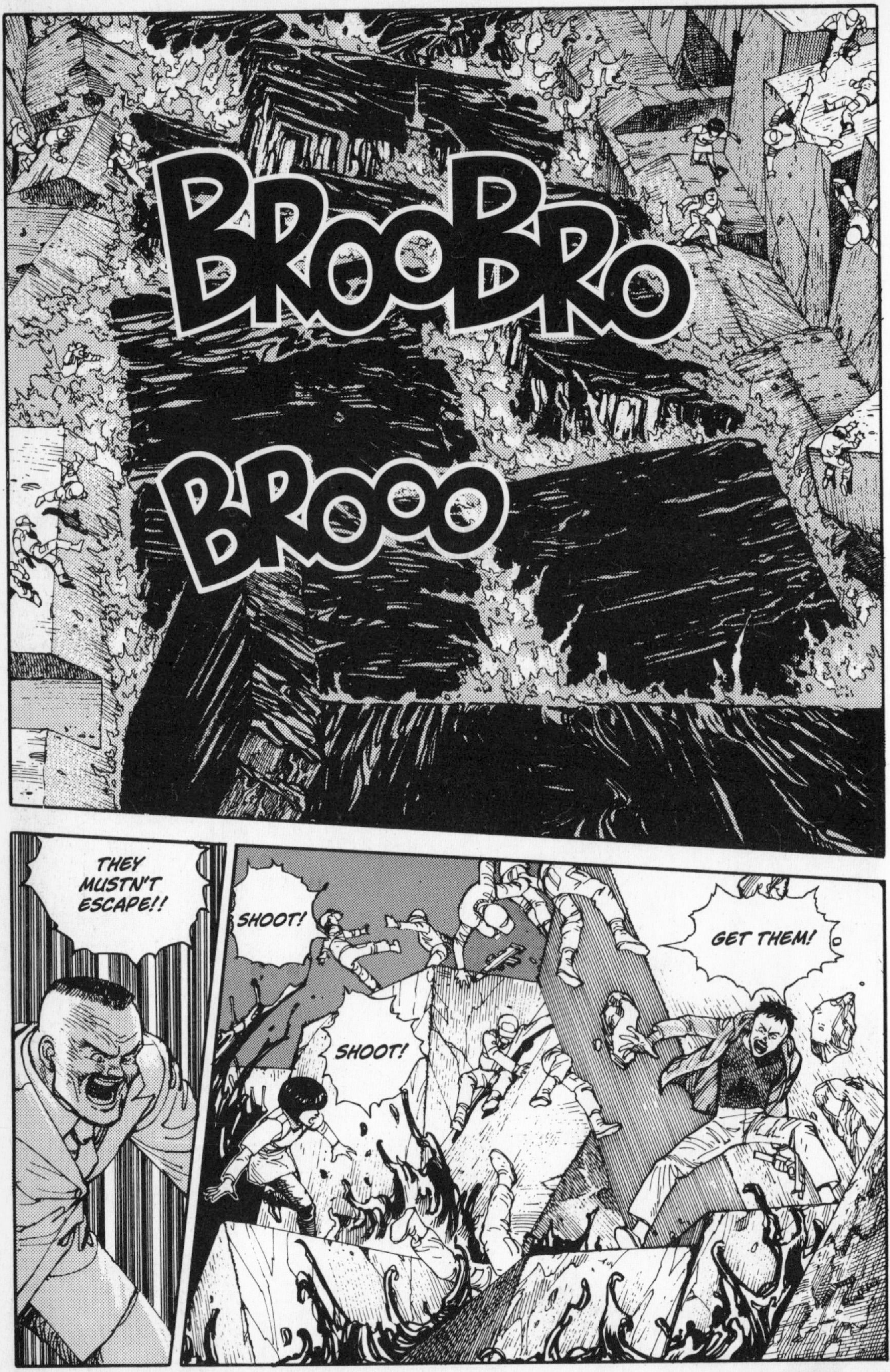
BROOBRO
BROOO
THEY MUSTN'T ESCAPE!!
SHOOT!
SHOOT!
GET THEM!

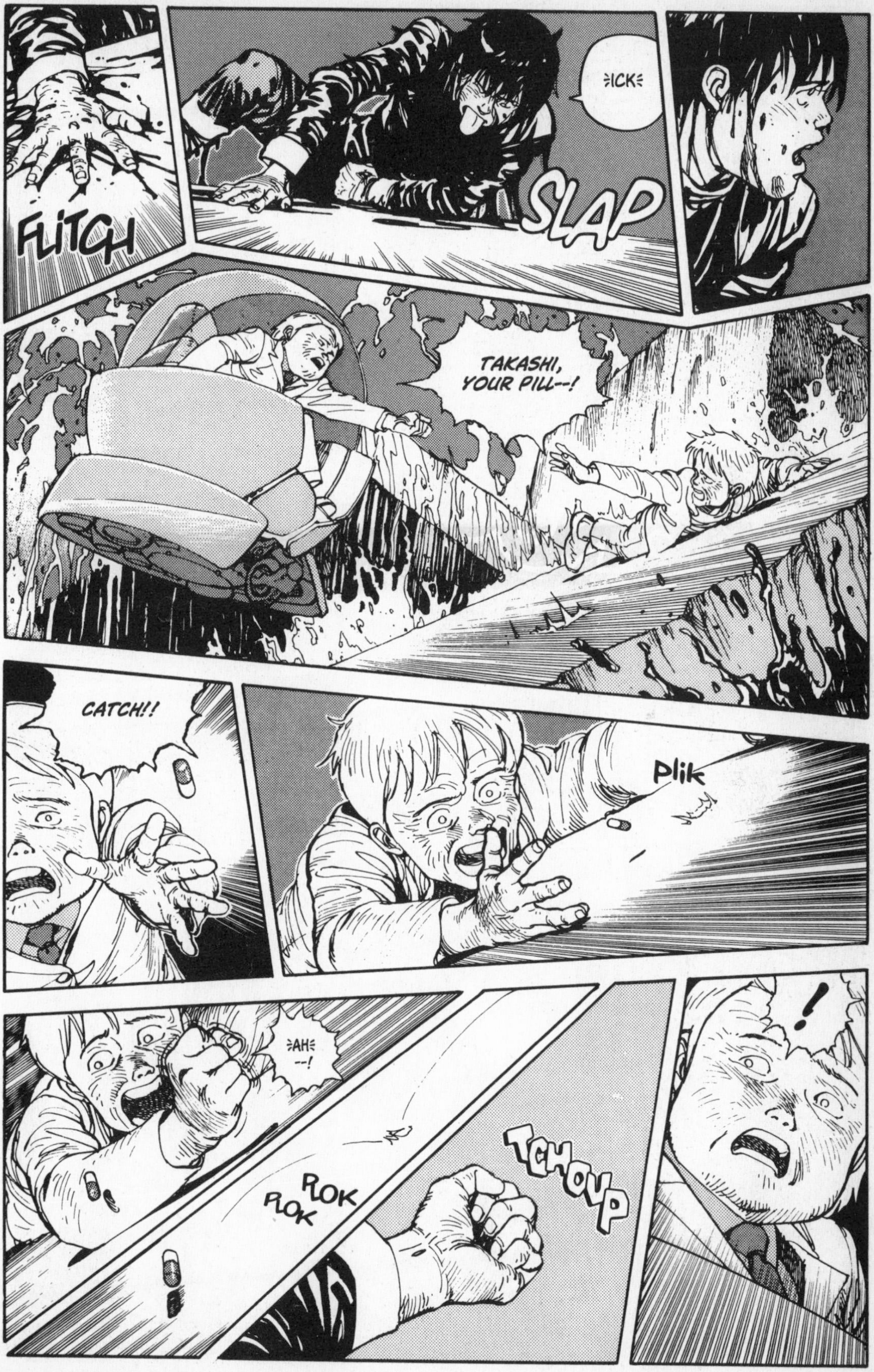
FLITCH
ICK
SLAP
TAKASHI, YOUR PILL--!
CATCH!!
Plik
AH --!
PLOK PLOK
TCHOUP
!

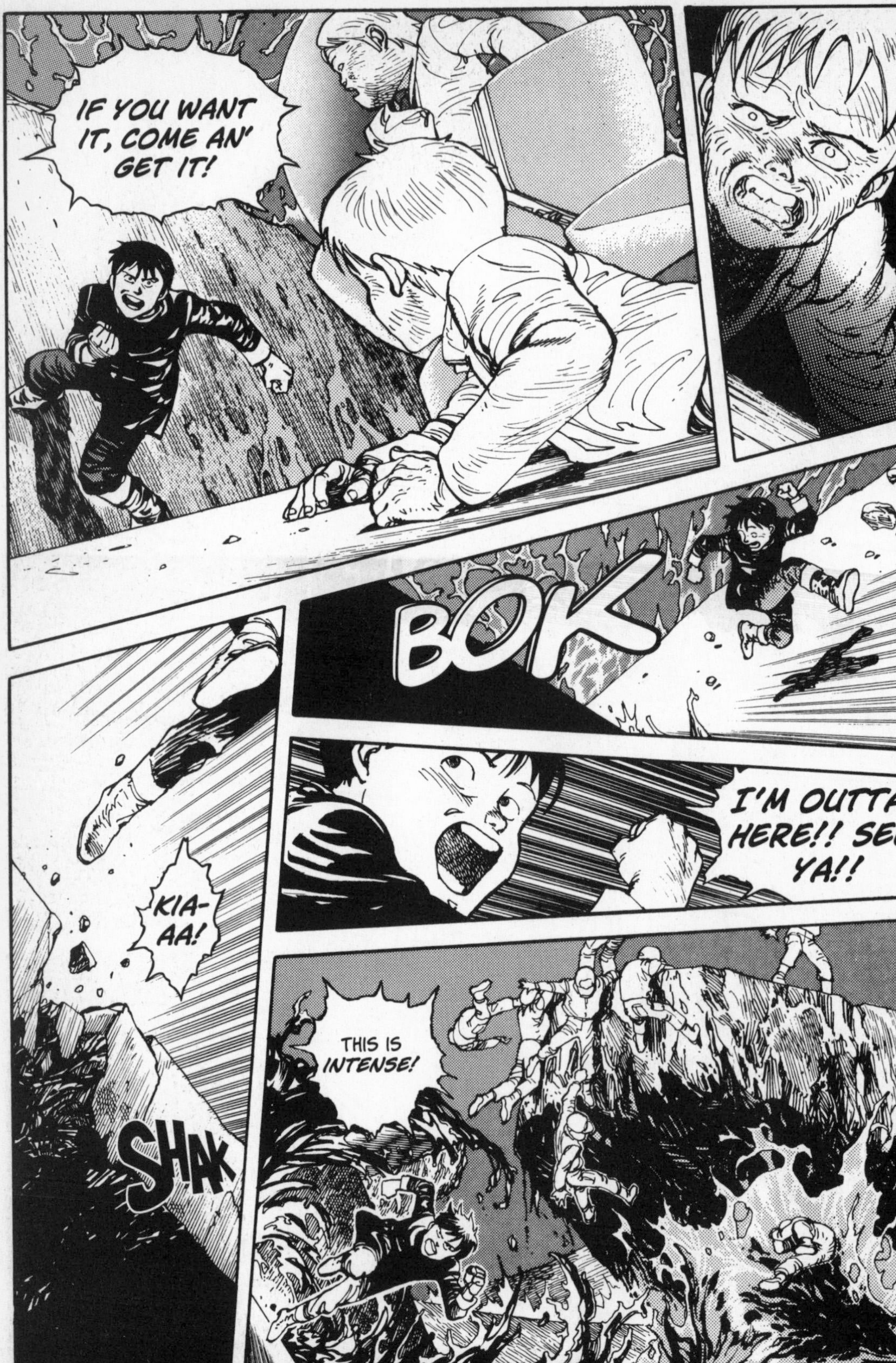
IF YOU WANT IT, COME AN' GET IT!
BOK
KIA-AA!
SHAK
I'M OUTTA HERE!! SEE YA!!
THIS IS INTENSE!

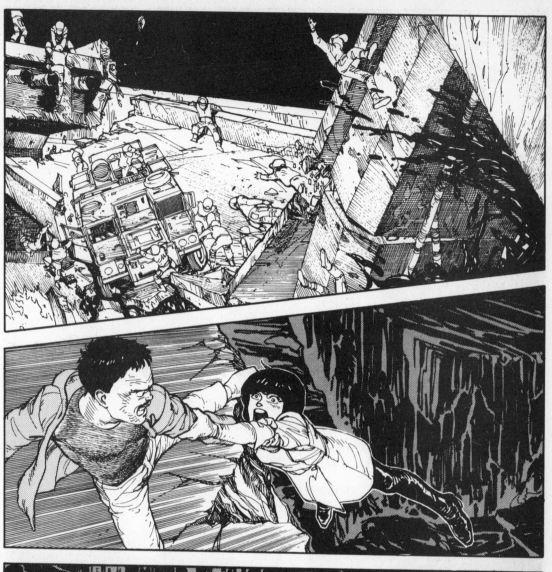

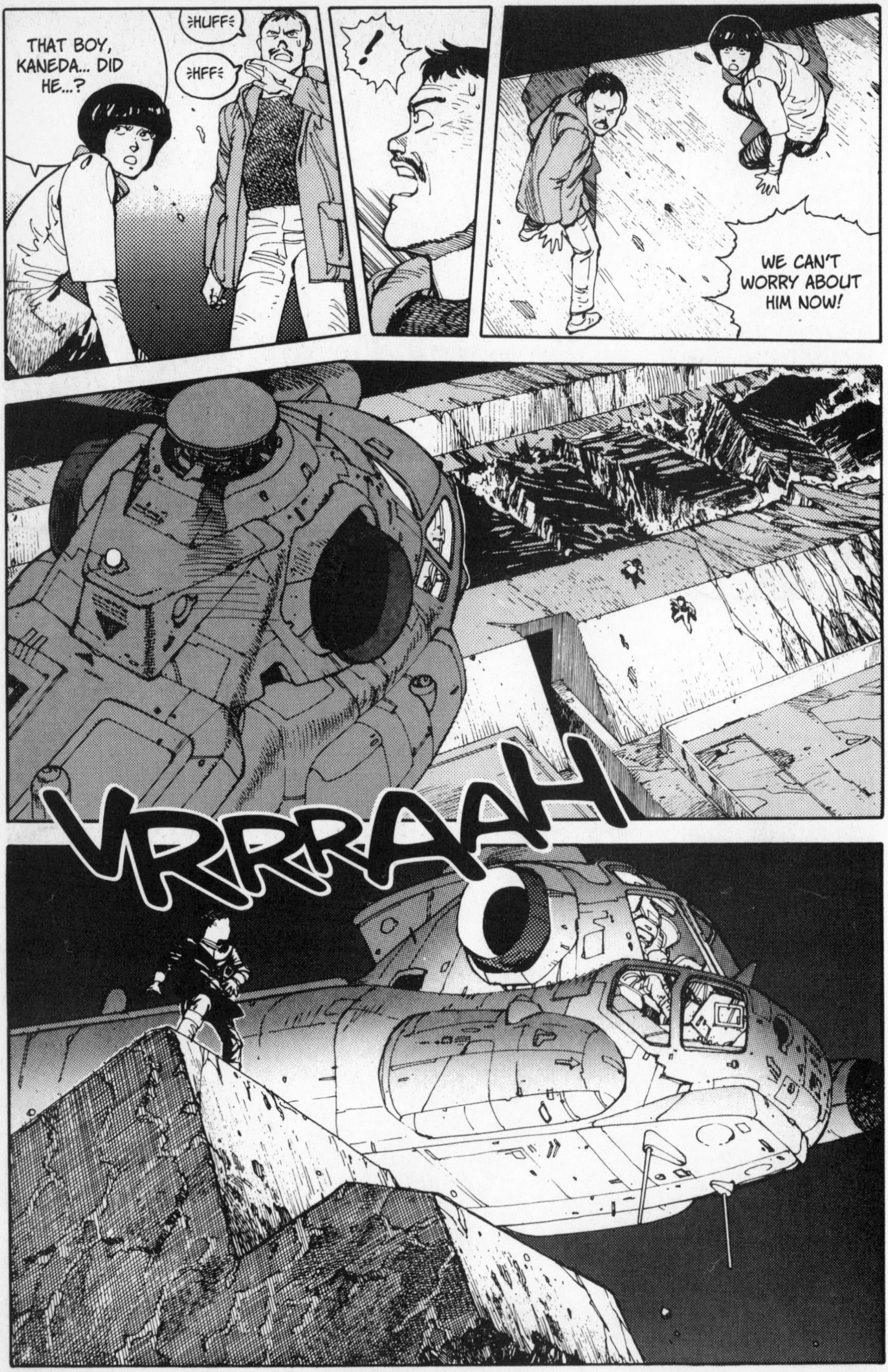
THAT BOY, KANEDA... DID HE...?
HUFF
HFF
!
WE CAN'T WORRY ABOUT HIM NOW!
VRRRAAH

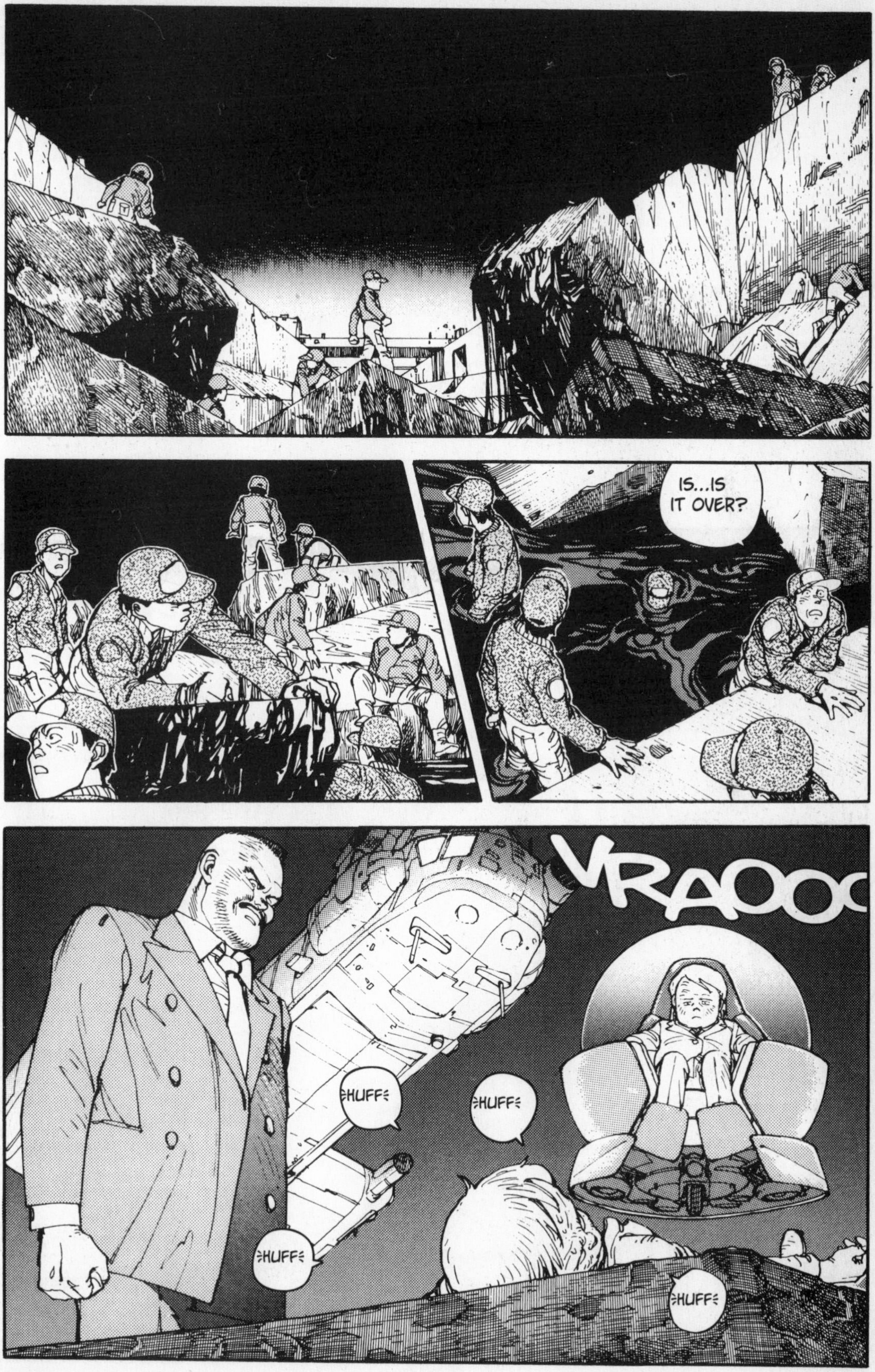
IS...IS IT OVER?
VRAOOO
HUFF
HUFF
HUFF
HUFF

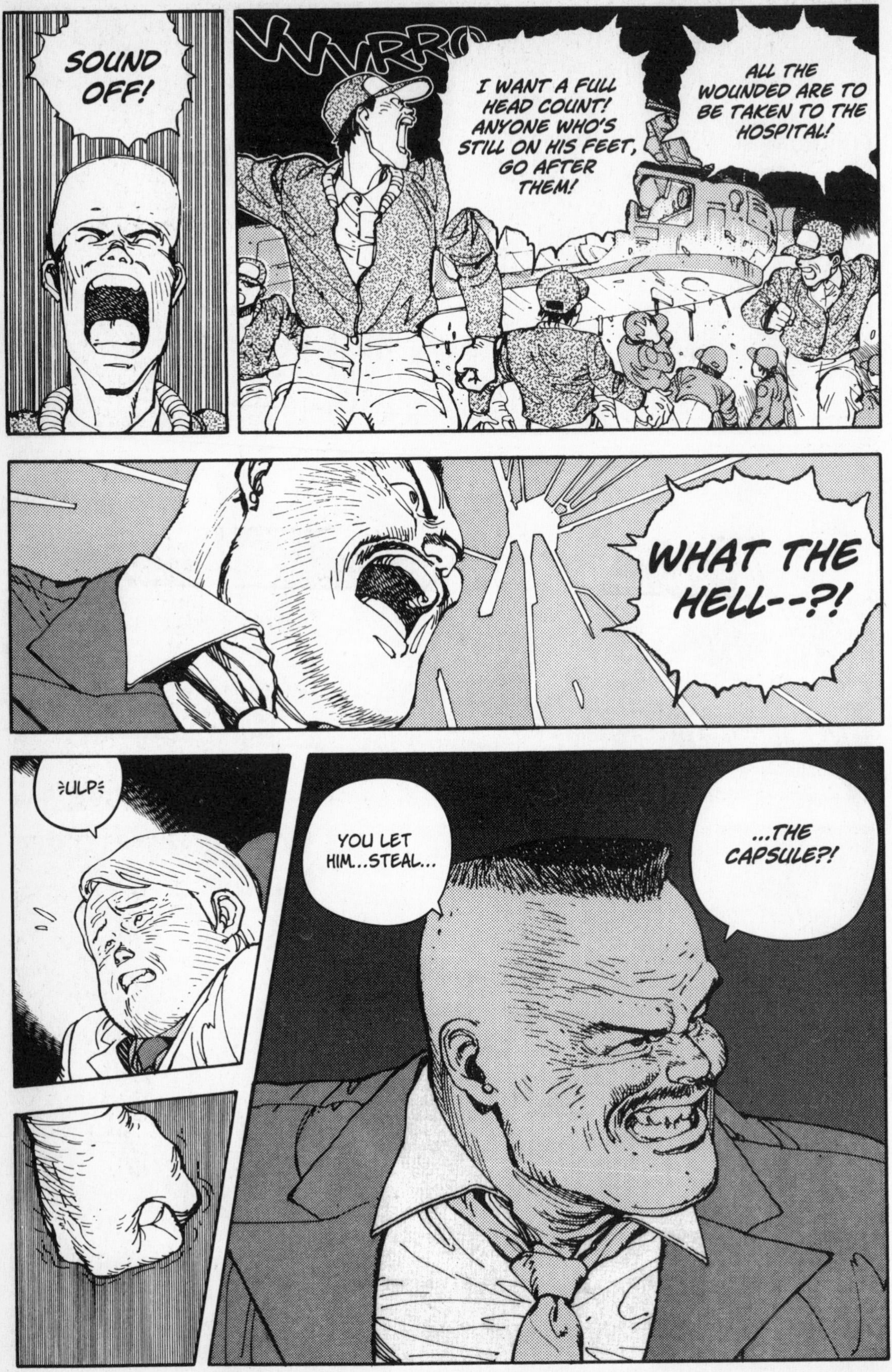
SOUND OFF!
VVVRRO
I WANT A FULL HEAD COUNT! ANYONE WHO'S STILL ON HIS FEET, GO AFTER THEM!
ALL THE WOUNDED ARE TO BE TAKEN TO THE HOSPITAL!
WHAT THE HELL--?!
ULP
YOU LET HIM...STEAL...
...THE CAPSULE?!

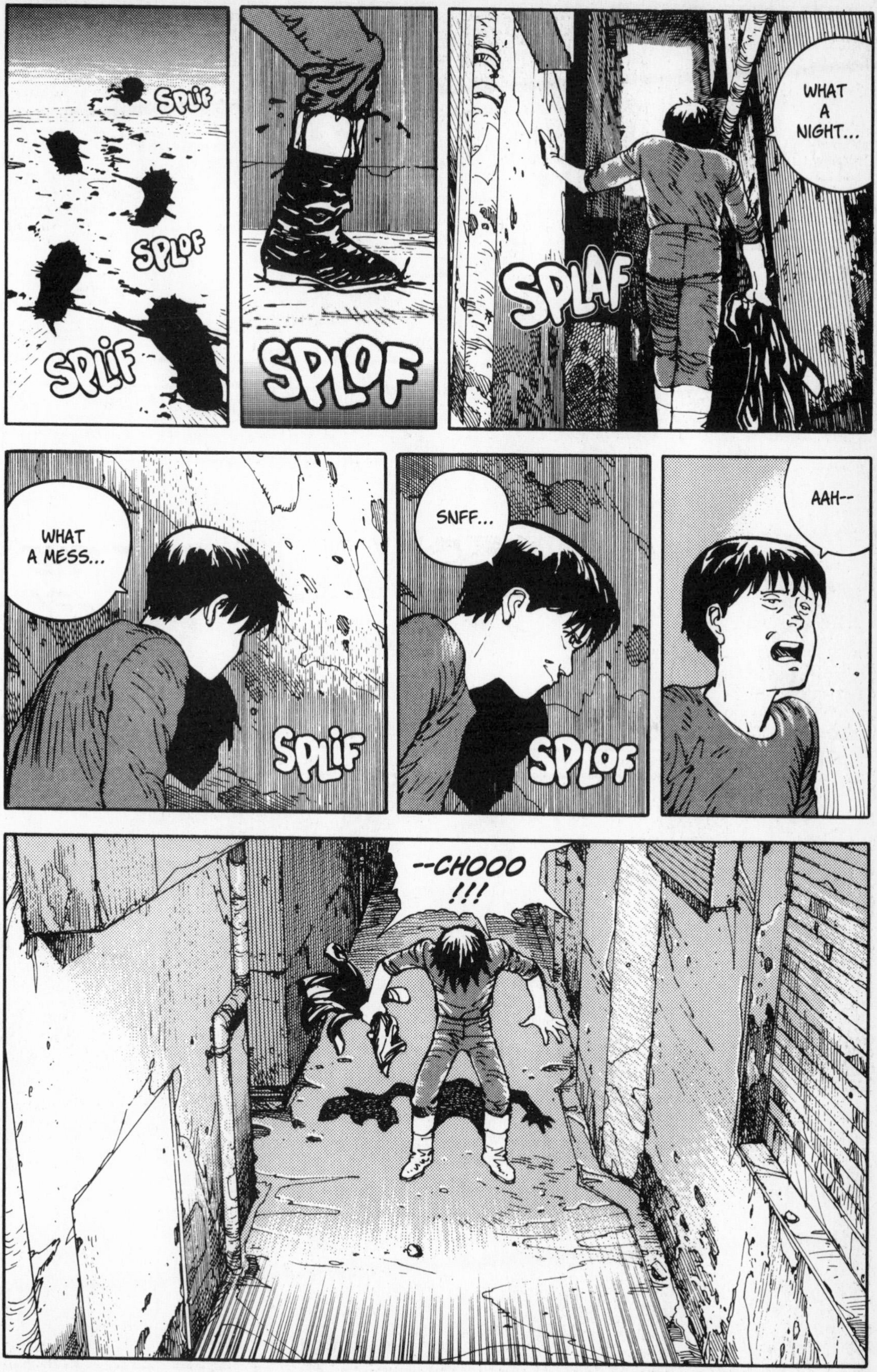
SPLIF
SPLOF
SPLIF
SPLOF
WHAT A NIGHT...
SPLAF
WHAT A MESS...
SPLIF
SNFF...
SPLOF
AAH--
--CHOOO !!!

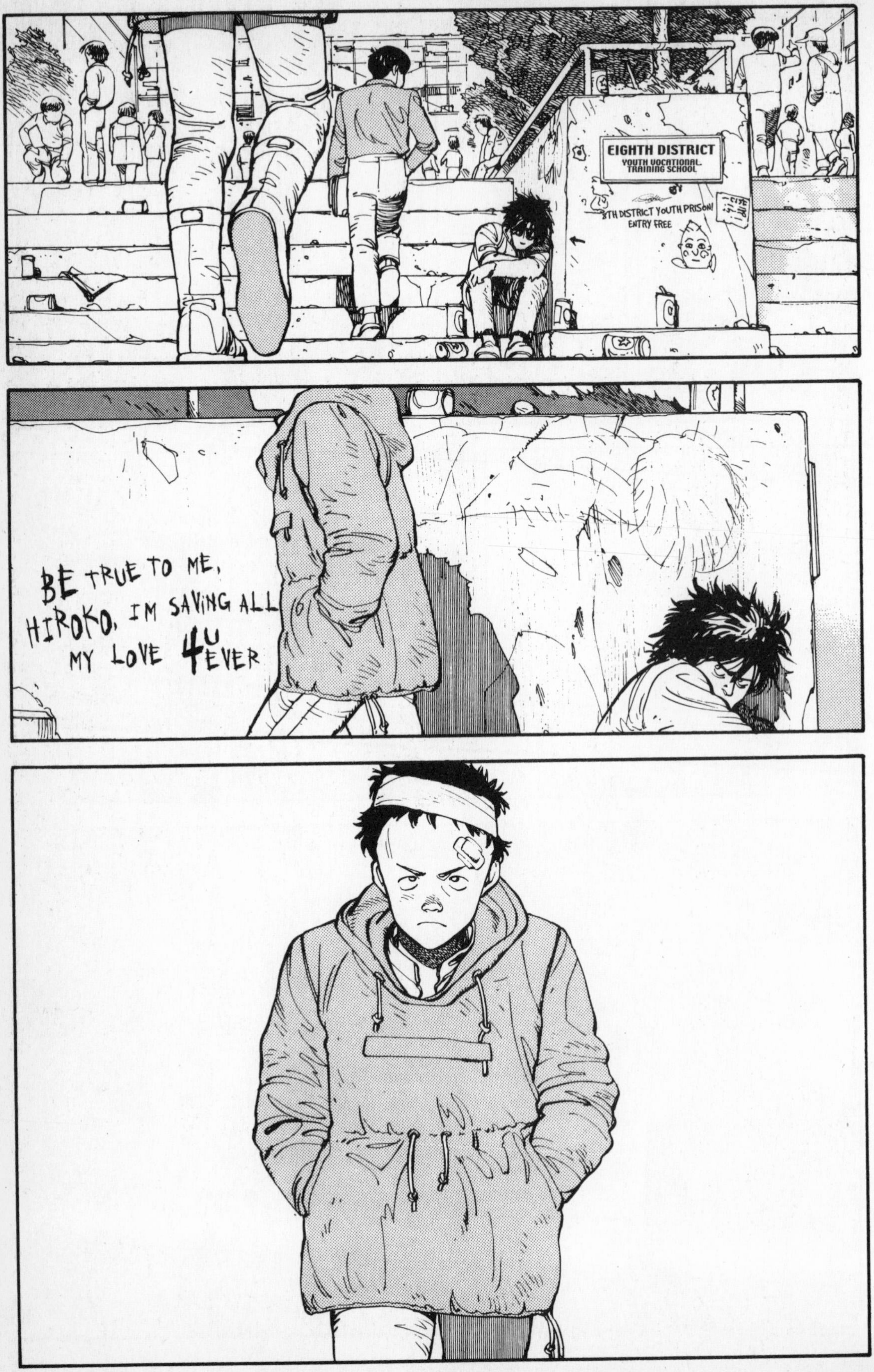
EIGHTH DISTRICT
YOUTH VOCATIONAL TRAINING SCHOOL
8TH DISTRICT YOUTH PRISON!
ENTRY FREE
BE TRUE TO ME, HIROKO, IM SAVING ALL MY LOVE 4U EVER

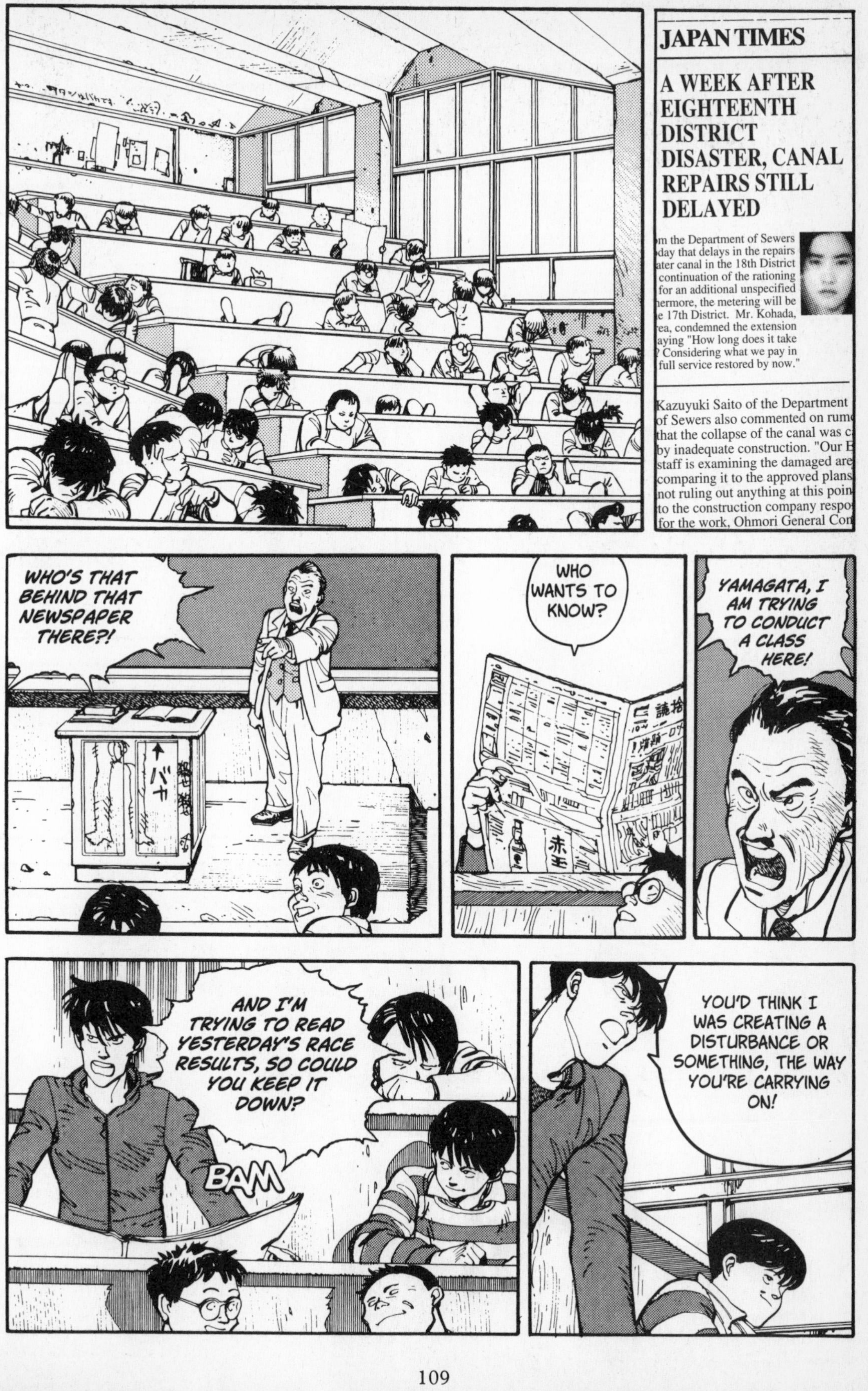
JAPAN TIMES
A WEEK AFTER EIGHTEENTH DISTRICT DISASTER, CANAL REPAIRS STILL DELAYED
m the Department of Sewers
day that delays in the repairs
ater canal in the 18th District
continuation of the rationing
for an additional unspecified
hermore, the metering will be
e 17th District. Mr. Kohada,
rea, condemned the extension
aying "How long does it take
? Considering what we pay in
full service restored by now."
Kazuyuki Saito of the Department
of Sewers also commented on rum
that the collapse of the canal was c
by inadequate construction. "Our E
staff is examining the damaged are
comparing it to the approved plans
not ruling out anything at this poin
to the construction company respo
for the work, Ohmori General Con
WHO'S THAT BEHIND THAT NEWSPAPER THERE?!
WHO WANTS TO KNOW?
YAMAGATA, I AM TRYING TO CONDUCT A CLASS HERE!
AND I'M TRYING TO READ YESTERDAY'S RACE RESULTS, SO COULD YOU KEEP IT DOWN?
BAM
YOU'D THINK I WAS CREATING A DISTURBANCE OR SOMETHING, THE WAY YOU'RE CARRYING ON!

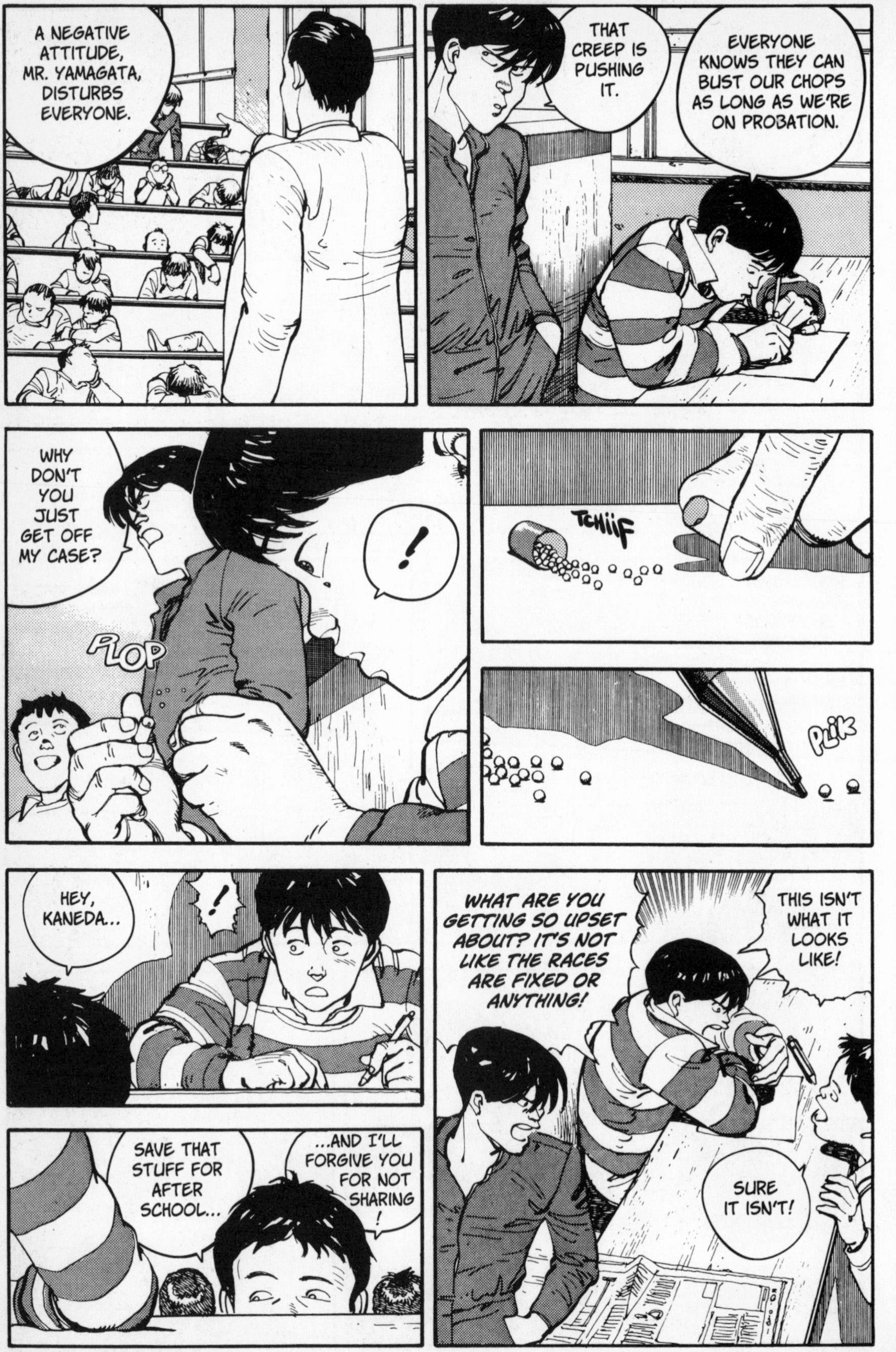
A NEGATIVE ATTITUDE, MR. YAMAGATA, DISTURBS EVERYONE.
THAT CREEP IS PUSHING IT.
EVERYONE KNOWS THEY CAN BUST OUR CHOPS AS LONG AS WE'RE ON PROBATION.
WHY DON'T YOU JUST GET OFF MY CASE?
!
PLOP
TCHIIF
PLIK
HEY, KANEDA...
!
SAVE THAT STUFF FOR AFTER SCHOOL...
...AND I'LL FORGIVE YOU FOR NOT SHARING!
WHAT ARE YOU GETTING SO UPSET ABOUT? IT'S NOT LIKE THE RACES ARE FIXED OR ANYTHING!
THIS ISN'T WHAT IT LOOKS LIKE!
SURE IT ISN'T!

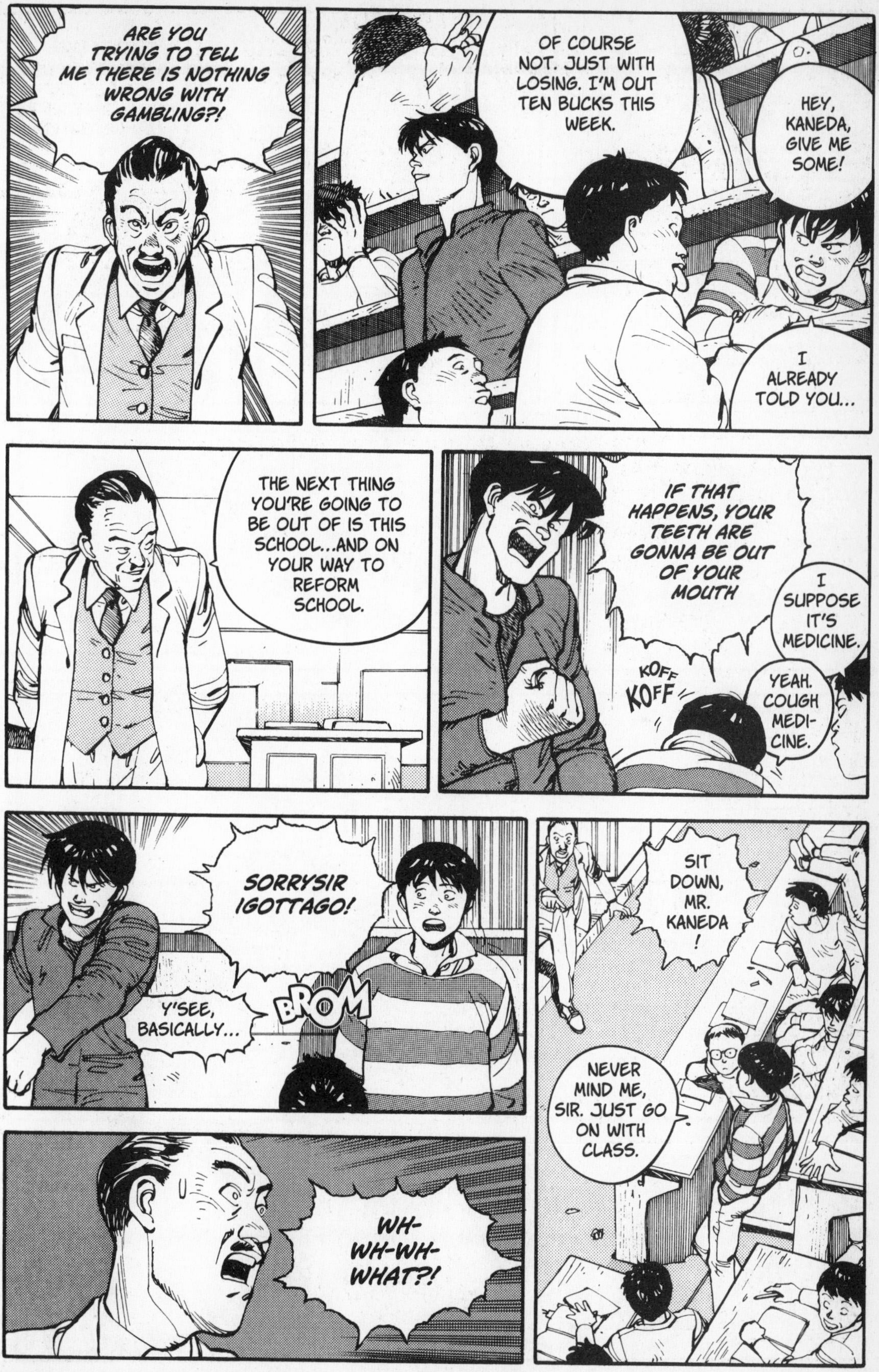
ARE YOU TRYING TO TELL ME THERE IS NOTHING WRONG WITH GAMBLING?!
OF COURSE NOT. JUST WITH LOSING. I'M OUT TEN BUCKS THIS WEEK.
HEY, KANEDA, GIVE ME SOME!
I ALREADY TOLD YOU...
THE NEXT THING YOU'RE GOING TO BE OUT OF IS THIS SCHOOL...AND ON YOUR WAY TO REFORM SCHOOL.
IF THAT HAPPENS, YOUR TEETH ARE GONNA BE OUT OF YOUR MOUTH
I SUPPOSE IT'S MEDICINE.
KOFF KOFF
YEAH. COUGH MEDI-CINE.
SORRYSIR IGOTTAGO!
Y'SEE, BASICALLY...
BROM
WH-WH-WH-WHAT?!
SIT DOWN, MR. KANEDA!
NEVER MIND ME, SIR. JUST GO ON WITH CLASS.

'BYE

GET BACK IN HERE, KANEDA!

I HAVE TO GO, TOO!

ME, TOO! ME, TOO!

MY PARENTS ARE BOTH DYING!

SHUT UP!

NO, SHE'S NOT!

MY MOTHER IS GOING TO HAVE A BABY...

YES SHE IS! AND I'M THE FATHER!

TANAKA LOOKS SICK, SIR. CAN I TAKE HIM TO THE INFIRMARY?

INFIRMARY

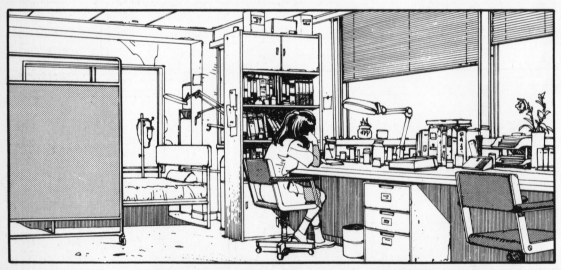

TOK TOK

!

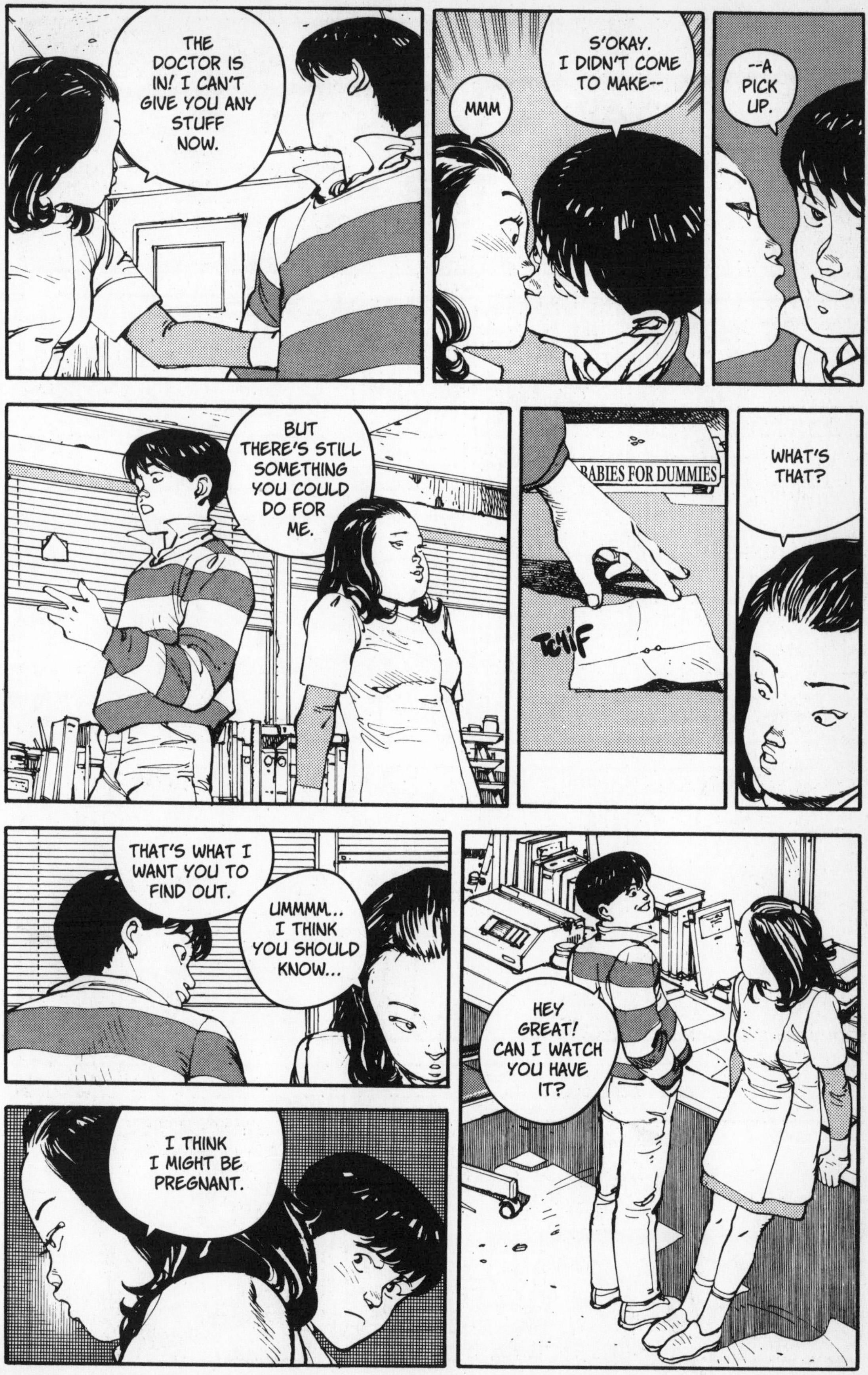
THE DOCTOR IS IN! I CAN'T GIVE YOU ANY STUFF NOW.
MMM
S'OKAY. I DIDN'T COME TO MAKE--
--A PICK UP.
BUT THERE'S STILL SOMETHING YOU COULD DO FOR ME.
BABIES FOR DUMMIES
TCHIF
WHAT'S THAT?
THAT'S WHAT I WANT YOU TO FIND OUT.
UMMMM... I THINK YOU SHOULD KNOW...
I THINK I MIGHT BE PREGNANT.
HEY GREAT! CAN I WATCH YOU HAVE IT?

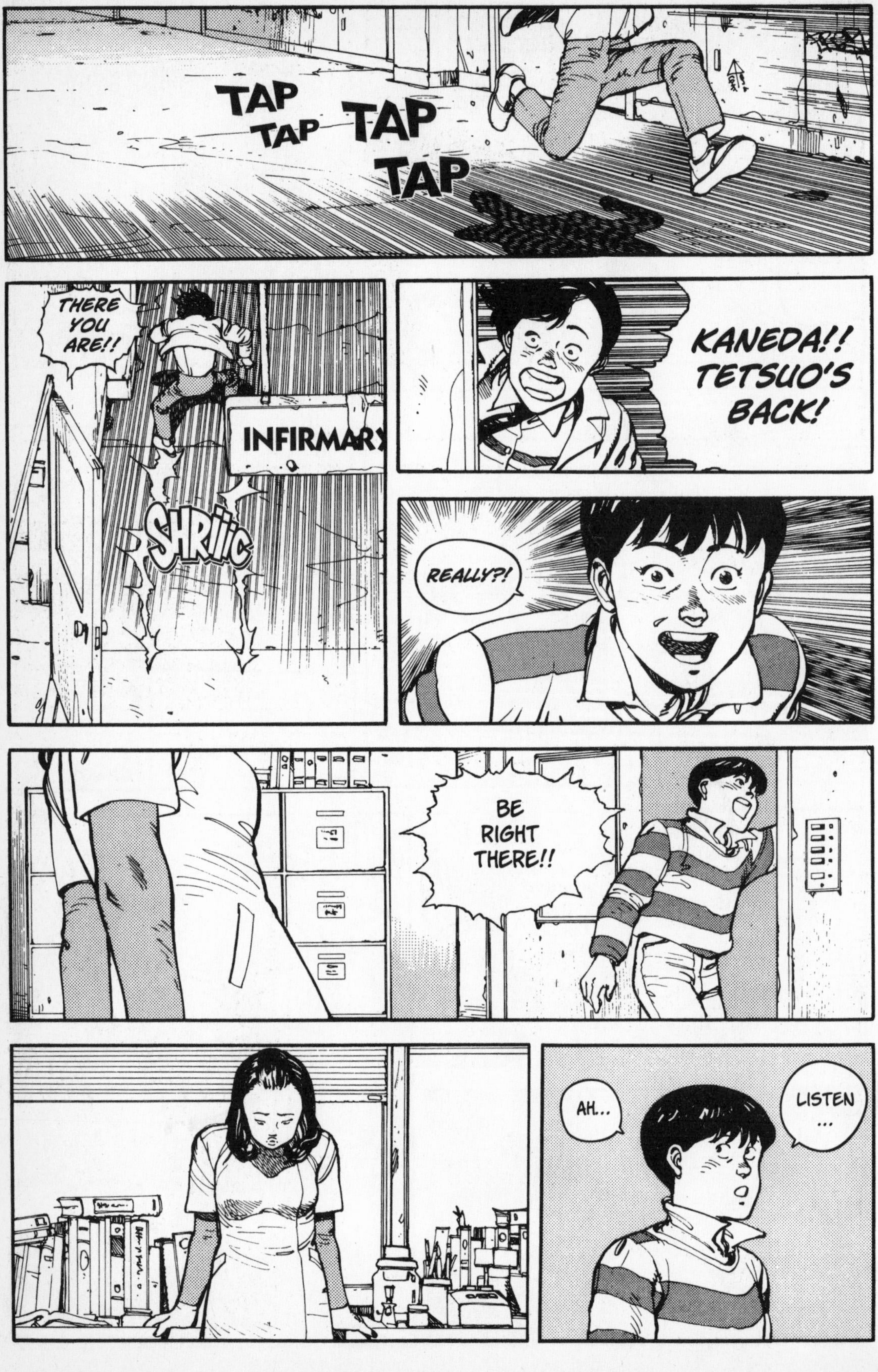
TAP
TAP
TAP
TAP
TAP
THERE YOU ARE!!
INFIRMARY
SHRIiic
KANEDA!! TETSUO'S BACK!
REALLY?!
BE RIGHT THERE!!
AH...
LISTEN ...

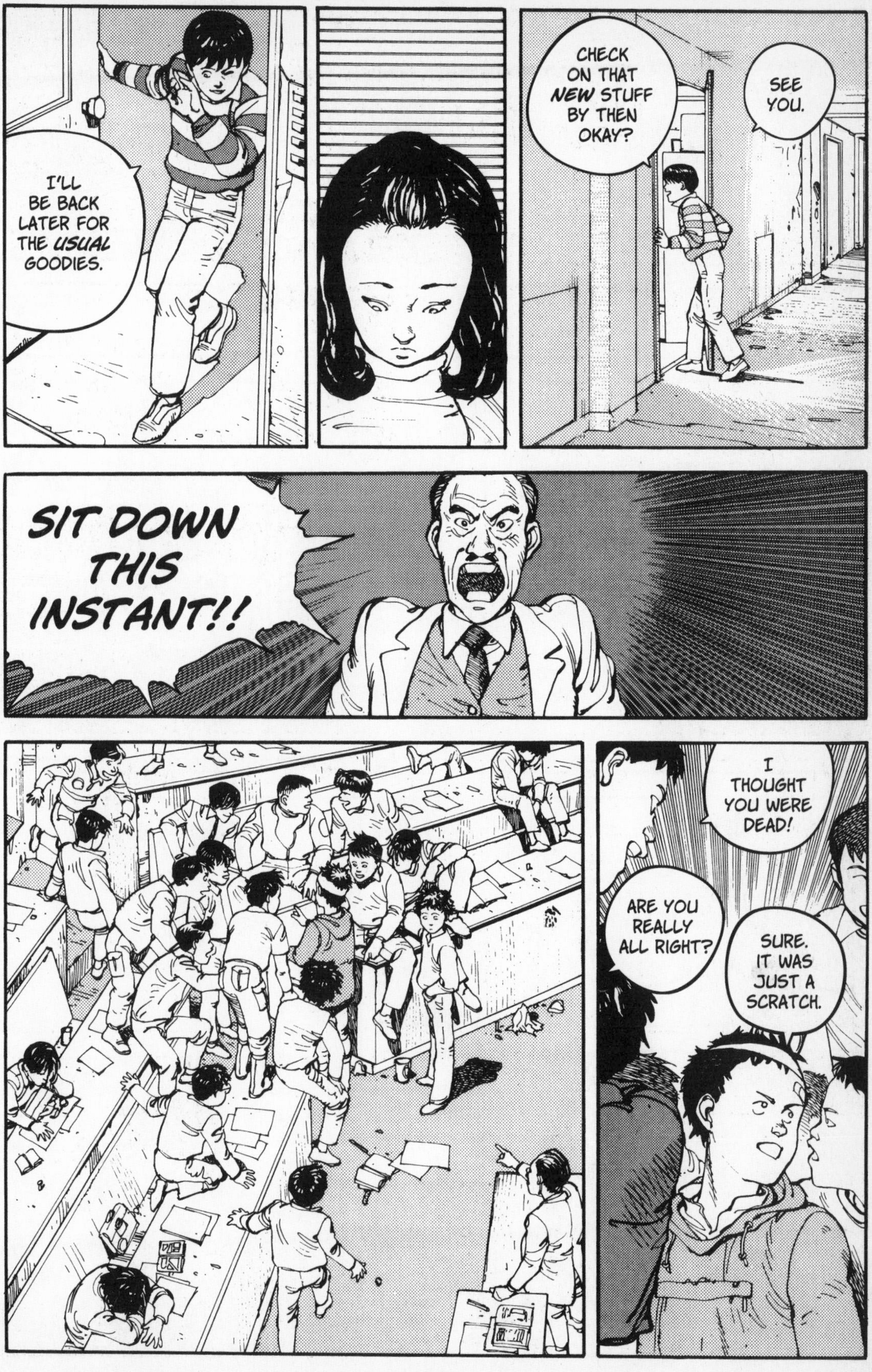

I'LL BE BACK LATER FOR THE *USUAL* GOODIES.
CHECK ON THAT *NEW* STUFF BY THEN OKAY?
SEE YOU.
SIT DOWN THIS INSTANT!!
I THOUGHT YOU WERE DEAD!
ARE YOU REALLY ALL RIGHT?
SURE. IT WAS JUST A SCRATCH.

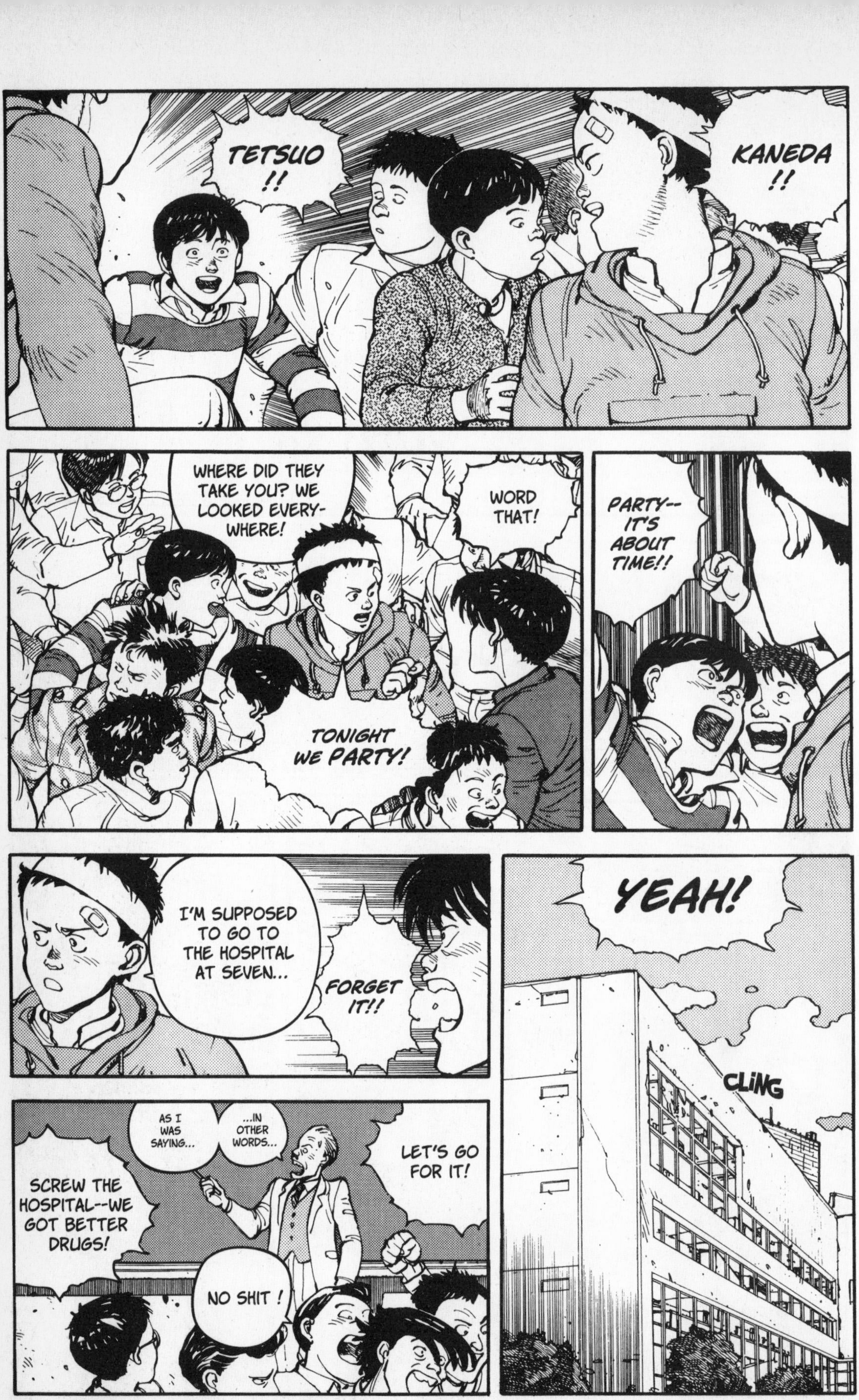

TETSUO !!
KANEDA !!
WHERE DID THEY TAKE YOU? WE LOOKED EVERY-WHERE!
WORD THAT!
TONIGHT WE PARTY!
PARTY-- IT'S ABOUT TIME!!
I'M SUPPOSED TO GO TO THE HOSPITAL AT SEVEN...
FORGET IT!!
AS I WAS SAYING...
...IN OTHER WORDS...
SCREW THE HOSPITAL--WE GOT BETTER DRUGS!
LET'S GO FOR IT!
NO SHIT !
YEAH!
CLING

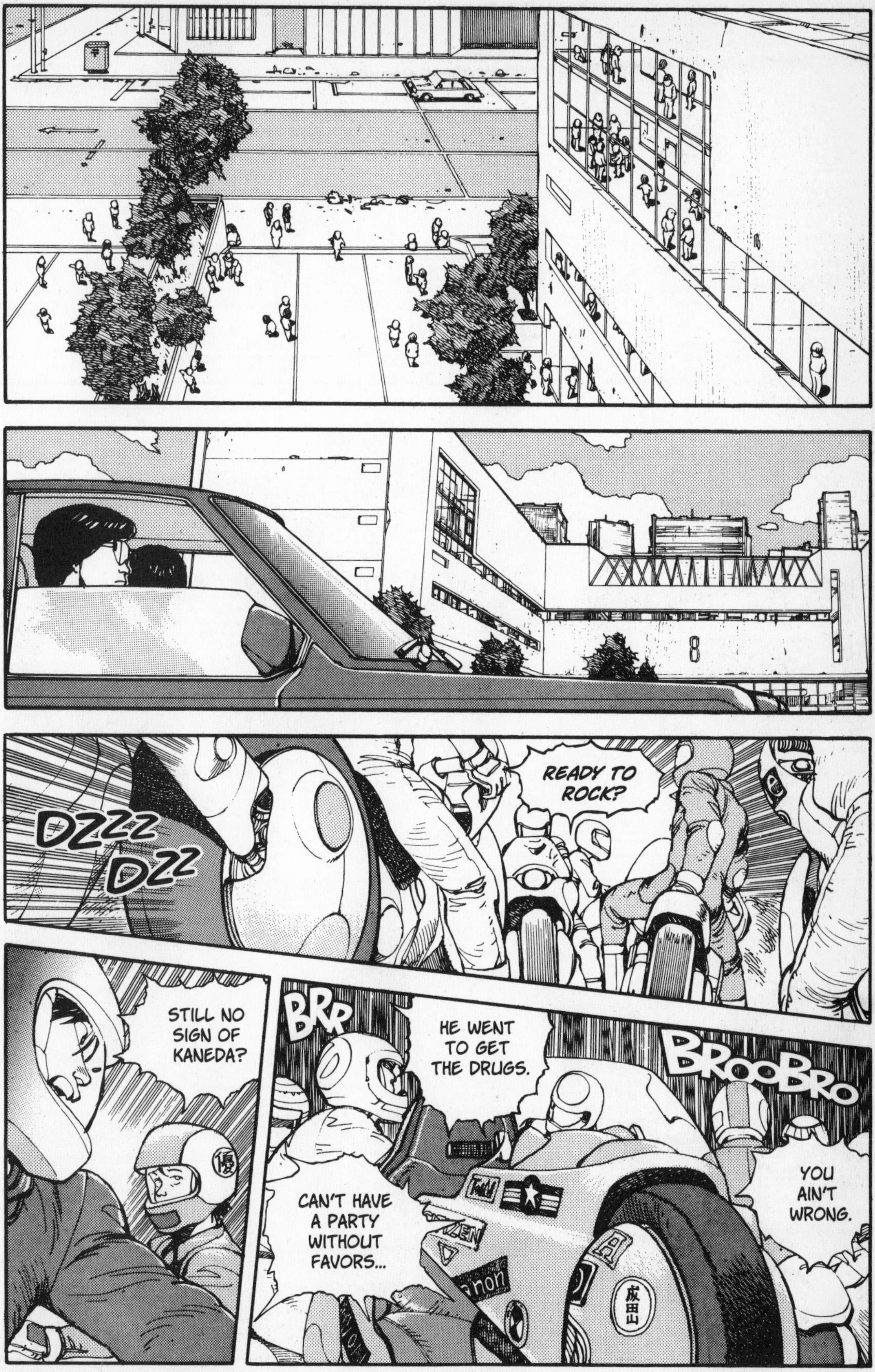
DZZZ DZZ
READY TO ROCK?
STILL NO SIGN OF KANEDA?
BRR
HE WENT TO GET THE DRUGS.
BROOBRO
CAN'T HAVE A PARTY WITHOUT FAVORS...
YOU AIN'T WRONG.

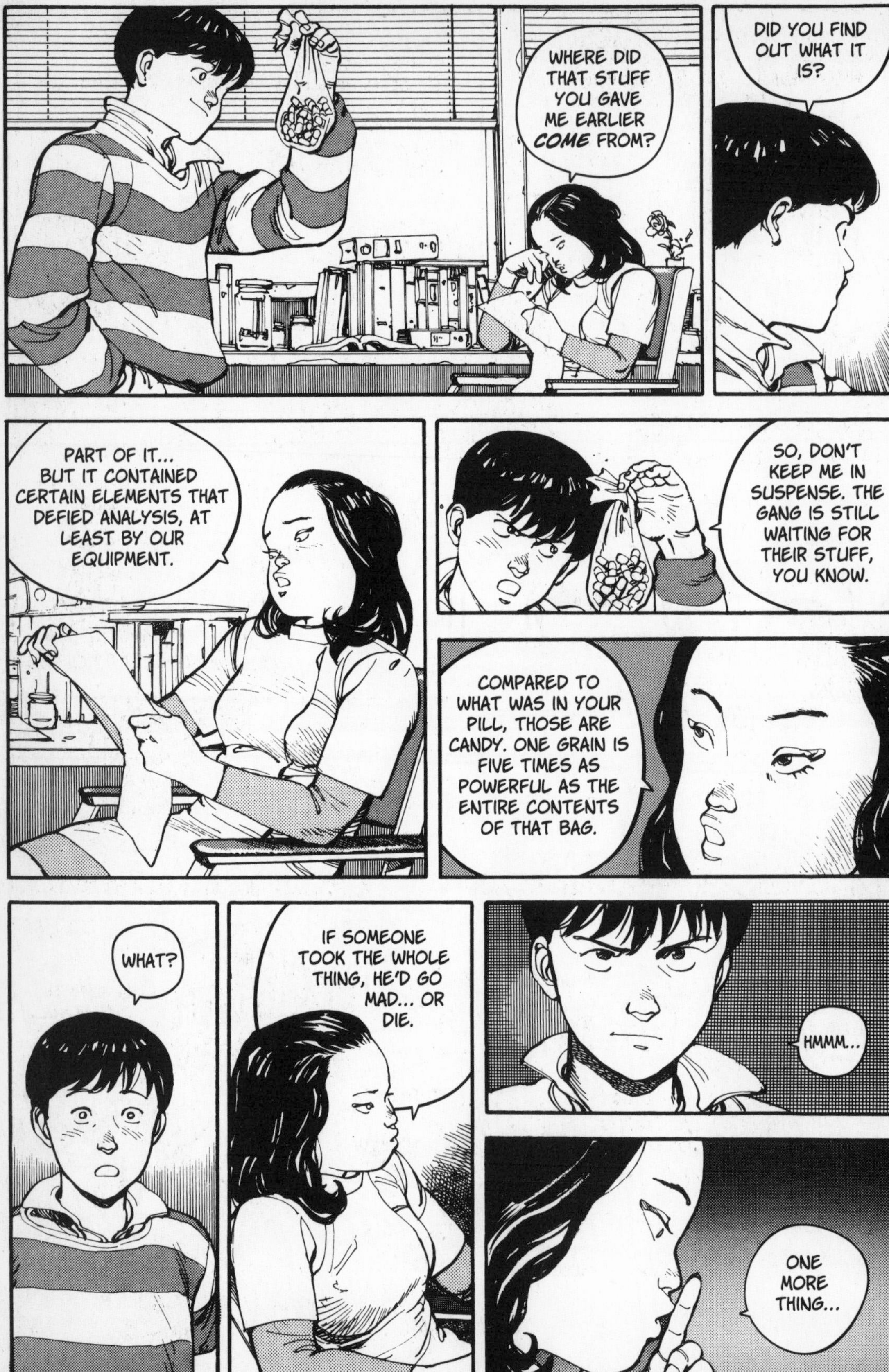
WHERE DID THAT STUFF YOU GAVE ME EARLIER COME FROM?
DID YOU FIND OUT WHAT IT IS?
PART OF IT... BUT IT CONTAINED CERTAIN ELEMENTS THAT DEFIED ANALYSIS, AT LEAST BY OUR EQUIPMENT.
SO, DON'T KEEP ME IN SUSPENSE. THE GANG IS STILL WAITING FOR THEIR STUFF, YOU KNOW.
COMPARED TO WHAT WAS IN YOUR PILL, THOSE ARE CANDY. ONE GRAIN IS FIVE TIMES AS POWERFUL AS THE ENTIRE CONTENTS OF THAT BAG.
WHAT?
IF SOMEONE TOOK THE WHOLE THING, HE'D GO MAD... OR DIE.
HMMM...
ONE MORE THING...

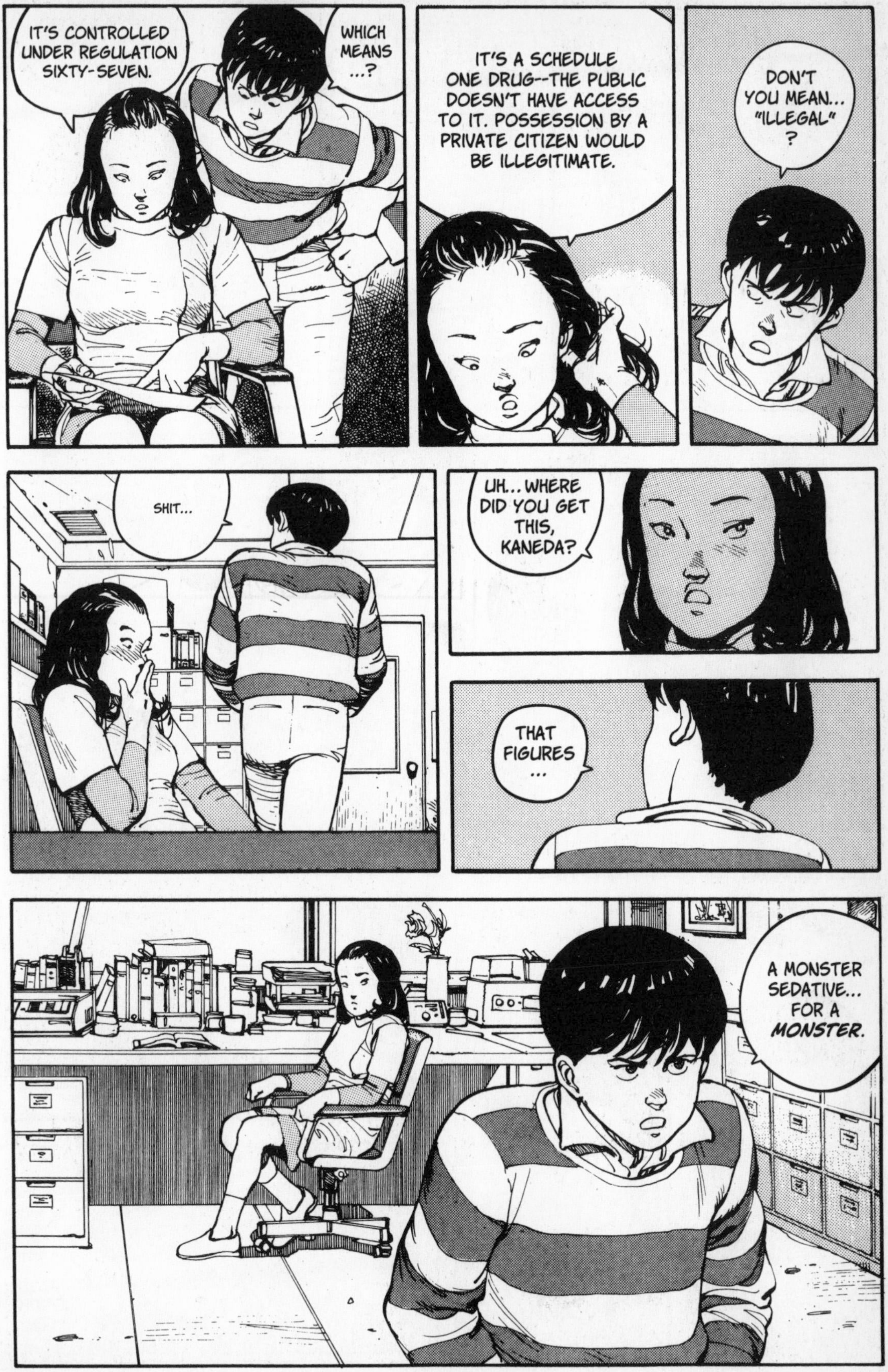
IT'S CONTROLLED UNDER REGULATION SIXTY-SEVEN.
WHICH MEANS ...?
IT'S A SCHEDULE ONE DRUG--THE PUBLIC DOESN'T HAVE ACCESS TO IT. POSSESSION BY A PRIVATE CITIZEN WOULD BE ILLEGITIMATE.
DON'T YOU MEAN... "ILLEGAL" ?
SHIT...
UH... WHERE DID YOU GET THIS, KANEDA?
THAT FIGURES ...
A MONSTER SEDATIVE... FOR A *MONSTER*.

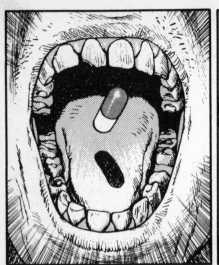

LET'S GO!!

VROOBRO

YEAAHH!!!

GULP

IT'S GREAT. WHERE'D YOU GET IT?

LIKE THE NEW BIKE?

OH... SOMEONE LEFT IT IN THE STREET.

THOUGHT SO.

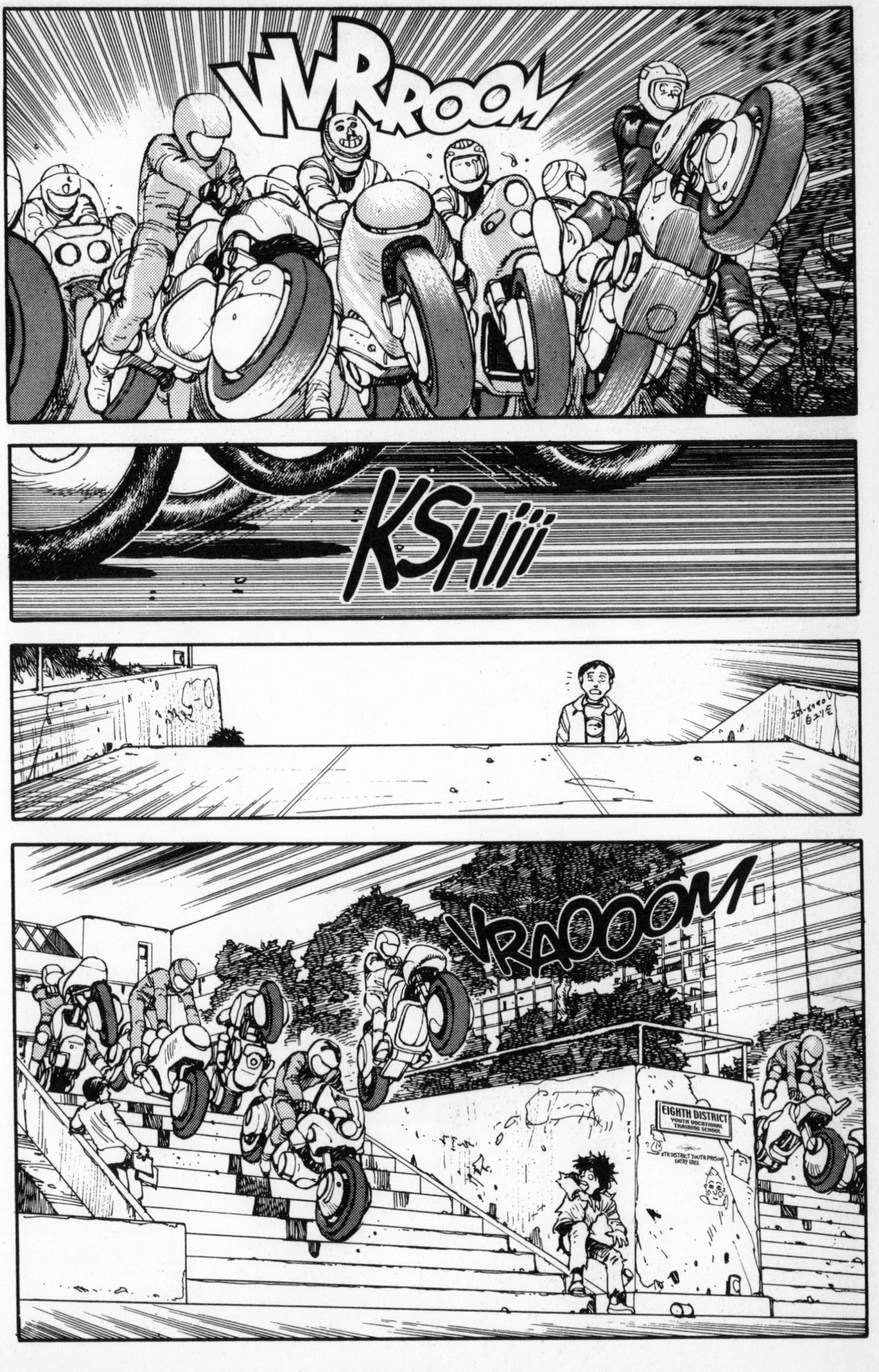
VVRROOM
KSHiii
VRAOOOM
EIGHTH DISTRICT
YOUTH VOCATIONAL TRAINING SCHOOL
8TH DISTRICT YOUTH PRISON
ENTRY FREE

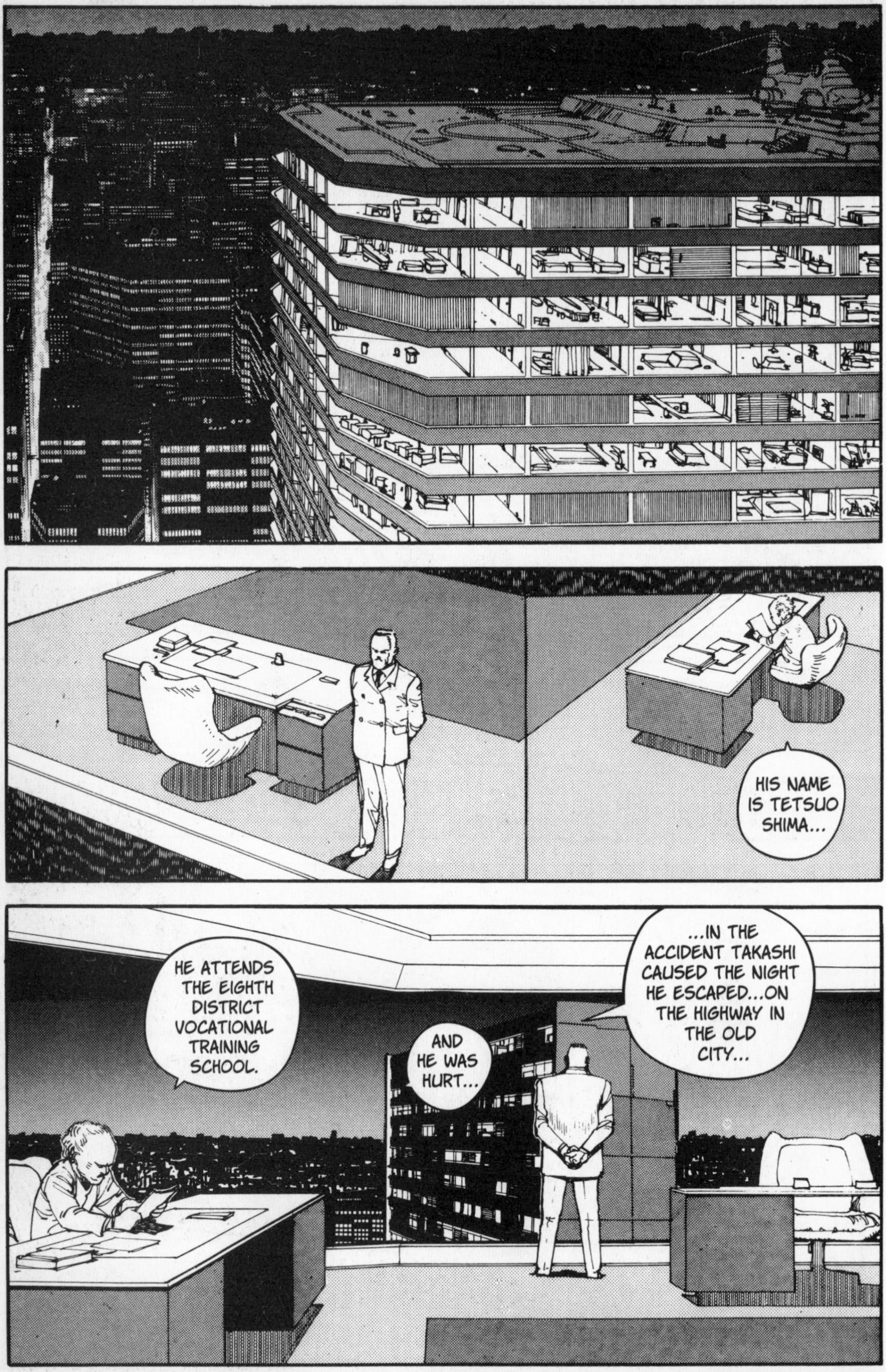
HIS NAME IS TETSUO SHIMA...
HE ATTENDS THE EIGHTH DISTRICT VOCATIONAL TRAINING SCHOOL.
AND HE WAS HURT...
...IN THE ACCIDENT TAKASHI CAUSED THE NIGHT HE ESCAPED...ON THE HIGHWAY IN THE OLD CITY...

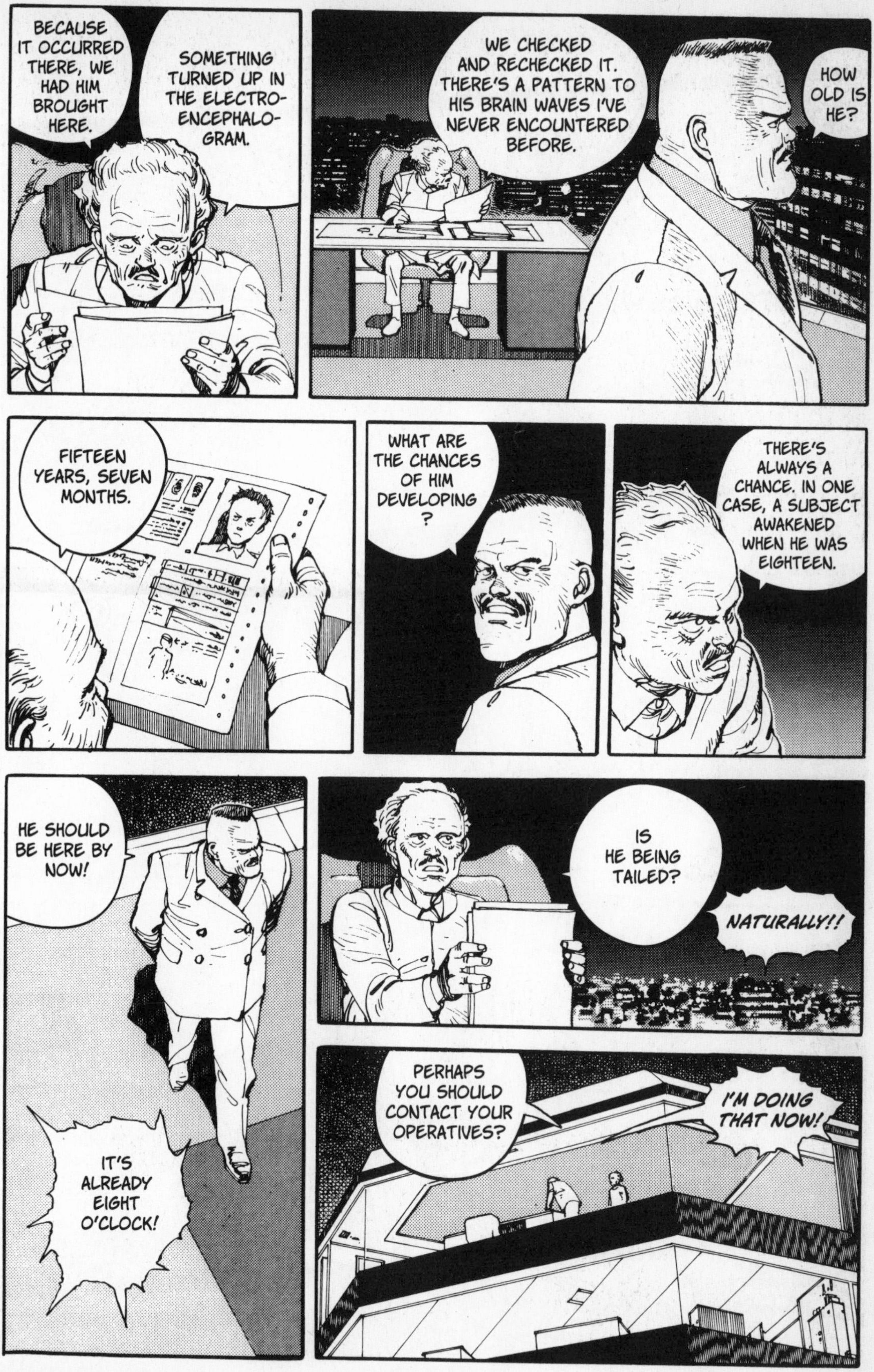
BECAUSE IT OCCURRED THERE, WE HAD HIM BROUGHT HERE.
SOMETHING TURNED UP IN THE ELECTRO-ENCEPHALOGRAM.
WE CHECKED AND RECHECKED IT. THERE'S A PATTERN TO HIS BRAIN WAVES I'VE NEVER ENCOUNTERED BEFORE.
HOW OLD IS HE?
FIFTEEN YEARS, SEVEN MONTHS.
WHAT ARE THE CHANCES OF HIM DEVELOPING ?
THERE'S ALWAYS A CHANCE. IN ONE CASE, A SUBJECT AWAKENED WHEN HE WAS EIGHTEEN.
HE SHOULD BE HERE BY NOW!
IT'S ALREADY EIGHT O'CLOCK!
IS HE BEING TAILED?
NATURALLY!!
PERHAPS YOU SHOULD CONTACT YOUR OPERATIVES?
I'M DOING THAT NOW!

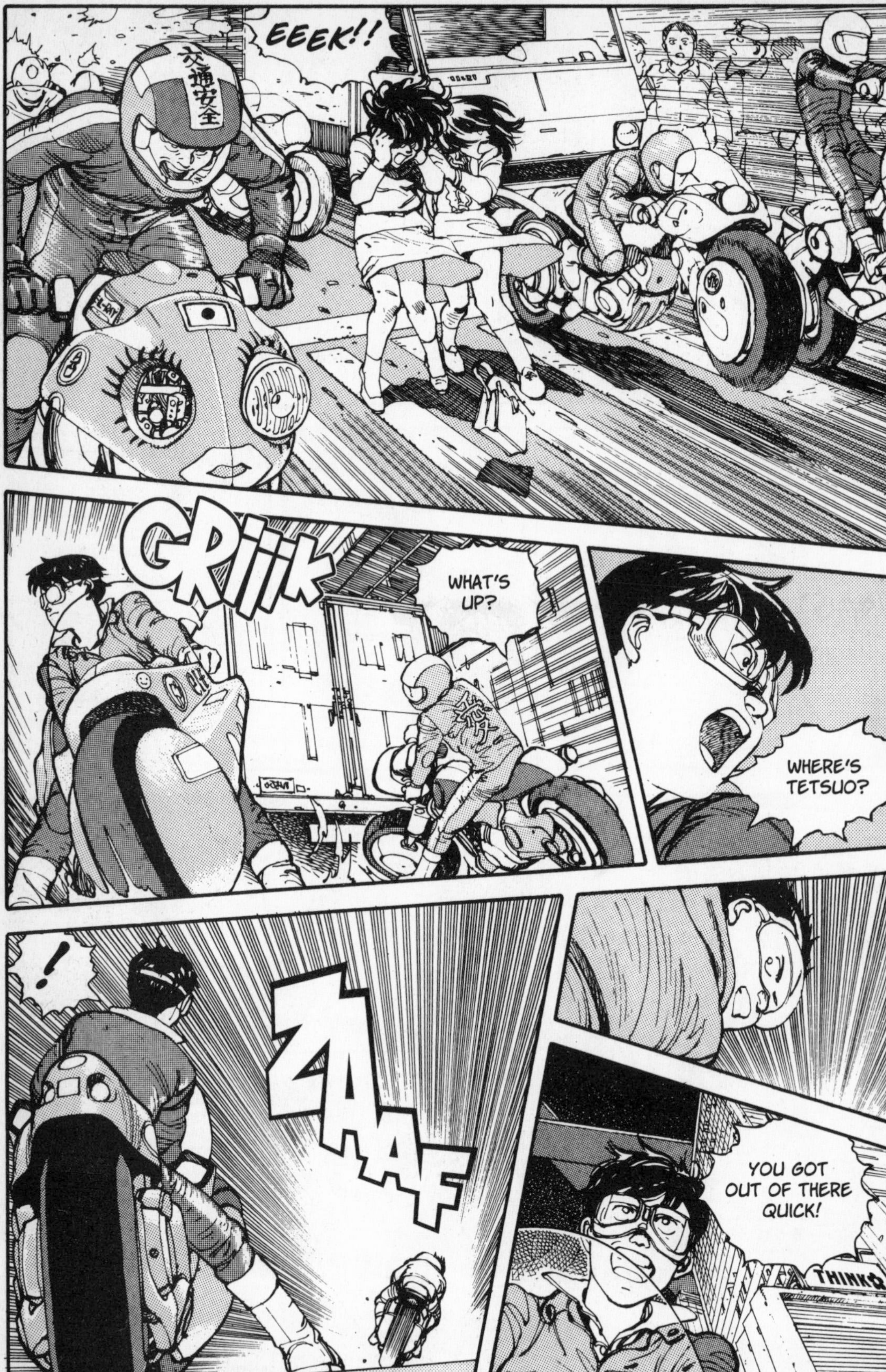
EEEK!!
GRIIIK
WHAT'S UP?
WHERE'S TETSUO?
!
ZAAF
YOU GOT OUT OF THERE QUICK!
THINK

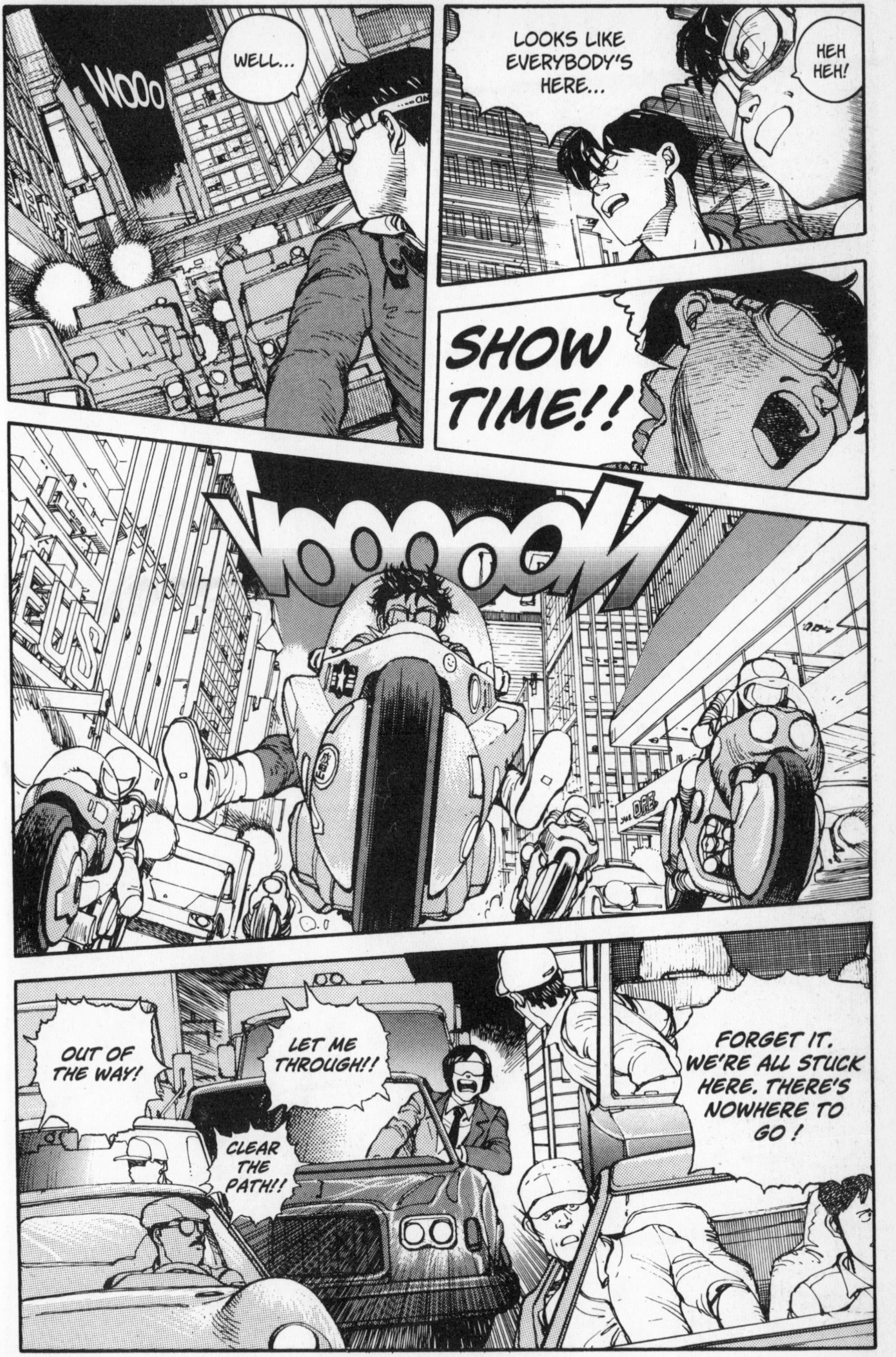
WOOO
WELL...
LOOKS LIKE EVERYBODY'S HERE...
HEH HEH!
SHOW TIME!!
VOOOOOM
OUT OF THE WAY!
LET ME THROUGH!!
CLEAR THE PATH!!
FORGET IT. WE'RE ALL STUCK HERE. THERE'S NOWHERE TO GO!

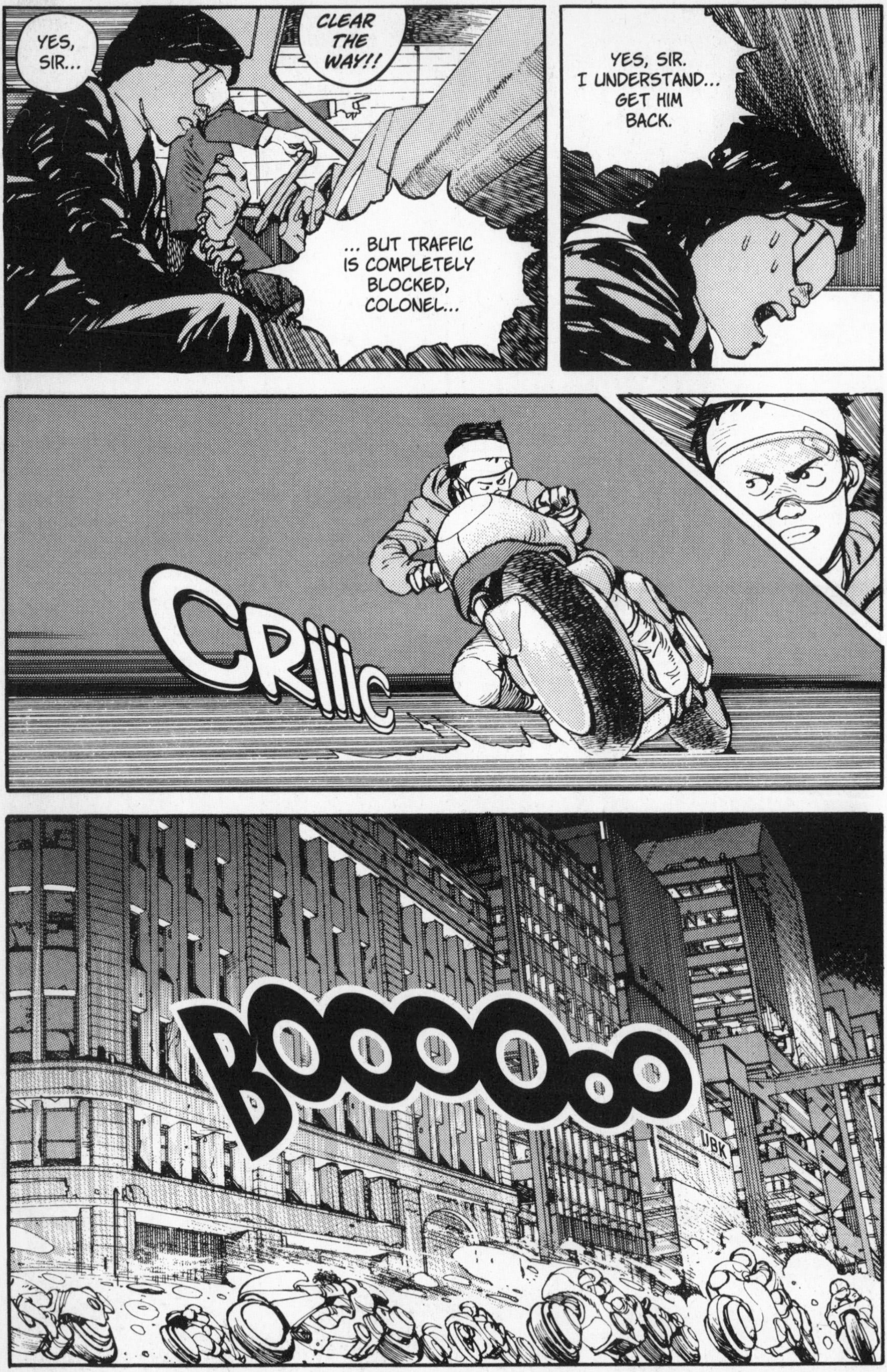
YES, SIR...
CLEAR THE WAY!!
... BUT TRAFFIC IS COMPLETELY BLOCKED, COLONEL...
YES, SIR. I UNDERSTAND... GET HIM BACK.
CRiiic
BOOOO..O
UBK

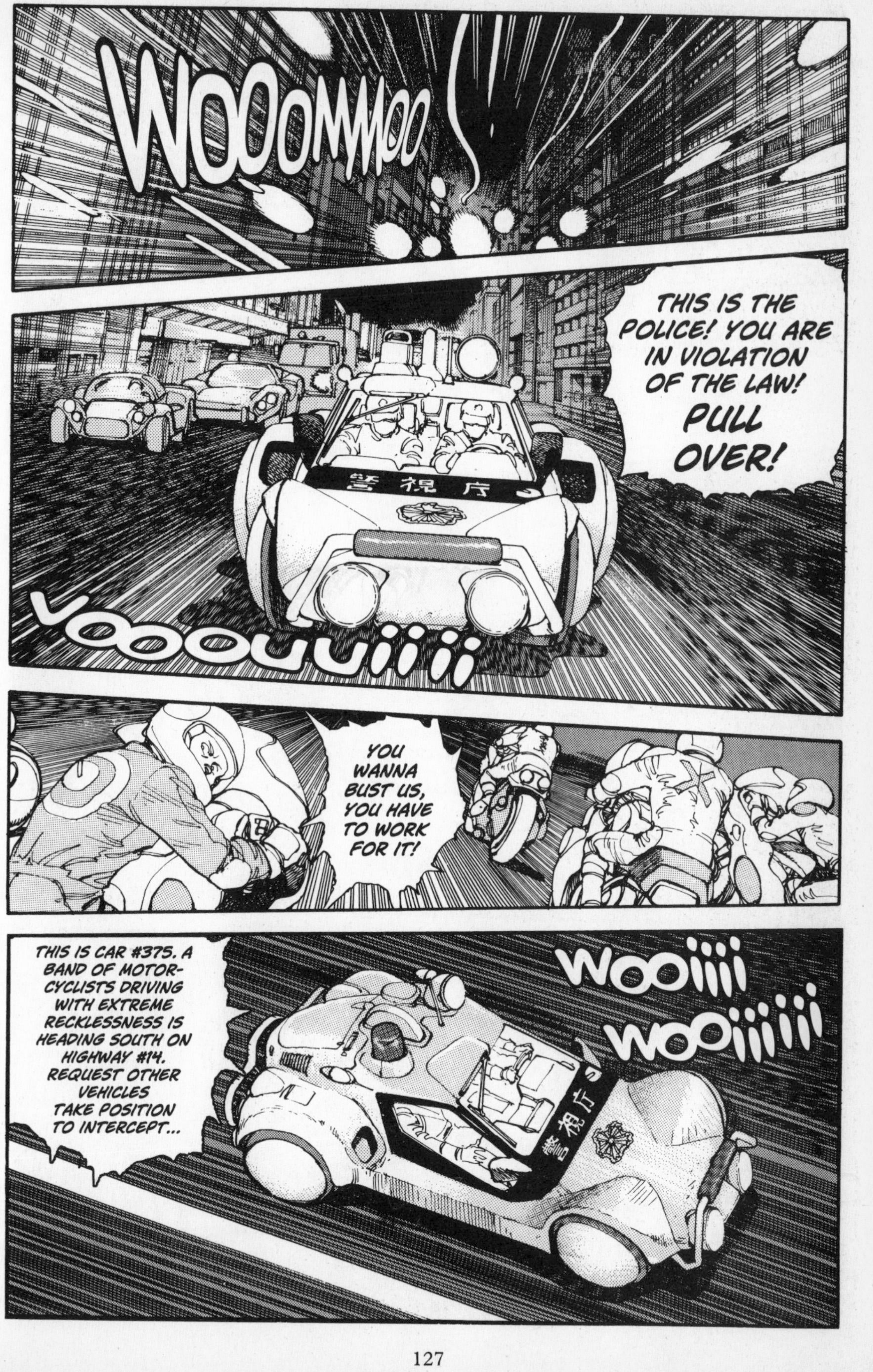
WOOOMMOO
THIS IS THE POLICE! YOU ARE IN VIOLATION OF THE LAW! PULL OVER!
警視庁
VOOOUUIIII
YOU WANNA BUST US, YOU HAVE TO WORK FOR IT!
THIS IS CAR #375. A BAND OF MOTOR-CYCLISTS DRIVING WITH EXTREME RECKLESSNESS IS HEADING SOUTH ON HIGHWAY #14. REQUEST OTHER VEHICLES TAKE POSITION TO INTERCEPT...
WOOIIII
WOOIIIIII
警視庁

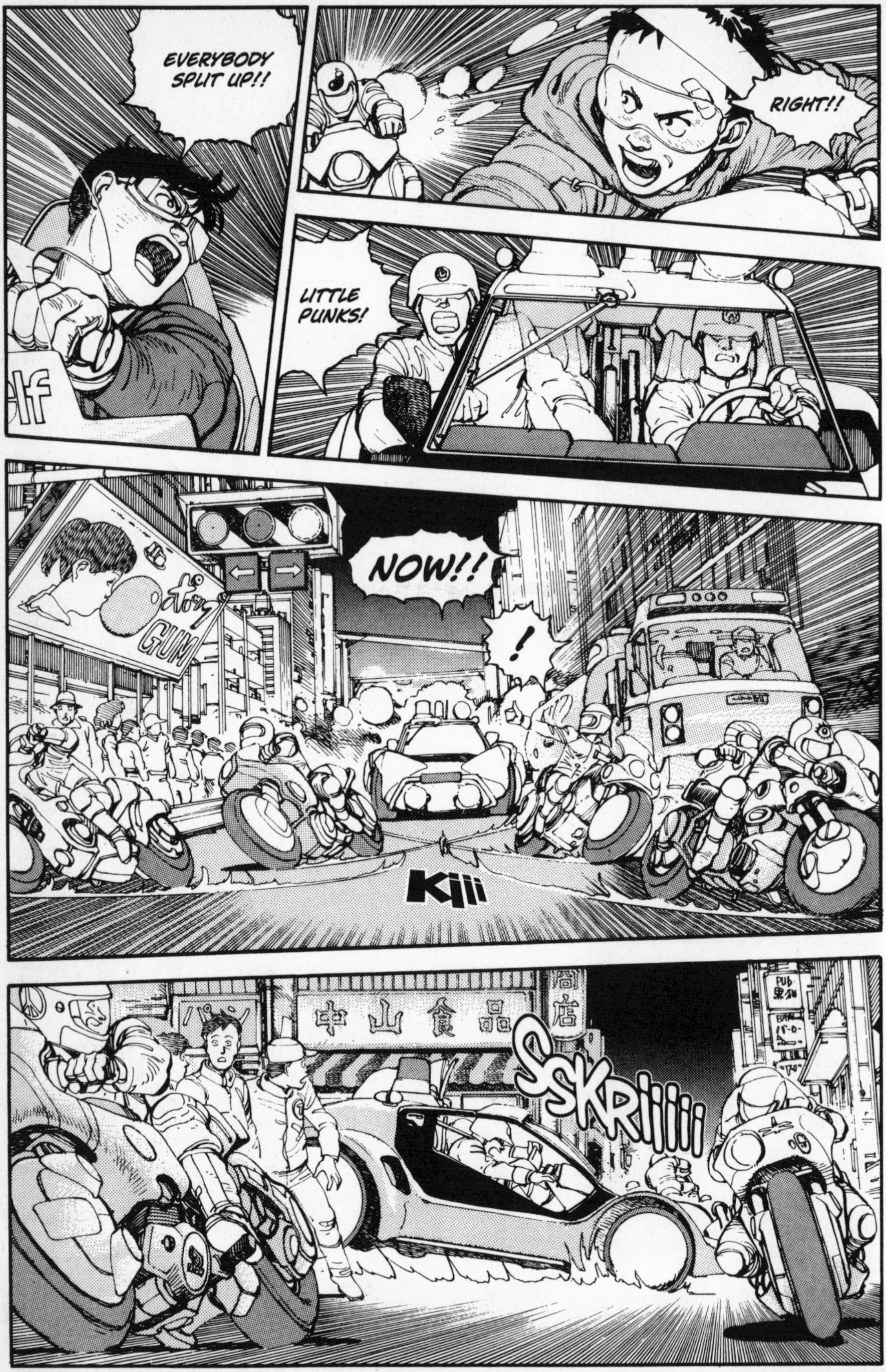
EVERYBODY SPLIT UP!!
RIGHT!!
LITTLE PUNKS!
NOW!!
!
GUM
Kiii
中山食品店
SSKRiiiii

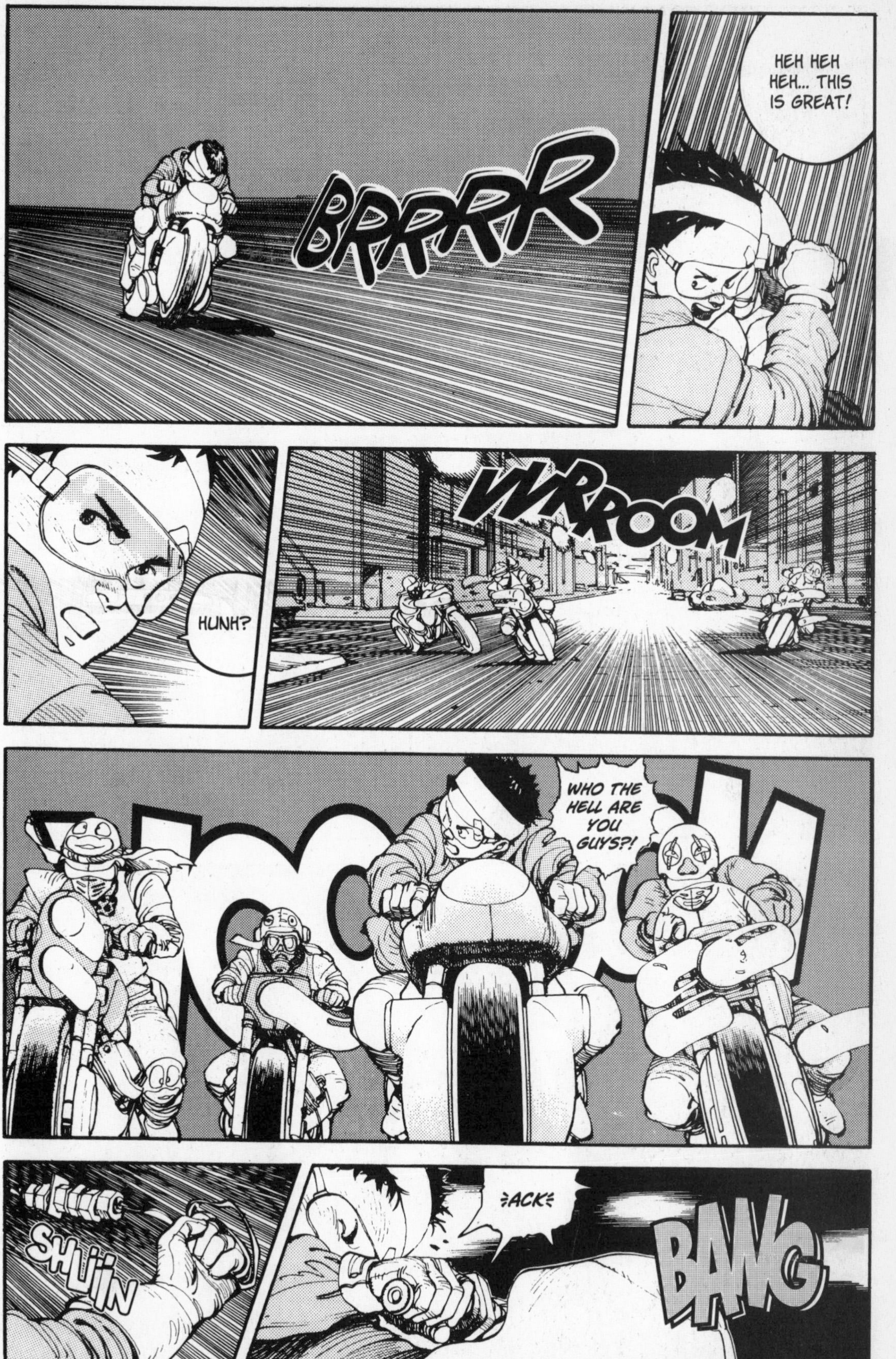
BRRRRR
HEH HEH HEH... THIS IS GREAT!
HUNH?
VVRROOM
WHO THE HELL ARE YOU GUYS?!
SHUIN
ACK
BAMG

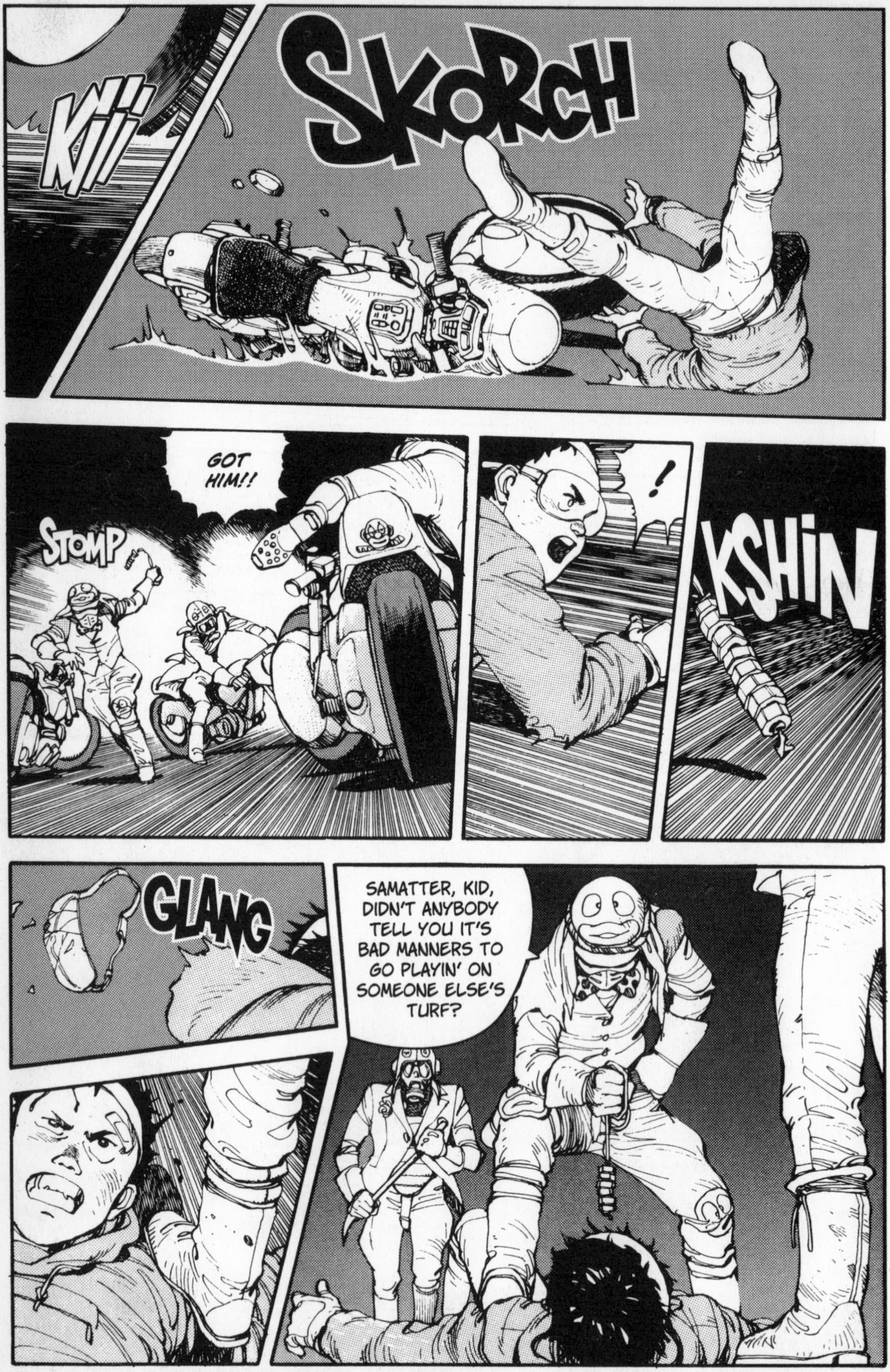

KIII
SKORCH
GOT HIM!!
STOMP
!
KSHIN
GLANG
SAMATTER, KID, DIDN'T ANYBODY TELL YOU IT'S BAD MANNERS TO GO PLAYIN' ON SOMEONE ELSE'S TURF?

≶UCK≶

PUNCH

工場西内 ≶OOCK≶ ストライキを潰せ！

HOLD IT!!

VRAOO

HERE COME THE REST OF THEM!

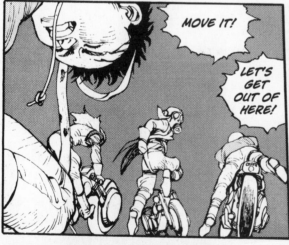

MOVE IT!

LET'S GET OUT OF HERE!

TETSUO!!

THAT WAS THE CLOWN GANG!!

!

?

!

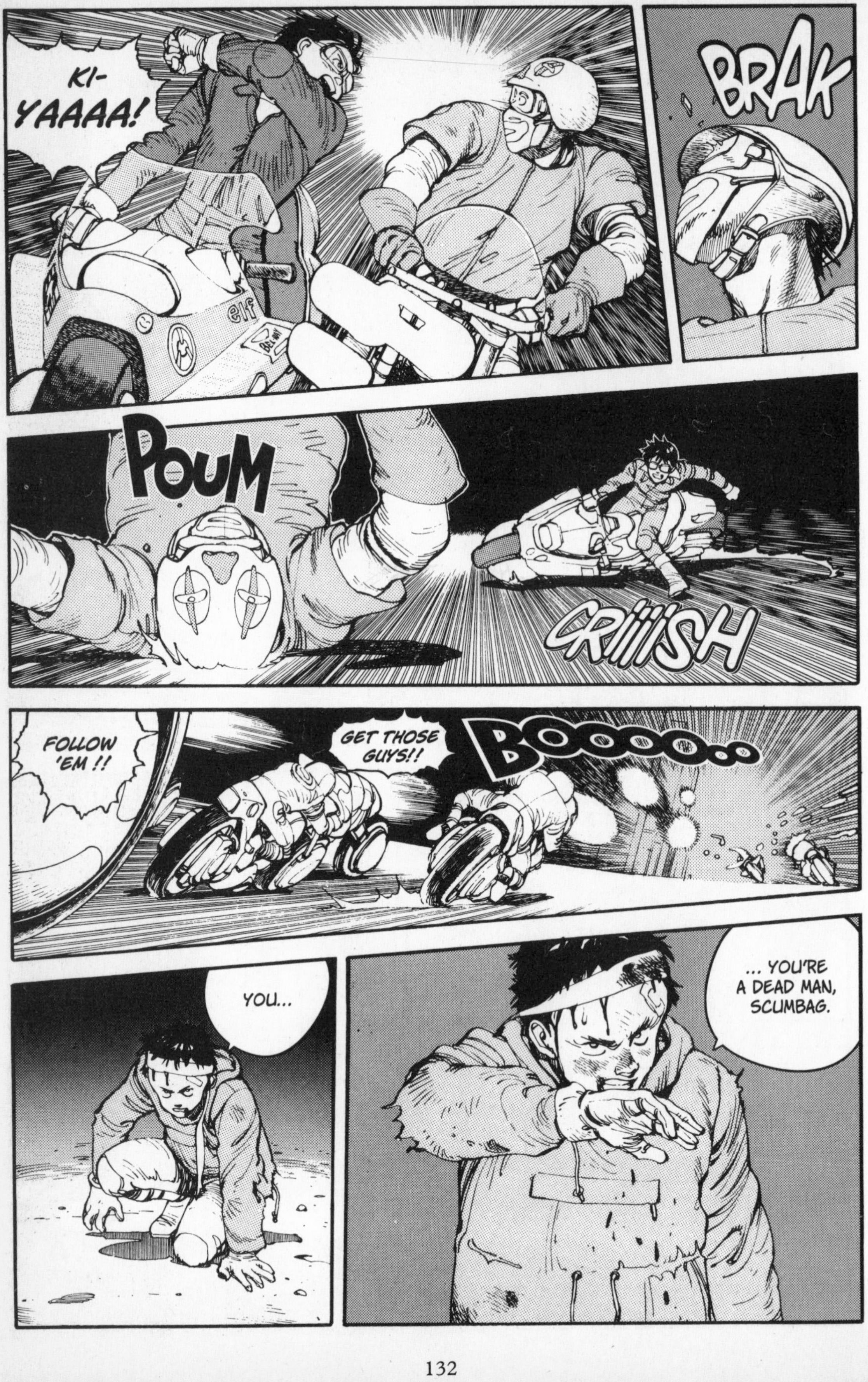
KI-
YAAAA!
BRAK
POUM
CRIIISH
FOLLOW 'EM !!
GET THOSE GUYS!!
BOOOOO...
YOU...
... YOU'RE A DEAD MAN, SCUMBAG.

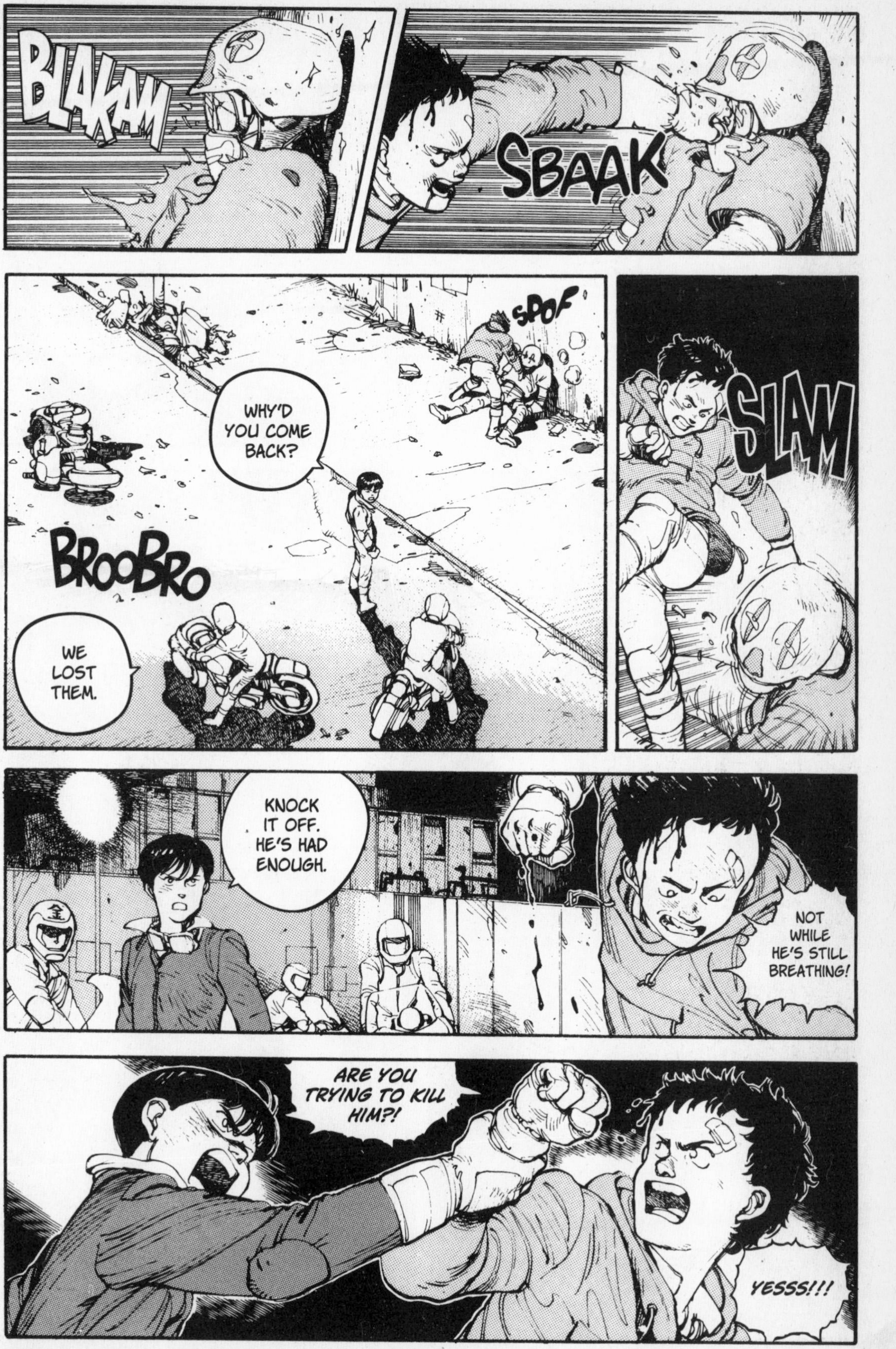

BLAKAM
SBAAK
SPOF
WHY'D YOU COME BACK?
BROOBRO
WE LOST THEM.
SLAM
KNOCK IT OFF. HE'S HAD ENOUGH.
NOT WHILE HE'S STILL BREATHING!
ARE YOU TRYING TO KILL HIM?!
YESSS!!!

I DON'T TAKE ORDERS FROM YOU.

SPLAT

SAY WHAT?!

I SAID I DON'T TAKE ORDERS FROM YOU, KANEDA, YOU GOT THAT?

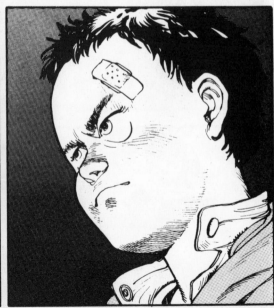

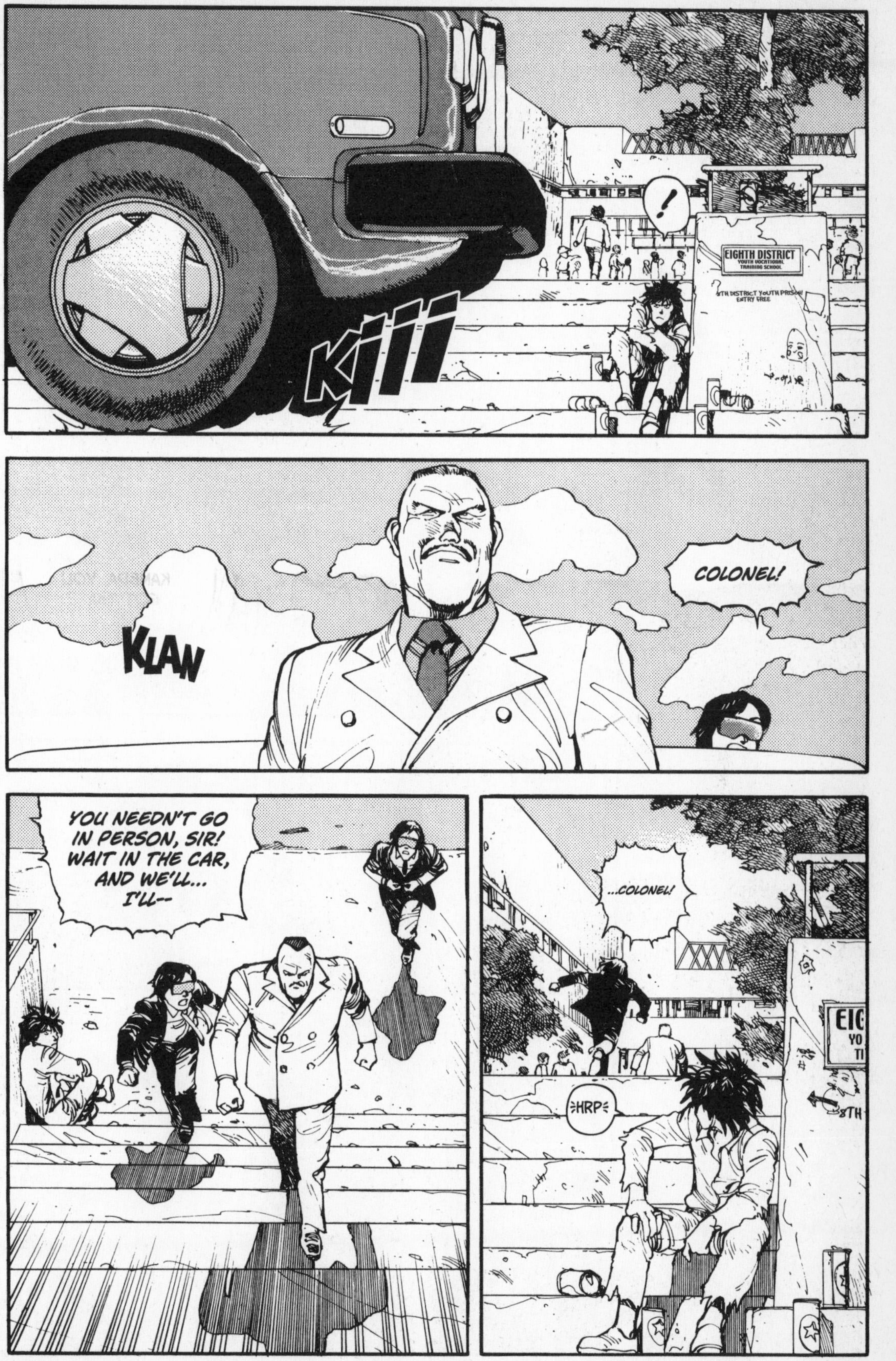
!
EIGHTH DISTRICT
YOUTH VOCATIONAL TRAINING SCHOOL
8TH DISTRICT YOUTH PRISON! ENTRY FREE
KIII
KLAN
COLONEL!
YOU NEEDN'T GO IN PERSON, SIR! WAIT IN THE CAR, AND WE'LL... I'LL--
...COLONEL!
HRP

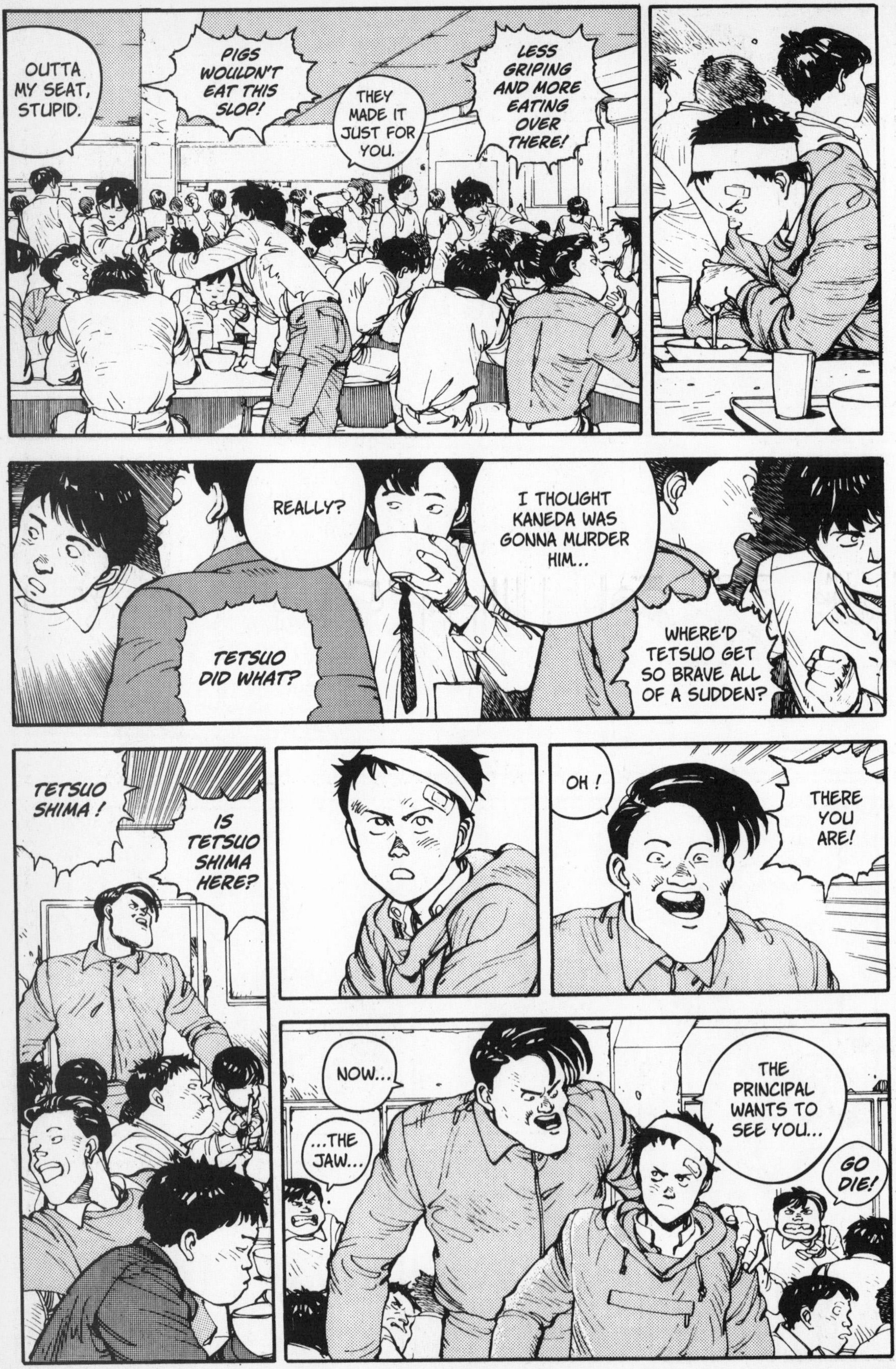
OUTTA MY SEAT, STUPID.
PIGS WOULDN'T EAT THIS SLOP!
THEY MADE IT JUST FOR YOU.
LESS GRIPING AND MORE EATING OVER THERE!
REALLY?
TETSUO DID WHAT?
I THOUGHT KANEDA WAS GONNA MURDER HIM...
WHERE'D TETSUO GET SO BRAVE ALL OF A SUDDEN?
TETSUO SHIMA!
IS TETSUO SHIMA HERE?
OH!
THERE YOU ARE!
NOW...
...THE JAW...
THE PRINCIPAL WANTS TO SEE YOU...
GO DIE!

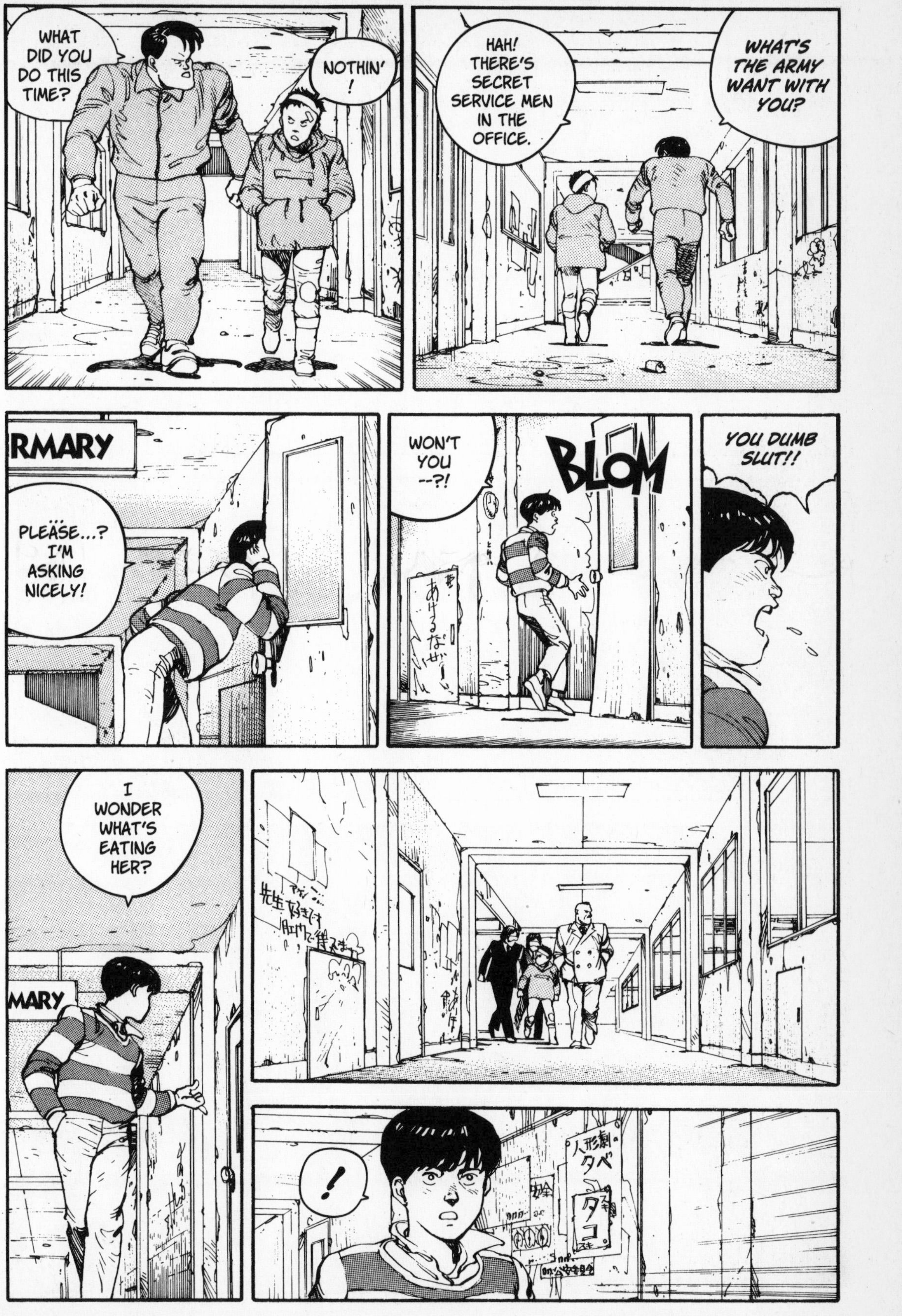
WHAT DID YOU DO THIS TIME?
NOTHIN'!
HAH! THERE'S SECRET SERVICE MEN IN THE OFFICE.
WHAT'S THE ARMY WANT WITH YOU?
RMARY
... PLEASE...? I'M ASKING NICELY!
WON'T YOU --?!
BLOM
YOU DUMB SLUT!!
I WONDER WHAT'S EATING HER?
MARY
!

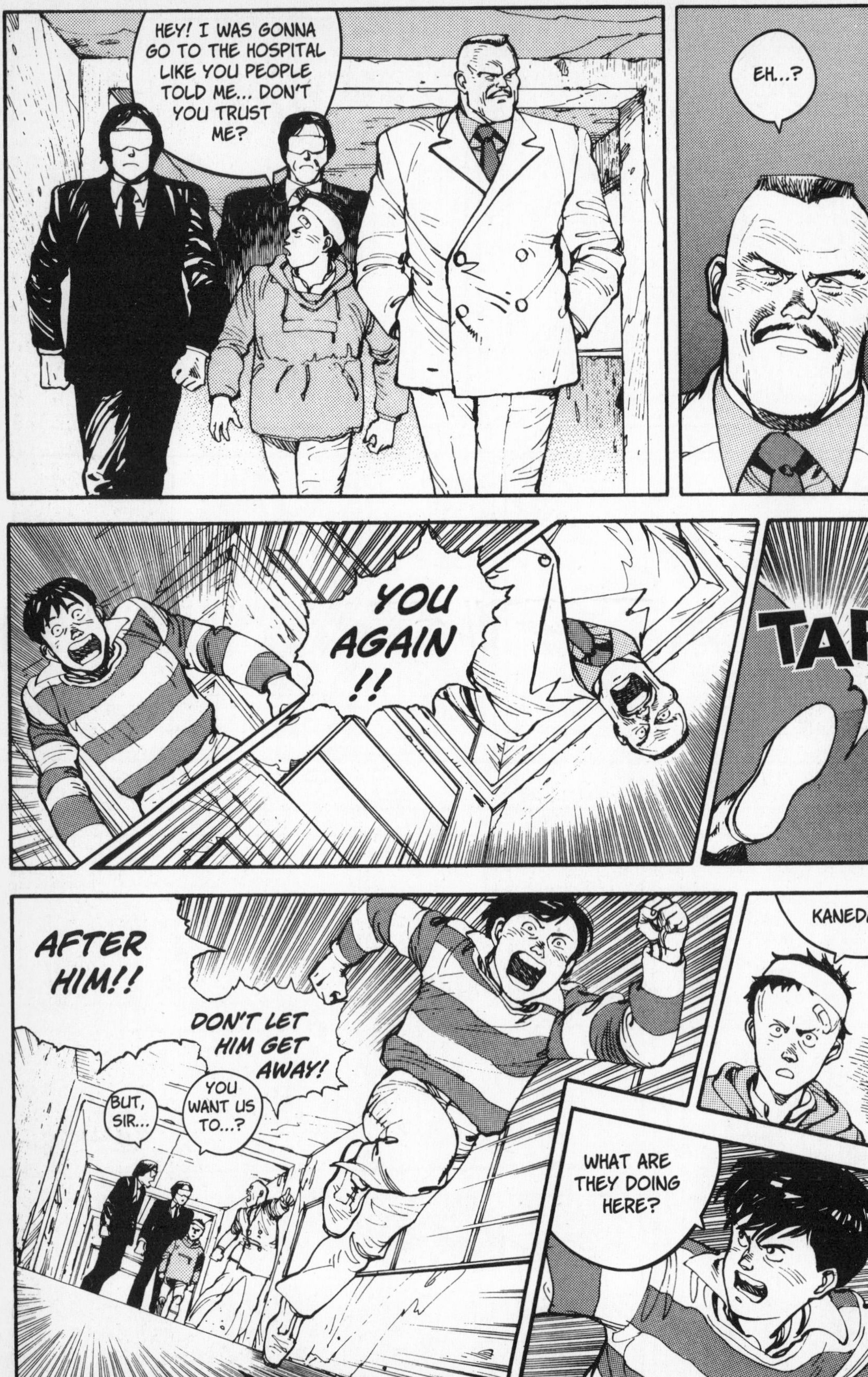
HEY! I WAS GONNA GO TO THE HOSPITAL LIKE YOU PEOPLE TOLD ME... DON'T YOU TRUST ME?
EH...?
YOU AGAIN !!
TAP
AFTER HIM!!
DON'T LET HIM GET AWAY!
BUT, SIR...
YOU WANT US TO...?
KANEDA?
WHAT ARE THEY DOING HERE?

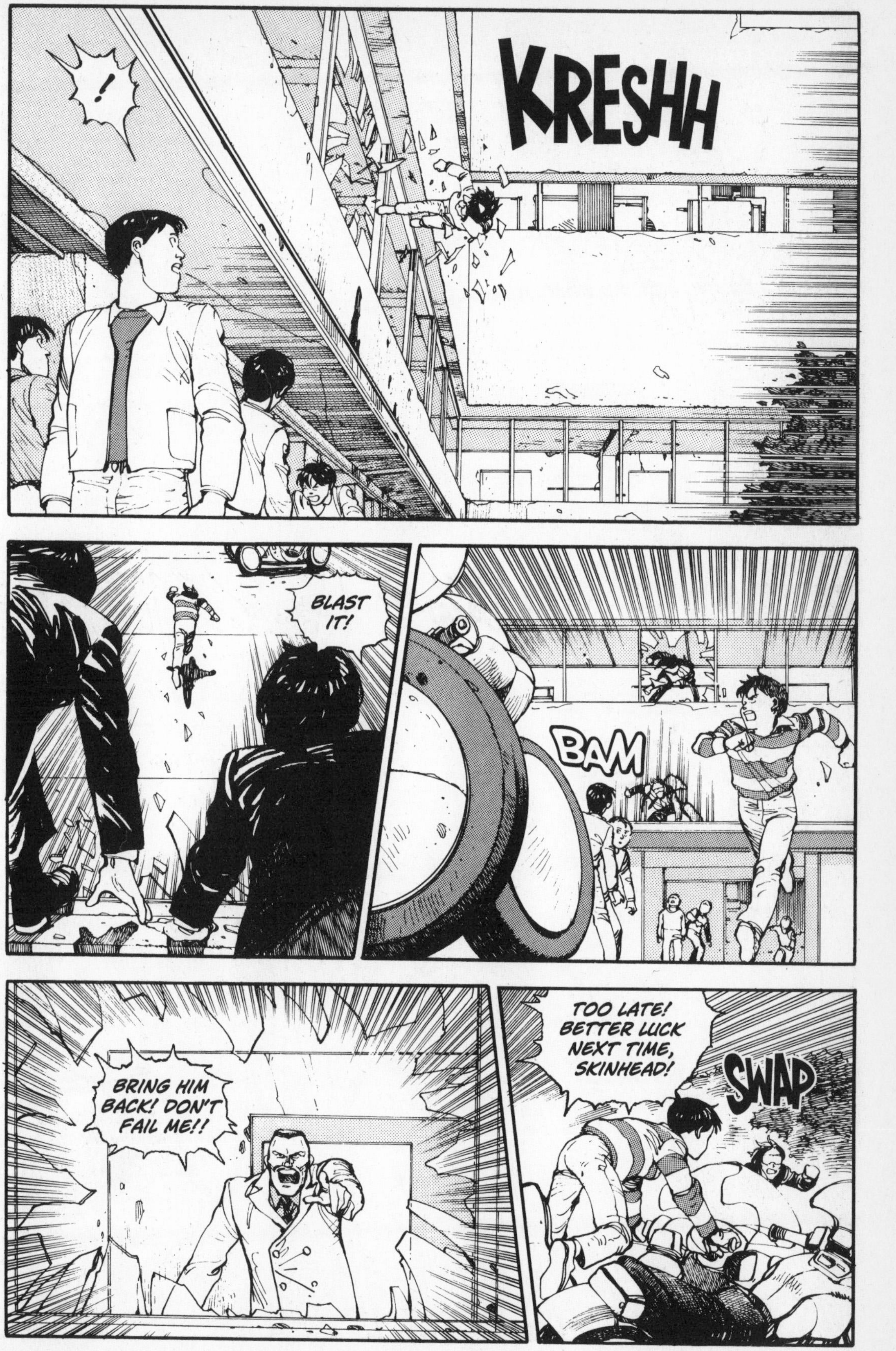
!
KRESHH
BLAST IT!
BAM
BRING HIM BACK! DON'T FAIL ME!!
TOO LATE! BETTER LUCK NEXT TIME, SKINHEAD!
SWAP

TCHOOF

VRRR

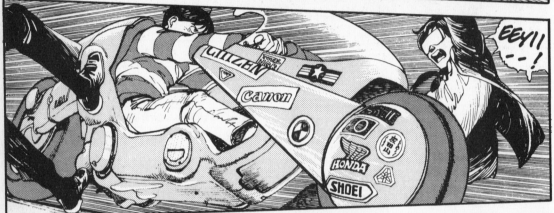

EEY!!
--!

VOOF

MISERABLE LITTLE UPSTART...

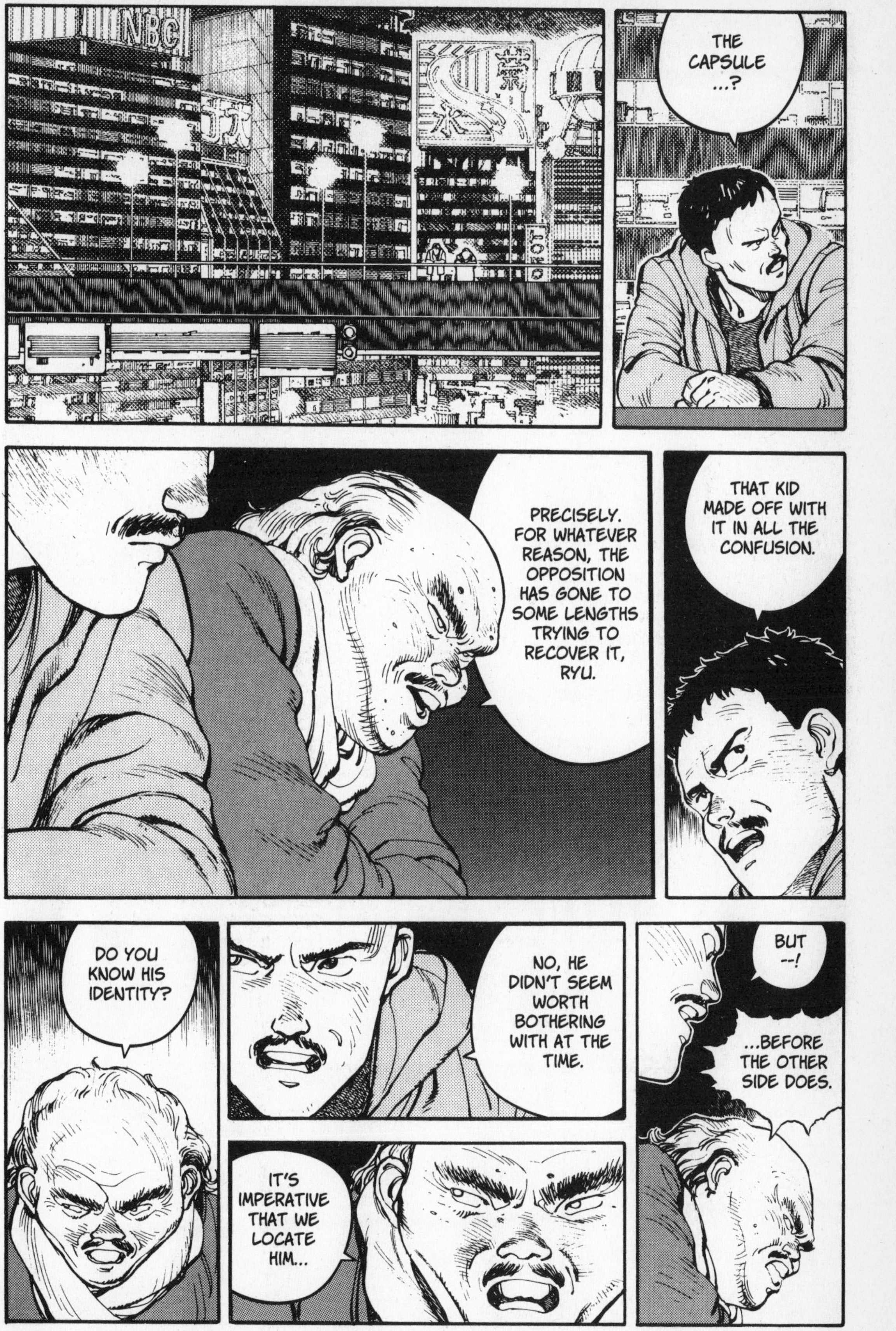
NBC
THE CAPSULE ...?
PRECISELY. FOR WHATEVER REASON, THE OPPOSITION HAS GONE TO SOME LENGTHS TRYING TO RECOVER IT, RYU.
THAT KID MADE OFF WITH IT IN ALL THE CONFUSION.
DO YOU KNOW HIS IDENTITY?
NO, HE DIDN'T SEEM WORTH BOTHERING WITH AT THE TIME.
IT'S IMPERATIVE THAT WE LOCATE HIM...
BUT --!
...BEFORE THE OTHER SIDE DOES.

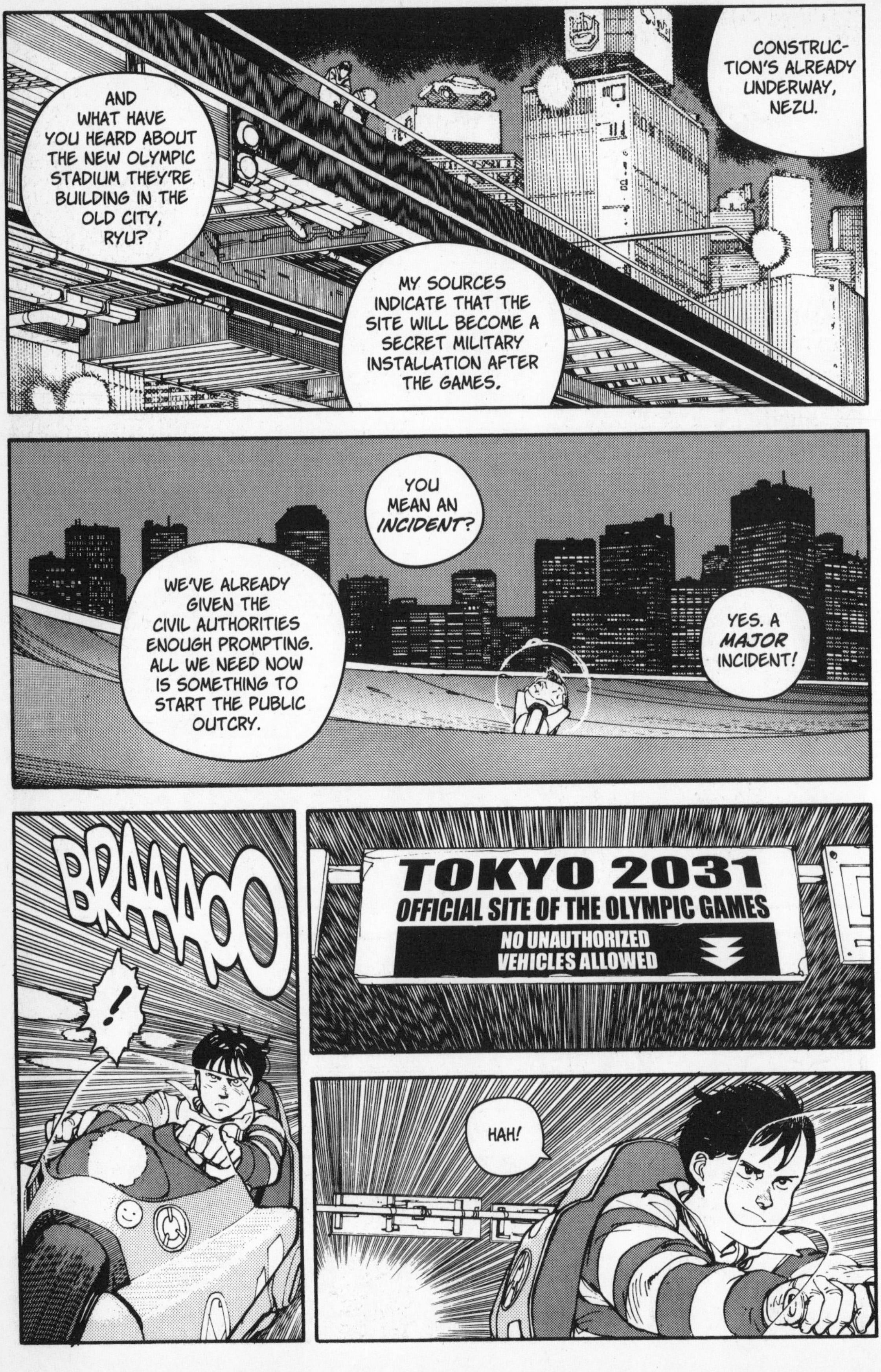
AND WHAT HAVE YOU HEARD ABOUT THE NEW OLYMPIC STADIUM THEY'RE BUILDING IN THE OLD CITY, RYU?
CONSTRUCTION'S ALREADY UNDERWAY, NEZU.
MY SOURCES INDICATE THAT THE SITE WILL BECOME A SECRET MILITARY INSTALLATION AFTER THE GAMES.
WE'VE ALREADY GIVEN THE CIVIL AUTHORITIES ENOUGH PROMPTING. ALL WE NEED NOW IS SOMETHING TO START THE PUBLIC OUTCRY.
YOU MEAN AN *INCIDENT*?
YES. A *MAJOR* INCIDENT!
BRAAAOO
!
TOKYO 2031
OFFICIAL SITE OF THE OLYMPIC GAMES
NO UNAUTHORIZED VEHICLES ALLOWED
HAH!

YOU INCOMPETENT IMBECILES!!!

BAKAM

YESSIR!

WE'RE SORRY, SIR!

NOT AS SORRY AS YOU'LL BE IF YOU FAIL ME AGAIN!

EXCUSE ME...

KLAP

NOW THE TWO OF YOU GET OUT!

WHAT WAS THAT ALL ABOUT?

NOTHING THAT CONCERNS YOU.

CLAK

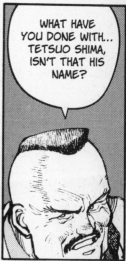

WHAT HAVE YOU DONE WITH... TETSUO SHIMA, ISN'T THAT HIS NAME?

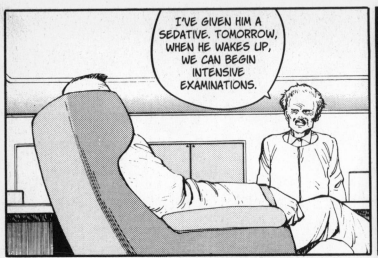

I'VE GIVEN HIM A SEDATIVE. TOMORROW, WHEN HE WAKES UP, WE CAN BEGIN INTENSIVE EXAMINATIONS.

WHEN MAY I EXPECT YOUR REPORT?

IT WILL TAKE ABOUT THREE WEEKS TO COMPILE ALL THE DATA.

DOOM

WHAT THE HELL...?!

IT CAME FROM THE OLD CITY.

COULD IT HAVE BEEN THE *OLYMPIC SITE?*

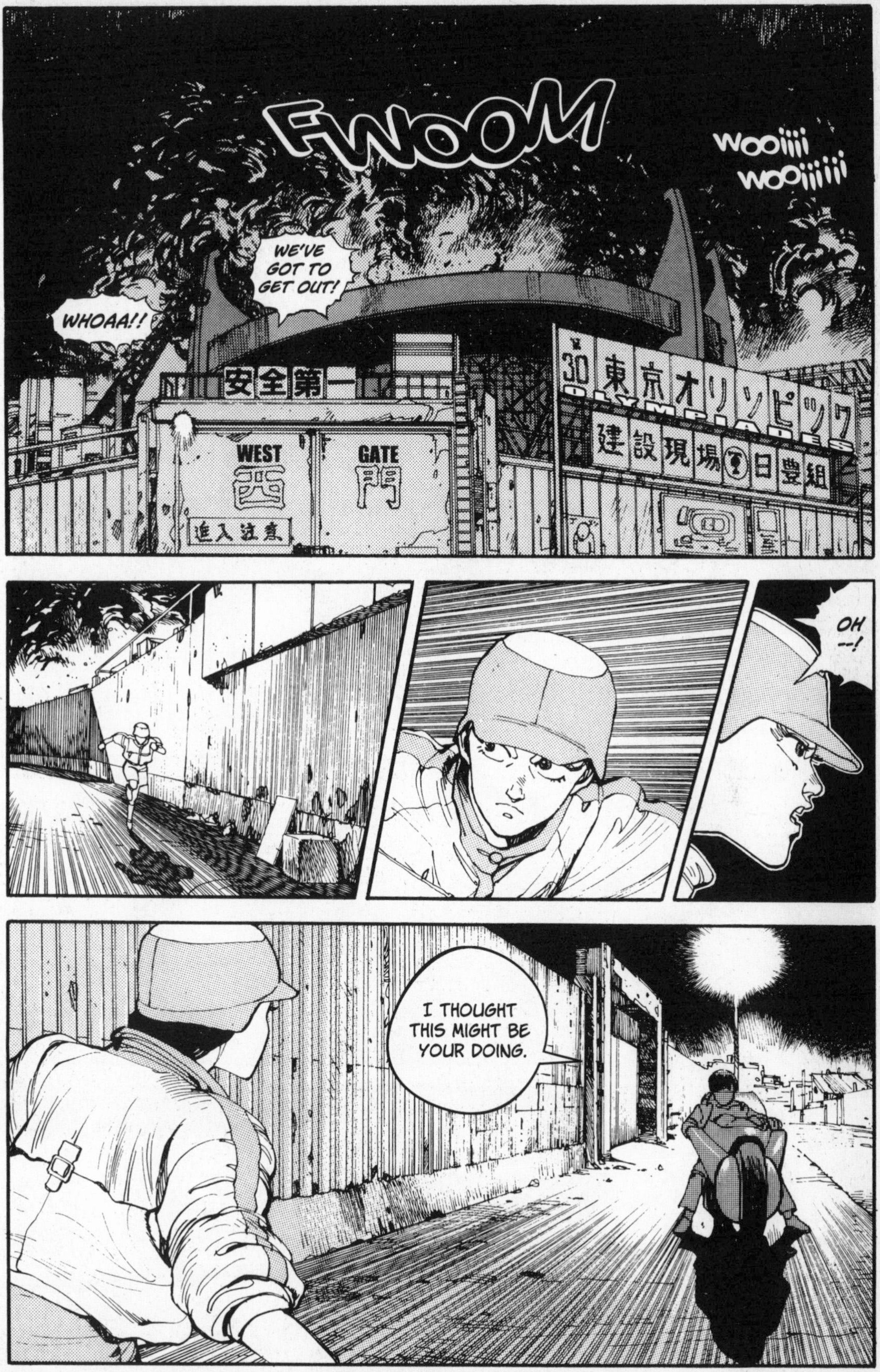
FWOOM
wooiiii
wooiiiiii
WHOAA!!
WE'VE GOT TO GET OUT!
安全第一
30 東京オリンピック
OLYMPIADES
建設現場 日豊組
WEST GATE
西 門
進入注意
OH --!
I THOUGHT THIS MIGHT BE YOUR DOING.

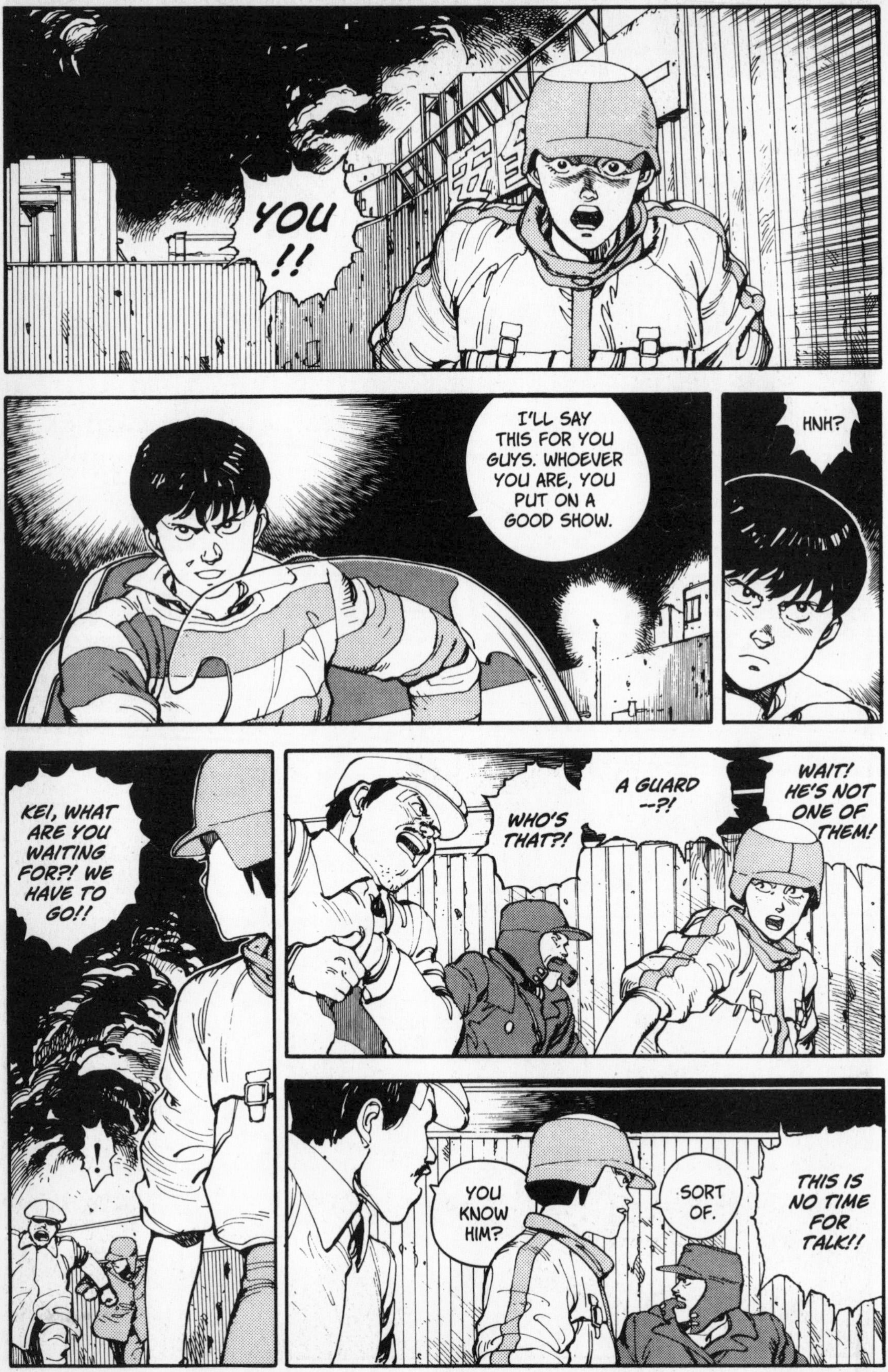
YOU !!
I'LL SAY THIS FOR YOU GUYS. WHOEVER YOU ARE, YOU PUT ON A GOOD SHOW.
HNH?
KEI, WHAT ARE YOU WAITING FOR?! WE HAVE TO GO!!
!
WHO'S THAT?!
A GUARD --?!
WAIT! HE'S NOT ONE OF THEM!
YOU KNOW HIM?
SORT OF.
THIS IS NO TIME FOR TALK!!

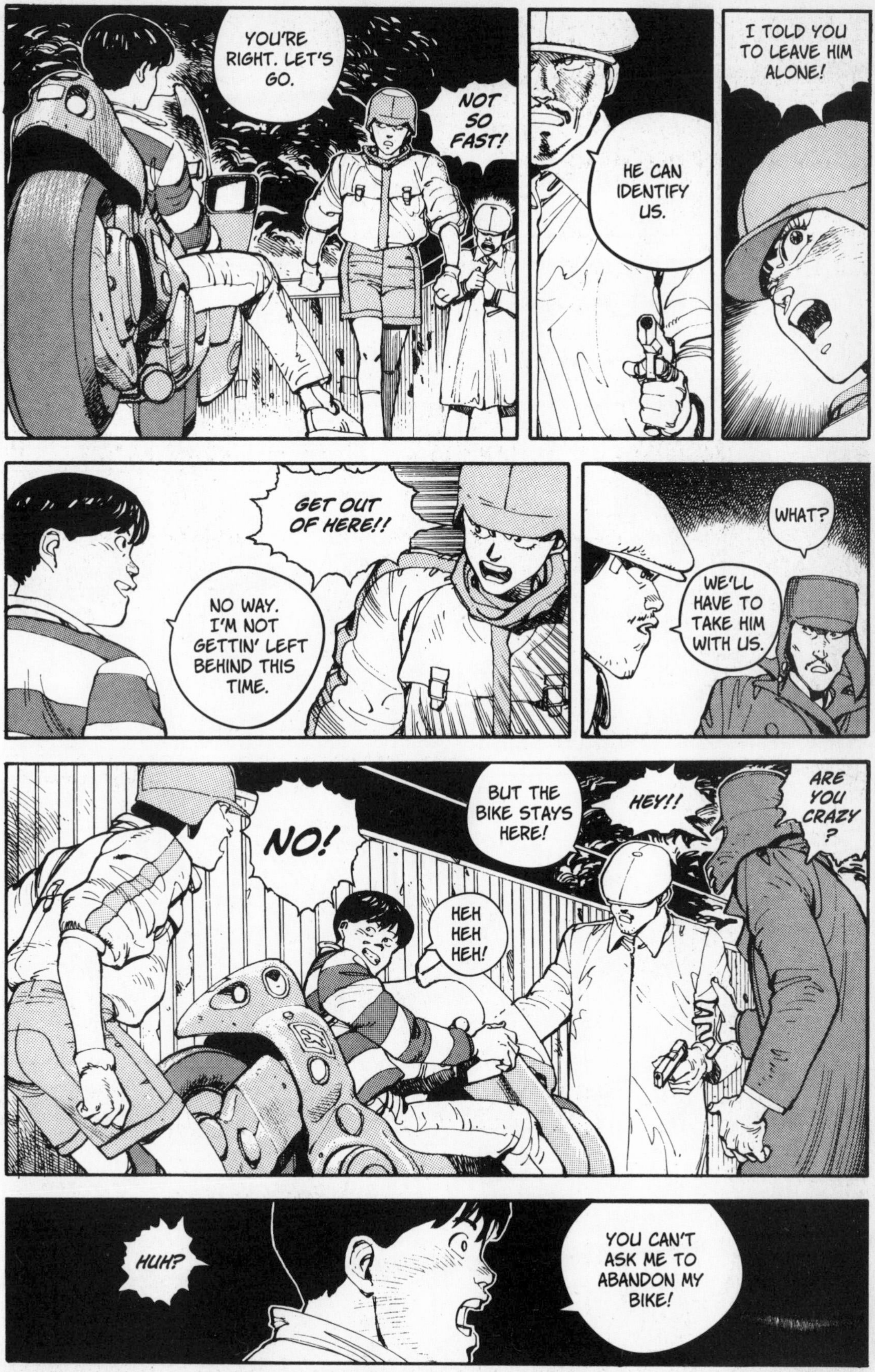
YOU'RE RIGHT. LET'S GO.
NOT SO FAST!
HE CAN IDENTIFY US.
I TOLD YOU TO LEAVE HIM ALONE!
GET OUT OF HERE!!
NO WAY. I'M NOT GETTIN' LEFT BEHIND THIS TIME.
WHAT?
WE'LL HAVE TO TAKE HIM WITH US.
NO!
BUT THE BIKE STAYS HERE!
HEY!!
ARE YOU CRAZY?
HEH HEH HEH!
HUH?
YOU CAN'T ASK ME TO ABANDON MY BIKE!

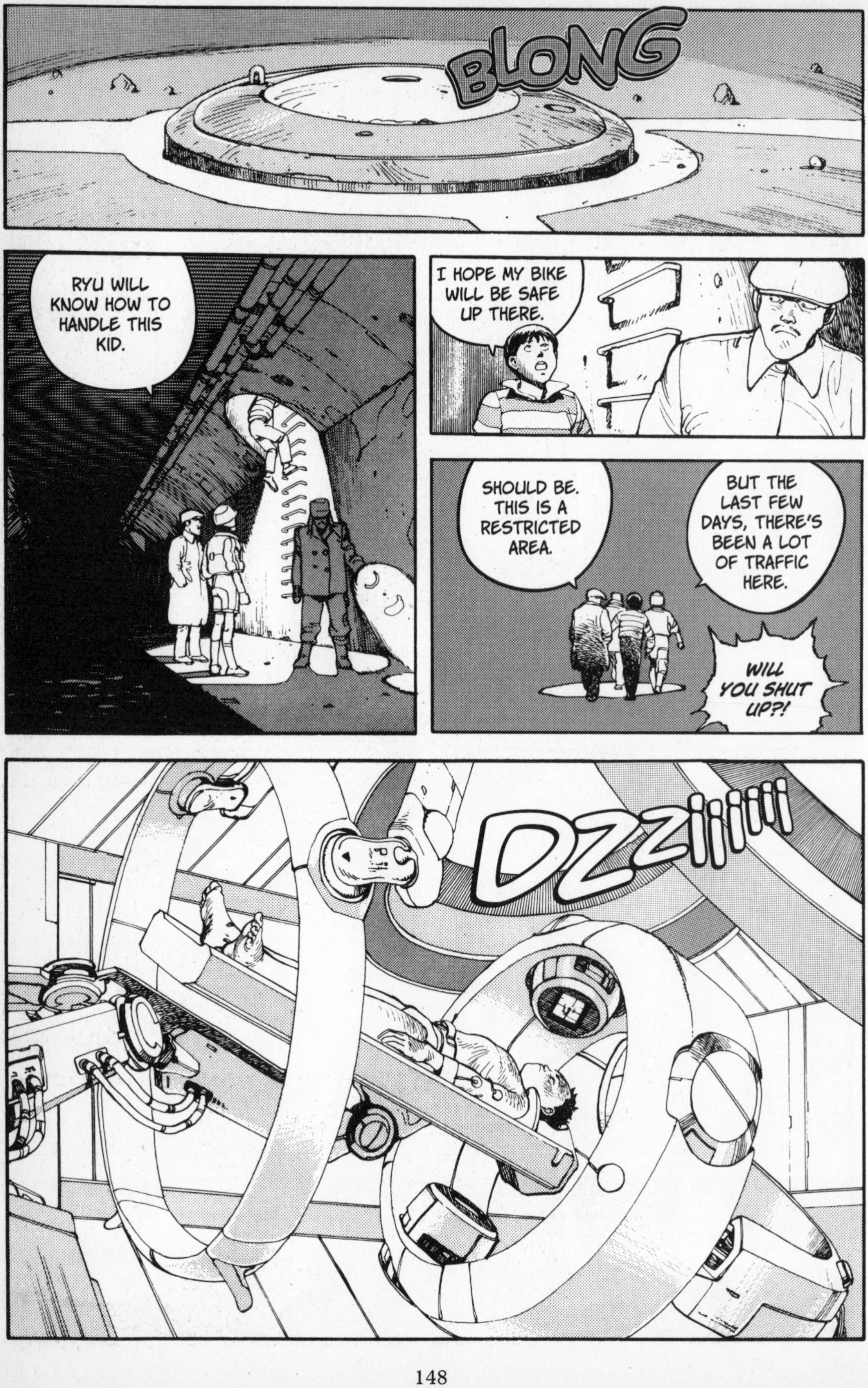
BLONG
RYU WILL KNOW HOW TO HANDLE THIS KID.
I HOPE MY BIKE WILL BE SAFE UP THERE.
SHOULD BE. THIS IS A RESTRICTED AREA.
BUT THE LAST FEW DAYS, THERE'S BEEN A LOT OF TRAFFIC HERE.
WILL YOU SHUT UP?!
DZZiiiiii

SOME TIME DURING THE PAST TWENTY-FOUR HOURS, HE TOOK SOME KIND OF ARTIFICIAL STIMULANT, COLONEL.

STIMULANT?

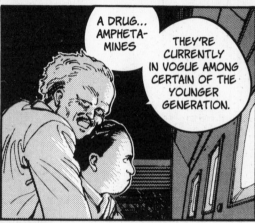

A DRUG... AMPHETA-MINES

THEY'RE CURRENTLY IN VOGUE AMONG CERTAIN OF THE YOUNGER GENERATION.

THIS ONE SEEMS TO BE A SIMPLE COMBINATION OF OVER-THE-COUNTER INGREDIENTS.

ANY REASONABLY SKILLED PHARMACIST COULD SYNTHESIZE IT.

IT'S NOT A HALLUCINOGEN, BUT IT MAY BE ADDICTIVE.

I BELIEVE IT ACCOUNTS FOR THE ALTERATION OF THE BRAINWAVE PATTERN.

WHICH MEANS, DOCTOR...?

DZZIIIIIII

THE FACT, SIR...

...IS THAT THIS IS THE FIRST SUCH CASE I'VE ENCOUNTERED, AND I'M AT A LOSS AS TO HOW TO PROCEED.

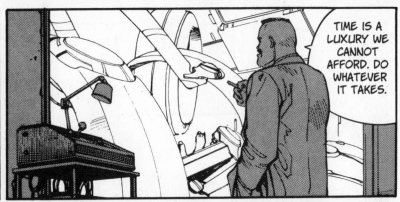

TIME IS A LUXURY WE CANNOT AFFORD. DO WHATEVER IT TAKES.

PLOK

UNREAL. THIS PLACE LOOKS THE WAY HIDEOUTS DO IN THE MOVIES!

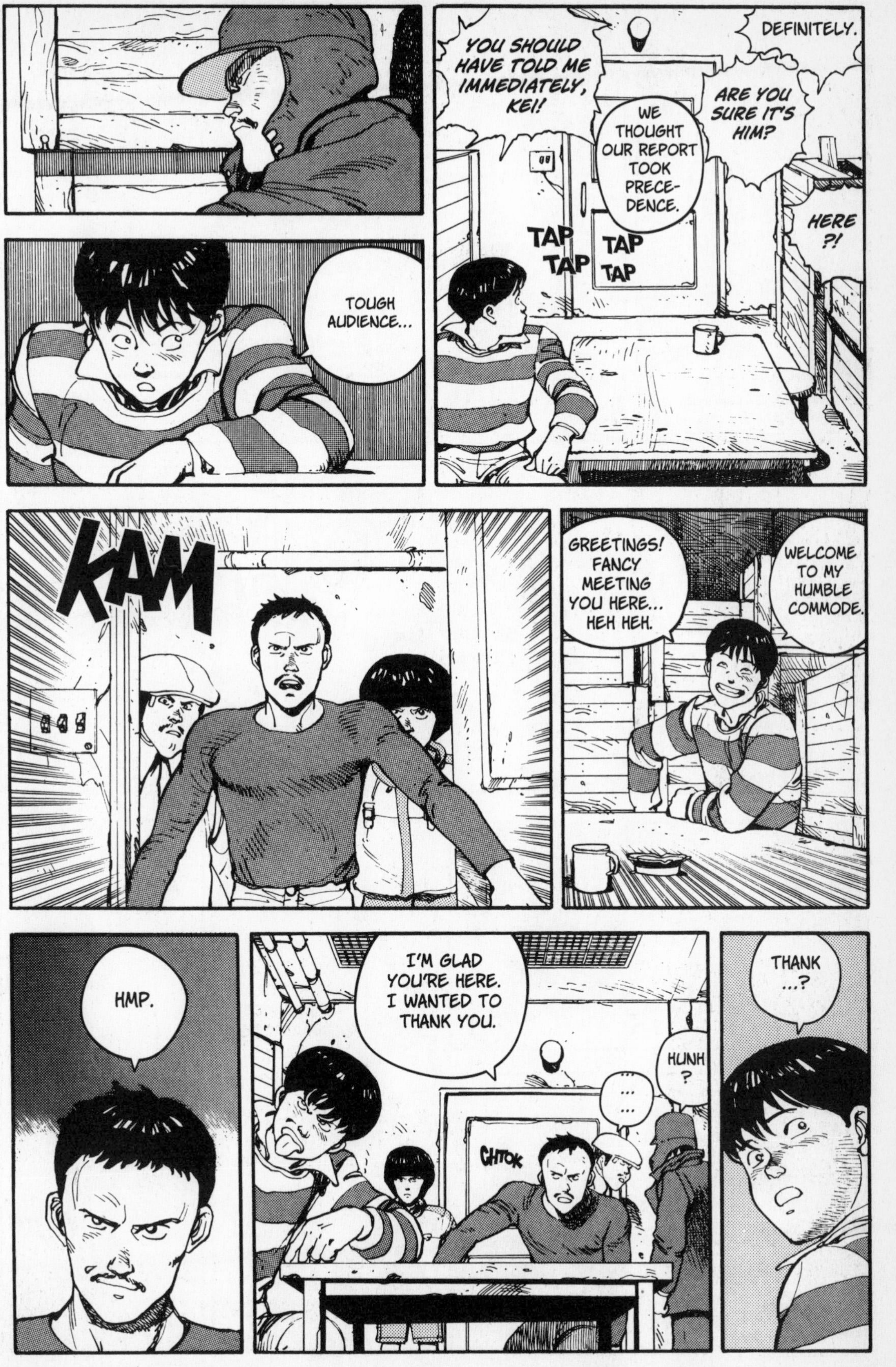
TOUGH AUDIENCE...
YOU SHOULD HAVE TOLD ME IMMEDIATELY, KEI!
WE THOUGHT OUR REPORT TOOK PRECE-DENCE.
ARE YOU SURE IT'S HIM?
DEFINITELY.
HERE ?!
TAP TAP TAP TAP
KAM
GREETINGS! FANCY MEETING YOU HERE... HEH HEH.
WELCOME TO MY HUMBLE COMMODE.
HMP.
I'M GLAD YOU'RE HERE. I WANTED TO THANK YOU.
HUNH ?
...
...
...
CHTOK
THANK ...?

SO...THAT PILL...HAVE YOU STILL GOT IT?

THE PILL? THAT PILL?

AH...NO. I LOST IT IN THE CANAL.

OH, YOU DID, HUNH? WELL, YOU LISTEN TO ME...

WE'RE PART OF AN UNDERGROUND RESISTANCE ORGANIZATION, AND--

DON'T, RYUSAKU! WE CAN'T TRUST--!

QUIET!!

LOOK, I'M SORRY. I PUT IT INTO MY POCKET, BUT THEN I LOST IT IN THE CANAL. *SPLASH!* REMEMBER?

I DON'T BELIEVE YOU.

THE WAY THAT WEIRD GUY, TAKASHI, KEPT GOING ON ABOUT IT, I HAD TO STEAL IT FROM HIM.

BUT WHAT WAS IT?

RYU, YOU'RE WASTING VALUABLE TIME!

KEI'S RIGHT. IT'S NOT LIKE YOU!

YOU REALLY DON'T KNOW, DO YOU?

I KEEP WORRYING ABOUT MY BIKE.

COULDN'T SOMEONE GO AND GET IT?

WE NEED THE TRUTH FROM HIM *NOW!*

GIMME A HALF HOUR WITH HIM!

DON'T WORRY... WE'VE GOT TIME.

≥HUH!≤

POOR BIKE, ALL ALONE IN THE DARK. DON'T CRY, MY POOR LITTLE BIKE.

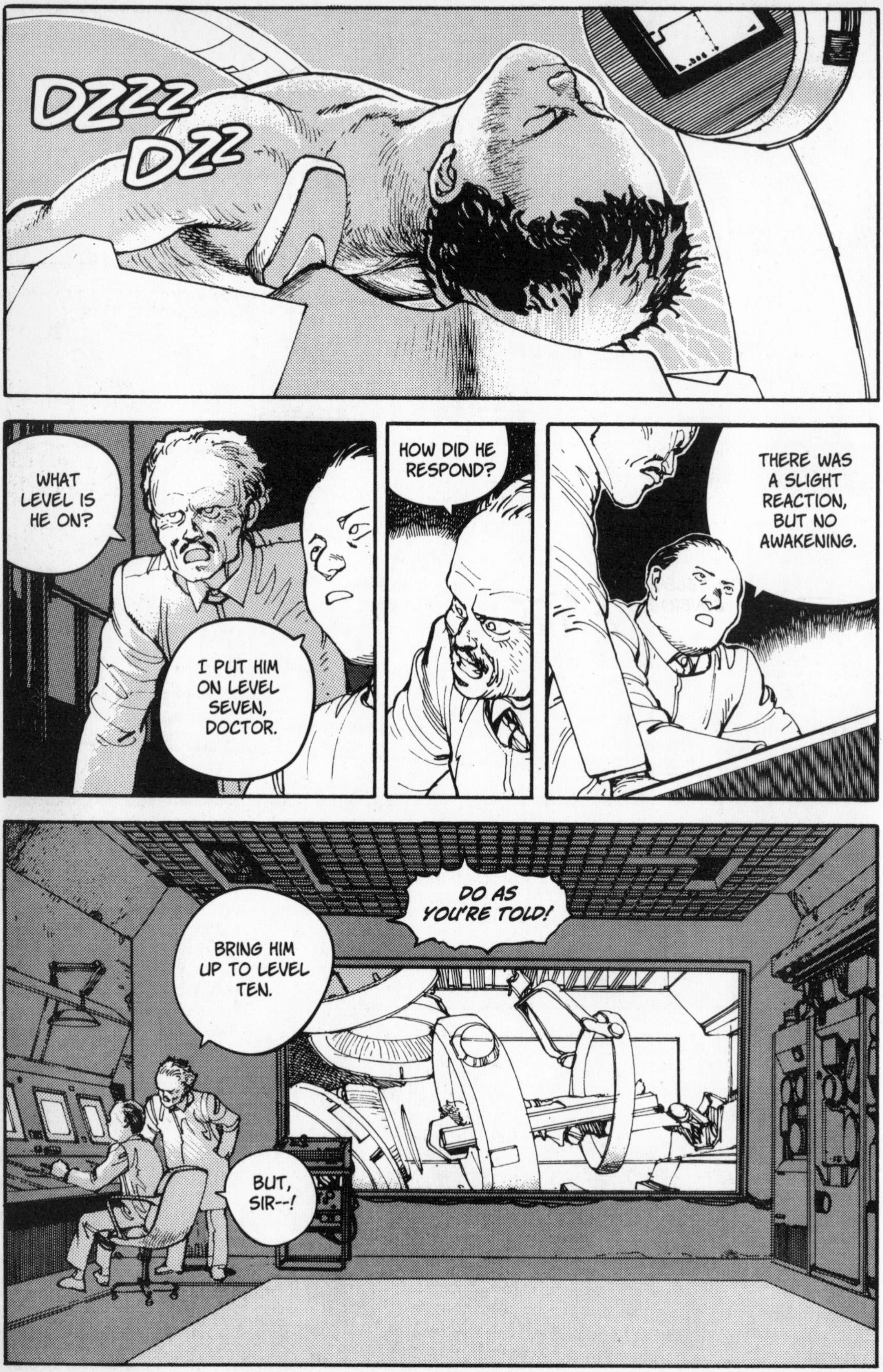
DZZZ DZZ
WHAT LEVEL IS HE ON?
I PUT HIM ON LEVEL SEVEN, DOCTOR.
HOW DID HE RESPOND?
THERE WAS A SLIGHT REACTION, BUT NO AWAKENING.
BRING HIM UP TO LEVEL TEN.
DO AS YOU'RE TOLD!
BUT, SIR--!

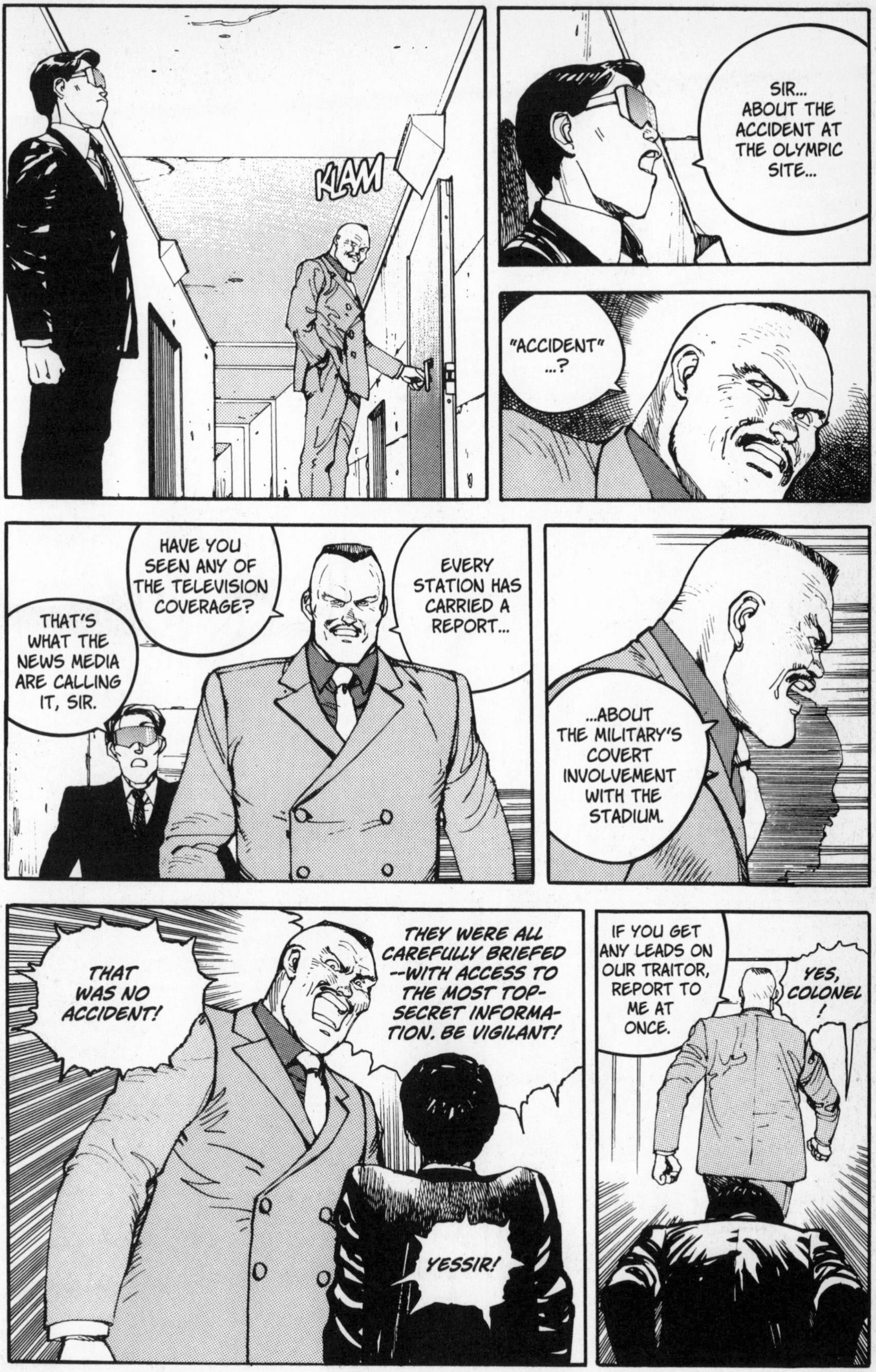
KLAM
SIR... ABOUT THE ACCIDENT AT THE OLYMPIC SITE...
"ACCIDENT" ...?
THAT'S WHAT THE NEWS MEDIA ARE CALLING IT, SIR.
HAVE YOU SEEN ANY OF THE TELEVISION COVERAGE?
EVERY STATION HAS CARRIED A REPORT...
...ABOUT THE MILITARY'S COVERT INVOLVEMENT WITH THE STADIUM.
THAT WAS NO ACCIDENT!
THEY WERE ALL CAREFULLY BRIEFED --WITH ACCESS TO THE MOST TOP-SECRET INFORMATION. BE VIGILANT!
YESSIR!
IF YOU GET ANY LEADS ON OUR TRAITOR, REPORT TO ME AT ONCE.
YES, COLONEL!

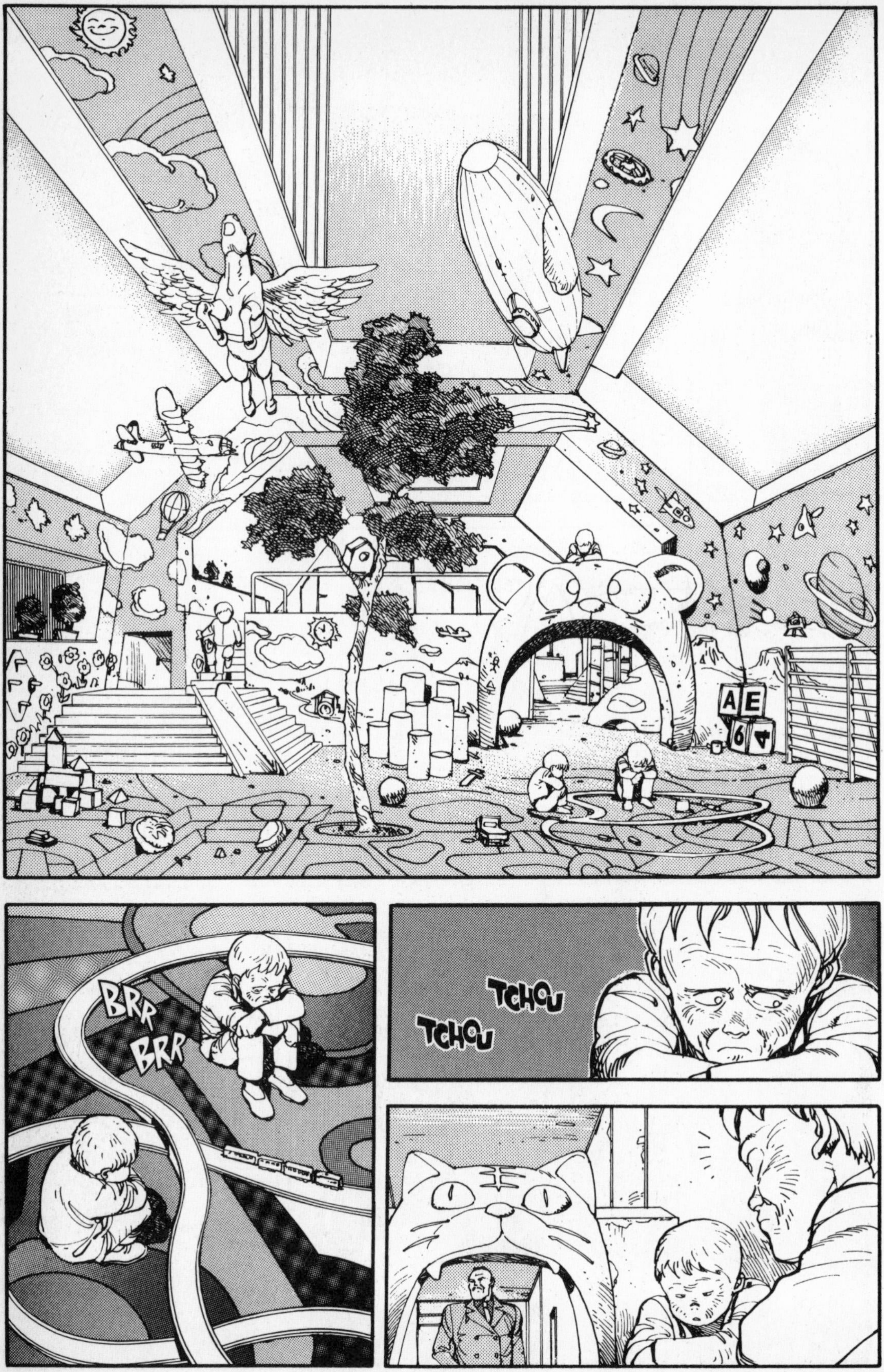
AE
64
BRR
BRR
TCHOU
TCHOU

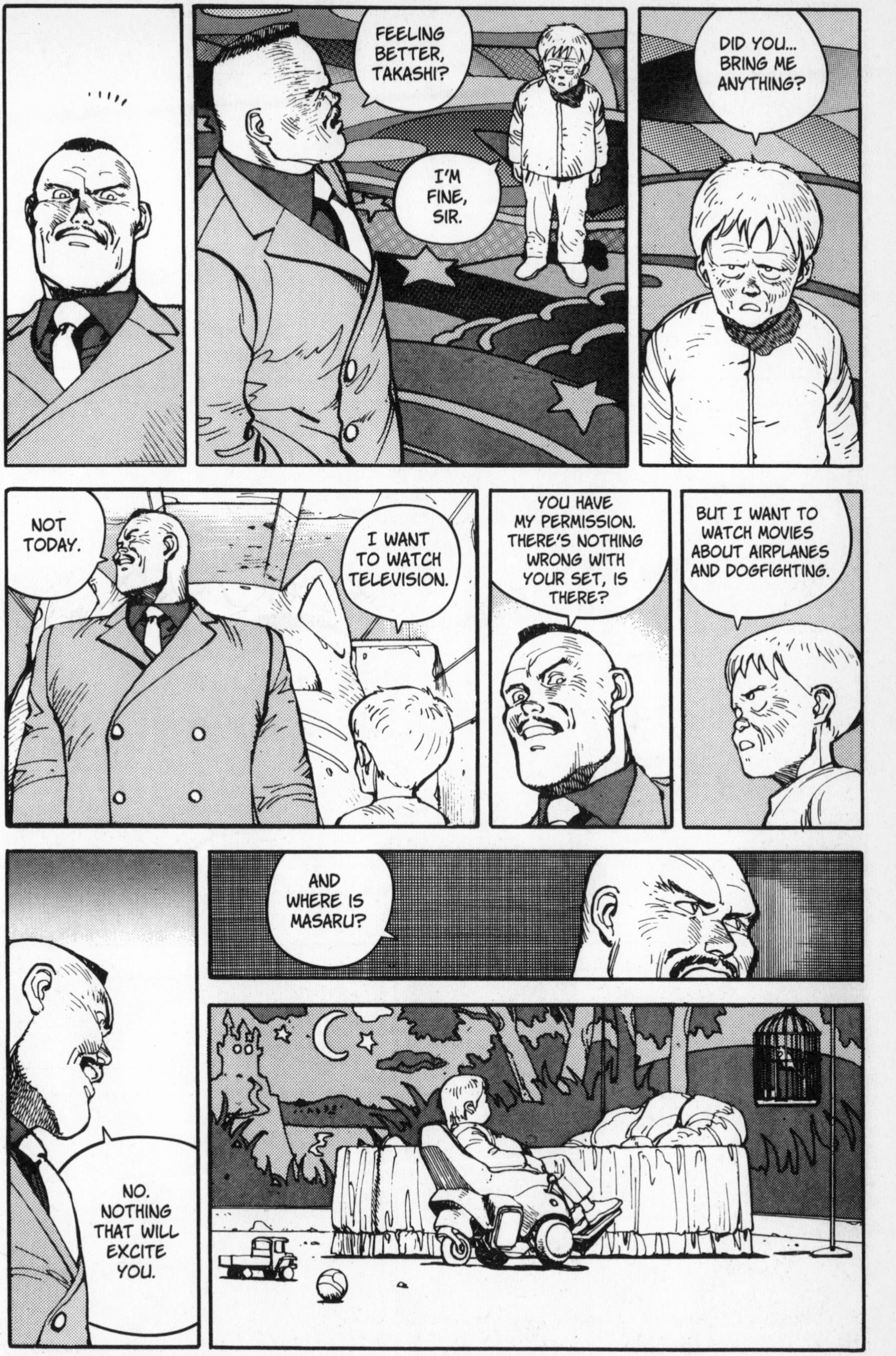

FEELING BETTER, TAKASHI?
I'M FINE, SIR.
DID YOU... BRING ME ANYTHING?
NOT TODAY.
I WANT TO WATCH TELEVISION.
YOU HAVE MY PERMISSION. THERE'S NOTHING WRONG WITH YOUR SET, IS THERE?
BUT I WANT TO WATCH MOVIES ABOUT AIRPLANES AND DOGFIGHTING.
NO. NOTHING THAT WILL EXCITE YOU.
AND WHERE IS MASARU?

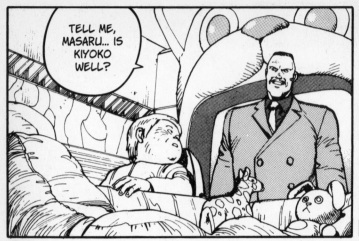

TELL ME, MASARU... IS KIYOKO WELL?

YES, SIR. SHE JUST WOKE UP.

I HAD A DREAM.

TELL ME ABOUT IT.

I DREAMED OF AKIRA.

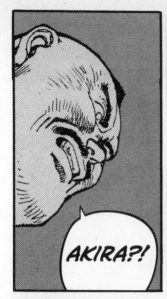

HE'LL AWAKEN SOON.

AKIRA?!

WHAT?! IS THIS THE TRUTH?!

WHEN? WHEN ?!?

SOON...

159

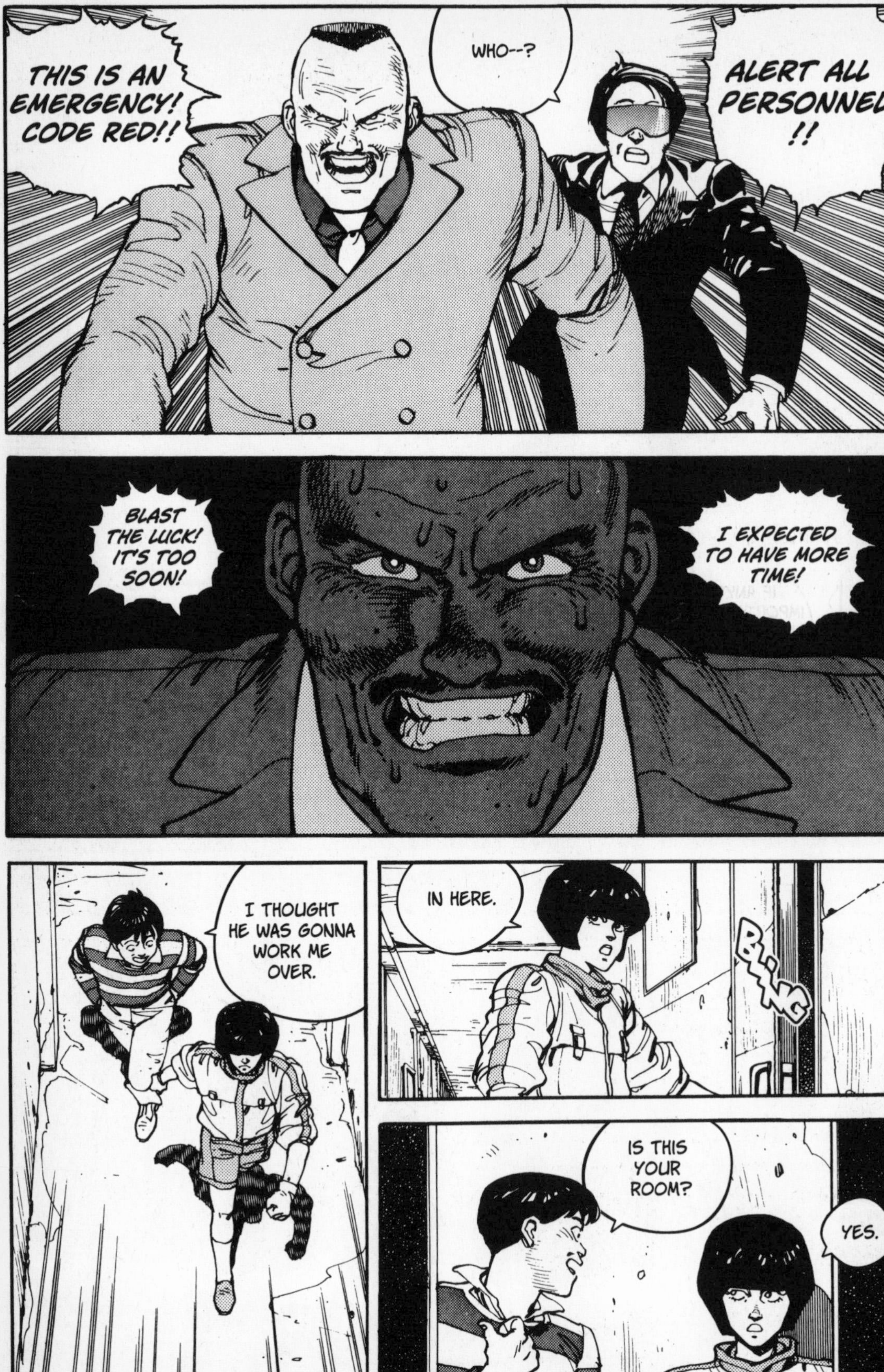
THIS IS AN EMERGENCY! CODE RED!!
WHO--?
ALERT ALL PERSONNEL !!
BLAST THE LUCK! IT'S TOO SOON!
I EXPECTED TO HAVE MORE TIME!
I THOUGHT HE WAS GONNA WORK ME OVER.
IN HERE.
BLING
IS THIS YOUR ROOM?
YES.

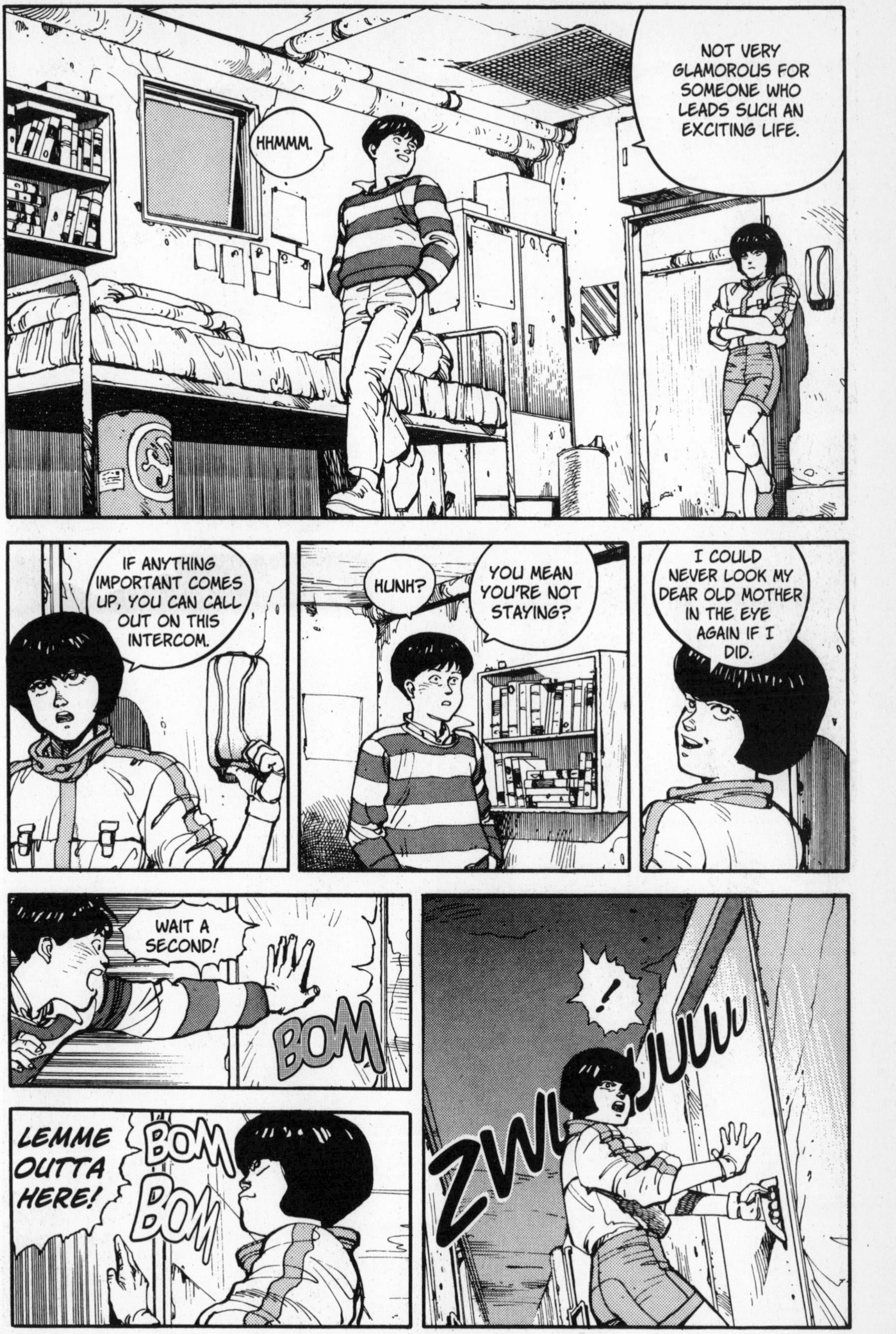
HHMMM.
NOT VERY GLAMOROUS FOR SOMEONE WHO LEADS SUCH AN EXCITING LIFE.
IF ANYTHING IMPORTANT COMES UP, YOU CAN CALL OUT ON THIS INTERCOM.
HUNH?
YOU MEAN YOU'RE NOT STAYING?
I COULD NEVER LOOK MY DEAR OLD MOTHER IN THE EYE AGAIN IF I DID.
WAIT A SECOND!
BOM
!
ZWUUUUU
LEMME OUTTA HERE!
BOM
BOM

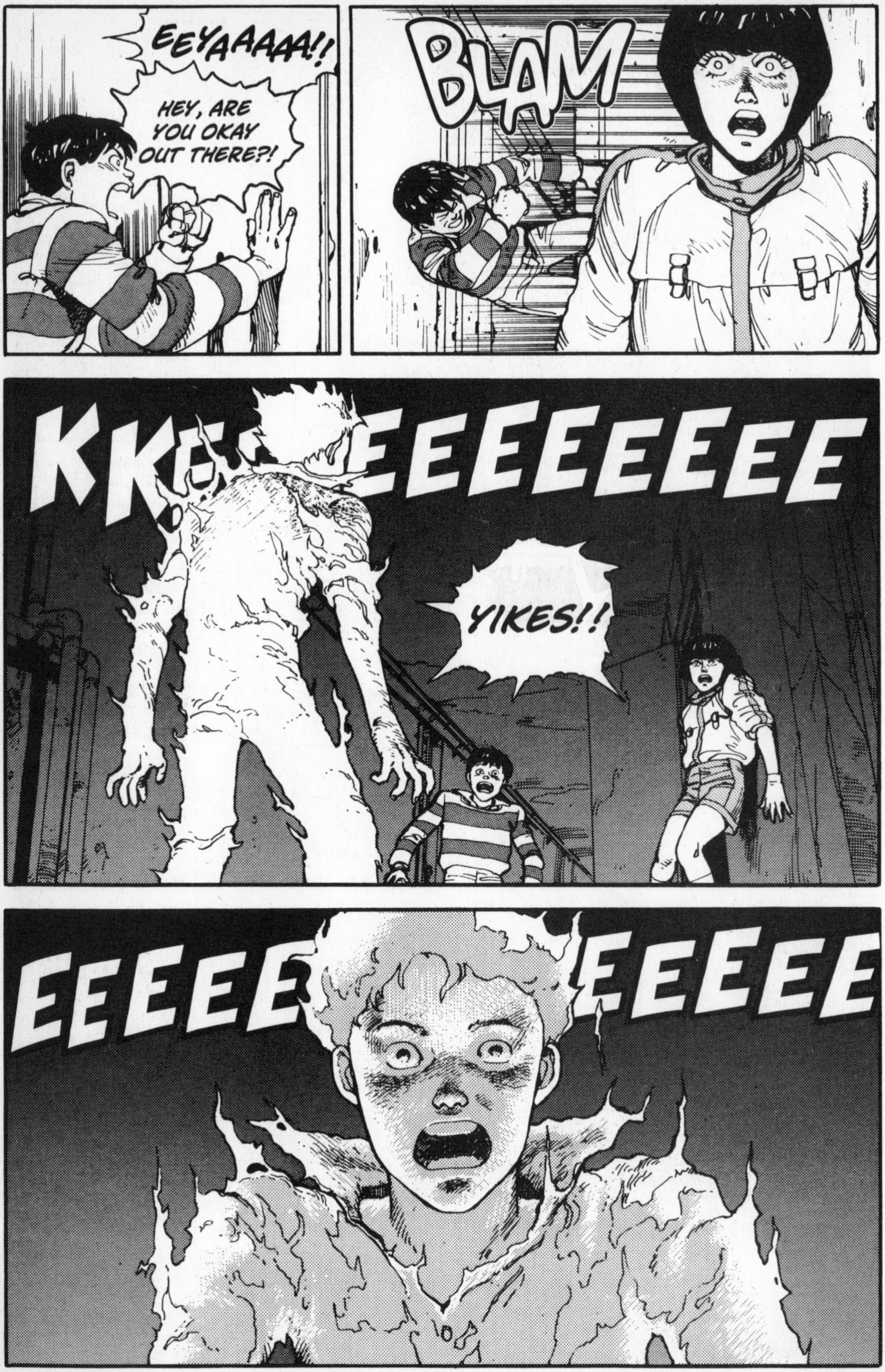
EEYAAAAA!!
HEY, ARE YOU OKAY OUT THERE?!
BLAM
KKEEEEEEEEEE
YIKES!!
EEEEEEEEE

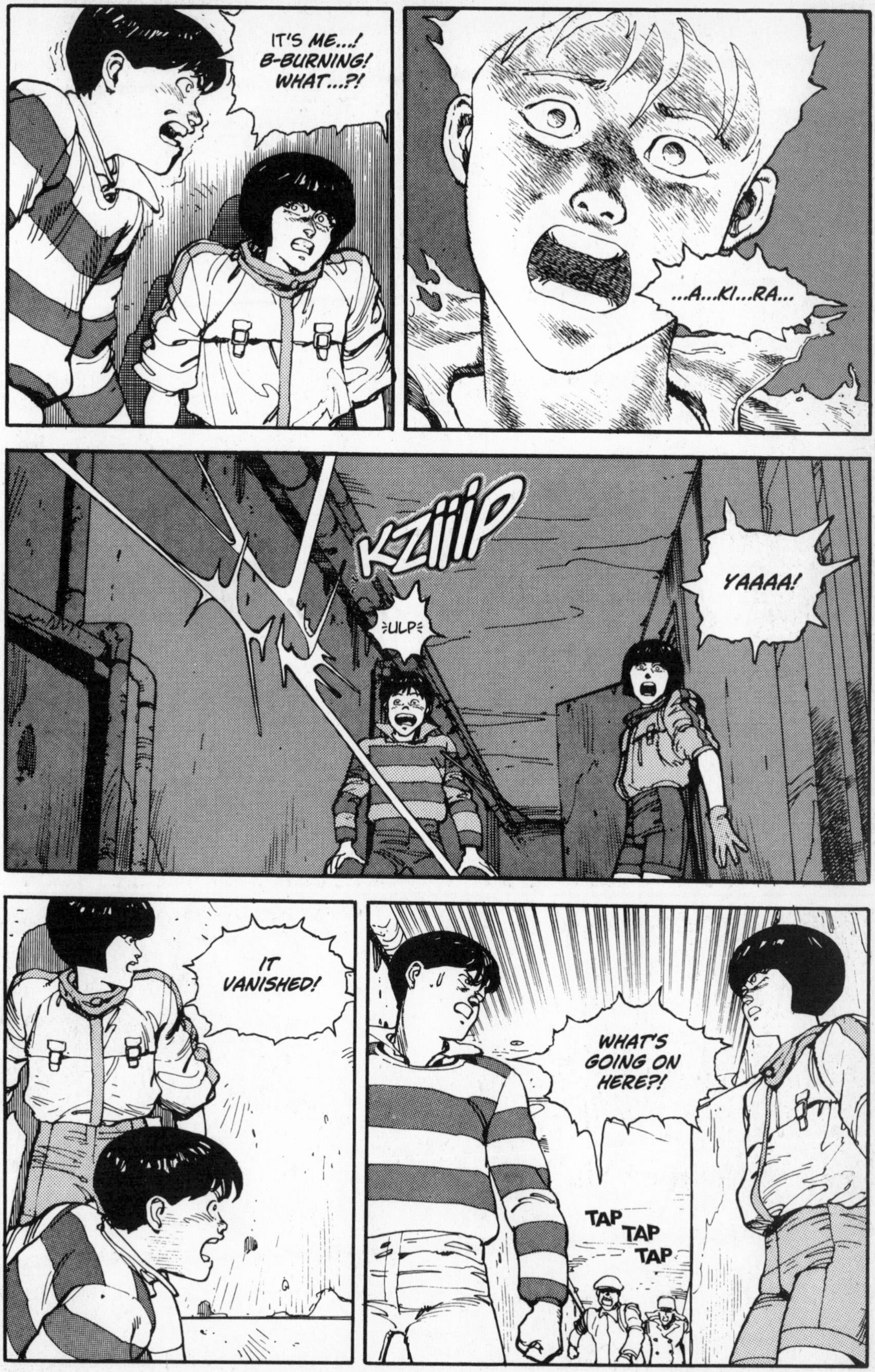
IT'S ME...! B-BURNING! WHAT...?!
...A...KI...RA...
KZIIIP
ULP
YAAAA!
IT VANISHED!
WHAT'S GOING ON HERE?!
TAP TAP TAP

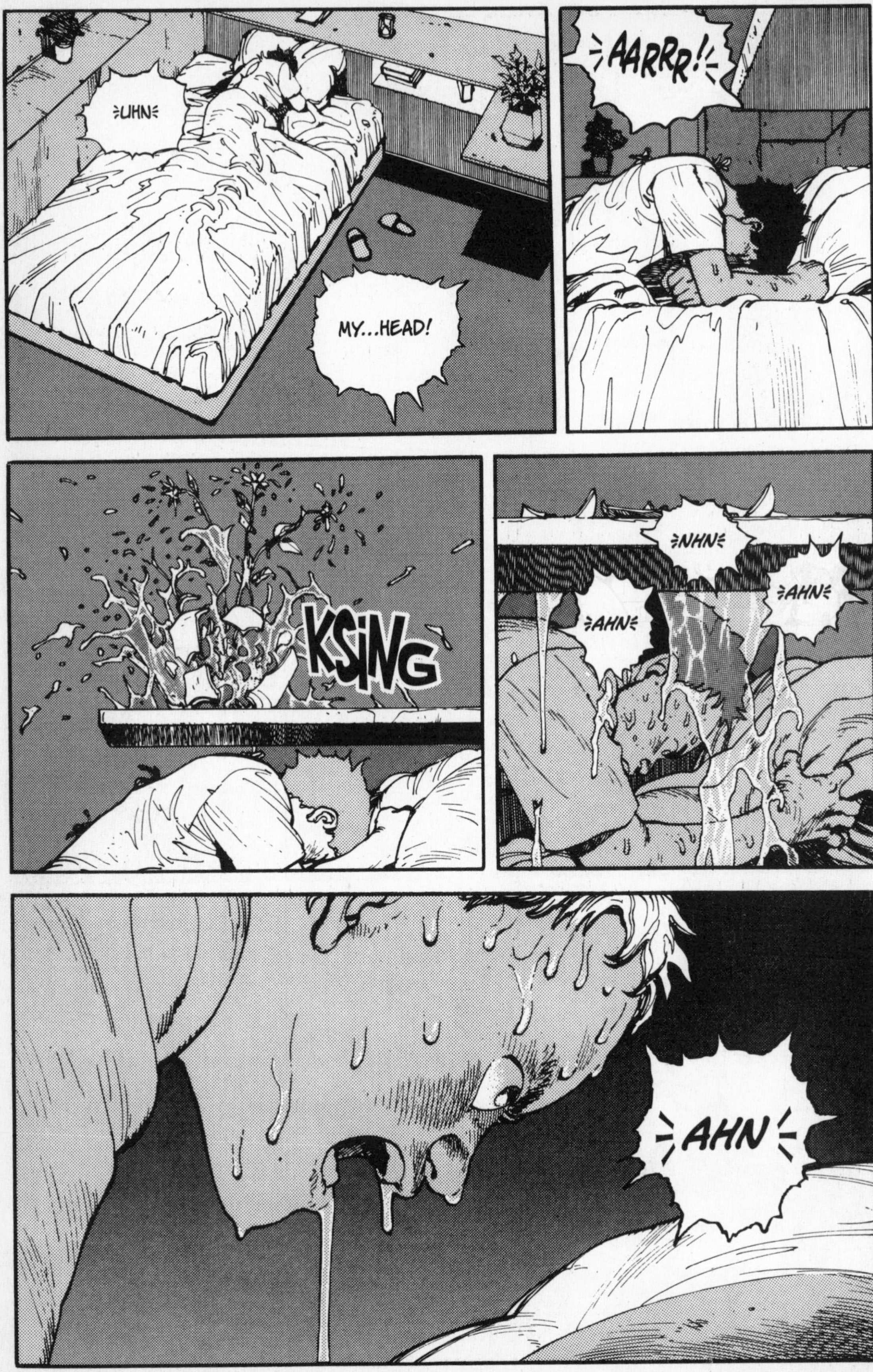
UHN
MY...HEAD!
AARRR!
KSING
NHN
AHN
AHN
AHN

COULD YOU BE MORE SPECIFIC THAN "SOON"?

NOT THAT WE BELIEVE A WORD OF IT!

WE'VE FINANCED THIS "AKIRA" OF YOURS, AND SO FAR NONE OF US EVEN KNOW WHAT IT IS.

THERE HAS BEEN NO PROGRESS IN THIRTY YEARS!

AND JUST WHERE ARE WE EXPECTED TO GET THE MONEY FOR ALL OF THIS?

THE COSTS HAVE BEEN EXORBITANT.

TO SAY THE LEAST.

ALL WE HAVE TO SHOW FOR OUR EXPENDITURES IS THAT GROTESQUE NURSERY.

AND THERE ARE THE UPCOMING OLYMPICS TO CONSIDER. WE MUST PUT THE WAR AND ITS MEMORIES BEHIND US. WE HAVE NO MONEY TO SPEND ON GHOSTS.

THAT'S WHAT I'VE SAID ALL ALONG!

THE MONEY COULD GO TO SOCIAL PROGRAMS!

OH, SHUT UP!

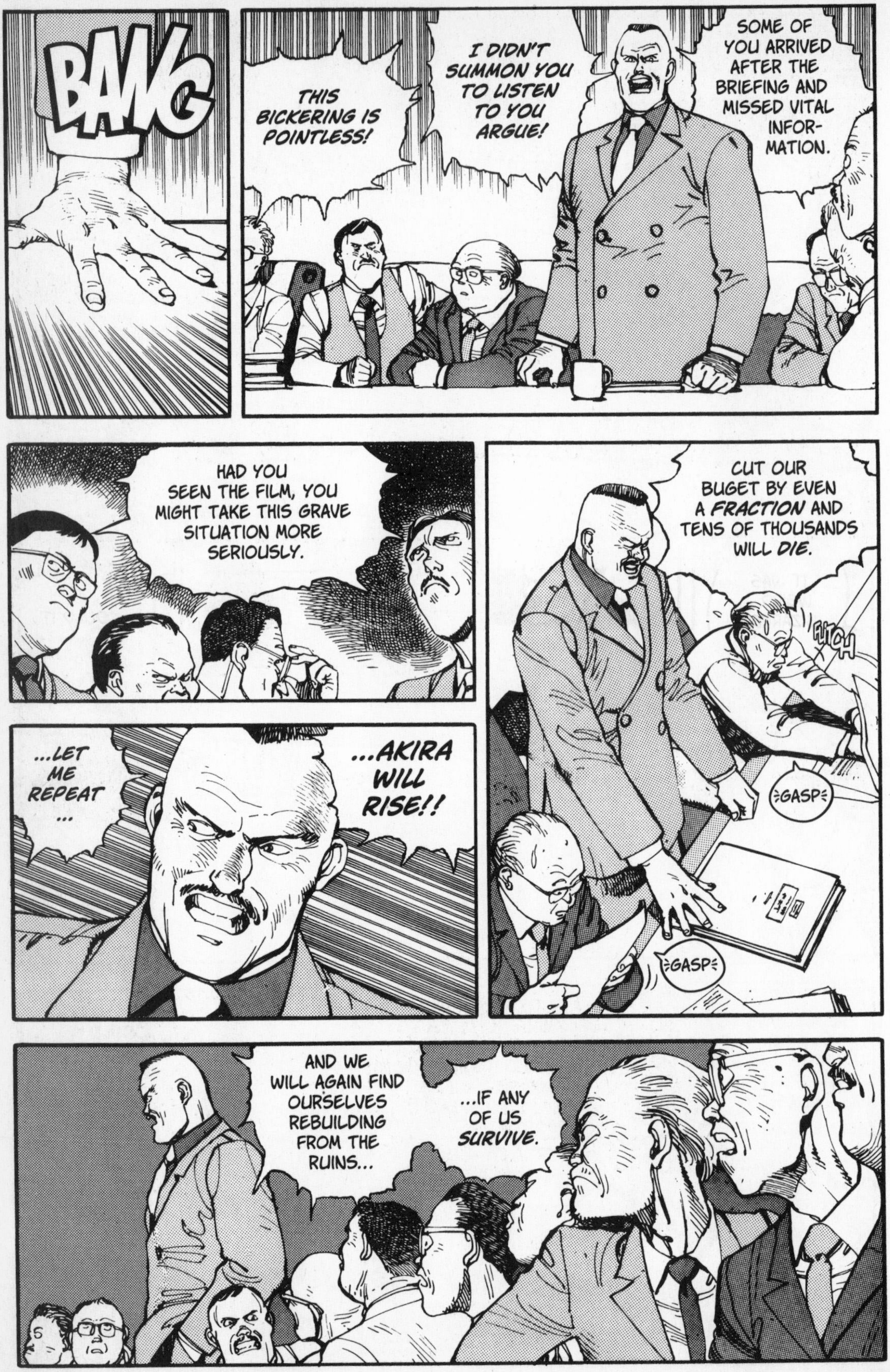
BANG
THIS BICKERING IS POINTLESS!
I DIDN'T SUMMON YOU TO LISTEN TO YOU ARGUE!
SOME OF YOU ARRIVED AFTER THE BRIEFING AND MISSED VITAL INFOR-MATION.
HAD YOU SEEN THE FILM, YOU MIGHT TAKE THIS GRAVE SITUATION MORE SERIOUSLY.
CUT OUR BUGET BY EVEN A *FRACTION* AND TENS OF THOUSANDS WILL *DIE*.
FLITCH
GASP
GASP
...LET ME REPEAT ...
...AKIRA WILL RISE!!
AND WE WILL AGAIN FIND OURSELVES REBUILDING FROM THE RUINS...
...IF ANY OF US *SURVIVE*.

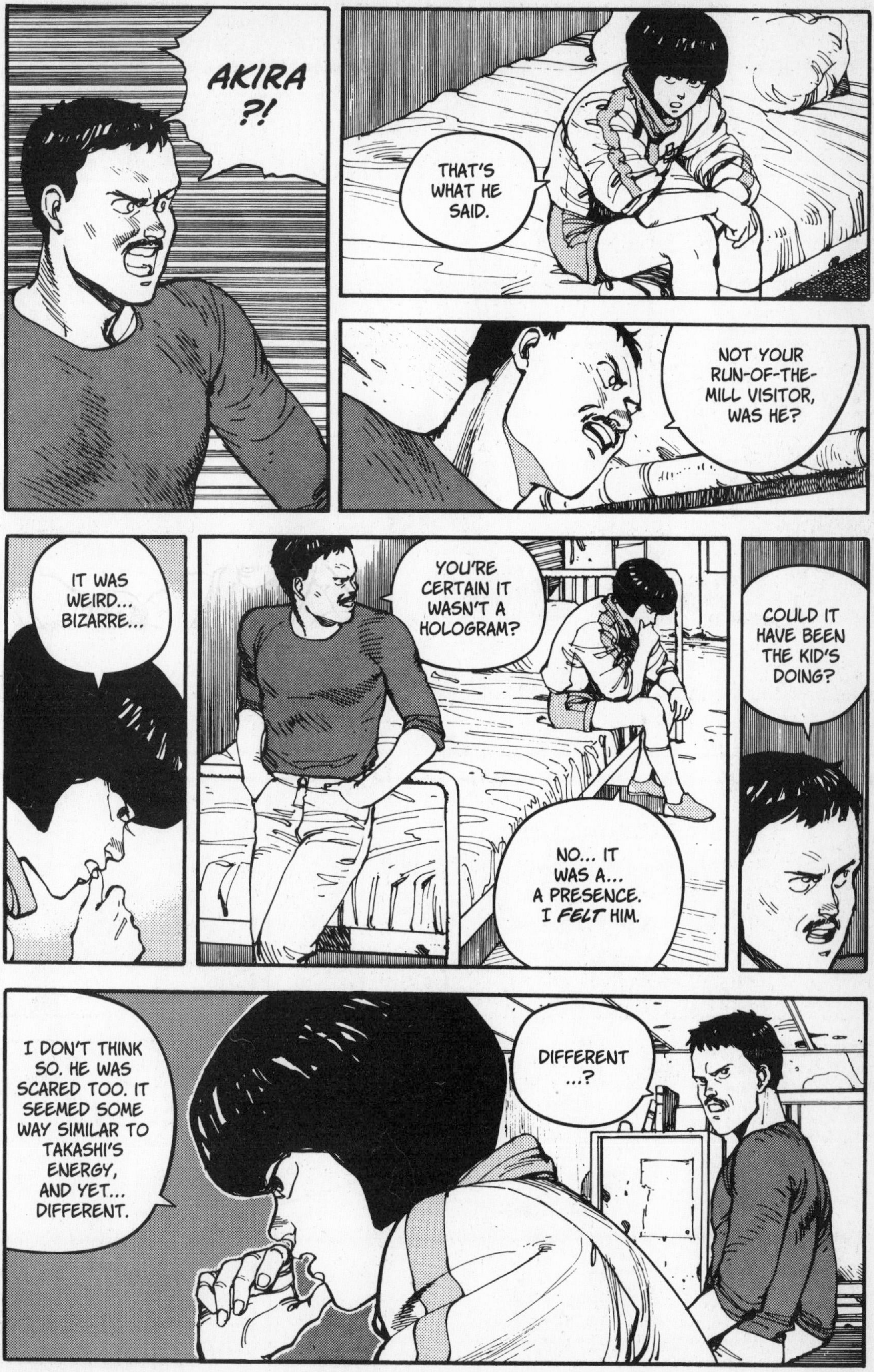
AKIRA ?!
THAT'S WHAT HE SAID.
NOT YOUR RUN-OF-THE-MILL VISITOR, WAS HE?
IT WAS WEIRD... BIZARRE...
YOU'RE CERTAIN IT WASN'T A HOLOGRAM?
NO... IT WAS A... A PRESENCE. I FELT HIM.
COULD IT HAVE BEEN THE KID'S DOING?
I DON'T THINK SO. HE WAS SCARED TOO. IT SEEMED SOME WAY SIMILAR TO TAKASHI'S ENERGY, AND YET... DIFFERENT.
DIFFERENT ...?

AKIRA..?

DON'T ASK ME...

JUST KEEP A CLOSE EYE ON OUR GUEST.

YOU BET.

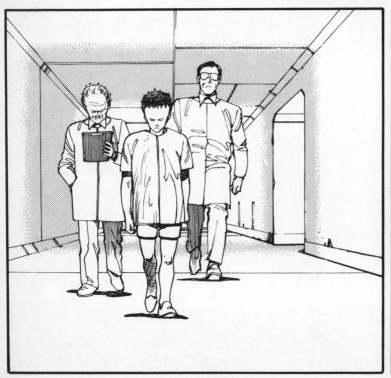

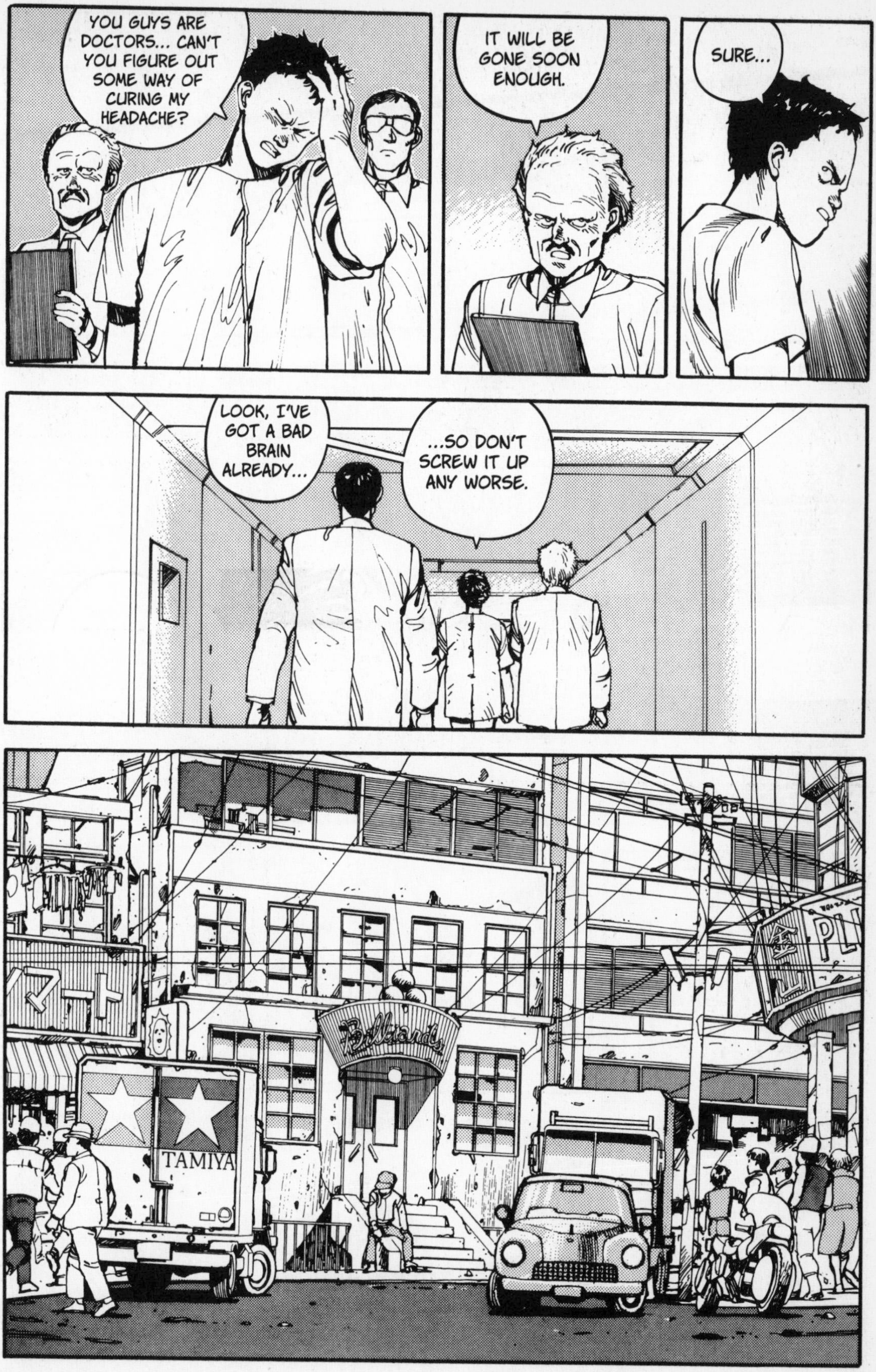
YOU GUYS ARE DOCTORS... CAN'T YOU FIGURE OUT SOME WAY OF CURING MY HEADACHE?
IT WILL BE GONE SOON ENOUGH.
SURE...
LOOK, I'VE GOT A BAD BRAIN ALREADY...
...SO DON'T SCREW IT UP ANY WORSE.
Billiards
TAMIYA

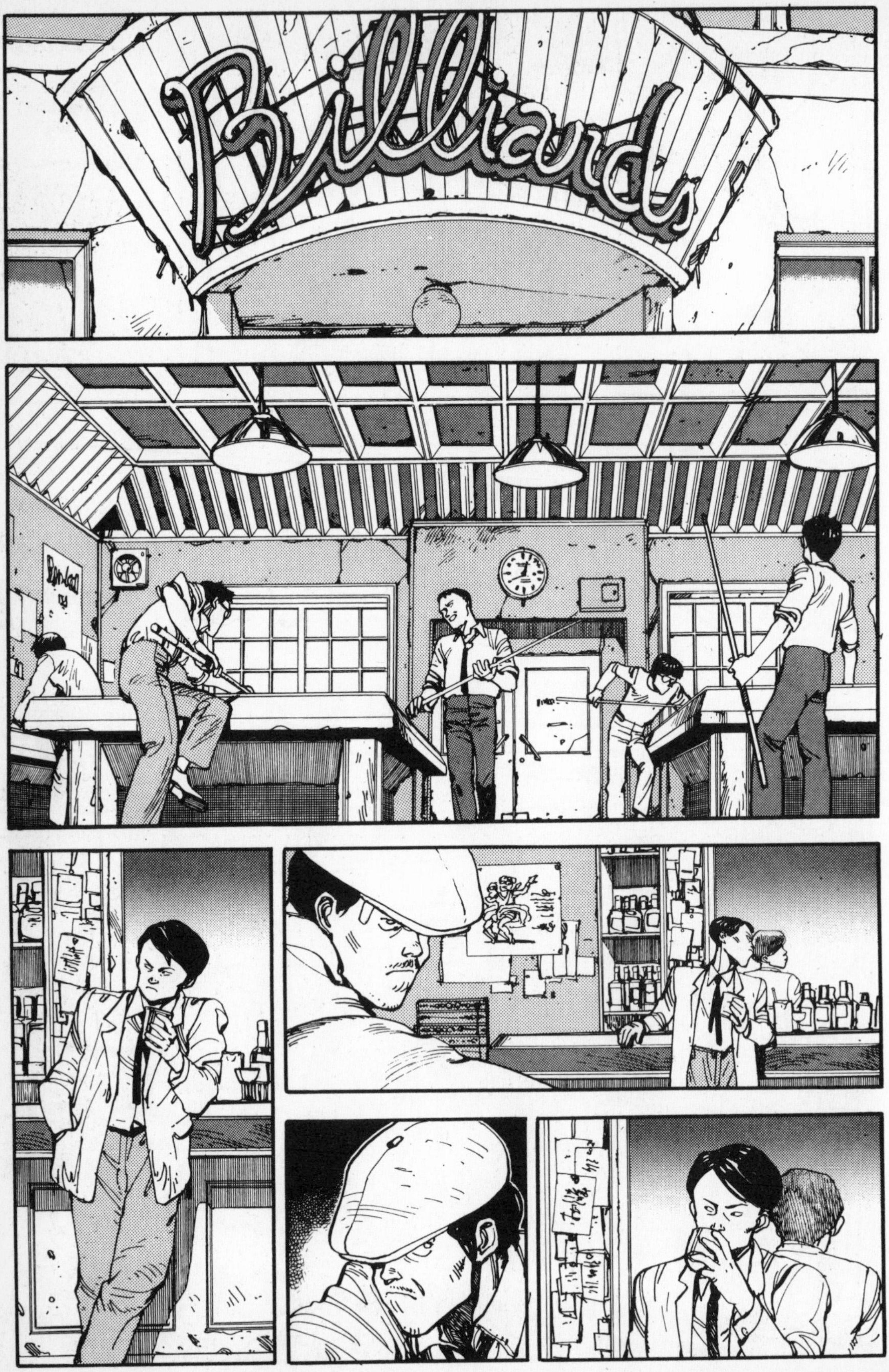
Billiards

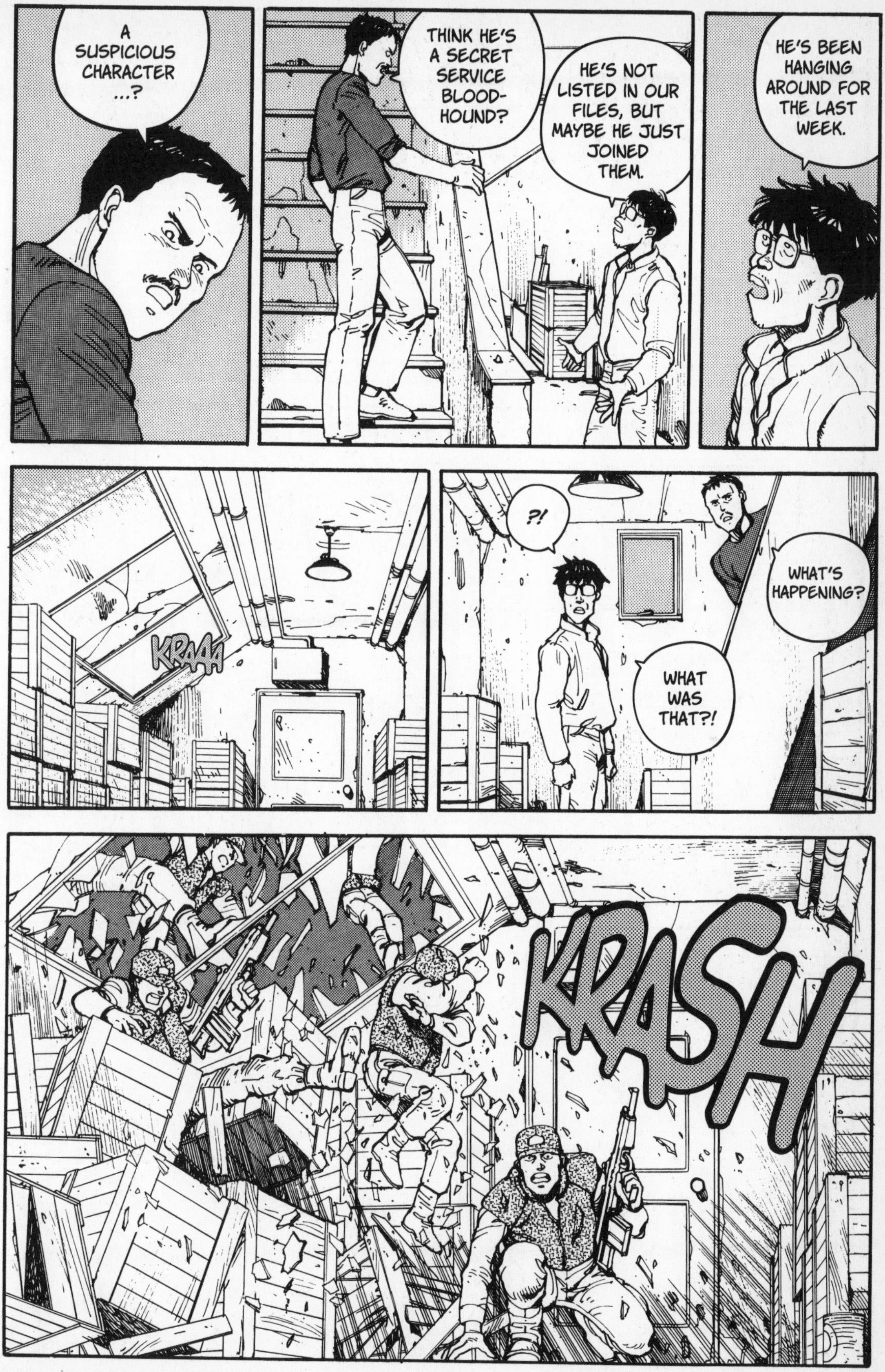
A SUSPICIOUS CHARACTER ...?
THINK HE'S A SECRET SERVICE BLOOD-HOUND?
HE'S NOT LISTED IN OUR FILES, BUT MAYBE HE JUST JOINED THEM.
HE'S BEEN HANGING AROUND FOR THE LAST WEEK.
KRAAA
?!
WHAT'S HAPPENING?
WHAT WAS THAT?!
KRASH

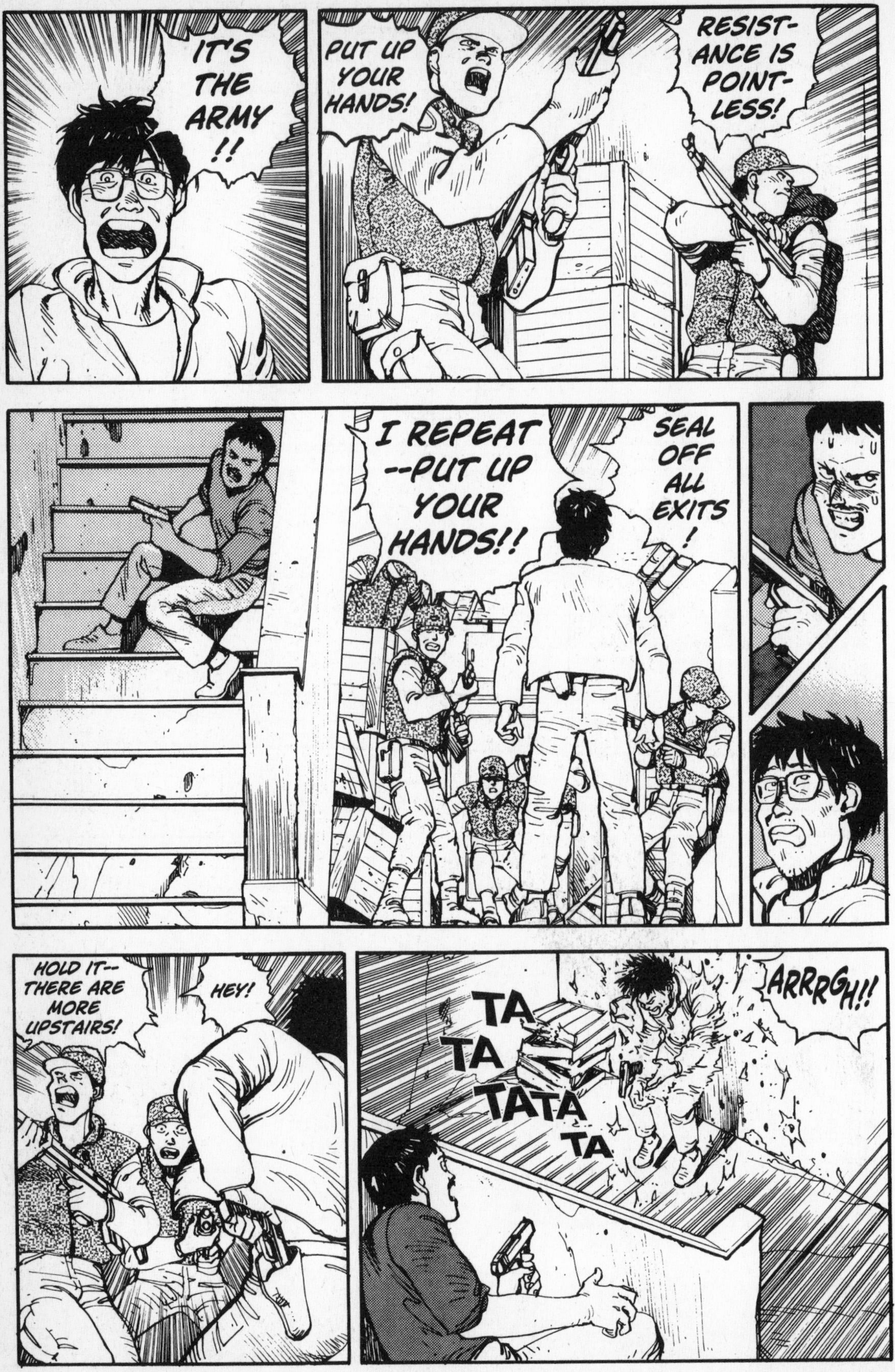
IT'S THE ARMY !!
PUT UP YOUR HANDS!
RESIST-ANCE IS POINT-LESS!
I REPEAT --PUT UP YOUR HANDS!!
SEAL OFF ALL EXITS !
HOLD IT-- THERE ARE MORE UPSTAIRS!
HEY!
TA TA TATA TA
ARRRGH!!

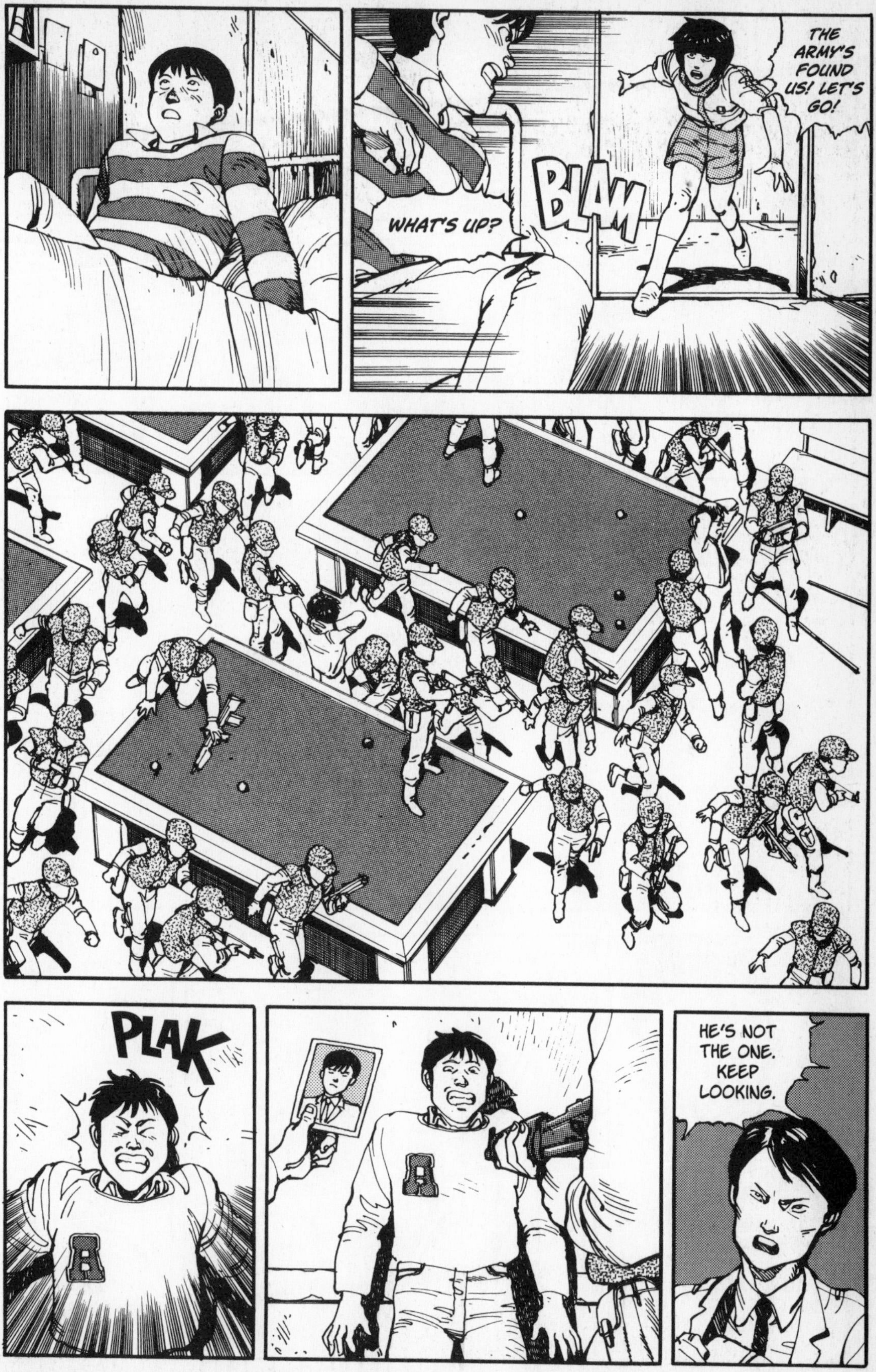
WHAT'S UP?
BLAM
THE ARMY'S FOUND US! LET'S GO!
PLAK
HE'S NOT THE ONE. KEEP LOOKING.

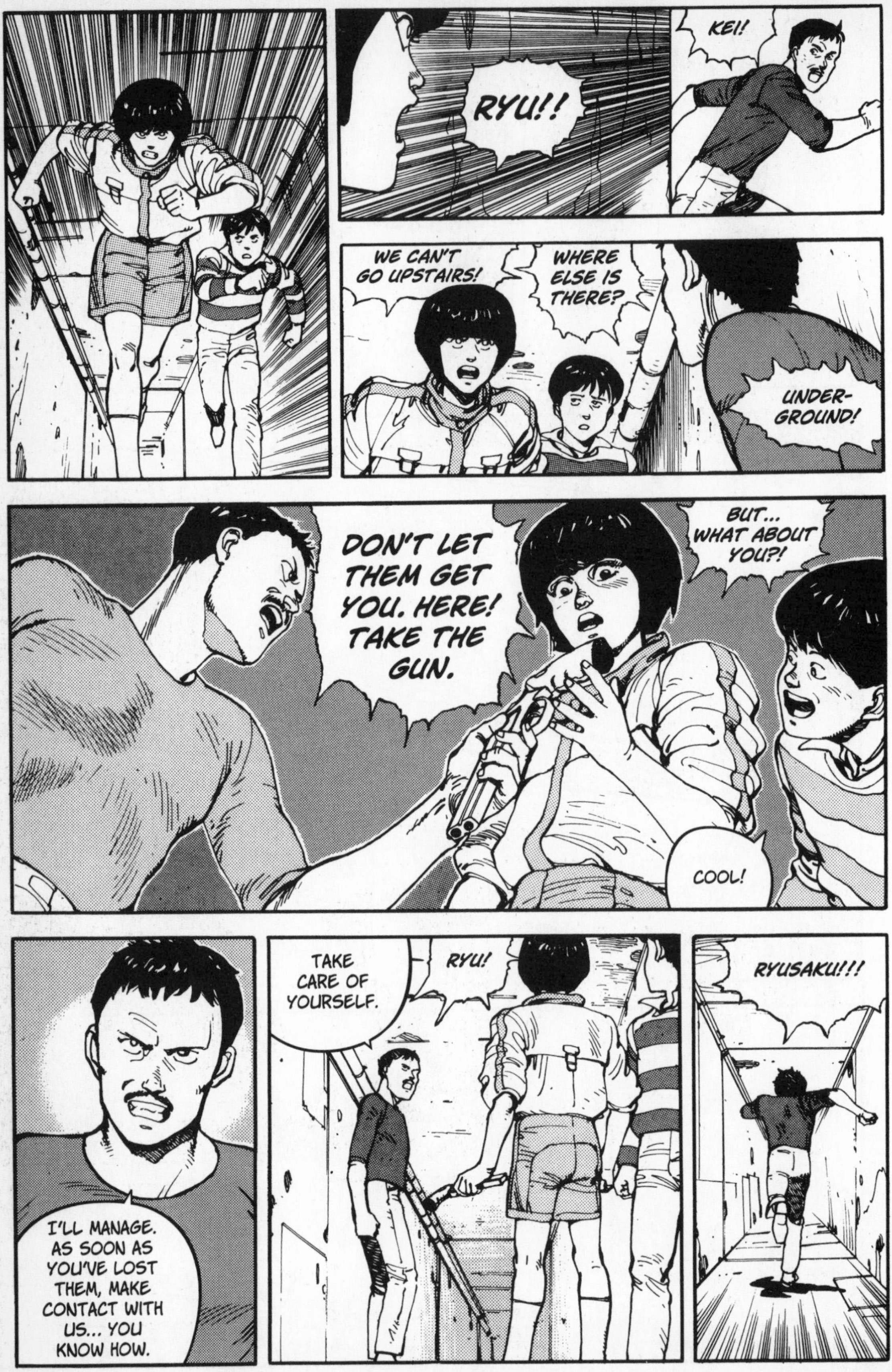
RYU!!
KEI!
WE CAN'T GO UPSTAIRS!
WHERE ELSE IS THERE?
UNDER-GROUND!
DON'T LET THEM GET YOU. HERE! TAKE THE GUN.
BUT... WHAT ABOUT YOU?!
COOL!
I'LL MANAGE. AS SOON AS YOU'VE LOST THEM, MAKE CONTACT WITH US... YOU KNOW HOW.
TAKE CARE OF YOURSELF.
RYU!
RYUSAKU!!!

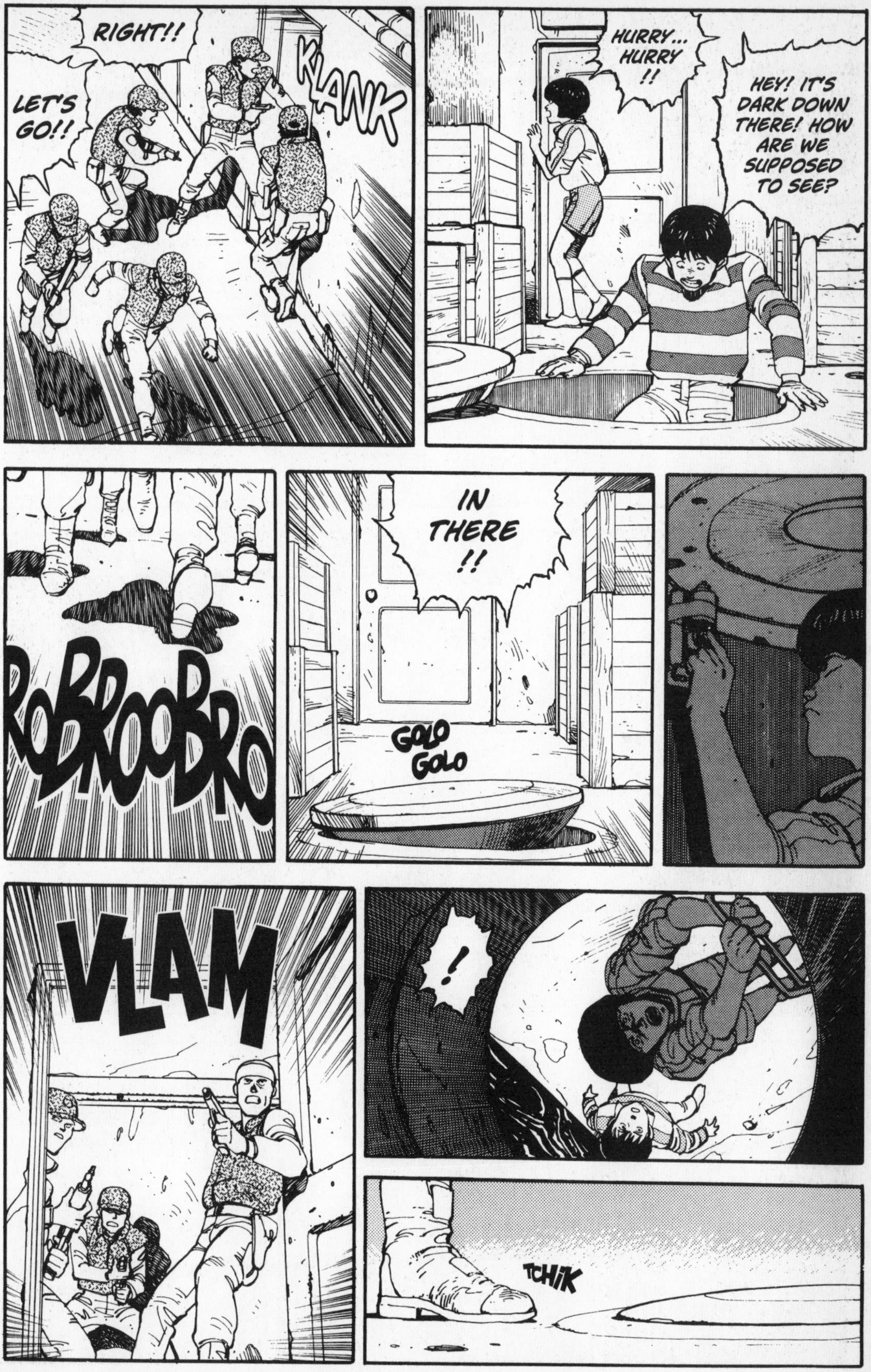
LET'S GO!!
RIGHT!!
KLANK
HURRY... HURRY !!
HEY! IT'S DARK DOWN THERE! HOW ARE WE SUPPOSED TO SEE?
ROBROOBRO
IN THERE !!
GOLO GOLO
VLAM
!
TCHIK

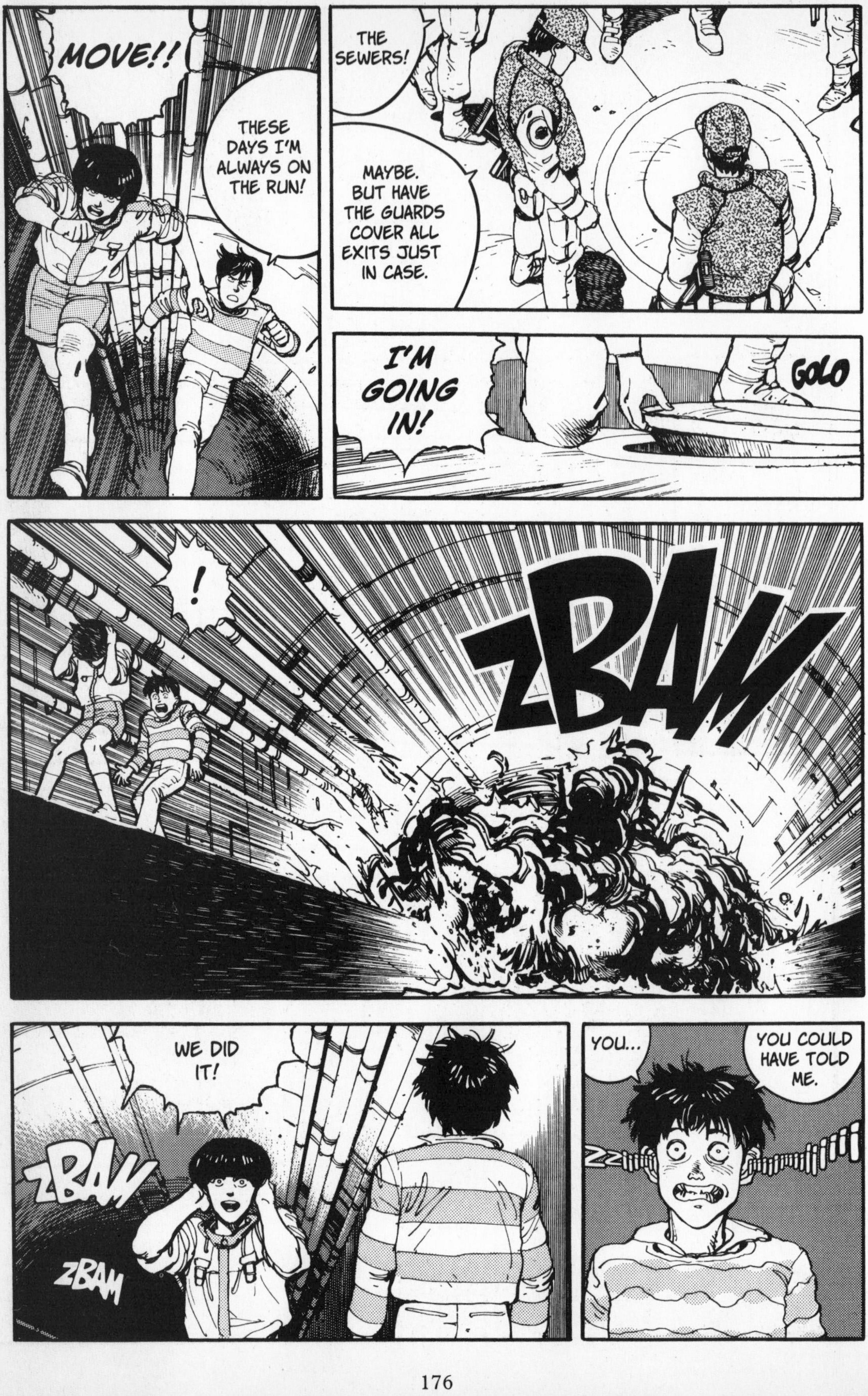
MOVE!!
THESE DAYS I'M ALWAYS ON THE RUN!
THE SEWERS!
MAYBE. BUT HAVE THE GUARDS COVER ALL EXITS JUST IN CASE.
I'M GOING IN!
GOLO
!
ZBAM
WE DID IT!
ZBAM
ZBAM
YOU...
YOU COULD HAVE TOLD ME.

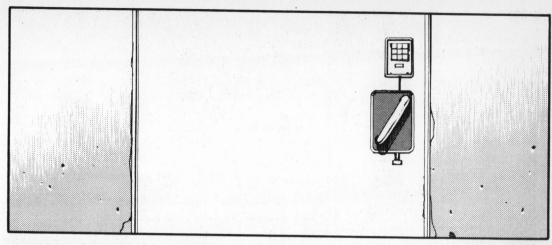

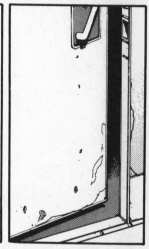

TH-THE
PAIN...
I CAN'T
STAND IT.

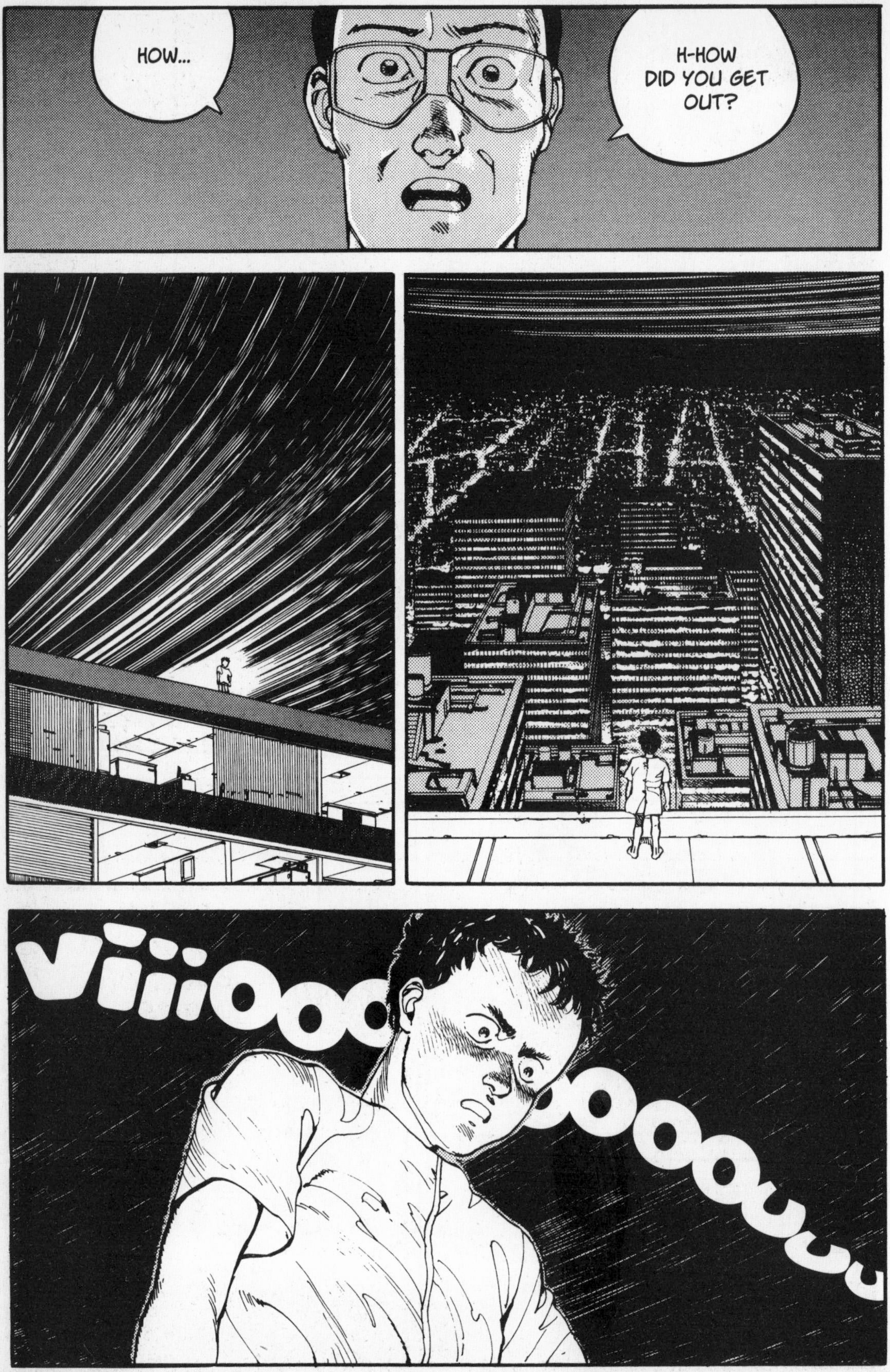
HOW...
H-HOW DID YOU GET OUT?
ViiiOOOOOOOOOUUUU

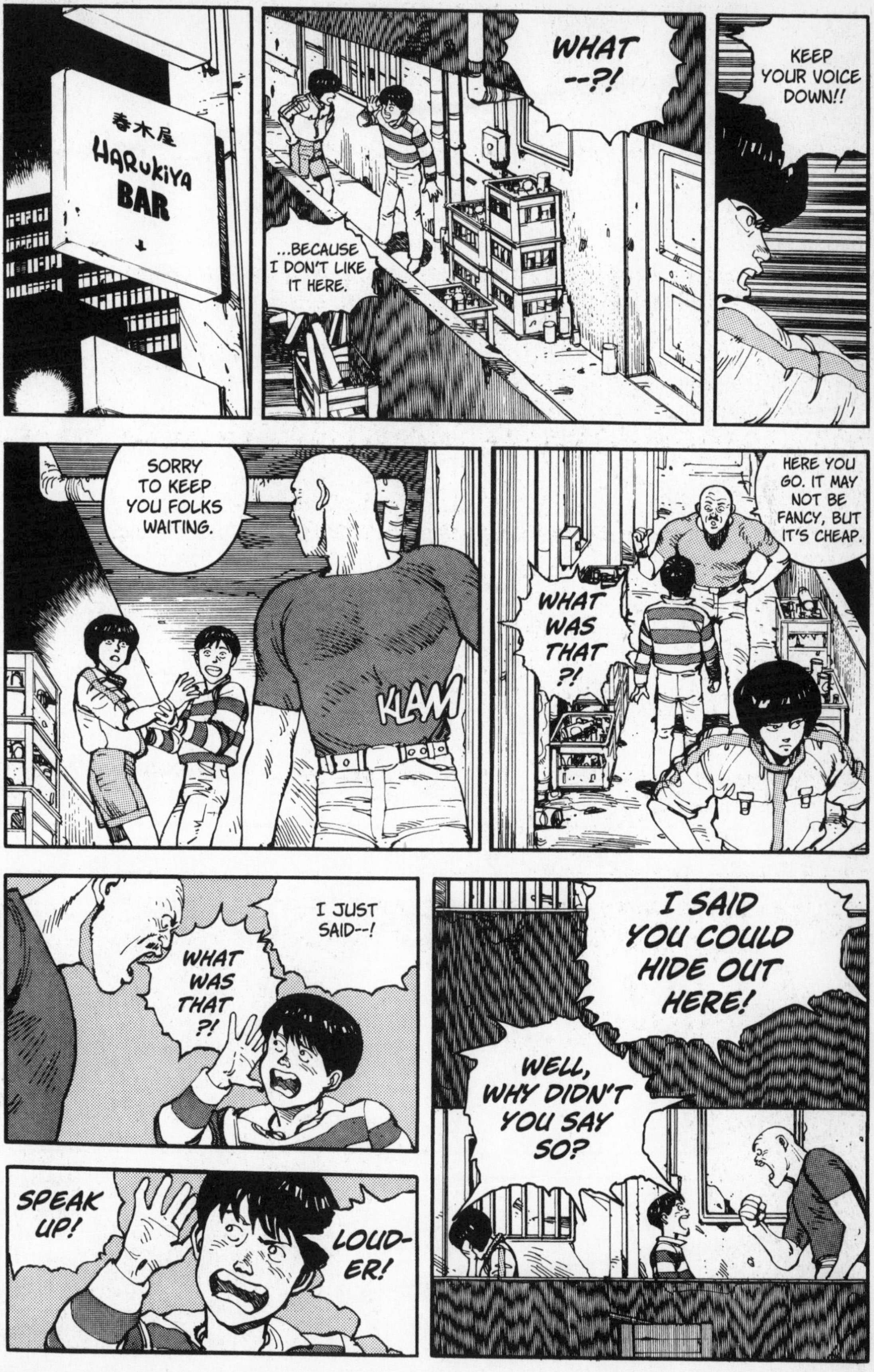

春木屋
HARukiYA
BAR
...BECAUSE I DON'T LIKE IT HERE.
WHAT --?!
KEEP YOUR VOICE DOWN!!
SORRY TO KEEP YOU FOLKS WAITING.
KLAM
HERE YOU GO. IT MAY NOT BE FANCY, BUT IT'S CHEAP.
WHAT WAS THAT ?!
I JUST SAID--!
WHAT WAS THAT ?!
SPEAK UP!
LOUD-ER!
I SAID YOU COULD HIDE OUT HERE!
WELL, WHY DIDN'T YOU SAY SO?

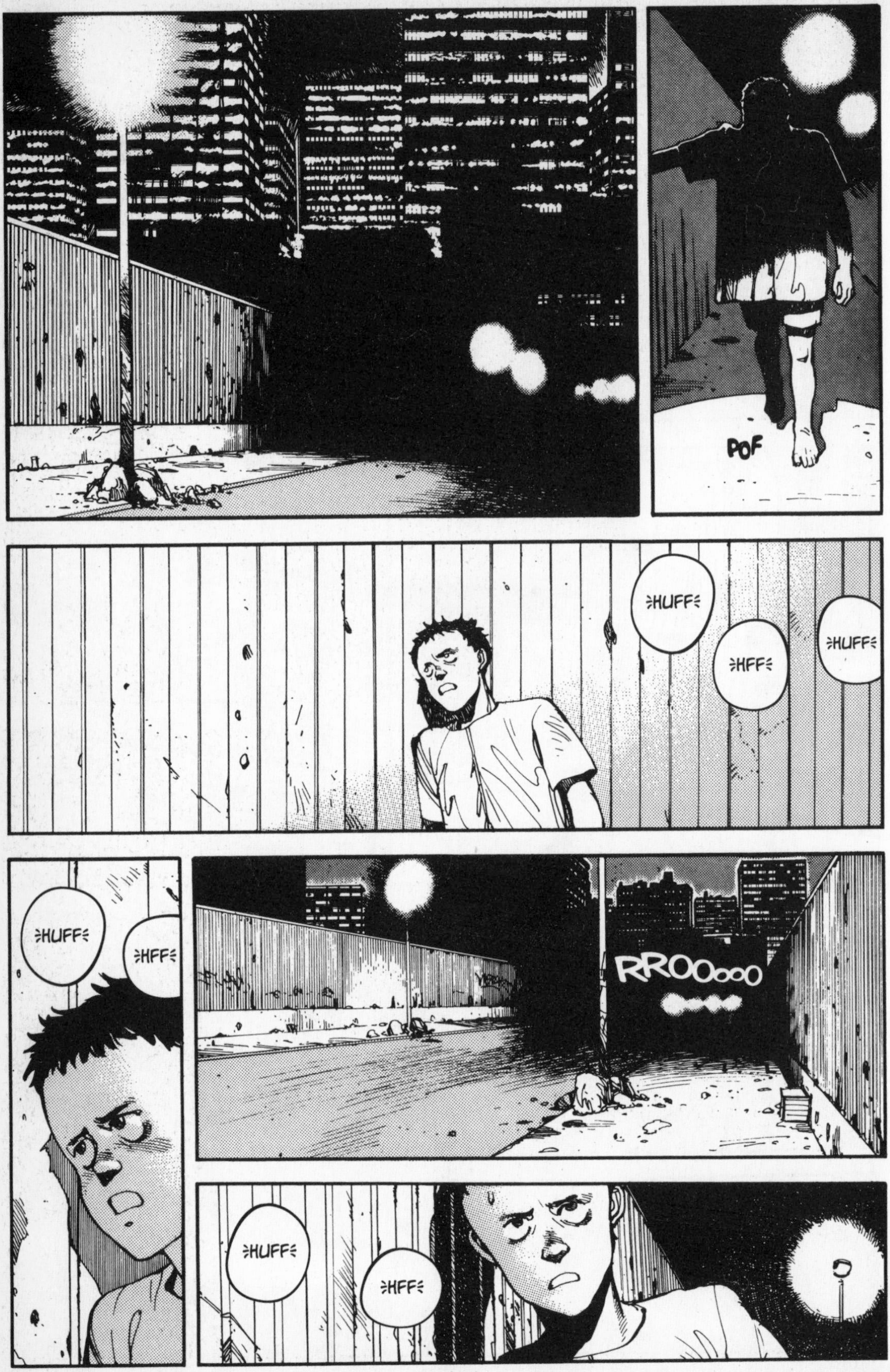
POF
HUFF
HFF
HUFF
HUFF
HFF
RROOooo
HUFF
HFF

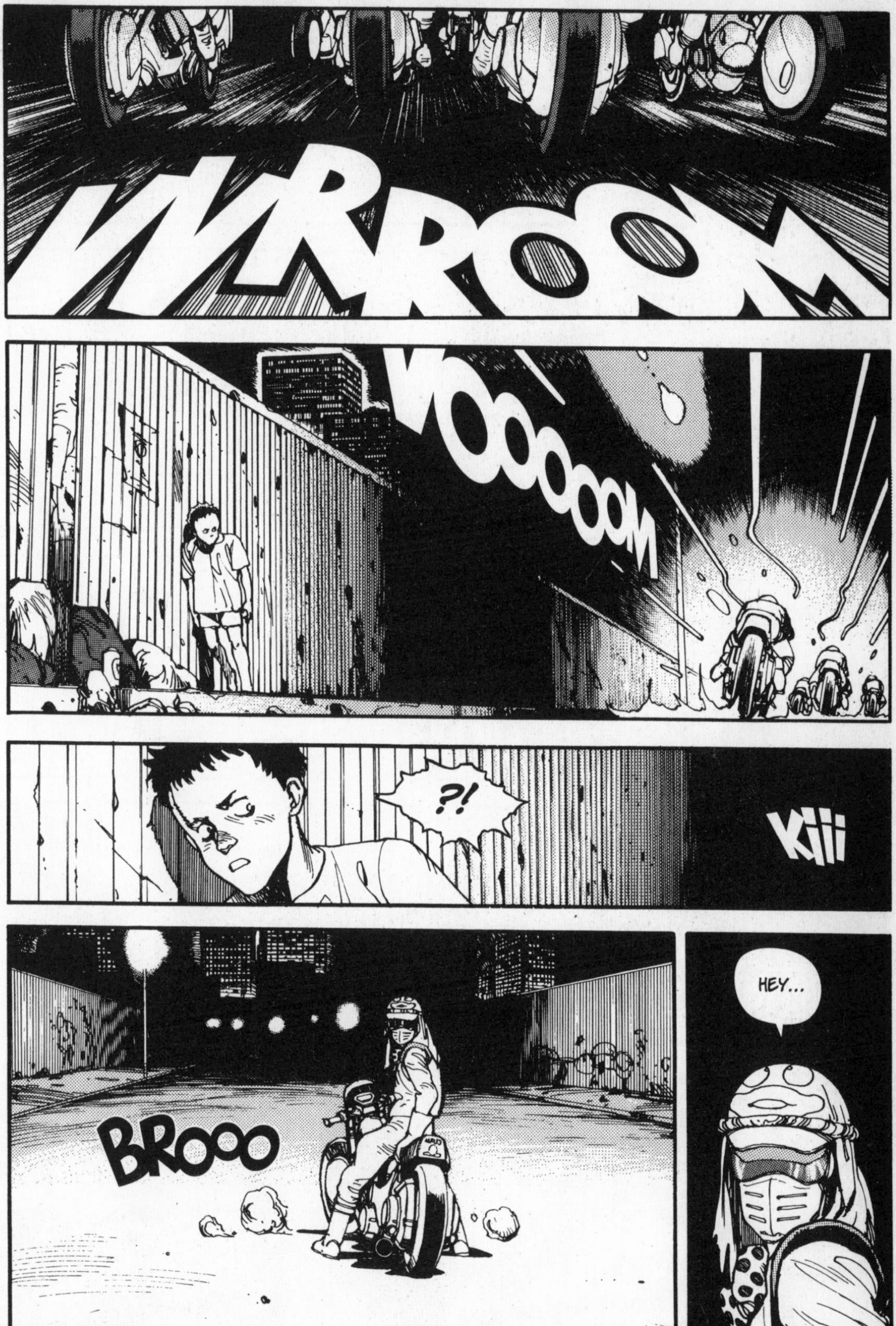
VVRROOM
VOOOOOM
?!
Kiii
BROOO
HEY...

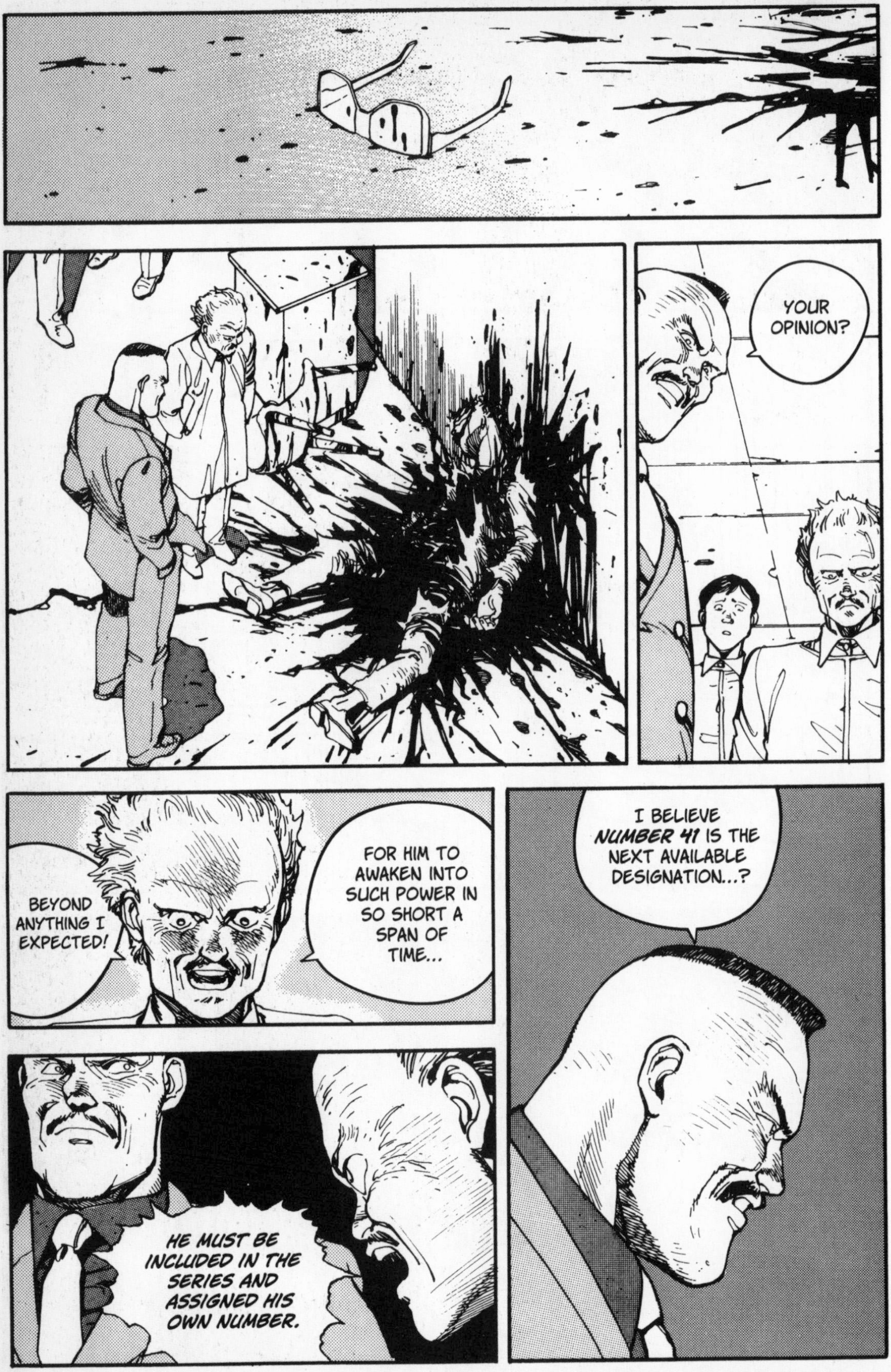
YOUR OPINION?
BEYOND ANYTHING I EXPECTED!
FOR HIM TO AWAKEN INTO SUCH POWER IN SO SHORT A SPAN OF TIME...
HE MUST BE INCLUDED IN THE SERIES AND ASSIGNED HIS OWN NUMBER.
I BELIEVE NUMBER 41 IS THE NEXT AVAILABLE DESIGNATION...?

VVVRROO

COME ON. HE'S ALL YOURS.

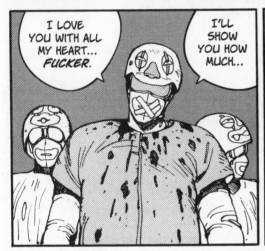

I LOVE YOU WITH ALL MY HEART... FUCKER.

I'LL SHOW YOU HOW MUCH...

TCHiK

YOU SHOULDA KILLED ME WHEN YOU HAD THE CHANCE...

...BUT IT'S TOO LATE NOW.

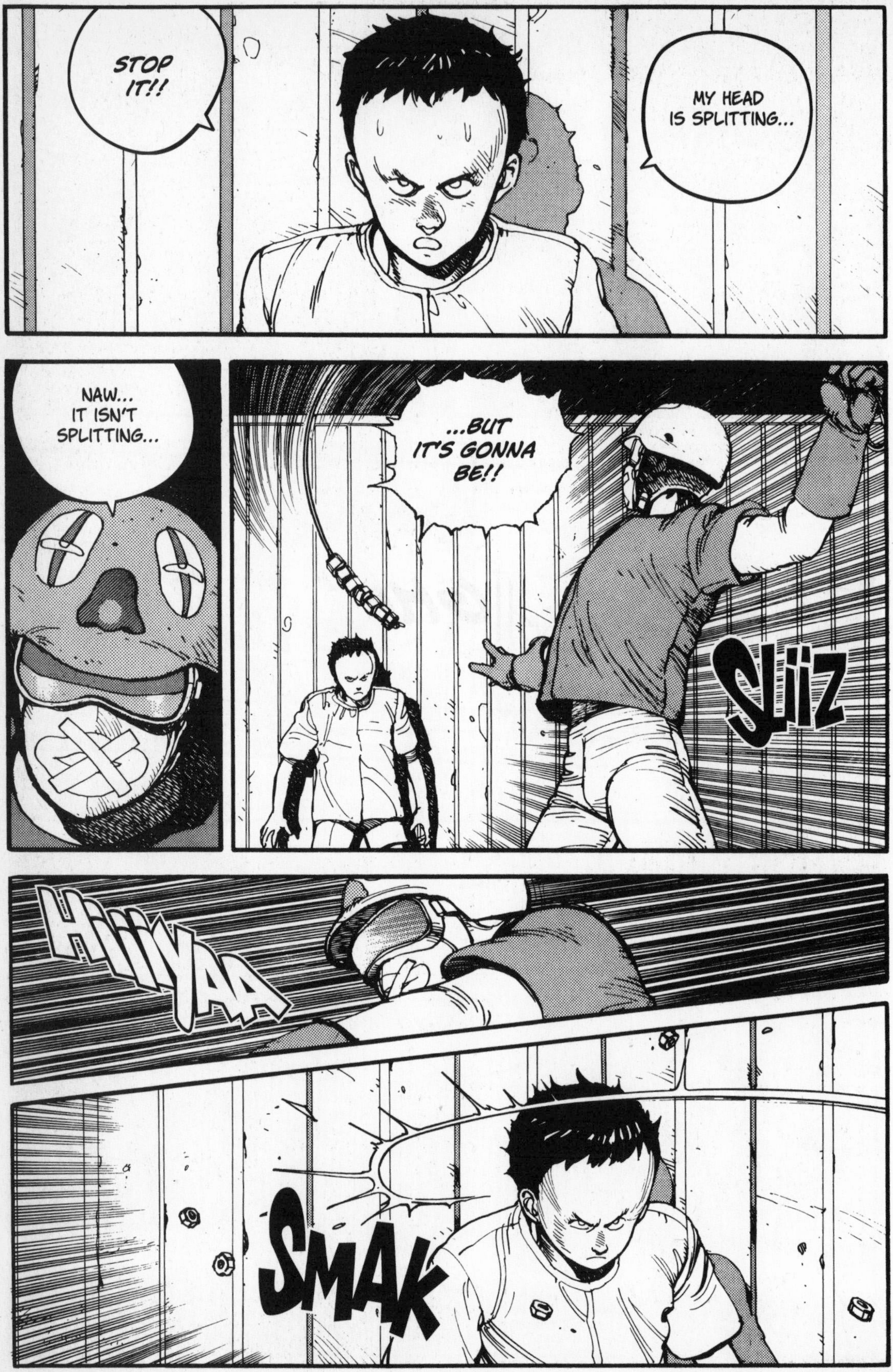
STOP IT!!
MY HEAD IS SPLITTING...
NAW... IT ISN'T SPLITTING...
...BUT IT'S GONNA BE!!
SLIIZ
HIIIIYAA
SMAK

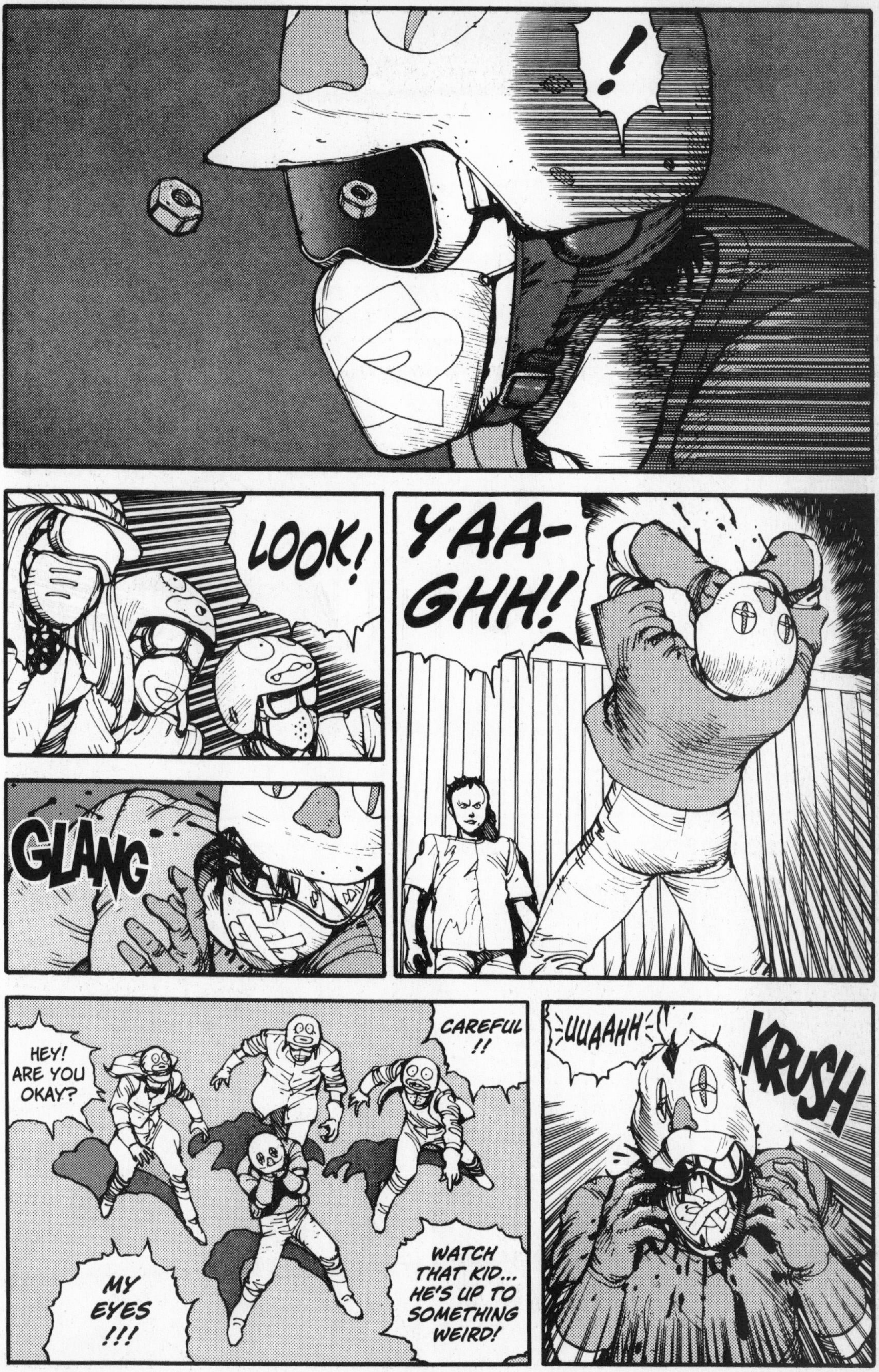
!
LOOK!
YAA-GHH!
GLANG
HEY! ARE YOU OKAY?
CAREFUL !!
MY EYES !!!
WATCH THAT KID... HE'S UP TO SOMETHING WEIRD!
UUAAHH
KRUSH

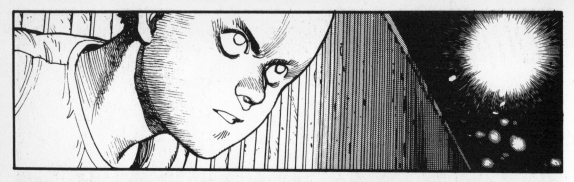

SPURT

≥AUGH≤
OH GOD!!

FLITCH

GROSS...

Y'KNOW... MY HEAD DOESN'T HURT ANY MORE. HOW'S YOURS?

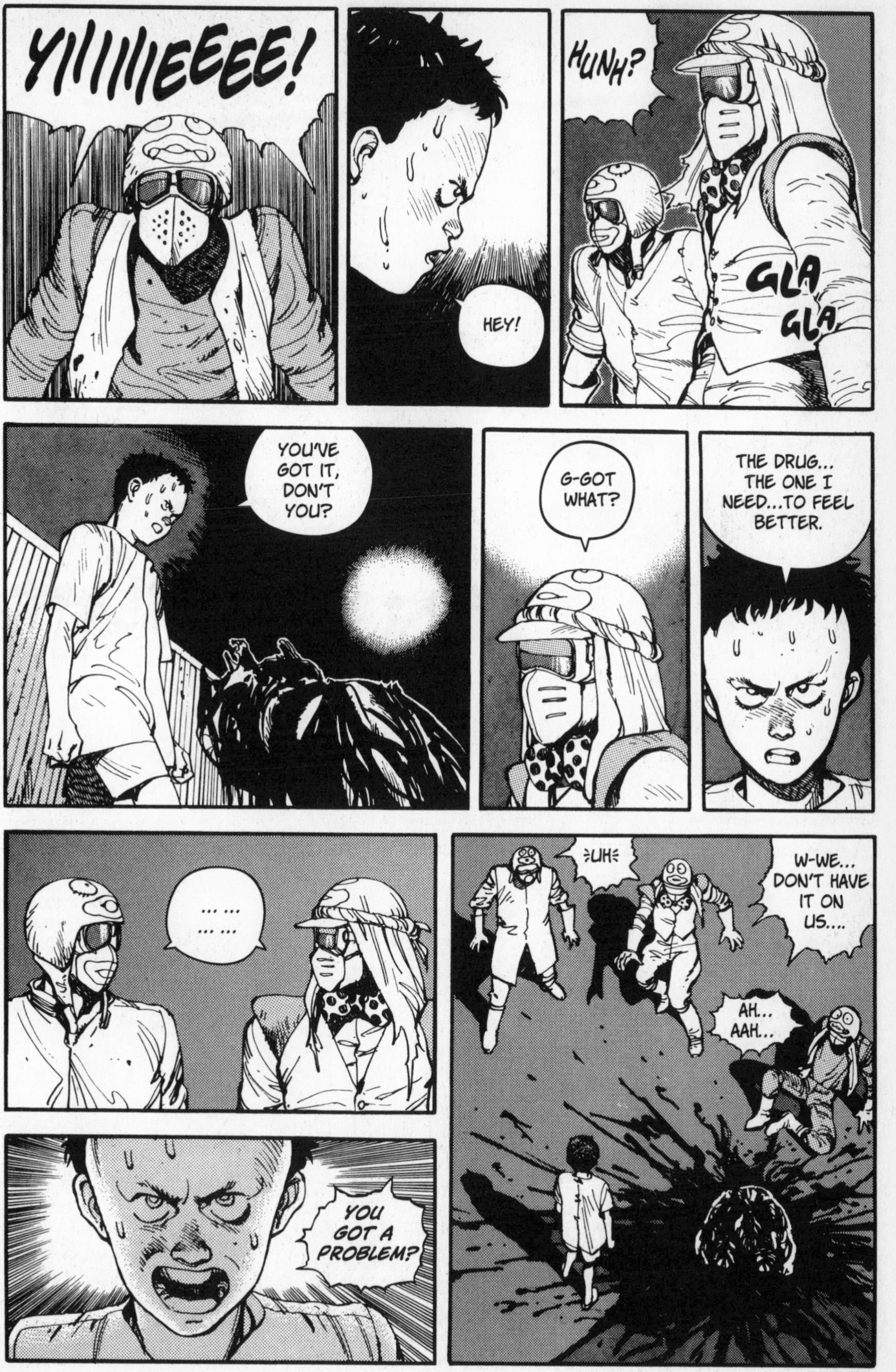
YIIIIIIEEEEE!
HEY!
HUNH?
GLA GLA
YOU'VE GOT IT, DON'T YOU?
G-GOT WHAT?
THE DRUG... THE ONE I NEED...TO FEEL BETTER.
... ...
UH
W-WE... DON'T HAVE IT ON US....
AH... AAH...
YOU GOT A PROBLEM?

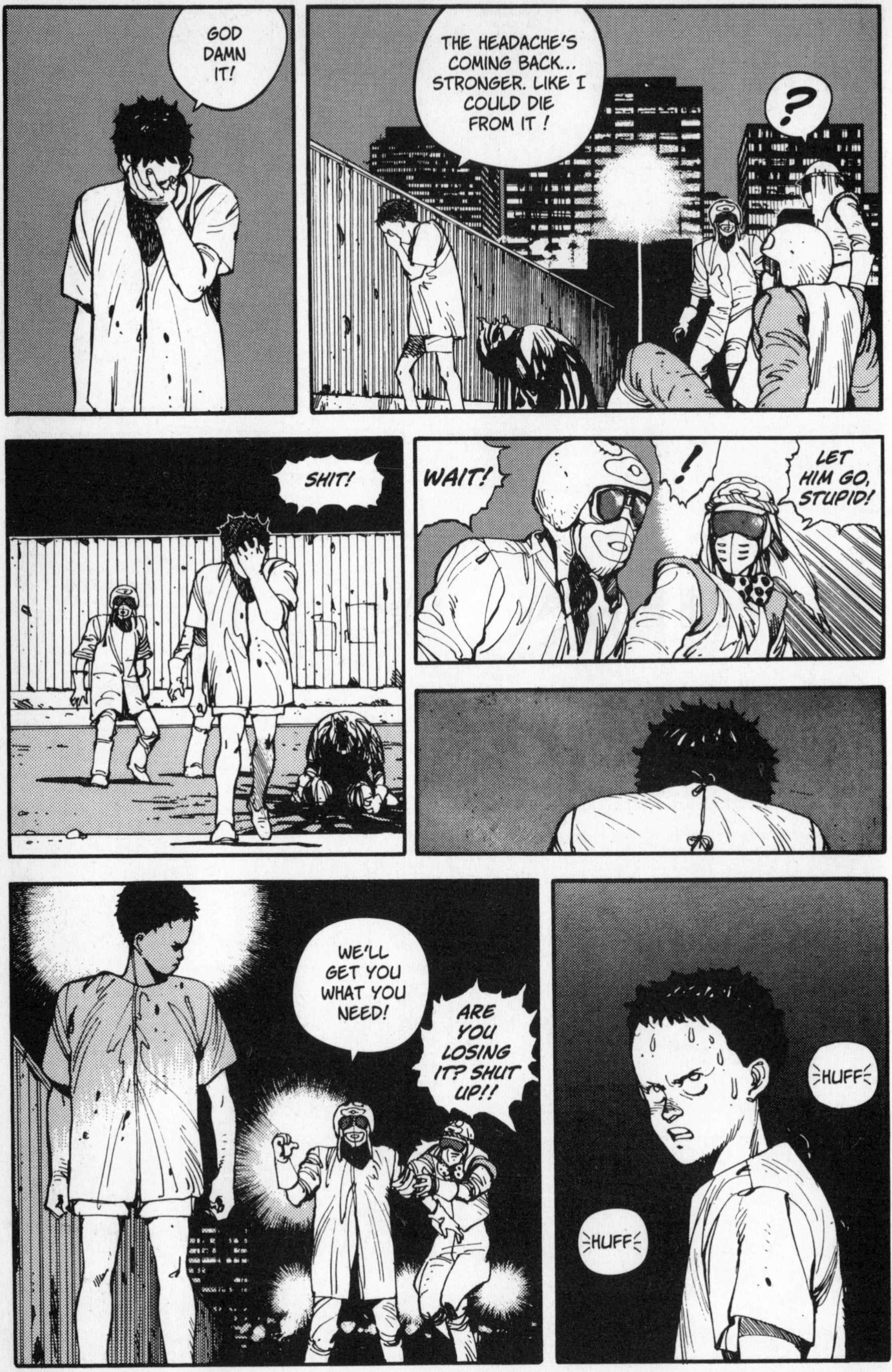
GOD DAMN IT!
THE HEADACHE'S COMING BACK... STRONGER. LIKE I COULD DIE FROM IT !
?
SHIT!
WAIT!
!
LET HIM GO, STUPID!
WE'LL GET YOU WHAT YOU NEED!
ARE YOU LOSING IT? SHUT UP!!
HUFF
HUFF

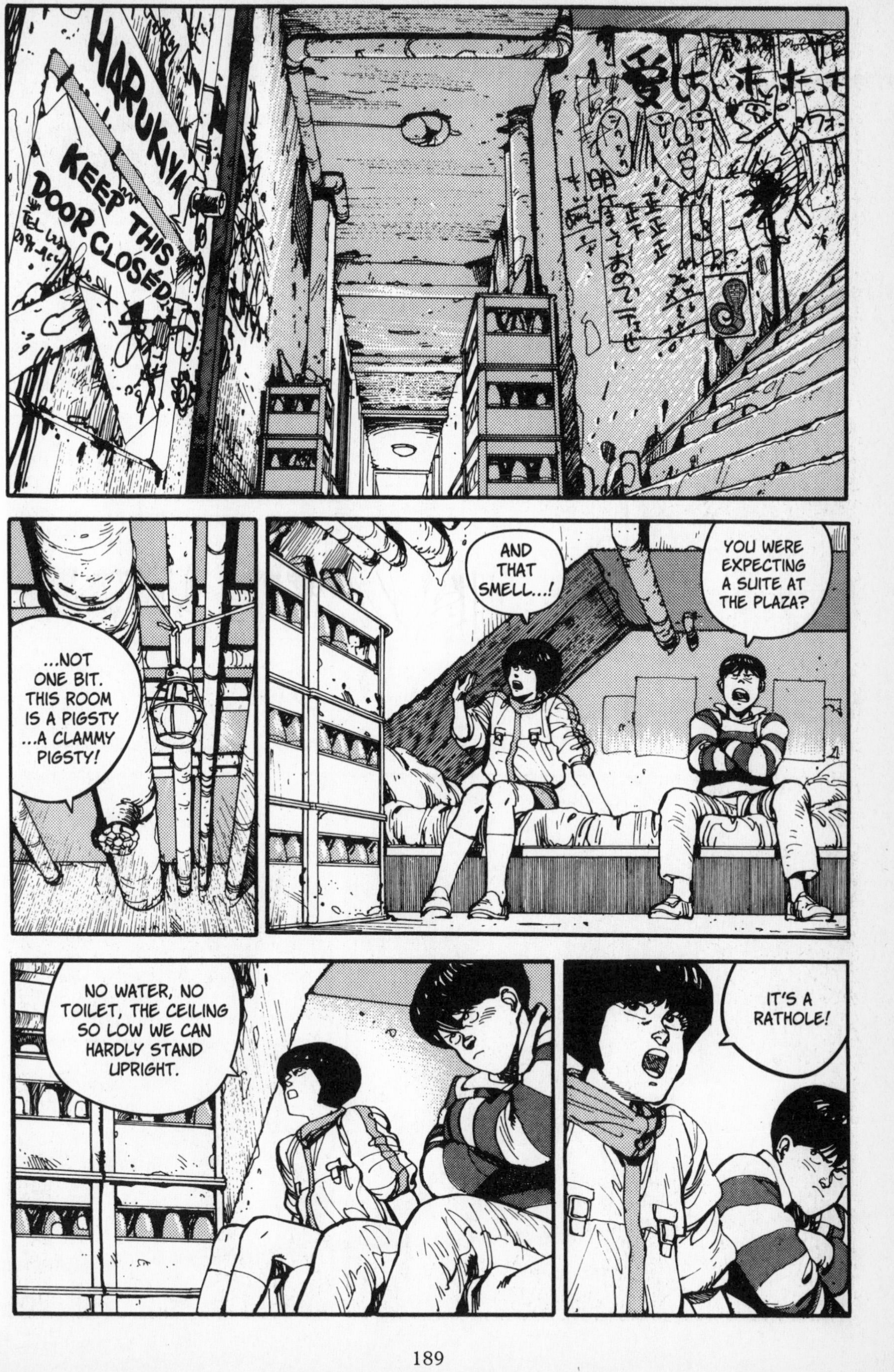
HARUKIYA
KEEP THIS DOOR CLOSED
...NOT ONE BIT. THIS ROOM IS A PIGSTY ...A CLAMMY PIGSTY!
AND THAT SMELL...!
YOU WERE EXPECTING A SUITE AT THE PLAZA?
NO WATER, NO TOILET, THE CEILING SO LOW WE CAN HARDLY STAND UPRIGHT.
IT'S A RATHOLE!

SO, WHAT'S THE STORY ON THAT RYU GUY?

WHAT'S HE TO YOU?

HE'S MY BROTHER.

BUT HE DOESN'T LOOK ANYTHING LIKE YOU.

THAT'S NONE OF YOUR BUSINESS.

OH, BUT IT IS. IF ONLY YOU KNEW THE THINGS I'D IMAGINED...

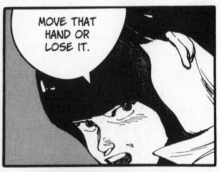

MOVE THAT HAND OR LOSE IT.

YOU DON'T MEAN THAT.

190

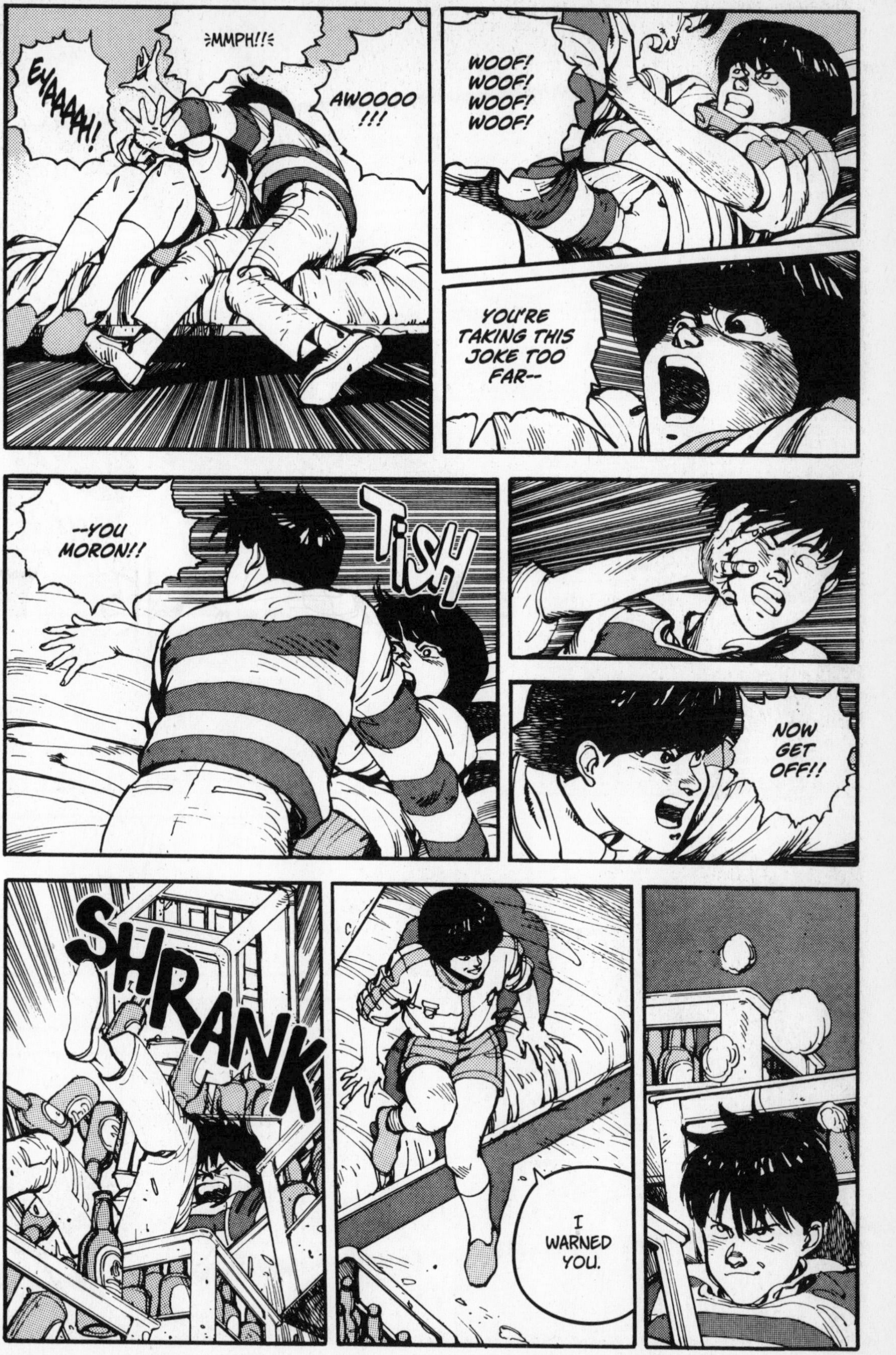
EYAAAAH!
MMPH!!
AWOOOO !!!
WOOF! WOOF! WOOF! WOOF!
YOU'RE TAKING THIS JOKE TOO FAR--
--YOU MORON!!
TISH
NOW GET OFF!!
SHRANK
I WARNED YOU.

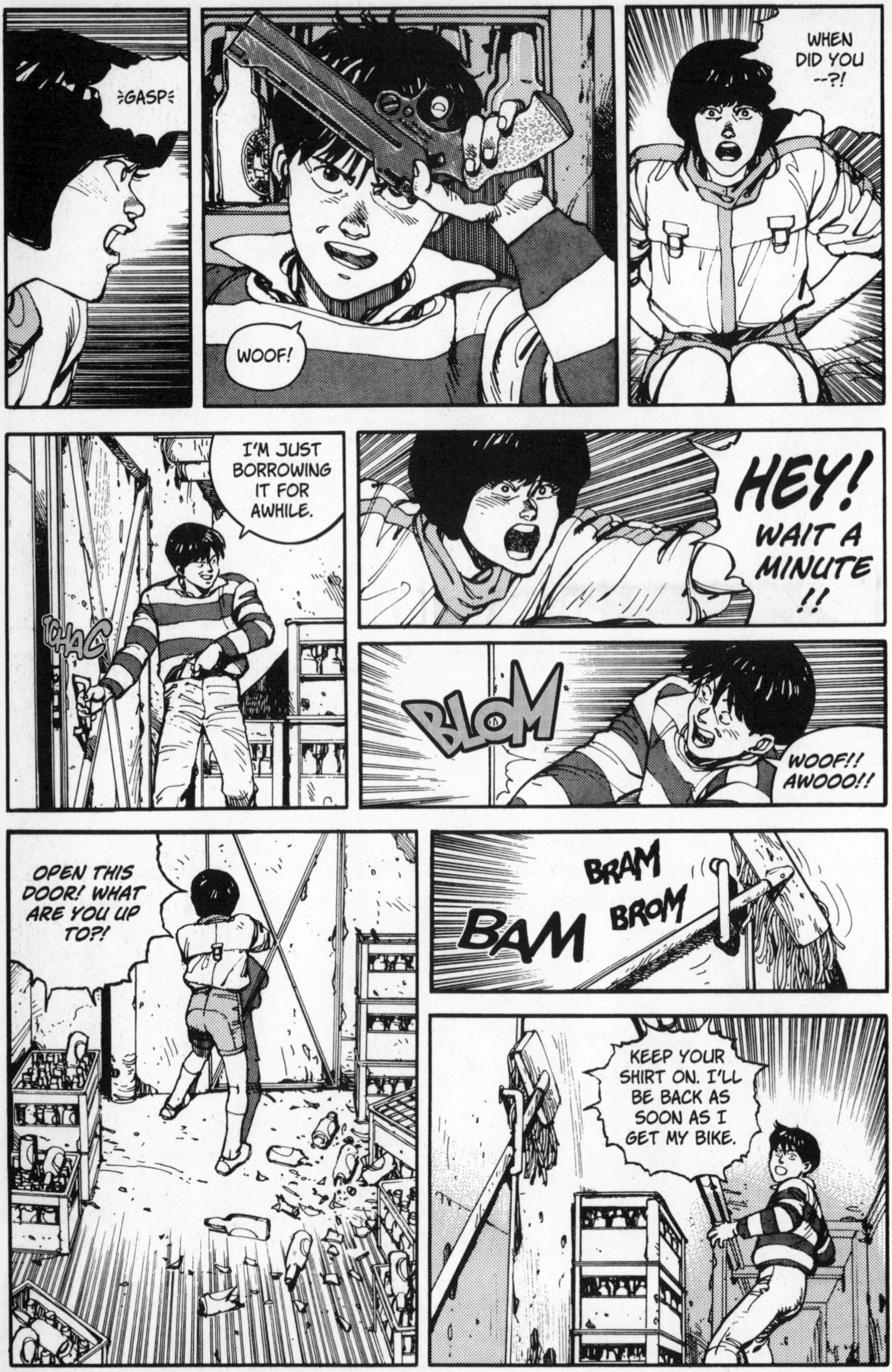
GASP
WOOF!
WHEN DID YOU --?!
I'M JUST BORROWING IT FOR AWHILE.
TCHAC
HEY! WAIT A MINUTE !!
BLOM
WOOF!! AWOOO!!
OPEN THIS DOOR! WHAT ARE YOU UP TO?!
BRAM
BAM
BROM
KEEP YOUR SHIRT ON. I'LL BE BACK AS SOON AS I GET MY BIKE.

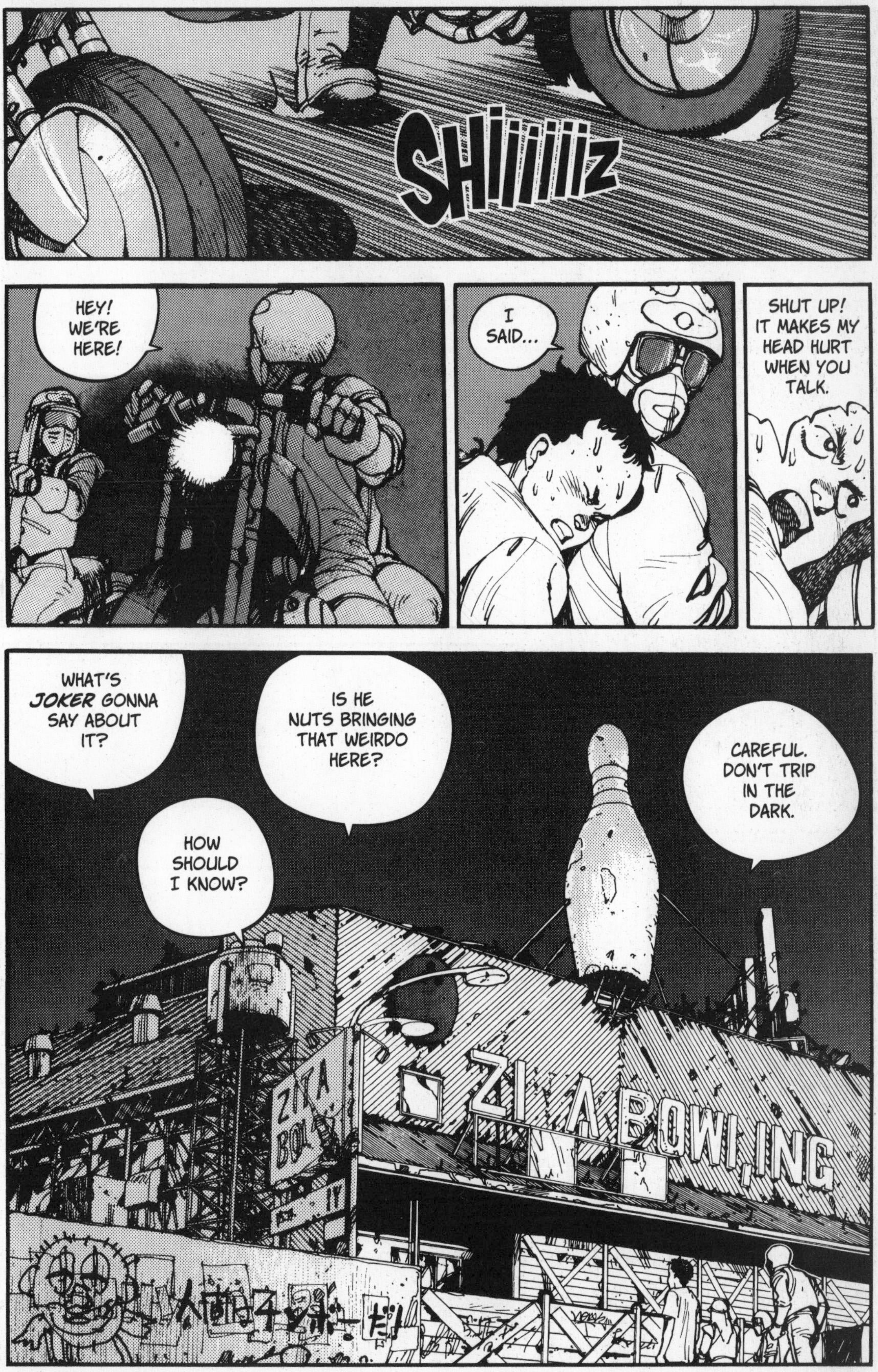
SHiiiiiz
HEY! WE'RE HERE!
I SAID...
SHUT UP! IT MAKES MY HEAD HURT WHEN YOU TALK.
WHAT'S *JOKER* GONNA SAY ABOUT IT?
IS HE NUTS BRINGING THAT WEIRDO HERE?
HOW SHOULD I KNOW?
CAREFUL. DON'T TRIP IN THE DARK.

WHAT DO YOU MEAN, CHIP'S HEAD EXPLODED?!

WHAT KINDA DRUGS YOU BEEN TAKING, HOMES?

SURE IT WASN'T HIS BALLS?

IT WAS HIS HEAD?

SO WHO KILLED HIM?

WELL...

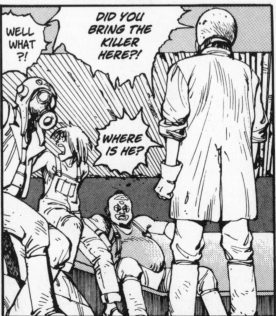

WELL WHAT?!

DID YOU BRING THE KILLER HERE?!

WHERE IS HE?

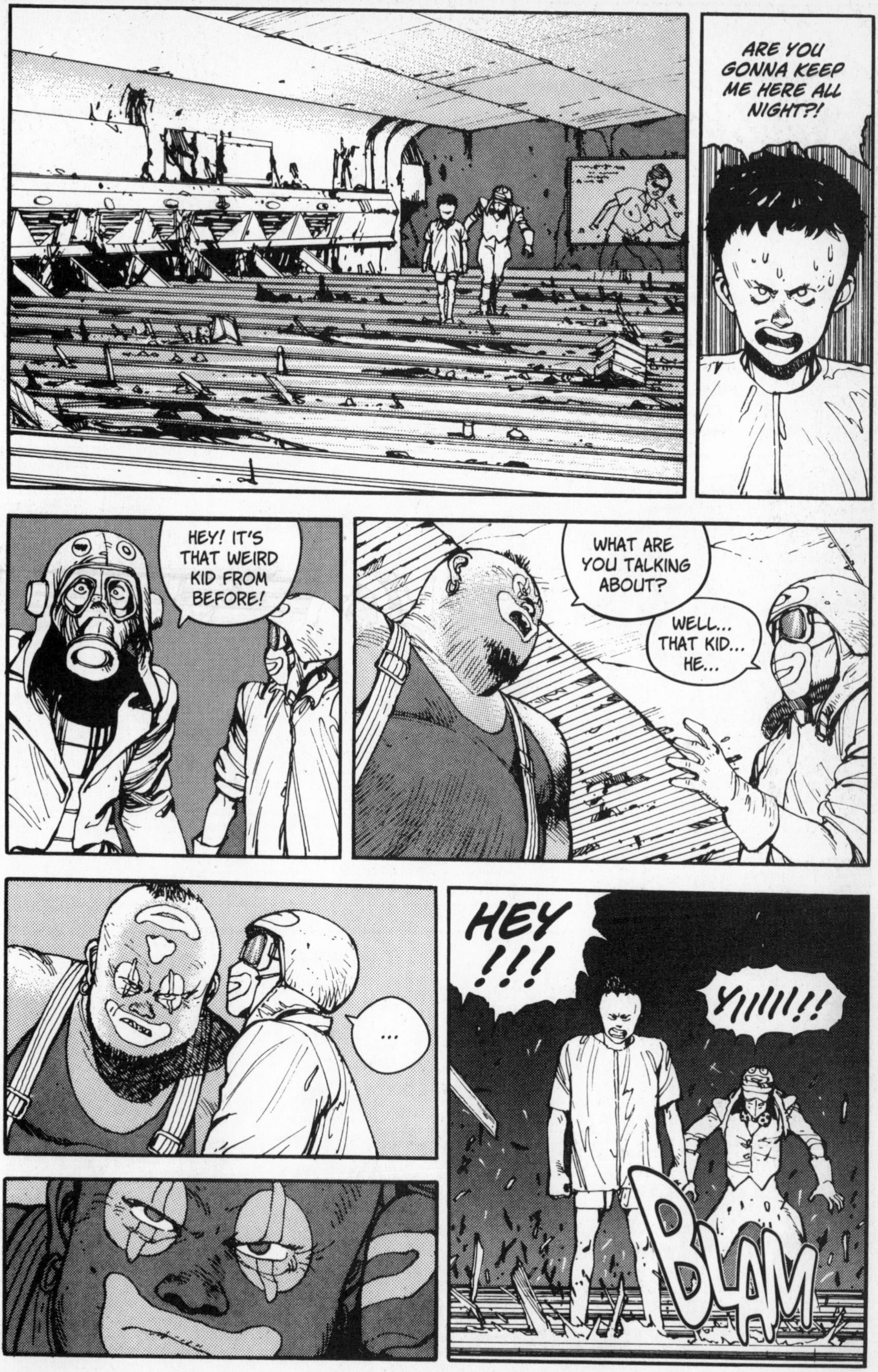

ARE YOU GONNA KEEP ME HERE ALL NIGHT?!
HEY! IT'S THAT WEIRD KID FROM BEFORE!
WHAT ARE YOU TALKING ABOUT?
WELL... THAT KID... HE...
...
HEY !!!
YIIIII!!
BLAM

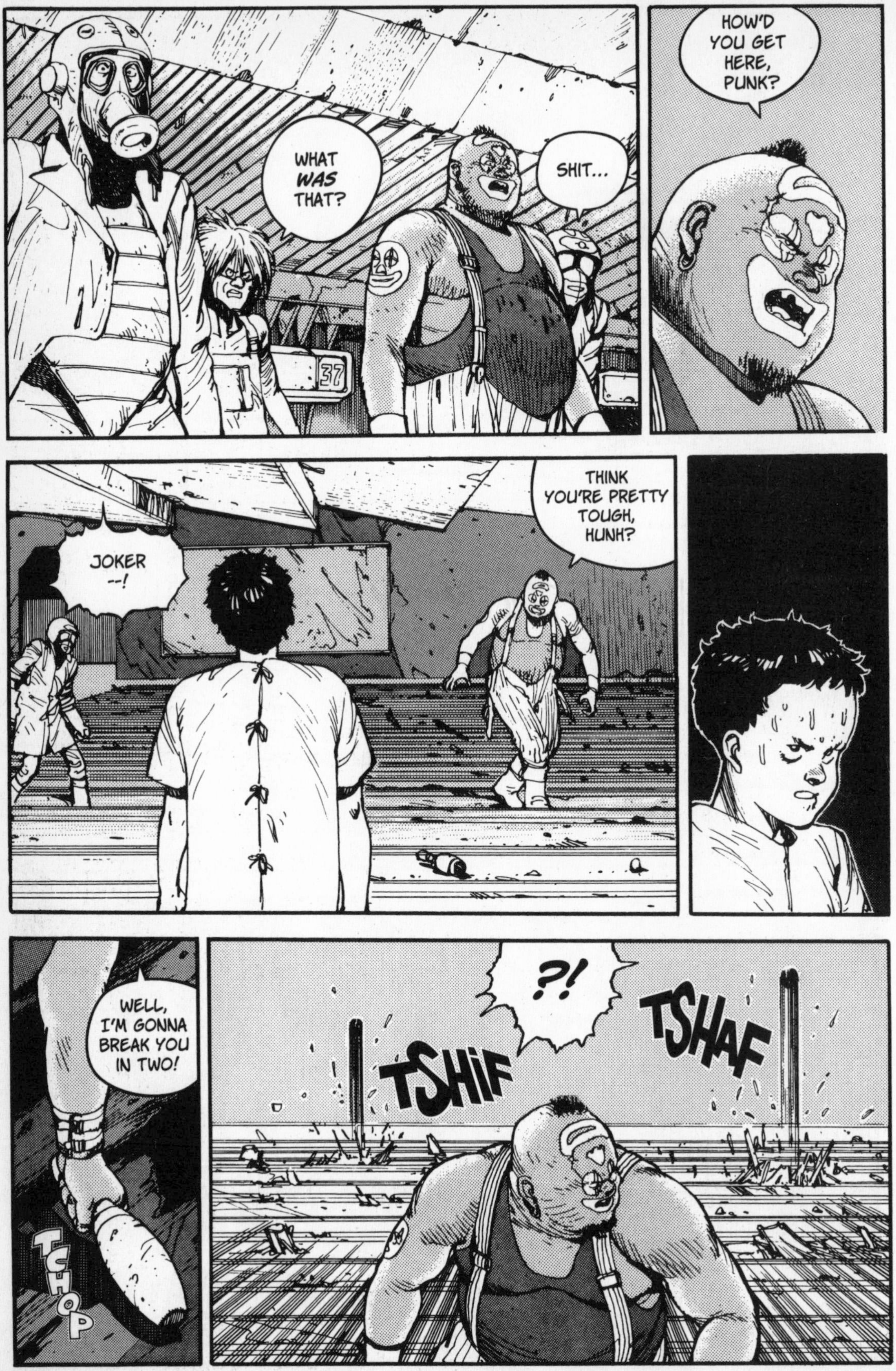
WHAT WAS THAT?
SHIT...
HOW'D YOU GET HERE, PUNK?
JOKER --!
THINK YOU'RE PRETTY TOUGH, HUNH?
WELL, I'M GONNA BREAK YOU IN TWO!
TCHOP
?!
TSHIF
TSHAF

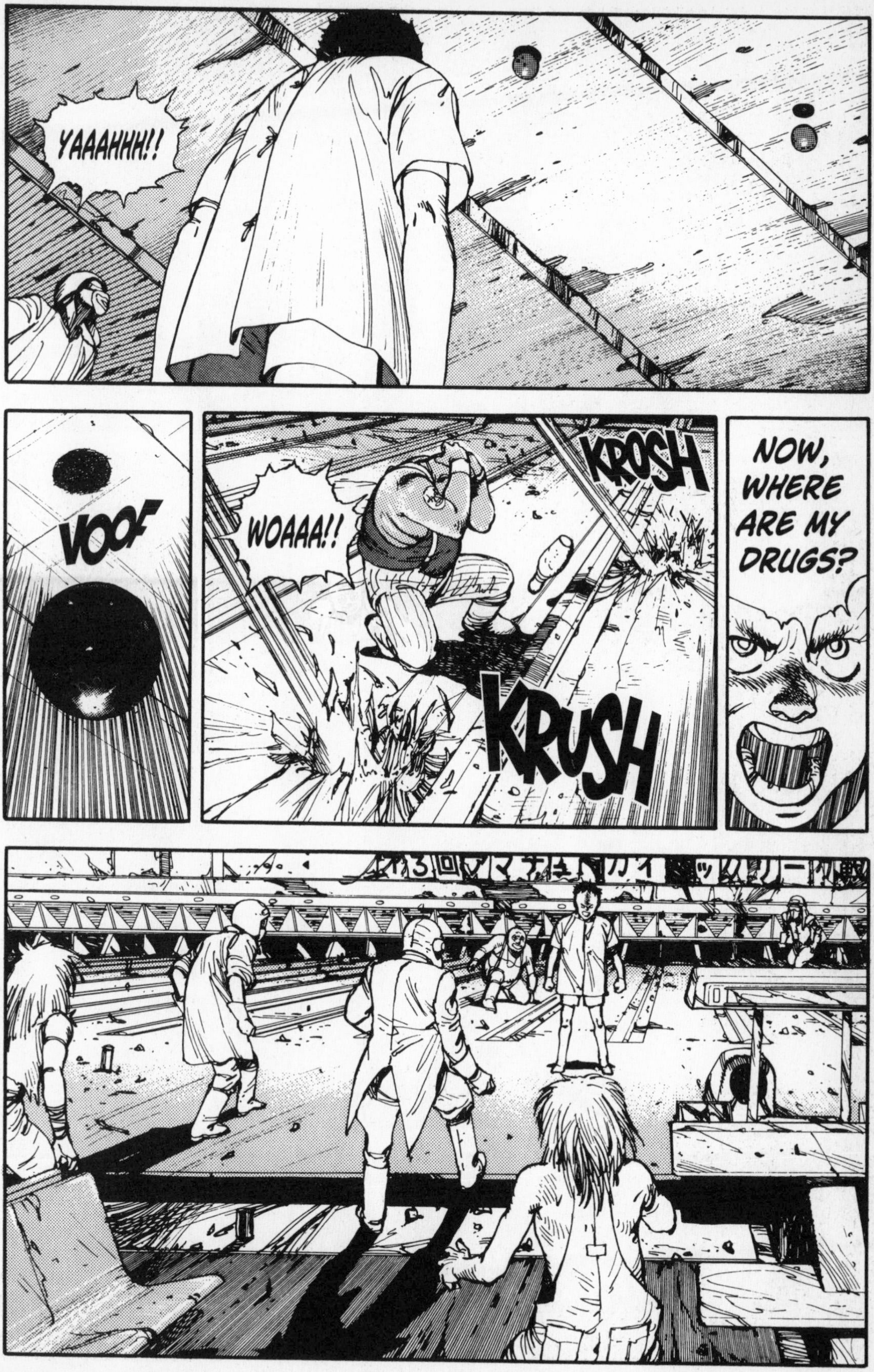
YAAAHHH!!
VOOF
WOAAA!!
KROSH
KRUSH
NOW, WHERE ARE MY DRUGS?

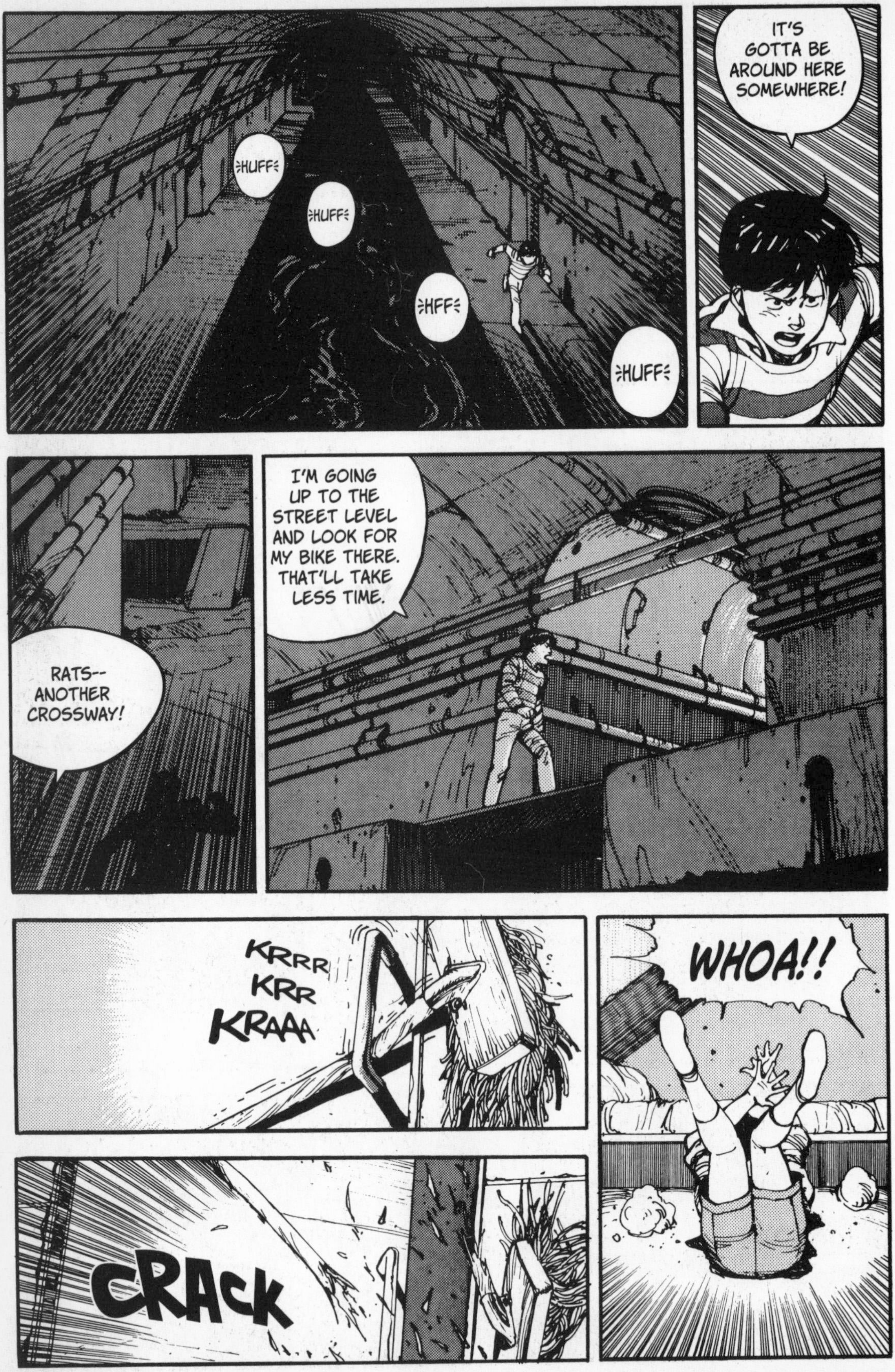
HUFF
HUFF
HFF
HUFF
IT'S GOTTA BE AROUND HERE SOMEWHERE!
RATS-- ANOTHER CROSSWAY!
I'M GOING UP TO THE STREET LEVEL AND LOOK FOR MY BIKE THERE. THAT'LL TAKE LESS TIME.
KRRRR KRR KRAAA
CRACK
WHOA!!

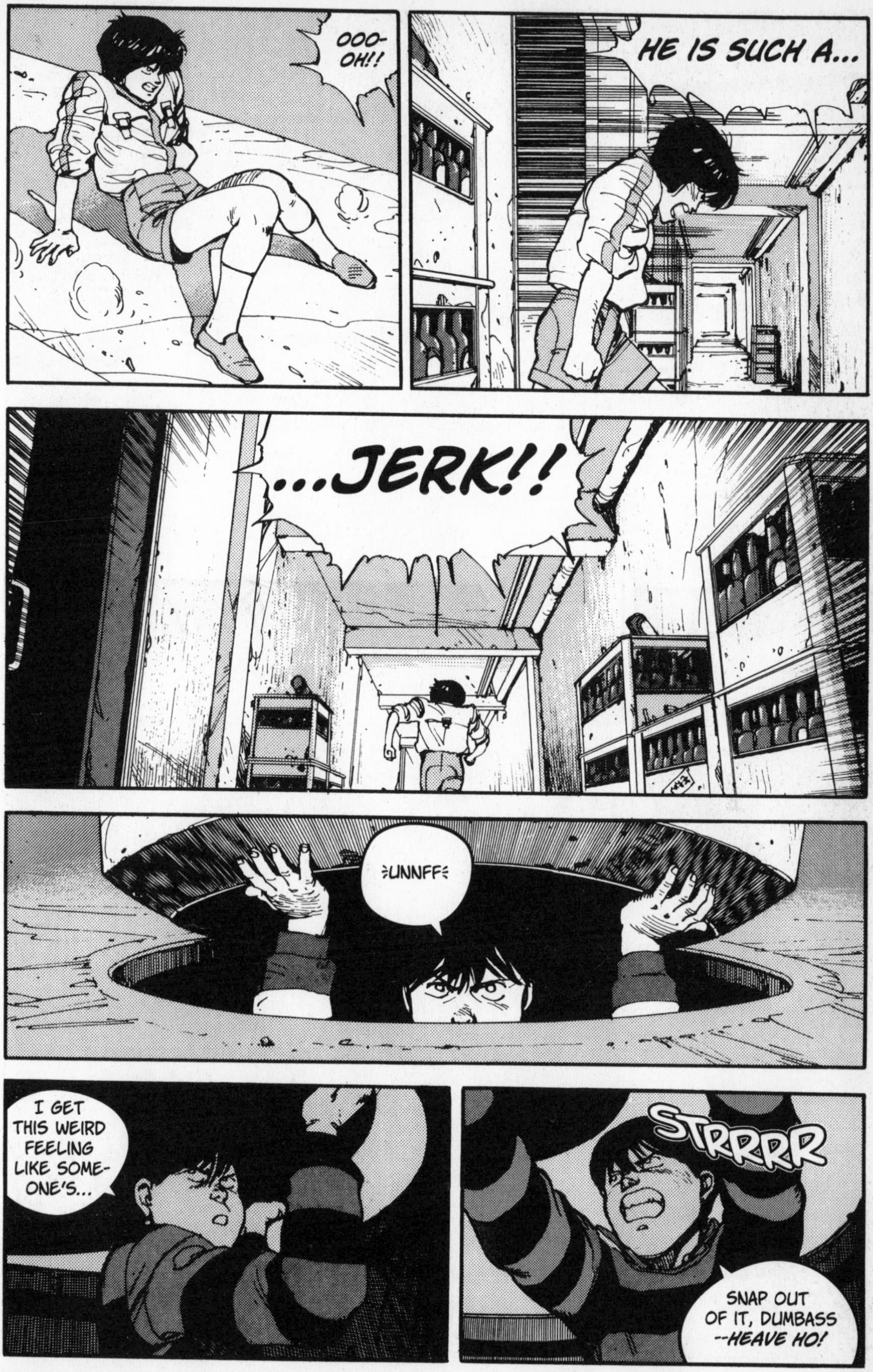
OOO-OH!!
HE IS SUCH A...
...JERK!!
UNNFF
I GET THIS WEIRD FEELING LIKE SOME-ONE'S...
STRRRR
SNAP OUT OF IT, DUMBASS --HEAVE HO!

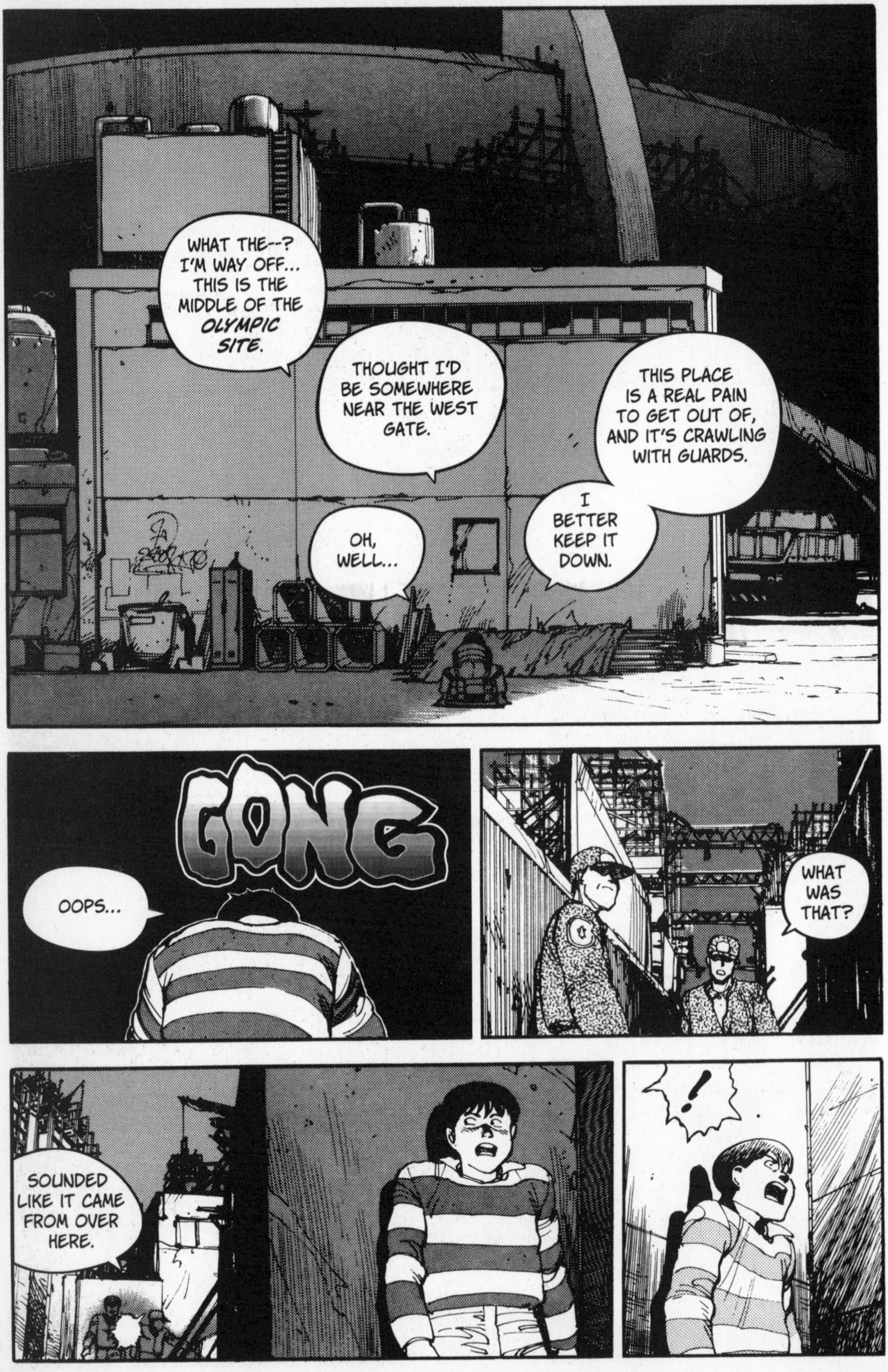
WHAT THE--? I'M WAY OFF... THIS IS THE MIDDLE OF THE *OLYMPIC SITE*.
THOUGHT I'D BE SOMEWHERE NEAR THE WEST GATE.
THIS PLACE IS A REAL PAIN TO GET OUT OF, AND IT'S CRAWLING WITH GUARDS.
OH, WELL...
I BETTER KEEP IT DOWN.
GONG
OOPS...
WHAT WAS THAT?
SOUNDED LIKE IT CAME FROM OVER HERE.
!

VRRRAAH

TAP TAP
TAP
TAP

THE COLONEL HAS LANDED!

THE COLONEL...

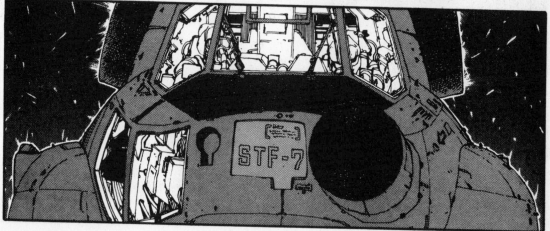

STF-7

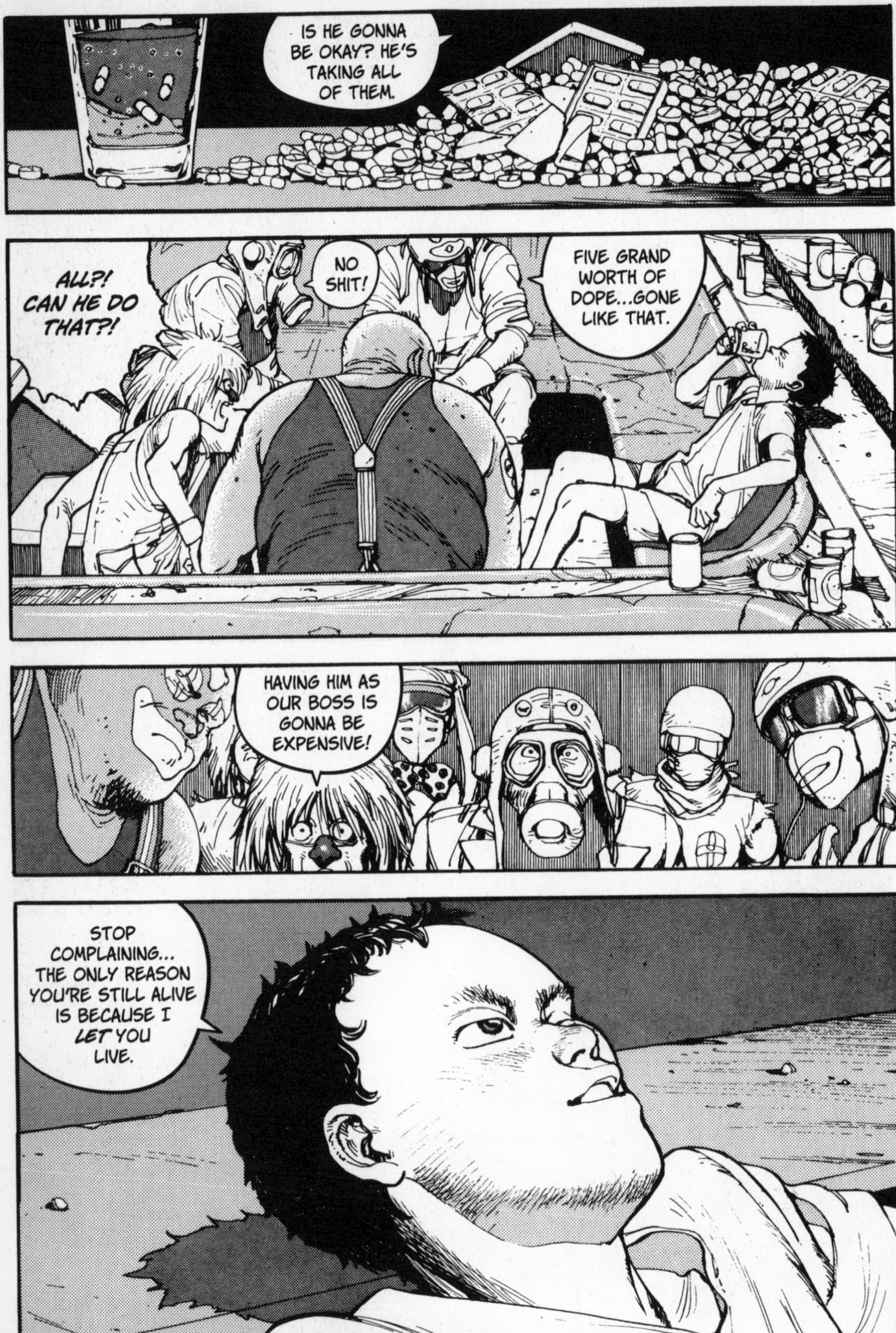

IS HE GONNA BE OKAY? HE'S TAKING ALL OF THEM.
ALL?! CAN HE DO THAT?!
NO SHIT!
FIVE GRAND WORTH OF DOPE...GONE LIKE THAT.
HAVING HIM AS OUR BOSS IS GONNA BE EXPENSIVE!
STOP COMPLAINING... THE ONLY REASON YOU'RE STILL ALIVE IS BECAUSE I *LET* YOU LIVE.

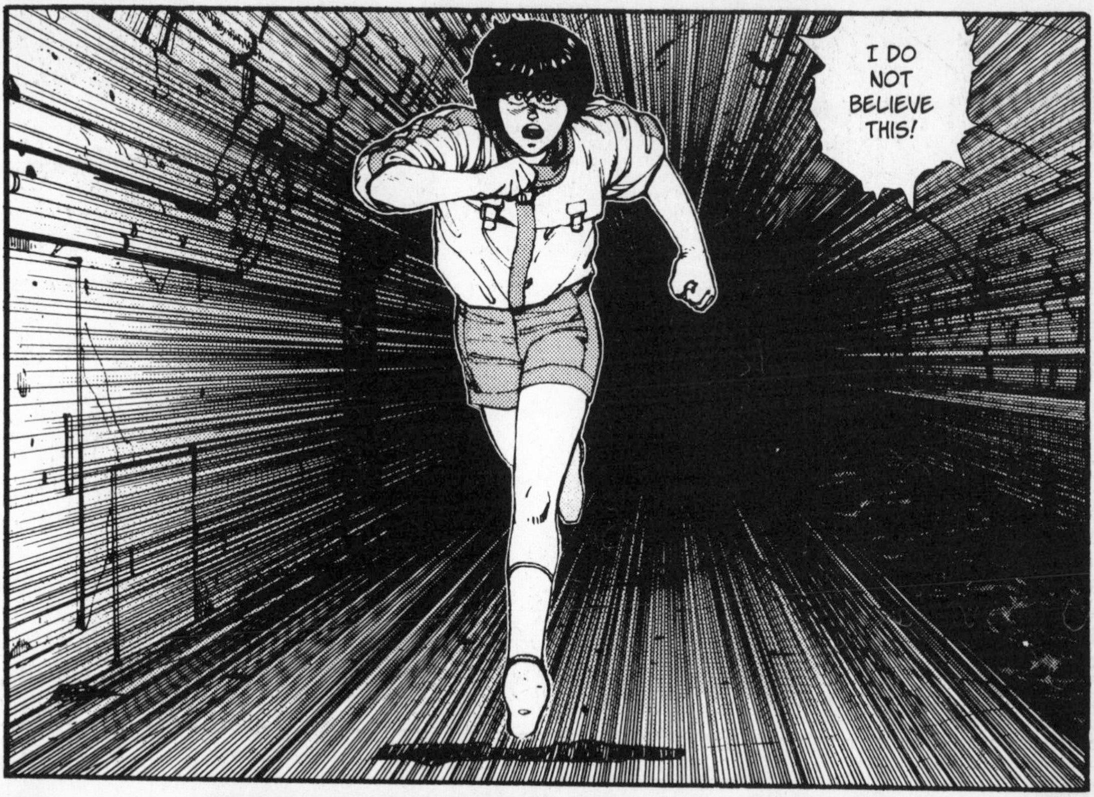
I DO NOT BELIEVE THIS!
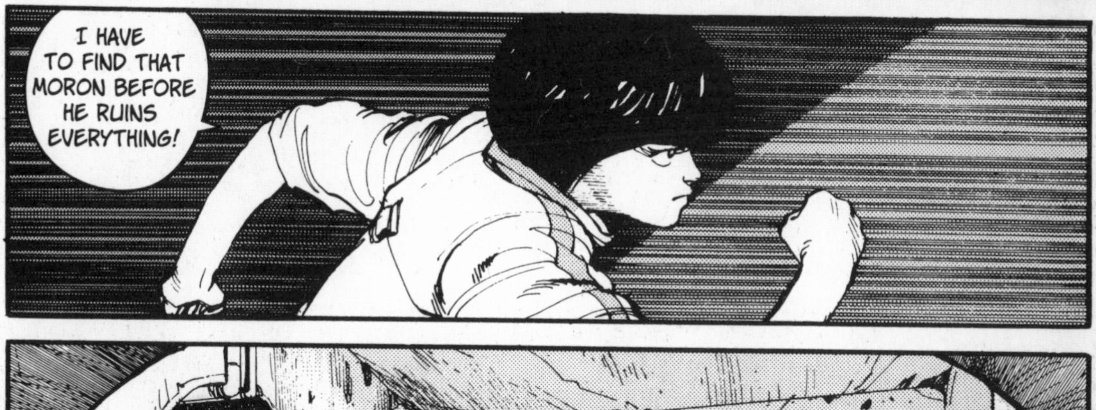
I HAVE TO FIND THAT MORON BEFORE HE RUINS EVERYTHING!
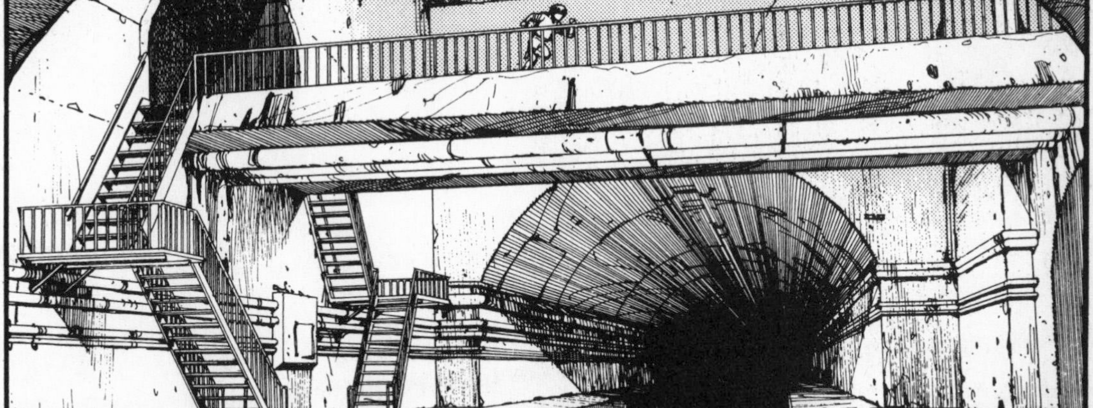

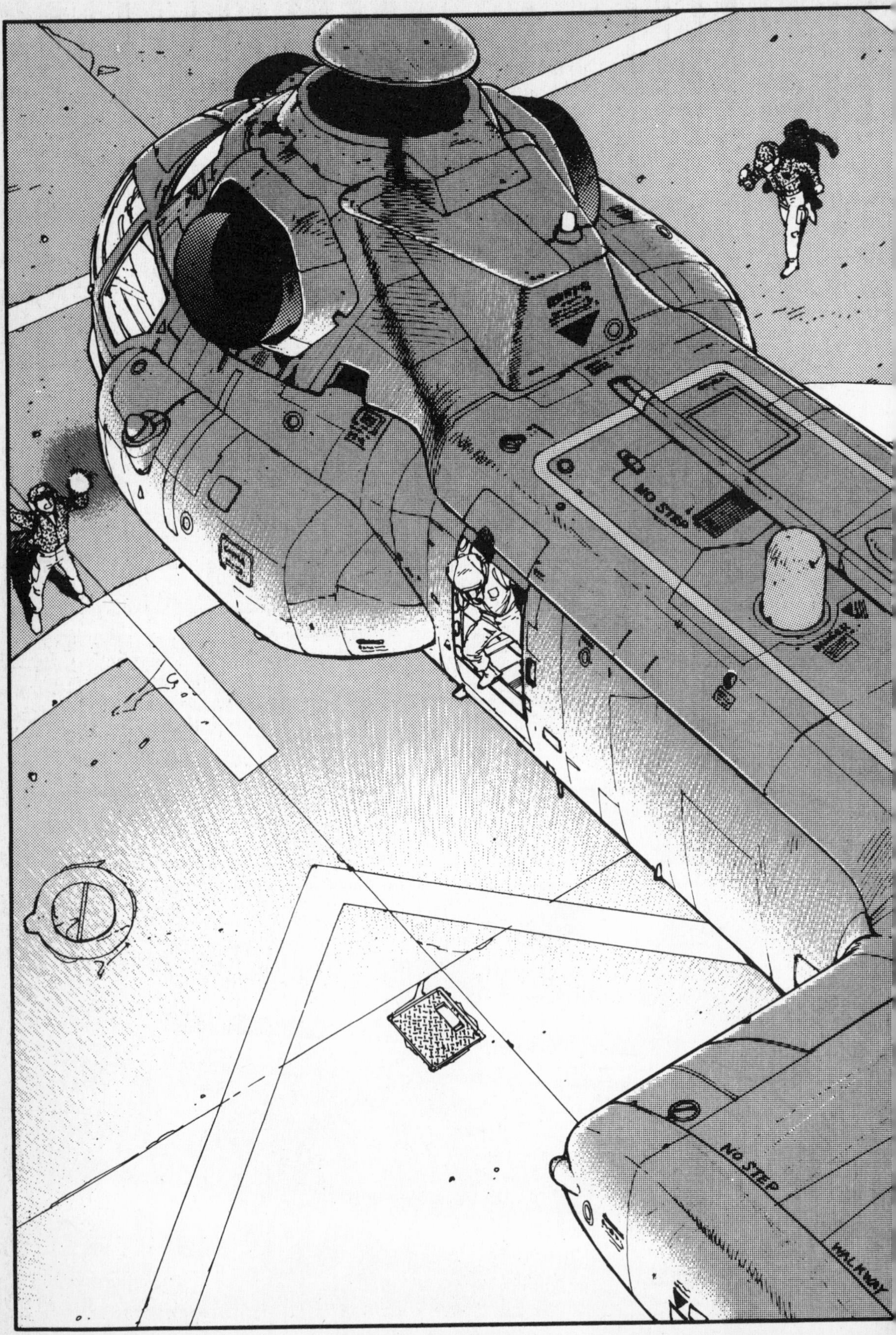
NO STEP
NO STEP
WALKWAY

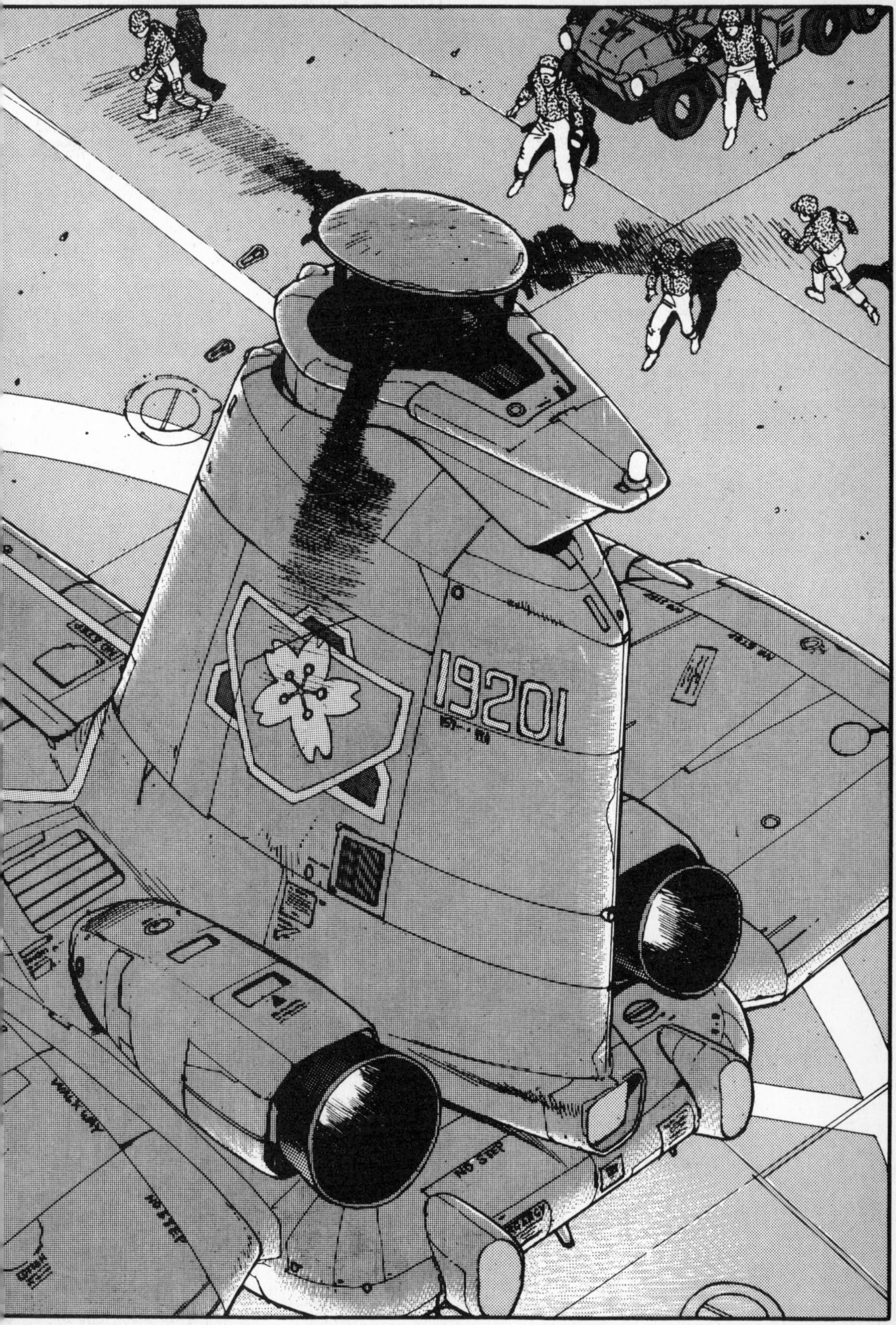
19201

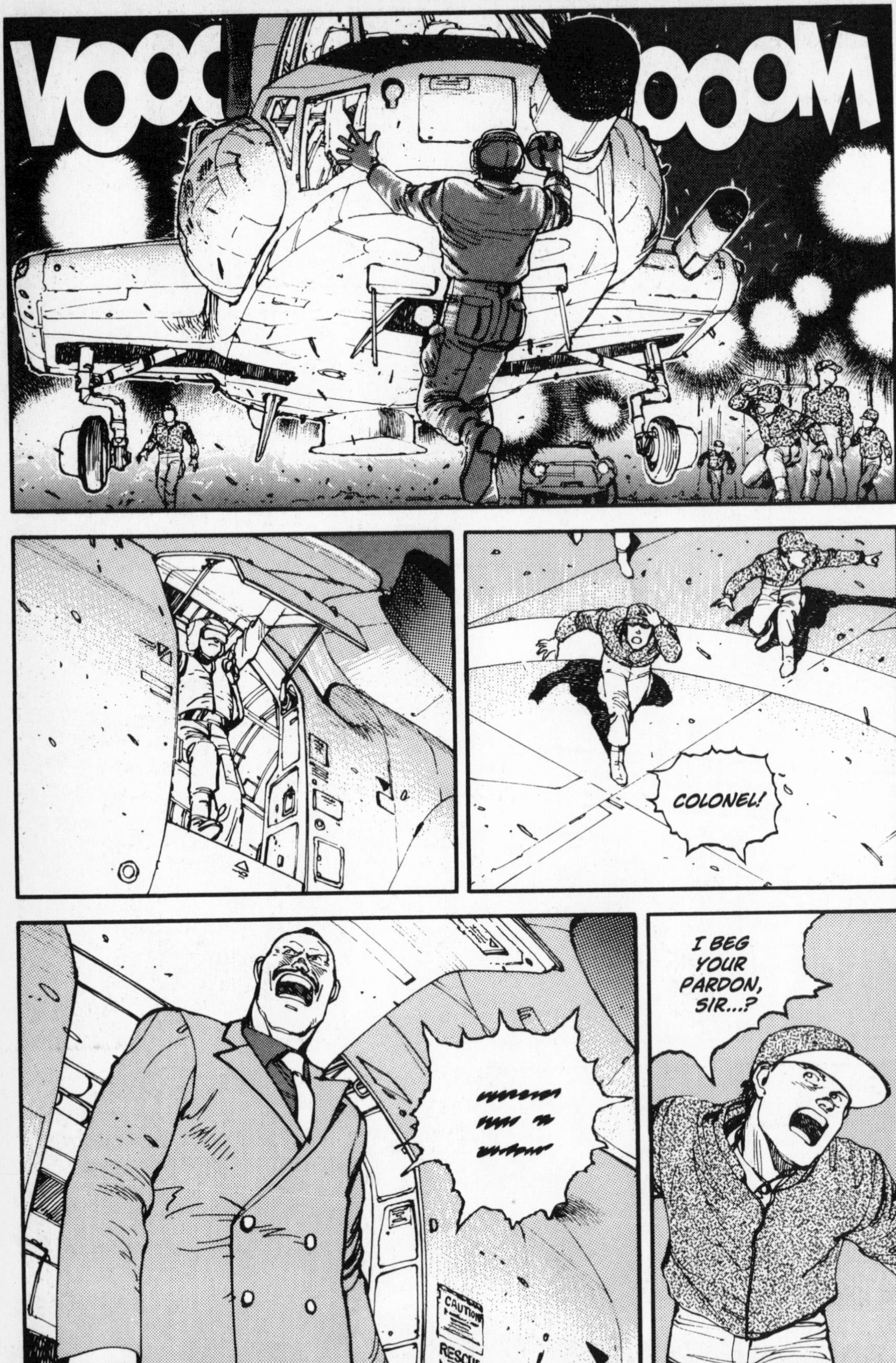
VOOO OOOOM
COLONEL!
I BEG YOUR PARDON, SIR...?

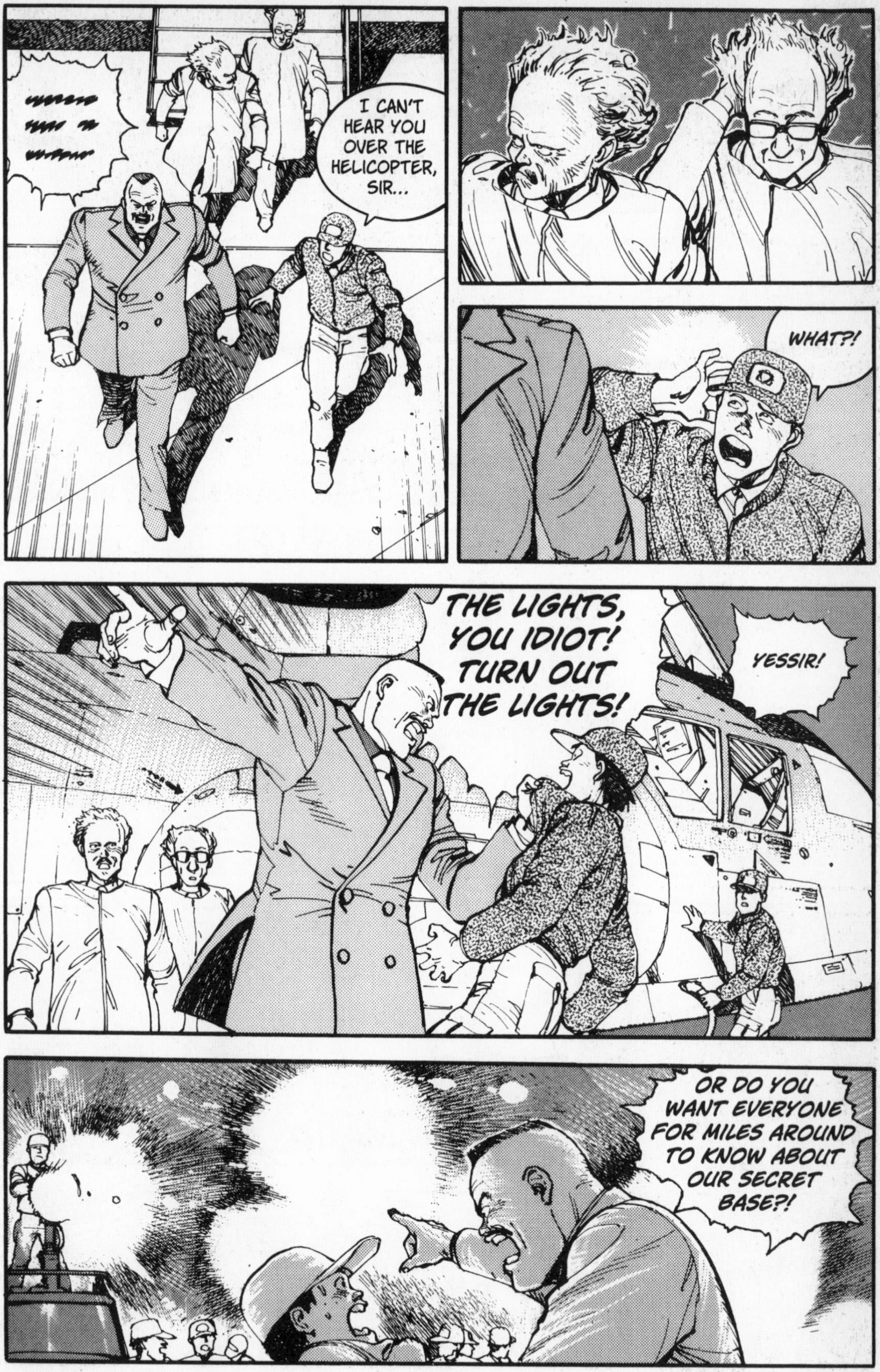
I CAN'T HEAR YOU OVER THE HELICOPTER, SIR...
WHAT?!
THE LIGHTS, YOU IDIOT! TURN OUT THE LIGHTS!
YESSIR!
OR DO YOU WANT EVERYONE FOR MILES AROUND TO KNOW ABOUT OUR SECRET BASE?!

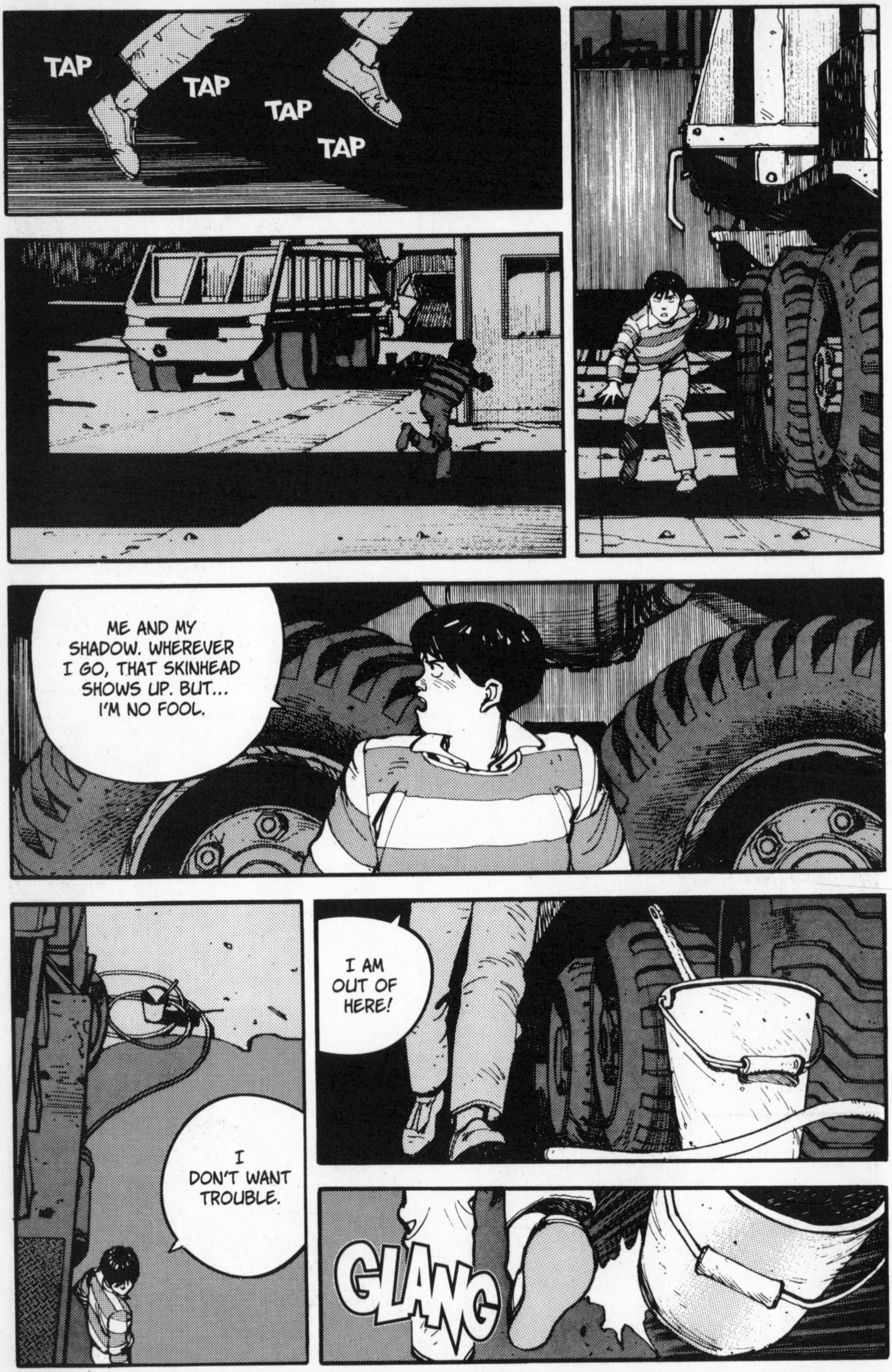
TAP
TAP
TAP
TAP
ME AND MY SHADOW. WHEREVER I GO, THAT SKINHEAD SHOWS UP. BUT... I'M NO FOOL.
I DON'T WANT TROUBLE.
I AM OUT OF HERE!
GLANG

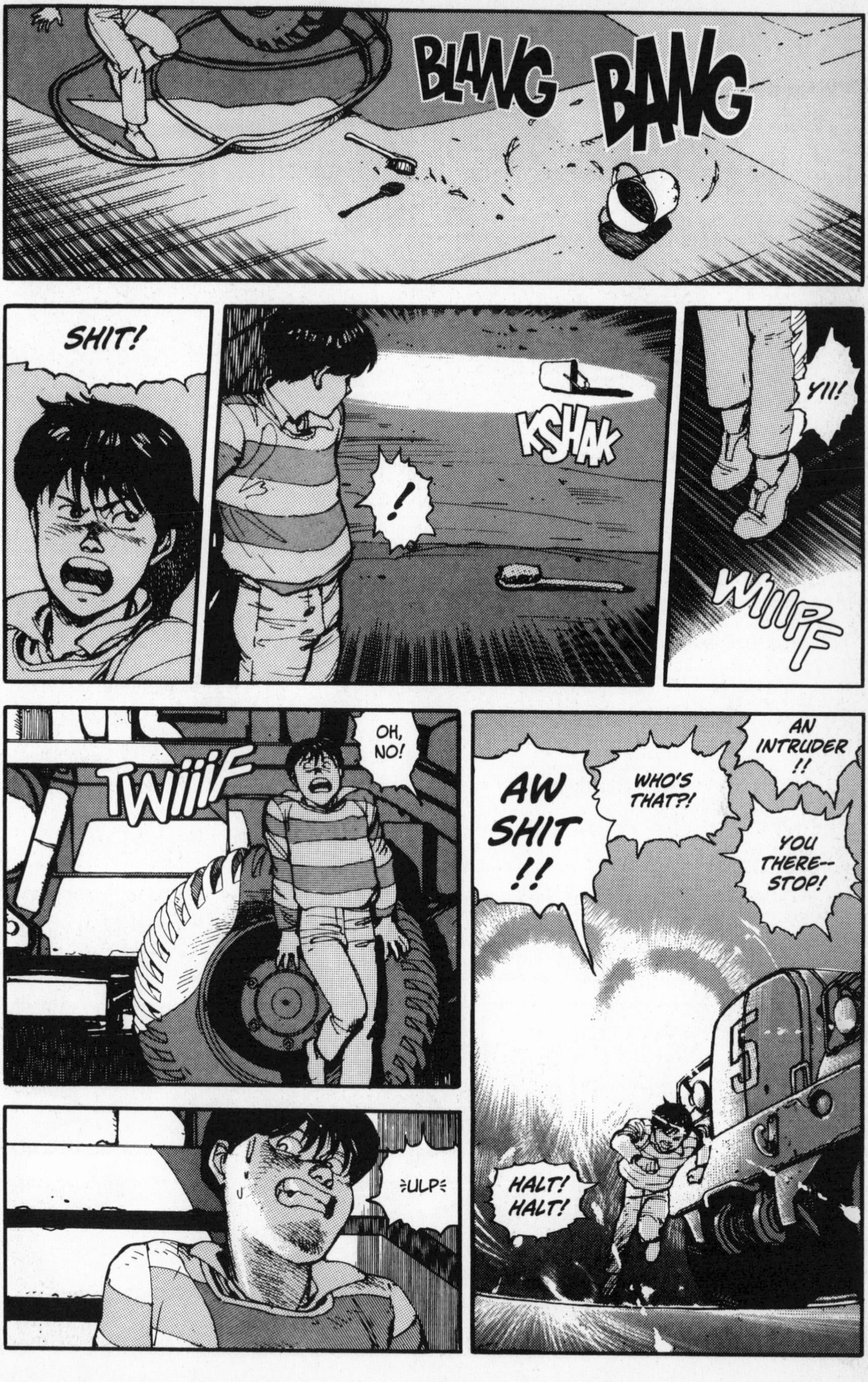
BLANG
BANG
SHIT!
KSHAK
!
YII!
WIIIPF
OH, NO!
TWiiiF
ULP
AW SHIT !!
WHO'S THAT?!
AN INTRUDER !!
YOU THERE-- STOP!
HALT! HALT!

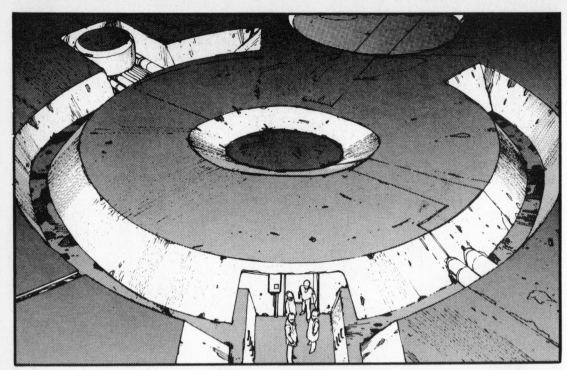

WHAT'S WRONG?

THERE'S AN INTRUDER ON THE GROUNDS, SIR.

IS THAT ALL?

KILL HIM!

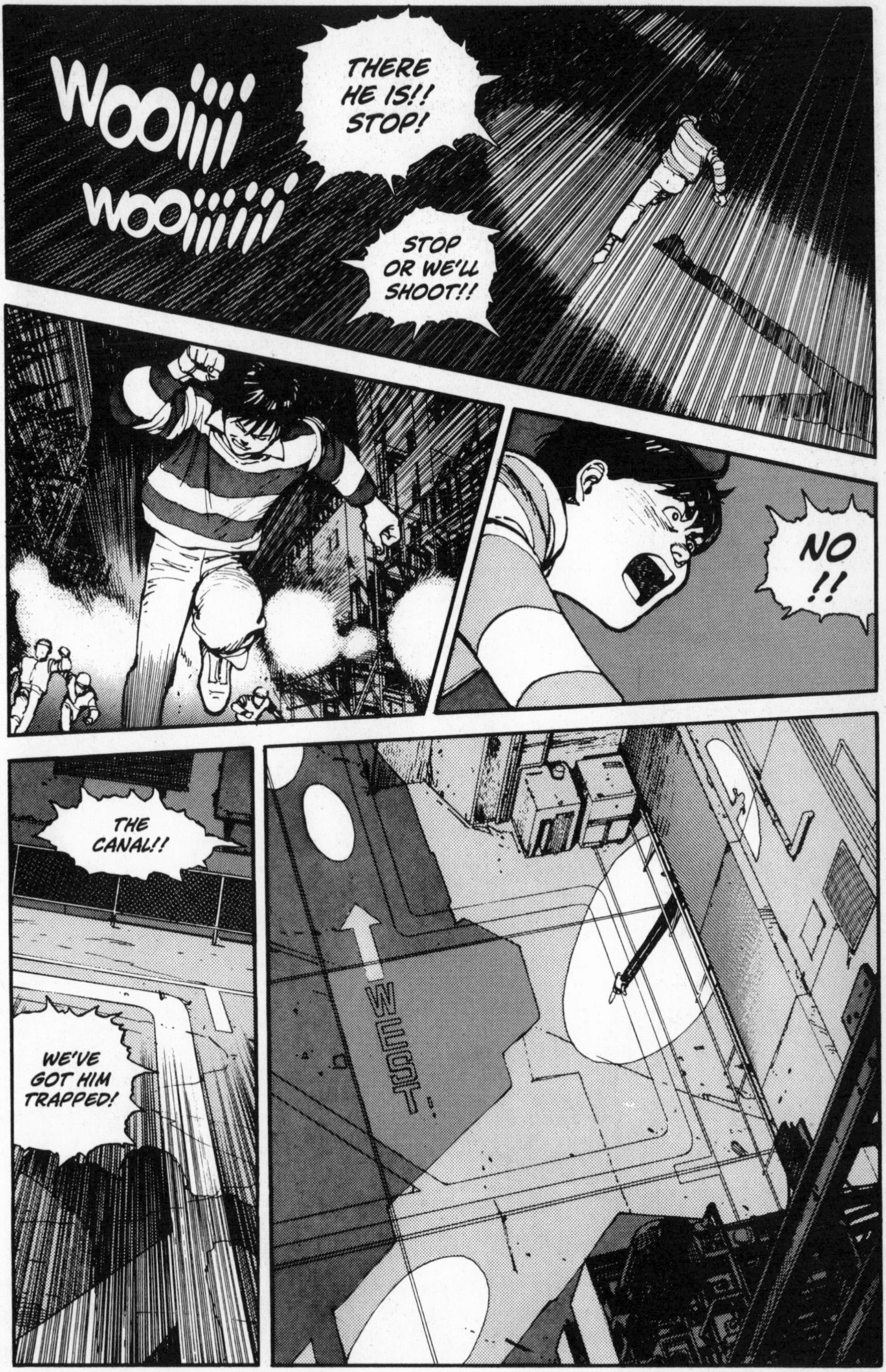
WOOiiii
WOOiiiiii
THERE HE IS!! STOP!
STOP OR WE'LL SHOOT!!
NO !!
THE CANAL!!
WE'VE GOT HIM TRAPPED!
WEST

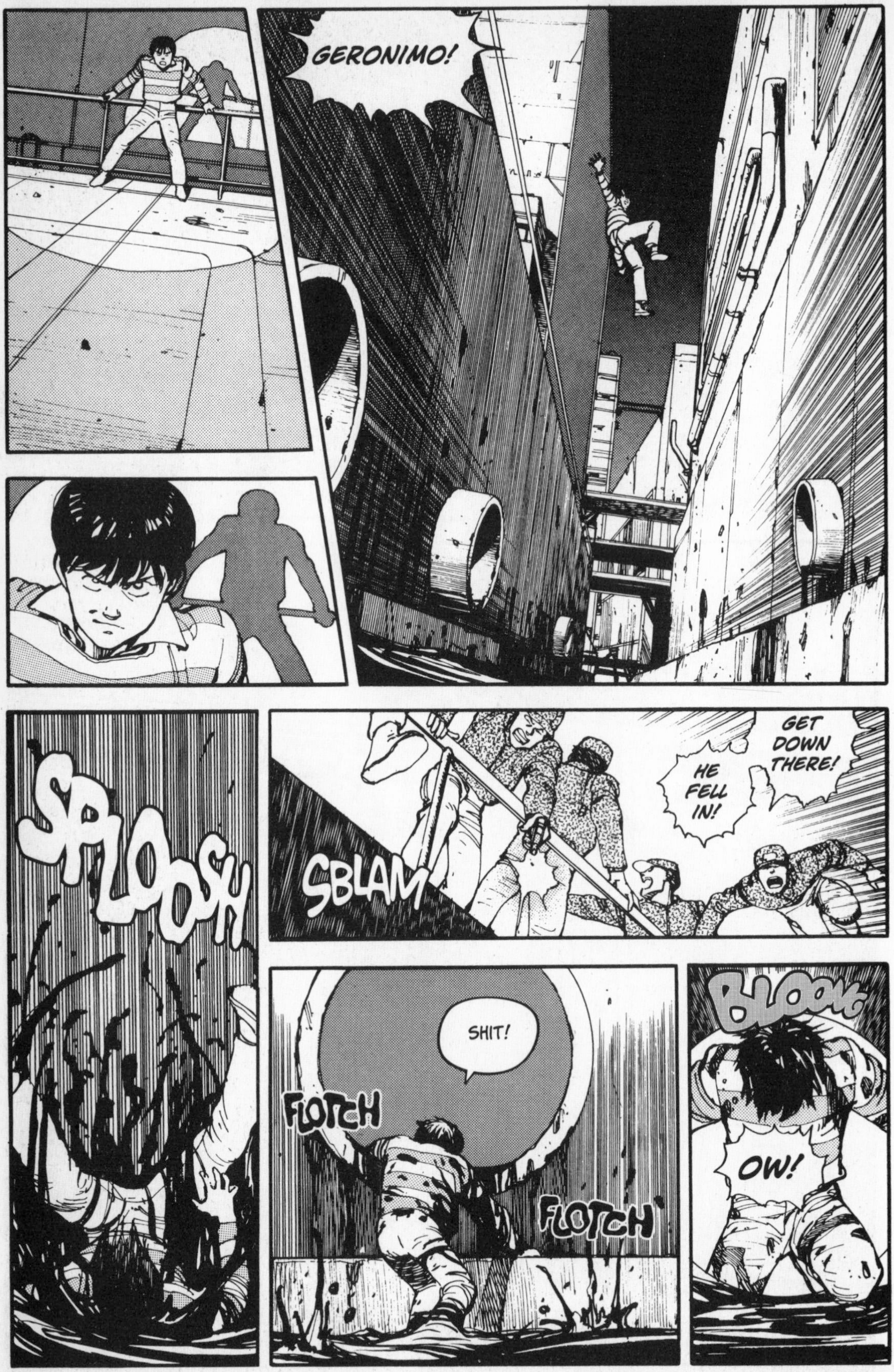
GERONIMO!
SPLOOSH
SBLAM
HE FELL IN!
GET DOWN THERE!
SHIT!
FLOTCH
FLOTCH
BLOONG
OW!

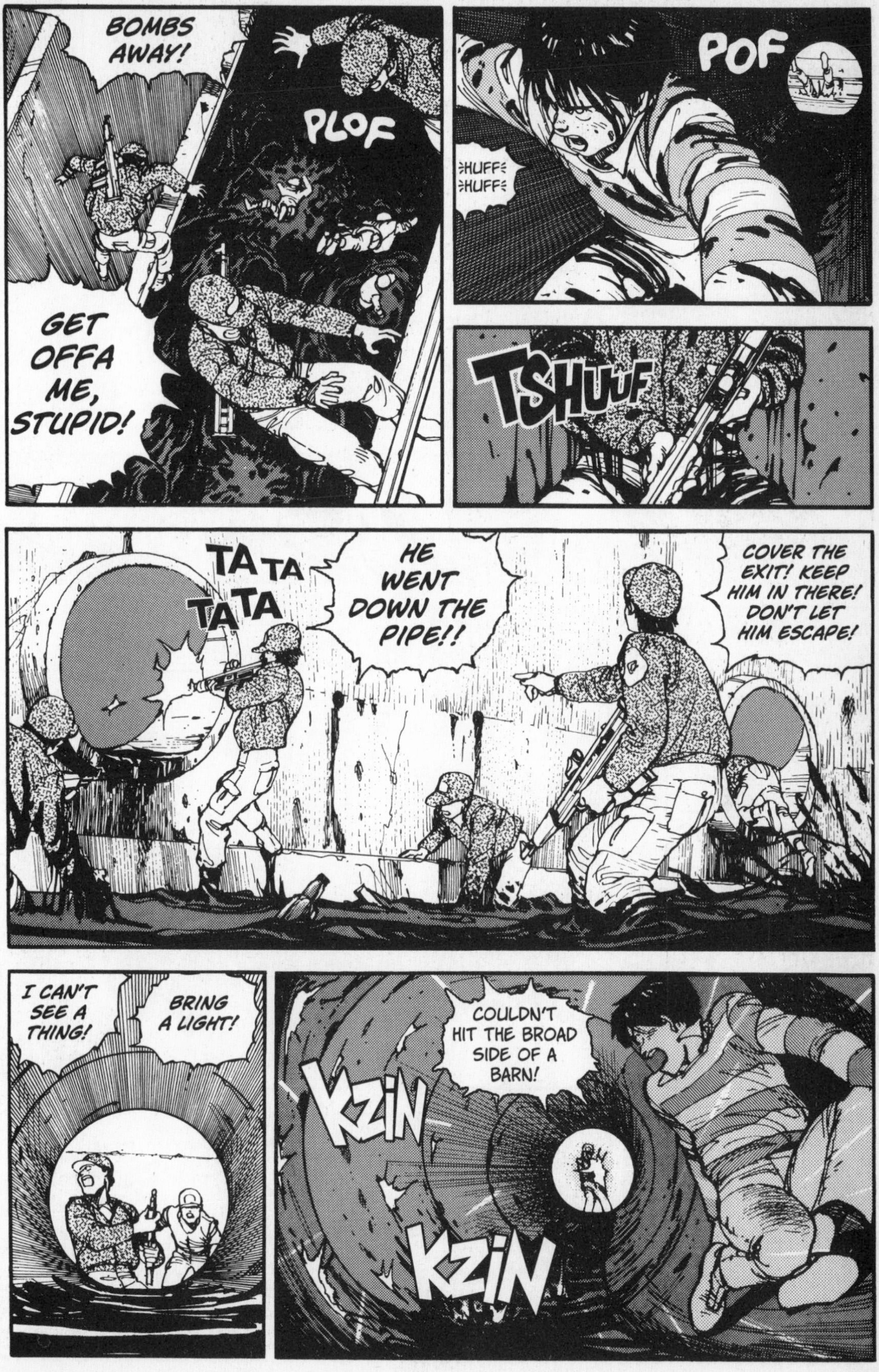
BOMBS AWAY!
PLOF
GET OFFA ME, STUPID!
POF
HUFF HUFF
TSHUUF
TA TA TA TA
HE WENT DOWN THE PIPE!!
COVER THE EXIT! KEEP HIM IN THERE! DON'T LET HIM ESCAPE!
I CAN'T SEE A THING!
BRING A LIGHT!
COULDN'T HIT THE BROAD SIDE OF A BARN!
KZIN
KZIN

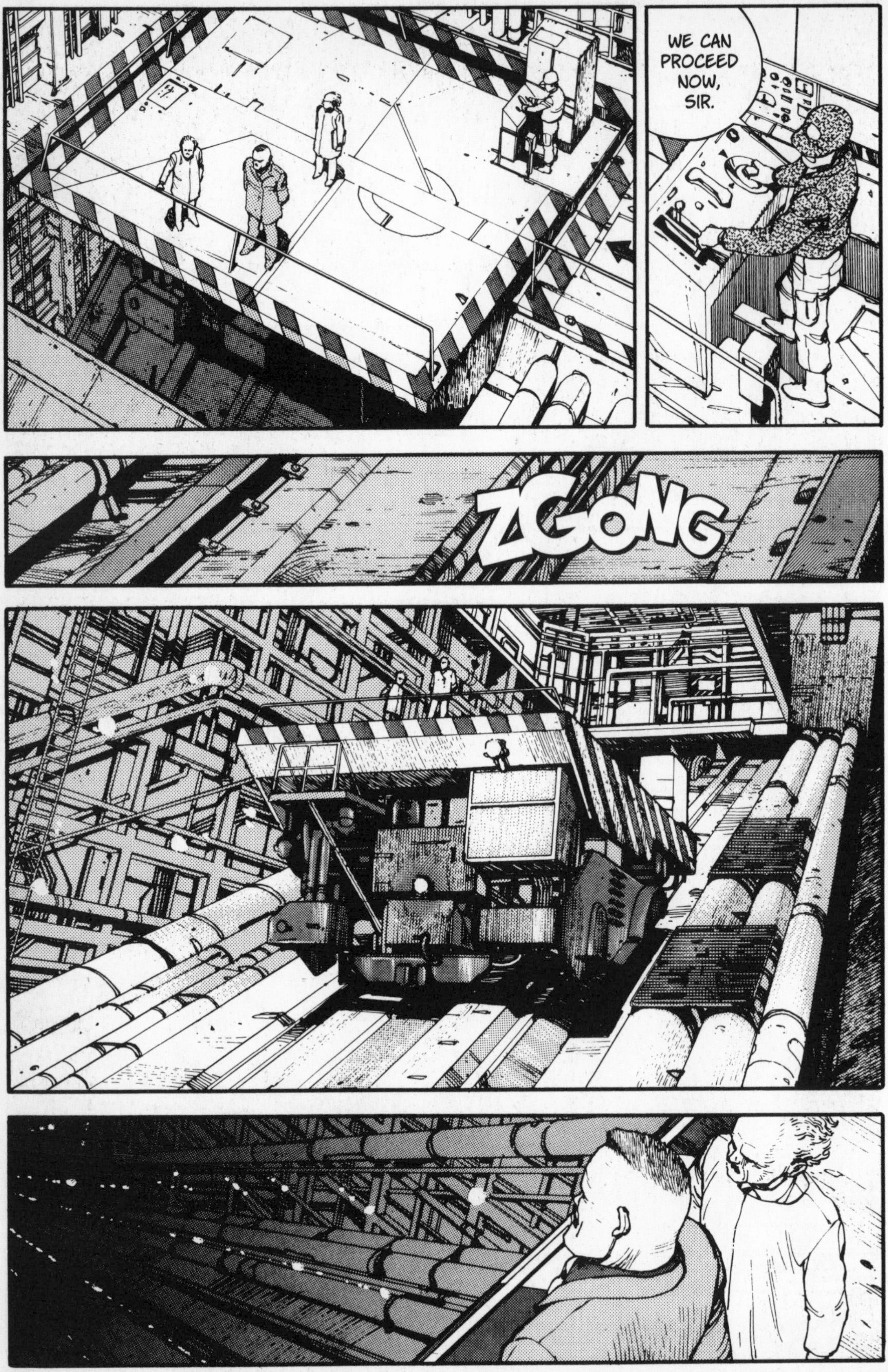
WE CAN PROCEED NOW, SIR.
ZGONG

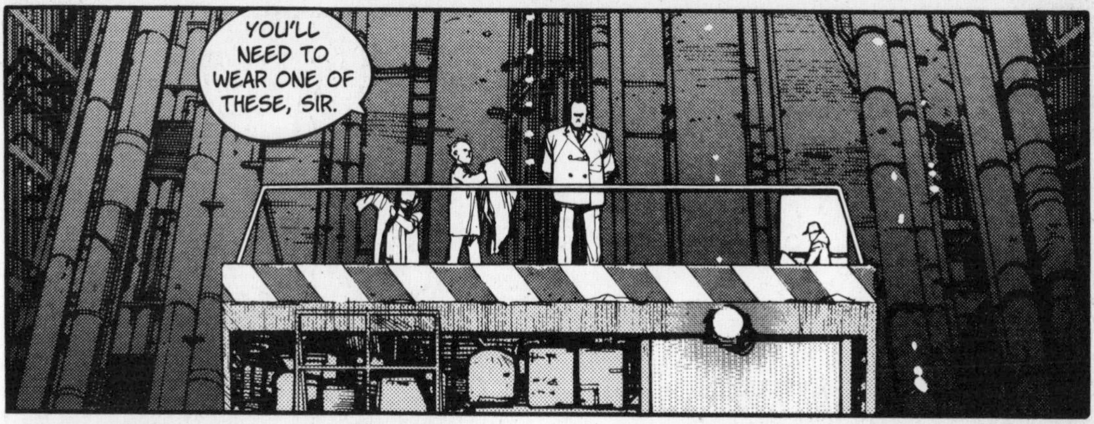
YOU'LL NEED TO WEAR ONE OF THESE, SIR.

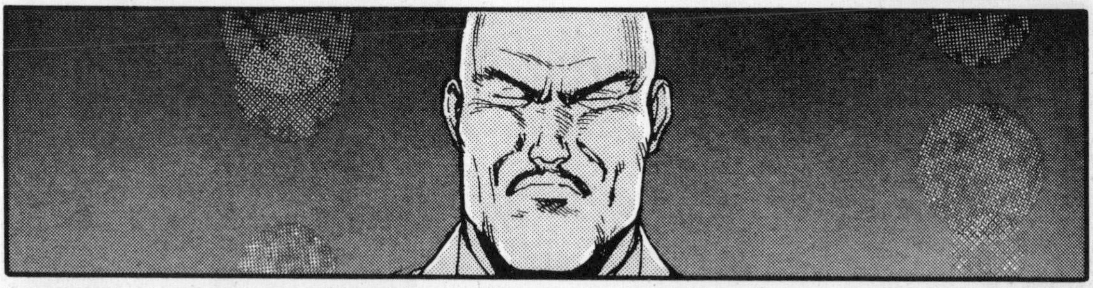

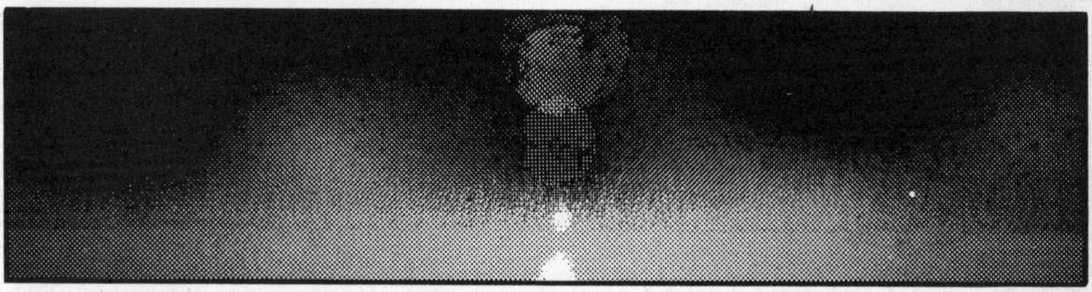

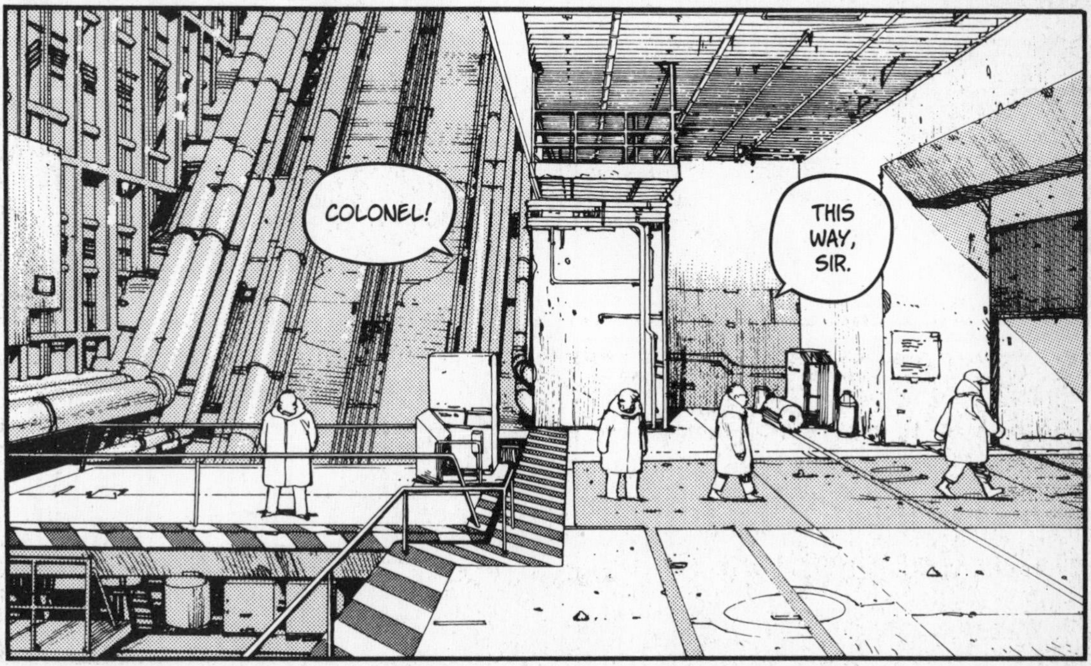
COLONEL!
THIS WAY, SIR.

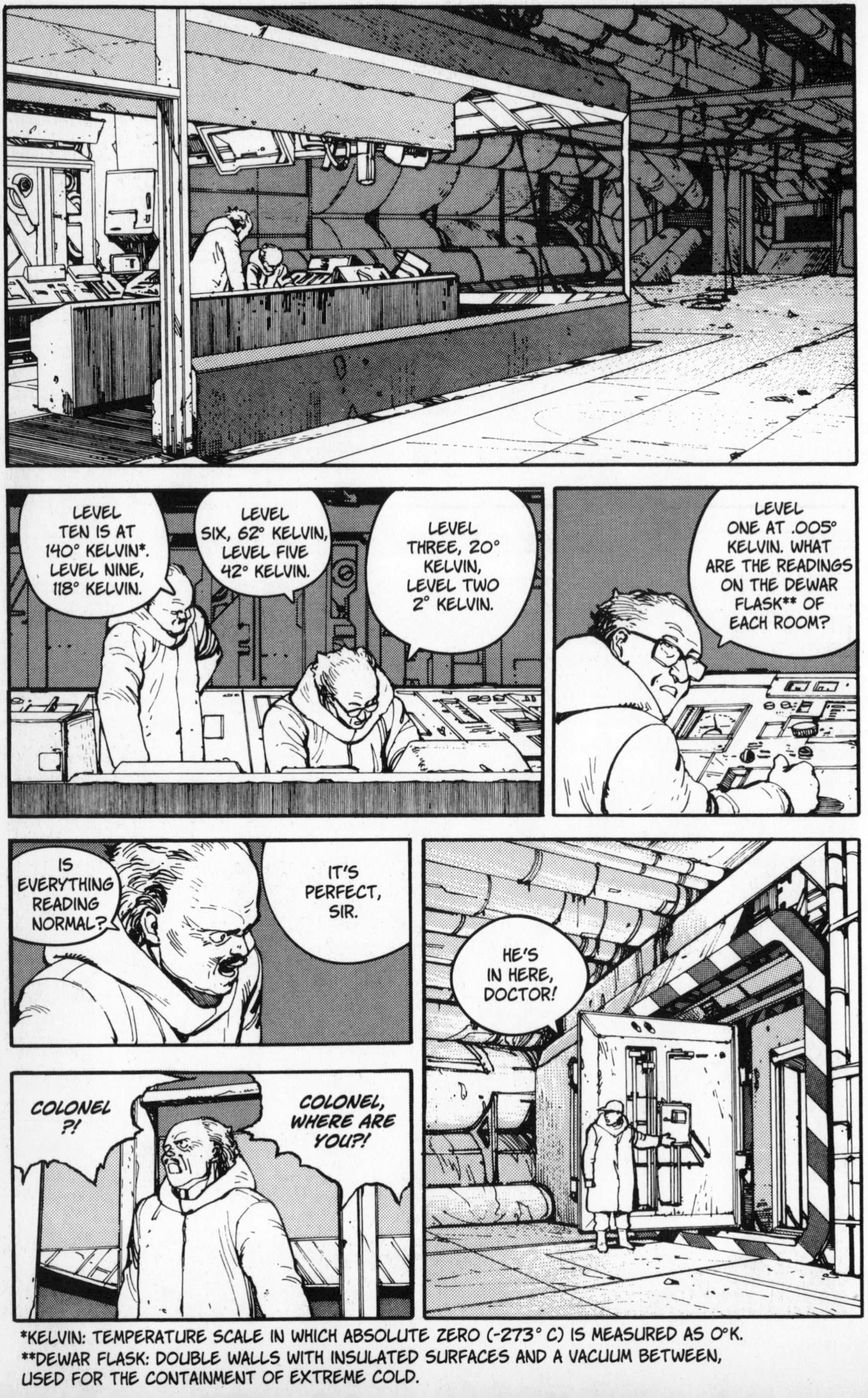
LEVEL TEN IS AT 140° KELVIN*. LEVEL NINE, 118° KELVIN.
LEVEL SIX, 62° KELVIN, LEVEL FIVE 42° KELVIN.
LEVEL THREE, 20° KELVIN, LEVEL TWO 2° KELVIN.
LEVEL ONE AT .005° KELVIN. WHAT ARE THE READINGS ON THE DEWAR FLASK** OF EACH ROOM?
IS EVERYTHING READING NORMAL?
IT'S PERFECT, SIR.
COLONEL ?!
COLONEL, WHERE ARE YOU?!
HE'S IN HERE, DOCTOR!

*KELVIN: TEMPERATURE SCALE IN WHICH ABSOLUTE ZERO (-273° C) IS MEASURED AS 0°K.

**DEWAR FLASK: DOUBLE WALLS WITH INSULATED SURFACES AND A VACUUM BETWEEN, USED FOR THE CONTAINMENT OF EXTREME COLD.

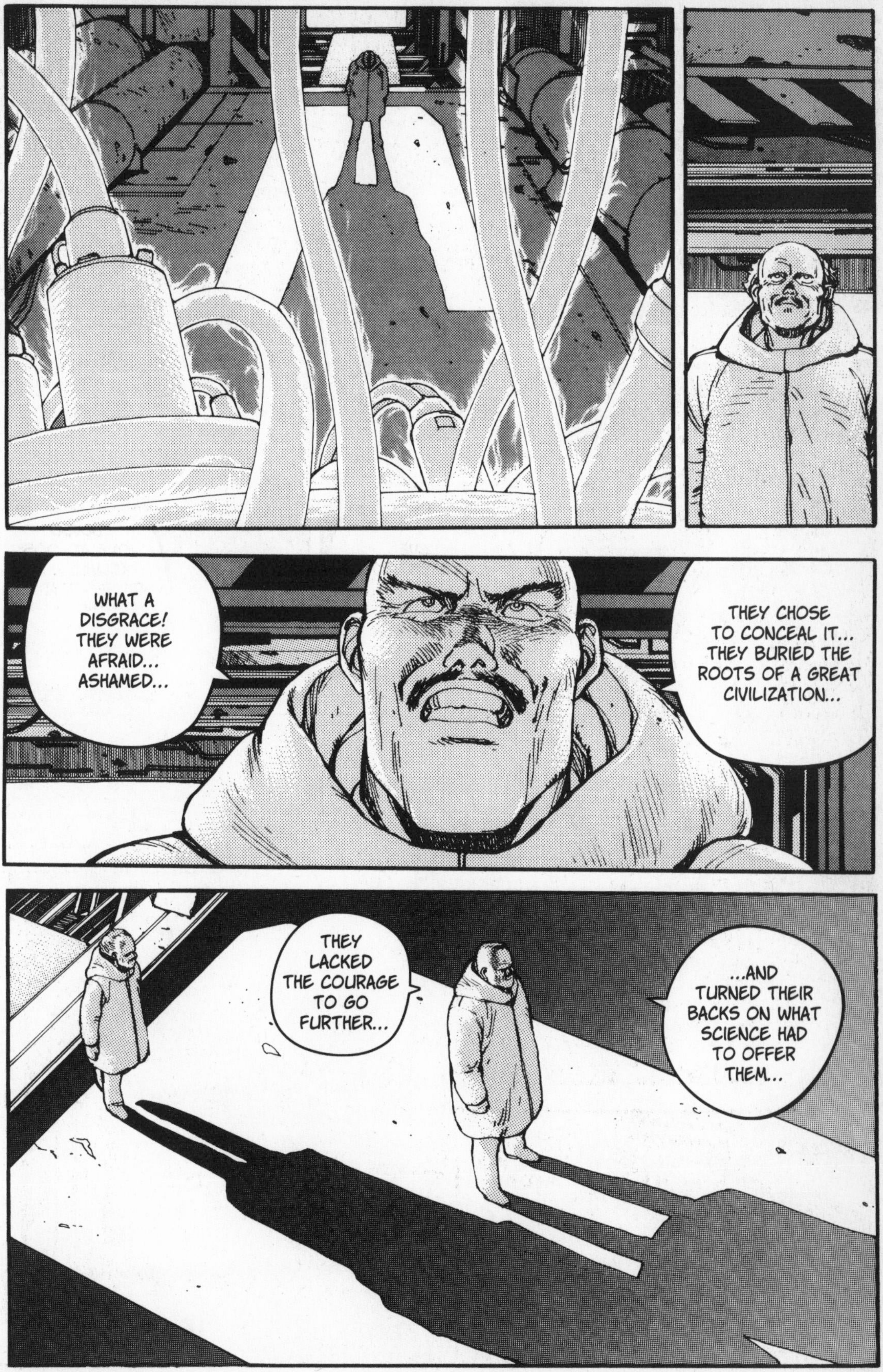
WHAT A DISGRACE! THEY WERE AFRAID... ASHAMED...
THEY CHOSE TO CONCEAL IT... THEY BURIED THE ROOTS OF A GREAT CIVILIZATION...
THEY LACKED THE COURAGE TO GO FURTHER...
...AND TURNED THEIR BACKS ON WHAT SCIENCE HAD TO OFFER THEM...

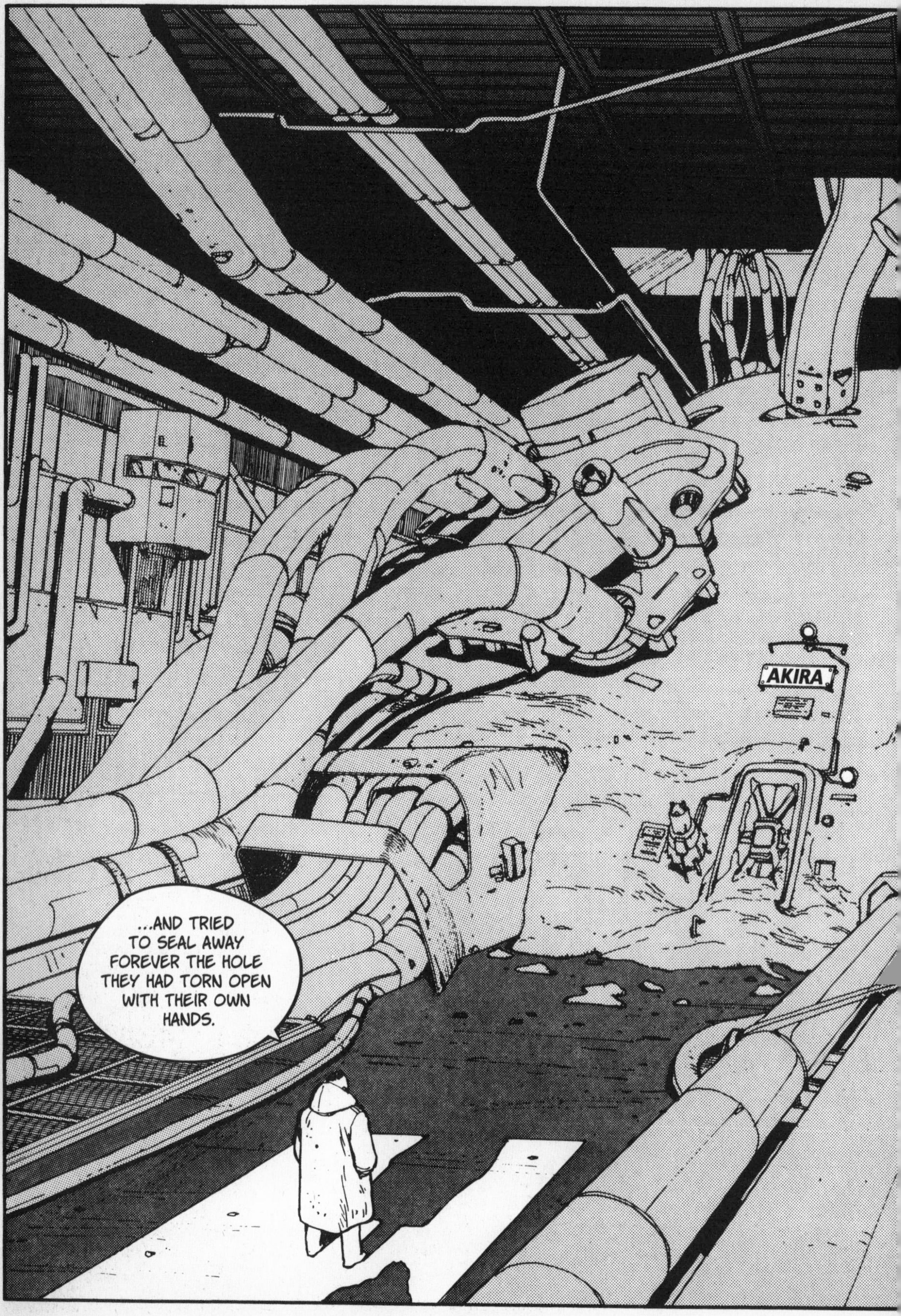
...AND TRIED TO SEAL AWAY FOREVER THE HOLE THEY HAD TORN OPEN WITH THEIR OWN HANDS.
AKIRA

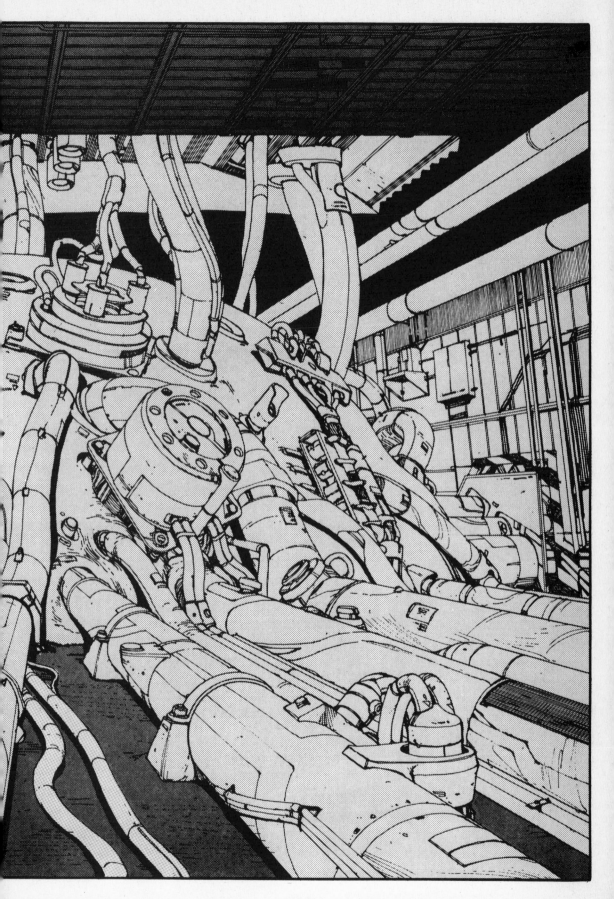

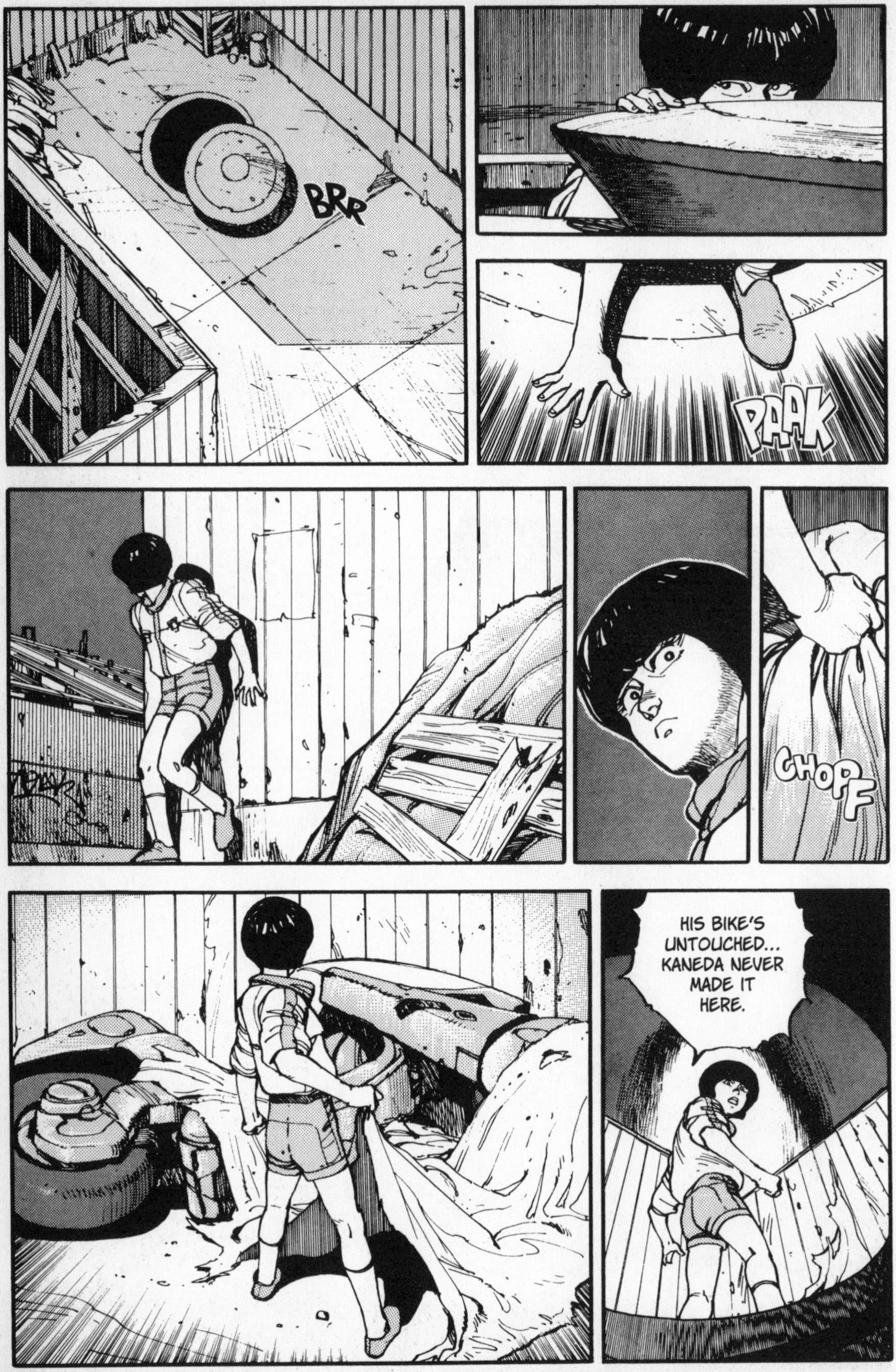
BRR
PAAK
CHOPF
HIS BIKE'S UNTOUCHED... KANEDA NEVER MADE IT HERE.

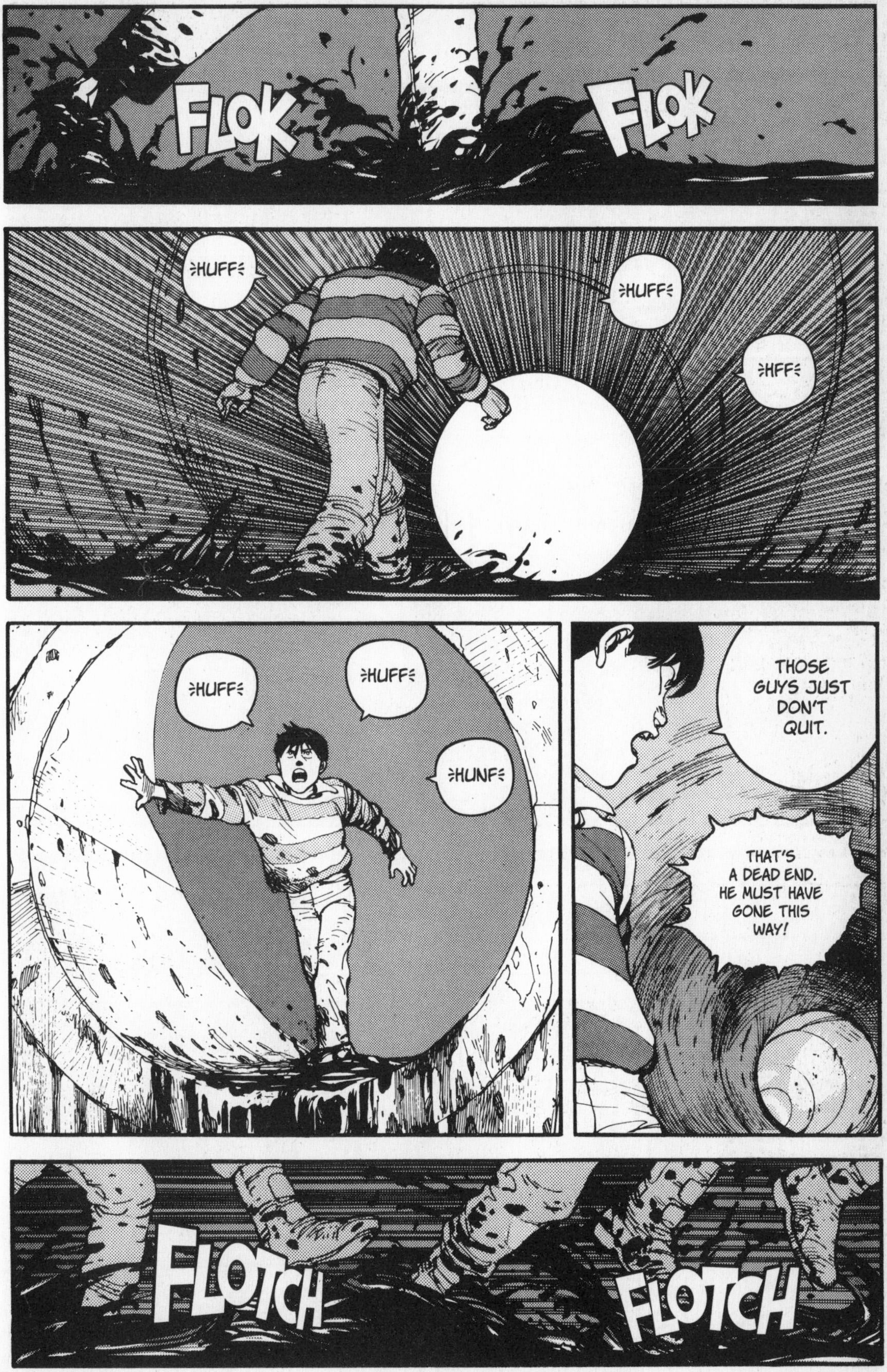
FLOK
FLOK
HUFF
HUFF
HFF
HUFF
HUFF
HUNF
THOSE GUYS JUST DON'T QUIT.
THAT'S A DEAD END. HE MUST HAVE GONE THIS WAY!
FLOTCH
FLOTCH

SPLUF

NOW WHERE DO I GO?

!

WHAT IS THAT ?!

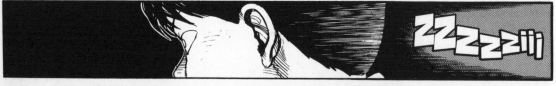

ZZZZZiii

WHAT --?!

GWiiiiz

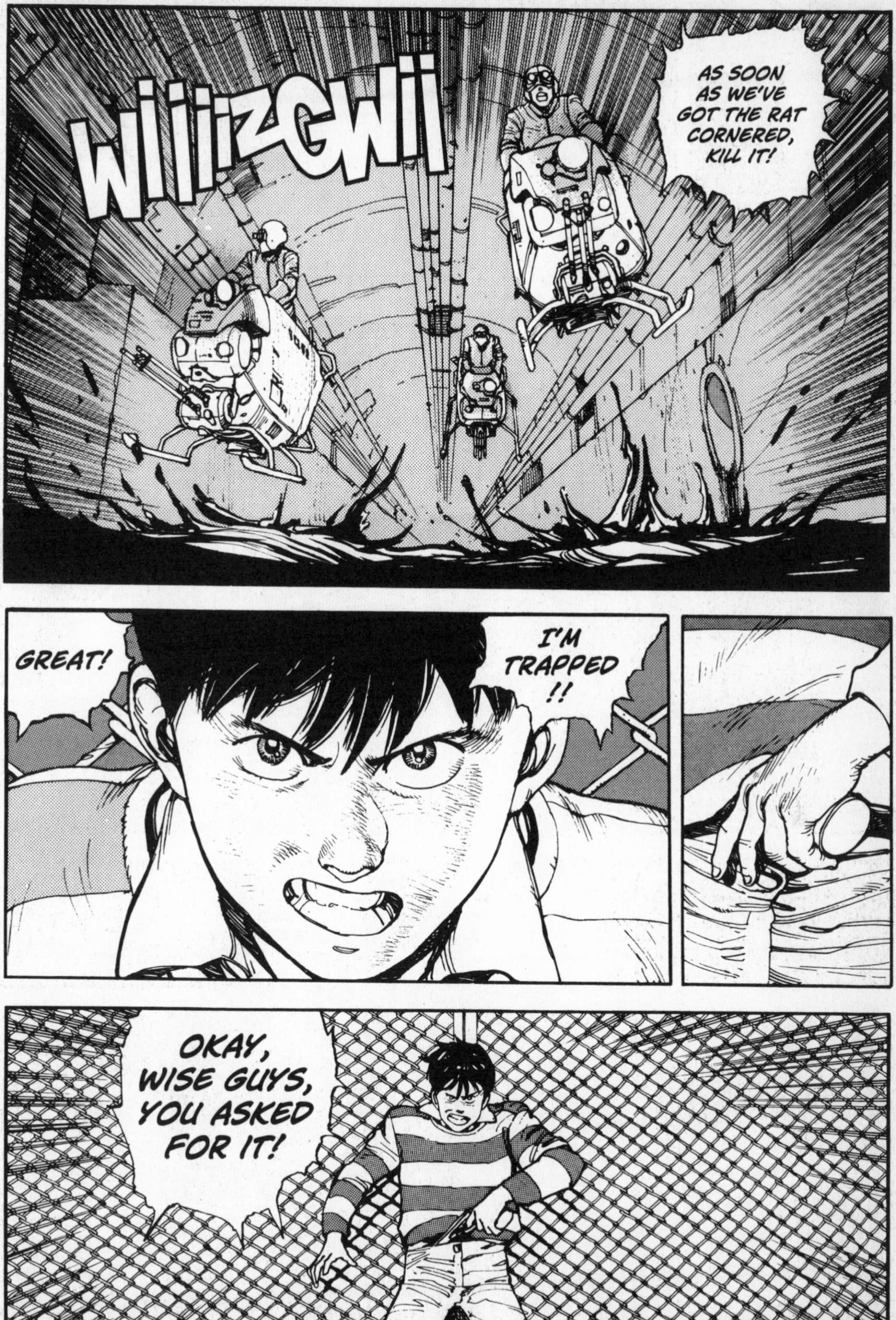
WIIIZGWII
AS SOON AS WE'VE GOT THE RAT CORNERED, KILL IT!
GREAT!
I'M TRAPPED !!
OKAY, WISE GUYS, YOU ASKED FOR IT!

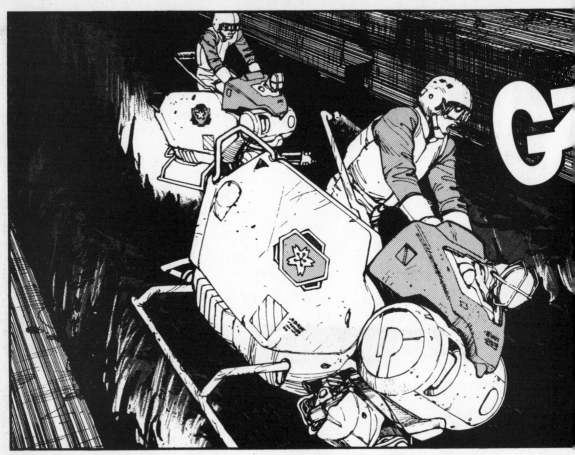

THERE HE IS!!

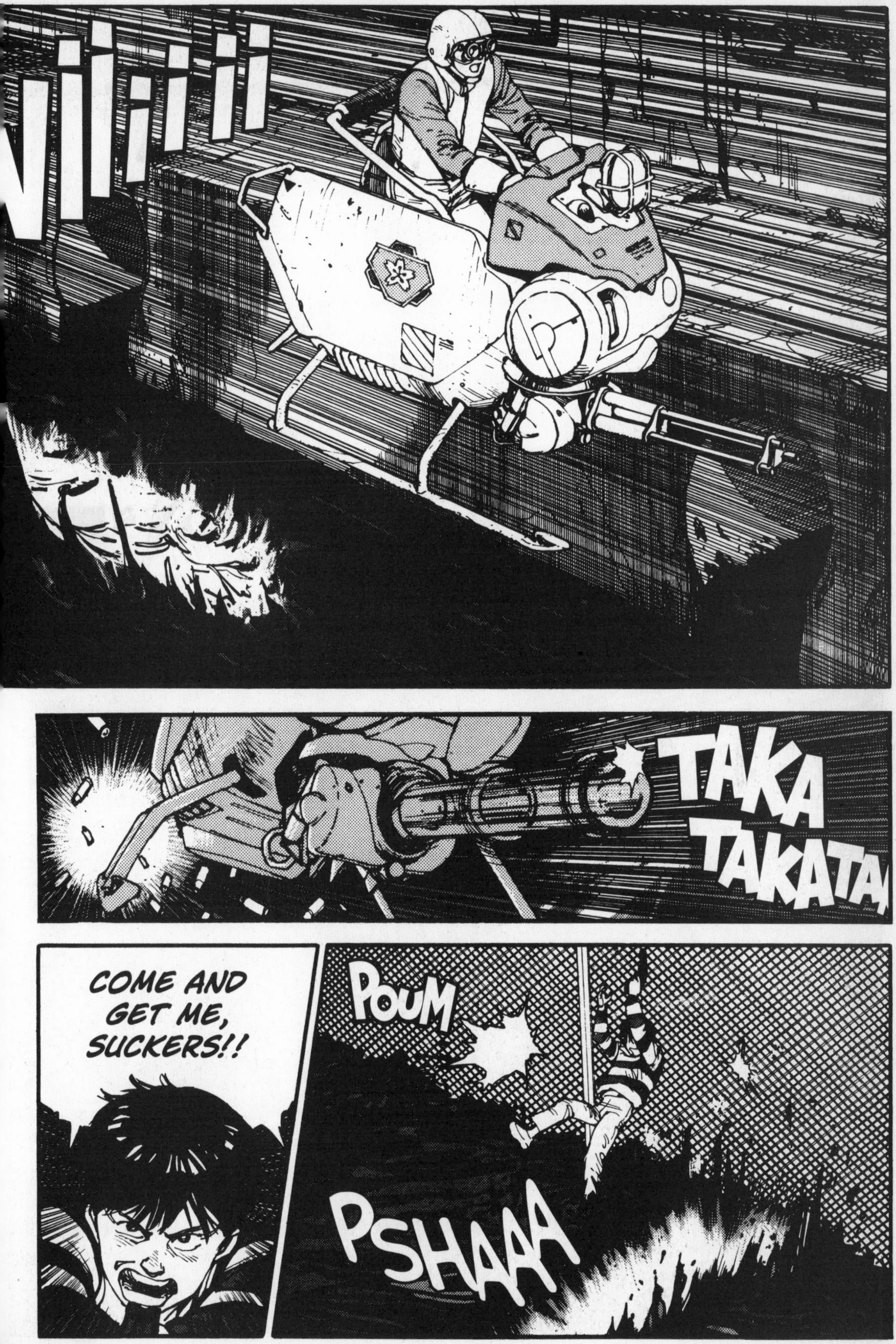
TAKA
TAKATA
POUM
PSHAAA
COME AND GET ME, SUCKERS!!

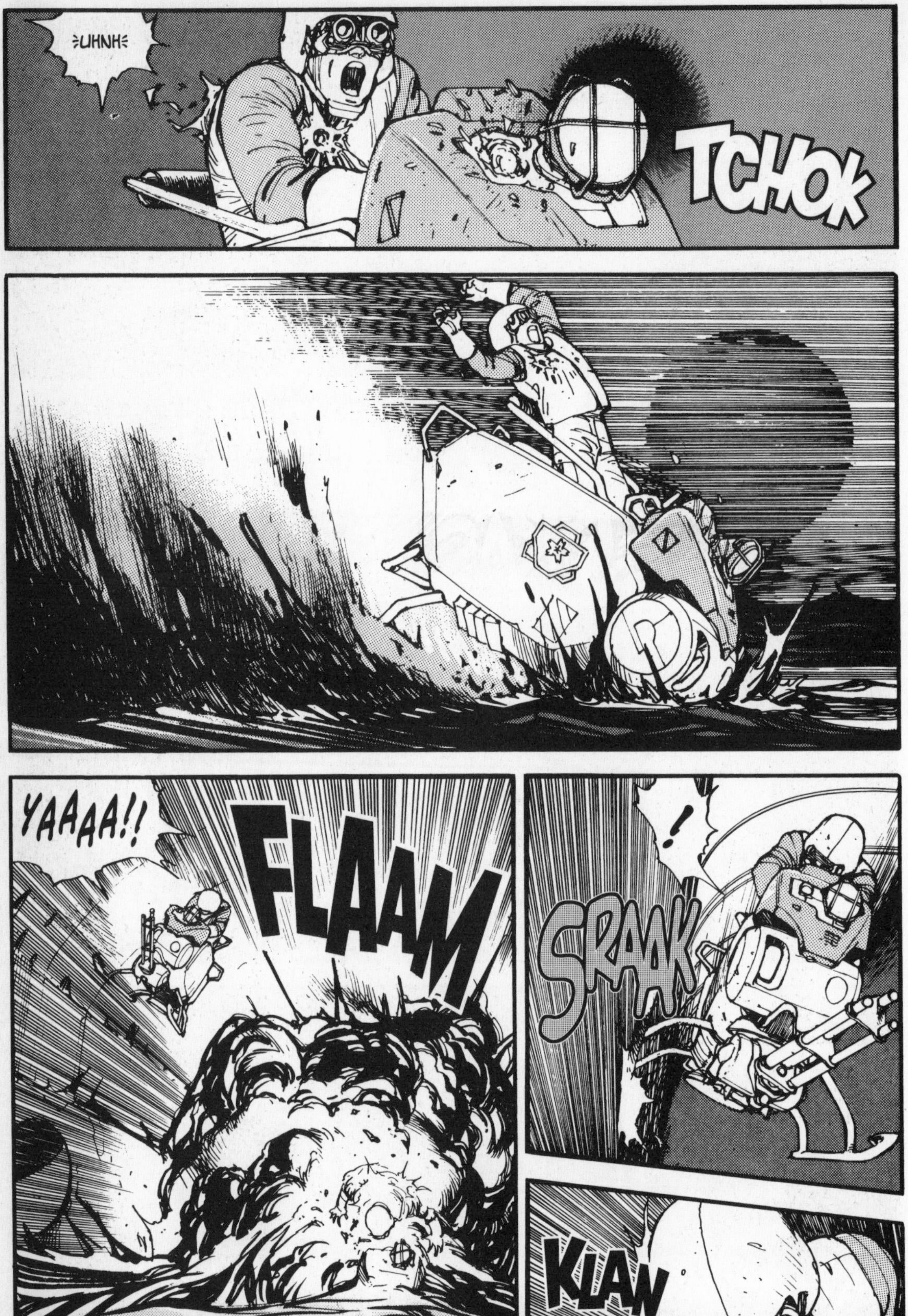
UHNH
TCHOK
YAAAA!!
FLAAM
!
SRAAK
KLAN

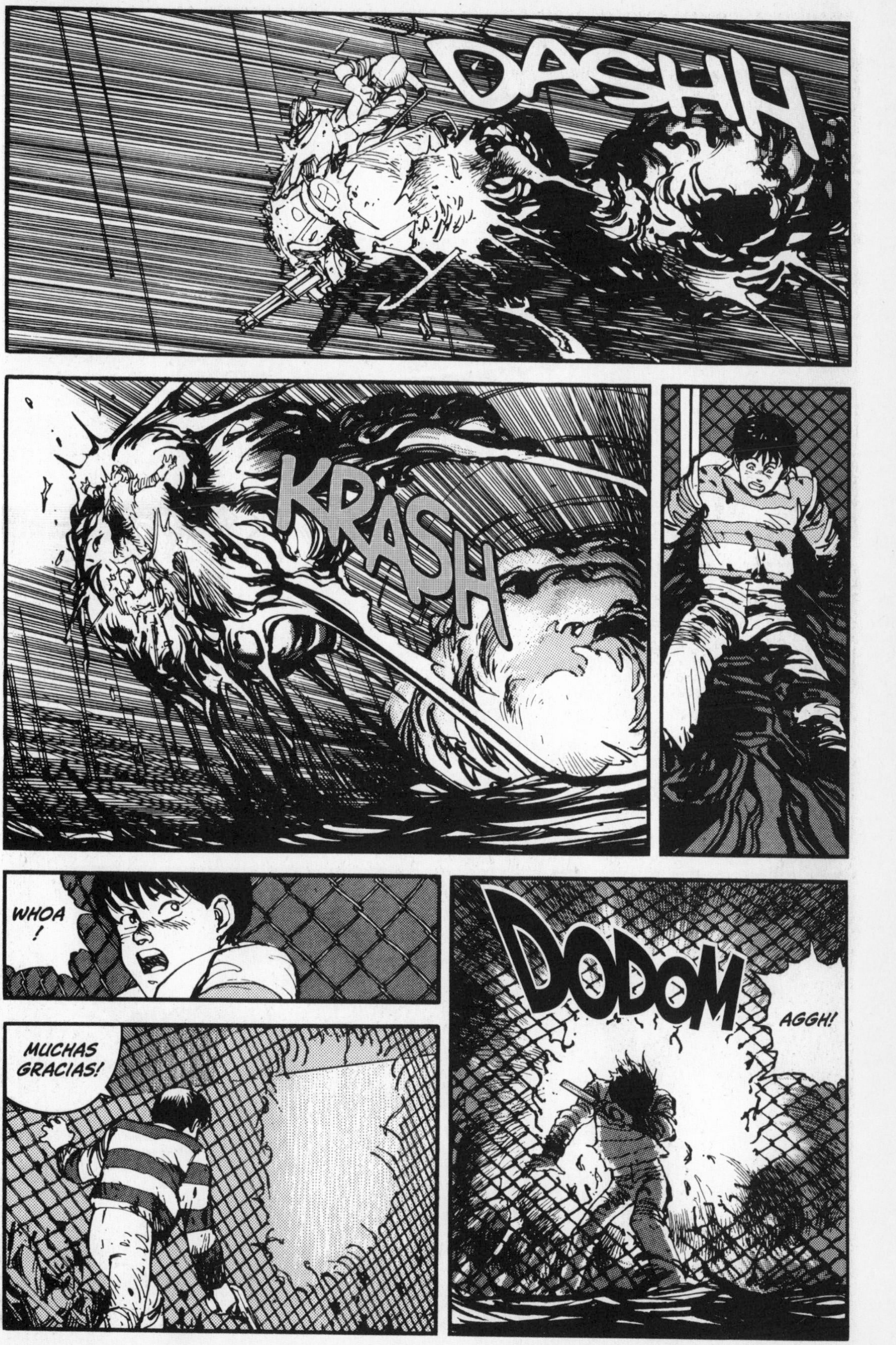
DASHH
KRASH
WHOA!
DODOM
AGGH!
MUCHAS GRACIAS!

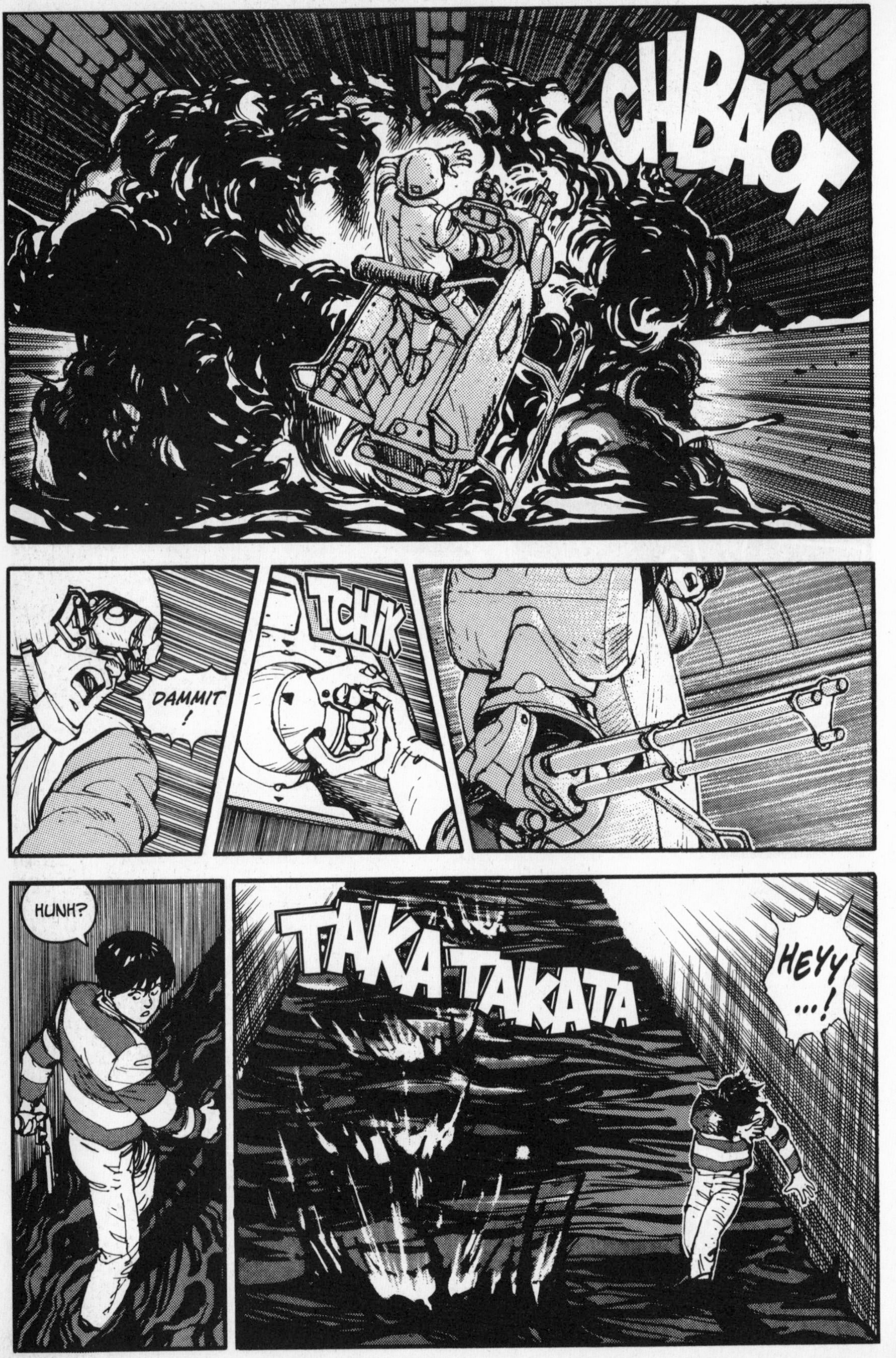
CHBAOF
DAMMIT!
TCHIK
HUNH?
TAKA TAKATA
HEYY ...!

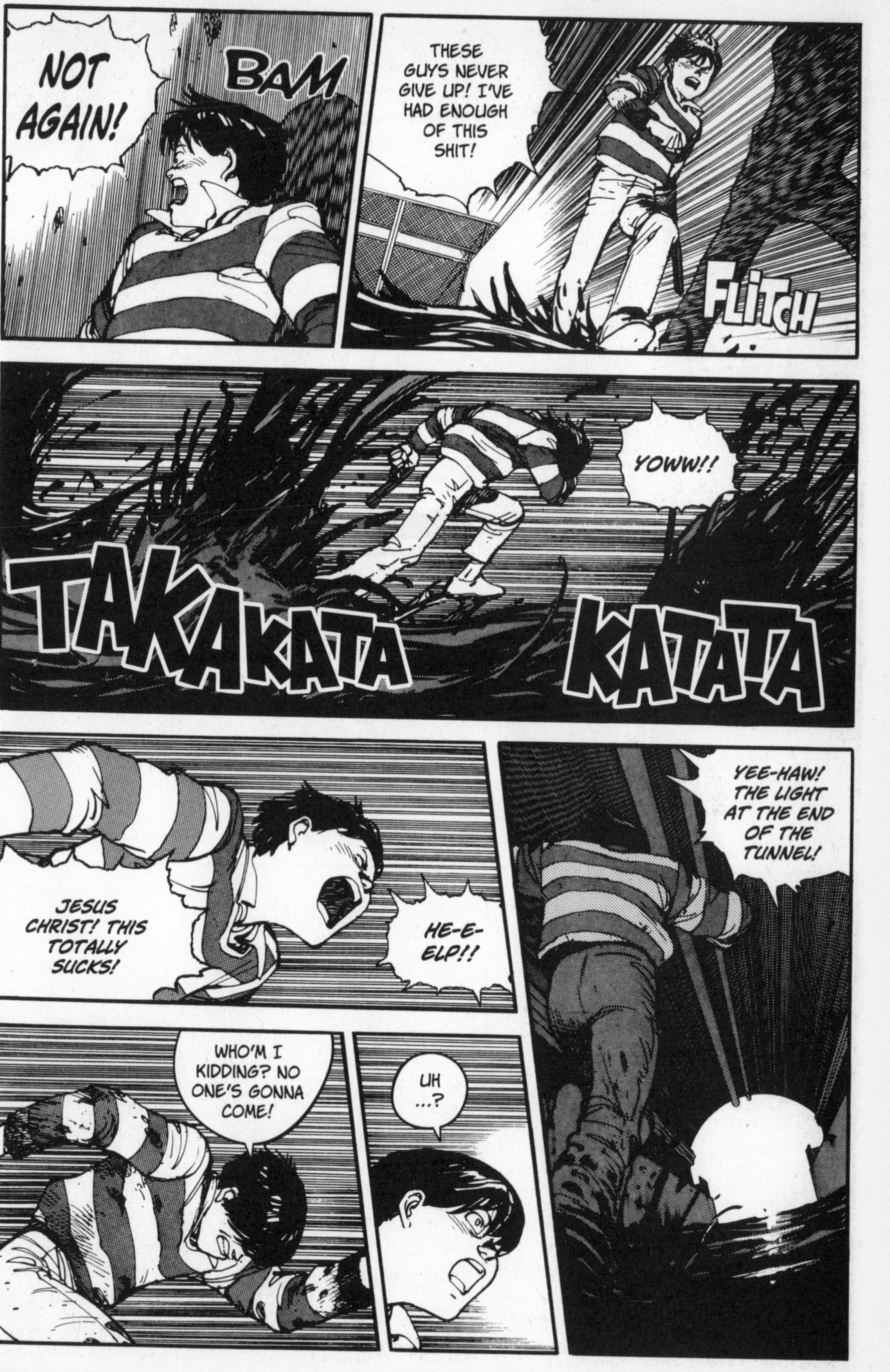
NOT AGAIN!
BAM
THESE GUYS NEVER GIVE UP! I'VE HAD ENOUGH OF THIS SHIT!
FLITCH
YOWW!!
TAKAKATA
KATATA
JESUS CHRIST! THIS TOTALLY SUCKS!
HE-E-ELP!!
WHO'M I KIDDING? NO ONE'S GONNA COME!
UH ...?
YEE-HAW! THE LIGHT AT THE END OF THE TUNNEL!

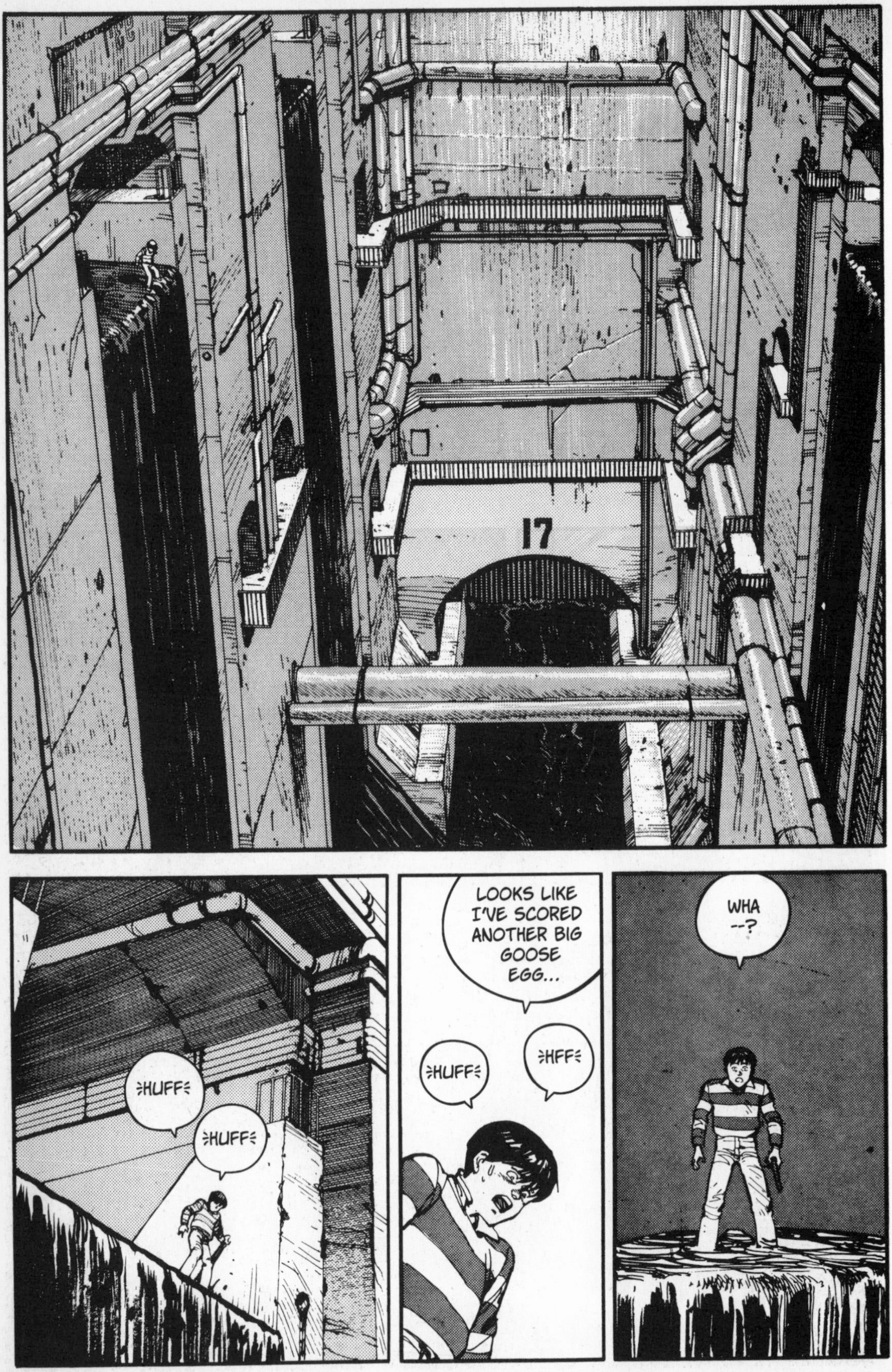
HUFF
HUFF
LOOKS LIKE I'VE SCORED ANOTHER BIG GOOSE EGG...
HUFF
HFF
WHA --?

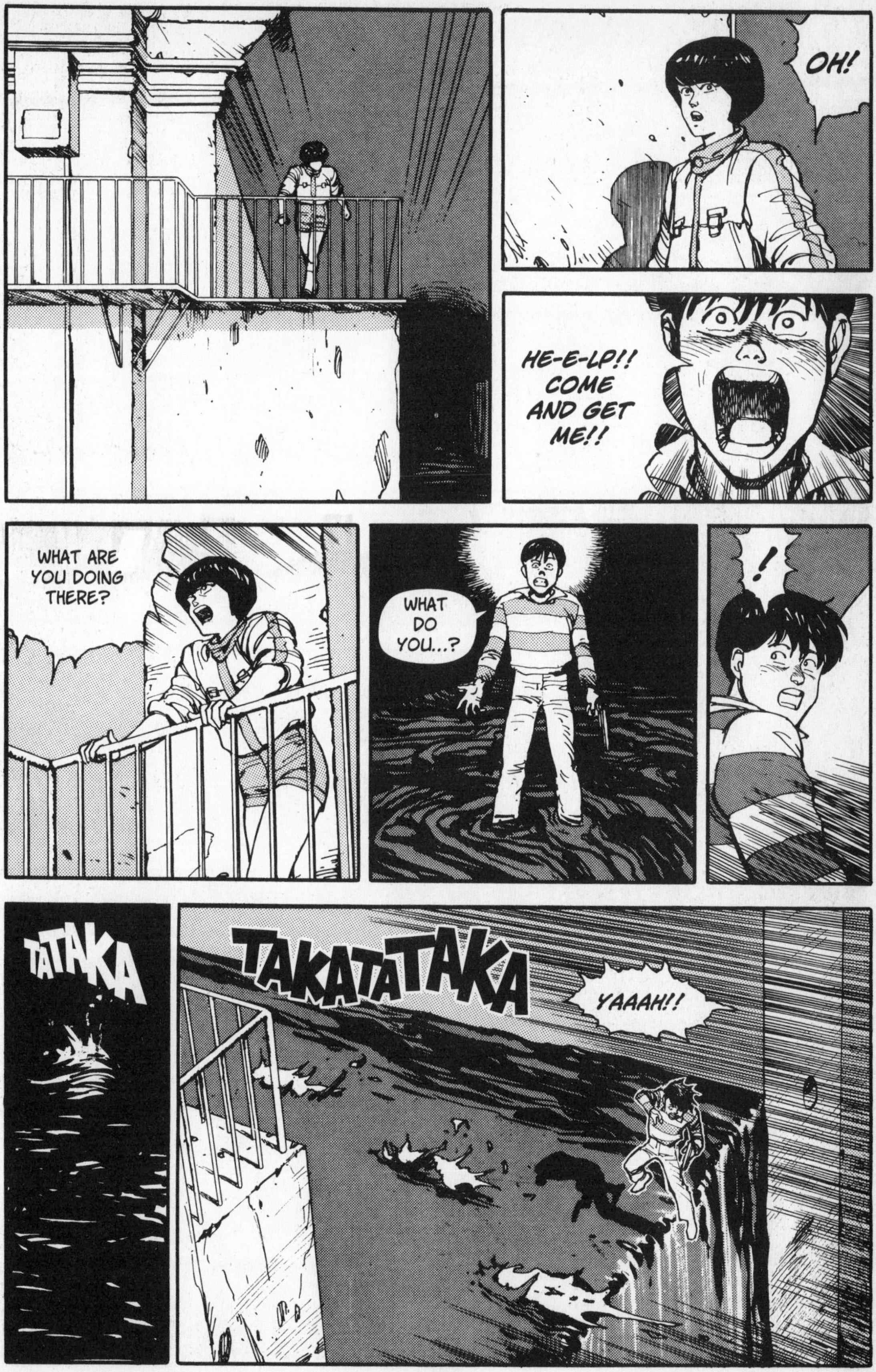
OH!
HE-E-LP!! COME AND GET ME!!
WHAT ARE YOU DOING THERE?
WHAT DO YOU...?
!
TATAKA
TAKATATAKA
YAAAH!!

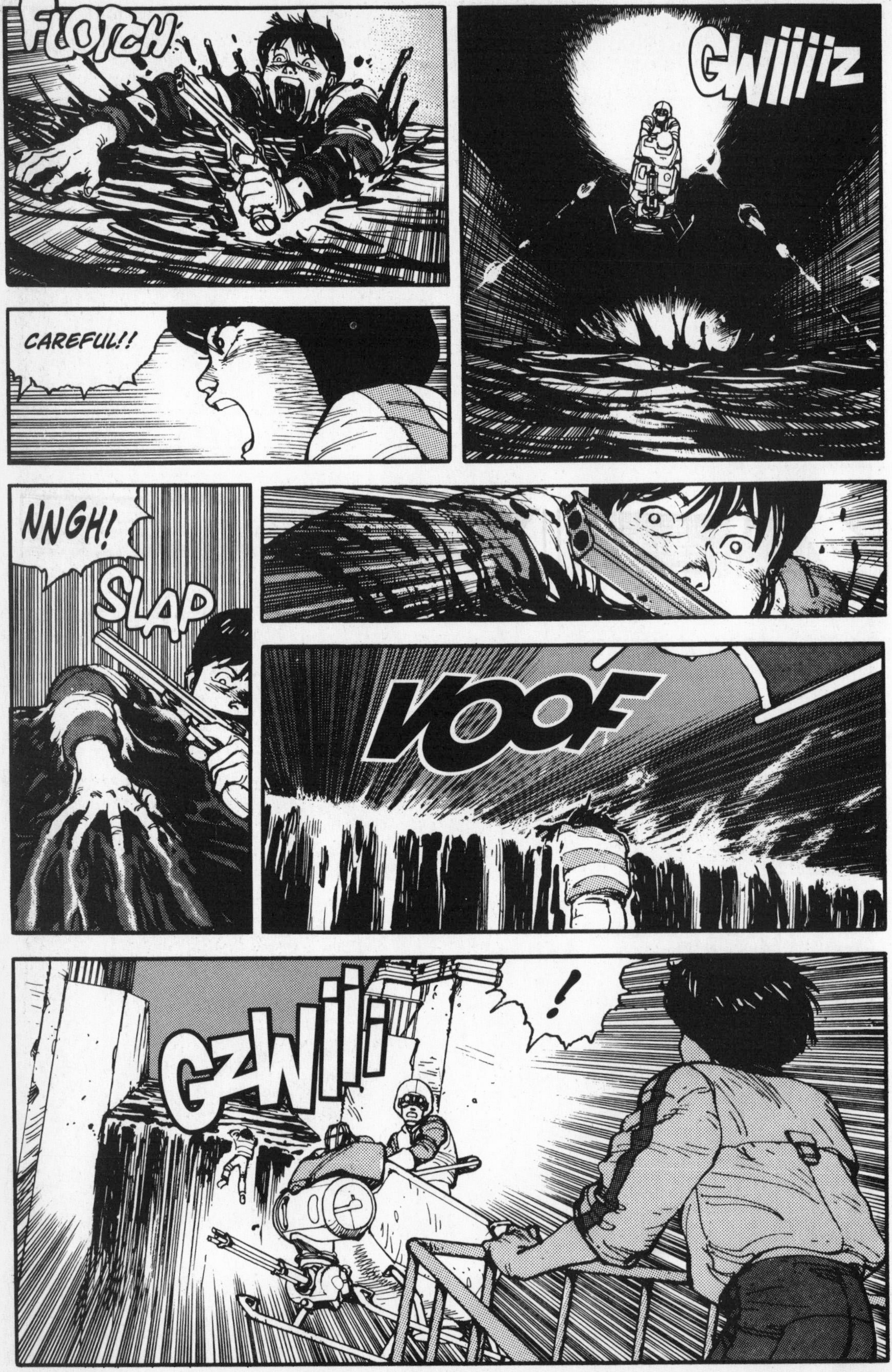
FLOTCH
GWIIIIIZ
CAREFUL!!
NNGH!
SLAP
VOOF
GZWIIII
!

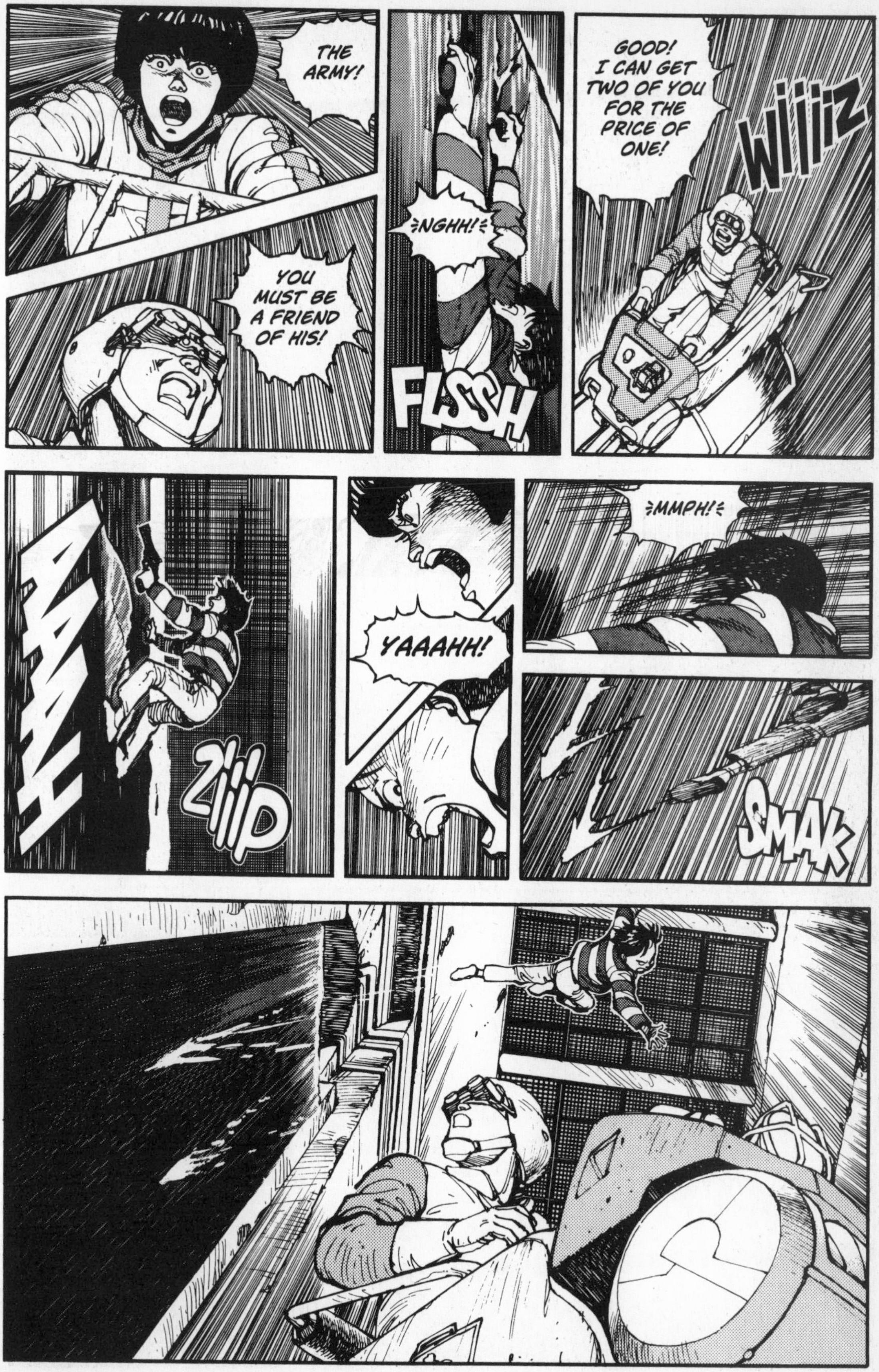
THE ARMY!
YOU MUST BE A FRIEND OF HIS!
NGHH!
FLSSH
GOOD! I CAN GET TWO OF YOU FOR THE PRICE OF ONE!
WIIIIZ
AAAAH
ZIIIP
YAAAHH!
MMPH!
SMAK

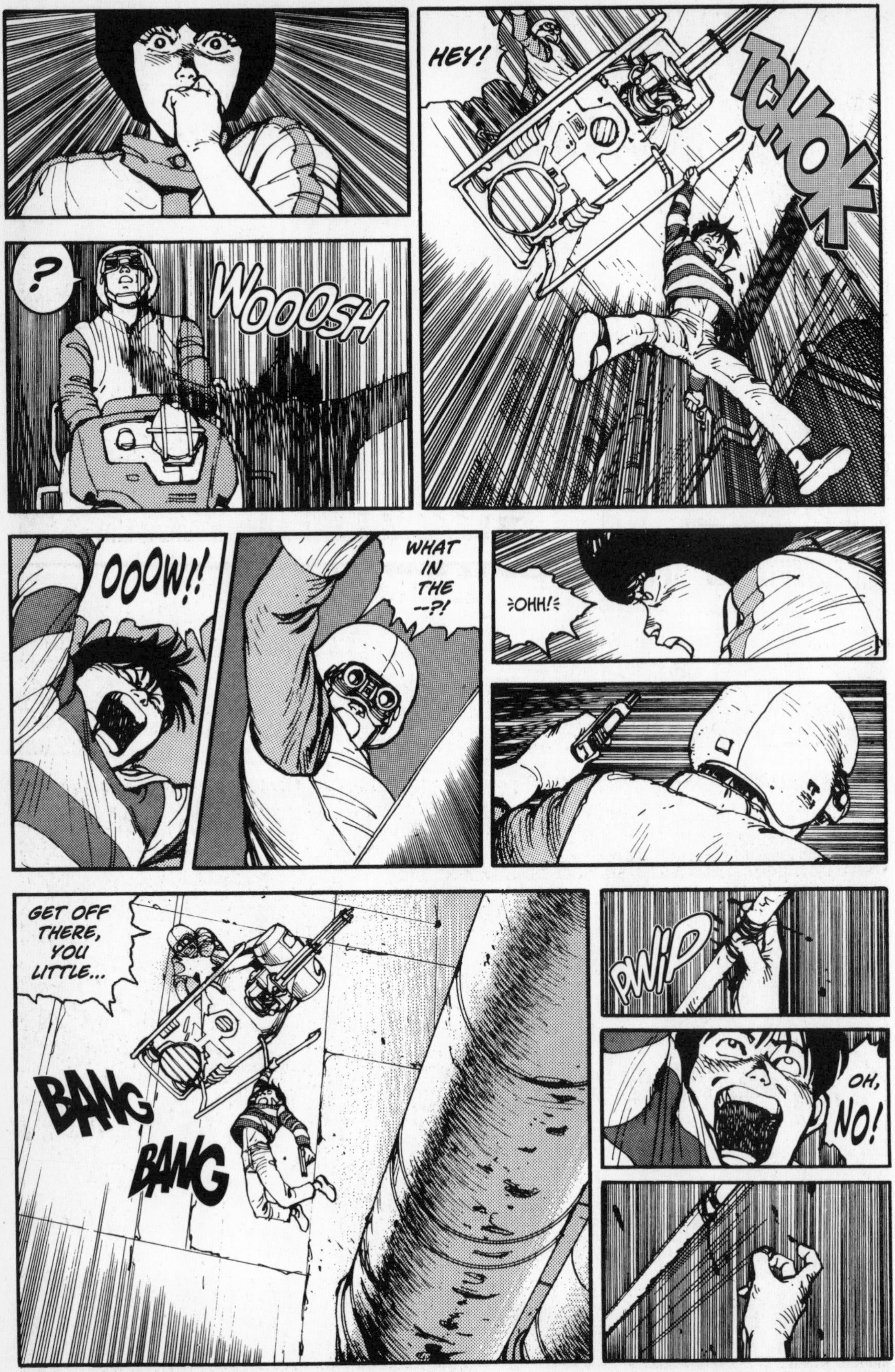
?
WOOOSH
HEY!
TCHOK
OOOW!!
WHAT IN THE --?!
OHH!
GET OFF THERE, YOU LITTLE...
BANG
BANG
PWIP
OH, NO!

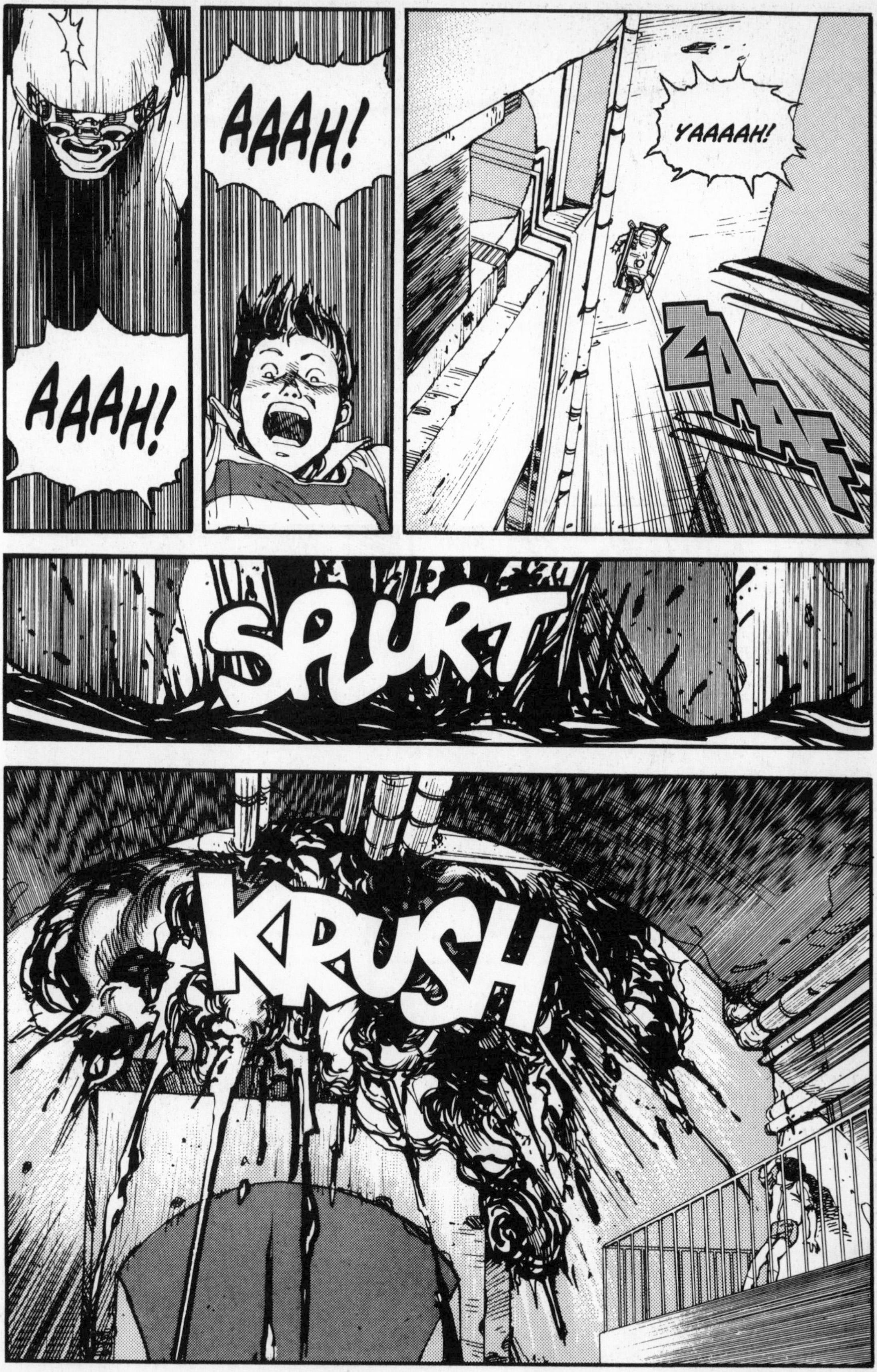
AAAH!
AAAH!
YAAAAH!
ZAAAF
SPLURT
KRUSH

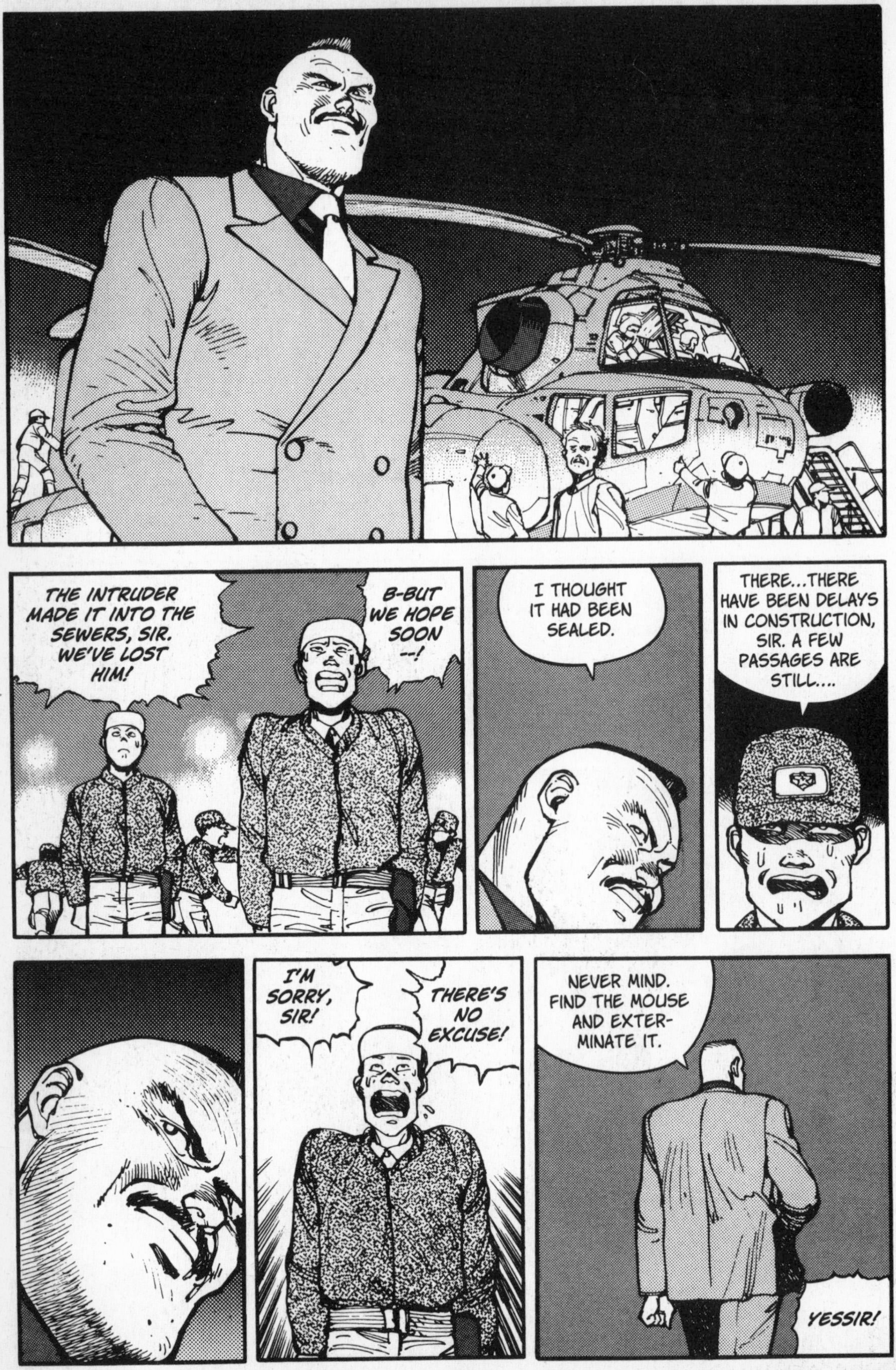
THE INTRUDER MADE IT INTO THE SEWERS, SIR. WE'VE LOST HIM!
B-BUT WE HOPE SOON --!
I THOUGHT IT HAD BEEN SEALED.
THERE...THERE HAVE BEEN DELAYS IN CONSTRUCTION, SIR. A FEW PASSAGES ARE STILL....
I'M SORRY, SIR!
THERE'S NO EXCUSE!
NEVER MIND. FIND THE MOUSE AND EXTER-MINATE IT.
YESSIR!

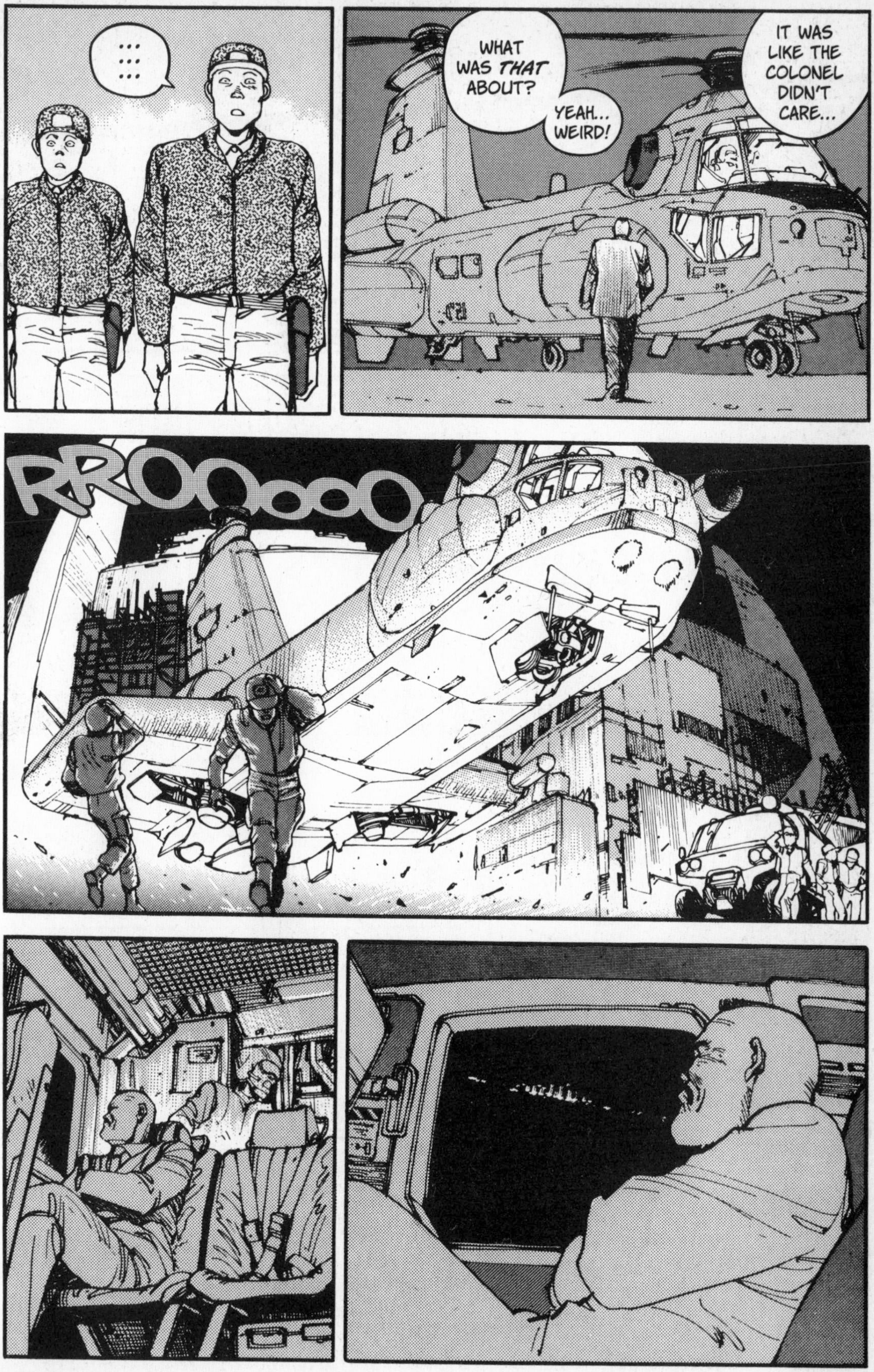
...
WHAT WAS *THAT* ABOUT?
YEAH... WEIRD!
IT WAS LIKE THE COLONEL DIDN'T CARE...
RROOooo

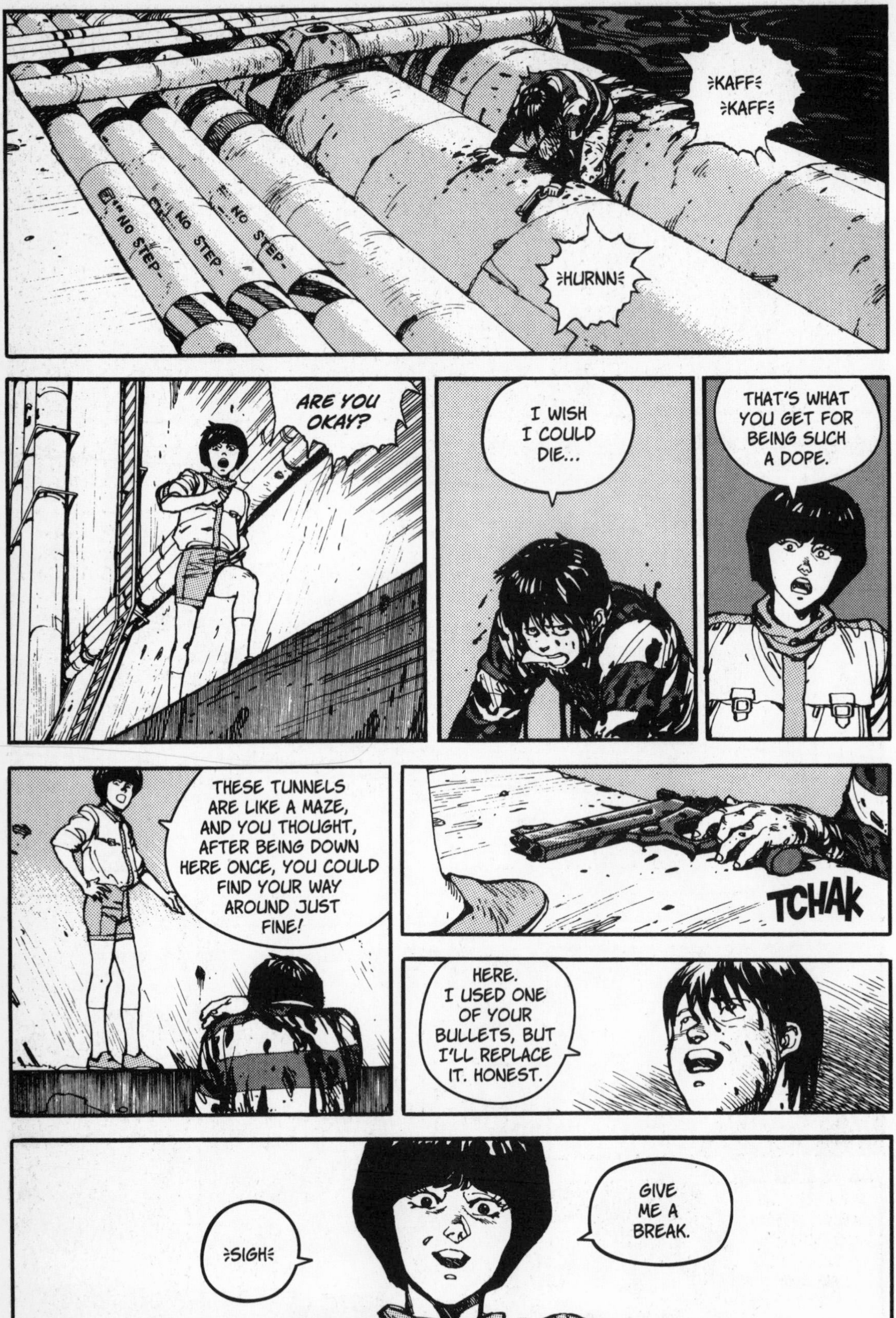

NO STEP
NO STEP
NO STEP
KAFF
KAFF
HURNN
ARE YOU OKAY?
I WISH I COULD DIE...
THAT'S WHAT YOU GET FOR BEING SUCH A DOPE.
THESE TUNNELS ARE LIKE A MAZE, AND YOU THOUGHT, AFTER BEING DOWN HERE ONCE, YOU COULD FIND YOUR WAY AROUND JUST FINE!
TCHAK
HERE. I USED ONE OF YOUR BULLETS, BUT I'LL REPLACE IT. HONEST.
SIGH
GIVE ME A BREAK.

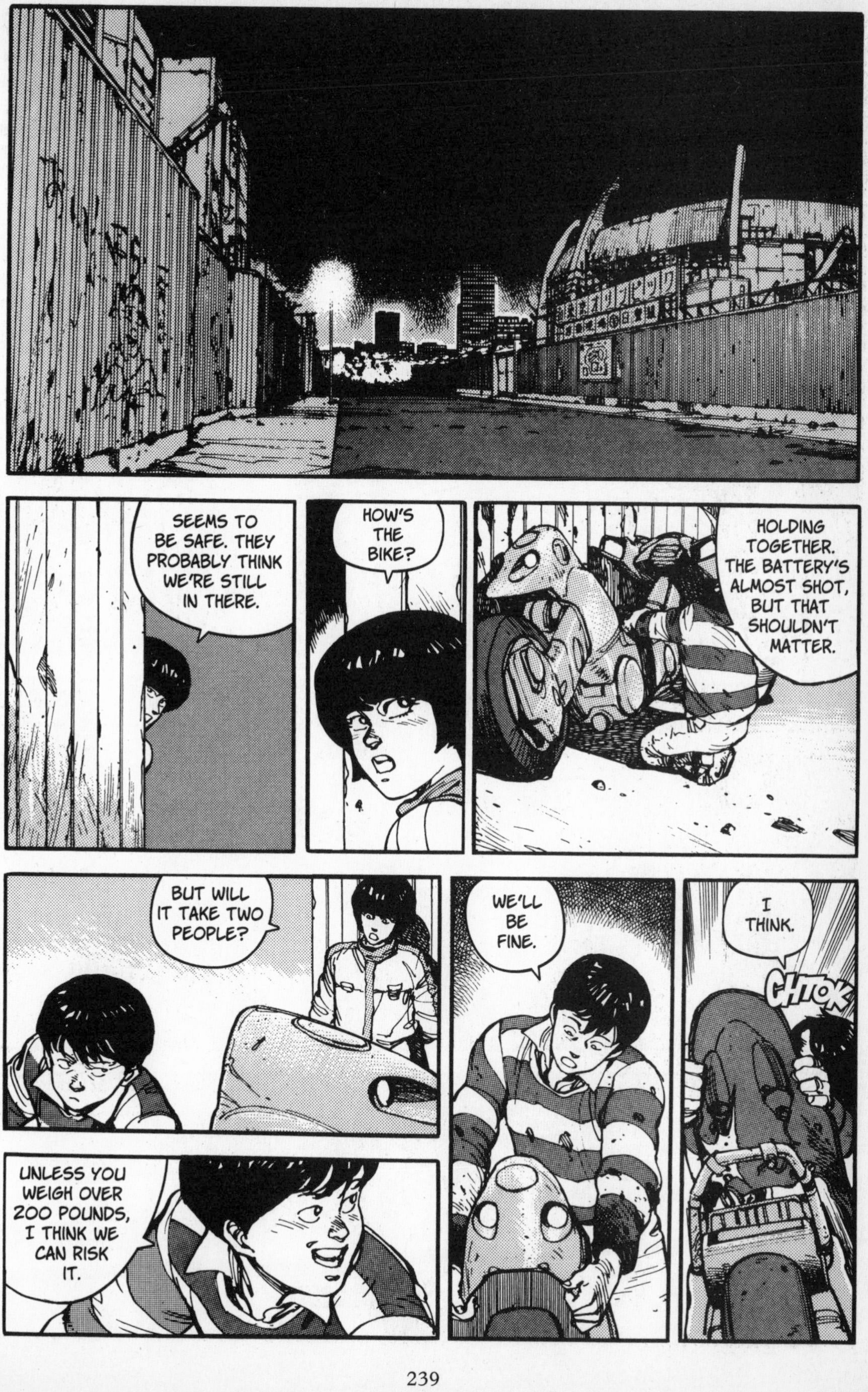

SEEMS TO BE SAFE. THEY PROBABLY THINK WE'RE STILL IN THERE.
HOW'S THE BIKE?
HOLDING TOGETHER. THE BATTERY'S ALMOST SHOT, BUT THAT SHOULDN'T MATTER.
BUT WILL IT TAKE TWO PEOPLE?
UNLESS YOU WEIGH OVER 200 POUNDS, I THINK WE CAN RISK IT.
WE'LL BE FINE.
I THINK.
CHTOK

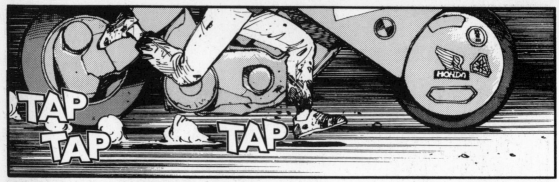

HERE GOES!

KLIC

COME ON, STUPID!!

PUNCH

KPOW

VVRROOM

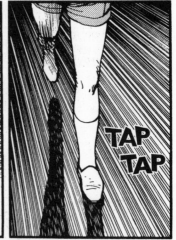

TAP
TAP

CAN WE PLEASE *ESCAPE* NOW?

WITH ME AT THE WHEEL, WE'RE AS GOOD AS GONE!

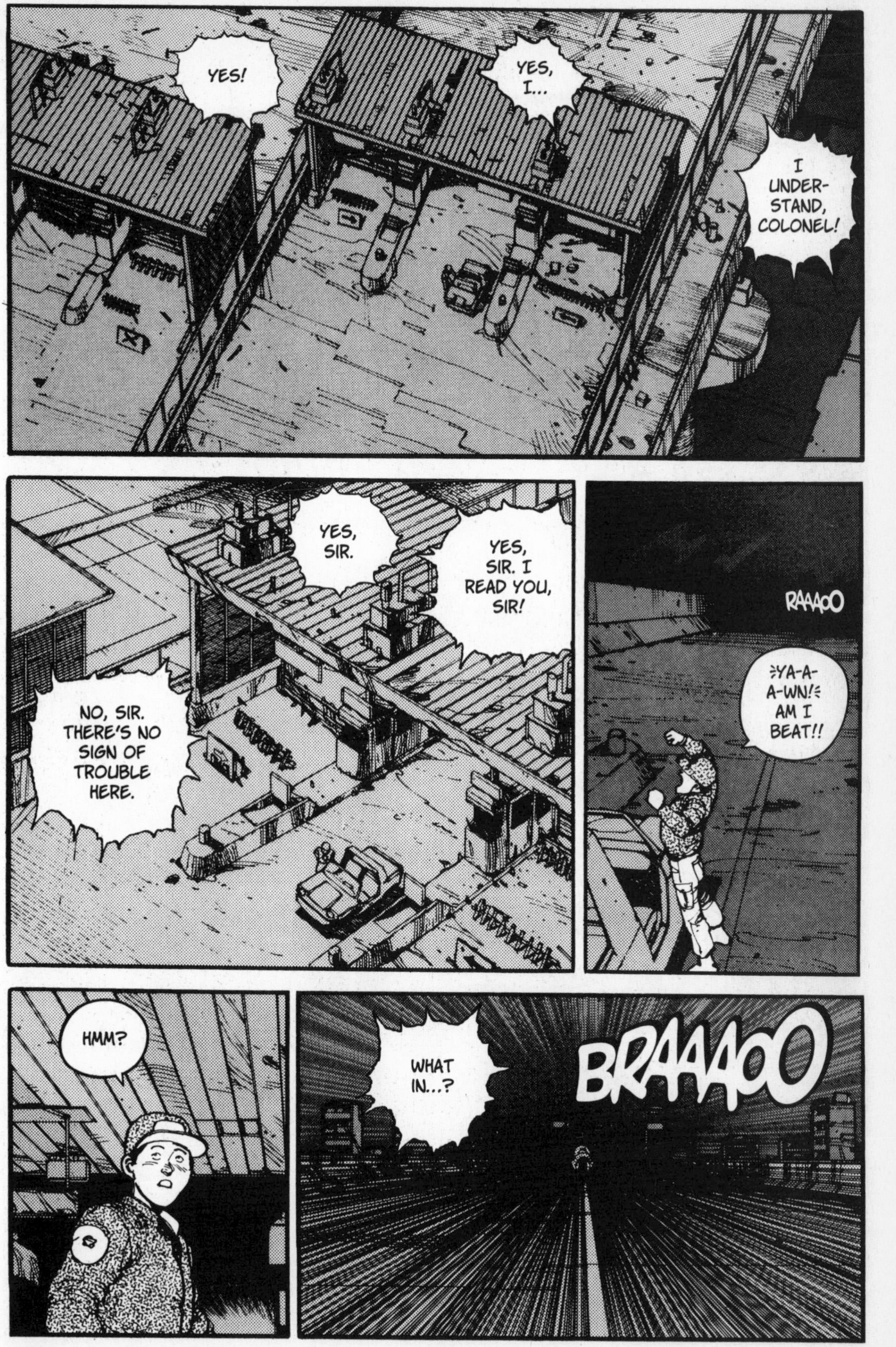
YES!
YES, I...
I UNDER-STAND, COLONEL!
YES, SIR.
YES, SIR. I READ YOU, SIR!
NO, SIR. THERE'S NO SIGN OF TROUBLE HERE.
RAAAOO
YA-A-A-WN! AM I BEAT!!
HMM?
WHAT IN...?
BRAAAOO

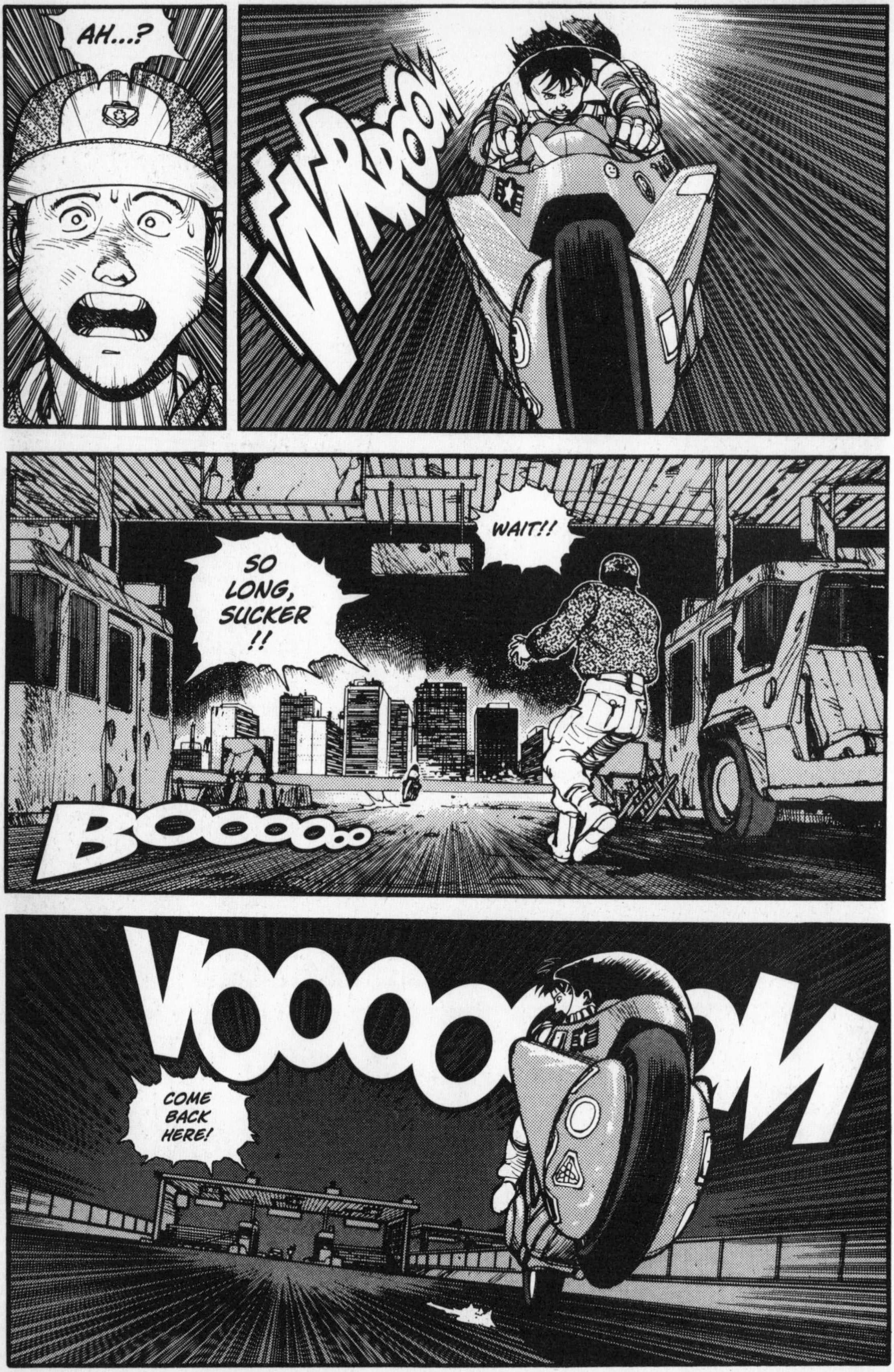
AH...?
VVRROOM
SO LONG, SUCKER !!
WAIT!!
BOOOO..
VOOOOOOM
COME BACK HERE!

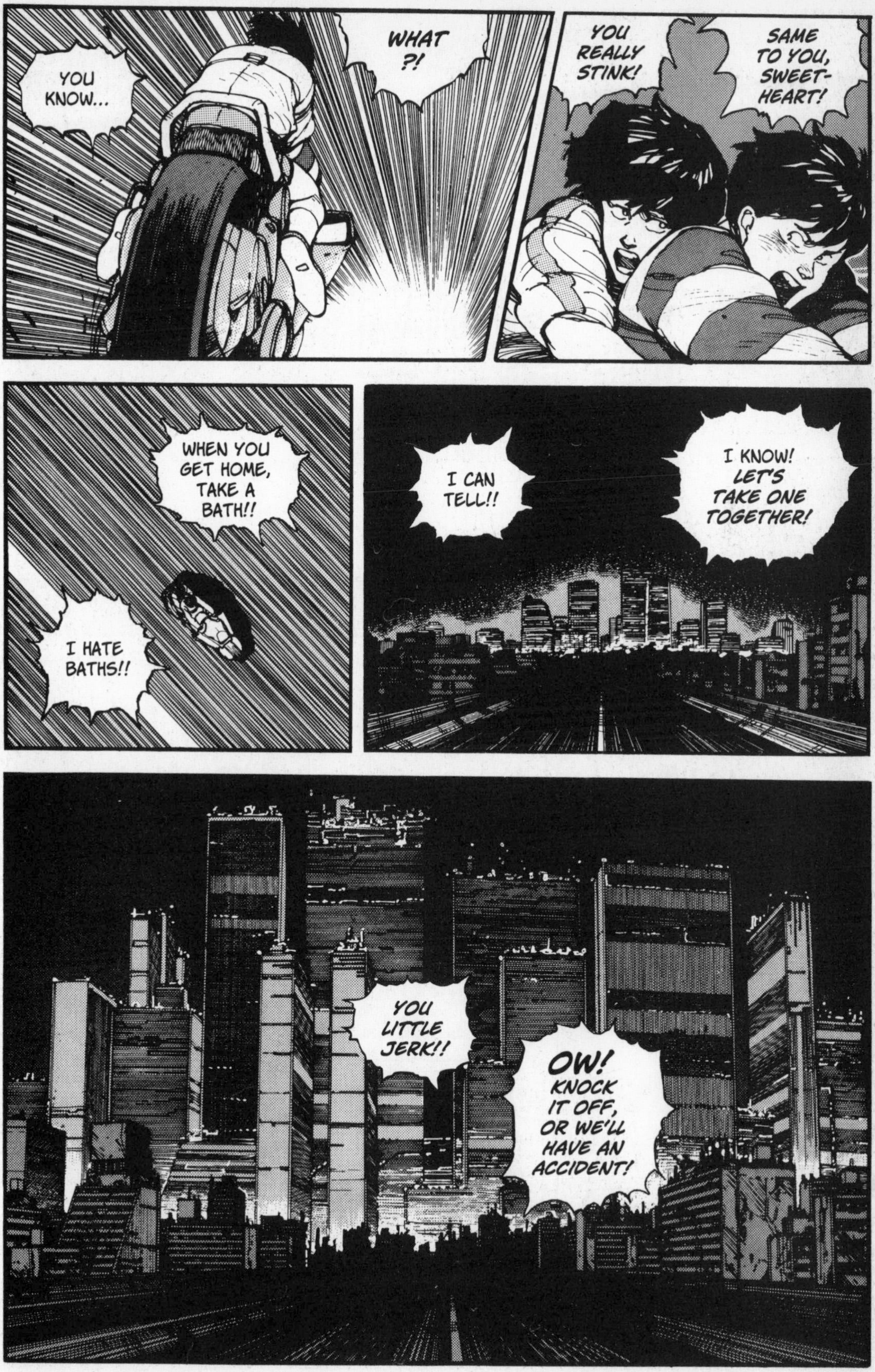
YOU KNOW...
WHAT ?!
YOU REALLY STINK!
SAME TO YOU, SWEET-HEART!
WHEN YOU GET HOME, TAKE A BATH!!
I HATE BATHS!!
I CAN TELL!!
I KNOW! LET'S TAKE ONE TOGETHER!
YOU LITTLE JERK!!
OW! KNOCK IT OFF, OR WE'LL HAVE AN ACCIDENT!

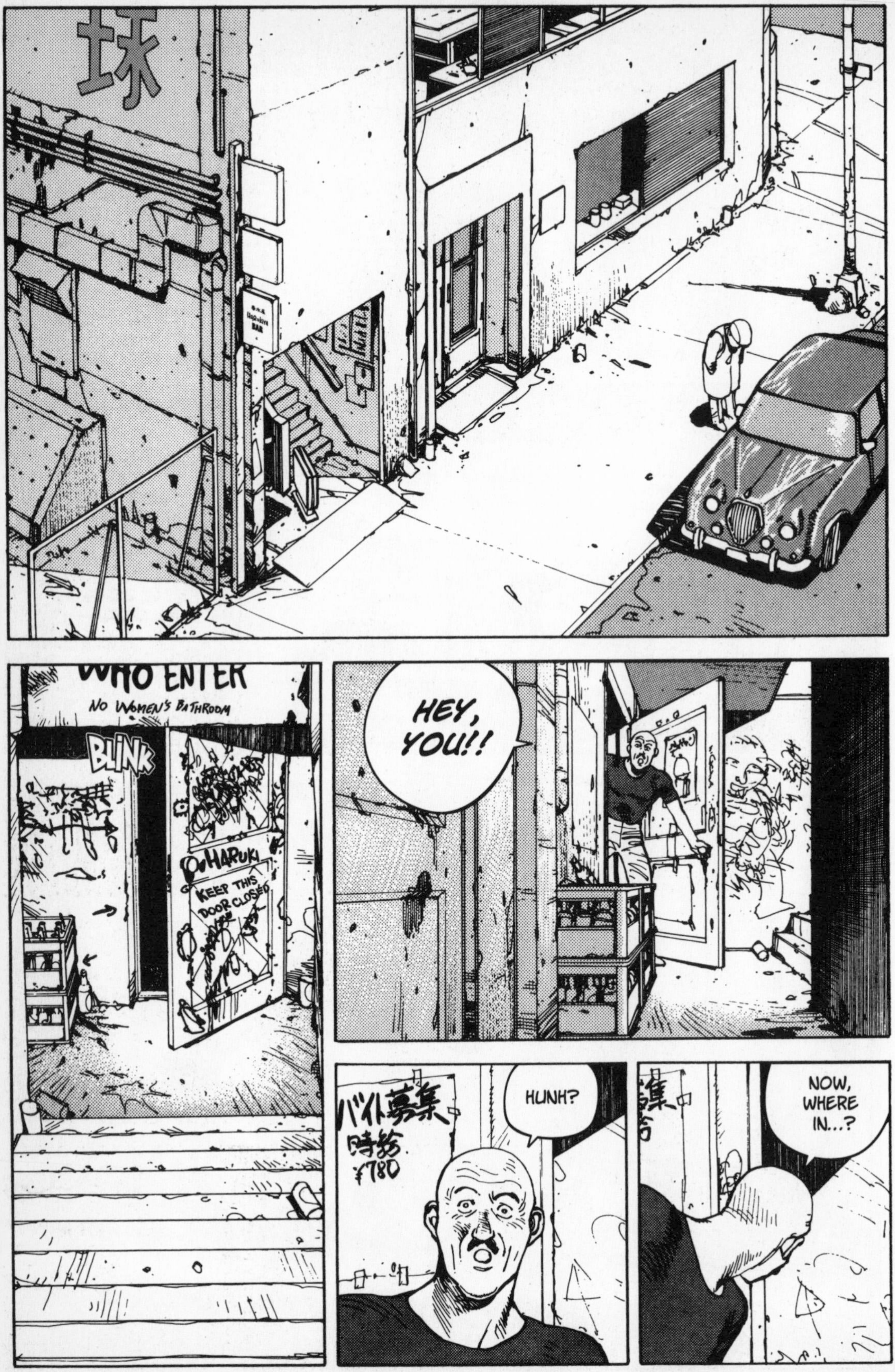
WHO ENTER
NO WOMEN'S BATHROOM
BLINK
HARUKI
KEEP THIS DOOR CLOSED
HEY, YOU!!
バイト募集
時給 ¥780
HUNH?
NOW, WHERE IN...?

TCHAK
TCHOK

DAMN! DAMN! DAMN! DAMN!

THE BLADE OF THIS SCREW-DRIVER IS BROKEN!

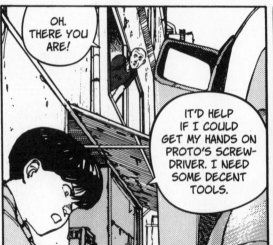

OH. THERE YOU ARE!

IT'D HELP IF I COULD GET MY HANDS ON PROTO'S SCREW-DRIVER. I NEED SOME DECENT TOOLS.

THIS PIECE OF SHIT THE BEST YOU GOT?

GET YOUR ASS UP HERE, KANEDA. YOU GOTTA CLEAN THE BAR BEFORE WE OPEN.

SO SINCE WHEN DID I BECOME YOUR SLAVE?

SINCE NOW. MOVE IT.

SKINHEAD BASTARD! DO I AT LEAST GET PAID?

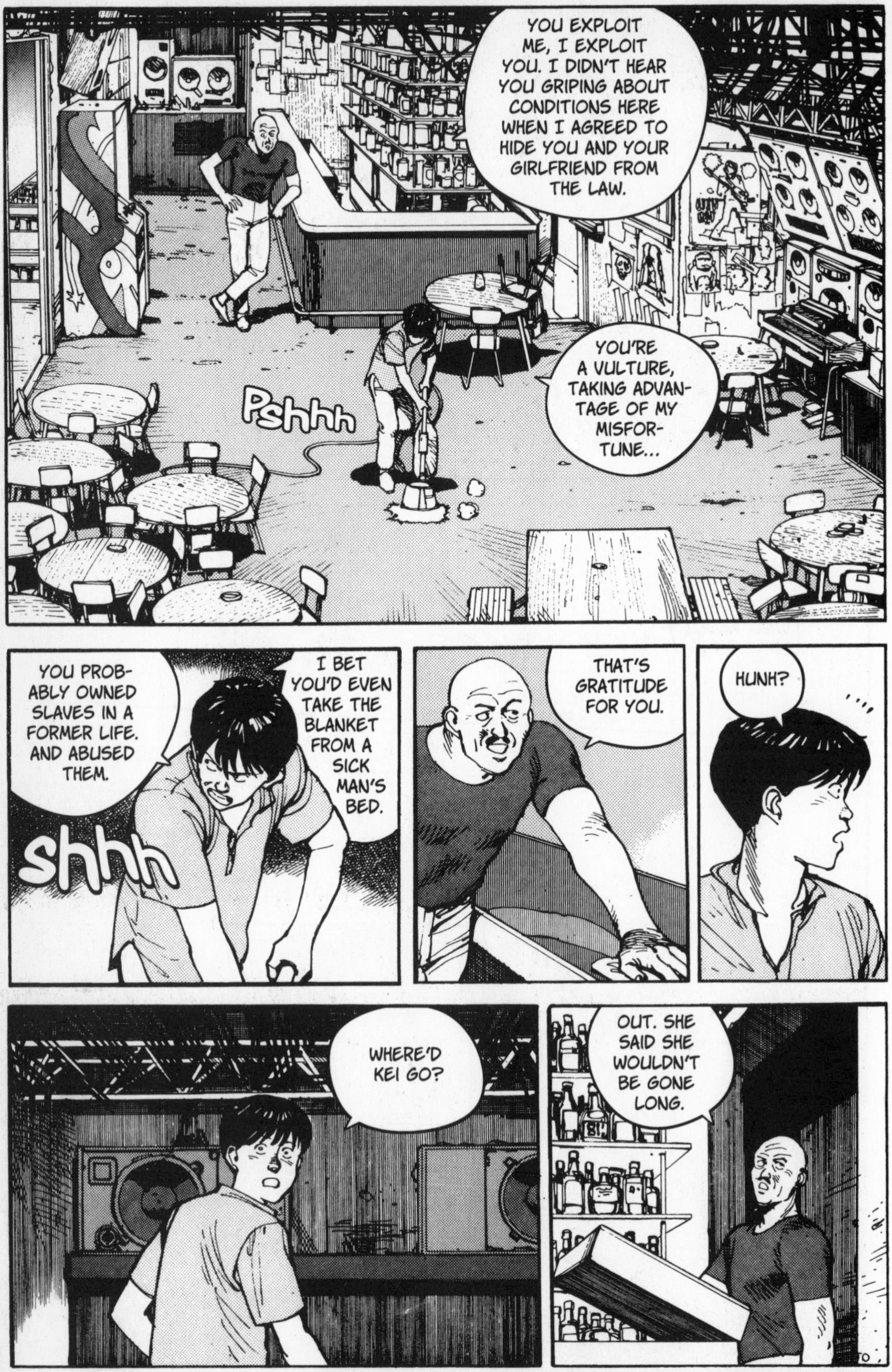
YOU EXPLOIT ME, I EXPLOIT YOU. I DIDN'T HEAR YOU GRIPING ABOUT CONDITIONS HERE WHEN I AGREED TO HIDE YOU AND YOUR GIRLFRIEND FROM THE LAW.
YOU'RE A VULTURE, TAKING ADVANTAGE OF MY MISFORTUNE...
Pshhh
YOU PROBABLY OWNED SLAVES IN A FORMER LIFE. AND ABUSED THEM.
I BET YOU'D EVEN TAKE THE BLANKET FROM A SICK MAN'S BED.
shhh
THAT'S GRATITUDE FOR YOU.
HUNH?
WHERE'D KEI GO?
OUT. SHE SAID SHE WOULDN'T BE GONE LONG.

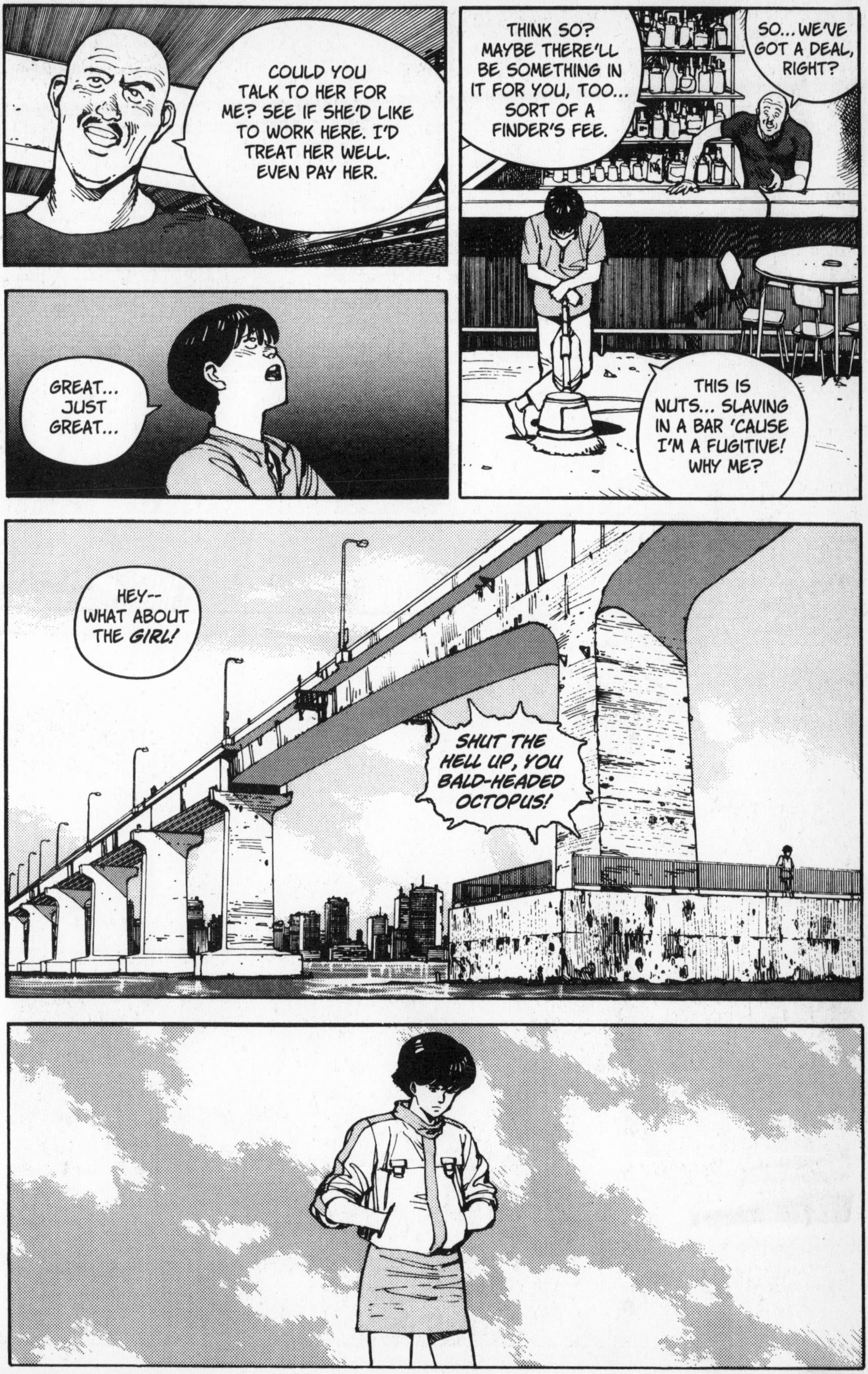
COULD YOU TALK TO HER FOR ME? SEE IF SHE'D LIKE TO WORK HERE. I'D TREAT HER WELL. EVEN PAY HER.
GREAT... JUST GREAT...
THINK SO? MAYBE THERE'LL BE SOMETHING IN IT FOR YOU, TOO... SORT OF A FINDER'S FEE.
SO... WE'VE GOT A DEAL, RIGHT?
THIS IS NUTS... SLAVING IN A BAR 'CAUSE I'M A FUGITIVE! WHY ME?
HEY-- WHAT ABOUT THE *GIRL!*
SHUT THE HELL UP, YOU BALD-HEADED OCTOPUS!

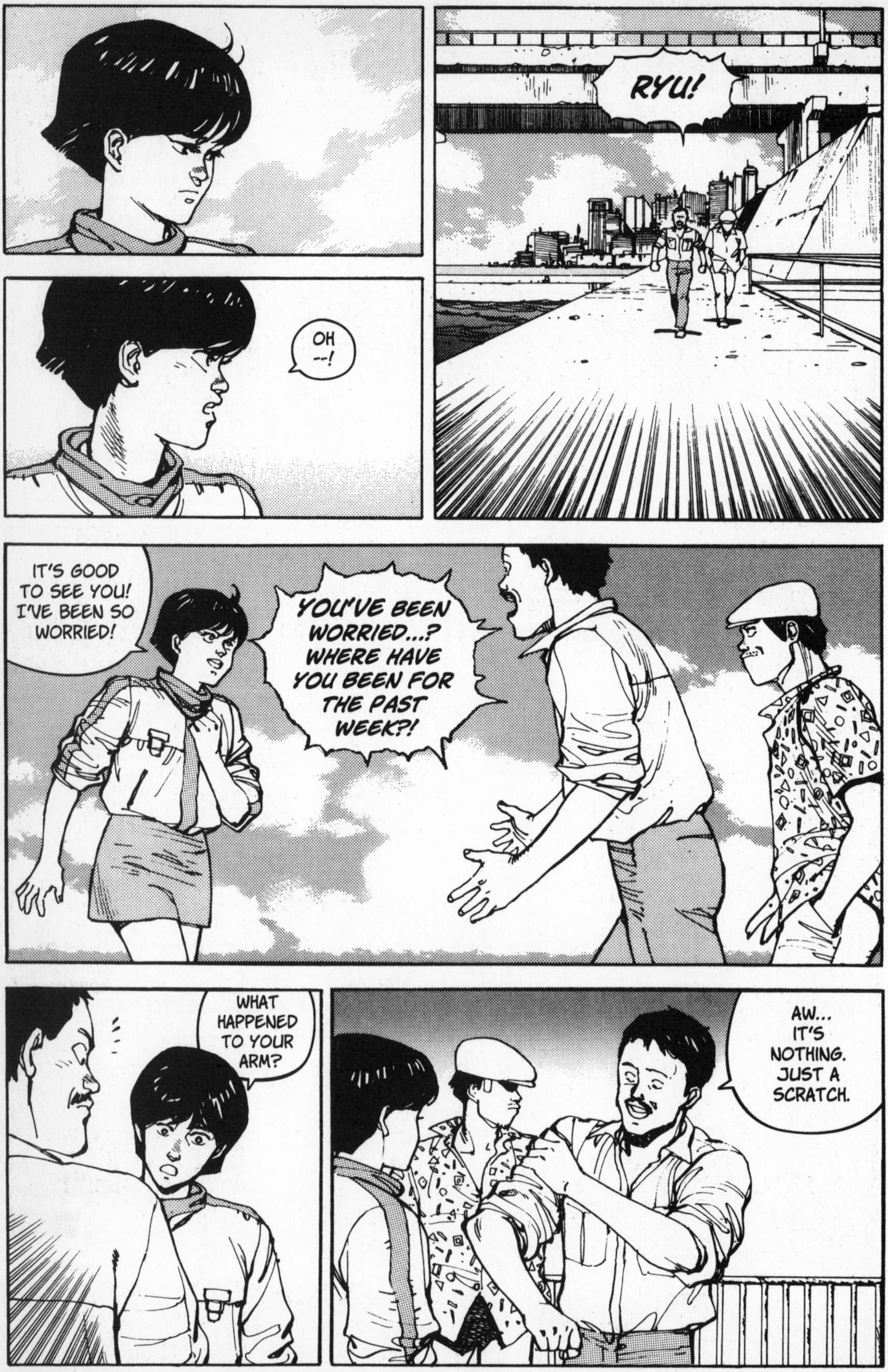
OH --!
RYU!
IT'S GOOD TO SEE YOU! I'VE BEEN SO WORRIED!
YOU'VE BEEN WORRIED...? WHERE HAVE YOU BEEN FOR THE PAST WEEK?!
WHAT HAPPENED TO YOUR ARM?
AW... IT'S NOTHING. JUST A SCRATCH.

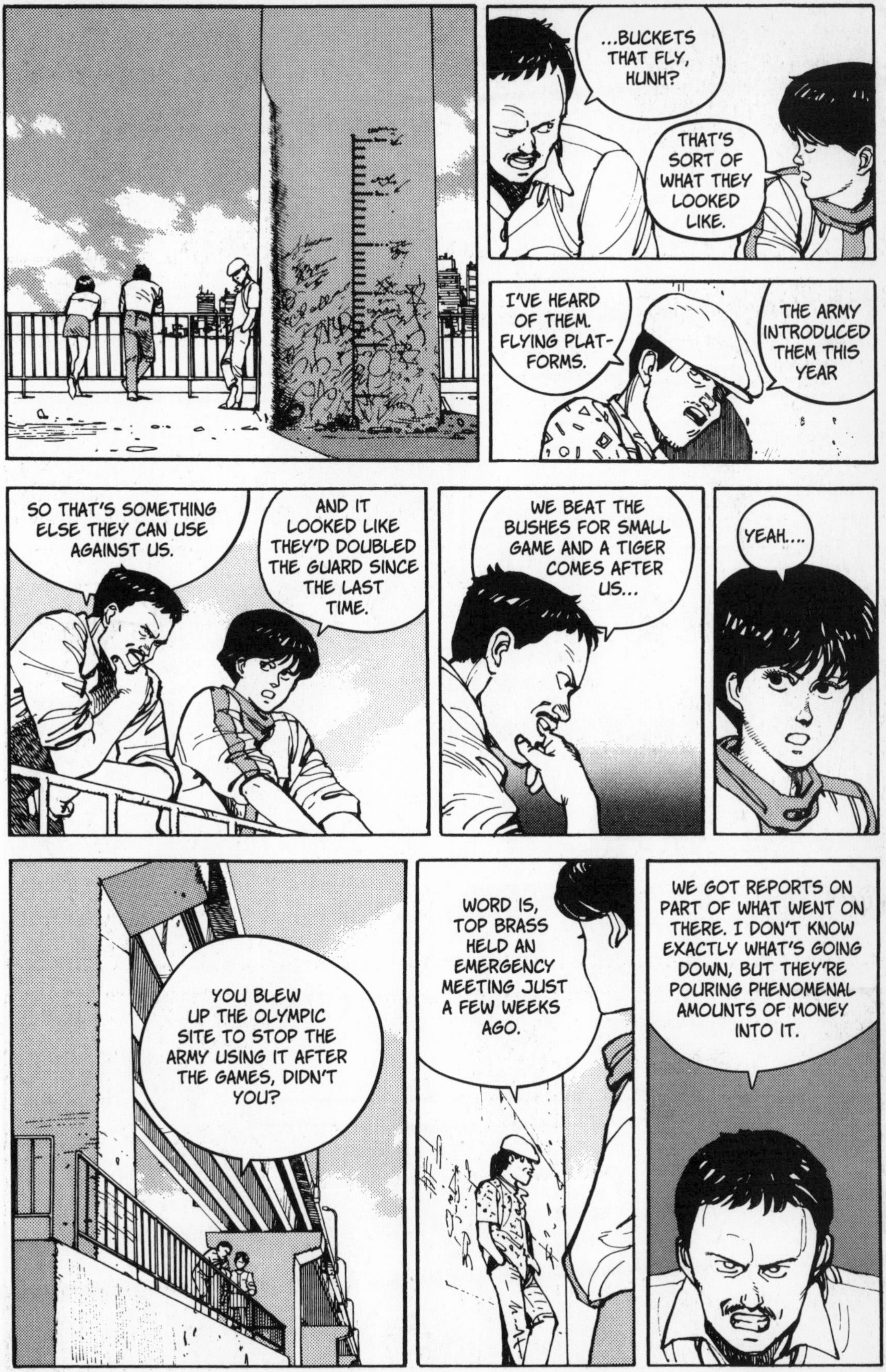
...BUCKETS THAT FLY, HUNH?
THAT'S SORT OF WHAT THEY LOOKED LIKE.
I'VE HEARD OF THEM. FLYING PLAT-FORMS.
THE ARMY INTRODUCED THEM THIS YEAR
SO THAT'S SOMETHING ELSE THEY CAN USE AGAINST US.
AND IT LOOKED LIKE THEY'D DOUBLED THE GUARD SINCE THE LAST TIME.
WE BEAT THE BUSHES FOR SMALL GAME AND A TIGER COMES AFTER US...
YEAH....
YOU BLEW UP THE OLYMPIC SITE TO STOP THE ARMY USING IT AFTER THE GAMES, DIDN'T YOU?
WORD IS, TOP BRASS HELD AN EMERGENCY MEETING JUST A FEW WEEKS AGO.
WE GOT REPORTS ON PART OF WHAT WENT ON THERE. I DON'T KNOW EXACTLY WHAT'S GOING DOWN, BUT THEY'RE POURING PHENOMENAL AMOUNTS OF MONEY INTO IT.

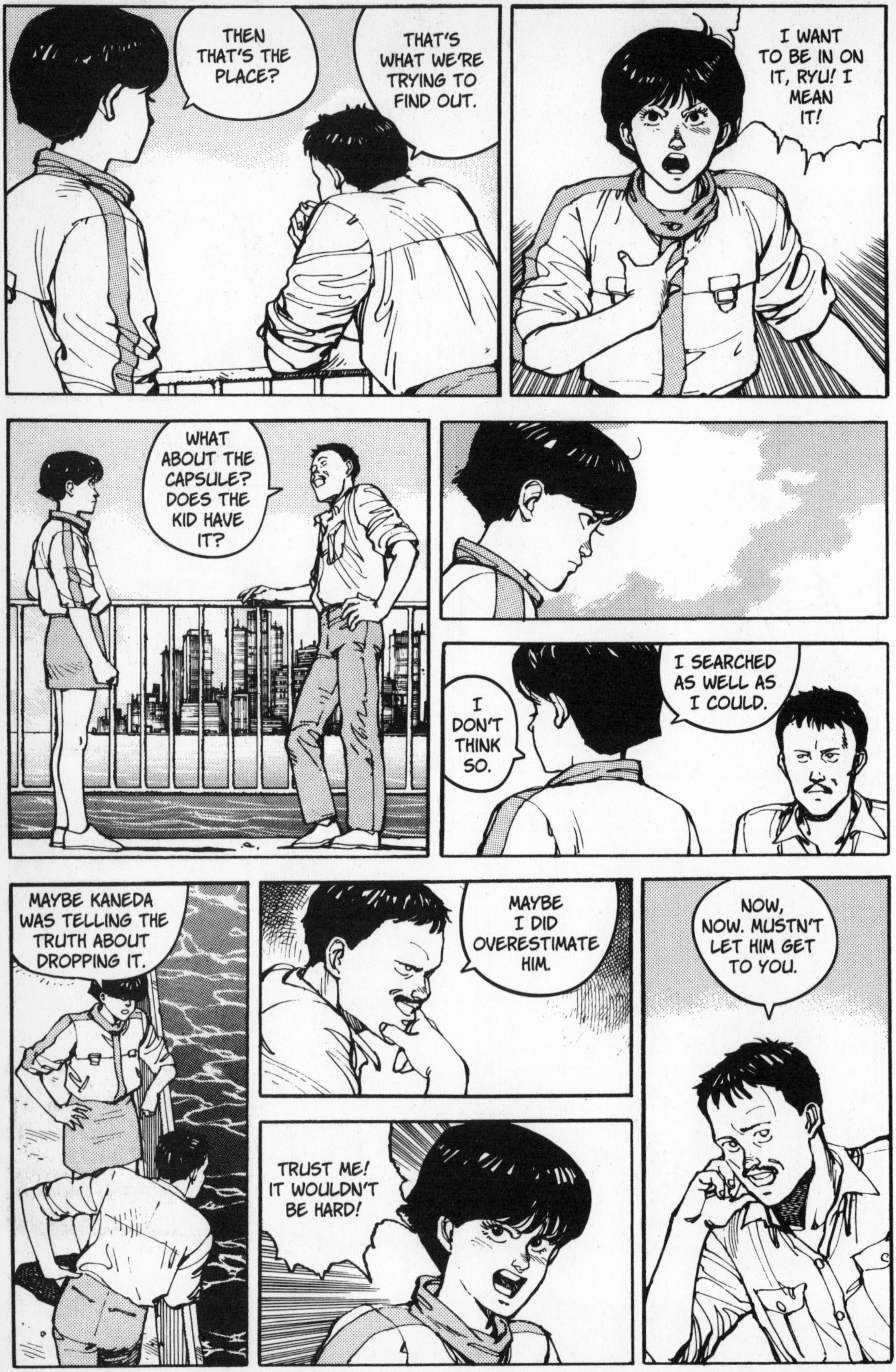
THEN THAT'S THE PLACE?
THAT'S WHAT WE'RE TRYING TO FIND OUT.
I WANT TO BE IN ON IT, RYU! I MEAN IT!
WHAT ABOUT THE CAPSULE? DOES THE KID HAVE IT?
I SEARCHED AS WELL AS I COULD.
I DON'T THINK SO.
MAYBE KANEDA WAS TELLING THE TRUTH ABOUT DROPPING IT.
MAYBE I DID OVERESTIMATE HIM.
TRUST ME! IT WOULDN'T BE HARD!
NOW, NOW. MUSTN'T LET HIM GET TO YOU.

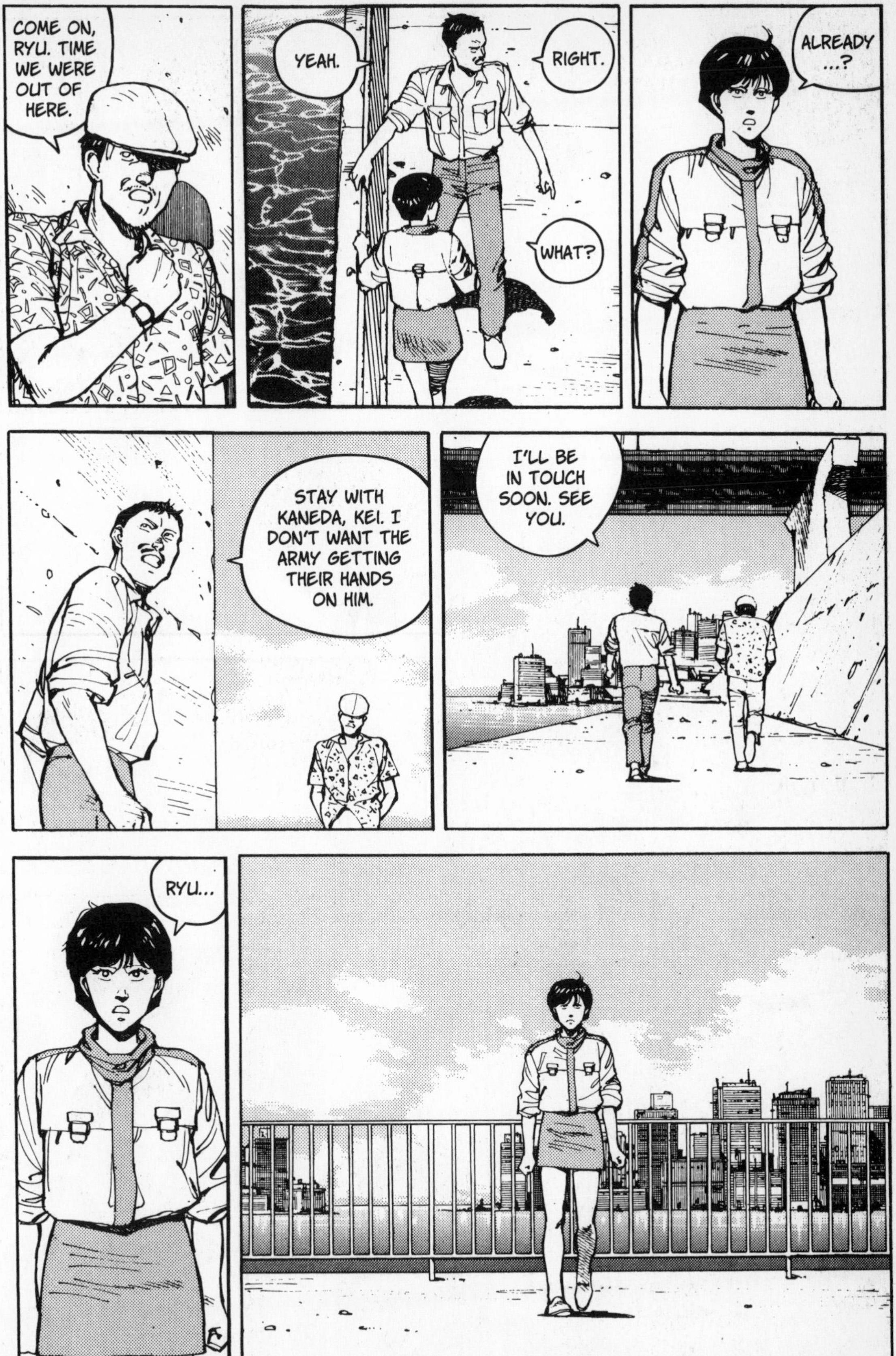
COME ON, RYU. TIME WE WERE OUT OF HERE.
YEAH.
RIGHT.
WHAT?
ALREADY ...?
STAY WITH KANEDA, KEI. I DON'T WANT THE ARMY GETTING THEIR HANDS ON HIM.
I'LL BE IN TOUCH SOON. SEE YOU.
RYU...

KRiiiiii

BOK

THE COAST IS CLEAR...

NOT EVEN *GOD* WILL KNOW WHAT I'M UP TO...

TCHiiF

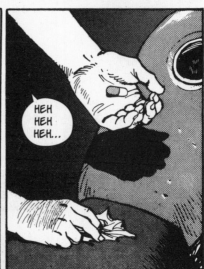

HEH HEH HEH...

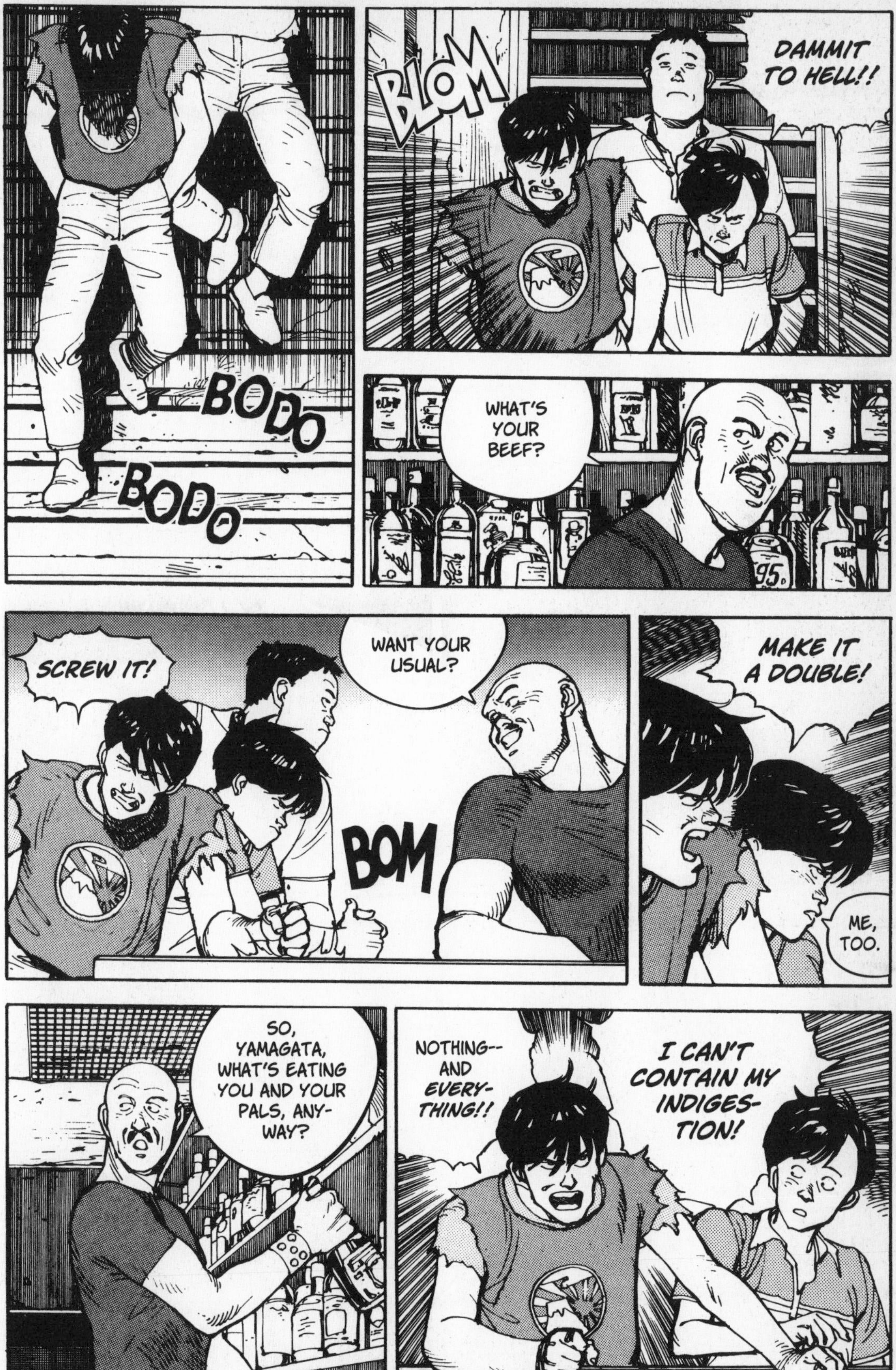
BODO
BODO
BLOM
DAMMIT TO HELL!!
WHAT'S YOUR BEEF?
SCREW IT!
WANT YOUR USUAL?
BOM
MAKE IT A DOUBLE!
ME, TOO.
SO, YAMAGATA, WHAT'S EATING YOU AND YOUR PALS, ANY-WAY?
NOTHING-- AND EVERY-THING!!
I CAN'T CONTAIN MY INDIGES-TION!

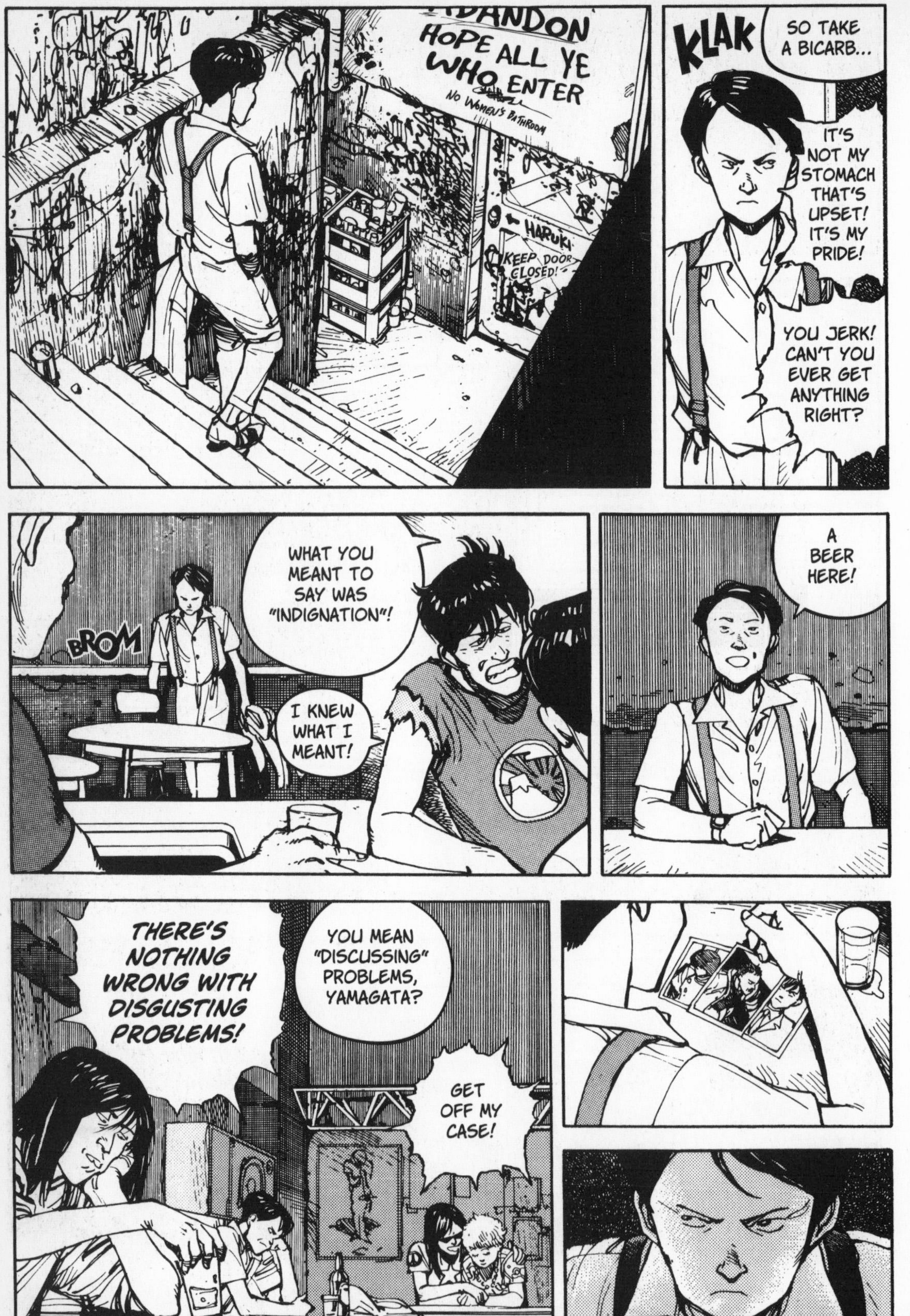
ABANDON HOPE ALL YE WHO ENTER
NO WOMEN'S BATHROOM
HARUKI
KEEP DOOR CLOSED!
KLAK
SO TAKE A BICARB...
IT'S NOT MY STOMACH THAT'S UPSET! IT'S MY PRIDE!
YOU JERK! CAN'T YOU EVER GET ANYTHING RIGHT?
BROM
WHAT YOU MEANT TO SAY WAS "INDIGNATION"!
I KNEW WHAT I MEANT!
A BEER HERE!
THERE'S NOTHING WRONG WITH DISGUSTING PROBLEMS!
YOU MEAN "DISCUSSING" PROBLEMS, YAMAGATA?
GET OFF MY CASE!

WE NEED KANEDA. WISH I KNEW WHERE HE IS...

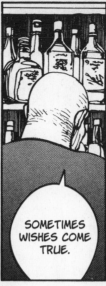

SOMETIMES WISHES COME TRUE.

WHAT'S THAT SUPPOSED TO MEAN?!

!

!

THERE YOU ARE!

HI.

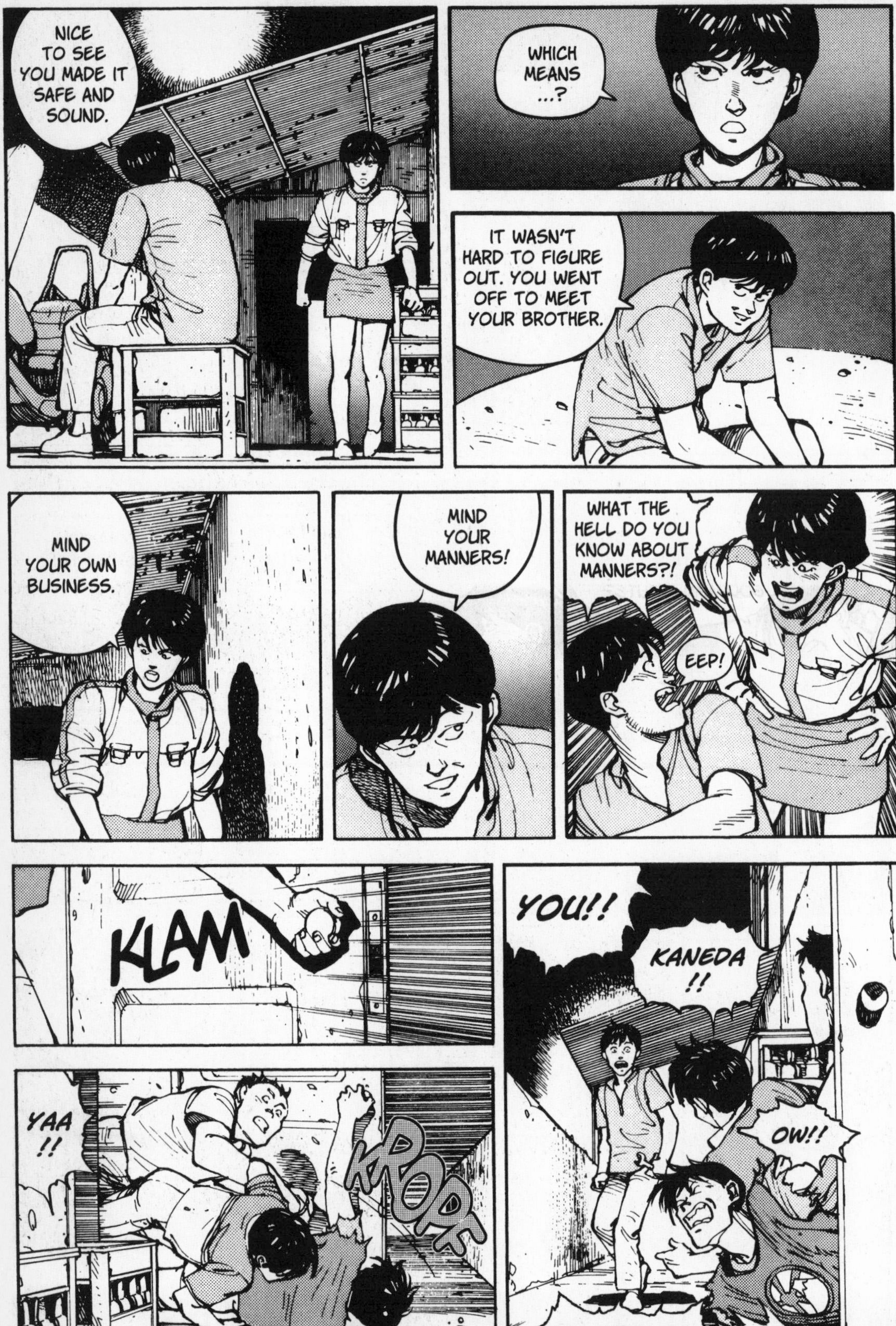
NICE TO SEE YOU MADE IT SAFE AND SOUND.
WHICH MEANS ...?
IT WASN'T HARD TO FIGURE OUT. YOU WENT OFF TO MEET YOUR BROTHER.
MIND YOUR OWN BUSINESS.
MIND YOUR MANNERS!
WHAT THE HELL DO YOU KNOW ABOUT MANNERS?!
EEP!
KLAM
YOU!!
KANEDA !!
YAA !!
KROOF
OW!!
GET OFFA ME, YOU MORON!

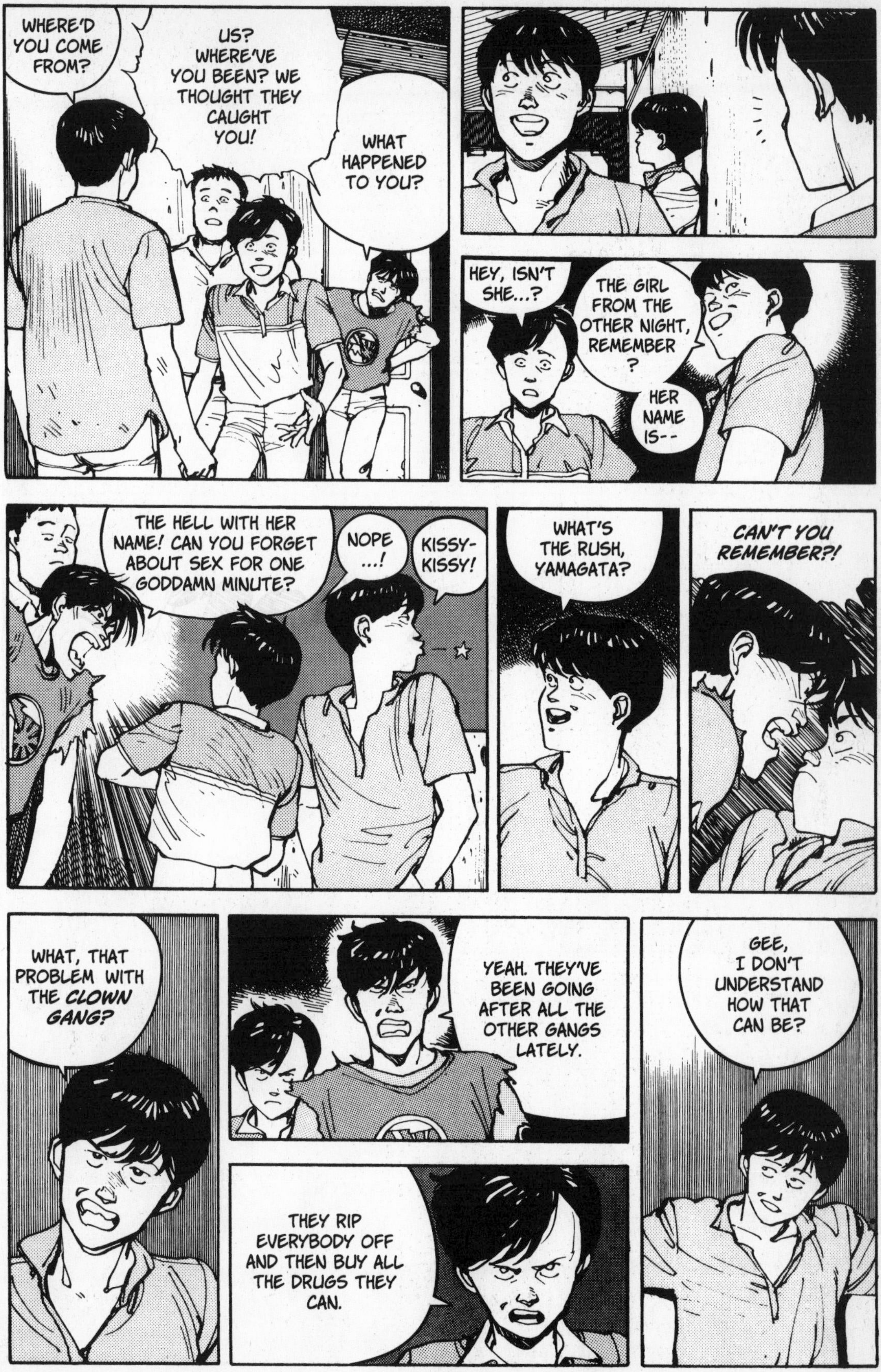
WHERE'D YOU COME FROM?
US? WHERE'VE YOU BEEN? WE THOUGHT THEY CAUGHT YOU!
WHAT HAPPENED TO YOU?
HEY, ISN'T SHE...?
THE GIRL FROM THE OTHER NIGHT, REMEMBER?
HER NAME IS--
THE HELL WITH HER NAME! CAN YOU FORGET ABOUT SEX FOR ONE GODDAMN MINUTE?
NOPE ...!
KISSY-KISSY!
WHAT'S THE RUSH, YAMAGATA?
CAN'T YOU REMEMBER?!
WHAT, THAT PROBLEM WITH THE CLOWN GANG?
YEAH. THEY'VE BEEN GOING AFTER ALL THE OTHER GANGS LATELY.
THEY RIP EVERYBODY OFF AND THEN BUY ALL THE DRUGS THEY CAN.
GEE, I DON'T UNDERSTAND HOW THAT CAN BE?

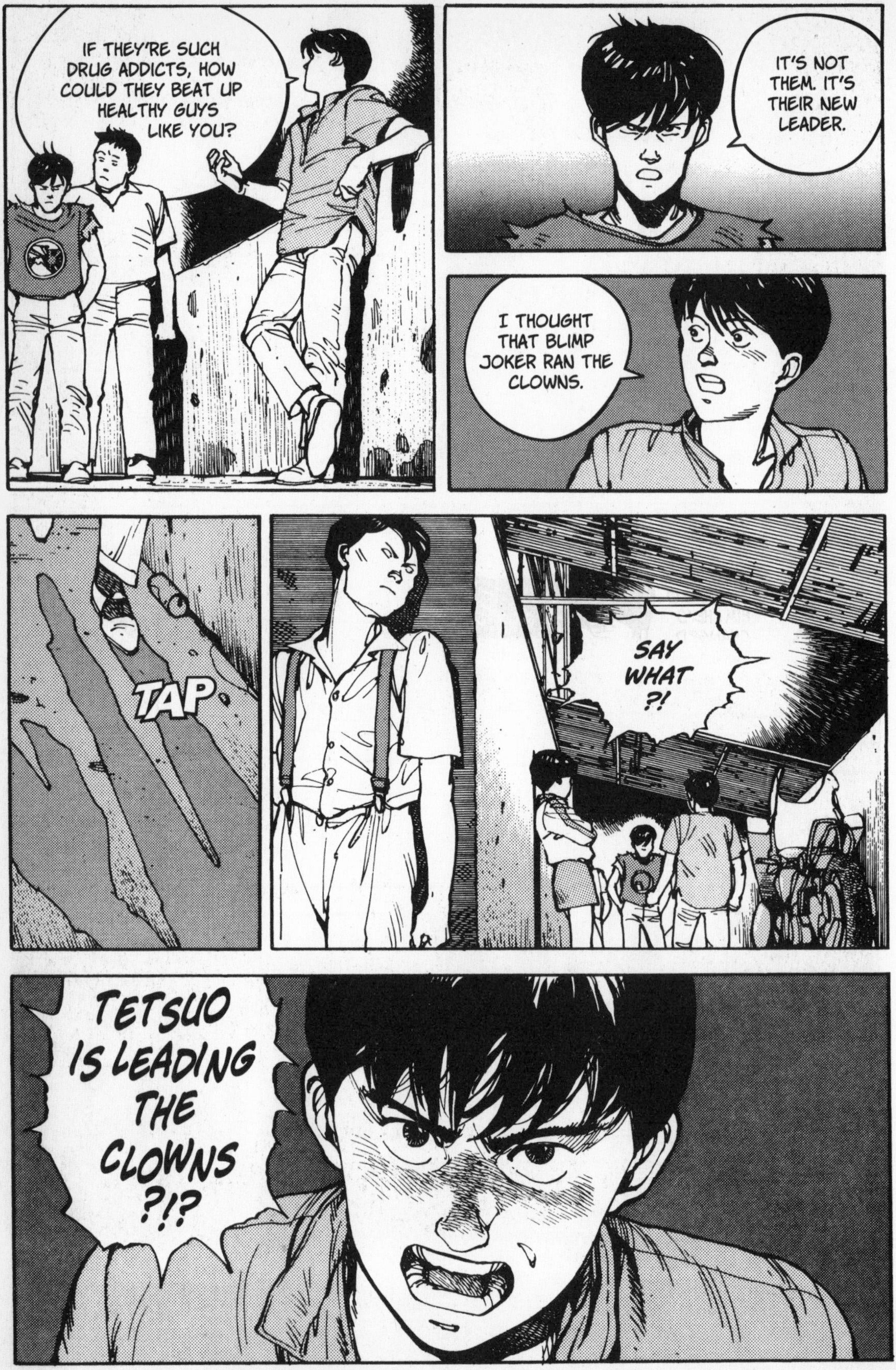
IF THEY'RE SUCH DRUG ADDICTS, HOW COULD THEY BEAT UP HEALTHY GUYS LIKE YOU?
IT'S NOT THEM. IT'S THEIR NEW LEADER.
I THOUGHT THAT BLIMP JOKER RAN THE CLOWNS.
TAP
SAY WHAT ?!
TETSUO IS LEADING THE CLOWNS ?!?

KANEDA...

BULLSHIT!

IT CAN'T BE TRUE!

I DIDN'T WANT TO BELIEVE IT EITHER, BUT I SAW WITH MY OWN EYES.

IT WAS DEFINITELY HIM, AND HE WAS DEFINITELY IN CHARGE!

I DIDN'T RECOGNIZE HIM AT FIRST. SOMETHING'S HAPPENED TO HIM. HE'S CHANGED.

BUT THERE'S NO DOUBT ABOUT IT!

IT WAS TETSUO, ALL RIGHT!

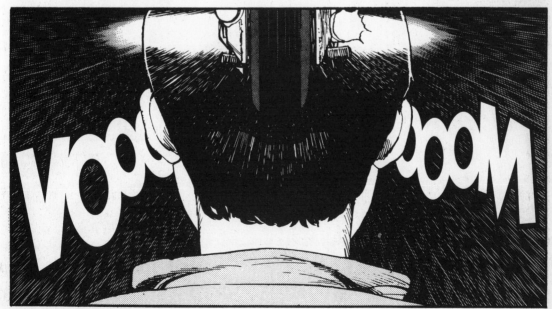

VOOOM

OOOM

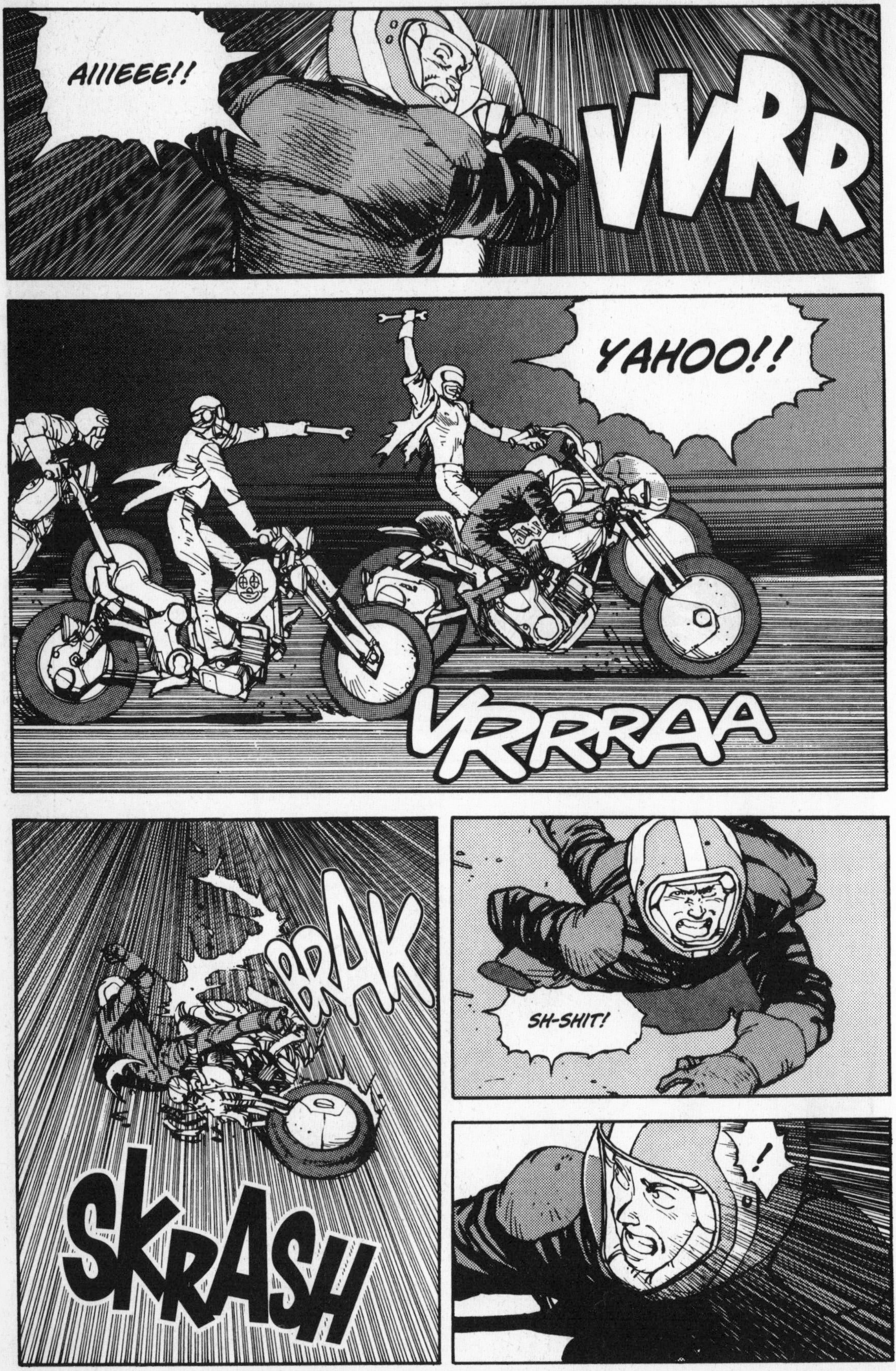
AIIIEEE!!
VVRR
YAHOO!!
VRRRAA
BRAK
SKRASH
SH-SHIT!
!

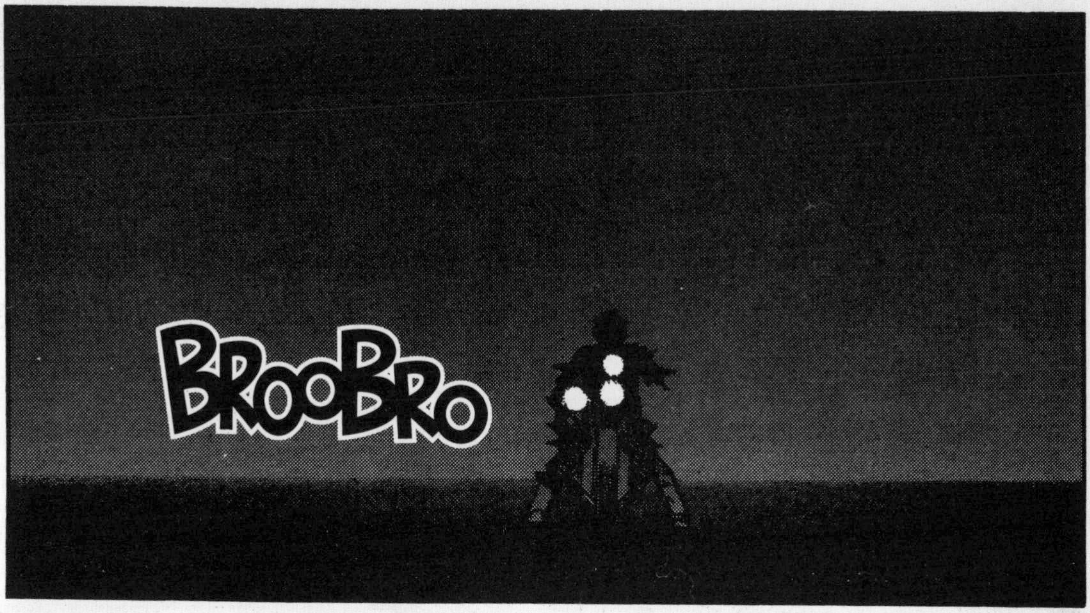
BROOBRO

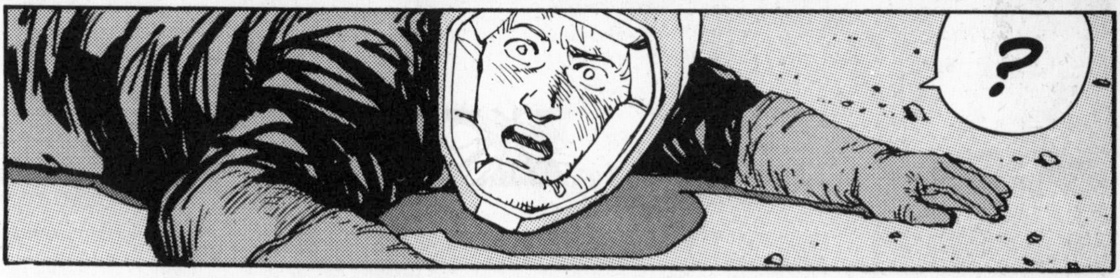
?

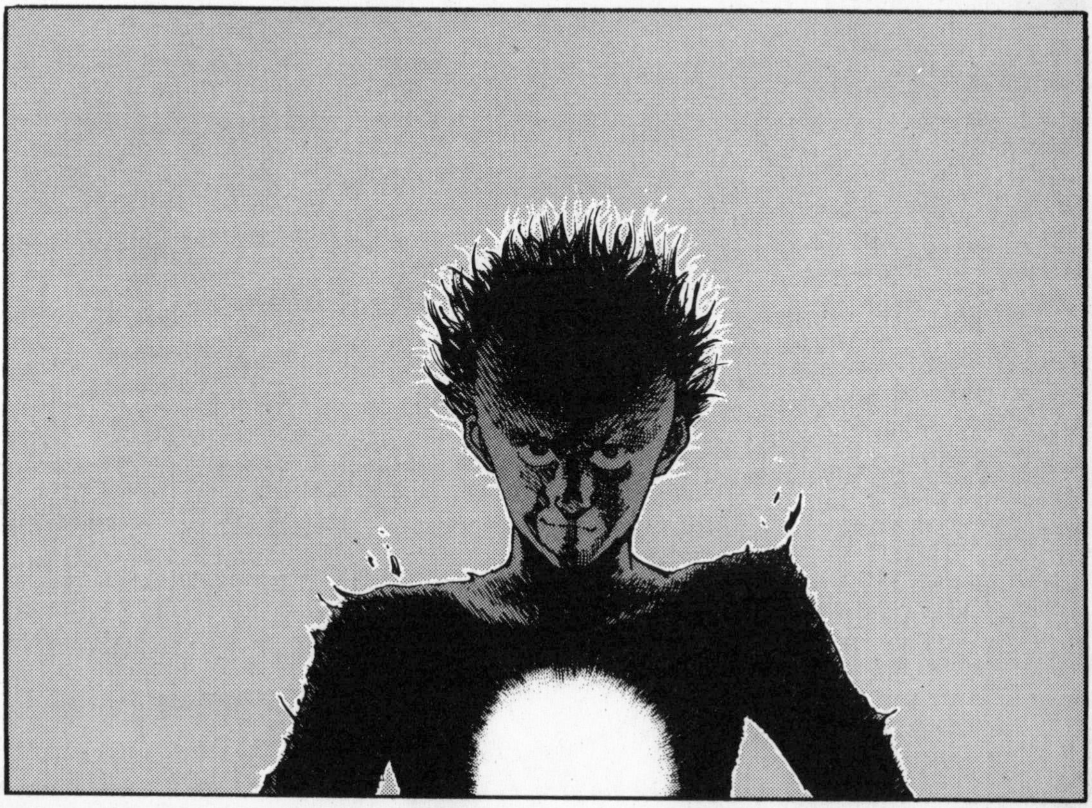

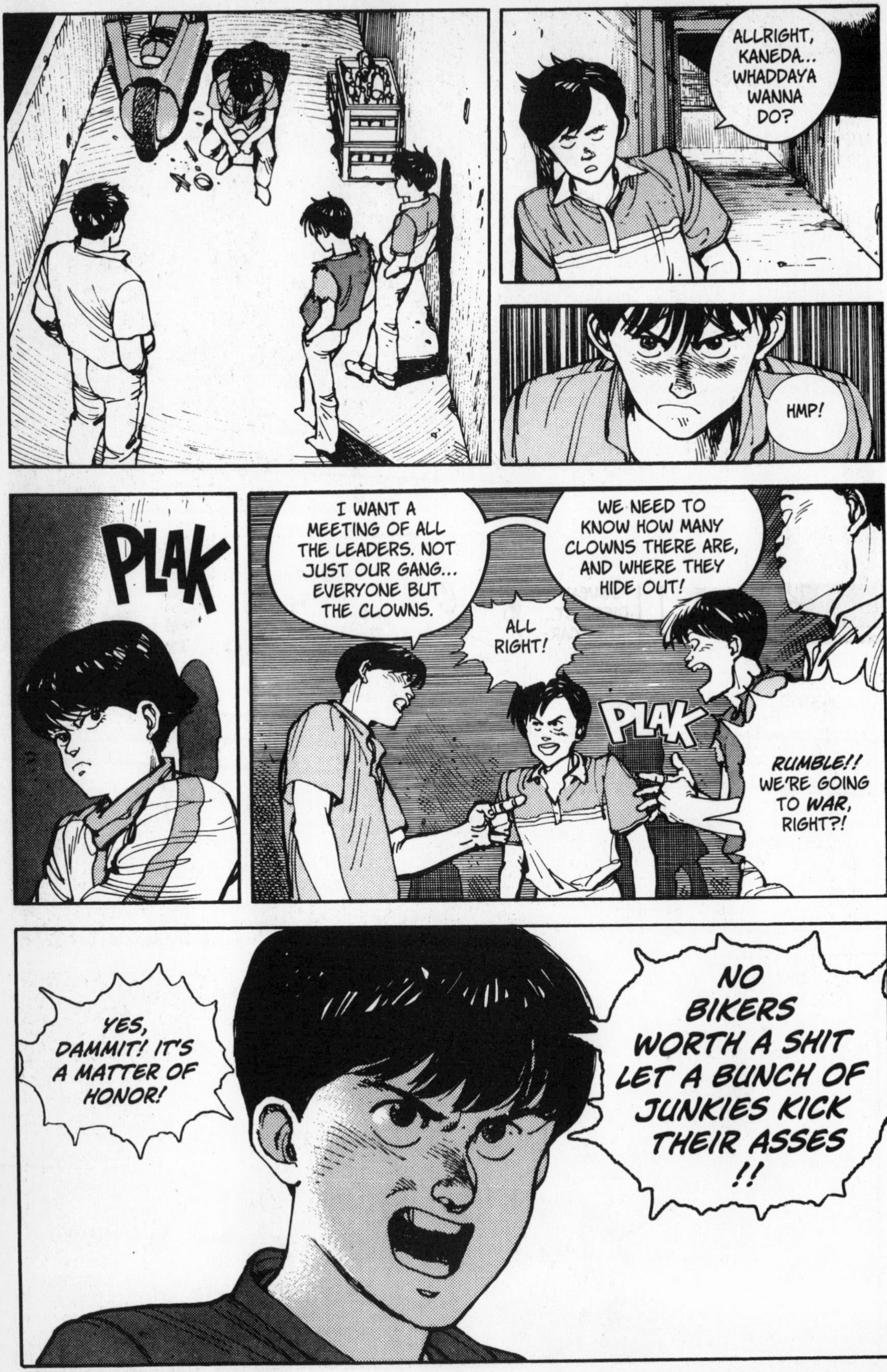
ALLRIGHT, KANEDA... WHADDAYA WANNA DO?
HMP!
PLAK
I WANT A MEETING OF ALL THE LEADERS. NOT JUST OUR GANG... EVERYONE BUT THE CLOWNS.
WE NEED TO KNOW HOW MANY CLOWNS THERE ARE, AND WHERE THEY HIDE OUT!
ALL RIGHT!
PLAK
RUMBLE!! WE'RE GOING TO WAR, RIGHT?!
YES, DAMMIT! IT'S A MATTER OF HONOR!
NO BIKERS WORTH A SHIT LET A BUNCH OF JUNKIES KICK THEIR ASSES !!

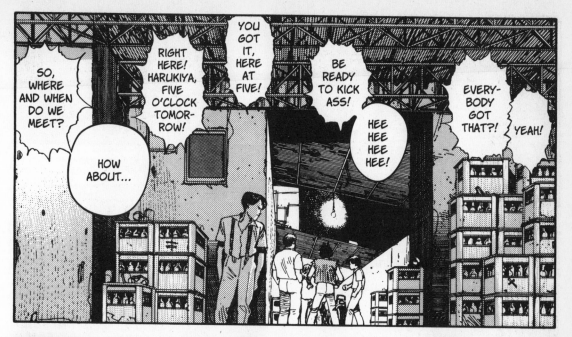

SO, WHERE AND WHEN DO WE MEET?

HOW ABOUT...

RIGHT HERE! HARUKIYA, FIVE O'CLOCK TOMORROW!

YOU GOT IT, HERE AT FIVE!

BE READY TO KICK ASS!

HEE HEE HEE HEE!

EVERY-BODY GOT THAT?!

YEAH!

SO WHERE DO WE BEGIN?

POF

I'LL TAKE THE SEVENTH DISTRICT... THE CARBURETOR BOYS!

TAP TAP TAP TAP

I CAN TALK TO MY CONTACTS IN THE WILD COCKS AND THE PRETTY BOMBERS.

REMEMBER, TOMORROW AT FIVE!

DON'T CATCH YOUR NUTS IN A VISE!

THEY CERTAINLY THINK A LOT OF YOU.

WELL...I'M A POPULAR KIND OF GUY.

YOU'RE NOT ACTUALLY PLANNING ON GOING THROUGH WITH IT, ARE YOU?

I'M GONNA GIVE THIS FIGHT EVERYTHING I'VE GOT!

BUT...

YOU BUTT-HEAD!!

HAVE YOU FORGOTTEN THAT YOU AND I ARE FUGITIVES?!

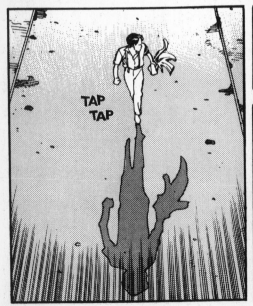

TAP TAP

HMM...

...
...
....

264

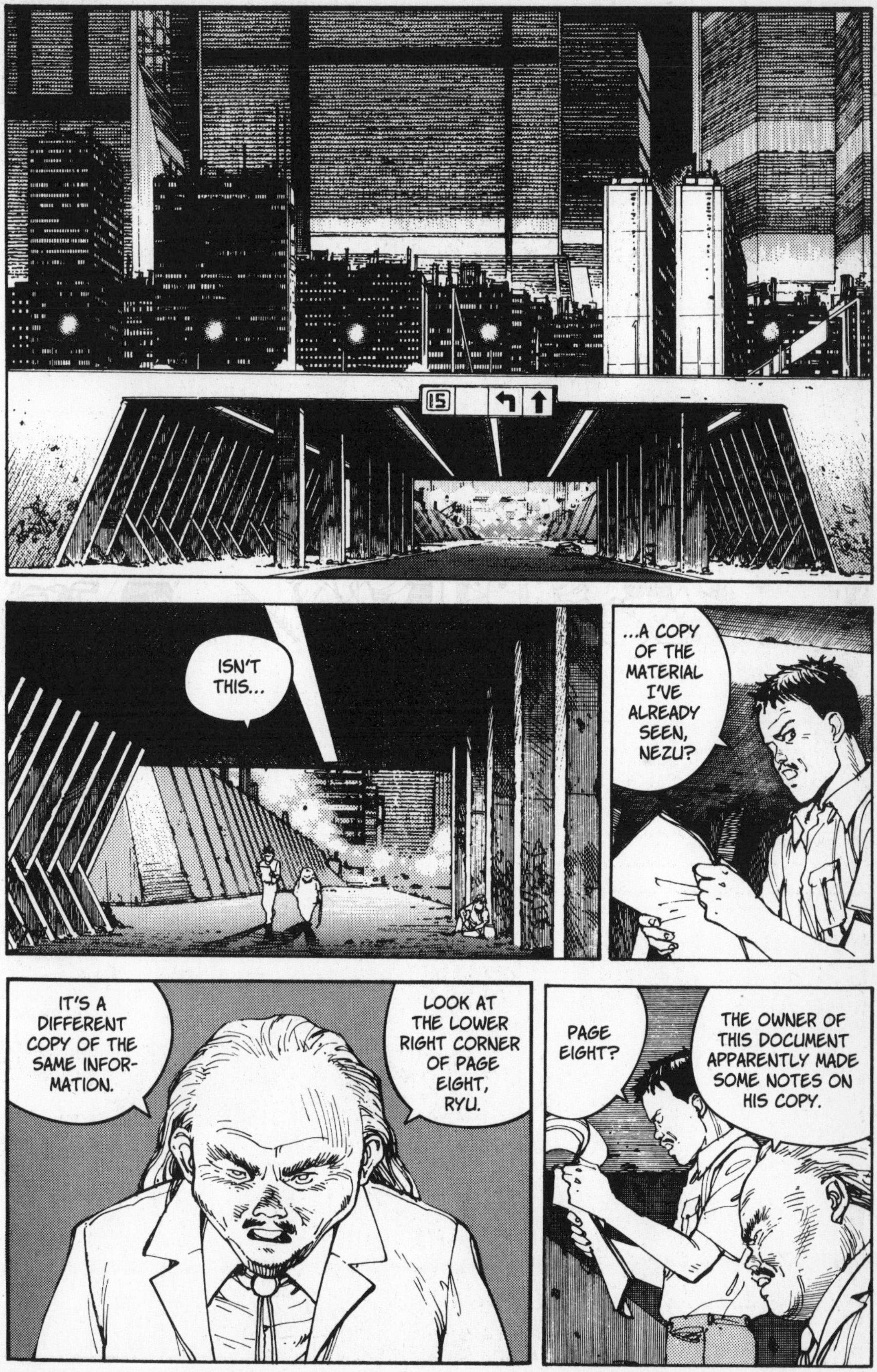
15
ISN'T THIS...
...A COPY OF THE MATERIAL I'VE ALREADY SEEN, NEZU?
IT'S A DIFFERENT COPY OF THE SAME INFORMATION.
LOOK AT THE LOWER RIGHT CORNER OF PAGE EIGHT, RYU.
PAGE EIGHT?
THE OWNER OF THIS DOCUMENT APPARENTLY MADE SOME NOTES ON HIS COPY.

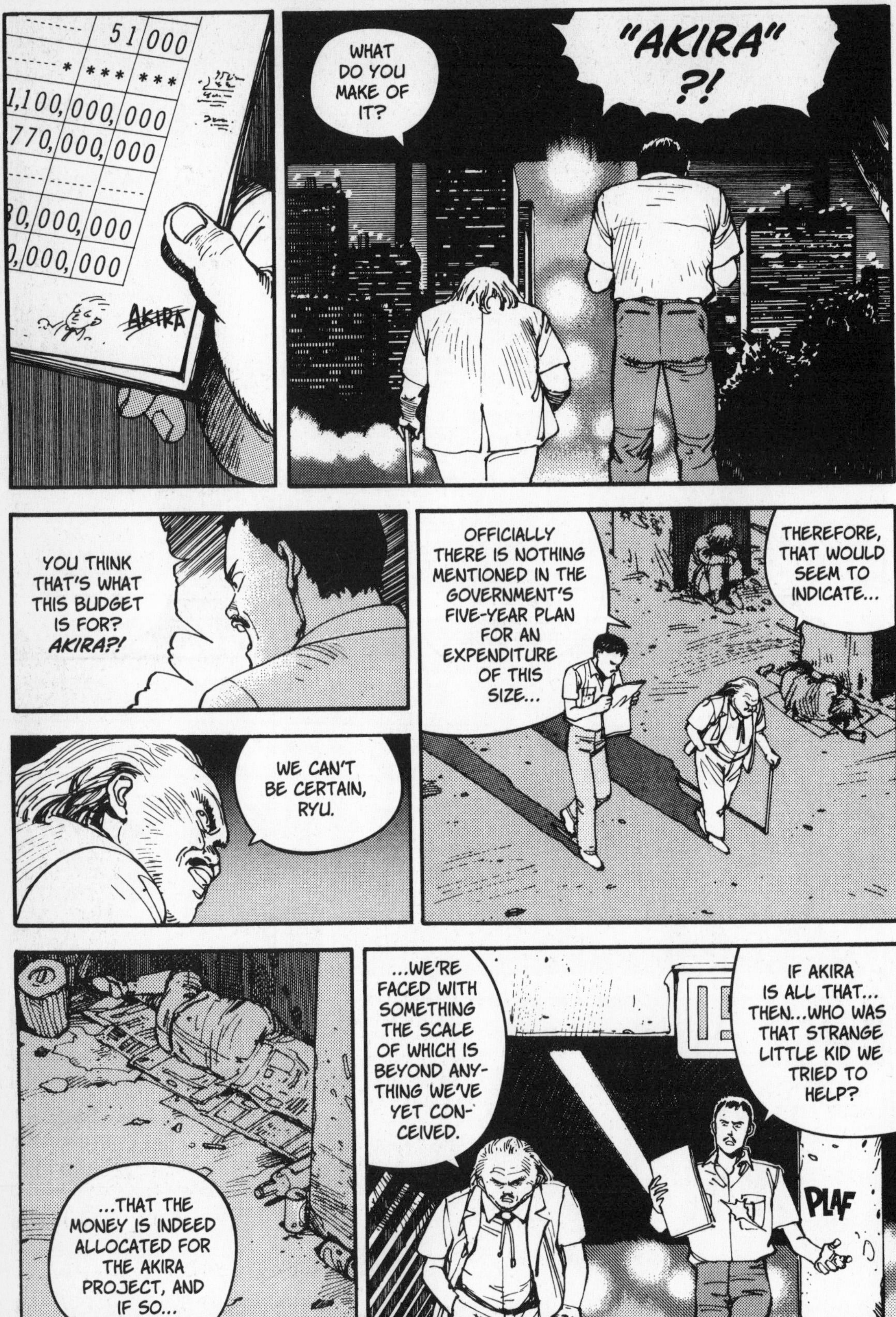

51 000
1,100,000,000
770,000,000
AKIRA
WHAT DO YOU MAKE OF IT?
"AKIRA" ?!
YOU THINK THAT'S WHAT THIS BUDGET IS FOR? *AKIRA?!*
WE CAN'T BE CERTAIN, RYU.
OFFICIALLY THERE IS NOTHING MENTIONED IN THE GOVERNMENT'S FIVE-YEAR PLAN FOR AN EXPENDITURE OF THIS SIZE...
THEREFORE, THAT WOULD SEEM TO INDICATE...
...THAT THE MONEY IS INDEED ALLOCATED FOR THE AKIRA PROJECT, AND IF SO...
...WE'RE FACED WITH SOMETHING THE SCALE OF WHICH IS BEYOND ANY-THING WE'VE YET CON-CEIVED.
IF AKIRA IS ALL THAT... THEN...WHO WAS THAT STRANGE LITTLE KID WE TRIED TO HELP?
PLAF

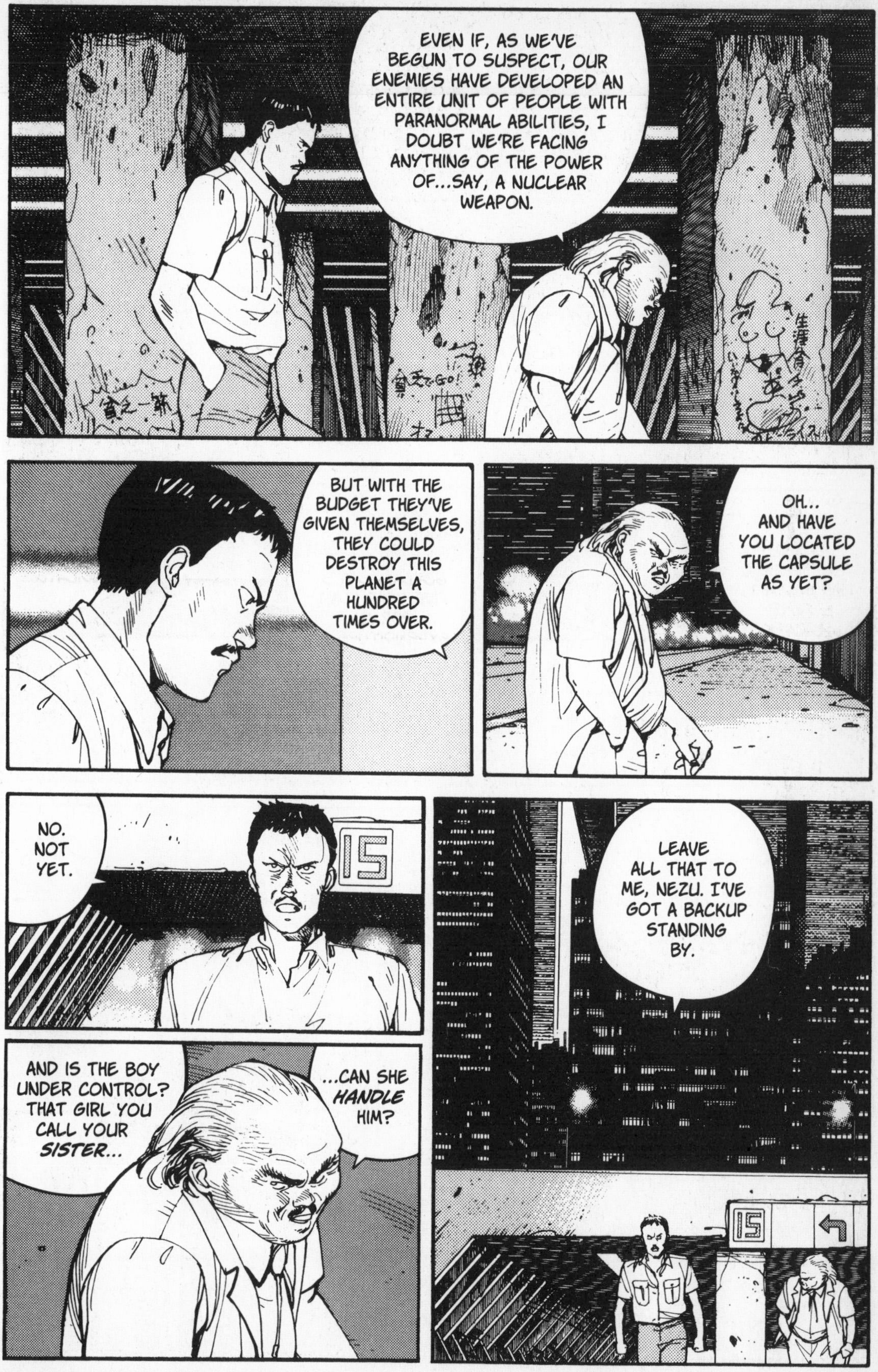
EVEN IF, AS WE'VE BEGUN TO SUSPECT, OUR ENEMIES HAVE DEVELOPED AN ENTIRE UNIT OF PEOPLE WITH PARANORMAL ABILITIES, I DOUBT WE'RE FACING ANYTHING OF THE POWER OF...SAY, A NUCLEAR WEAPON.
BUT WITH THE BUDGET THEY'VE GIVEN THEMSELVES, THEY COULD DESTROY THIS PLANET A HUNDRED TIMES OVER.
OH... AND HAVE YOU LOCATED THE CAPSULE AS YET?
NO. NOT YET.
AND IS THE BOY UNDER CONTROL? THAT GIRL YOU CALL YOUR *SISTER*...
...CAN SHE *HANDLE* HIM?
LEAVE ALL THAT TO ME, NEZU. I'VE GOT A BACKUP STANDING BY.

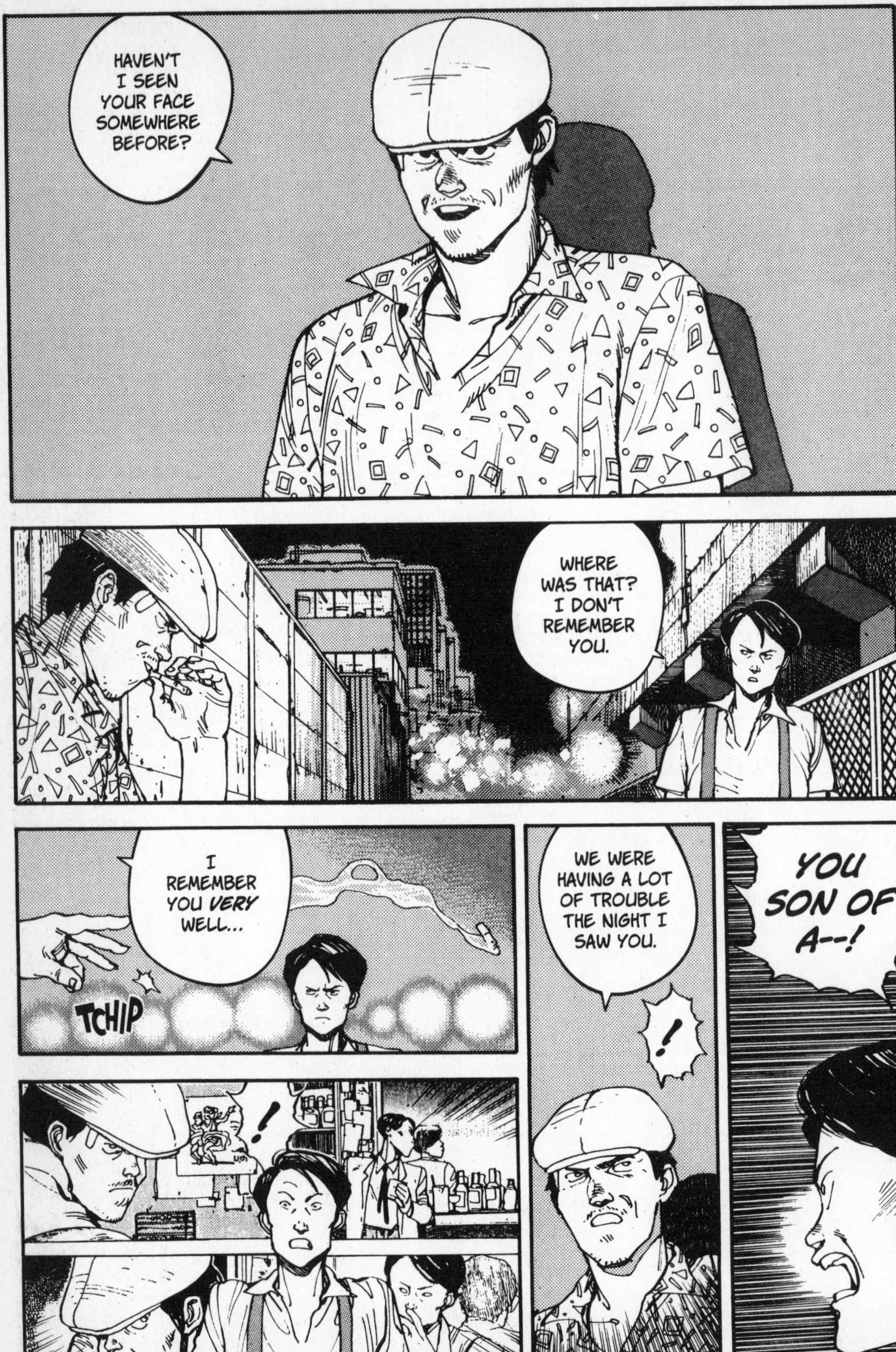
HAVEN'T I SEEN YOUR FACE SOMEWHERE BEFORE?
WHERE WAS THAT? I DON'T REMEMBER YOU.
I REMEMBER YOU *VERY* WELL...
TCHIP
!
WE WERE HAVING A LOT OF TROUBLE THE NIGHT I SAW YOU.
!
YOU SON OF A--!

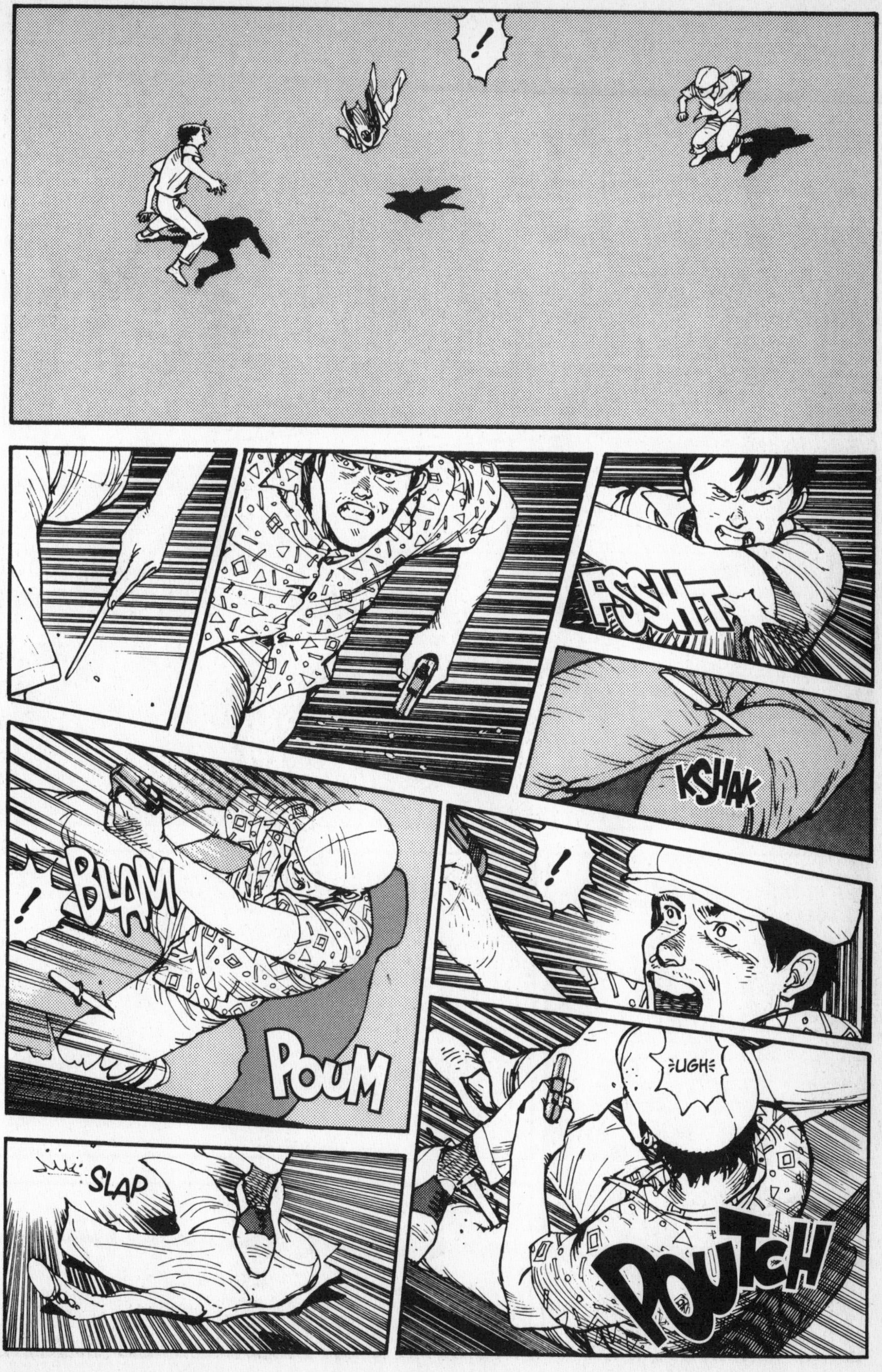
!
FSSHT
KSHAK
!
BLAM
POUM
!
SLAP
UGH
POUTCH

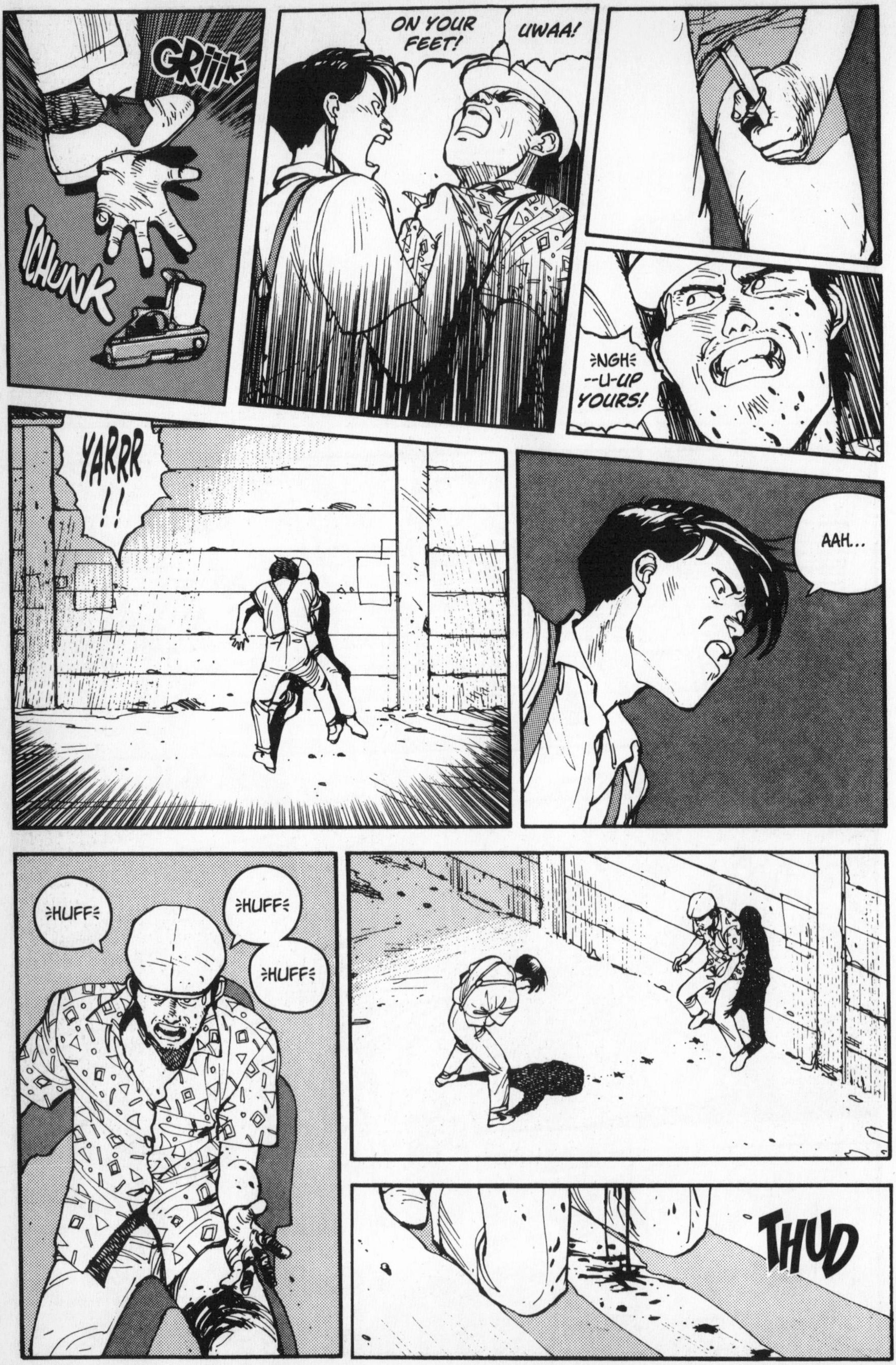
GRiiik
THUNK
ON YOUR FEET!
UWAA!
NGH --U-UP YOURS!
YARRR !!
AAH...
HUFF
HUFF
HUFF
THUD

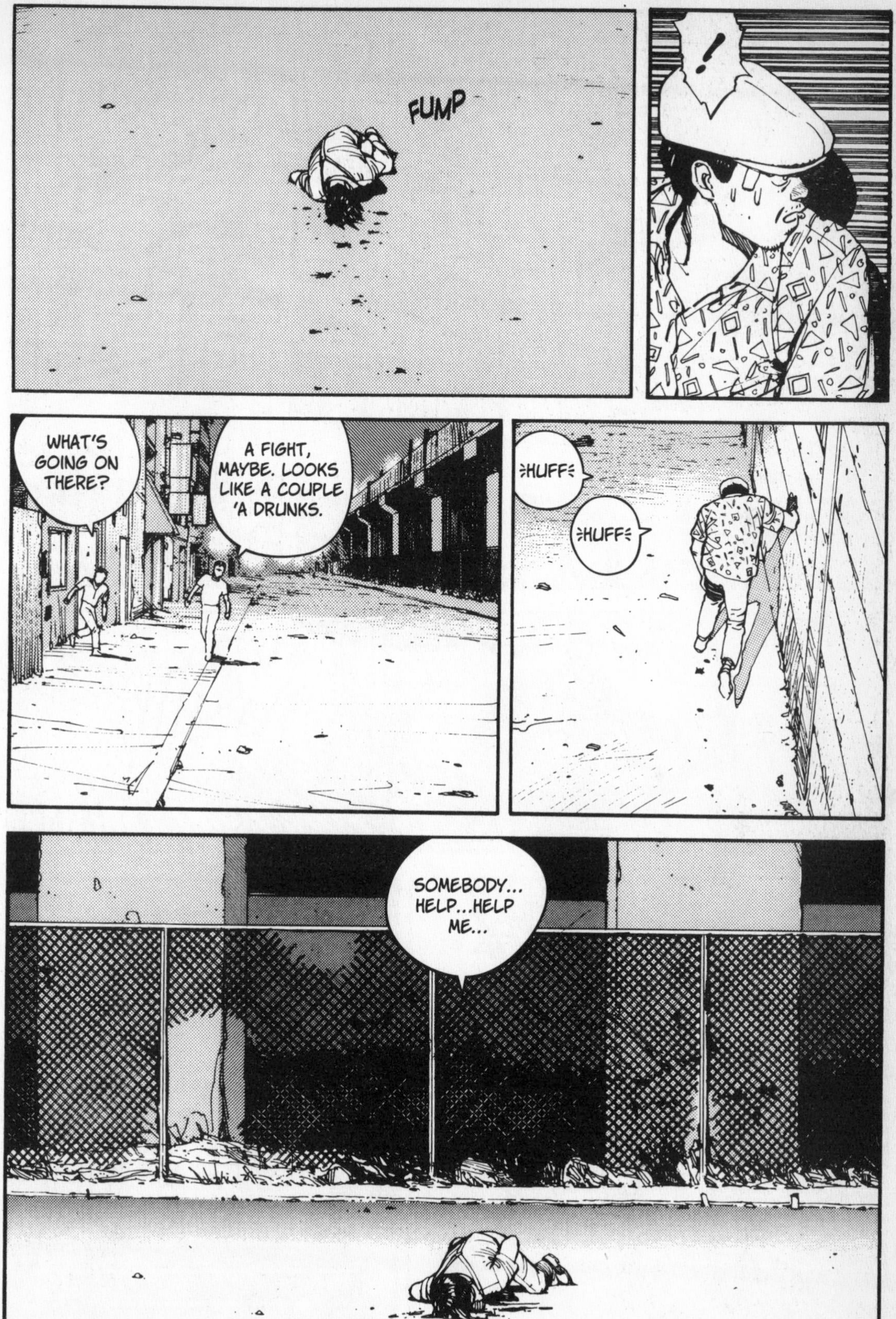
FUMP
!
WHAT'S GOING ON THERE?
A FIGHT, MAYBE. LOOKS LIKE A COUPLE 'A DRUNKS.
HUFF
HUFF
SOMEBODY... HELP...HELP ME...

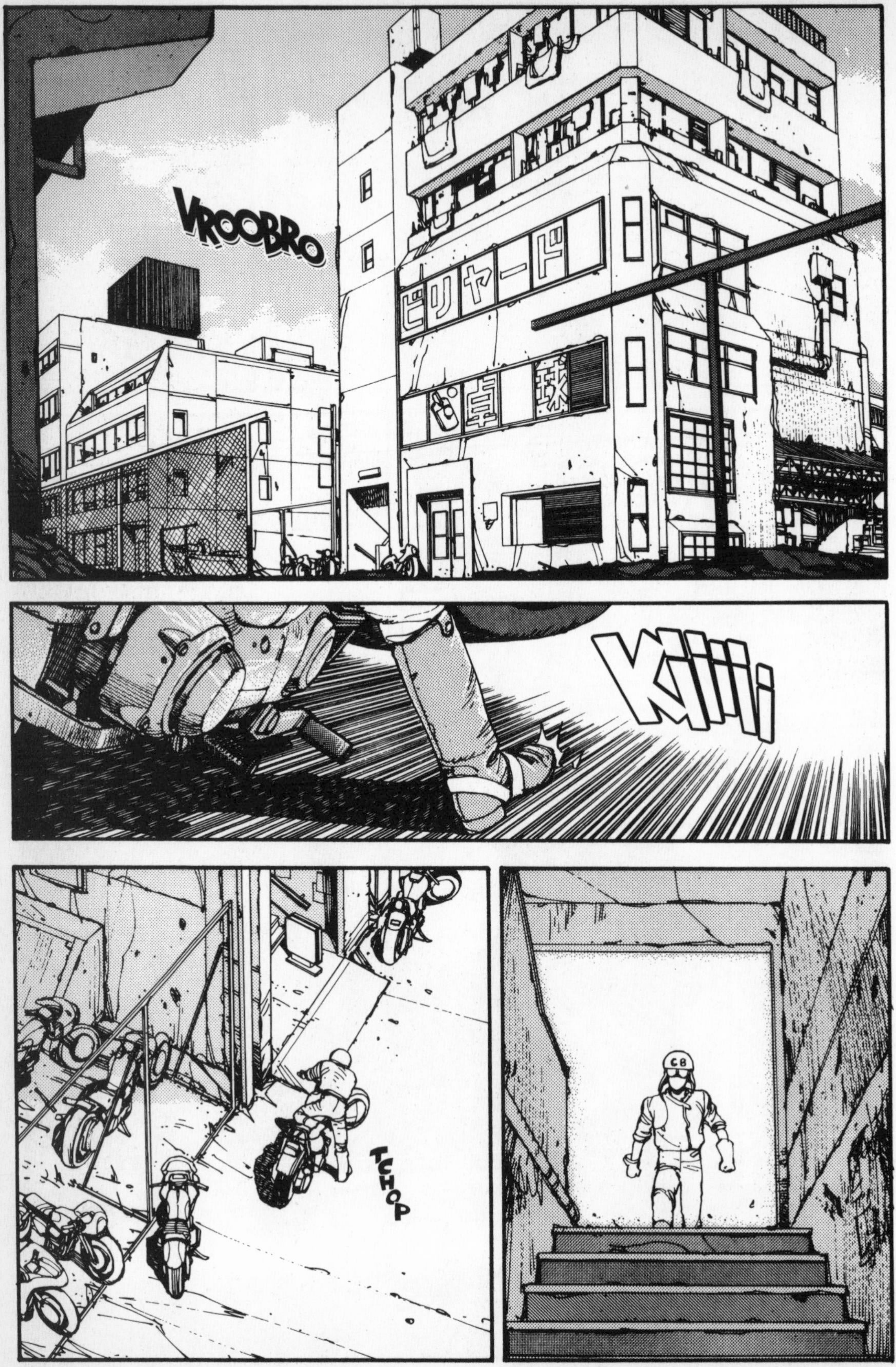
VROOBRO
ビリヤード
卓
球
Kiiiii
TCHOP
CB

IF THAT'S EVERYBODY, LET'S GET STARTED.

HEY! I'M RUNNING A BUSINESS. YOU'RE NOT PLANNING ON TURNING THIS PLACE INTO A MEETING HALL, ARE YOU?

WE'LL BE OUT OF HERE BEFORE YOU KNOW IT.

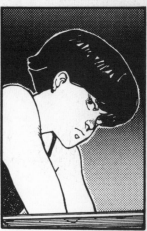

WE WANT THEM TO RUN ALONG THE ROUTE WE'VE LAID OUT, STRAIGHT TO PIER TWELVE.

ALONG THE WAY, YOU GUYS WILL BE PICKING OFF ALL THE WEAKER ONES.

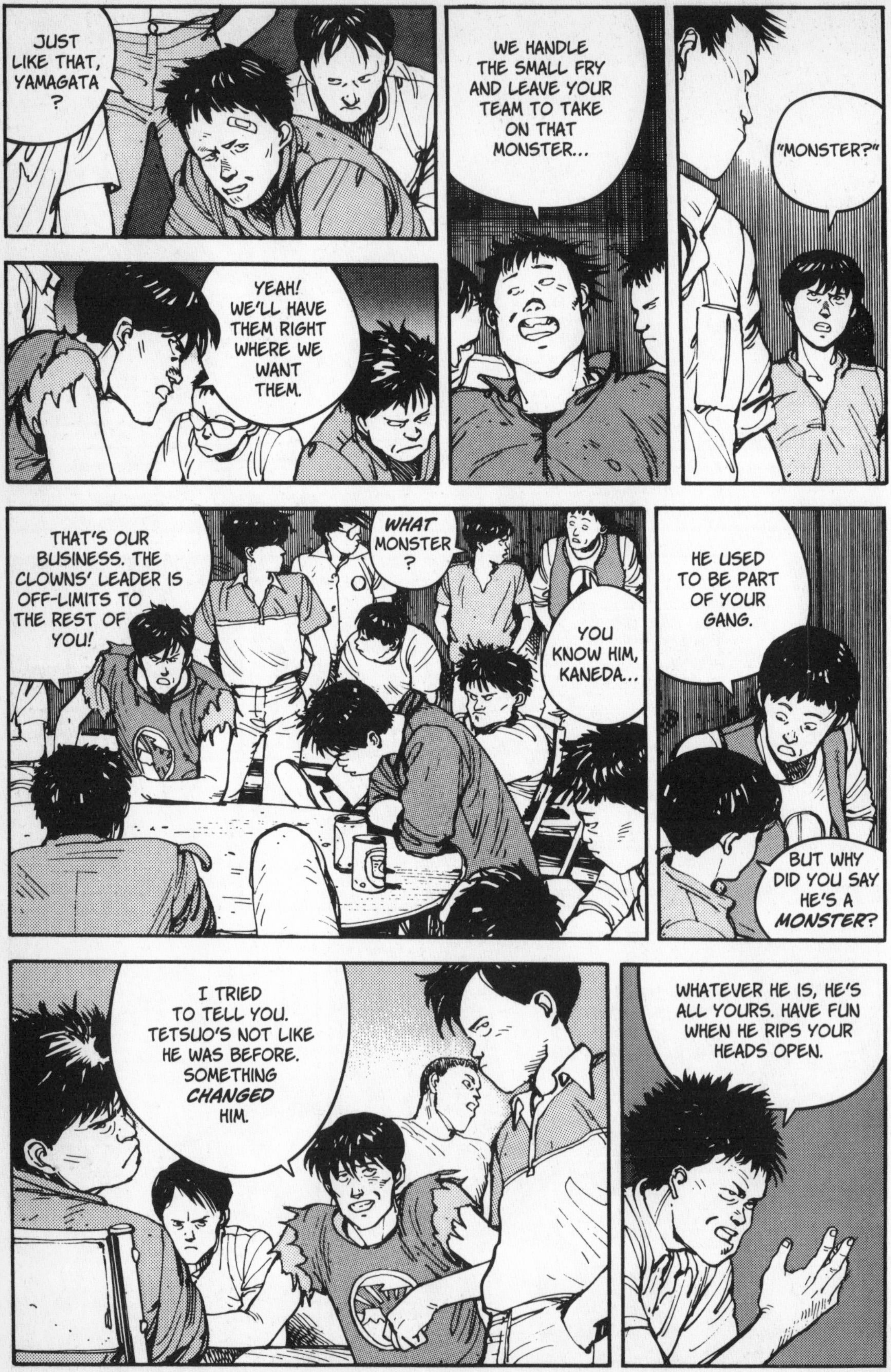
JUST LIKE THAT, YAMAGATA ?
YEAH! WE'LL HAVE THEM RIGHT WHERE WE WANT THEM.
WE HANDLE THE SMALL FRY AND LEAVE YOUR TEAM TO TAKE ON THAT MONSTER...
"MONSTER?"
THAT'S OUR BUSINESS. THE CLOWNS' LEADER IS OFF-LIMITS TO THE REST OF YOU!
WHAT MONSTER ?
YOU KNOW HIM, KANEDA...
HE USED TO BE PART OF YOUR GANG.
BUT WHY DID YOU SAY HE'S A *MONSTER*?
I TRIED TO TELL YOU. TETSUO'S NOT LIKE HE WAS BEFORE. SOMETHING *CHANGED* HIM.
WHATEVER HE IS, HE'S ALL YOURS. HAVE FUN WHEN HE RIPS YOUR HEADS OPEN.

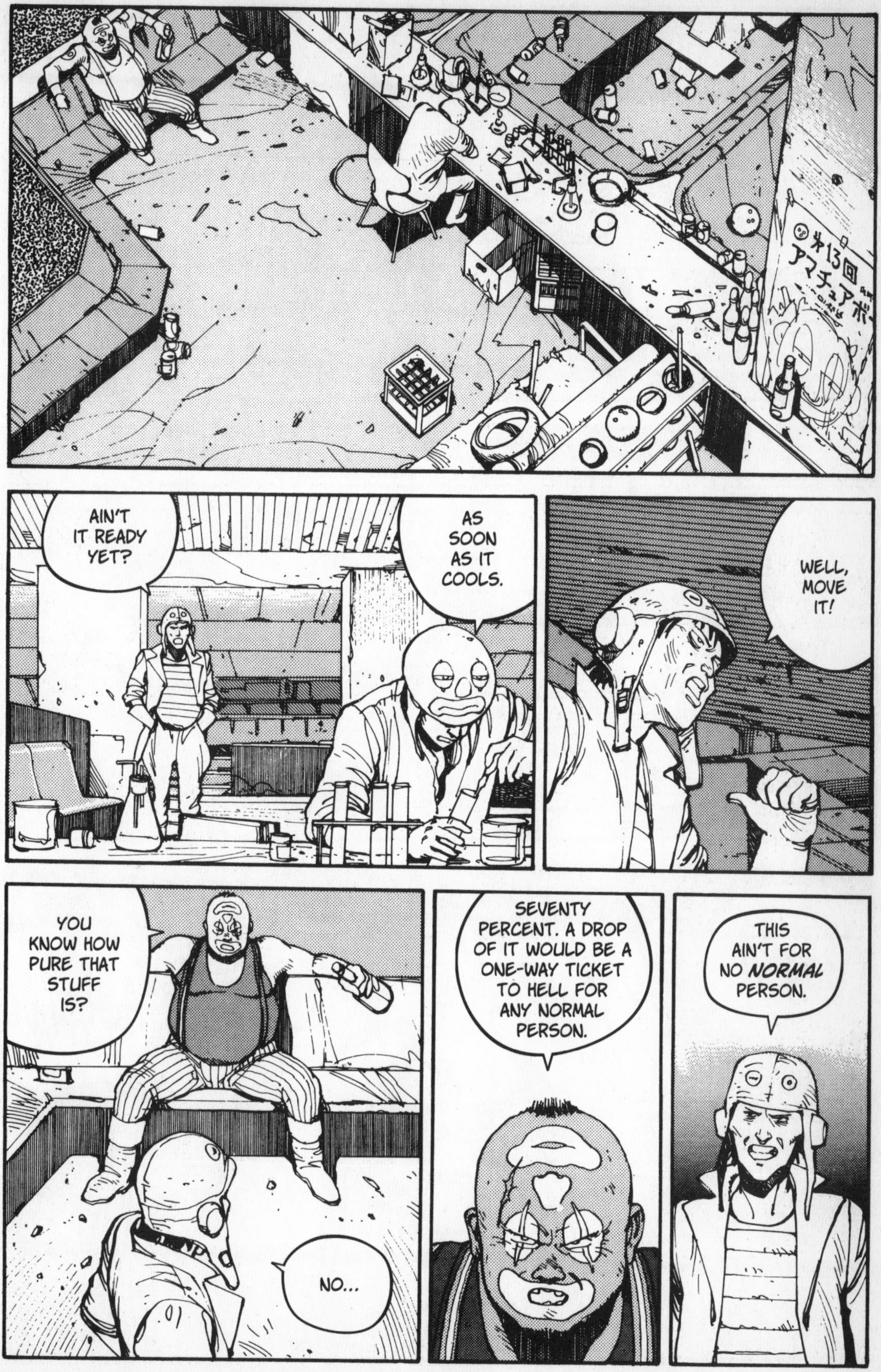
第13回
アマチュアボ
AIN'T IT READY YET?
AS SOON AS IT COOLS.
WELL, MOVE IT!
YOU KNOW HOW PURE THAT STUFF IS?
NO...
SEVENTY PERCENT. A DROP OF IT WOULD BE A ONE-WAY TICKET TO HELL FOR ANY NORMAL PERSON.
THIS AIN'T FOR NO ***NORMAL*** PERSON.

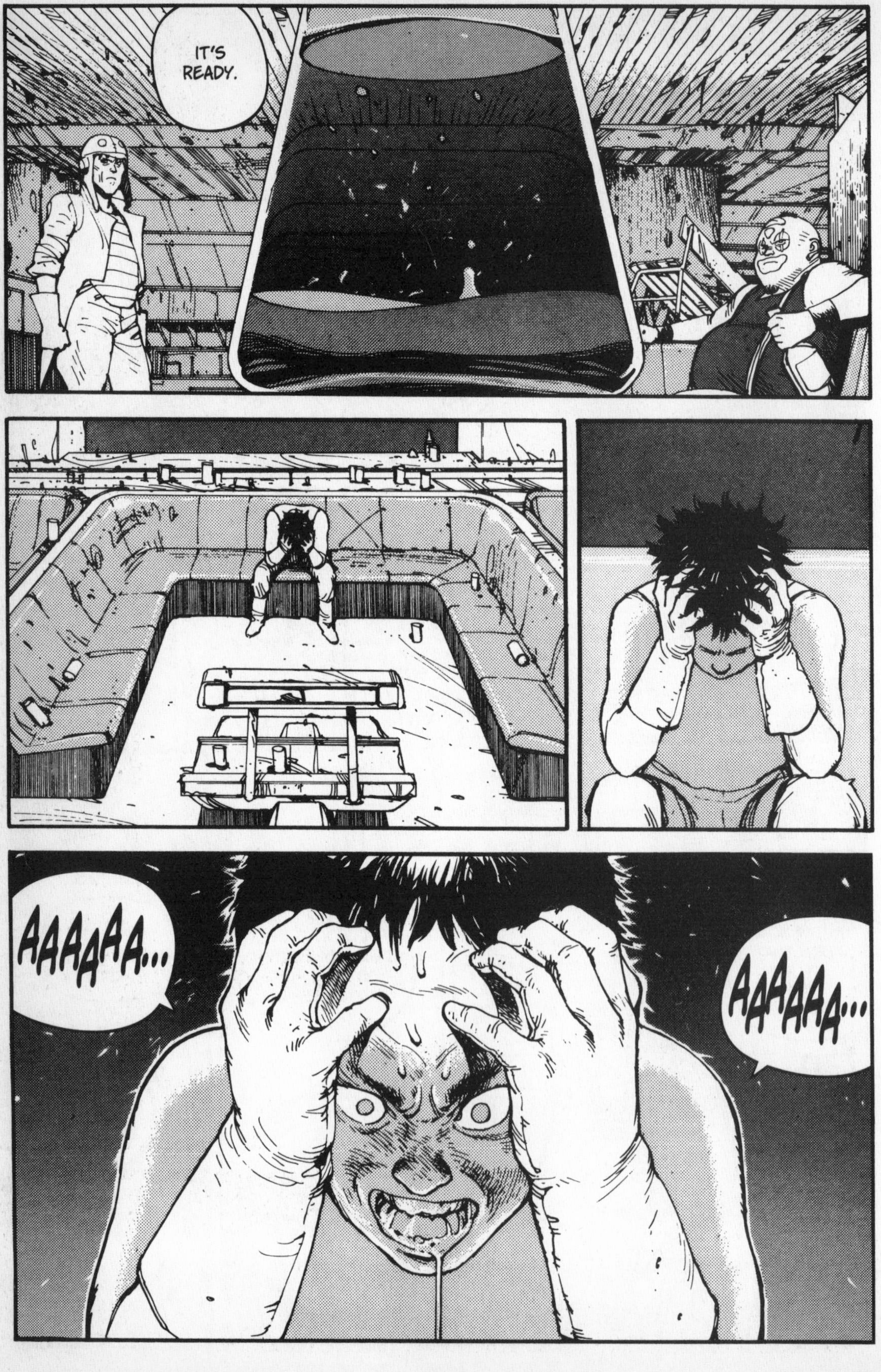

IT'S READY.
AAAAAA...
AAAAAA...

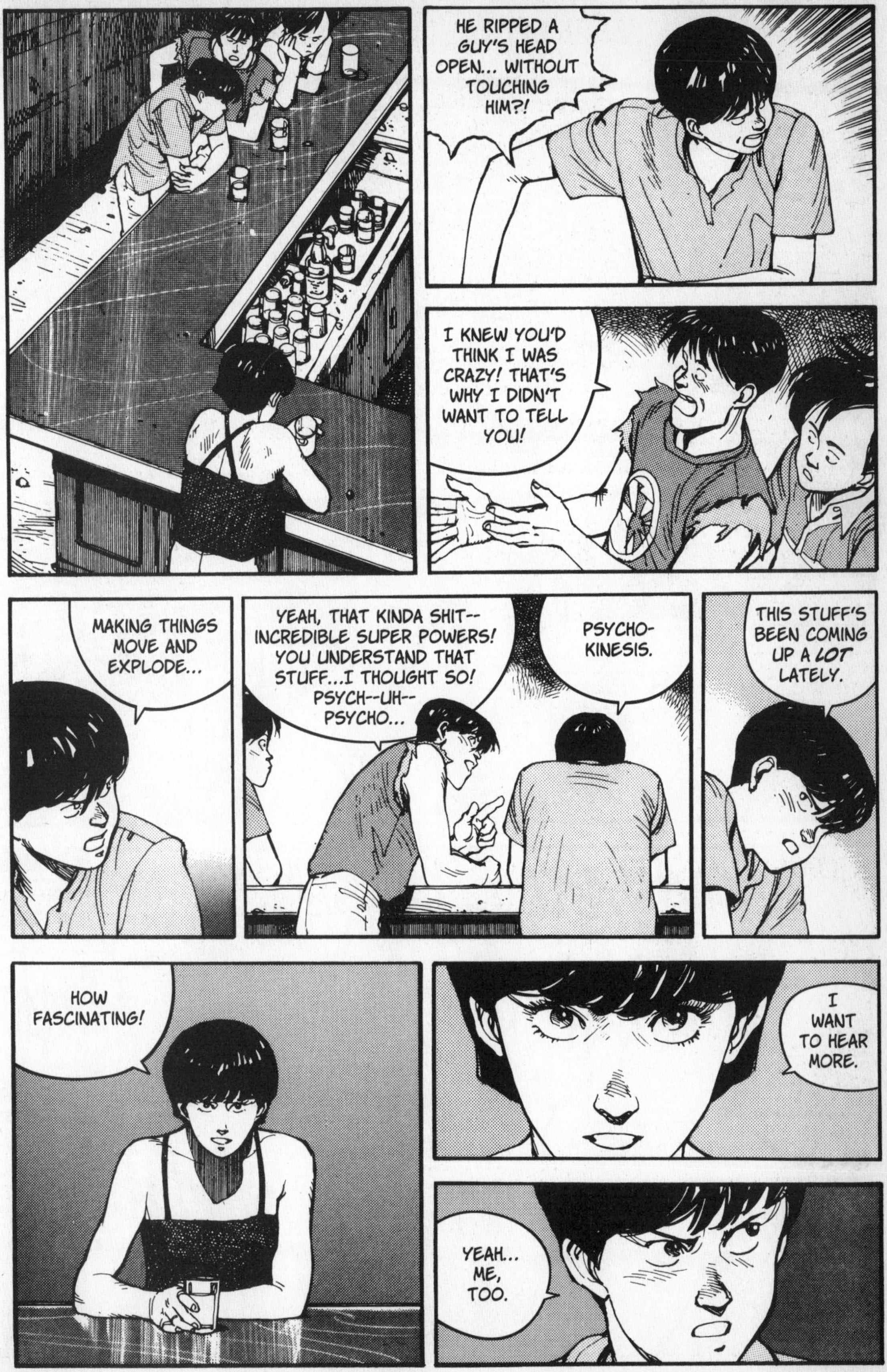
HE RIPPED A GUY'S HEAD OPEN... WITHOUT TOUCHING HIM?!
I KNEW YOU'D THINK I WAS CRAZY! THAT'S WHY I DIDN'T WANT TO TELL YOU!
MAKING THINGS MOVE AND EXPLODE...
YEAH, THAT KINDA SHIT--INCREDIBLE SUPER POWERS! YOU UNDERSTAND THAT STUFF...I THOUGHT SO! PSYCH--UH--PSYCHO...
PSYCHO-KINESIS.
THIS STUFF'S BEEN COMING UP A LOT LATELY.
HOW FASCINATING!
I WANT TO HEAR MORE.
YEAH... ME, TOO.

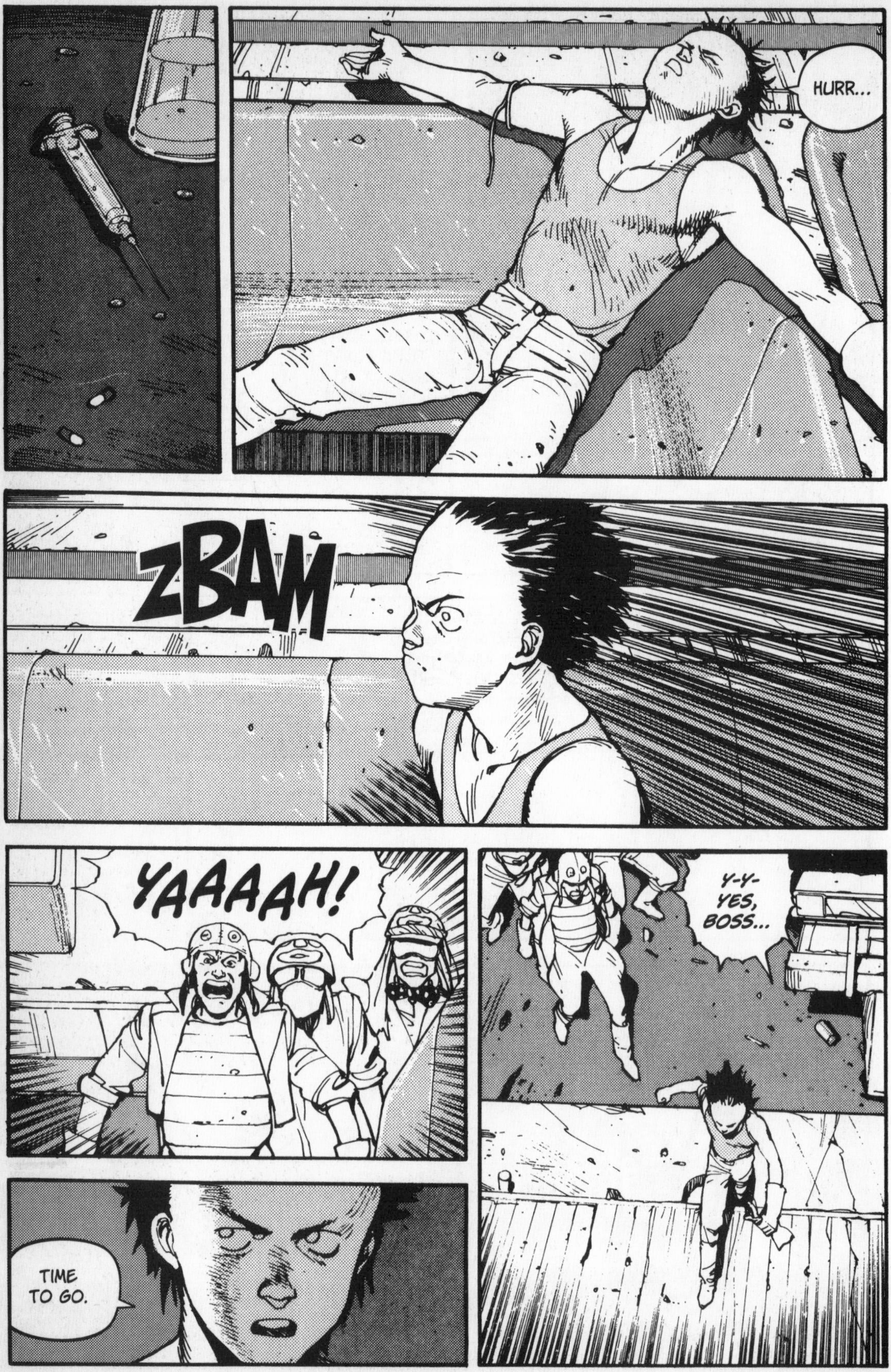
HURR...
ZBAM
YAAAAH!
Y-Y-YES, BOSS...
TIME TO GO.

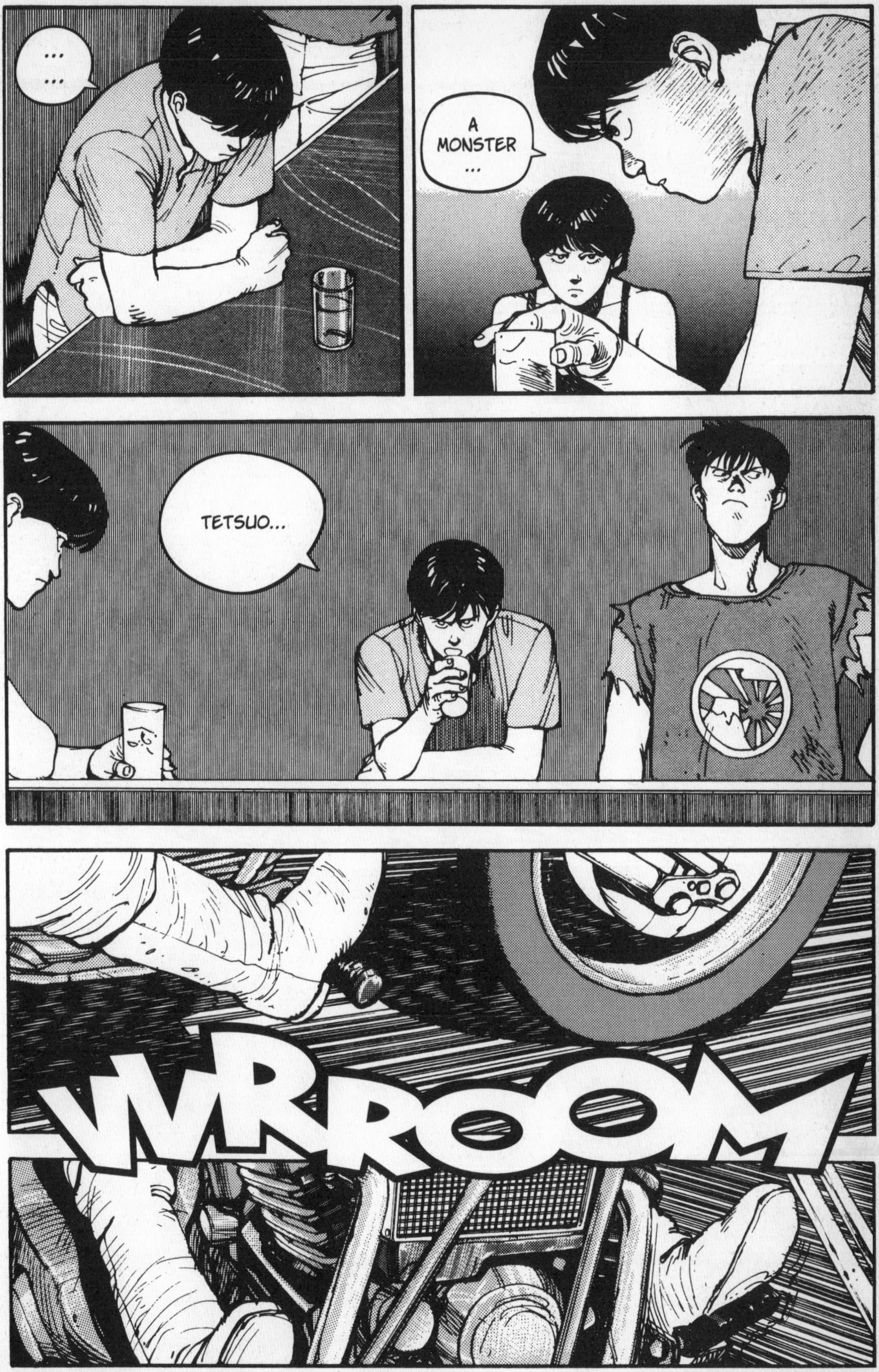
... ...
A MONSTER ...
TETSUO...
VVRROOM

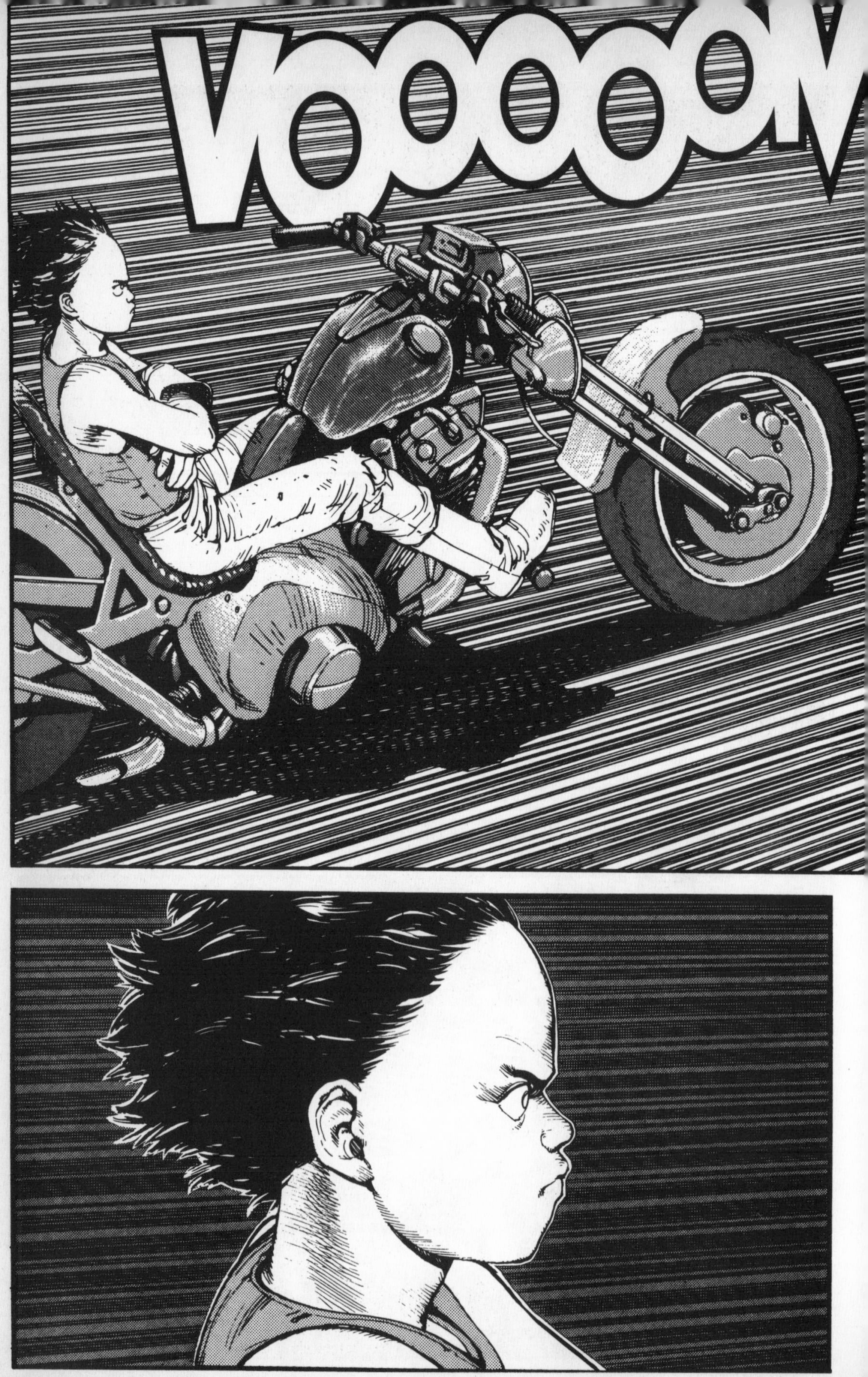
VOOOOOM

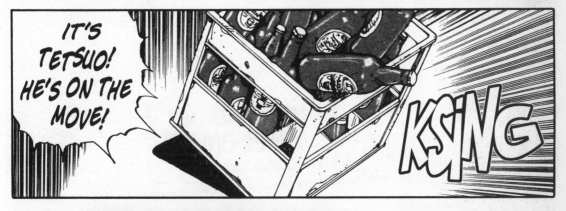

IT'S TETSUO! HE'S ON THE MOVE!

KSING

!

WAIT! I'M COMING TOO!!

HE ENTERED ROUTE SEVENTEEN IN THE BAY AREA TEN MINUTES AGO!

YOU MEAN UP NORTH?

YEAH, HEADING SOUTH. IF HE KEEPS ON THAT WAY, IT WILL BE PER-FECT!

LET'S GO!

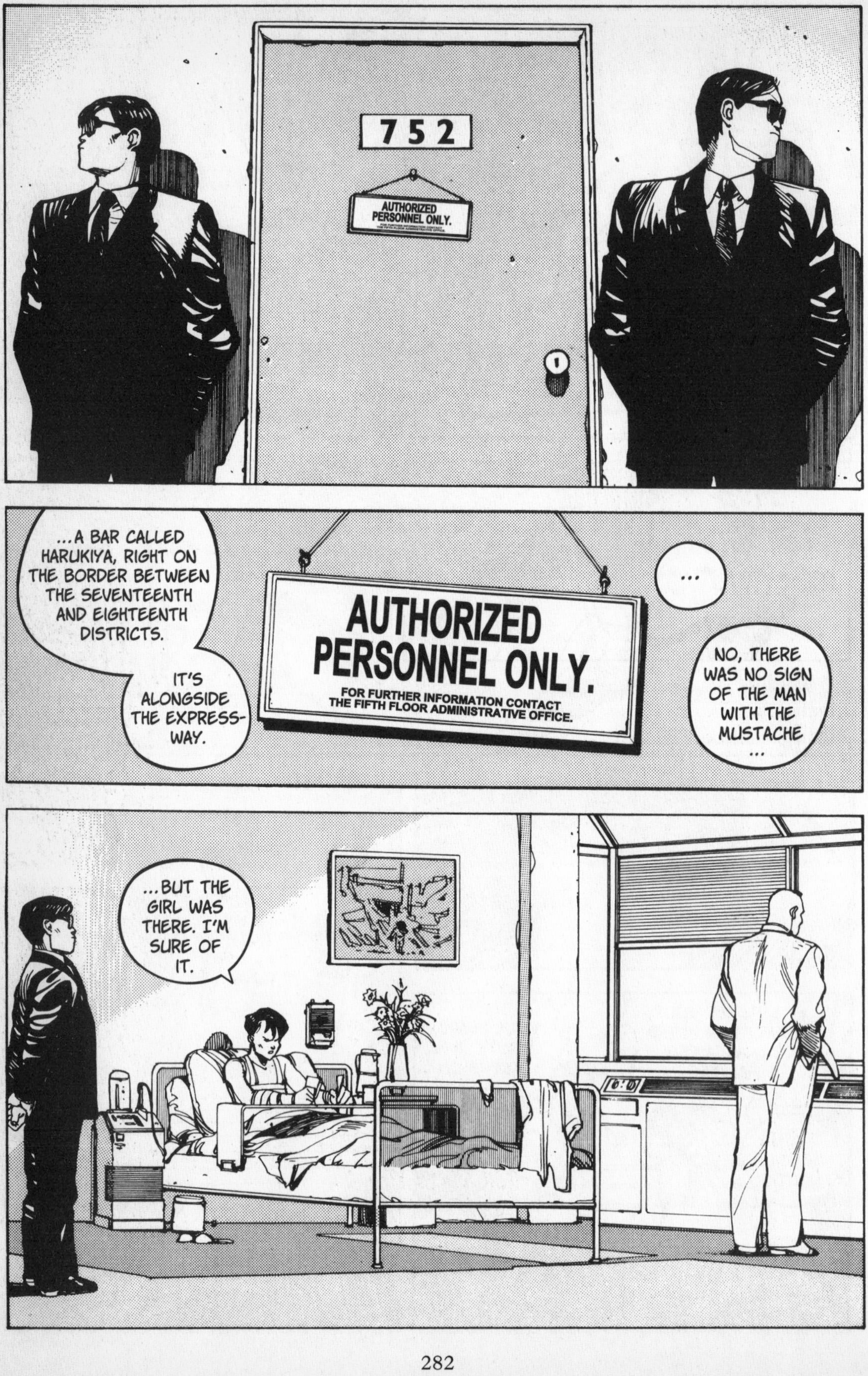
752
AUTHORIZED PERSONNEL ONLY.
...A BAR CALLED HARUKIYA, RIGHT ON THE BORDER BETWEEN THE SEVENTEENTH AND EIGHTEENTH DISTRICTS.
IT'S ALONGSIDE THE EXPRESS-WAY.
AUTHORIZED PERSONNEL ONLY.
FOR FURTHER INFORMATION CONTACT THE FIFTH FLOOR ADMINISTRATIVE OFFICE.
...
NO, THERE WAS NO SIGN OF THE MAN WITH THE MUSTACHE ...
...BUT THE GIRL WAS THERE. I'M SURE OF IT.

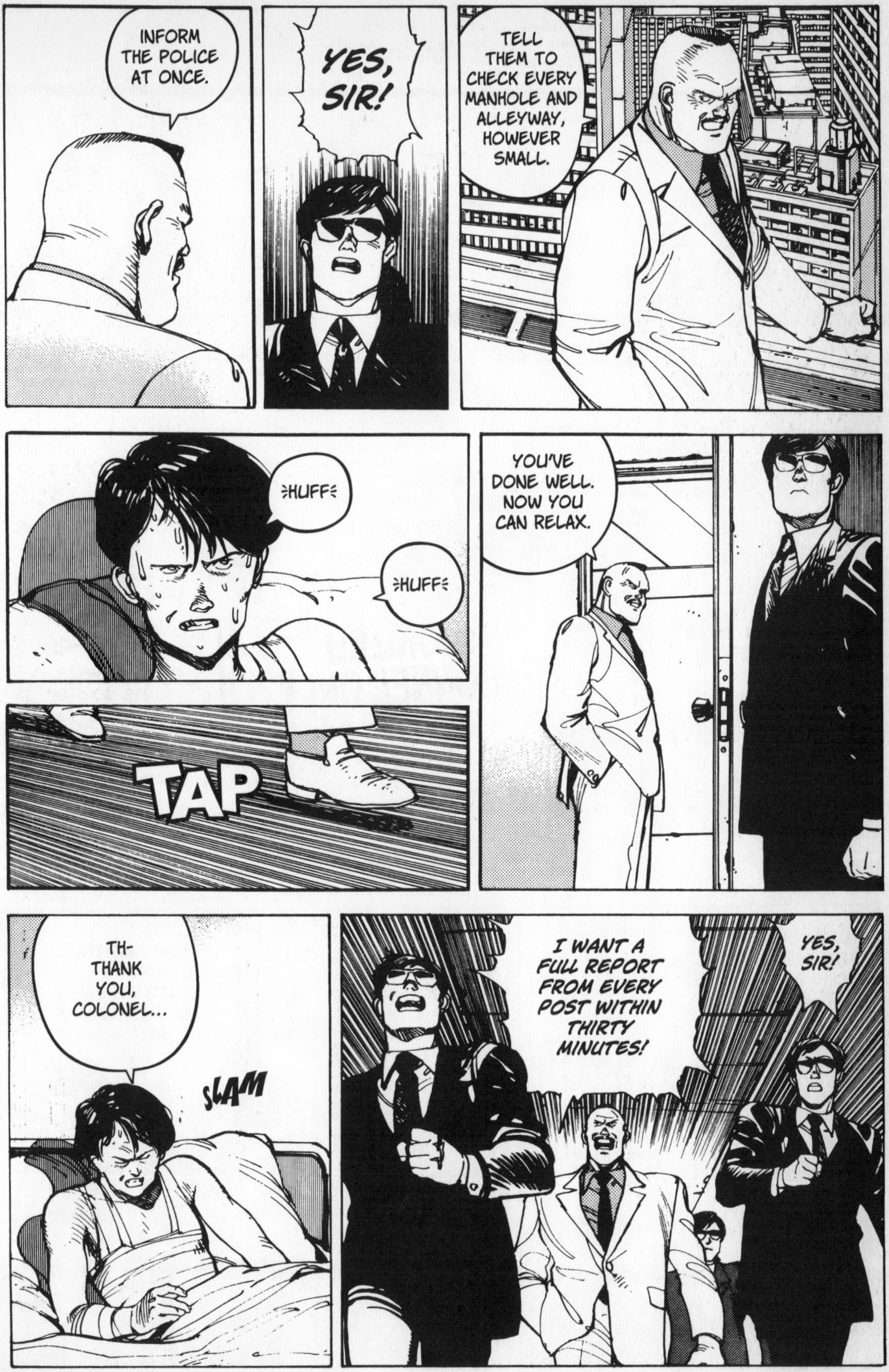

INFORM THE POLICE AT ONCE.
YES, SIR!
TELL THEM TO CHECK EVERY MANHOLE AND ALLEYWAY, HOWEVER SMALL.
HUFF
HUFF
TAP
YOU'VE DONE WELL. NOW YOU CAN RELAX.
TH-THANK YOU, COLONEL...
SLAM
I WANT A FULL REPORT FROM EVERY POST WITHIN THIRTY MINUTES!
YES, SIR!

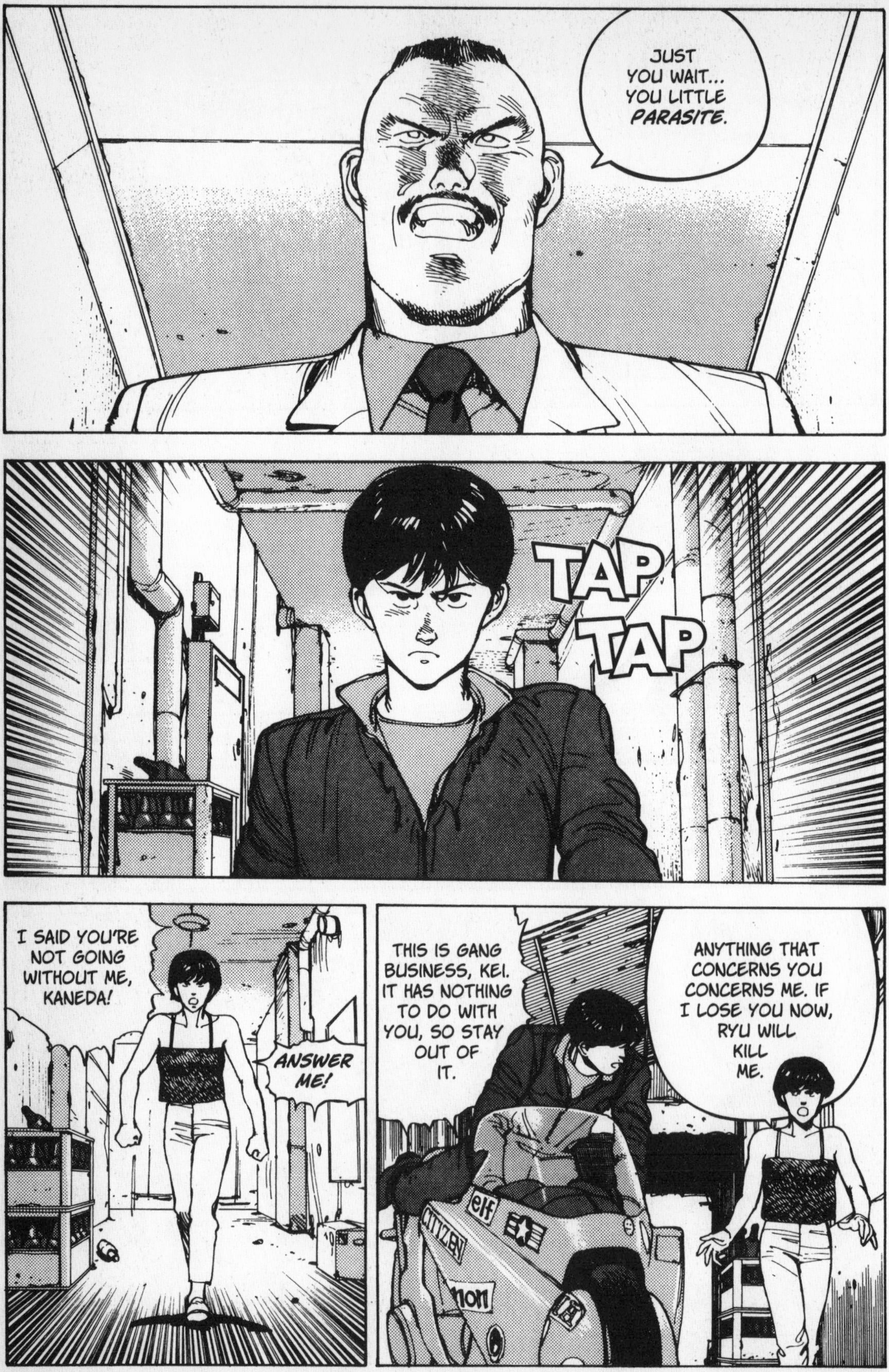
JUST YOU WAIT... YOU LITTLE *PARASITE*.
TAP
TAP
I SAID YOU'RE NOT GOING WITHOUT ME, KANEDA!
ANSWER ME!
THIS IS GANG BUSINESS, KEI. IT HAS NOTHING TO DO WITH YOU, SO STAY OUT OF IT.
ANYTHING THAT CONCERNS YOU CONCERNS ME. IF I LOSE YOU NOW, RYU WILL KILL ME.
elf
CITIZEN

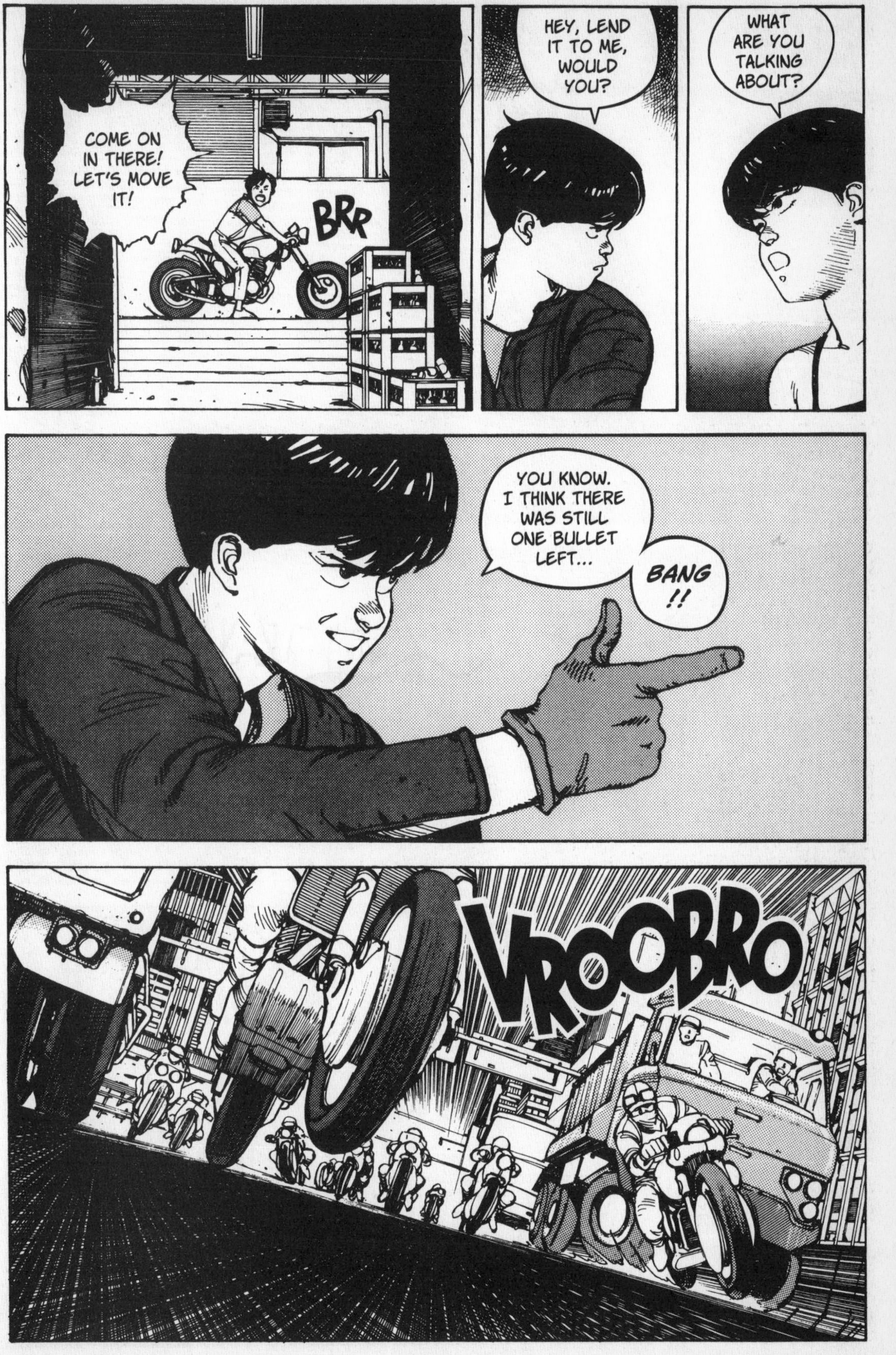
COME ON IN THERE! LET'S MOVE IT!
BRR
HEY, LEND IT TO ME, WOULD YOU?
WHAT ARE YOU TALKING ABOUT?
YOU KNOW. I THINK THERE WAS STILL ONE BULLET LEFT...
BANG !!
VROOBRO

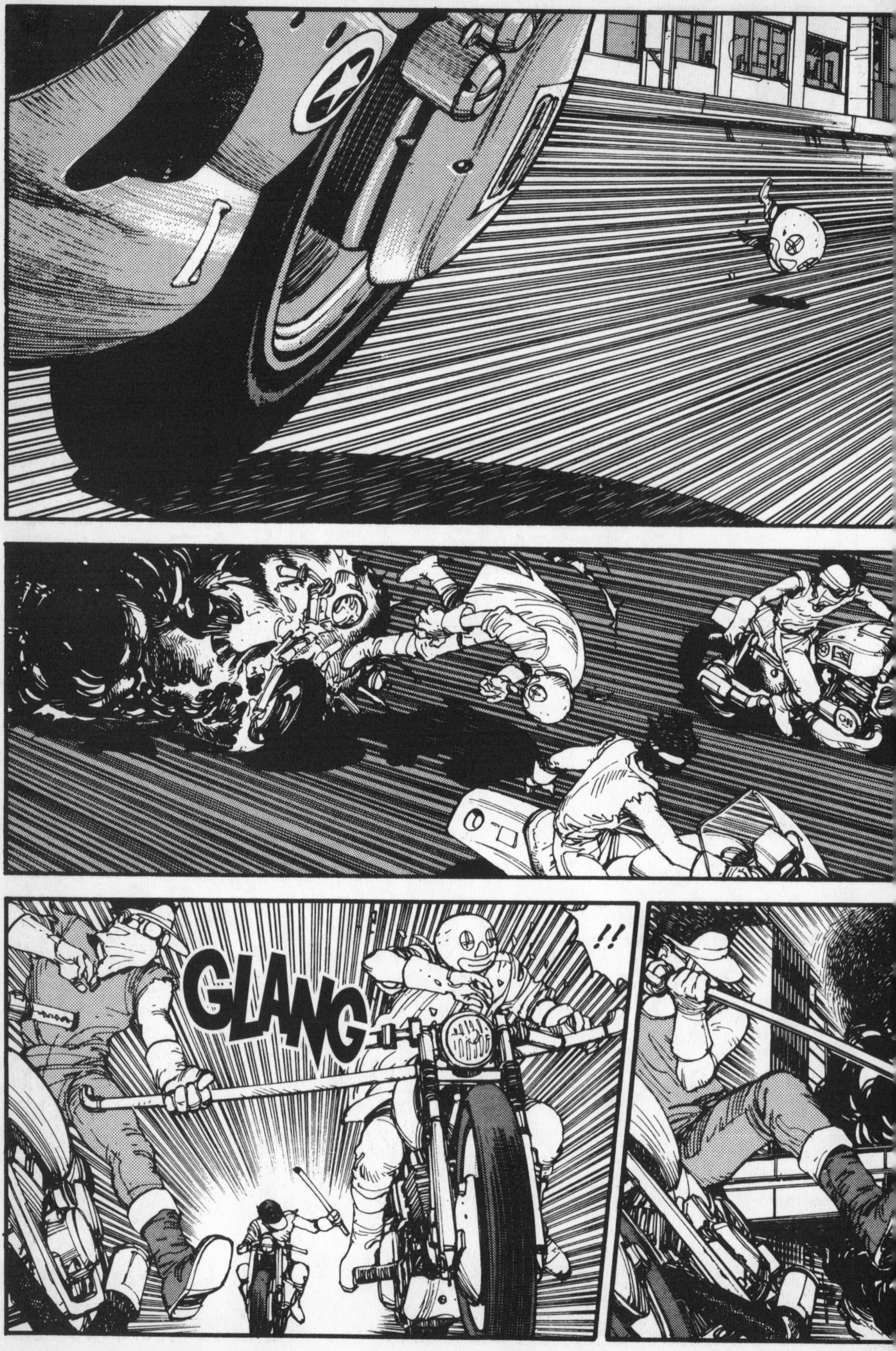
GLANG
!!

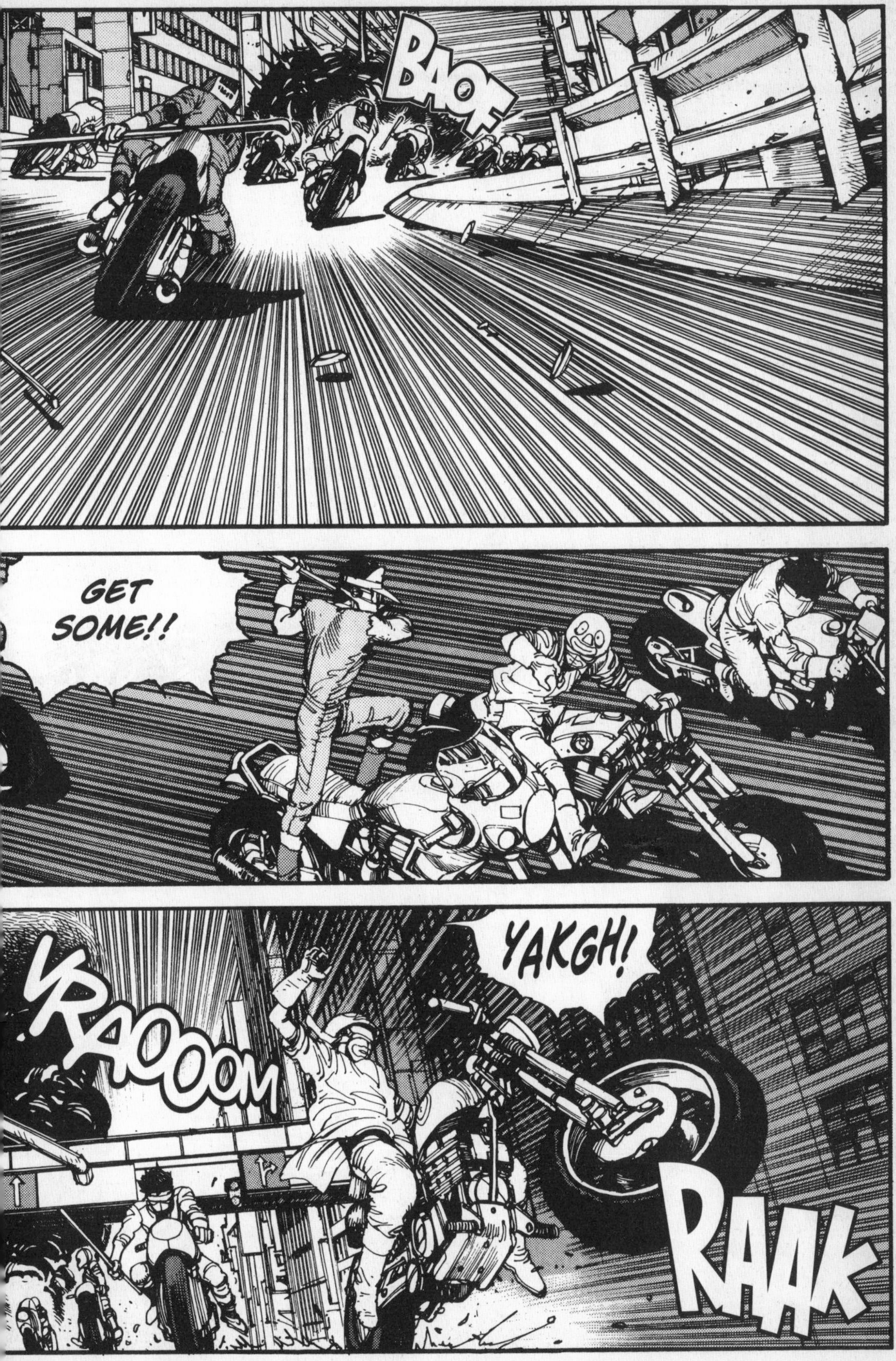
BAOF
GET SOME!!
VRAOOOM
YAKGH!
RAAK

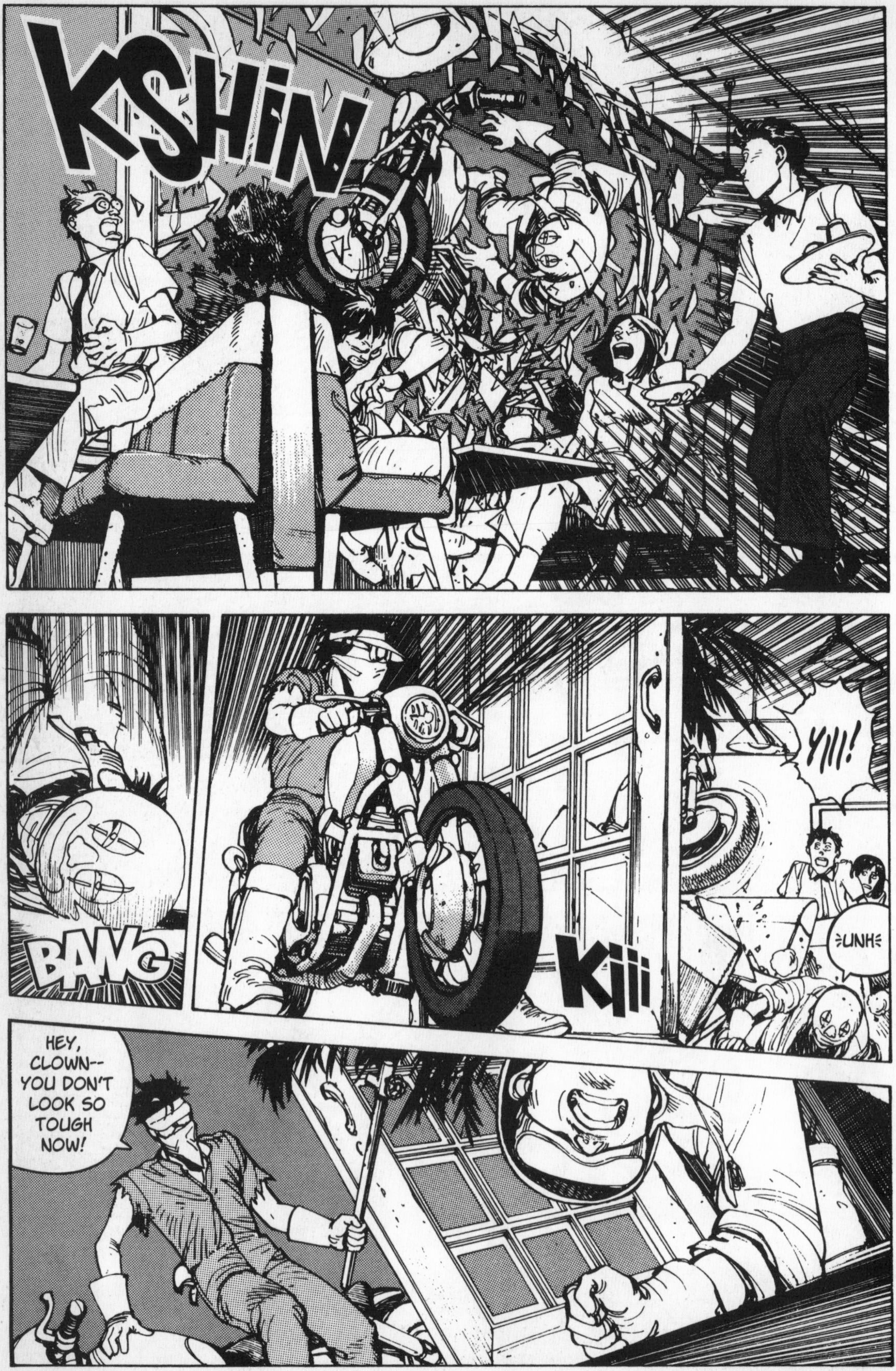
KSHIN
BANG
Kiii
YIII!
UNH
HEY, CLOWN-- YOU DON'T LOOK SO TOUGH NOW!

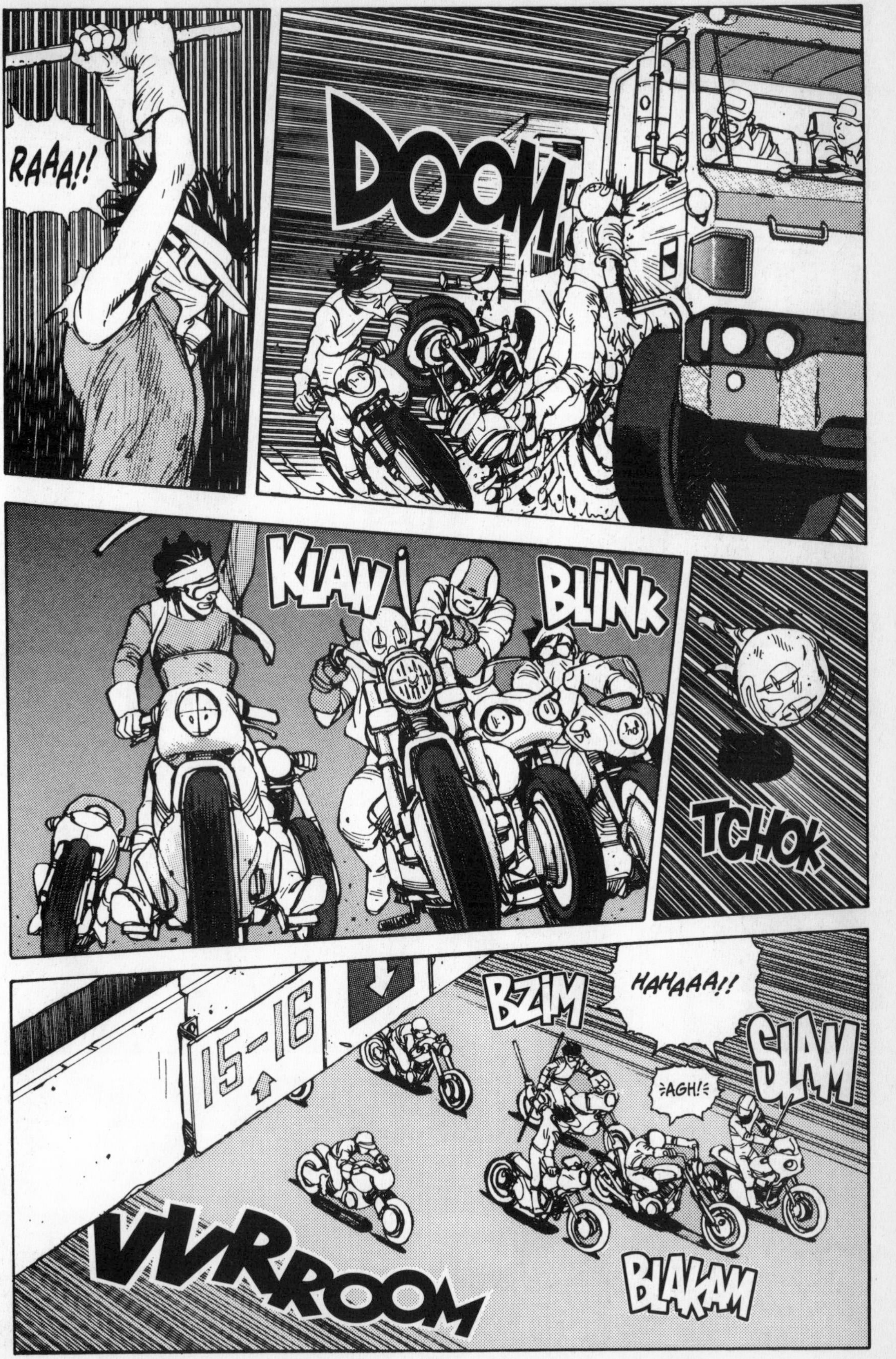
RAAA!!
DOOM
KLAN
BLINK
TCHOK
15-16
BZIM
HAHAAA!!
SLAM
AGH!
VVRROOM
BLAKAM

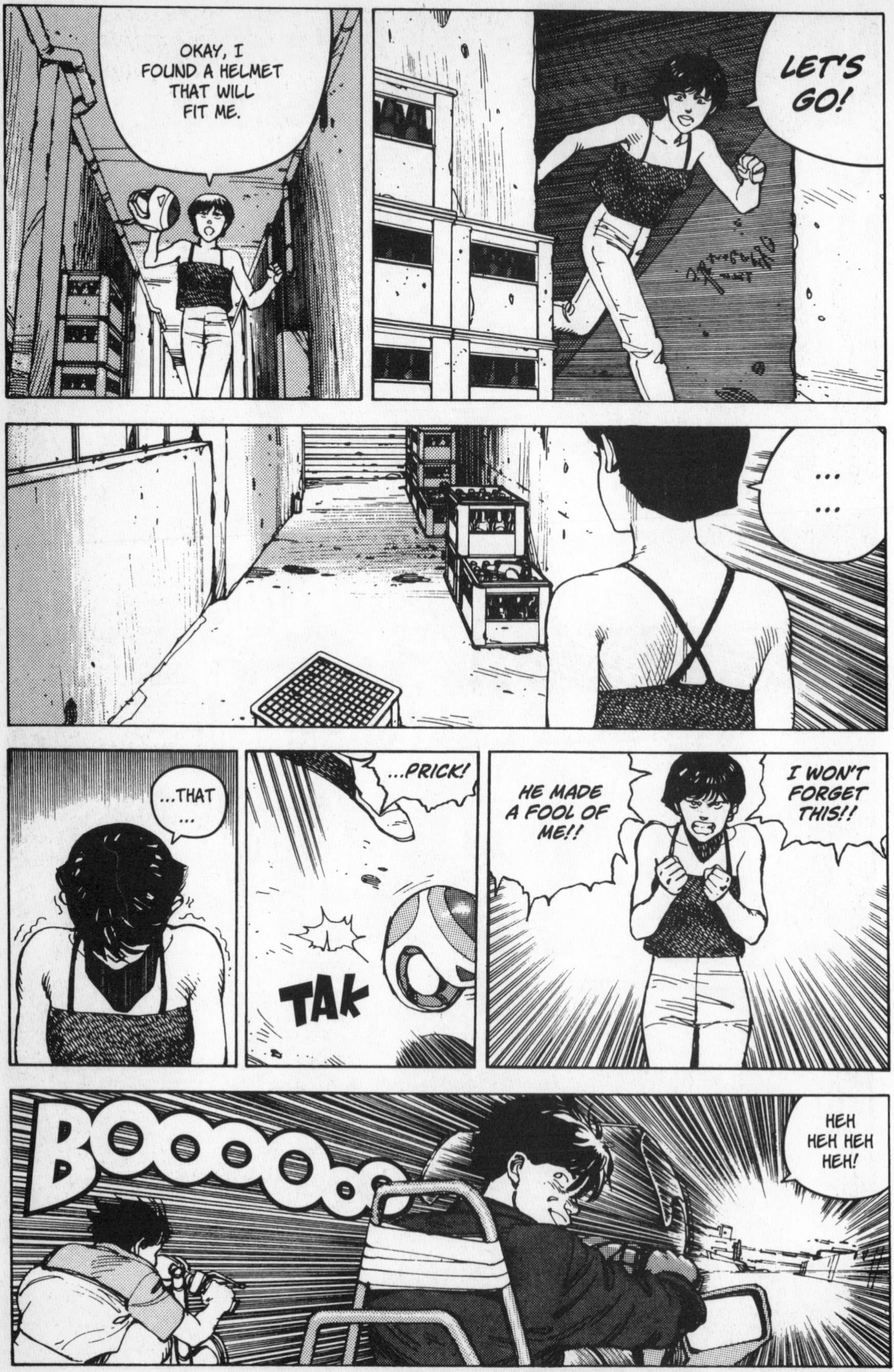
OKAY, I FOUND A HELMET THAT WILL FIT ME.
LET'S GO!
... ...
...THAT ...
...PRICK!
TAK
HE MADE A FOOL OF ME!!
I WON'T FORGET THIS!!
BOOOOO..
HEH HEH HEH HEH!

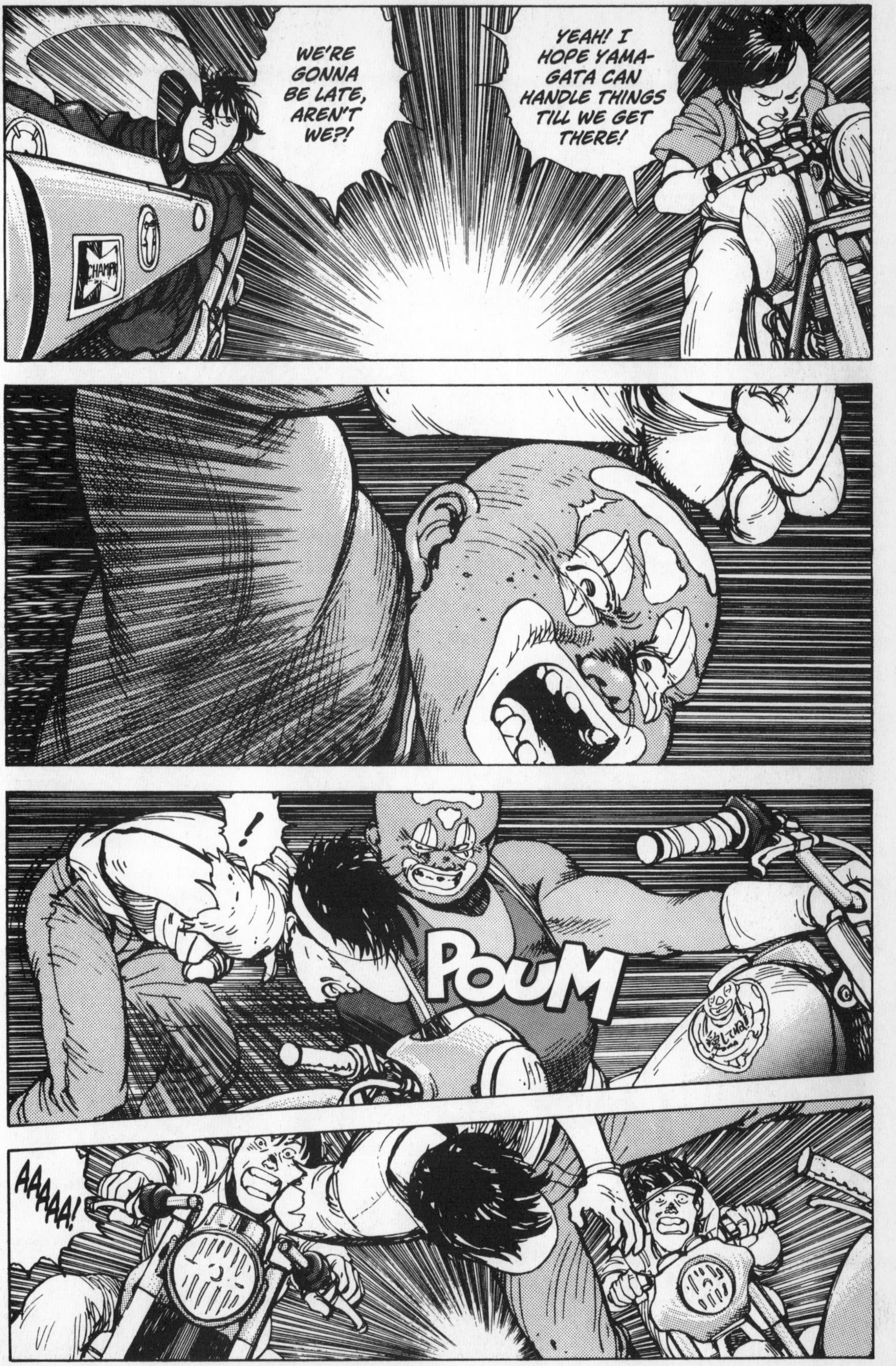
WE'RE GONNA BE LATE, AREN'T WE?!
YEAH! I HOPE YAMAGATA CAN HANDLE THINGS TILL WE GET THERE!
!
POUM
AAAAA!

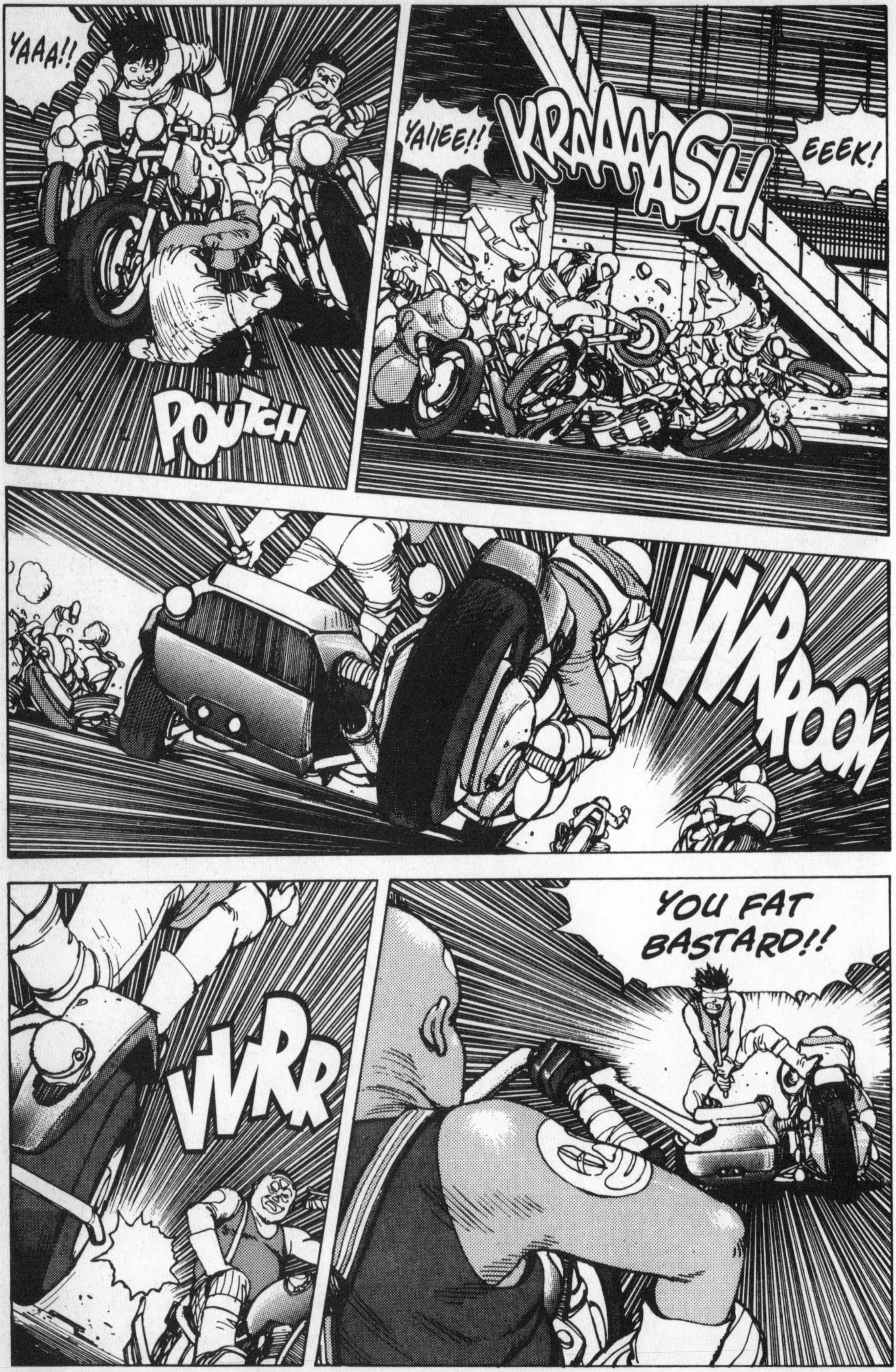
YAAA!!
POUTCH
YAIIEE!!
KRAAAAASH
EEEK!
VVRROOM
VVRR
YOU FAT BASTARD!!

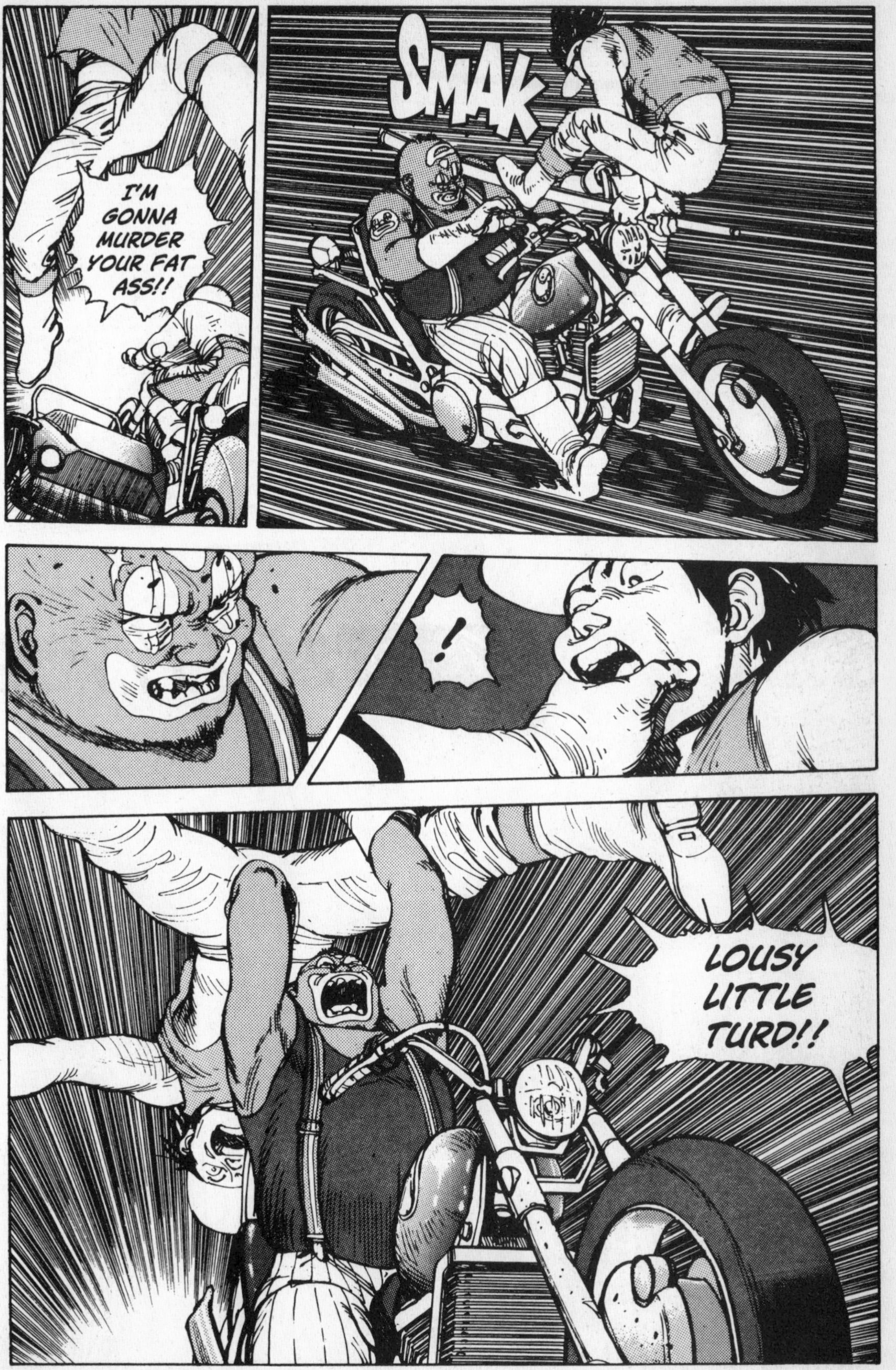
I'M GONNA MURDER YOUR FAT ASS!!
SMAK
!
LOUSY LITTLE TURD!!

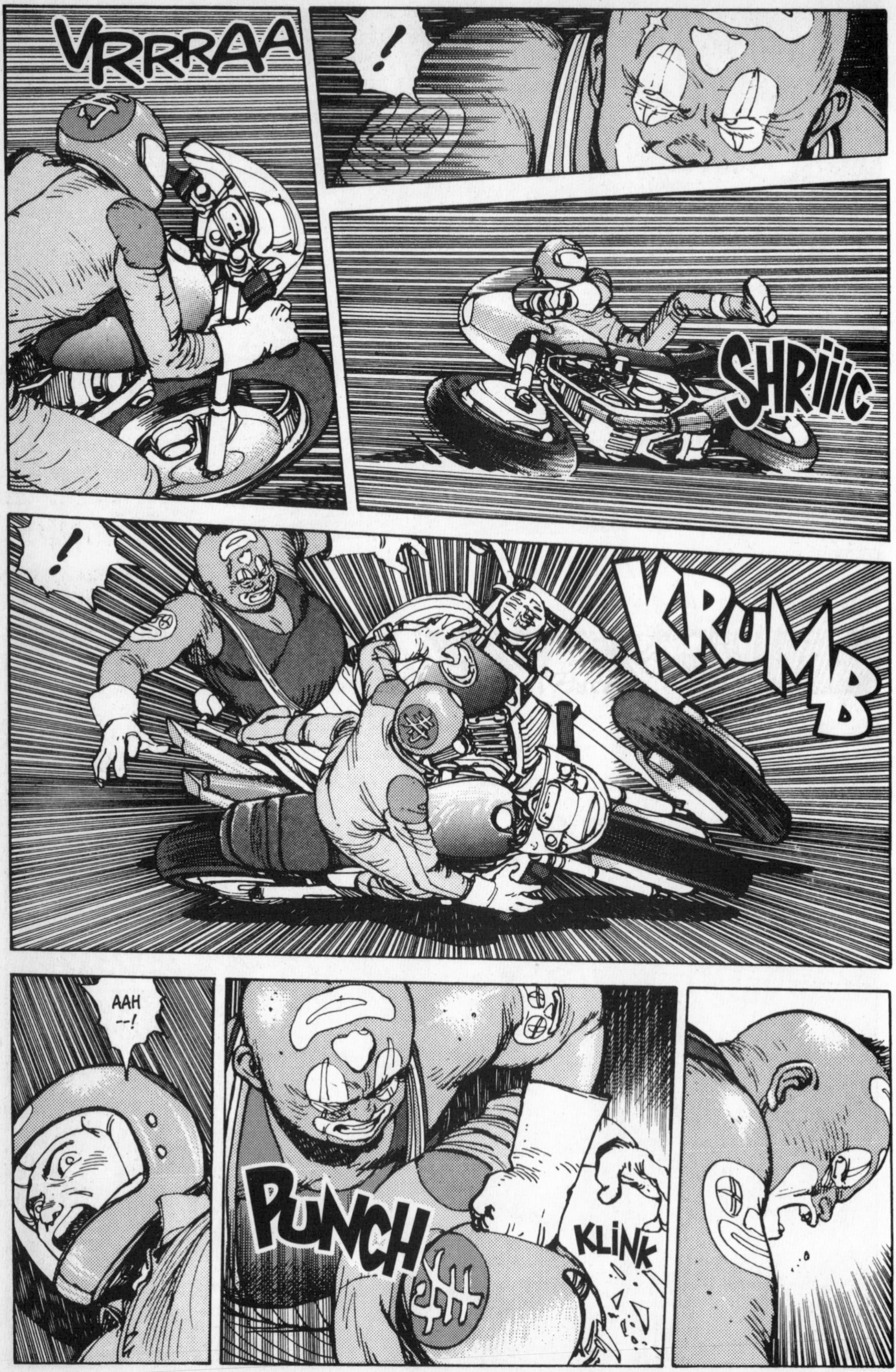
VRRRAA
!
SHRiiic
!
KRUMB
AAH --!
PUNCH
KLINK

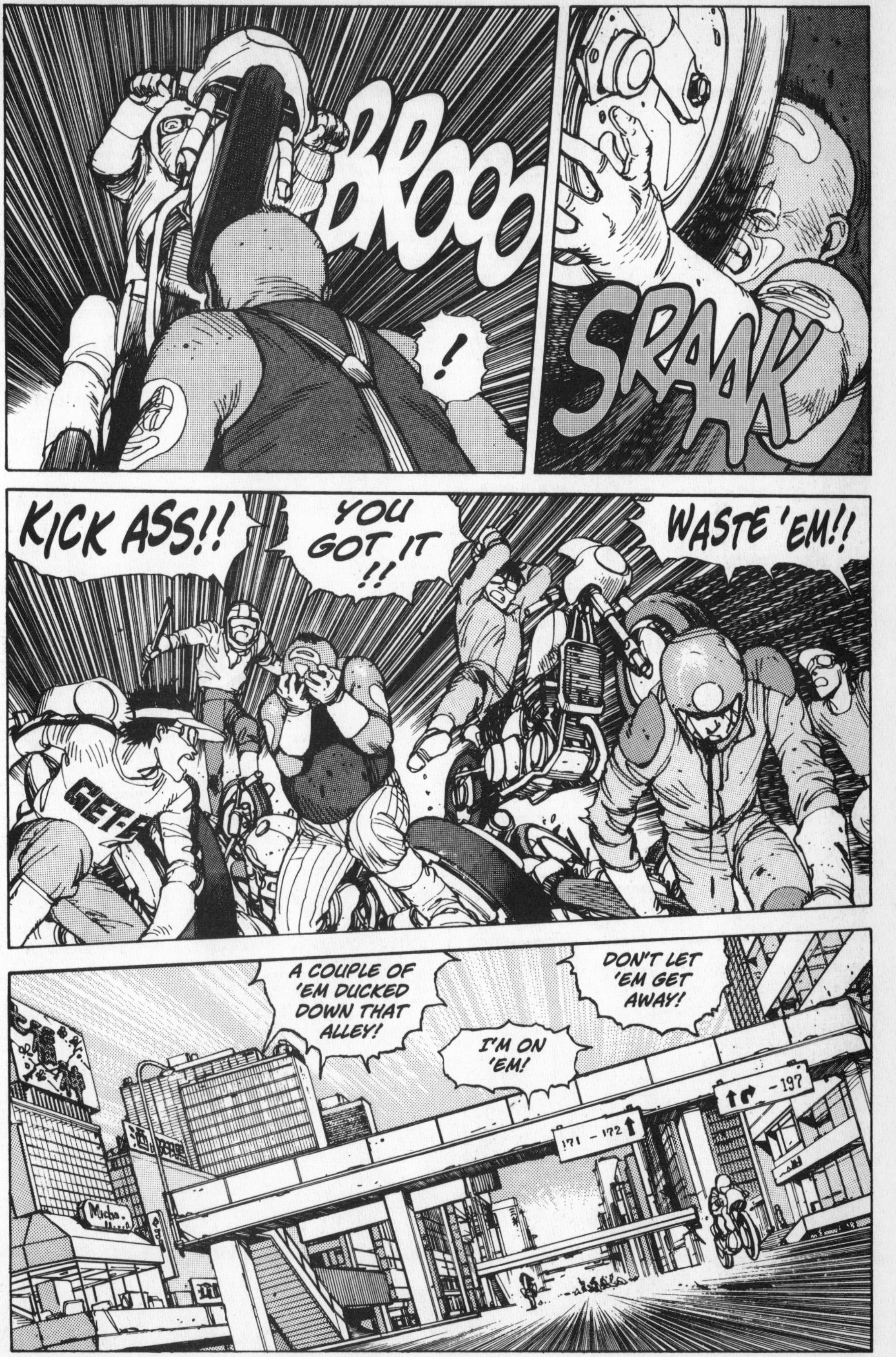
BROOOO
!
SRAAK
KICK ASS!!
YOU GOT IT !!
WASTE 'EM!!
A COUPLE OF 'EM DUCKED DOWN THAT ALLEY!
DON'T LET 'EM GET AWAY!
I'M ON 'EM!
171 - 172
-197

MY, MY, MY, ISN'T THIS *CUTE?*

AND WITH THE *KEY* STILL IN THE IGNITION!

HEY! WHAT ARE YOU DOING WITH MY--?

THANKS SO MUCH FOR THE USE OF YOUR BIKE, MA'AM! I'LL HAVE IT BACK IN NO TIME! PROMISE!

YEEEEK!

Wiiiiiiiiz

KPOW

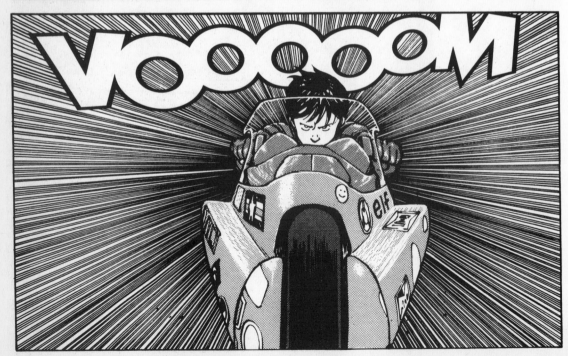

VOOOOOM

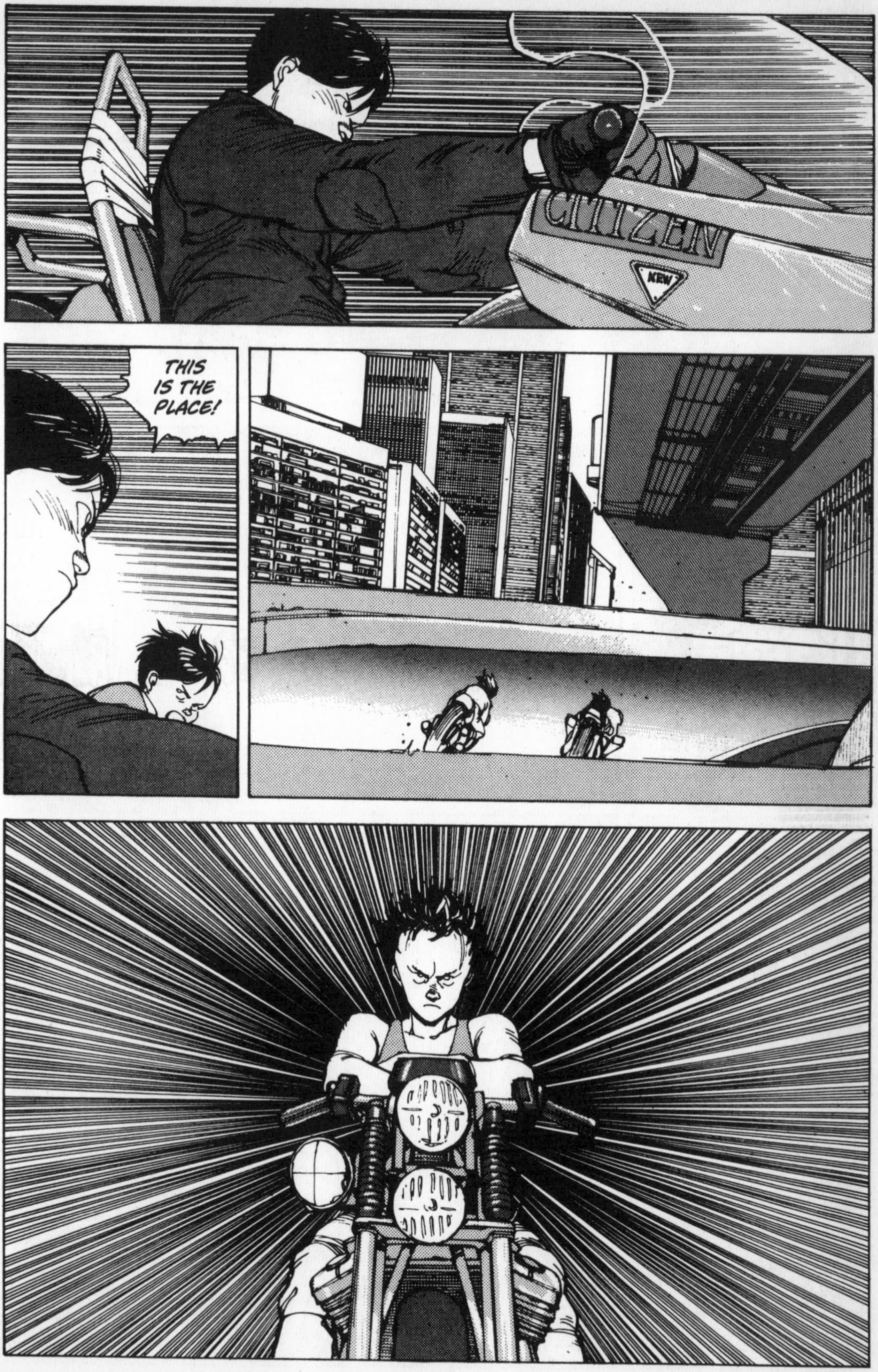
CITIZEN
KEW
THIS IS THE PLACE!

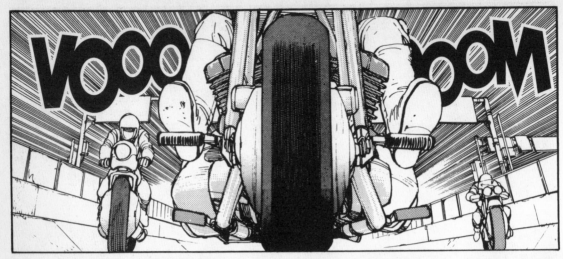

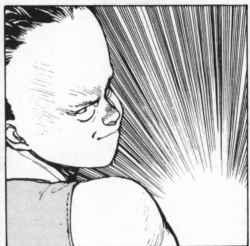

HOLD IT RIGHT THERE, YOU SONOFA-BITCH!

LAST WEEK YOU KILLED MY BEST FRIEND!!

NOW IT'S YOUR TURN!!

298

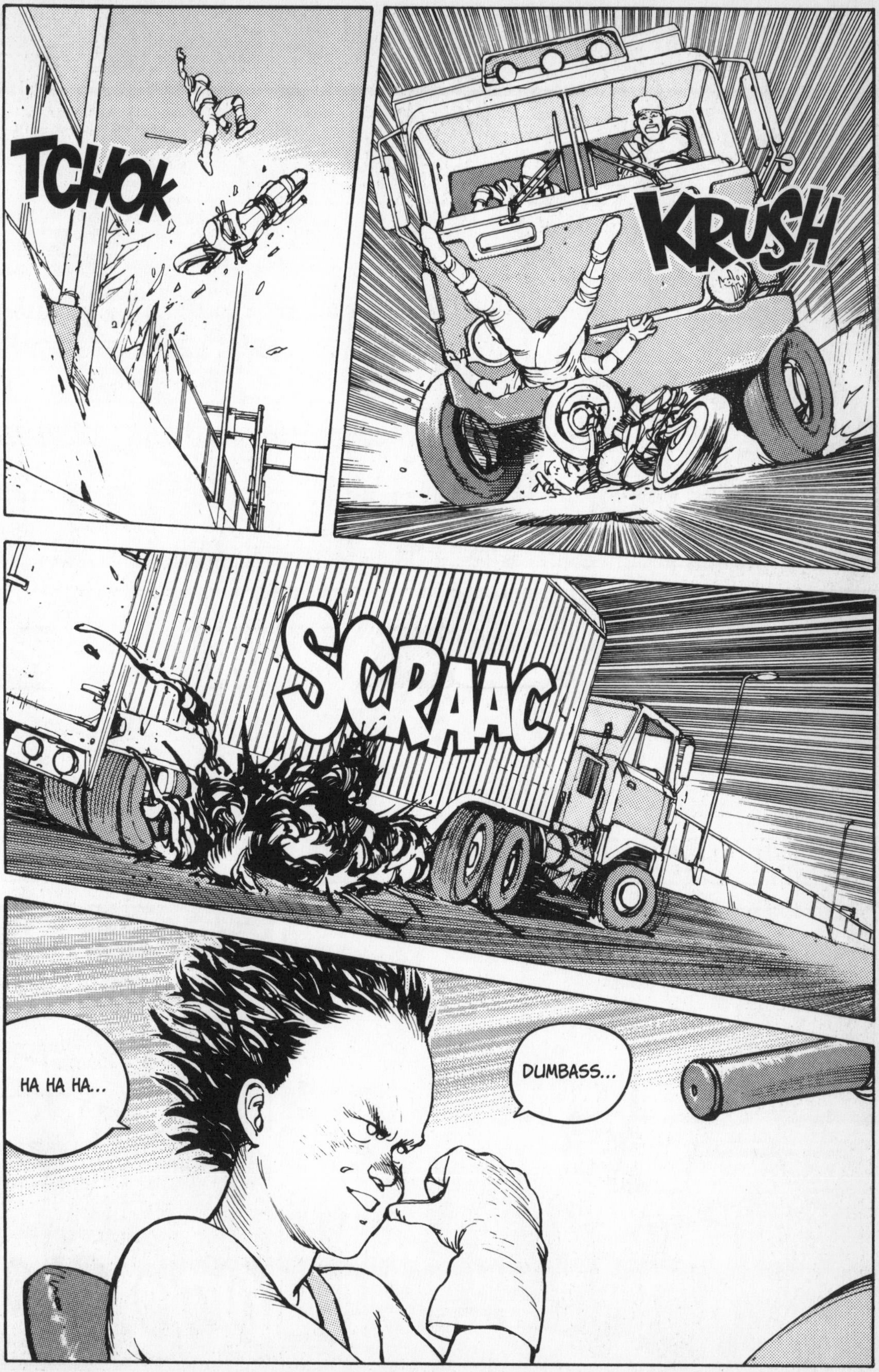
TCHOK
KRUSH
SCRAAC
HA HA HA...
DUMBASS...

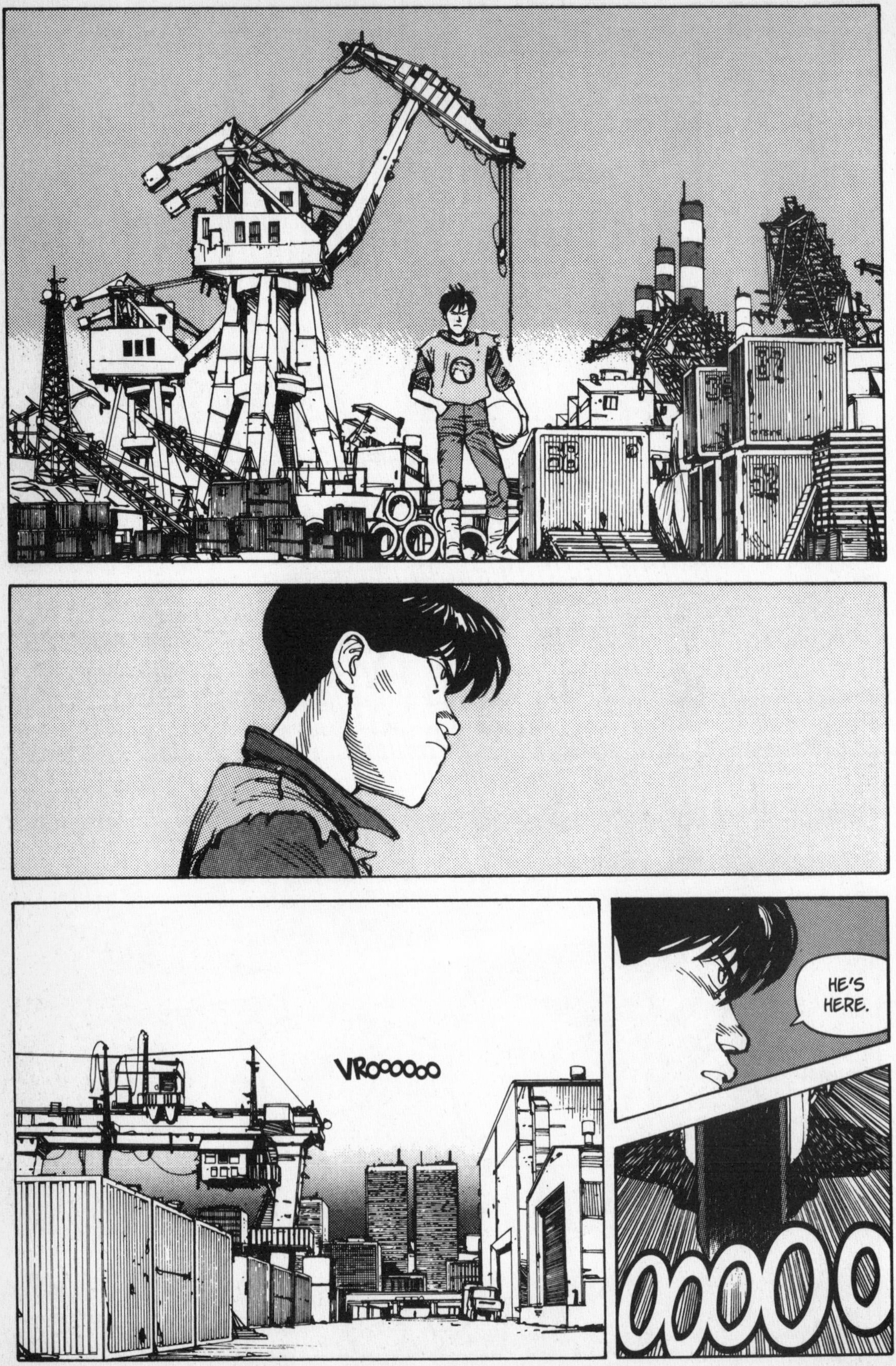
VROOOOOO
HE'S HERE.
OOOOO

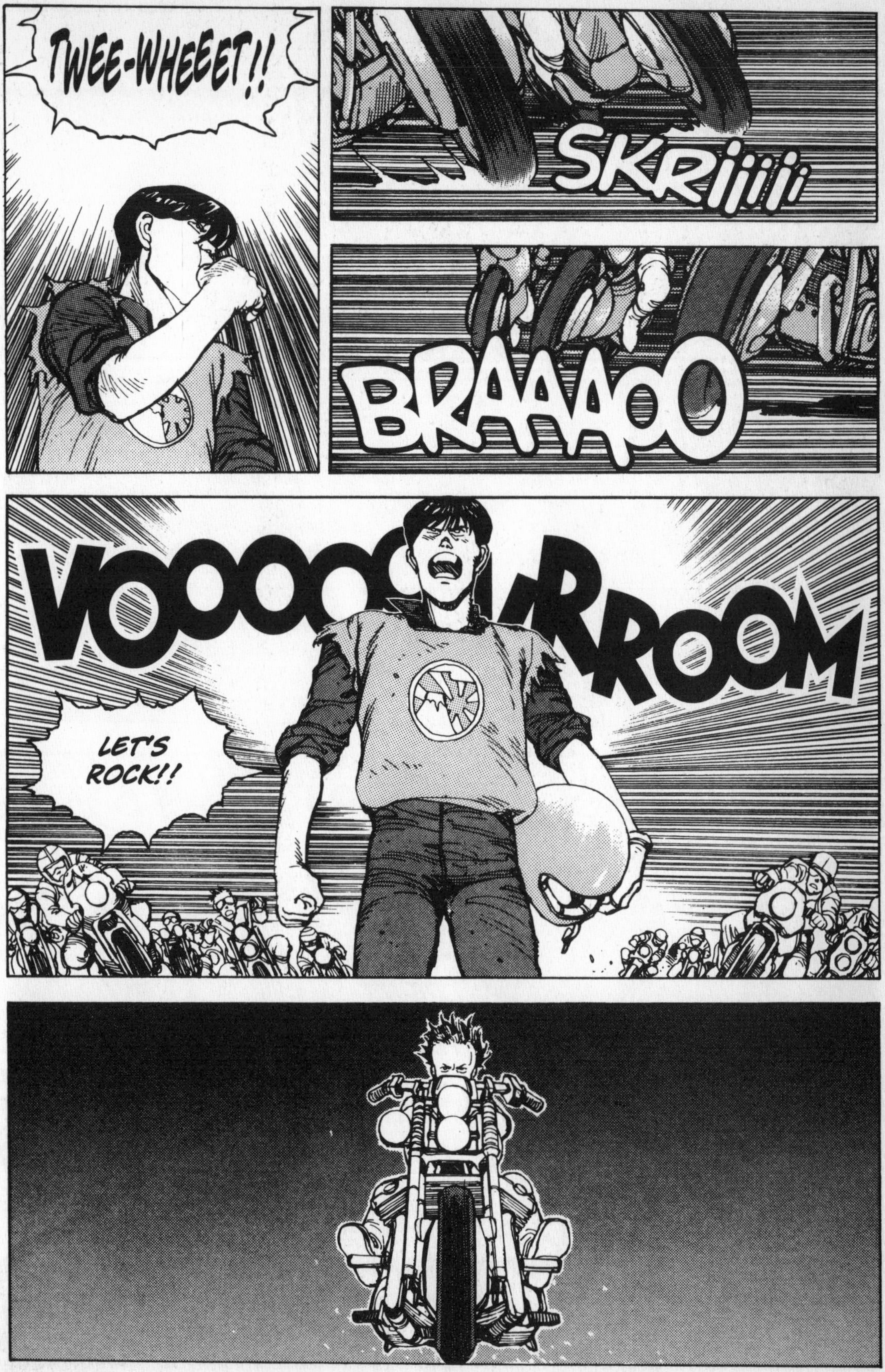
TWEE-WHEEET!!
SKRiiiii
BRAAAOO
VOOOOVRROOM
LET'S ROCK!!

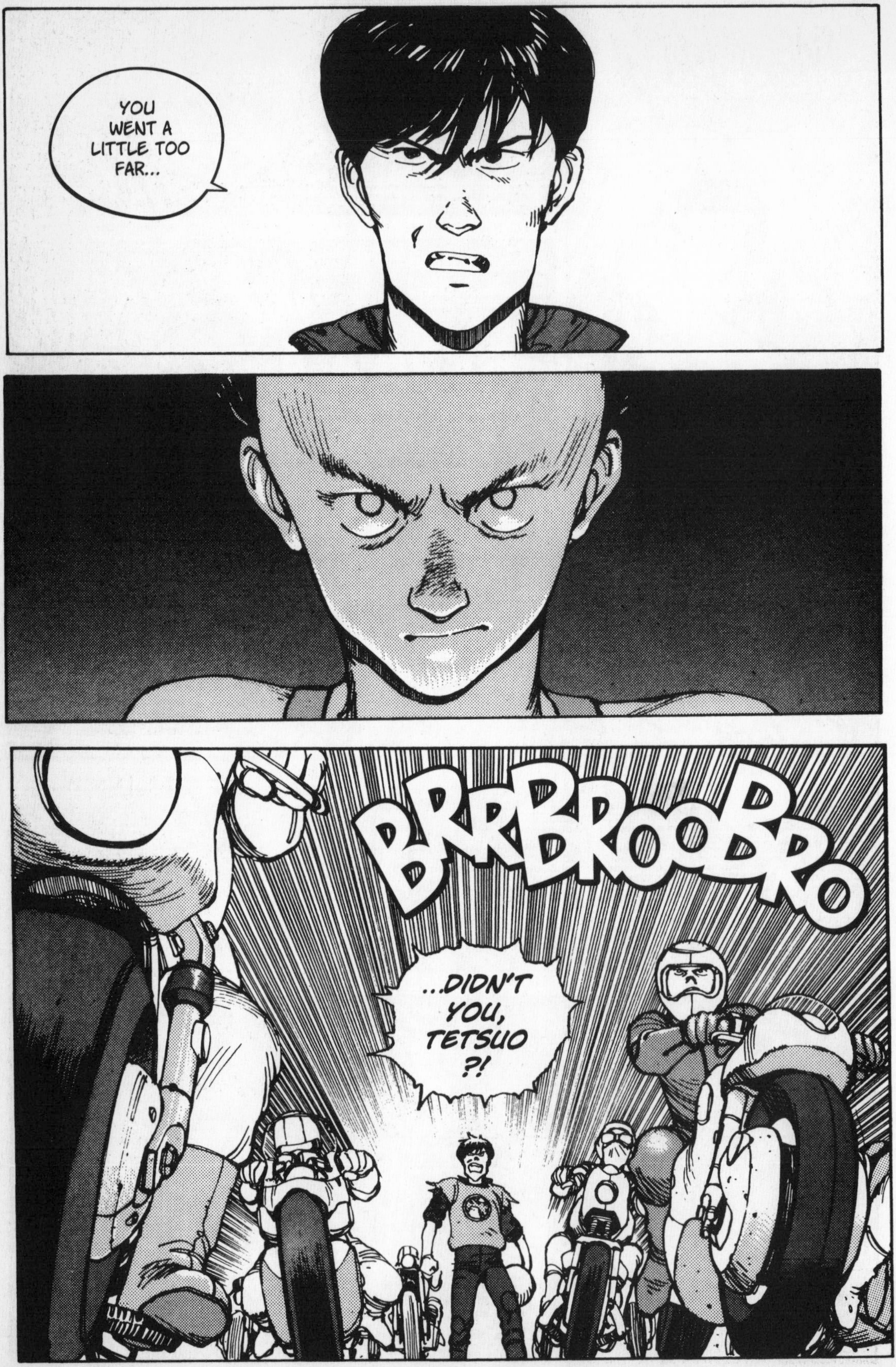
YOU WENT A LITTLE TOO FAR...
BRRBROOBRO
...DIDN'T YOU, TETSUO ?!

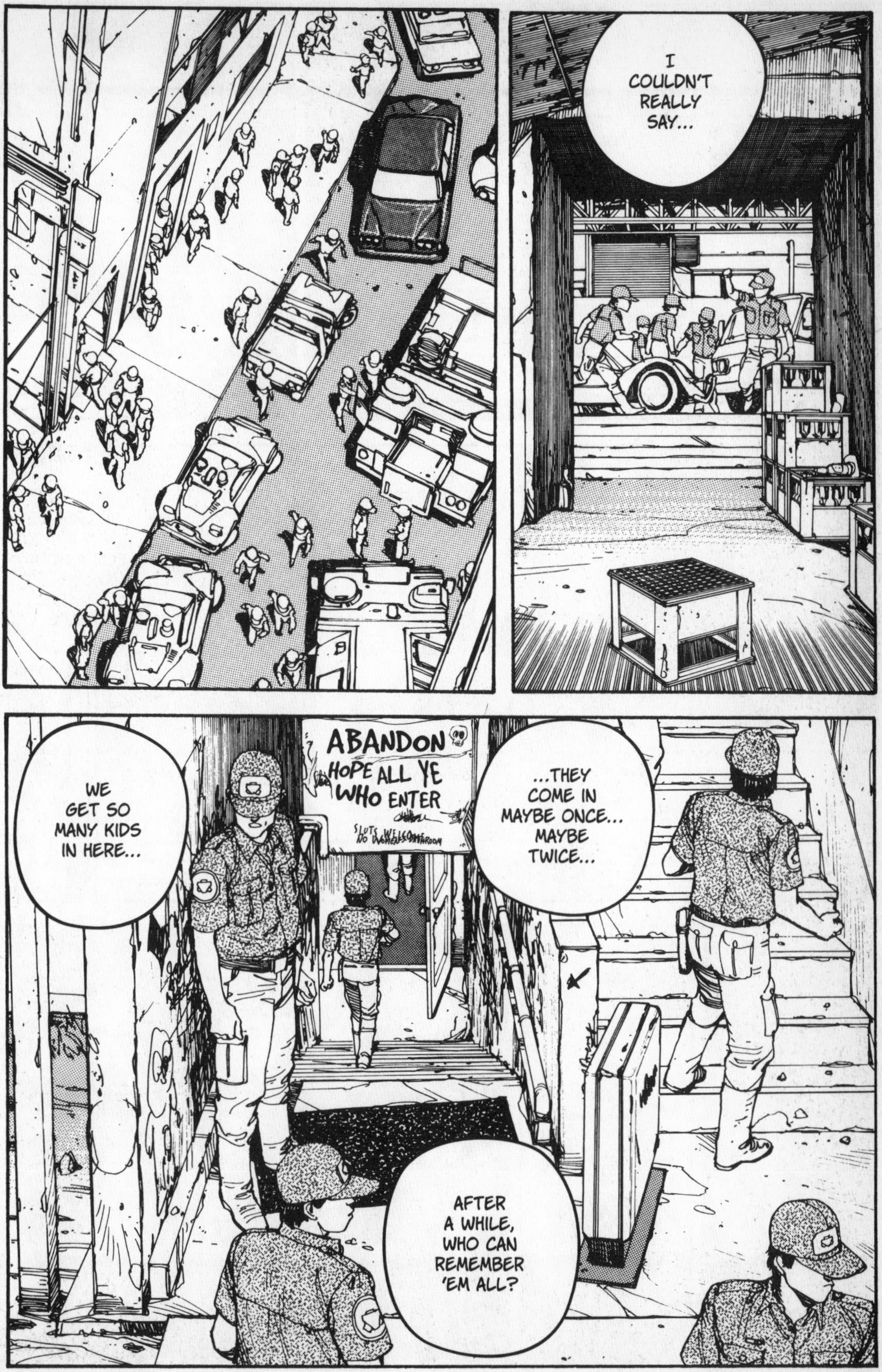
I COULDN'T REALLY SAY...
WE GET SO MANY KIDS IN HERE...
ABANDON HOPE ALL YE WHO ENTER
...THEY COME IN MAYBE ONCE... MAYBE TWICE...
AFTER A WHILE, WHO CAN REMEMBER 'EM ALL?

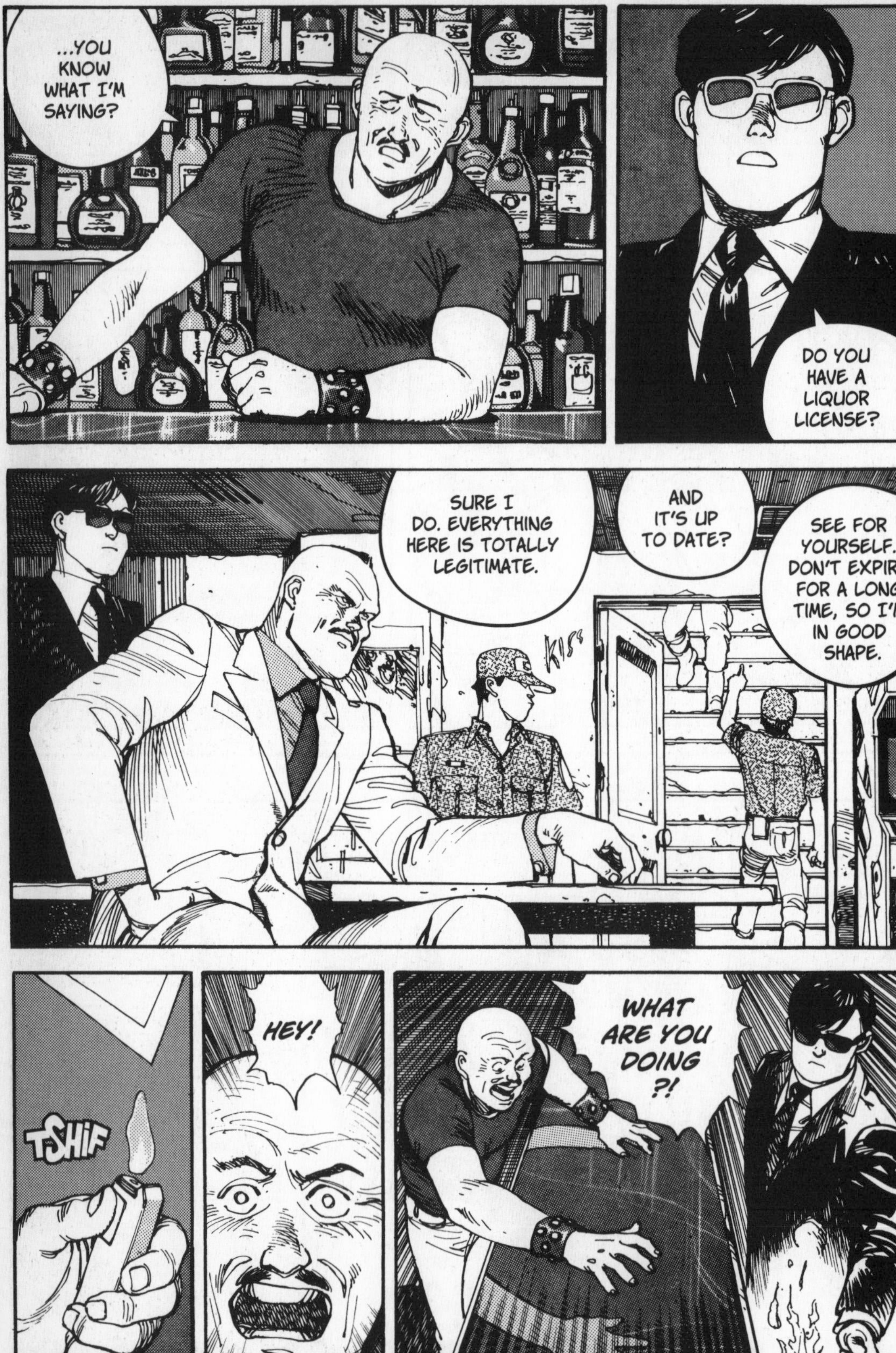
...YOU KNOW WHAT I'M SAYING?
DO YOU HAVE A LIQUOR LICENSE?
SURE I DO. EVERYTHING HERE IS TOTALLY LEGITIMATE.
AND IT'S UP TO DATE?
KISS
SEE FOR YOURSELF. DON'T EXPIRE FOR A LONG TIME, SO I'M IN GOOD SHAPE.
TSHIF
HEY!
WHAT ARE YOU DOING ?!

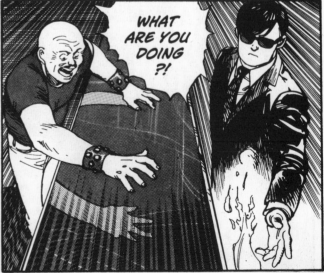

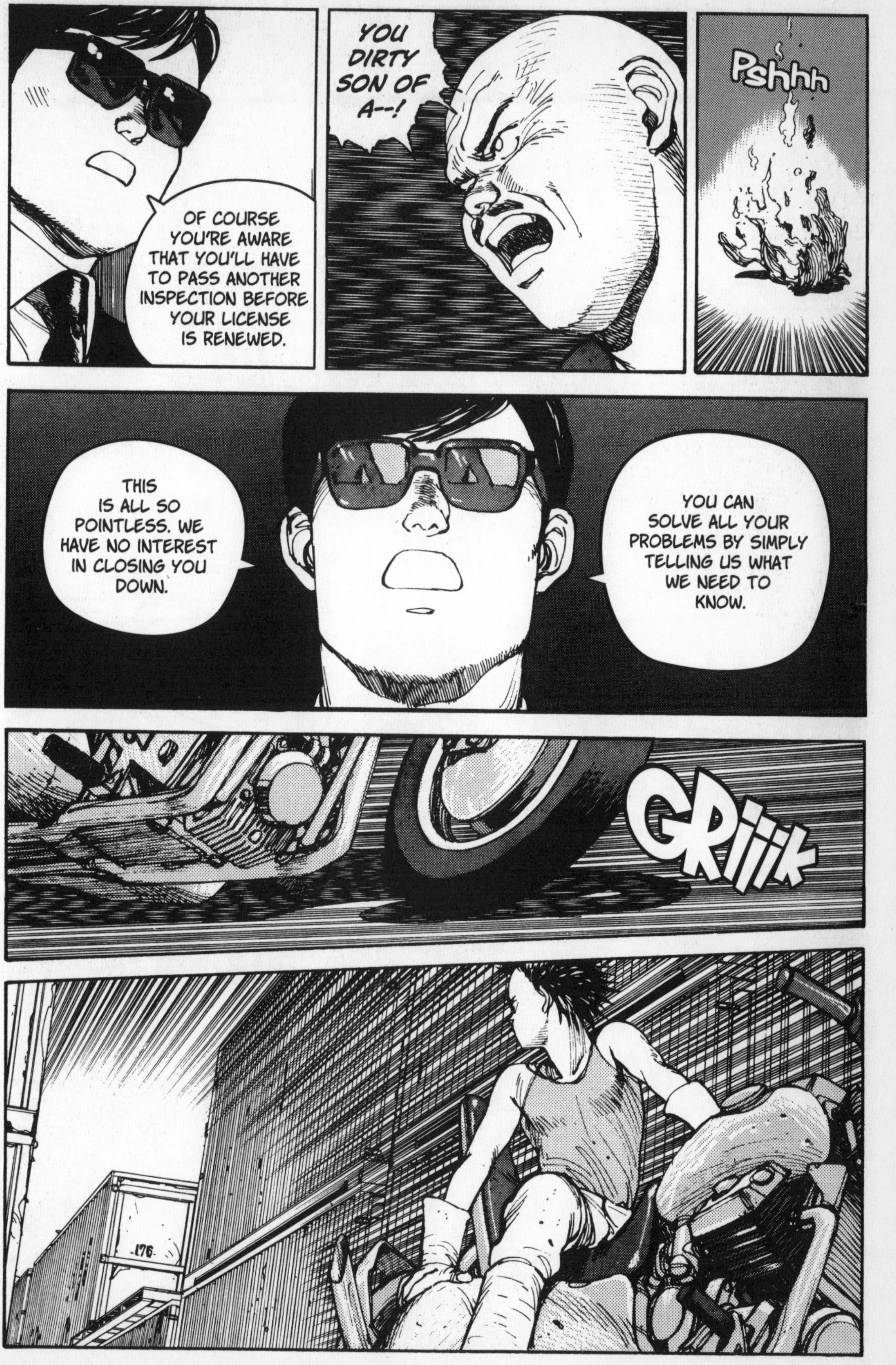
OF COURSE YOU'RE AWARE THAT YOU'LL HAVE TO PASS ANOTHER INSPECTION BEFORE YOUR LICENSE IS RENEWED.
YOU DIRTY SON OF A--!
Pshhh
THIS IS ALL SO POINTLESS. WE HAVE NO INTEREST IN CLOSING YOU DOWN.
YOU CAN SOLVE ALL YOUR PROBLEMS BY SIMPLY TELLING US WHAT WE NEED TO KNOW.
GRiiik
176

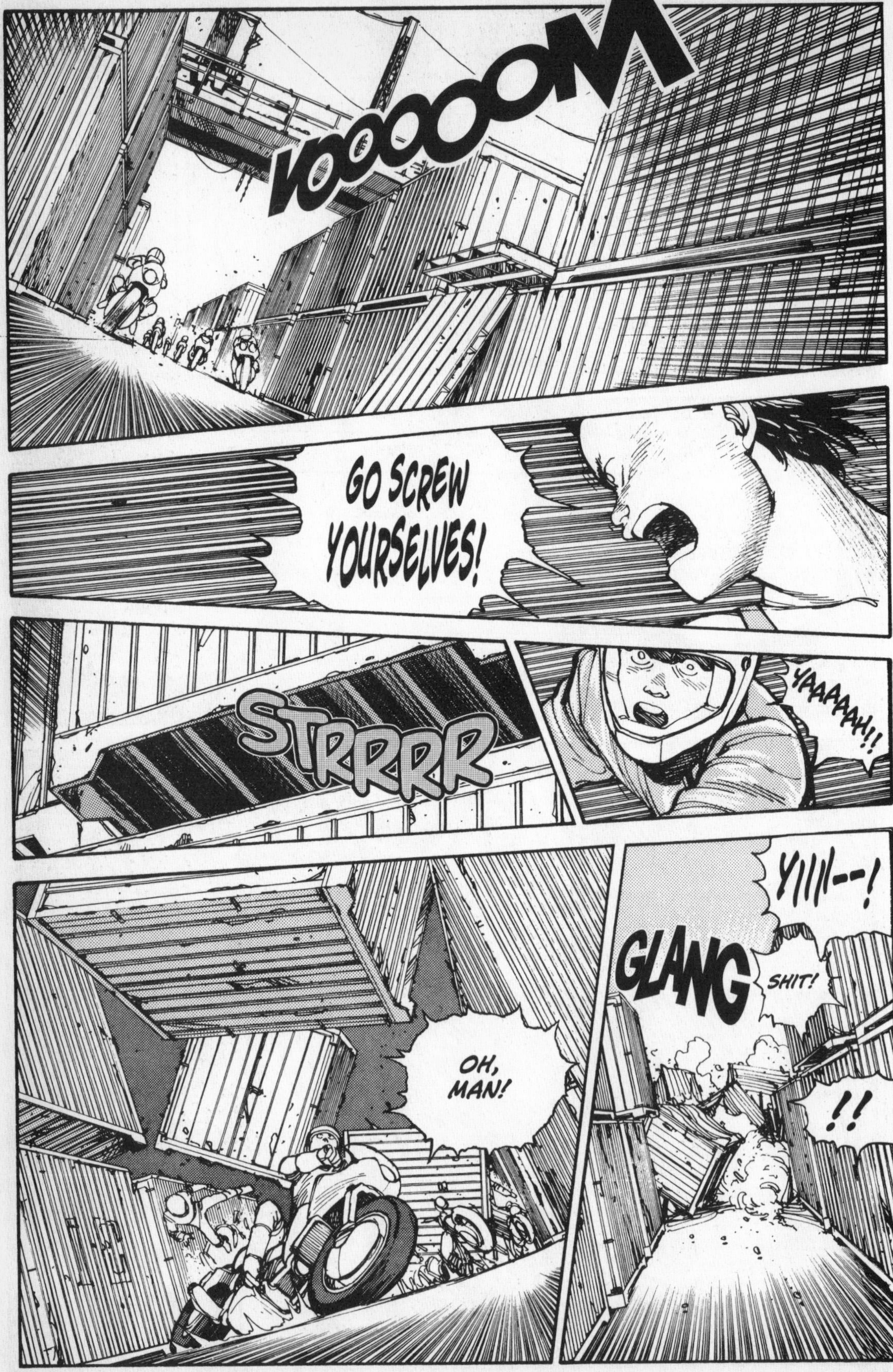
VOOOOOM
GO SCREW YOURSELVES!
STRRRR
YAAAAAH!!
OH, MAN!
YIIII--!
GLANG
SHIT!
!!

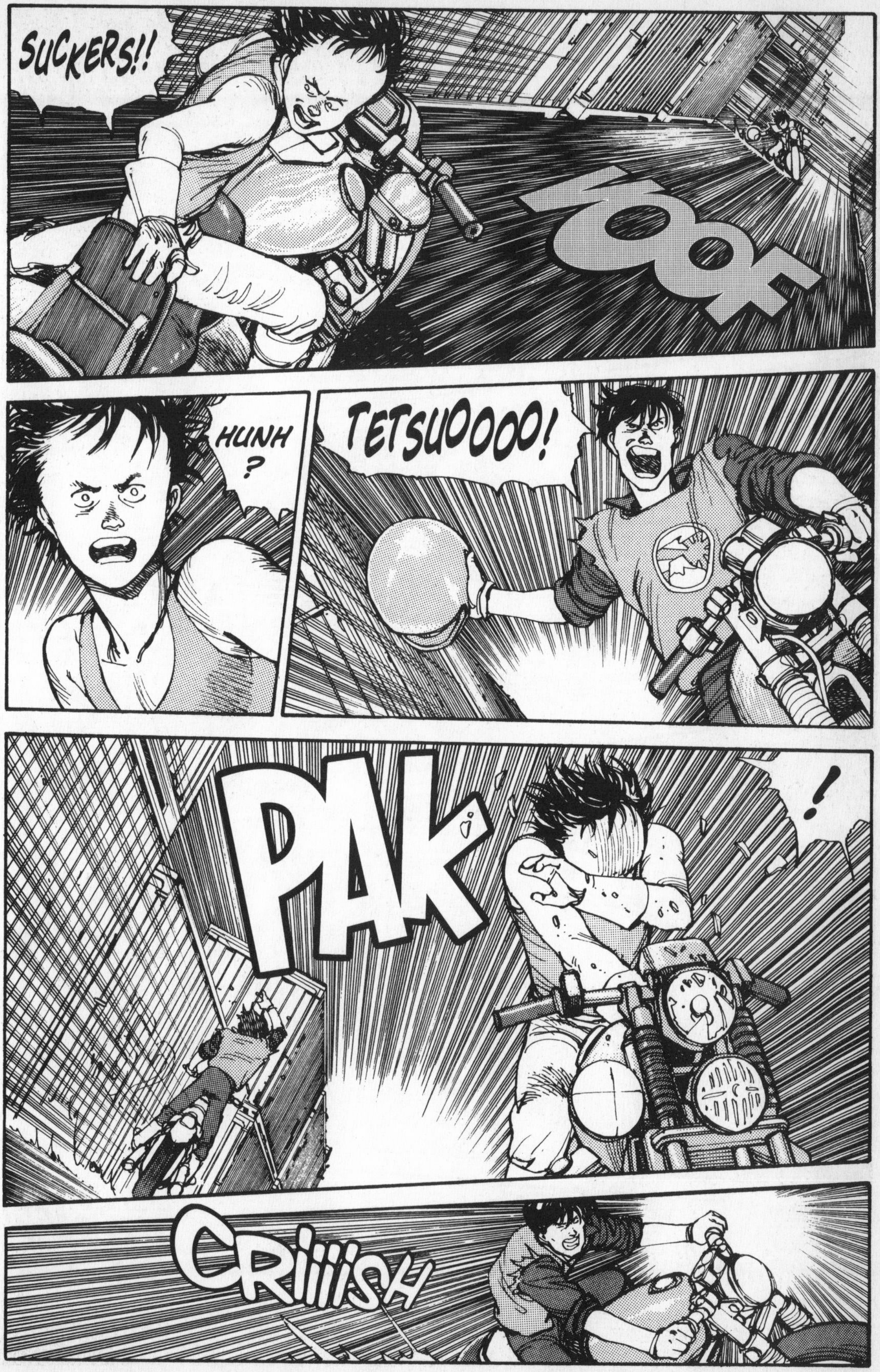
SUCKERS!!
VOOF
HUNH ?
TETSUOOOO!
PAK
!
CRiiiiSH

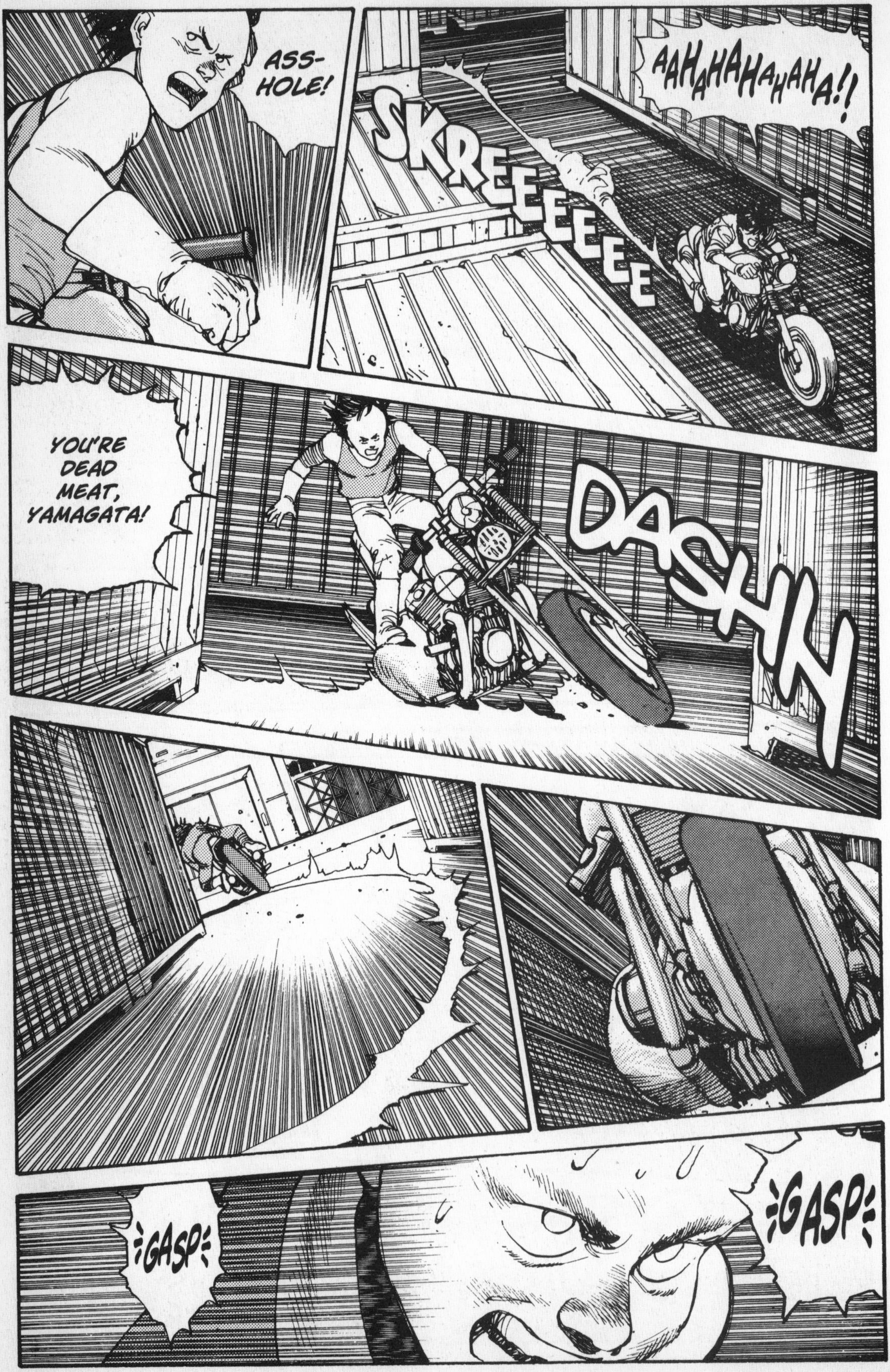
ASS-HOLE!
SKREEEEEEEE
AAHAHAHAHAHAHA!!
YOU'RE DEAD MEAT, YAMAGATA!
DASHH
GASP
GASP

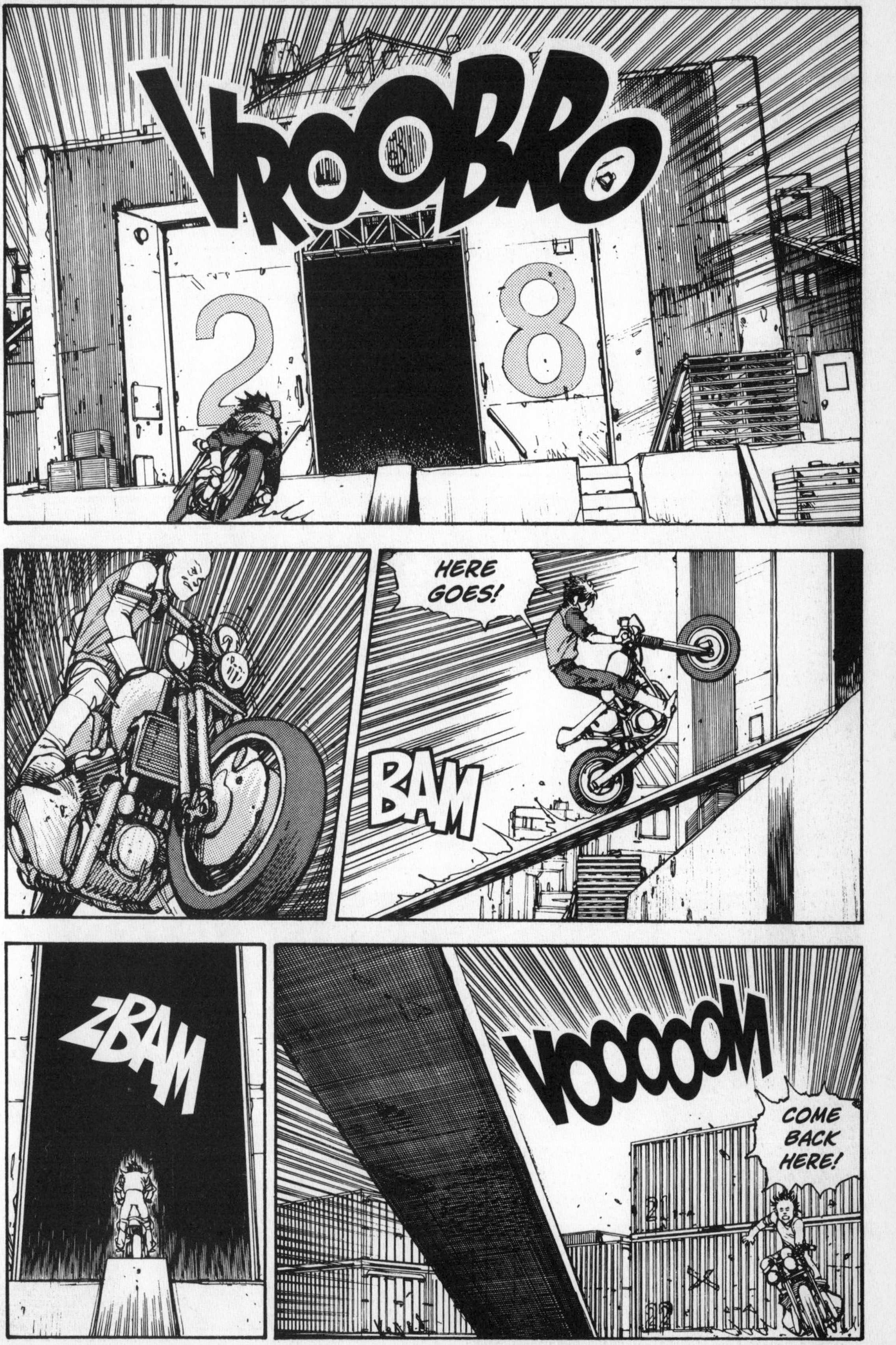
VROOBRO
2
8
HERE GOES!
BAM
ZBAM
VOOOOOM
COME BACK HERE!

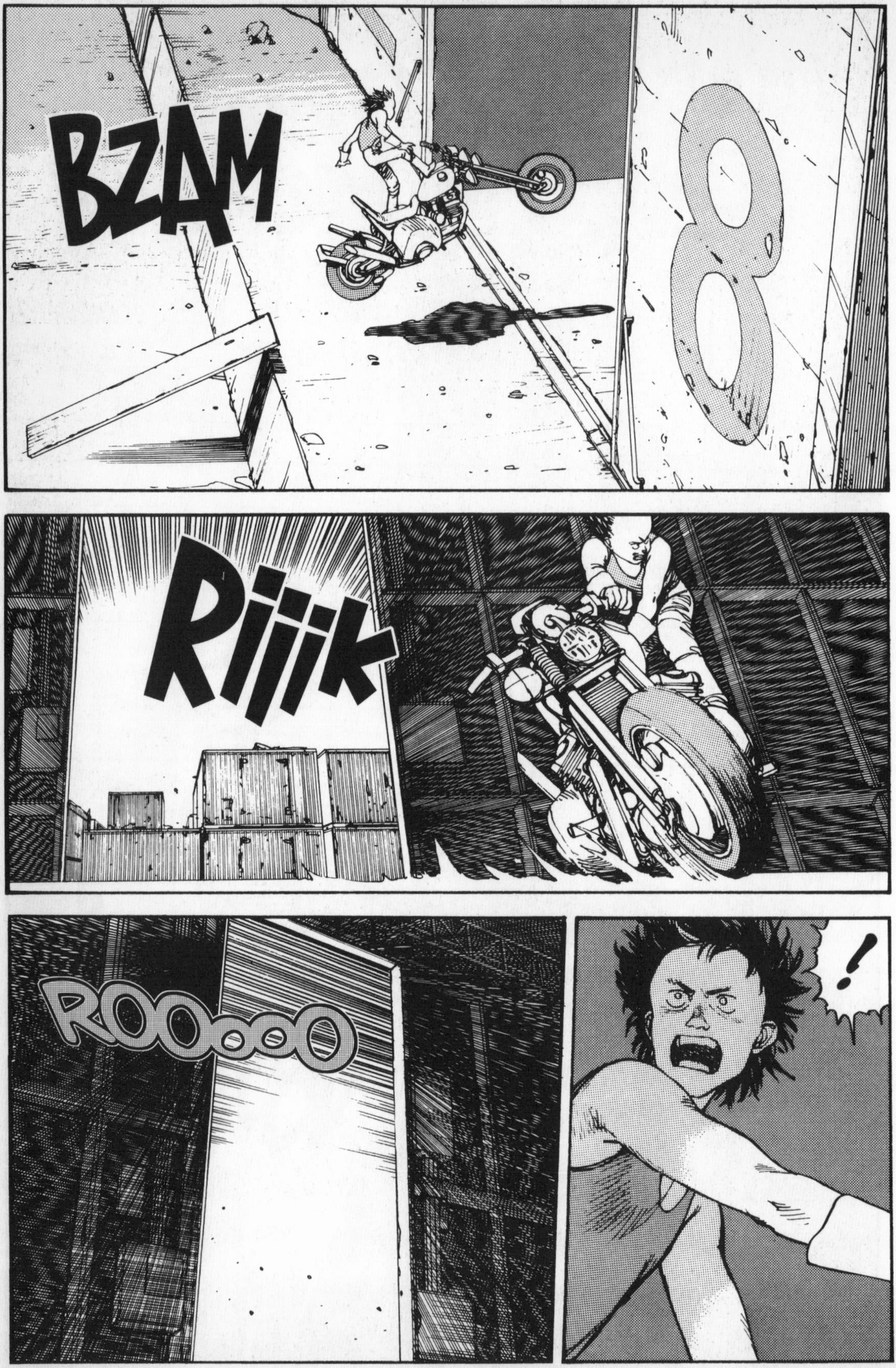
BZAM
Riiik
ROOooO
!

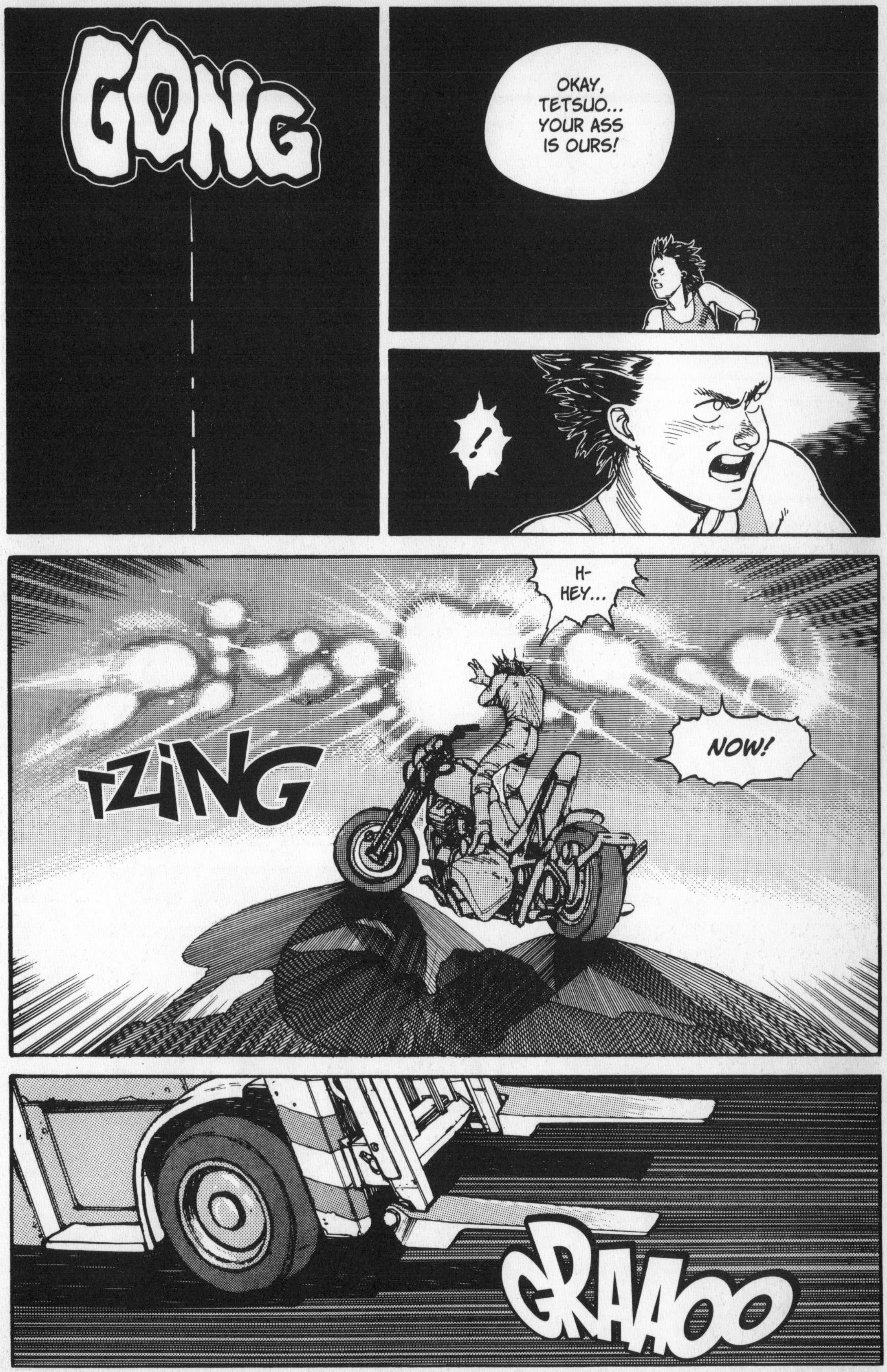
GONG
OKAY, TETSUO... YOUR ASS IS OURS!
!
H- HEY...
NOW!
TZING
GRAAOO

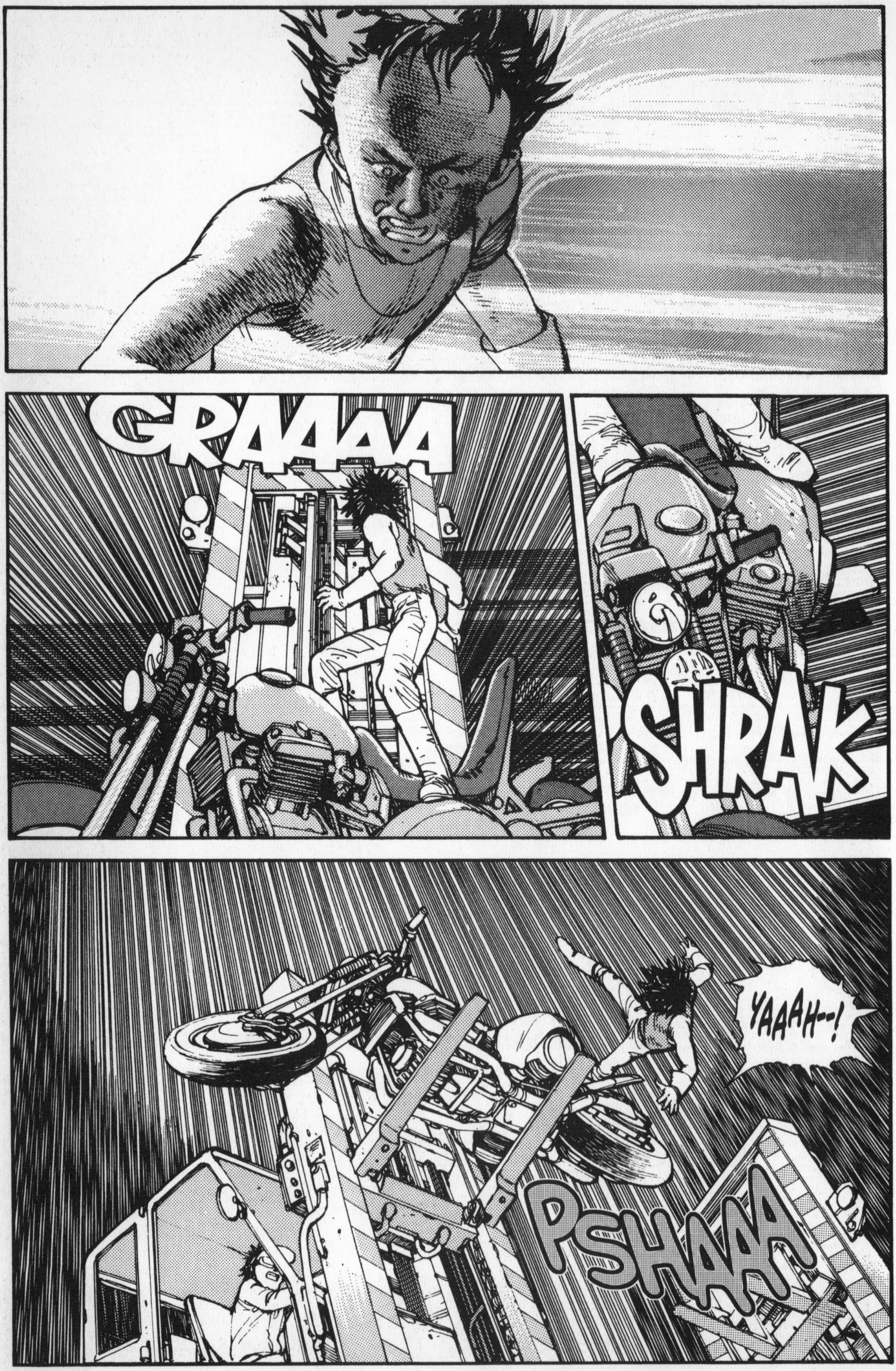
GRAAAA
SHRAK
YAAAH--!
PSHAAAA

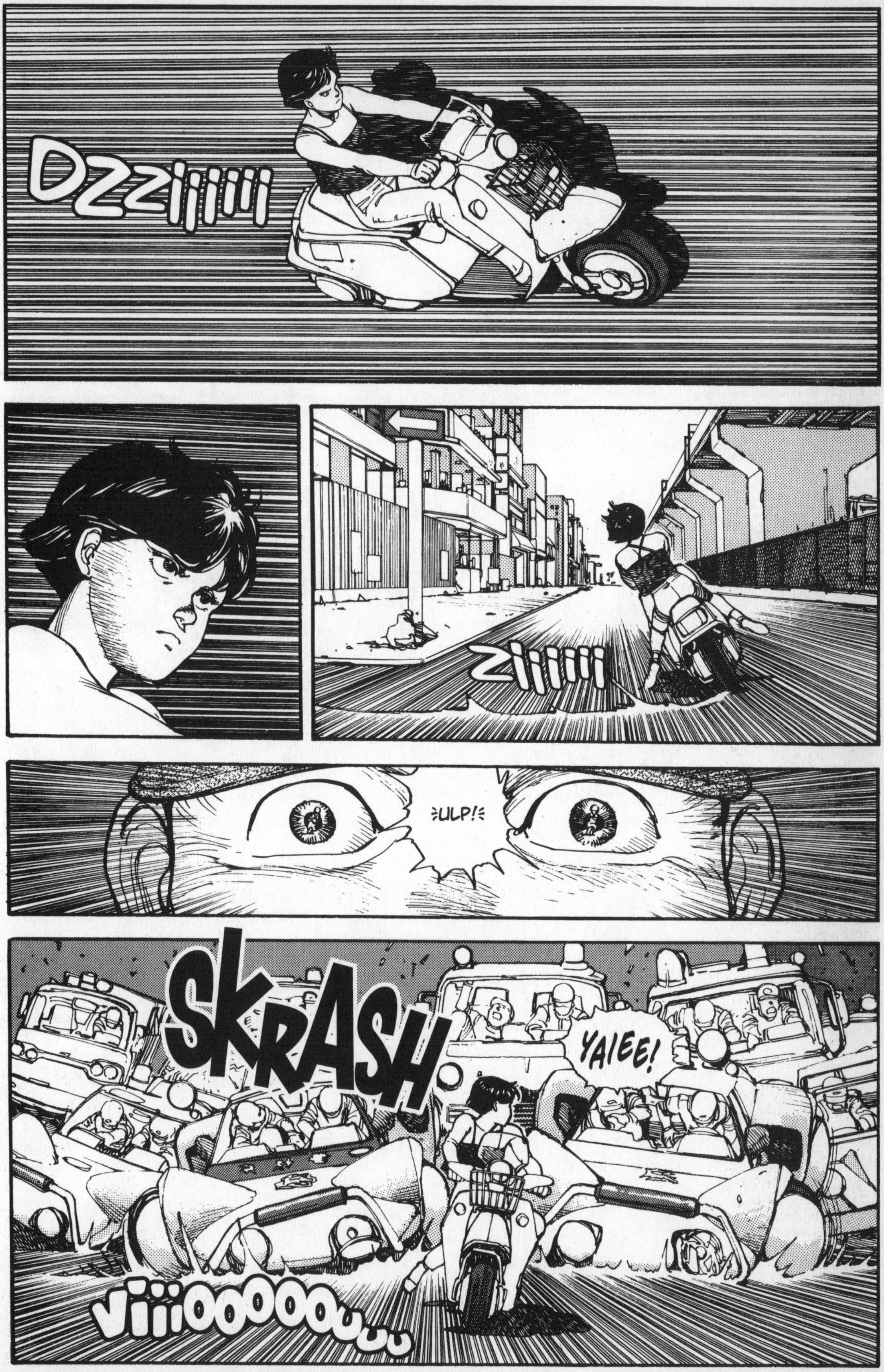
DZZiiiiii
Ziiiiii
ULP!
SKRASH
YAIEE!
Viiioooooouuu

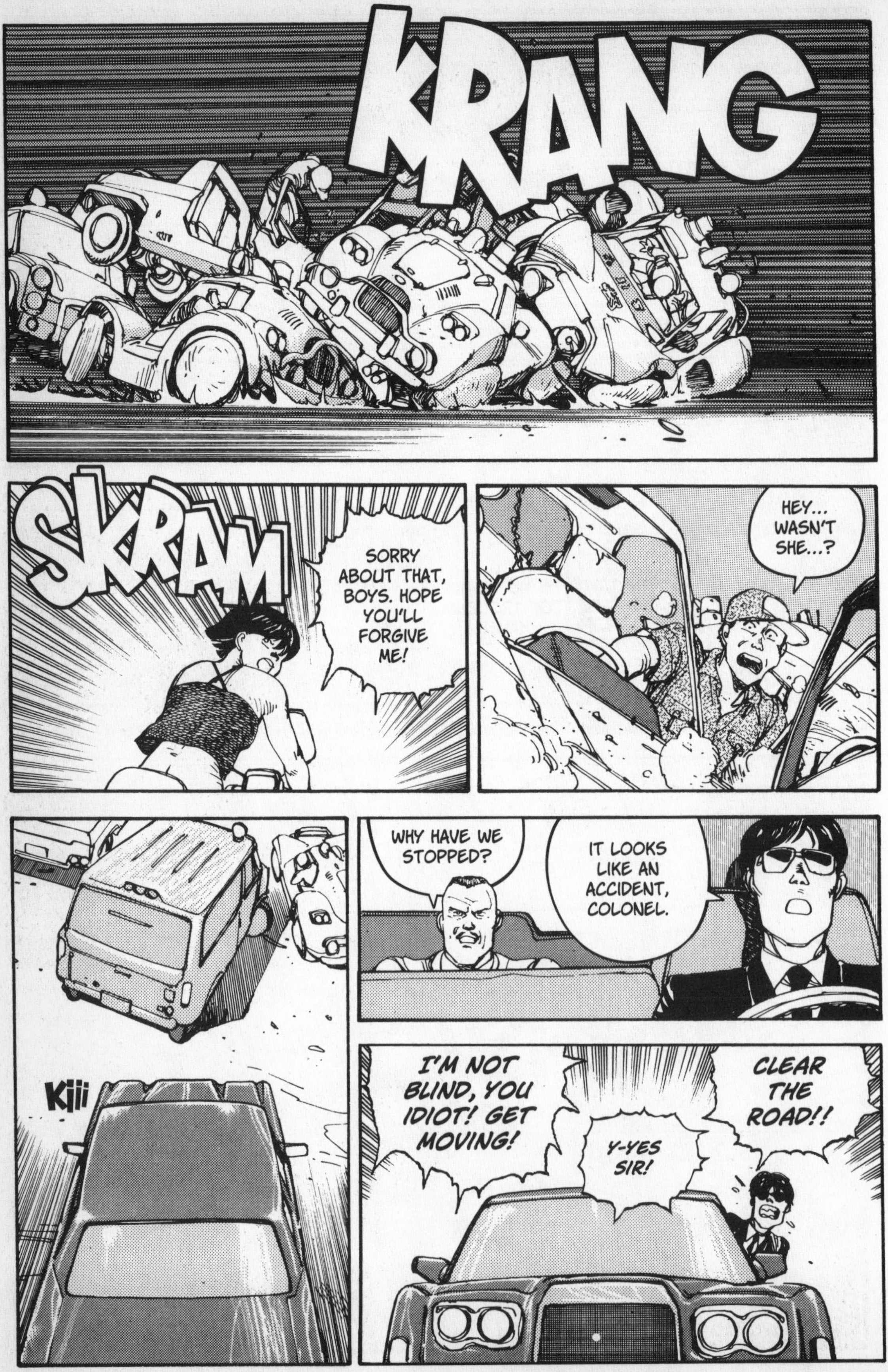
KRANG
SKRAM
SORRY ABOUT THAT, BOYS. HOPE YOU'LL FORGIVE ME!
HEY... WASN'T SHE...?
KIII
WHY HAVE WE STOPPED?
IT LOOKS LIKE AN ACCIDENT, COLONEL.
I'M NOT BLIND, YOU IDIOT! GET MOVING!
CLEAR THE ROAD!!
Y-YES SIR!

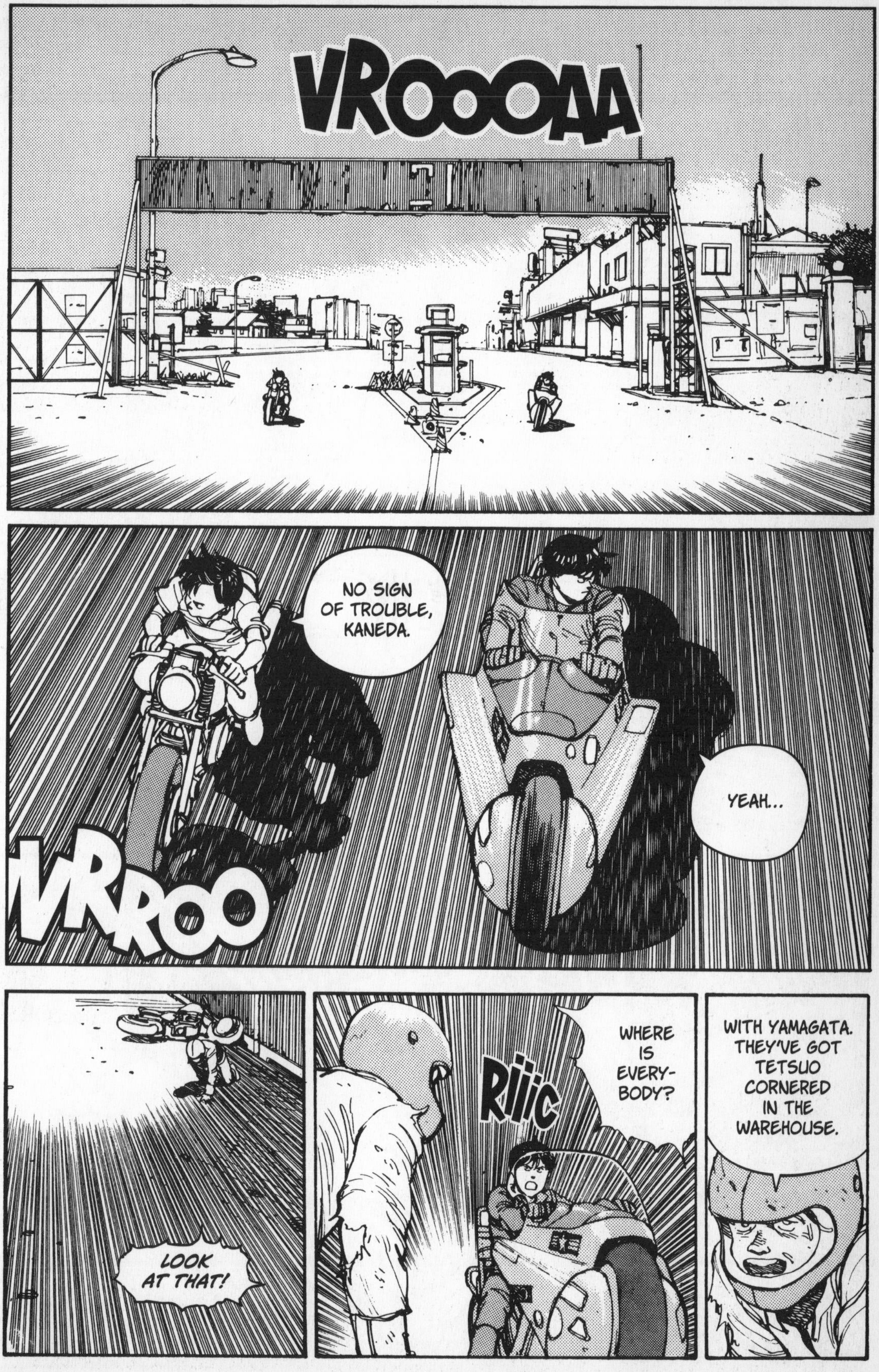
VROOOAA
NO SIGN OF TROUBLE, KANEDA.
YEAH...
VRROO
LOOK AT THAT!
RIIIC
WHERE IS EVERY-BODY?
WITH YAMAGATA. THEY'VE GOT TETSUO CORNERED IN THE WAREHOUSE.

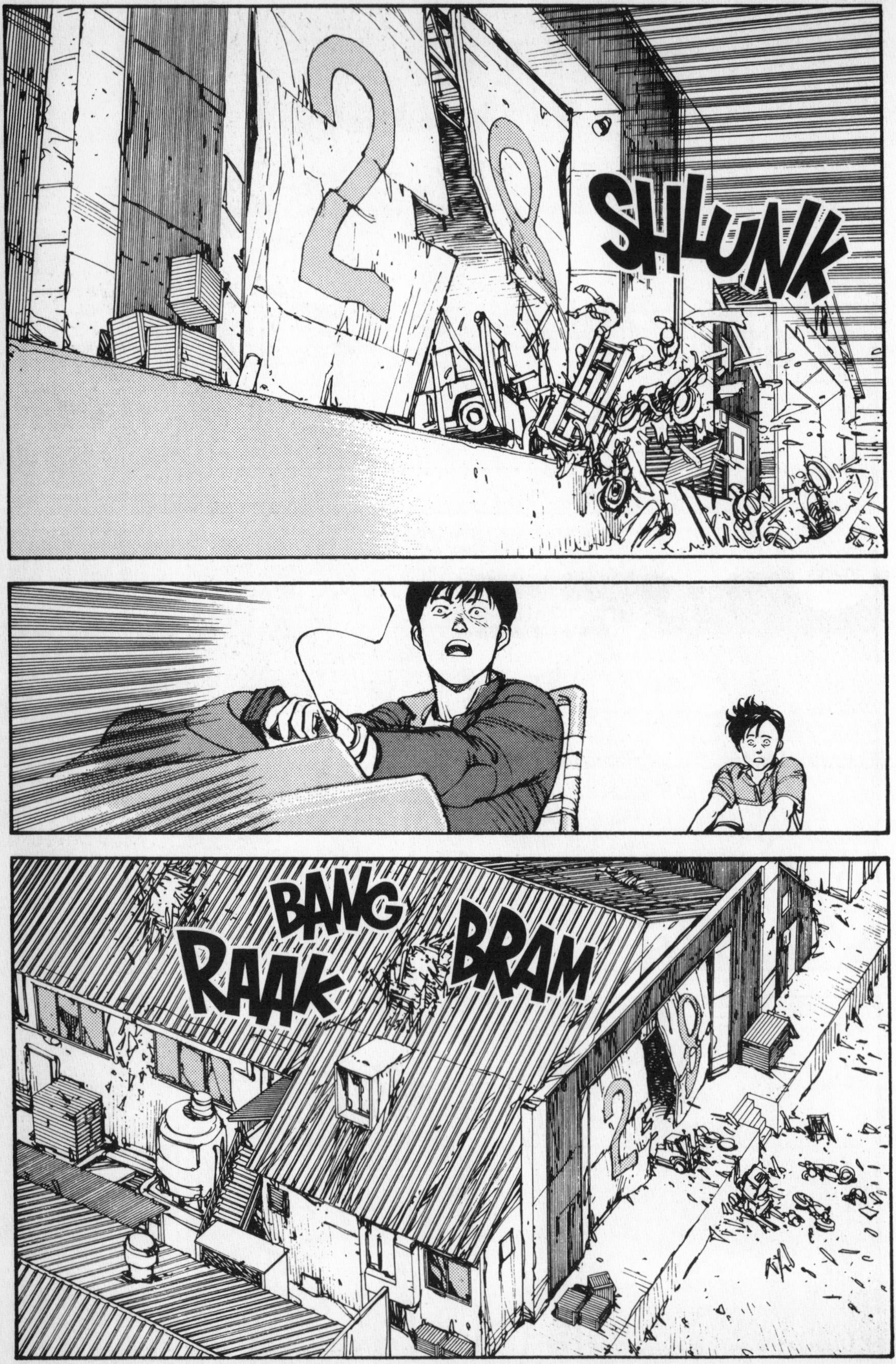
SHLUNK
BANG
RAAK
BRAM

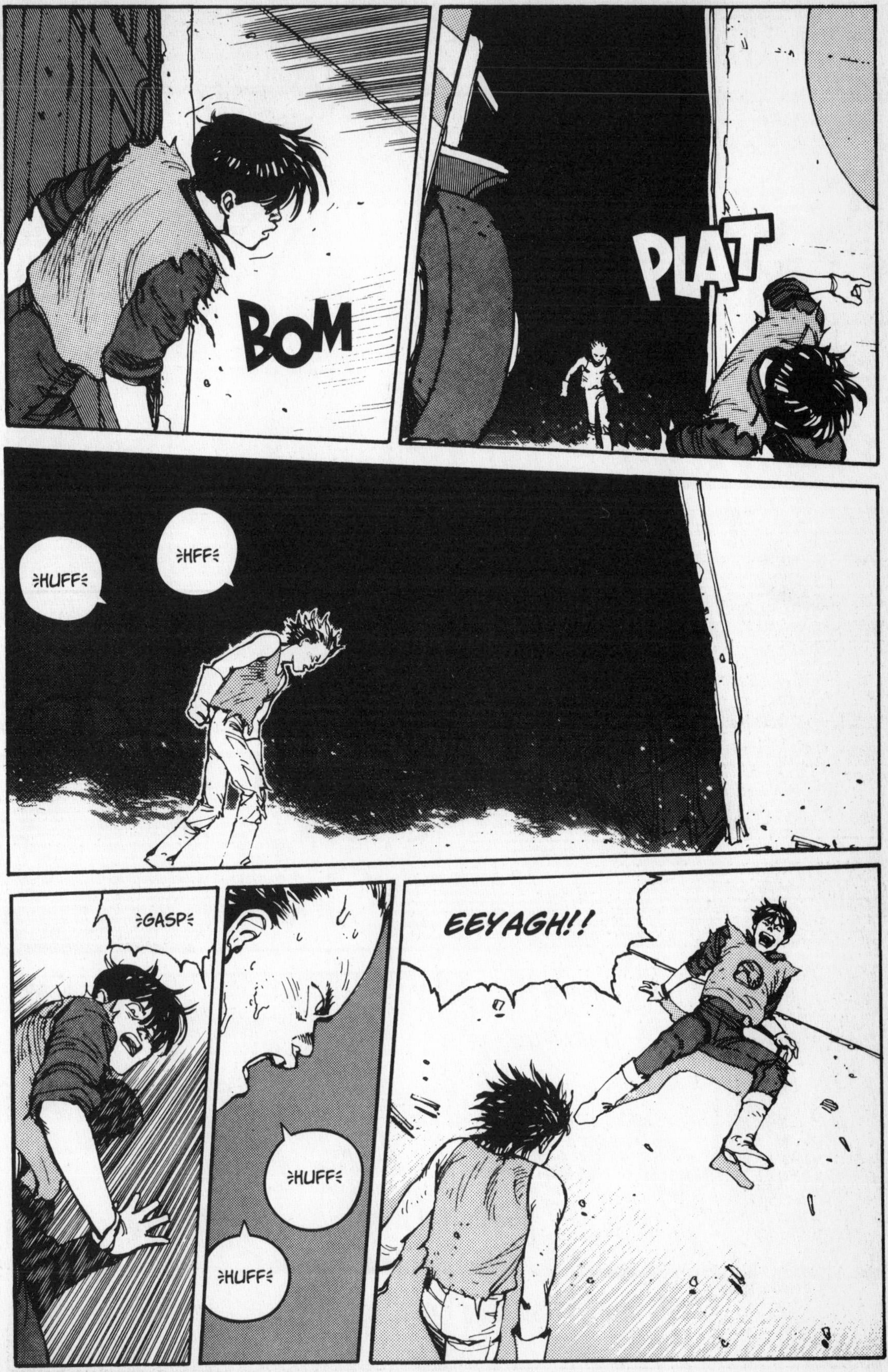
BOM
PLAT
HUFF
HFF
GASP
HUFF
HUFF
EEYAGH!!

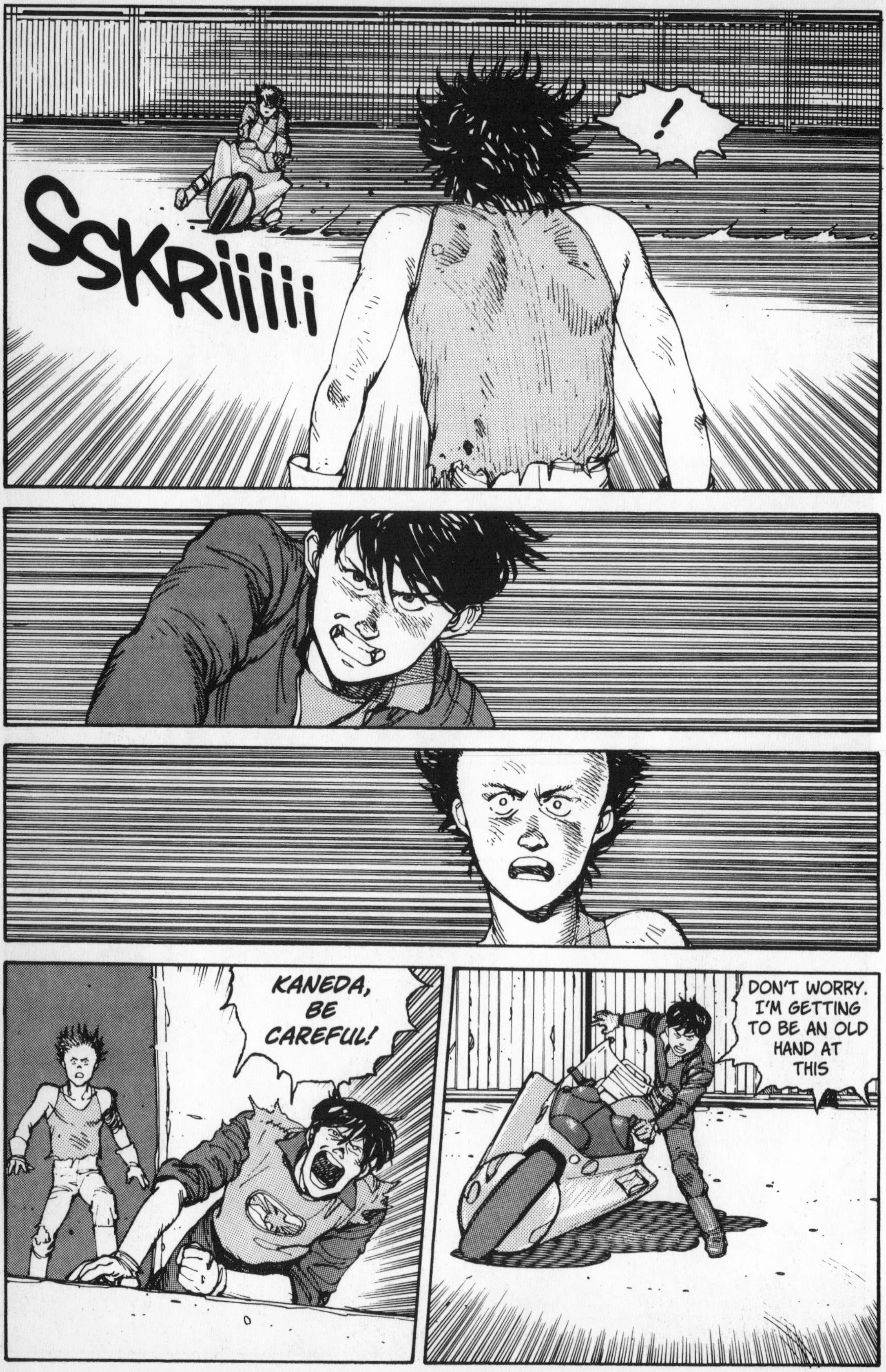
SSKRiiiiii
!
KANEDA, BE CAREFUL!
DON'T WORRY. I'M GETTING TO BE AN OLD HAND AT THIS

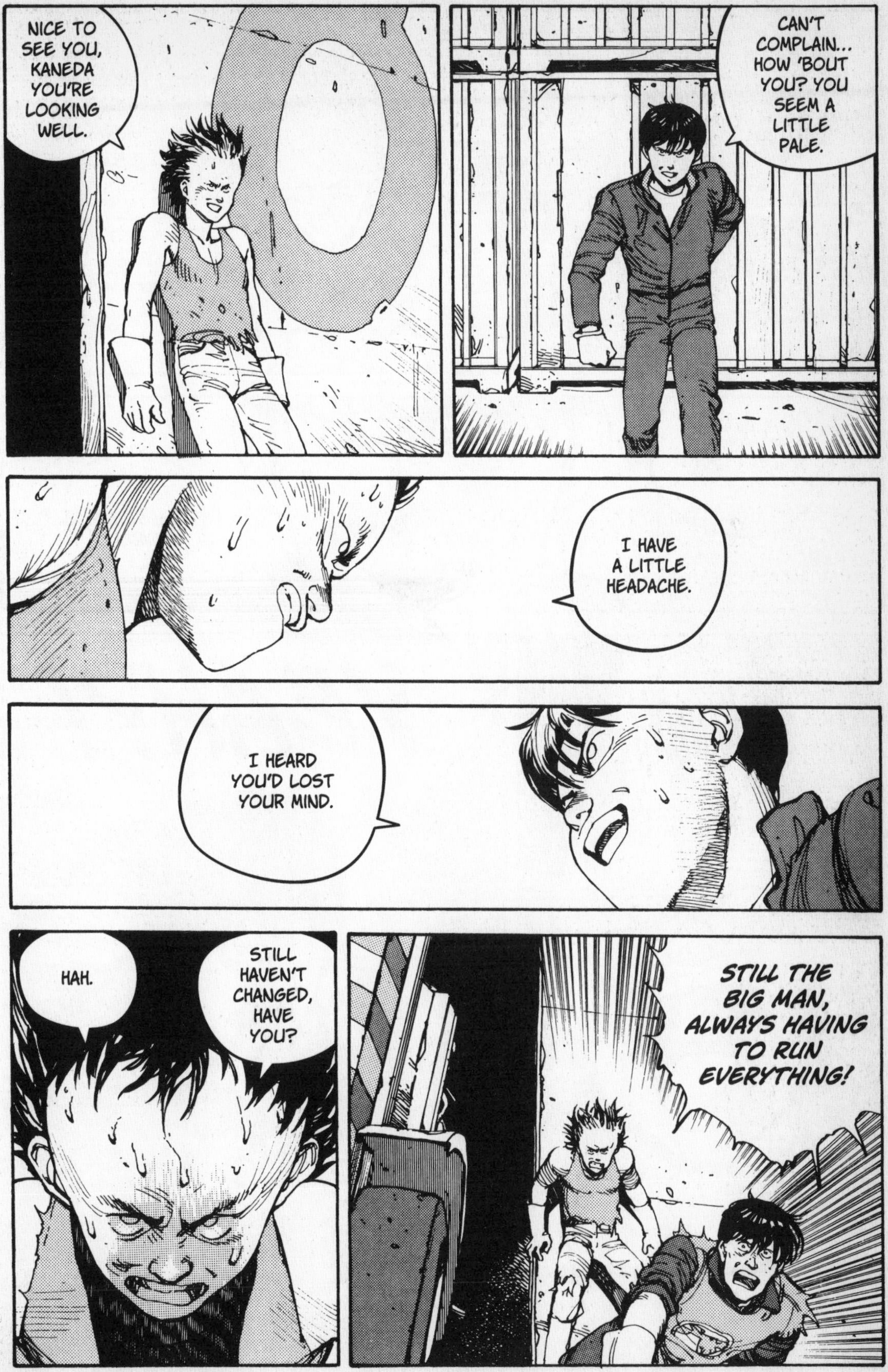
NICE TO SEE YOU, KANEDA YOU'RE LOOKING WELL.
CAN'T COMPLAIN... HOW 'BOUT YOU? YOU SEEM A LITTLE PALE.
I HAVE A LITTLE HEADACHE.
I HEARD YOU'D LOST YOUR MIND.
HAH.
STILL HAVEN'T CHANGED, HAVE YOU?
STILL THE BIG MAN, ALWAYS HAVING TO RUN EVERYTHING!

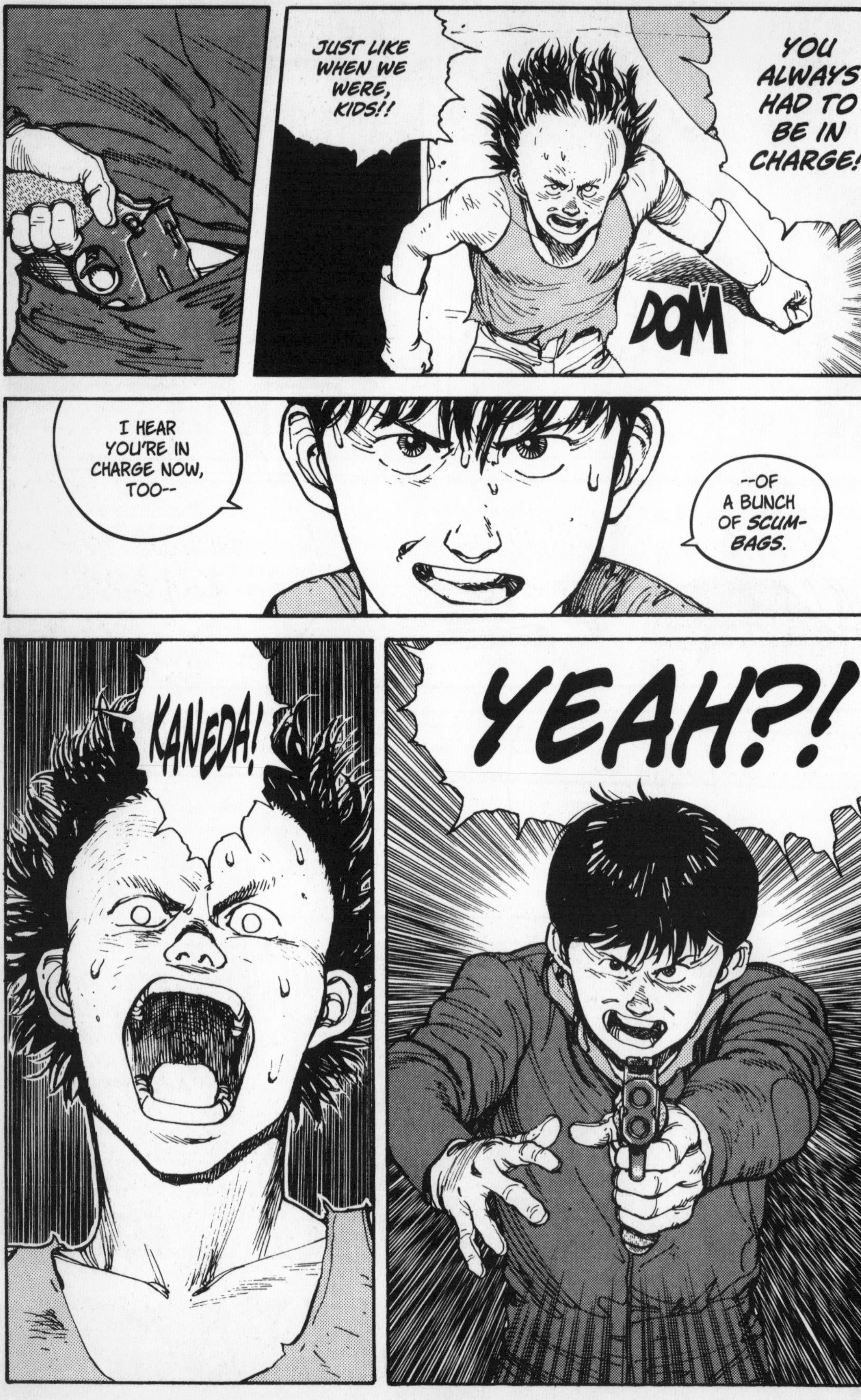
JUST LIKE WHEN WE WERE, KIDS!!
YOU ALWAYS HAD TO BE IN CHARGE!
DOM
I HEAR YOU'RE IN CHARGE NOW, TOO--
--OF A BUNCH OF SCUM-BAGS.
KANEDA!
YEAH?!

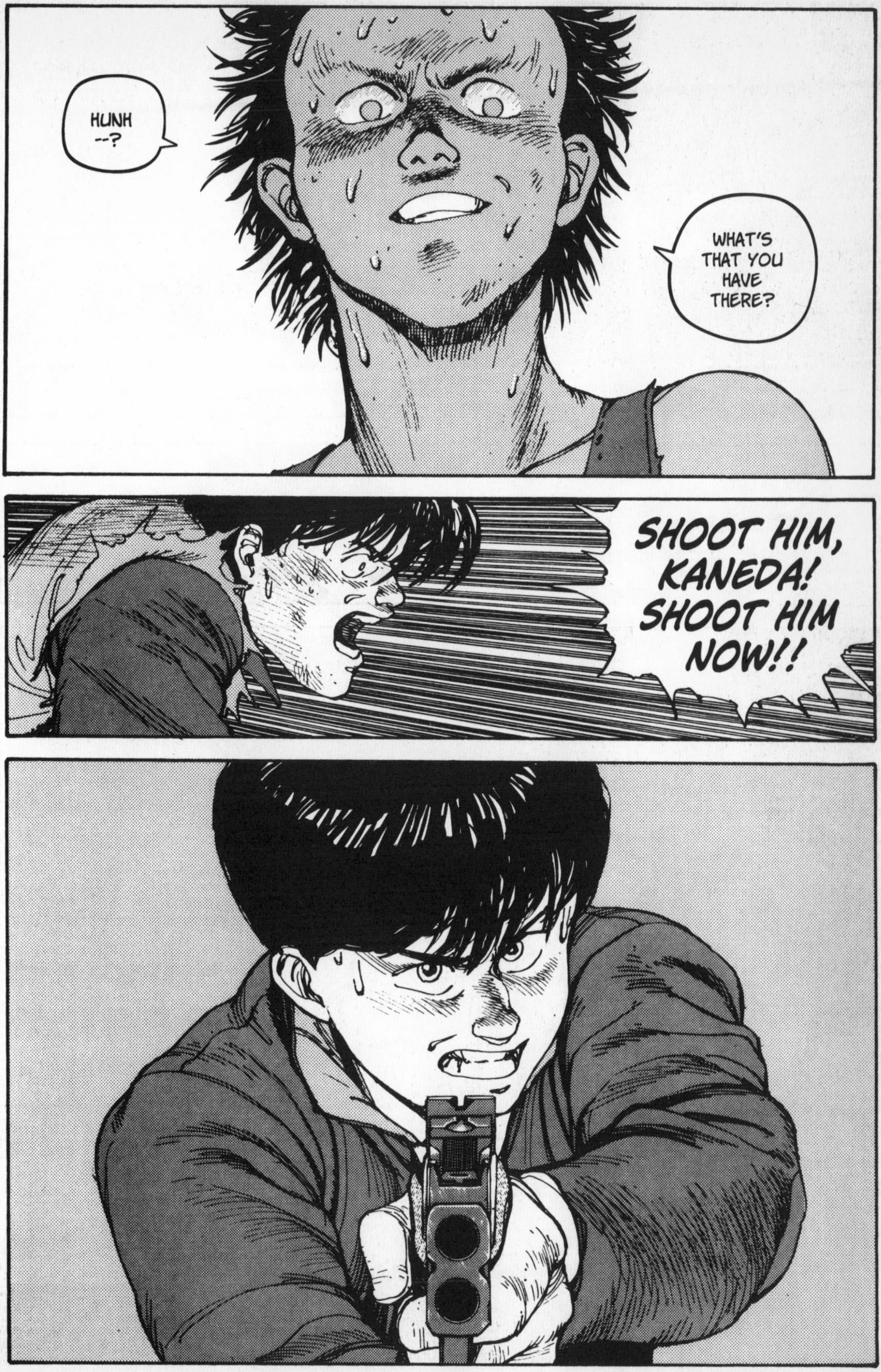
HUNH --?
WHAT'S THAT YOU HAVE THERE?
SHOOT HIM, KANEDA! SHOOT HIM NOW!!

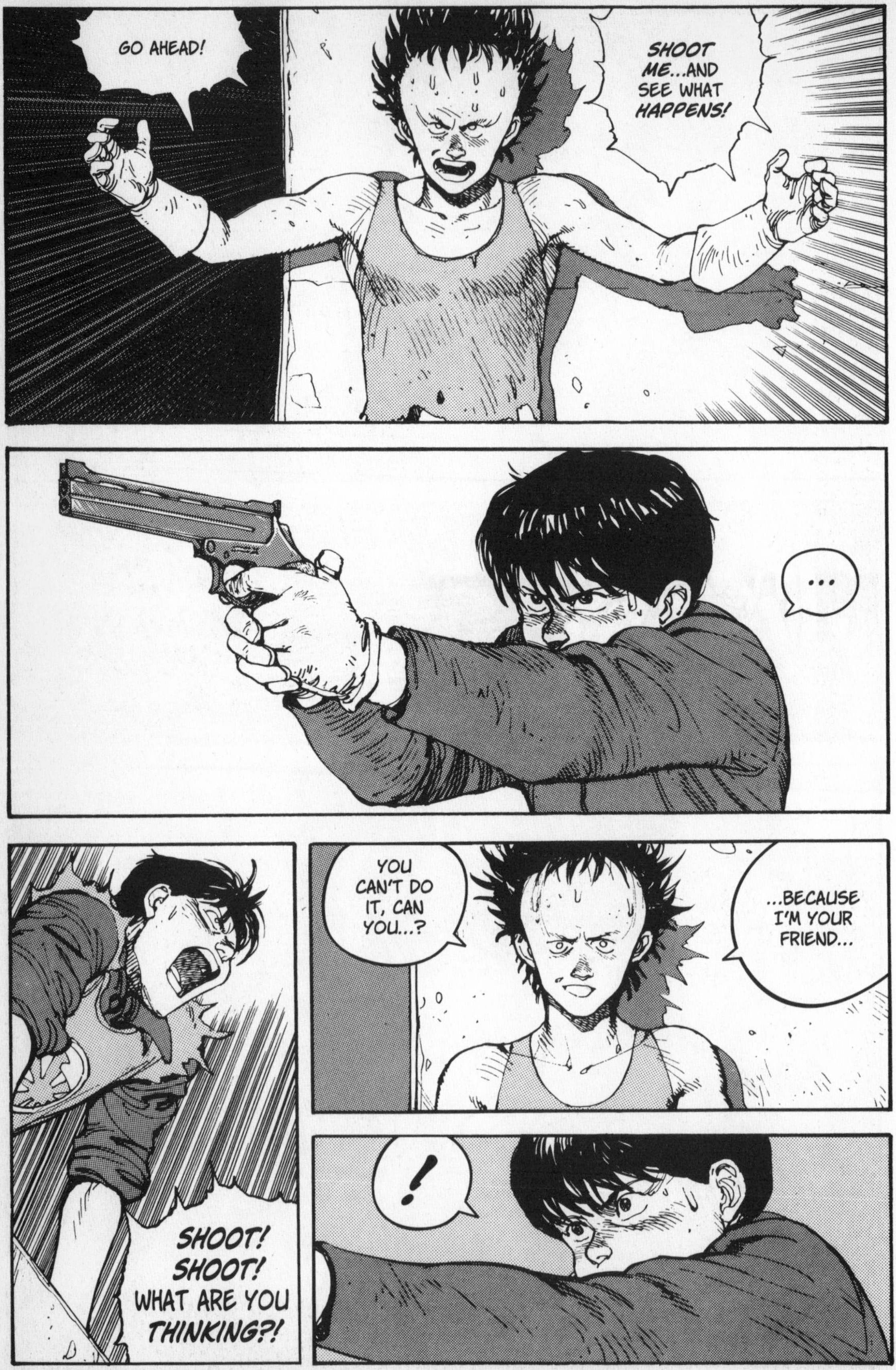
GO AHEAD!
SHOOT ME...AND SEE WHAT HAPPENS!
...
SHOOT! SHOOT! WHAT ARE YOU THINKING?!
YOU CAN'T DO IT, CAN YOU...?
...BECAUSE I'M YOUR FRIEND...
!

...ISN'T THAT RIGHT...

...KANEDA?

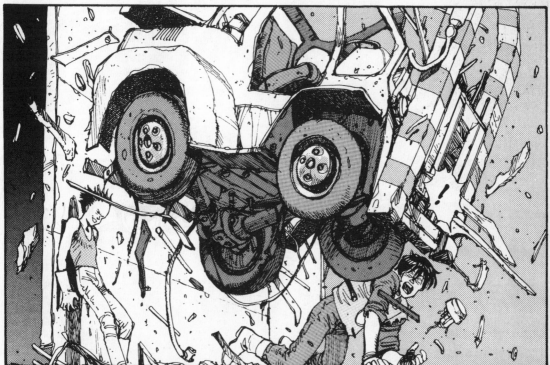

NOOOO!

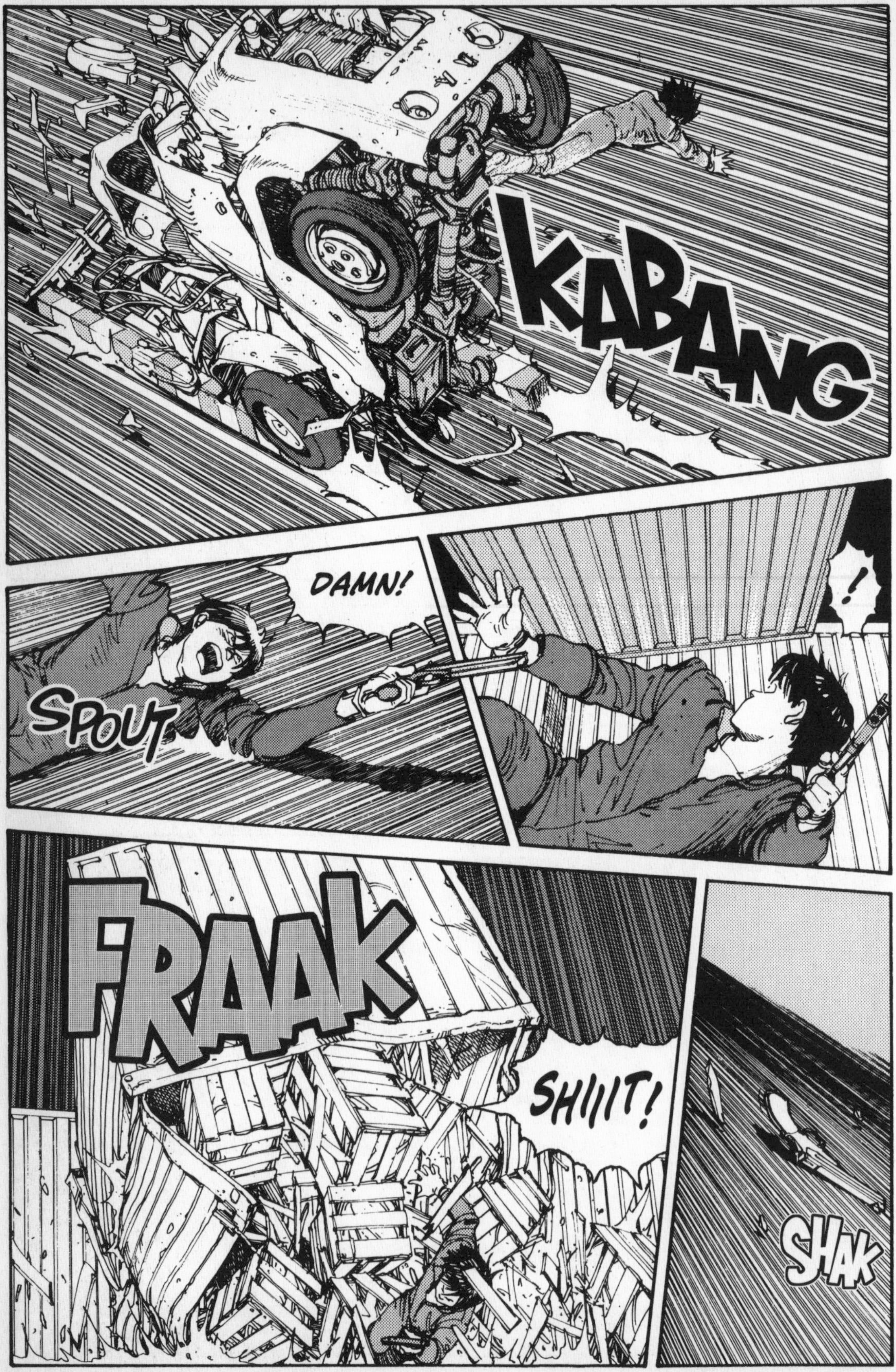
KABANG
DAMN!
SPOUT
!
FRAAK
SHIIIT!
SHAK

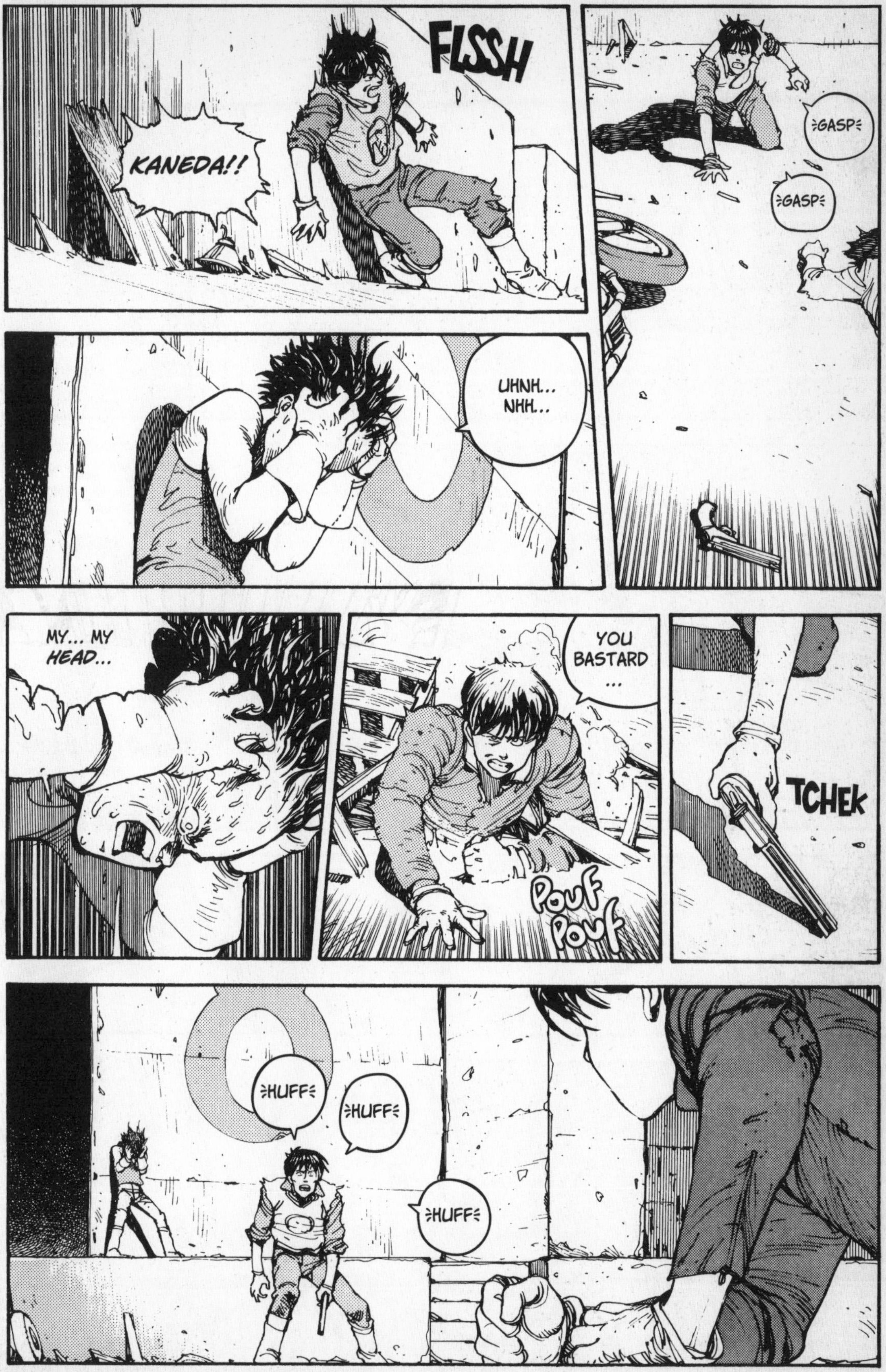
FLSSH
KANEDA!!
GASP
GASP
UHNH... NHH...
MY... MY HEAD...
YOU BASTARD ...
POUF POUF
TCHEK
HUFF
HUFF
HUFF

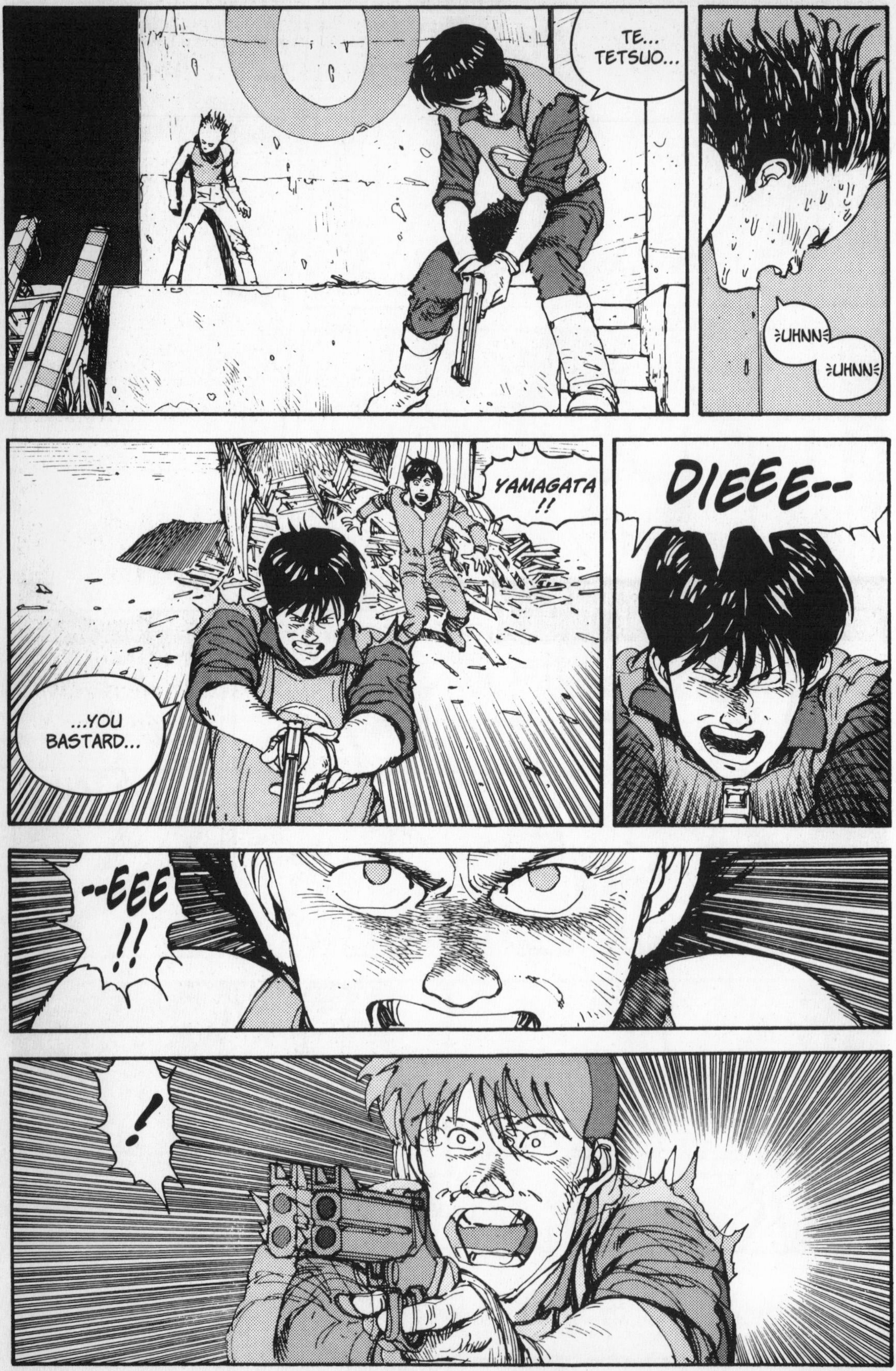
TE... TETSUO...
UHNN
UHNN
YAMAGATA !!
...YOU BASTARD...
DIEEE--
--EEE !!
!

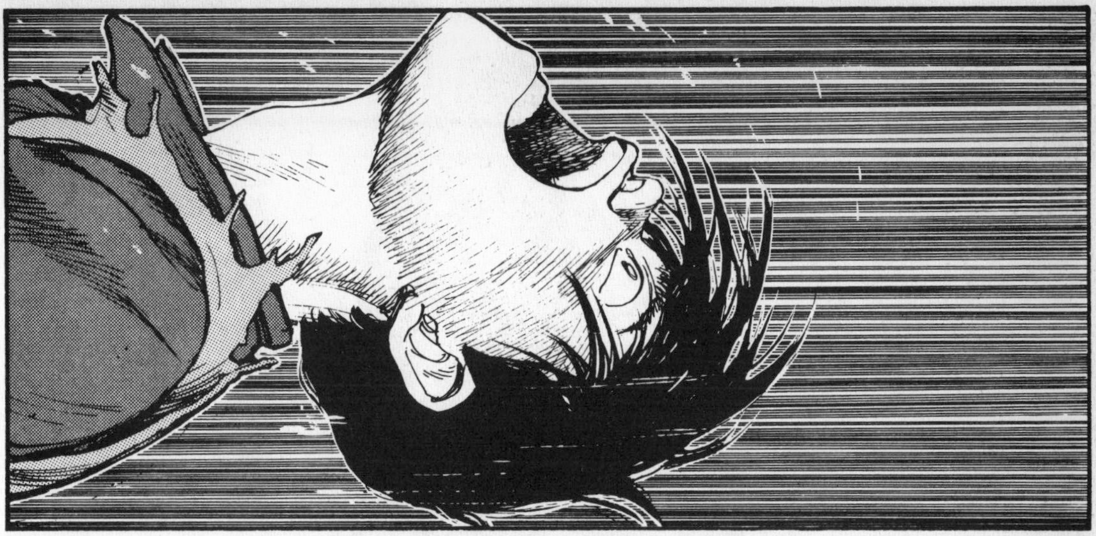

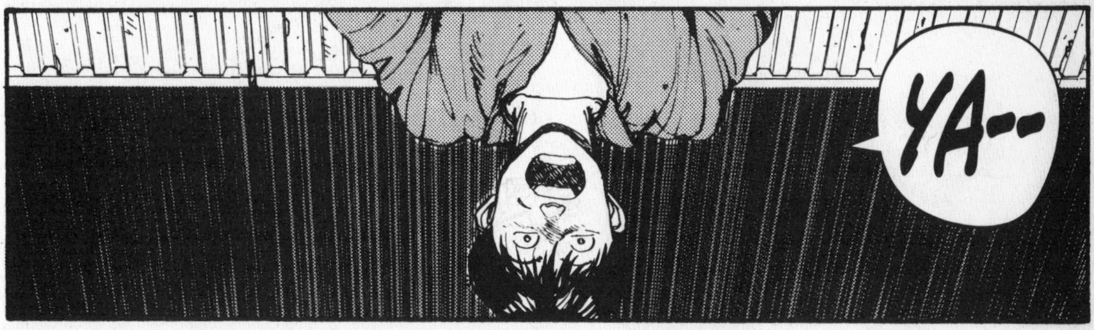
YA--

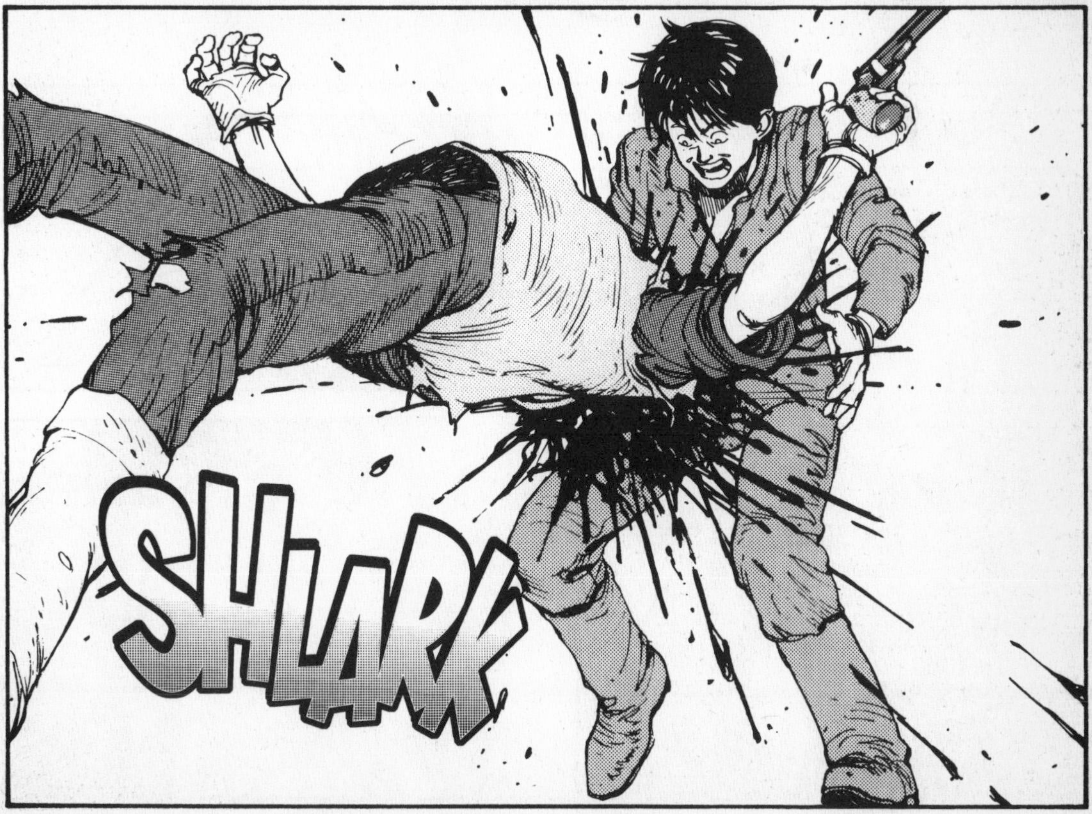
SHLARK

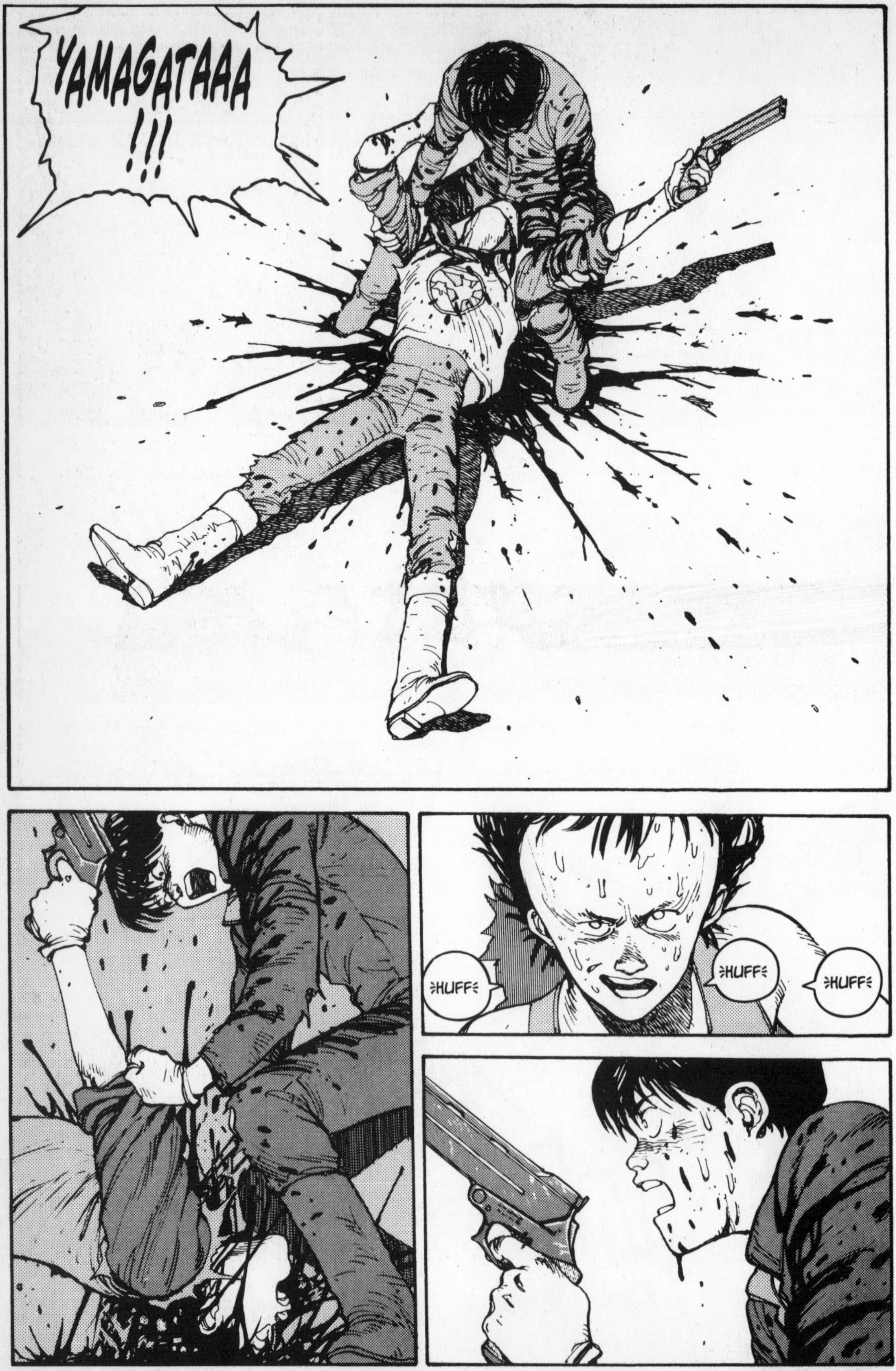
YAMAGATAAA !!!
HUFF
HUFF
HUFF

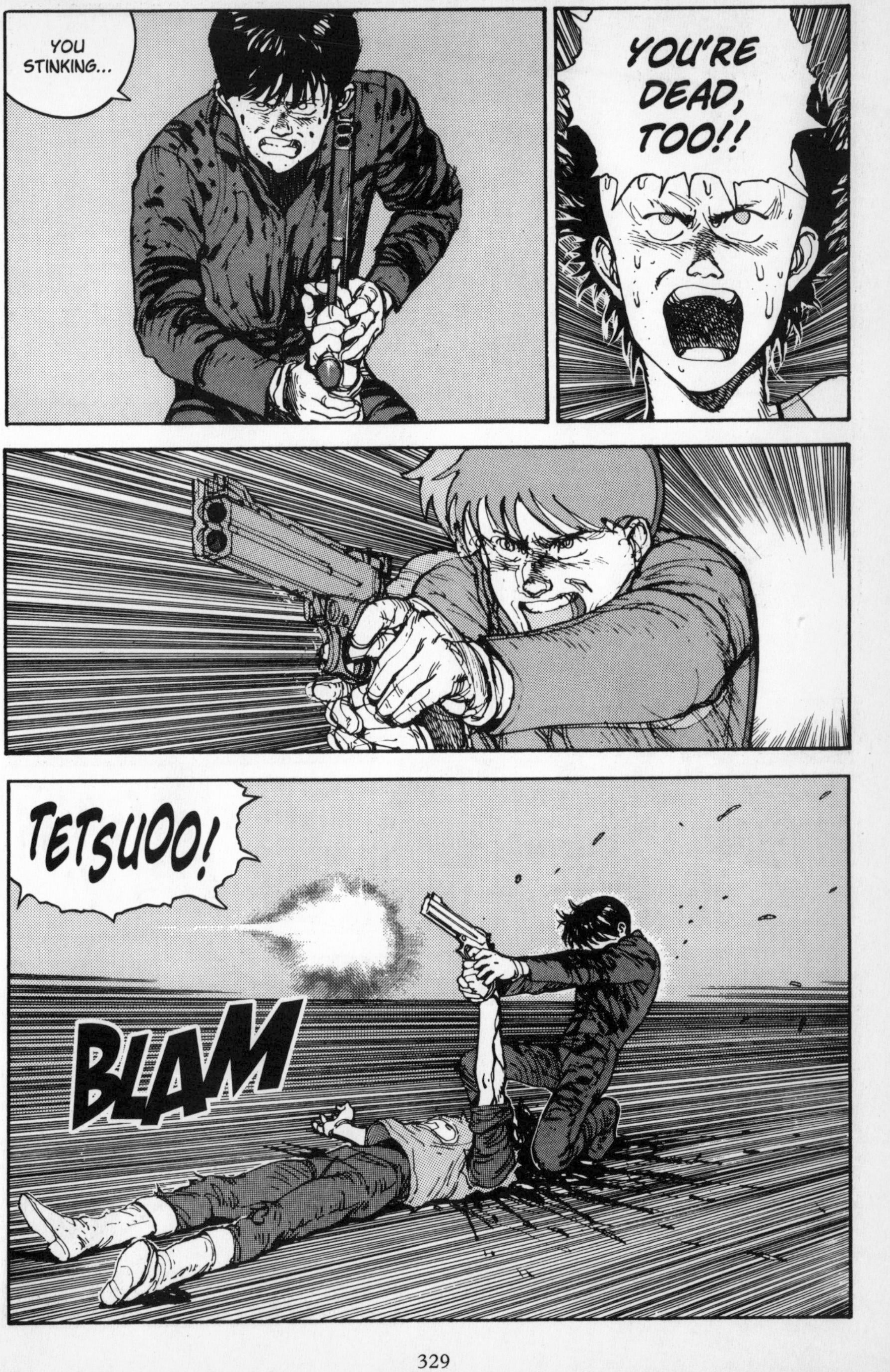
YOU STINKING...
YOU'RE DEAD, TOO!!
TETSUOO!
BLAM

EEYAAAA!!

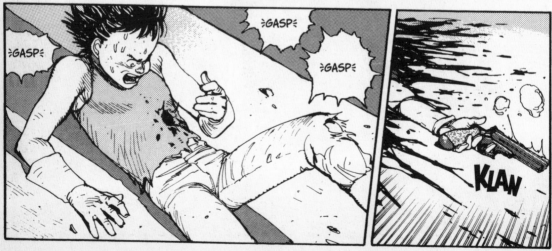

≶GASP≶

≶GASP≶

≶GASP≶

KLAN

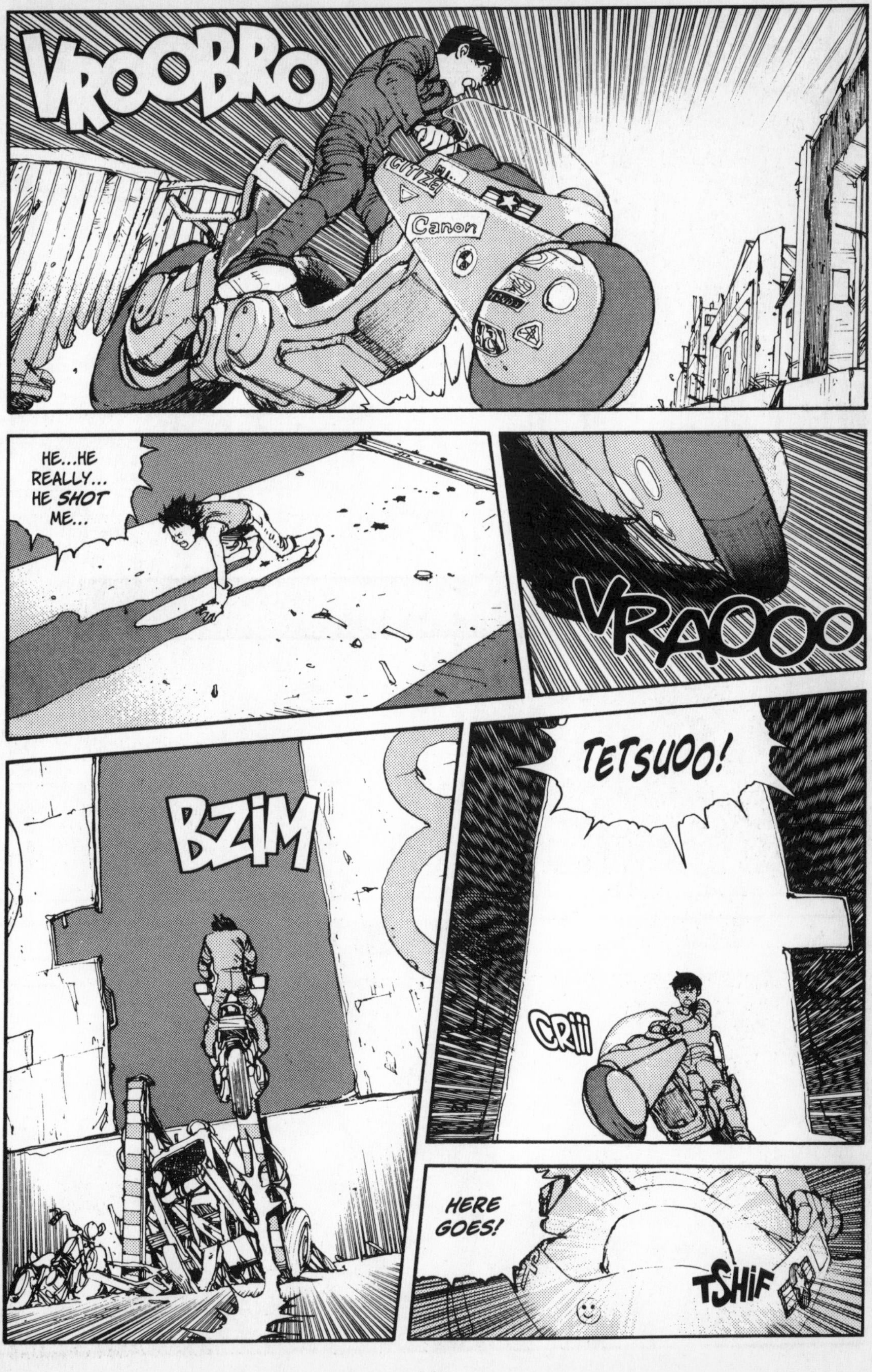
VROOBRO
HE...HE REALLY... HE SHOT ME...
VRAOOO
BZIM
TETSUOO!
CRiii
HERE GOES!
TSHIF

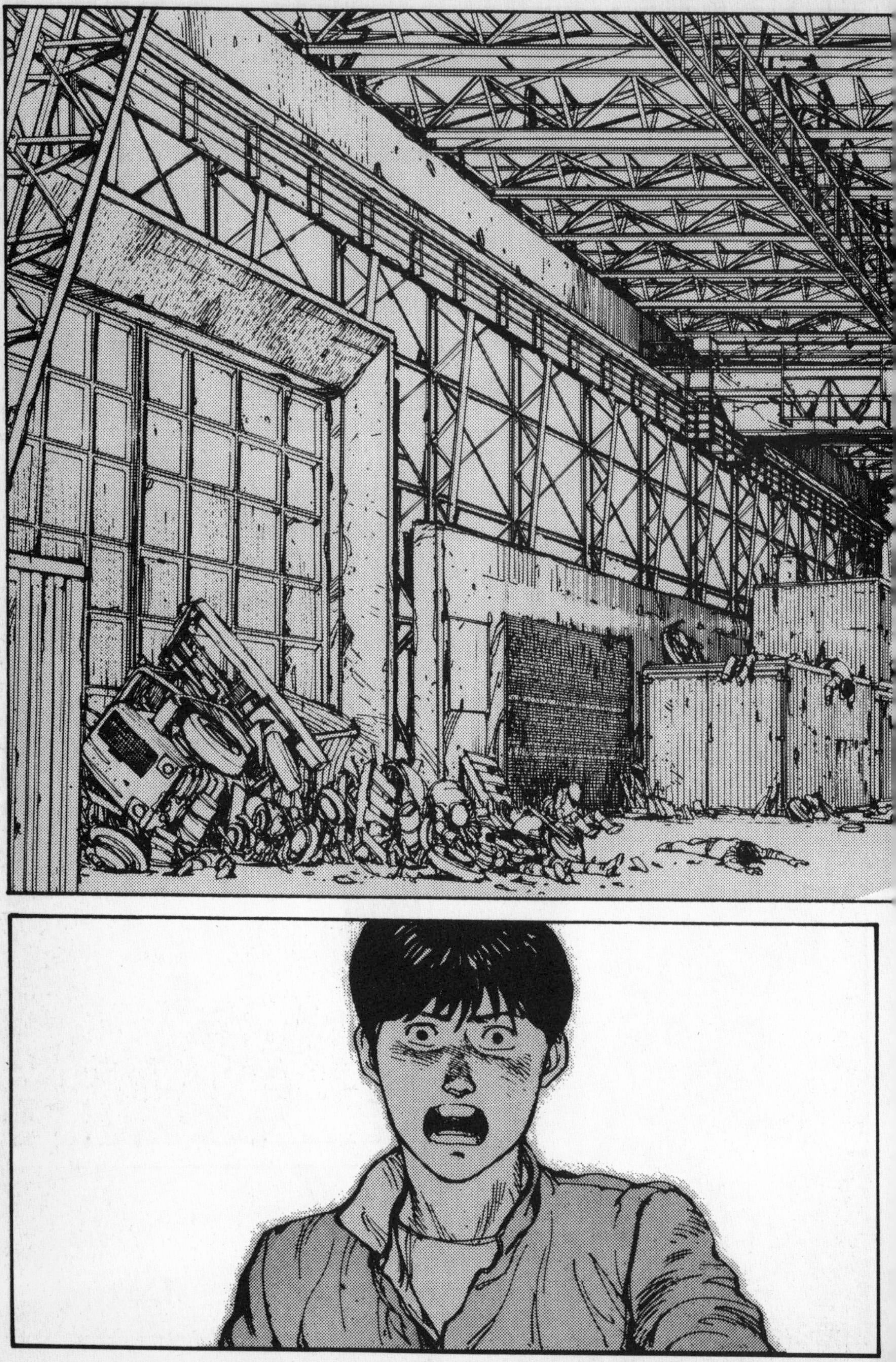

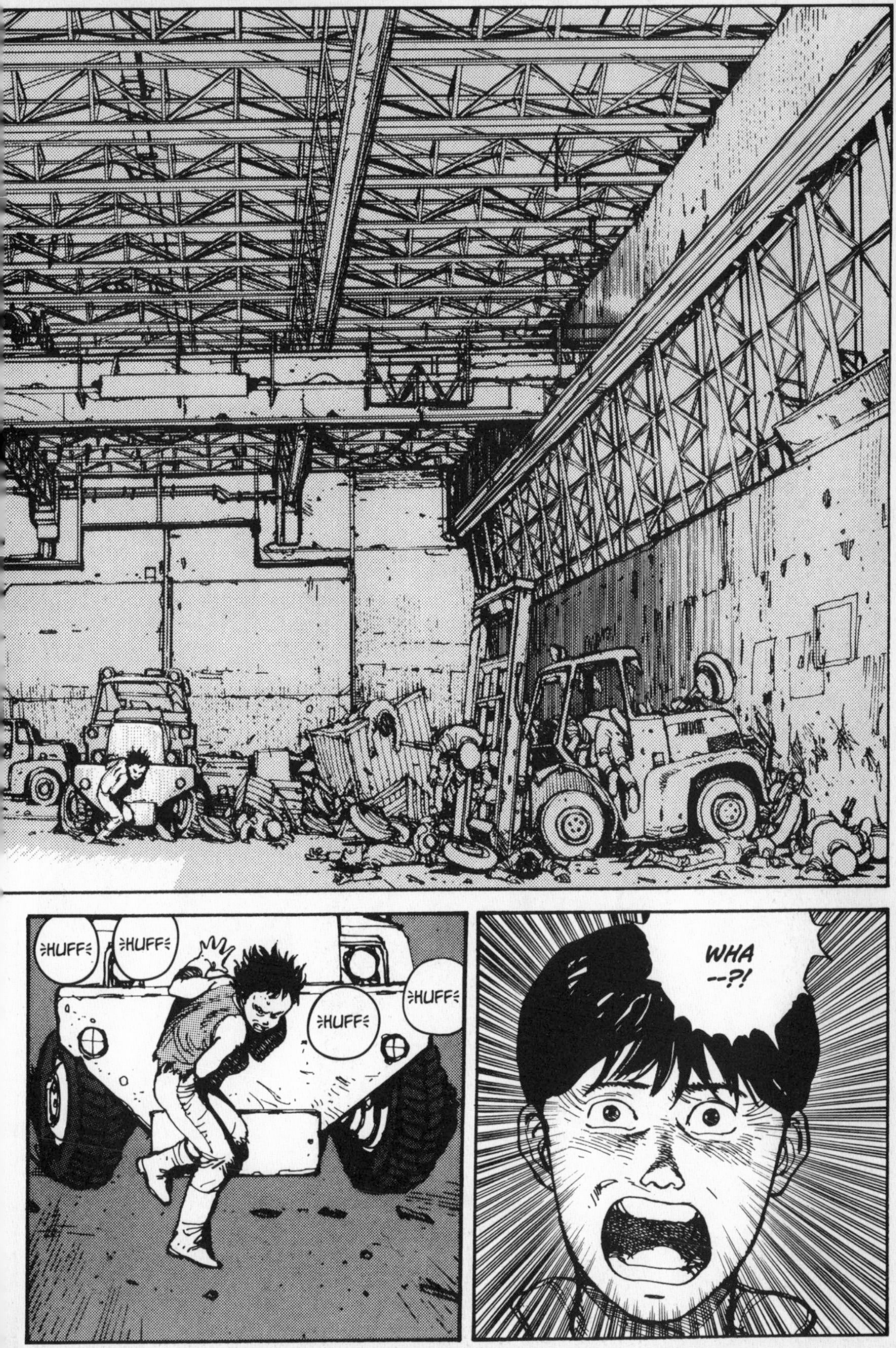
HUFF
HUFF
HUFF
HUFF
WHA --?!

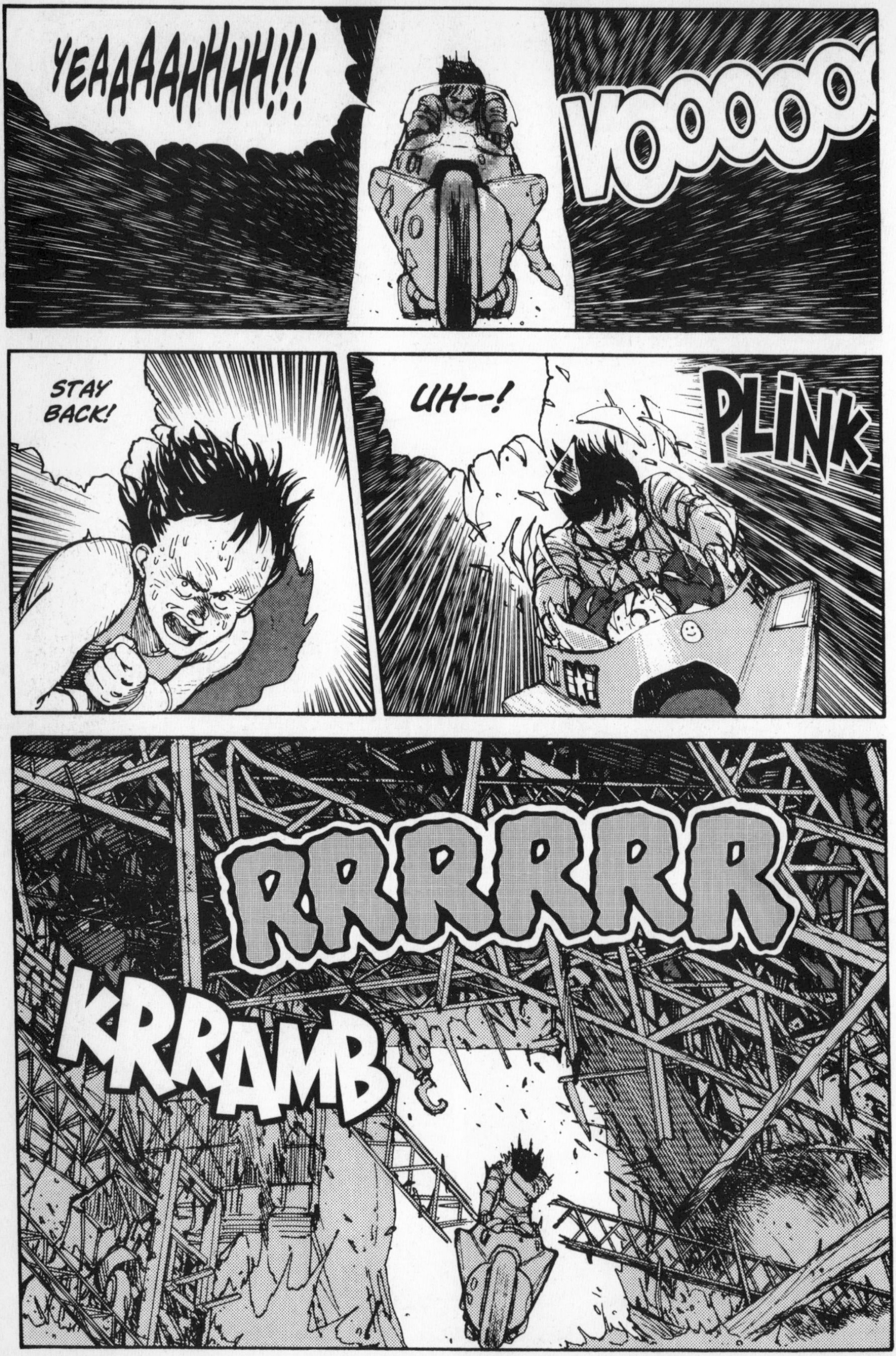
YEAAAAHHHH!!!
VOOOOOO
STAY BACK!
UH--!
PLINK
RRRRRR
KRRAMB

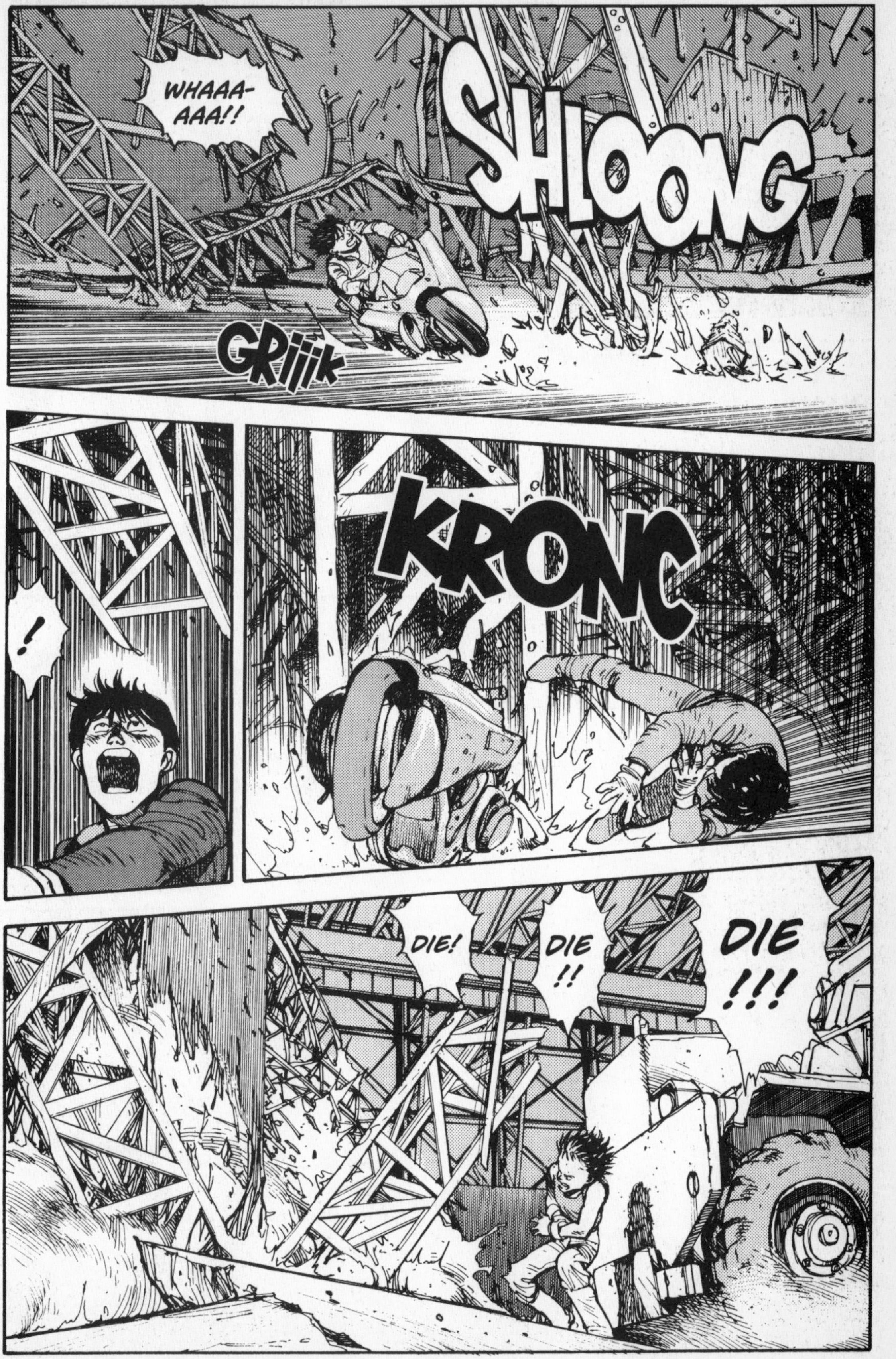
WHAAA-
AAA!!
SHLOONG
GRiiik
!
KRONC
DIE!
DIE
!!
DIE
!!!

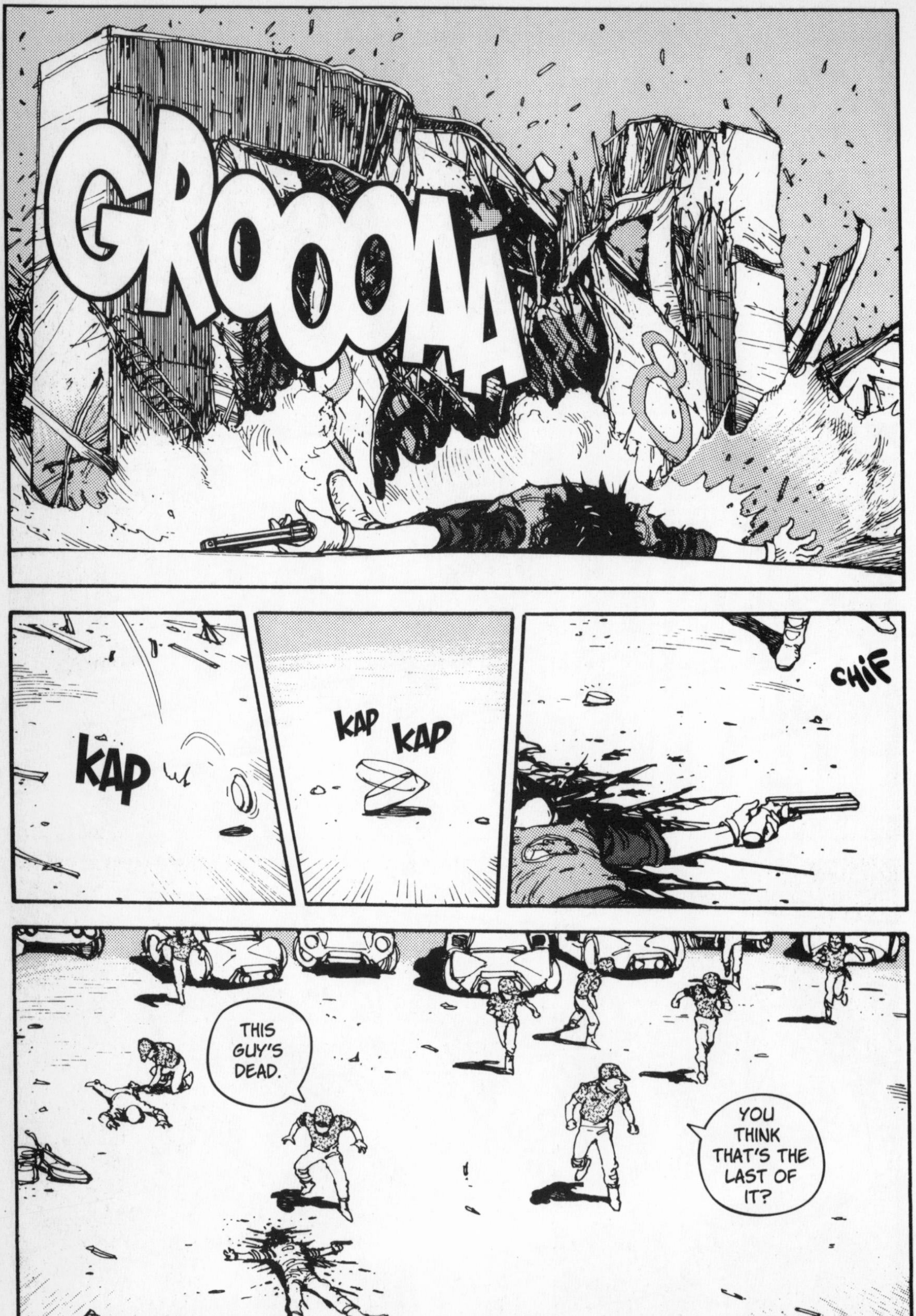
GROOOAA
KAP
KAP KAP
CHIF
THIS GUY'S DEAD.
YOU THINK THAT'S THE LAST OF IT?

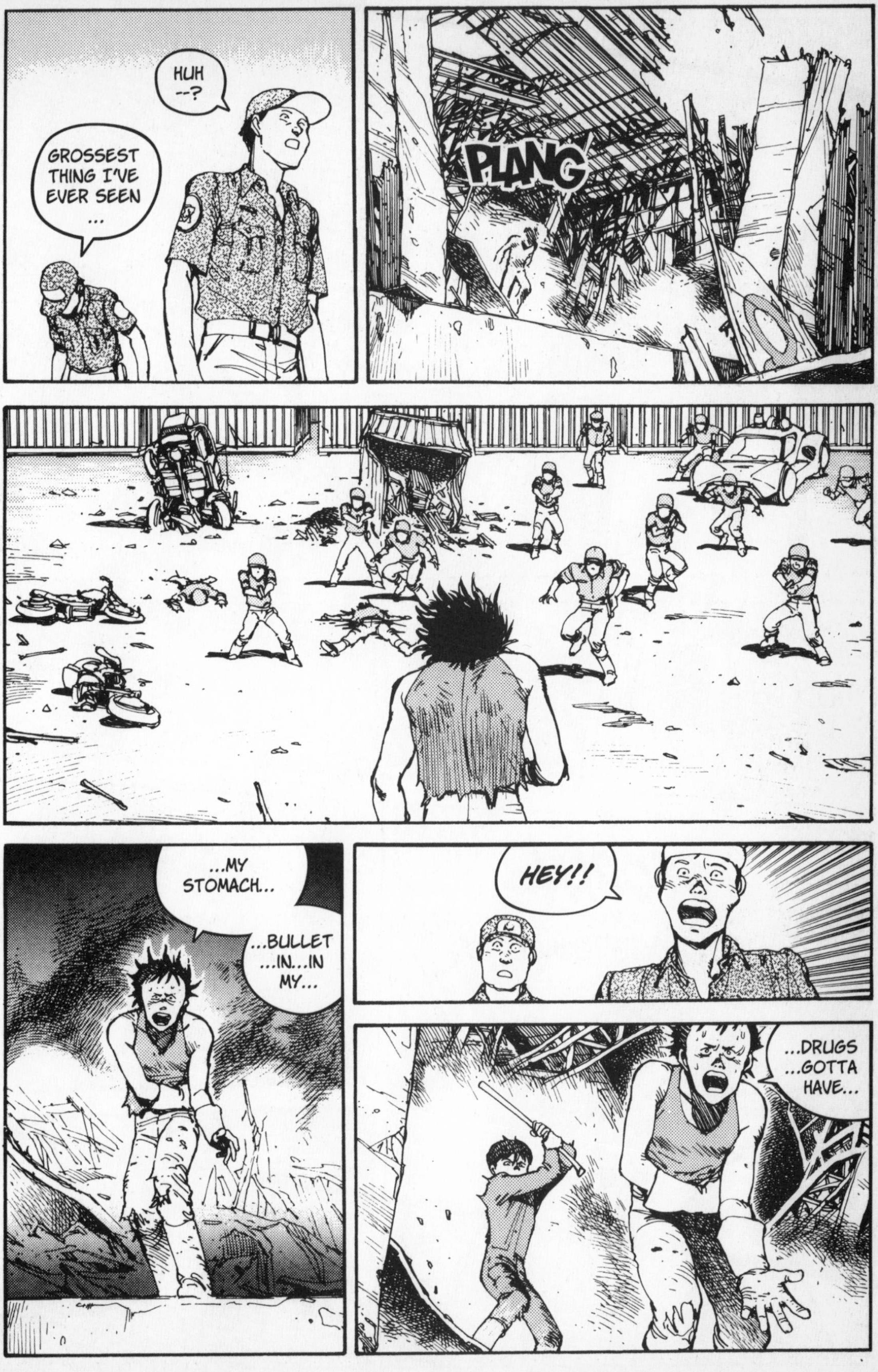
HUH --?
GROSSEST THING I'VE EVER SEEN ...
PLANG
...MY STOMACH...
...BULLET ...IN...IN MY...
HEY!!
...DRUGS ...GOTTA HAVE...

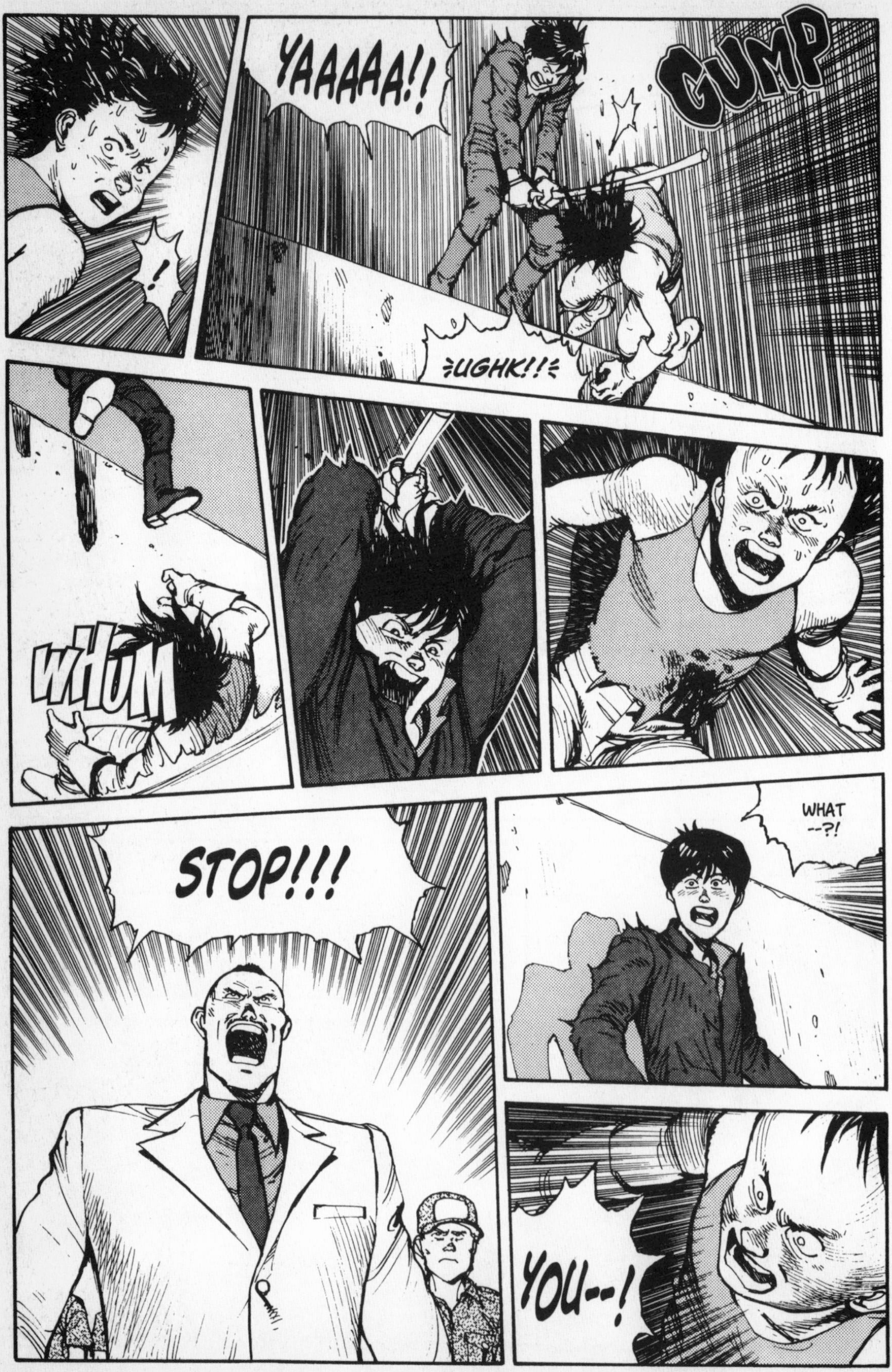
!
YAAAAA!!
GUMP
UGHK!!
WHUM
STOP!!!
WHAT --?!
YOU--!

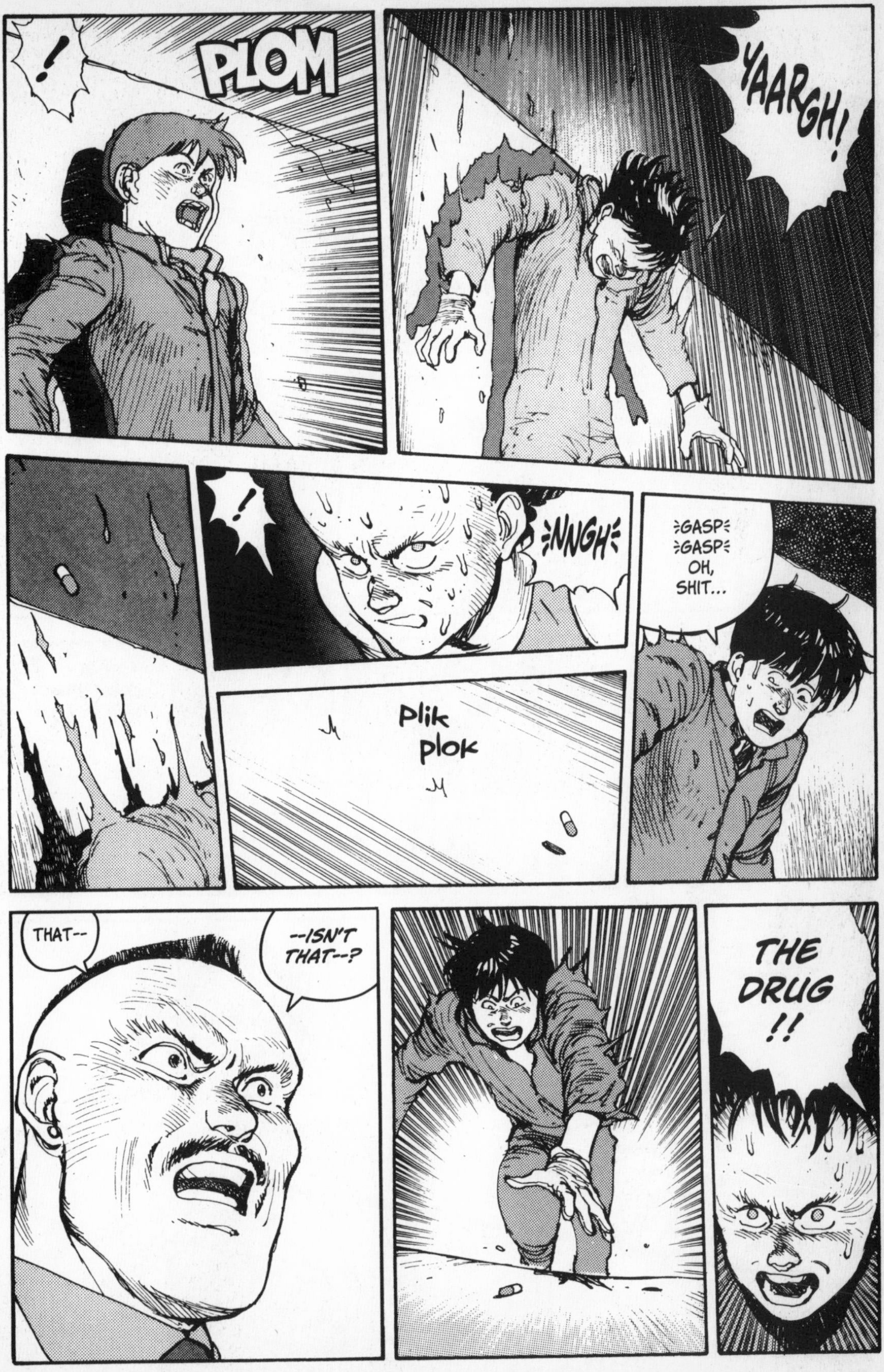

!
PLOM
YAARGH!
!
NNGH
GASP
GASP
OH,
SHIT...
plik
plok
THAT--
--ISN'T THAT--?
THE DRUG !!

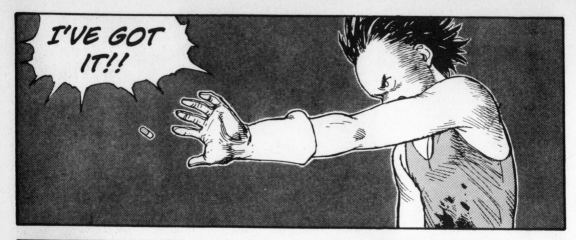

I'VE GOT IT!!

THAT'S THE CAPSULE THAT--

IT WAS YOU, WASN'T IT?

THANKS FOR SAVING IT FOR ME!

HEH...

IF YOU WANT IT SO BAD, IT'S ALL YOURS!

FIRST I'M TAKING THIS, THEN I'M TAKING CARE OF YOU

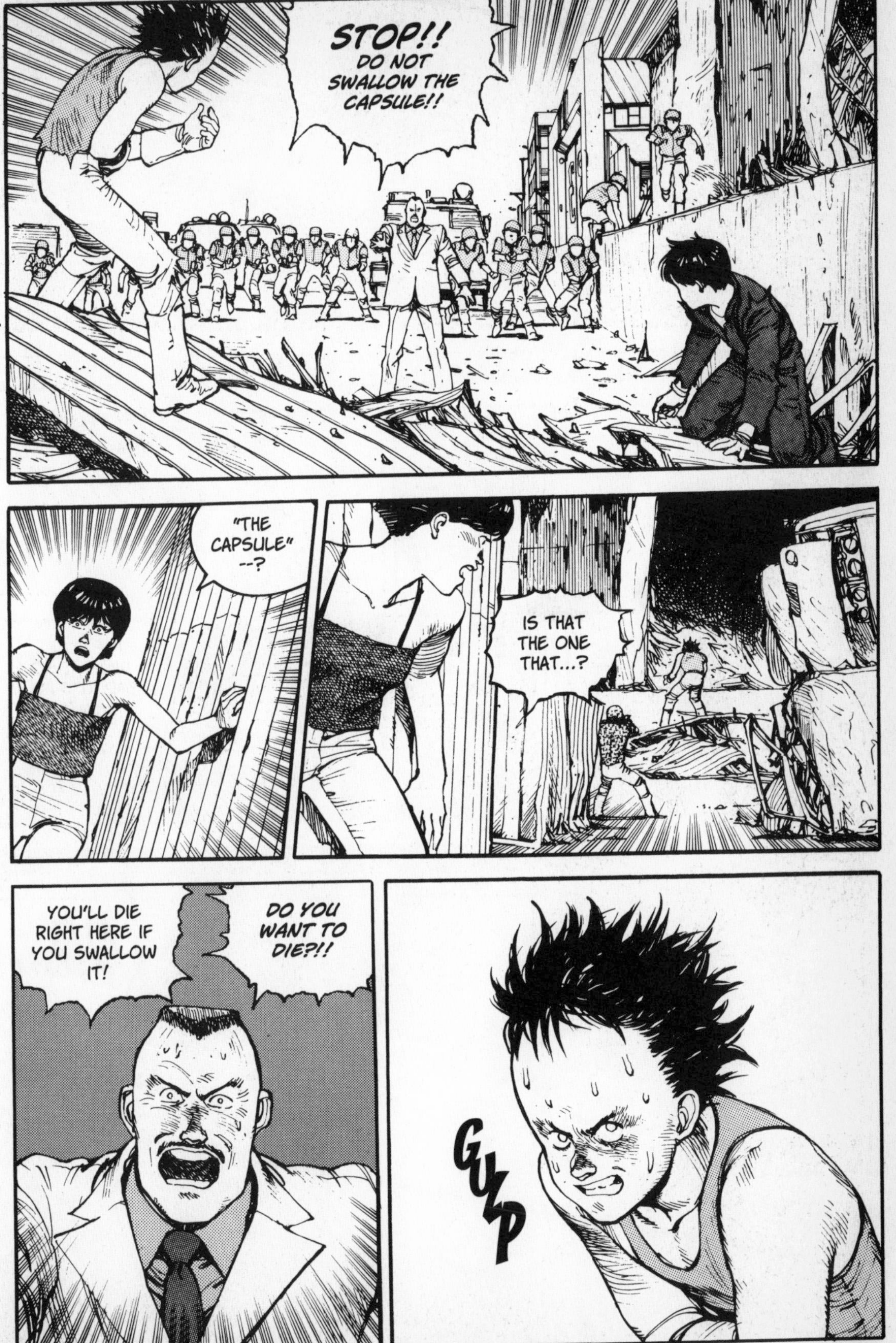
STOP!! DO NOT SWALLOW THE CAPSULE!!
"THE CAPSULE" --?
IS THAT THE ONE THAT...?
YOU'LL DIE RIGHT HERE IF YOU SWALLOW IT!
DO YOU WANT TO DIE?!!
GULP

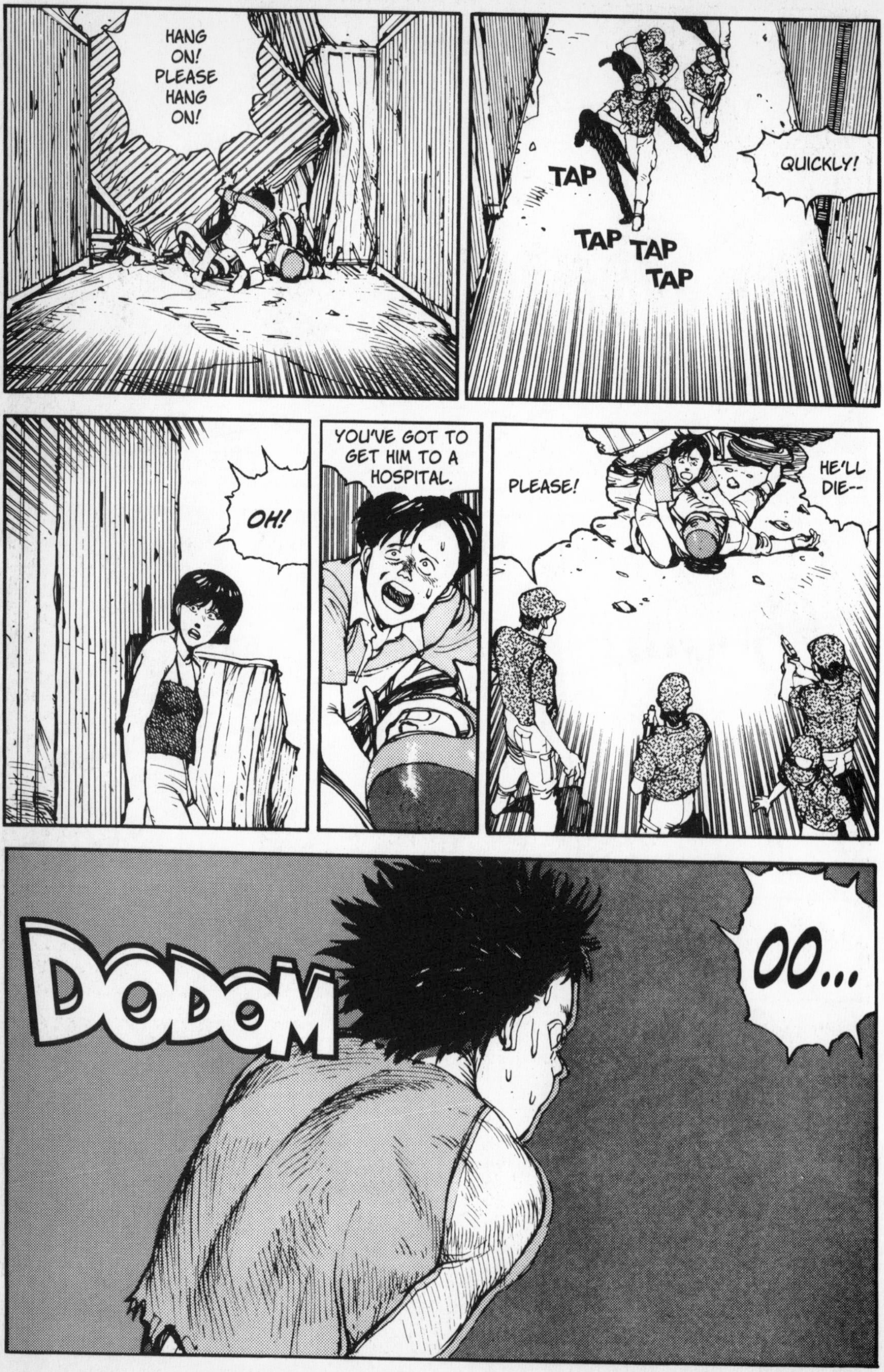
HANG ON! PLEASE HANG ON!
TAP
TAP TAP
TAP
QUICKLY!
OH!
YOU'VE GOT TO GET HIM TO A HOSPITAL.
PLEASE!
HE'LL DIE--
DODOM
OO...

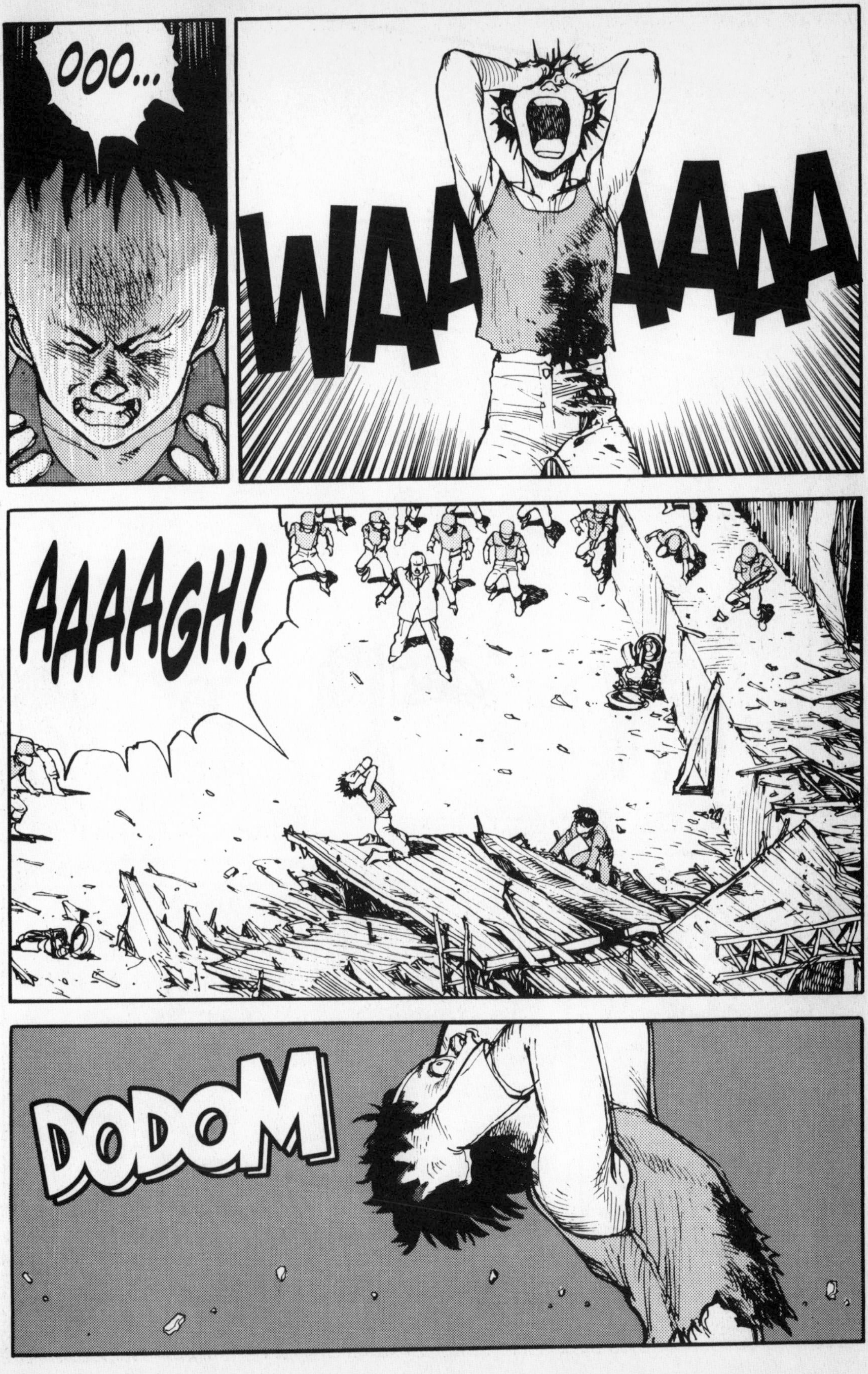
OOO...
WAAAAAAA
AAAAGH!
DODOM

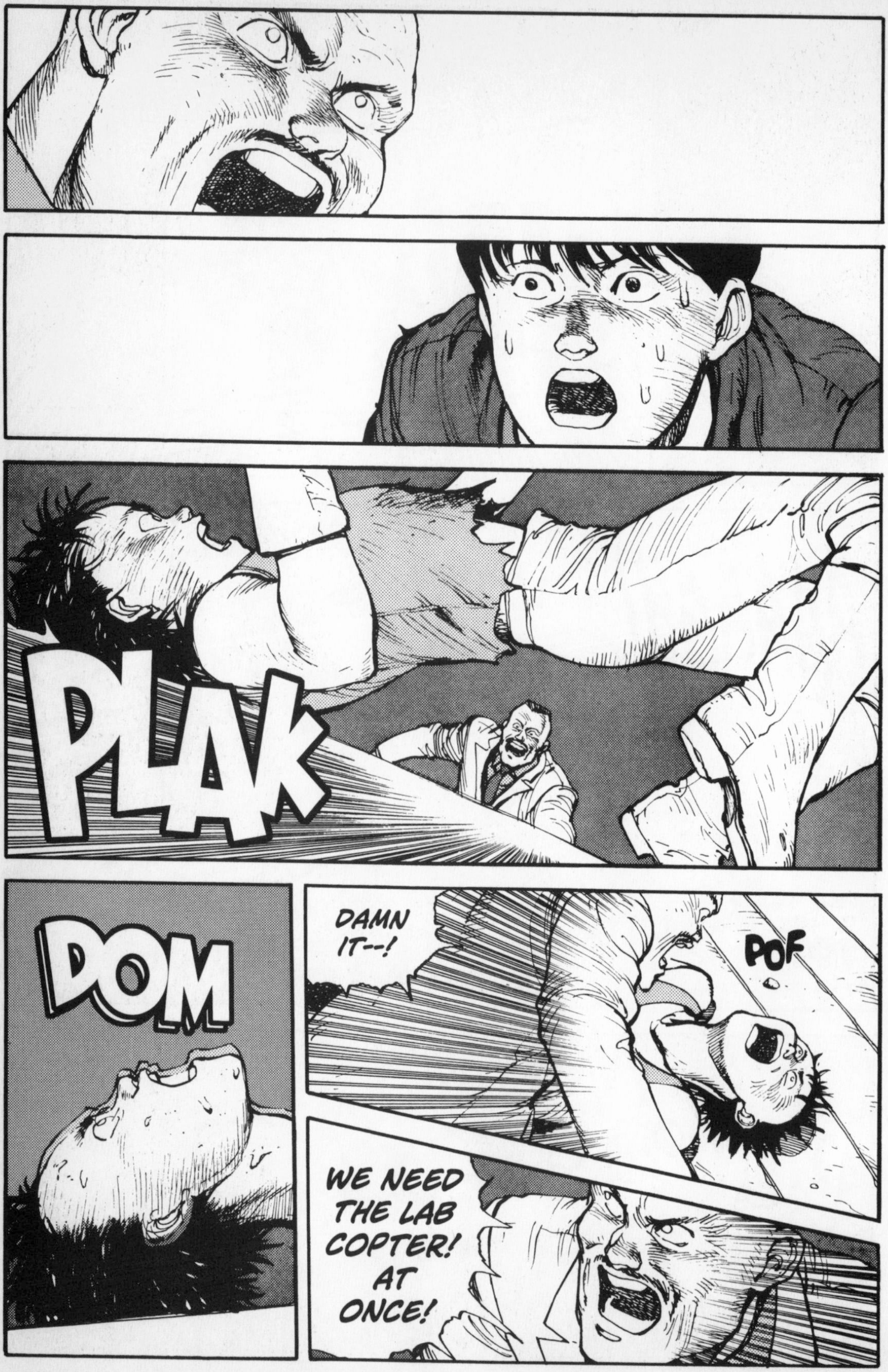
PLAK
DOM
DAMN IT--!
POF
WE NEED THE LAB COPTER! AT ONCE!

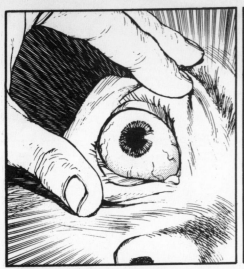

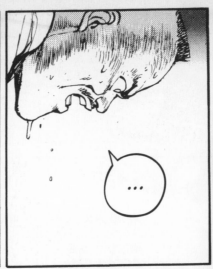

I HOPE YOU BURN IN HELL !!

WHAT'RE *YOU* LOOKIN' AT, BALDY?!

SHUT YOUR INSOLENT MOUTH!

TOO BAD ABOUT THAT PILL. YOU WERE COUNTING ON GETTING IT BACK, HUNH?

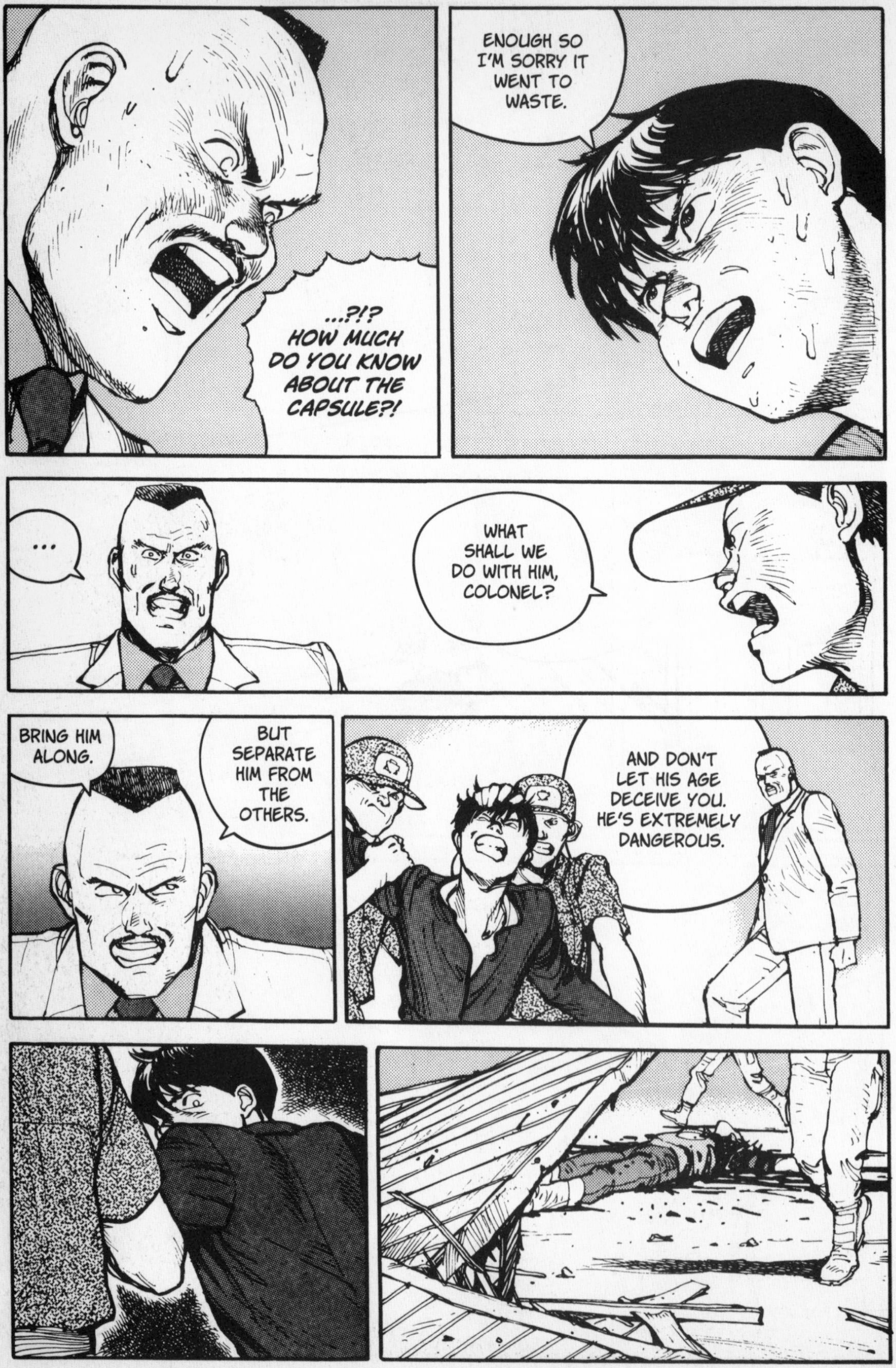
...?!? HOW MUCH DO YOU KNOW ABOUT THE CAPSULE?!
ENOUGH SO I'M SORRY IT WENT TO WASTE.
...
WHAT SHALL WE DO WITH HIM, COLONEL?
BRING HIM ALONG.
BUT SEPARATE HIM FROM THE OTHERS.
AND DON'T LET HIS AGE DECEIVE YOU. HE'S EXTREMELY DANGEROUS.

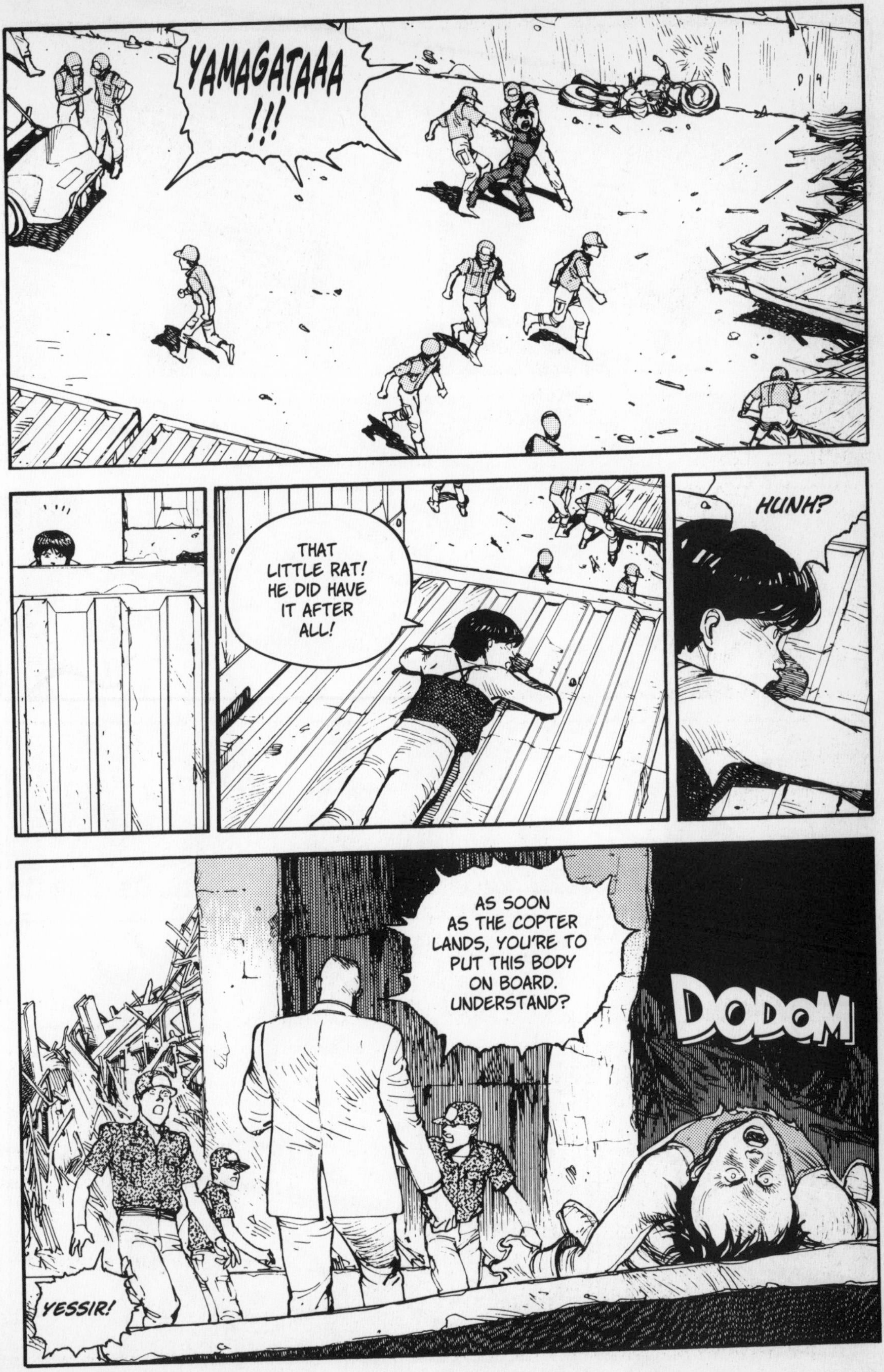
YAMAGATAAA !!!
THAT LITTLE RAT! HE DID HAVE IT AFTER ALL!
HUNH?
AS SOON AS THE COPTER LANDS, YOU'RE TO PUT THIS BODY ON BOARD. UNDERSTAND?
DODOM
YESSIR!

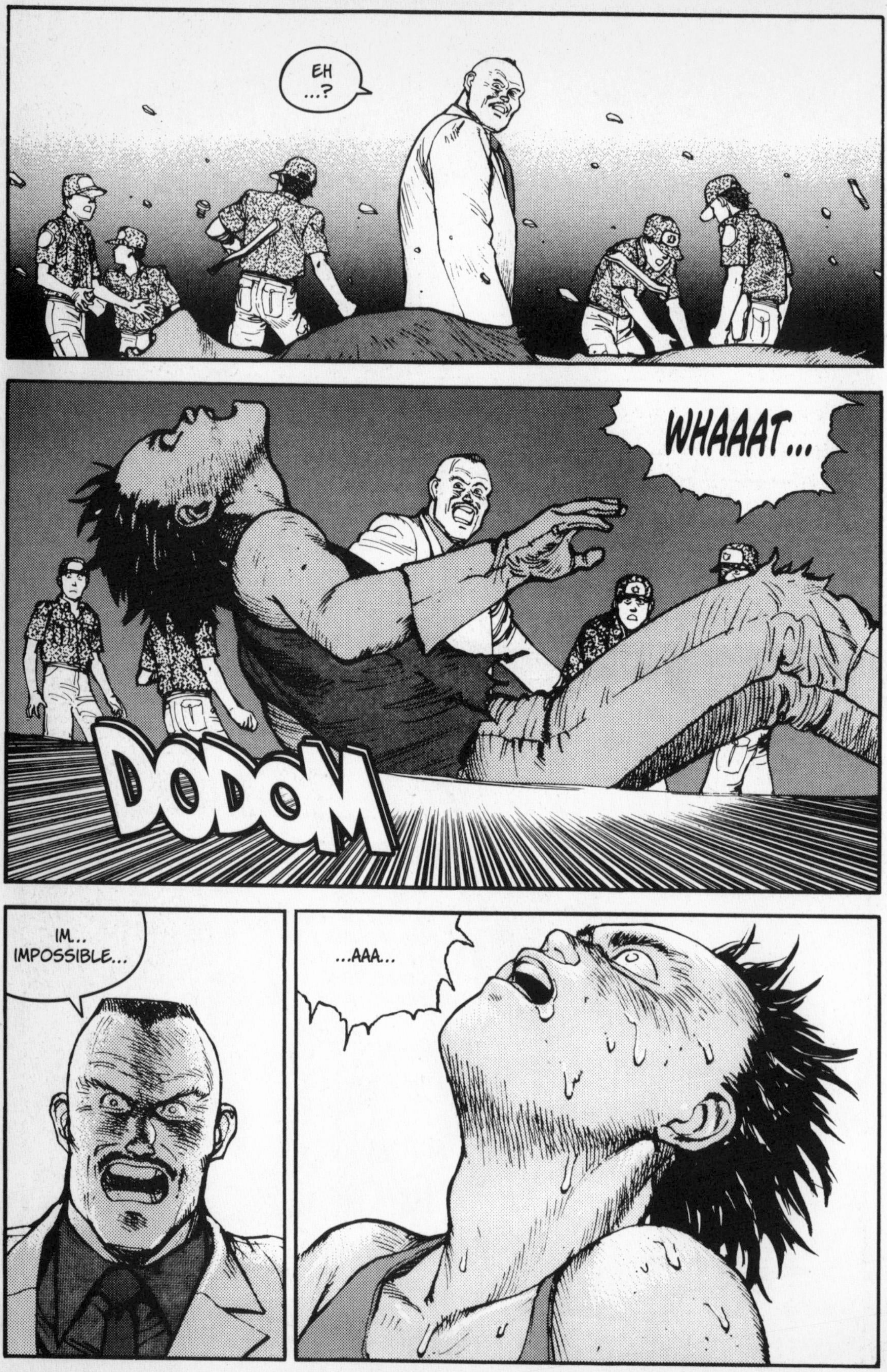
EH ...?
WHAAAT...
DODOM
IM... IMPOSSIBLE...
...AAA...

HUNH?

WHA --?!

TE...

TETSUO!

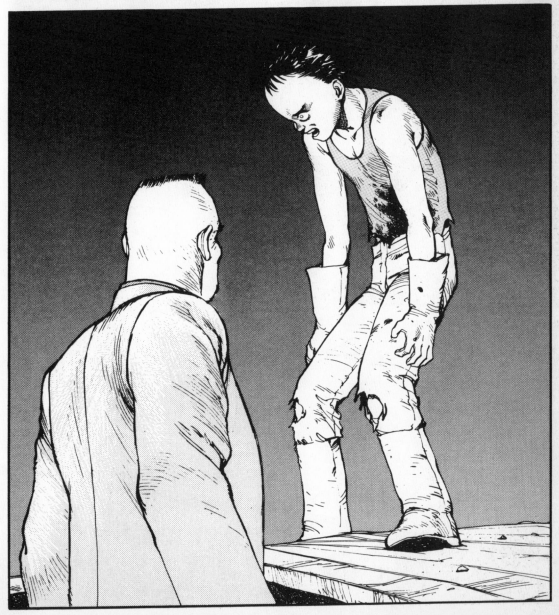

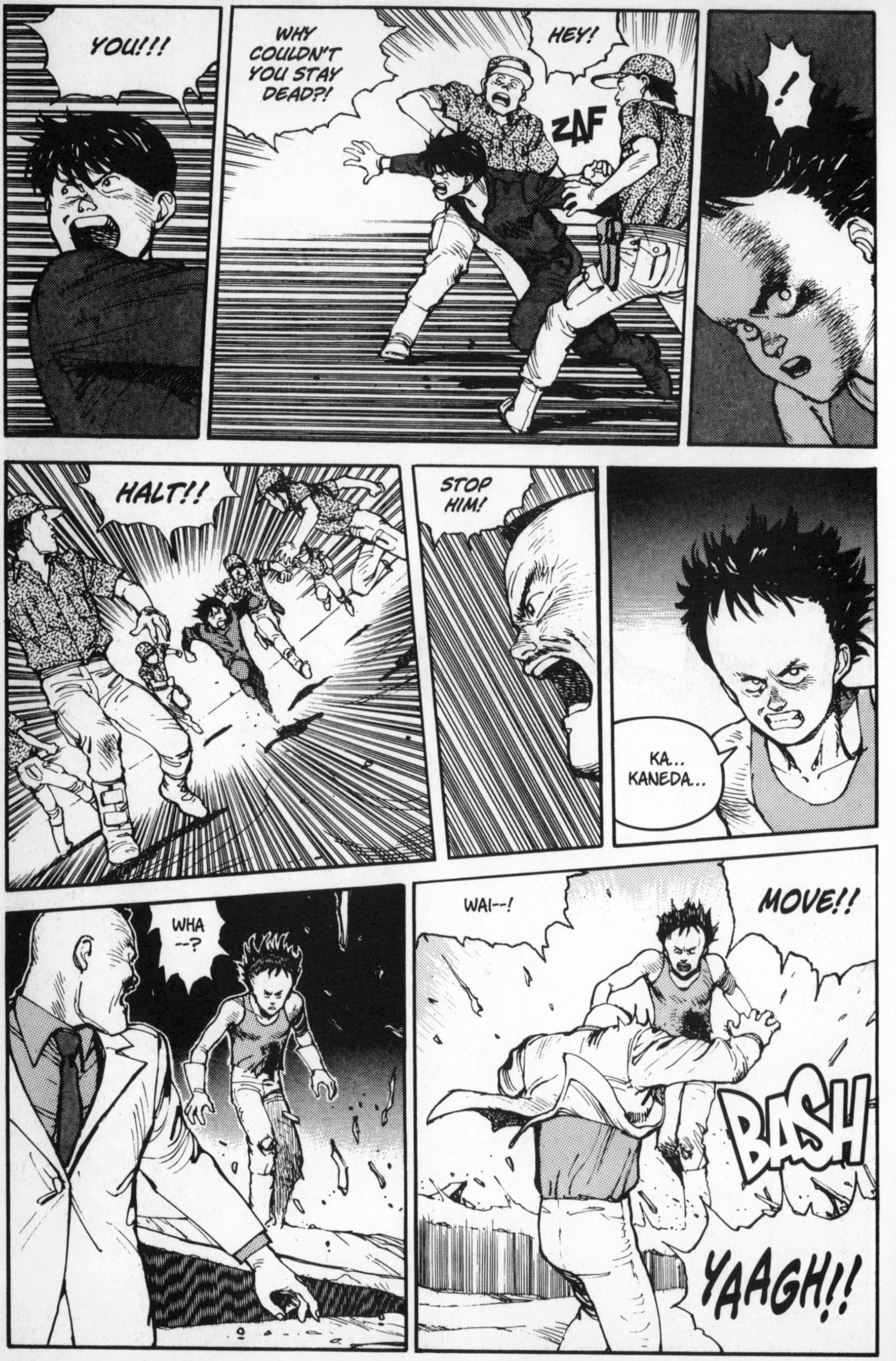

YOU!!!
WHY COULDN'T YOU STAY DEAD?!
HEY!
ZAF
!
HALT!!
STOP HIM!
KA... KANEDA...
WHA --?
WAI--!
MOVE!!
BASH
YAAGH!!

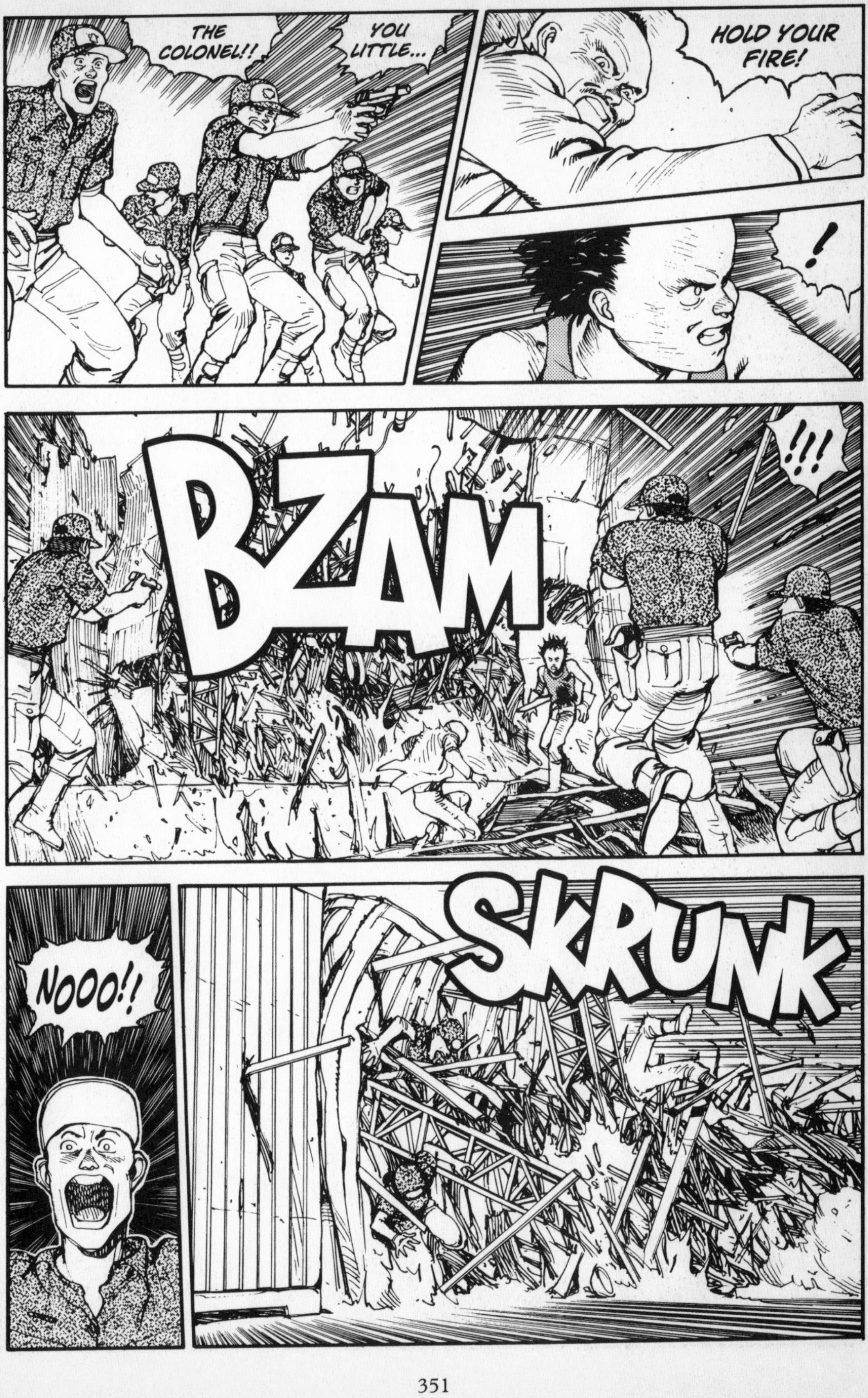
THE COLONEL!!
YOU LITTLE...
HOLD YOUR FIRE!
!
BZAM
!!!
NOOO!!
SKRUNK

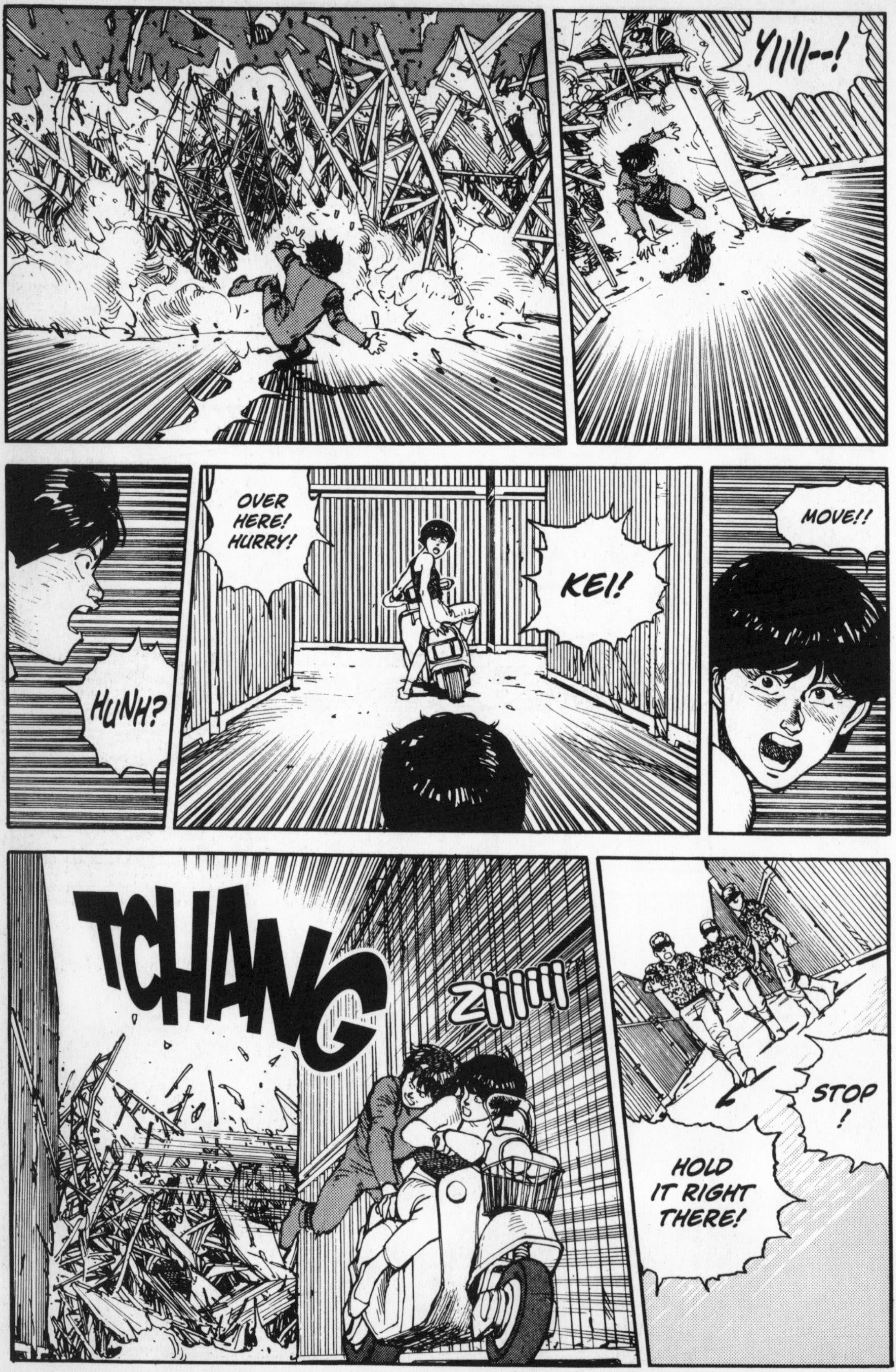

YIIII--!
HUNH?
OVER HERE! HURRY!
KEI!
MOVE!!
TCHANG
ZIIIIII
STOP!
HOLD IT RIGHT THERE!

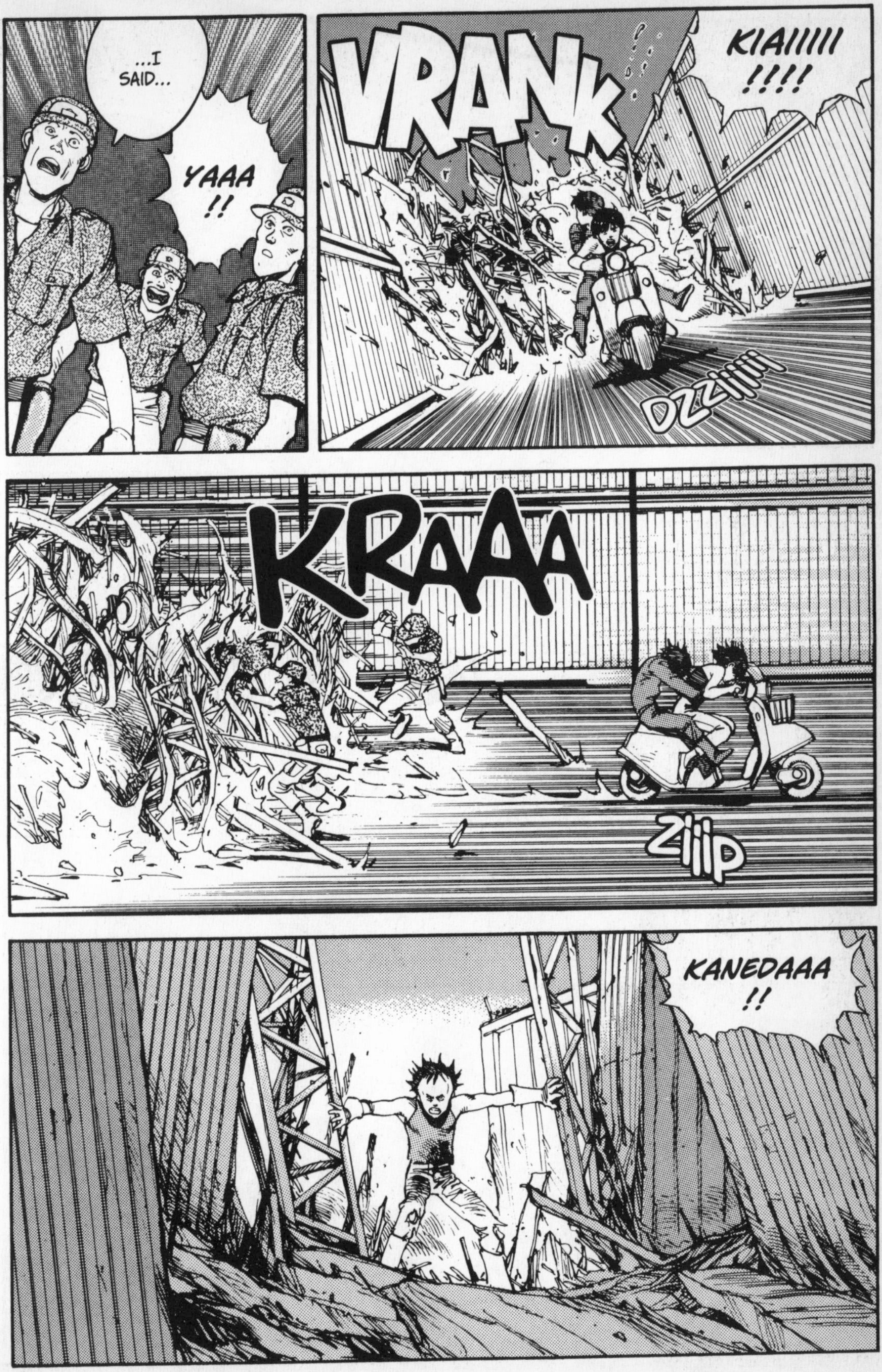
...I SAID...
YAAA !!
VRANK
KIAIIIII !!!!
DZZIIIII
KRAAA
ZIIIP
KANEDAAA !!

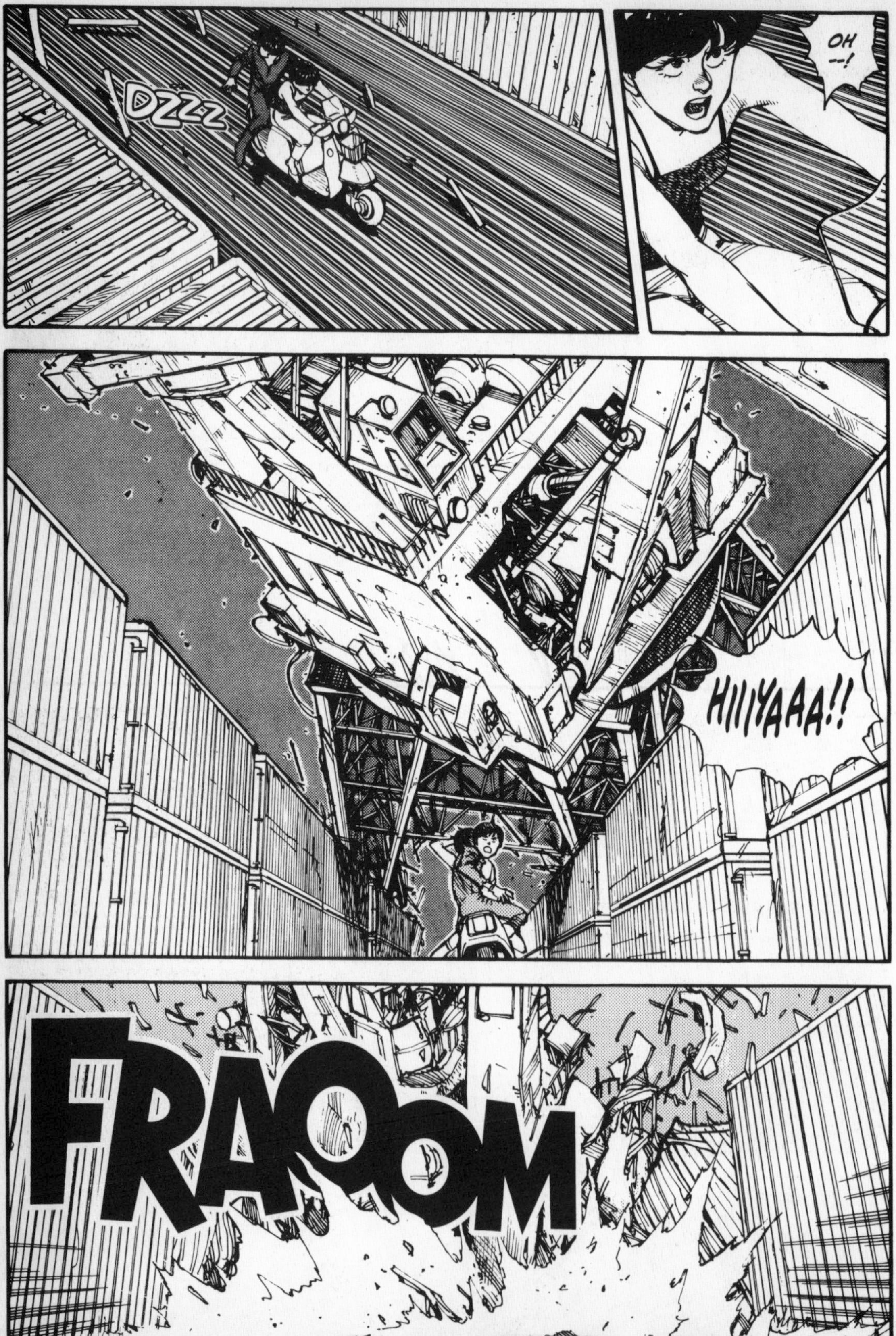
DZZZ
OH --!
HIIIYAAA!!
FRAOOM

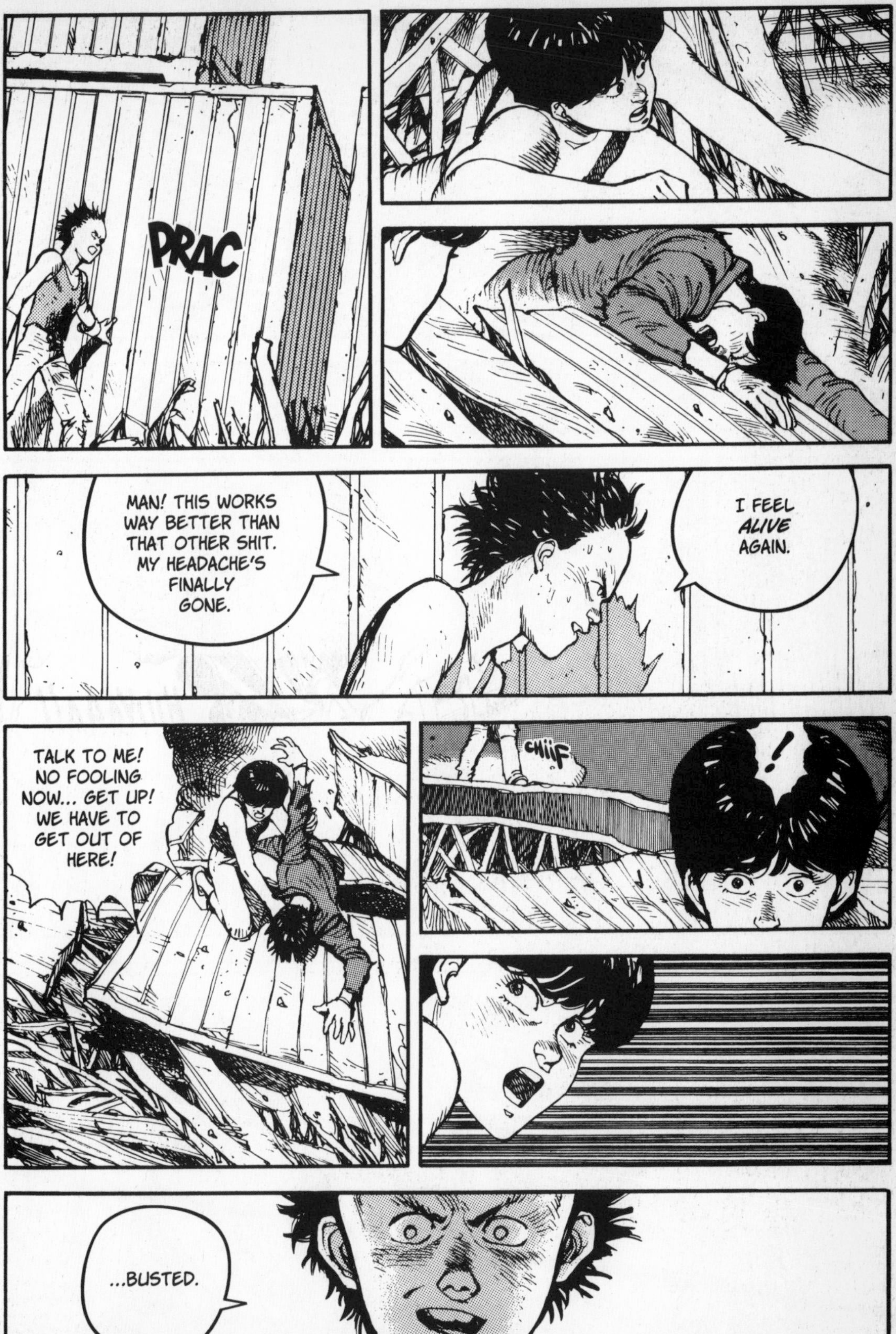
PRAC
MAN! THIS WORKS WAY BETTER THAN THAT OTHER SHIT. MY HEADACHE'S FINALLY GONE.
I FEEL *ALIVE* AGAIN.
TALK TO ME! NO FOOLING NOW... GET UP! WE HAVE TO GET OUT OF HERE!
CHIIF
!
...BUSTED.

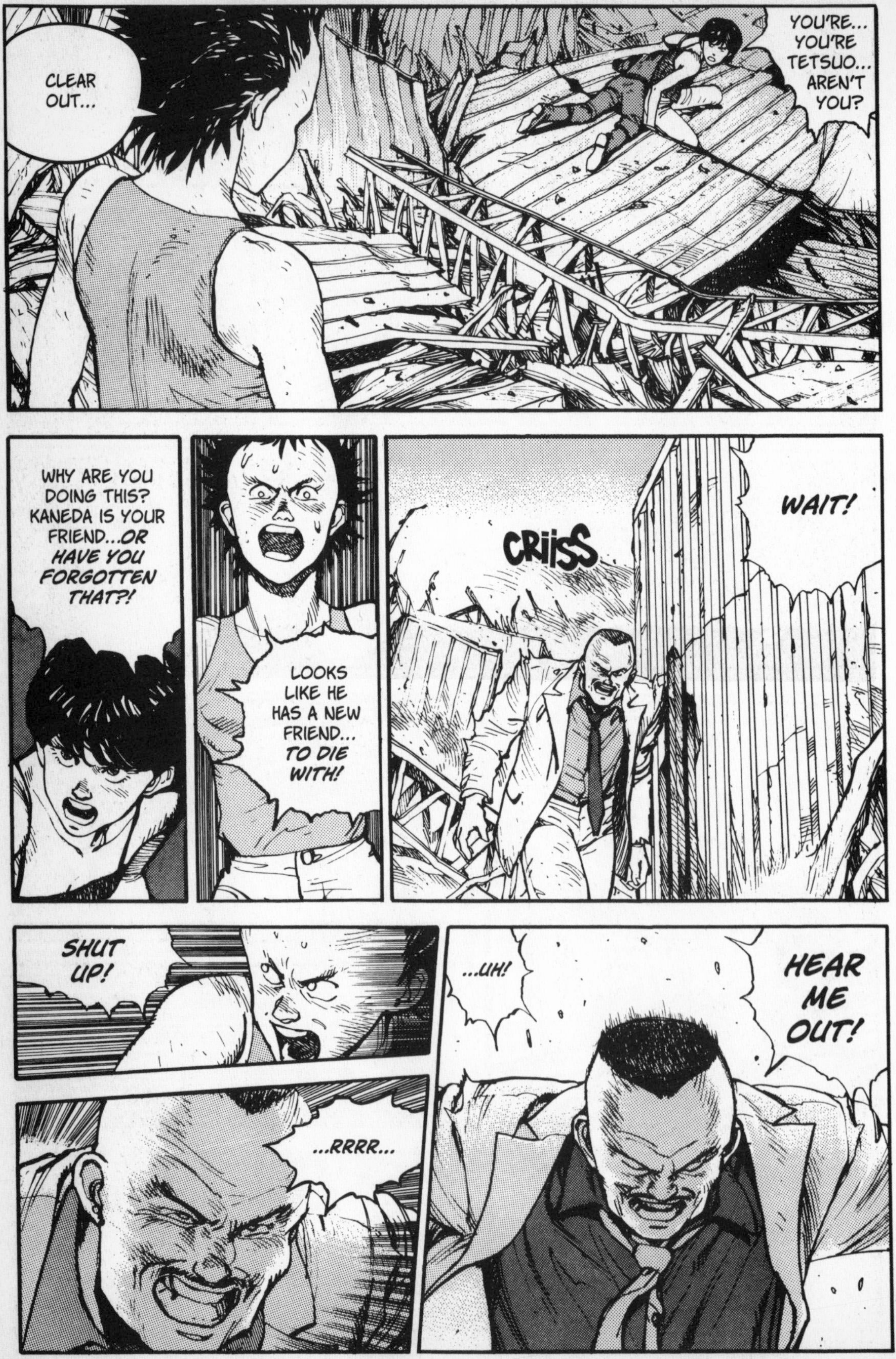
CLEAR OUT...
YOU'RE... YOU'RE TETSUO... AREN'T YOU?
WHY ARE YOU DOING THIS? KANEDA IS YOUR FRIEND...OR HAVE YOU FORGOTTEN THAT?!
LOOKS LIKE HE HAS A NEW FRIEND... TO DIE WITH!
CRIISS
WAIT!
SHUT UP!
...UH!
HEAR ME OUT!
...RRRR...

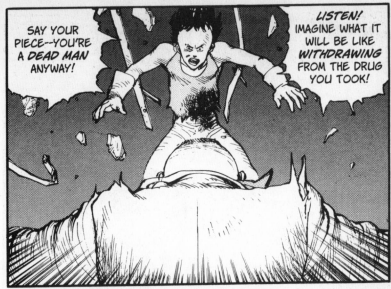

SAY YOUR PIECE--YOU'RE A *DEAD MAN* ANYWAY!

LISTEN! IMAGINE WHAT IT WILL BE LIKE *WITHDRAWING* FROM THE DRUG YOU TOOK!

USE YOUR HEAD! WHERE DO YOU THINK THE DRUG CAME FROM?!

≋HUFF≋

≋HUFF≋

THINK... THINK ABOUT IT.

THINK OF HOW MUCH POWER YOU COULD HAVE IF YOU LET US TRAIN YOU!

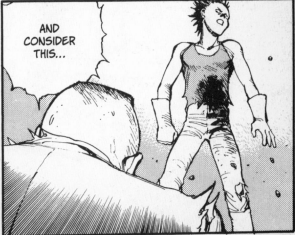

AND CONSIDER THIS...

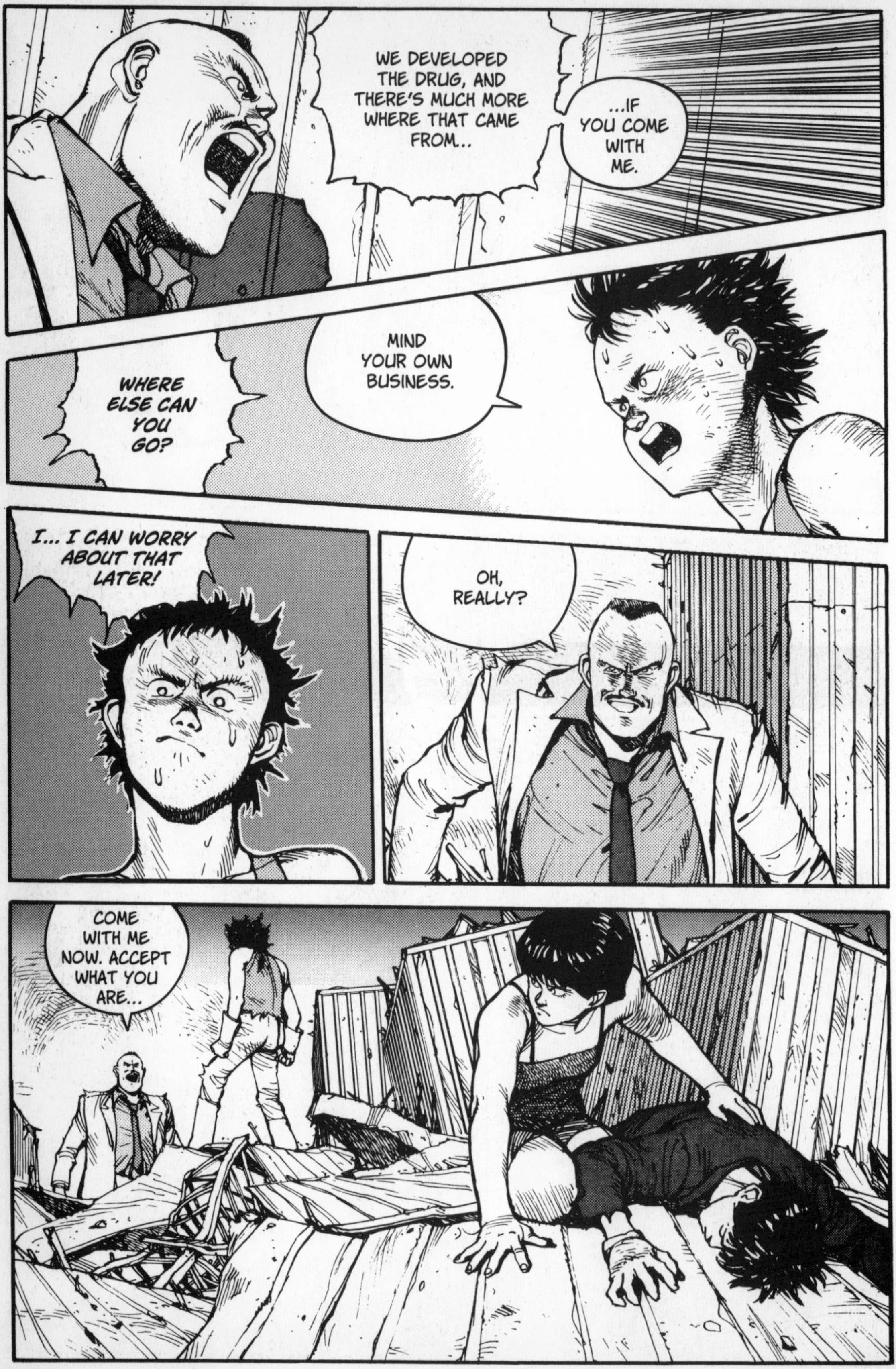
WE DEVELOPED THE DRUG, AND THERE'S MUCH MORE WHERE THAT CAME FROM...
...IF YOU COME WITH ME.
WHERE ELSE CAN YOU GO?
MIND YOUR OWN BUSINESS.
I... I CAN WORRY ABOUT THAT LATER!
OH, REALLY?
COME WITH ME NOW. ACCEPT WHAT YOU ARE...

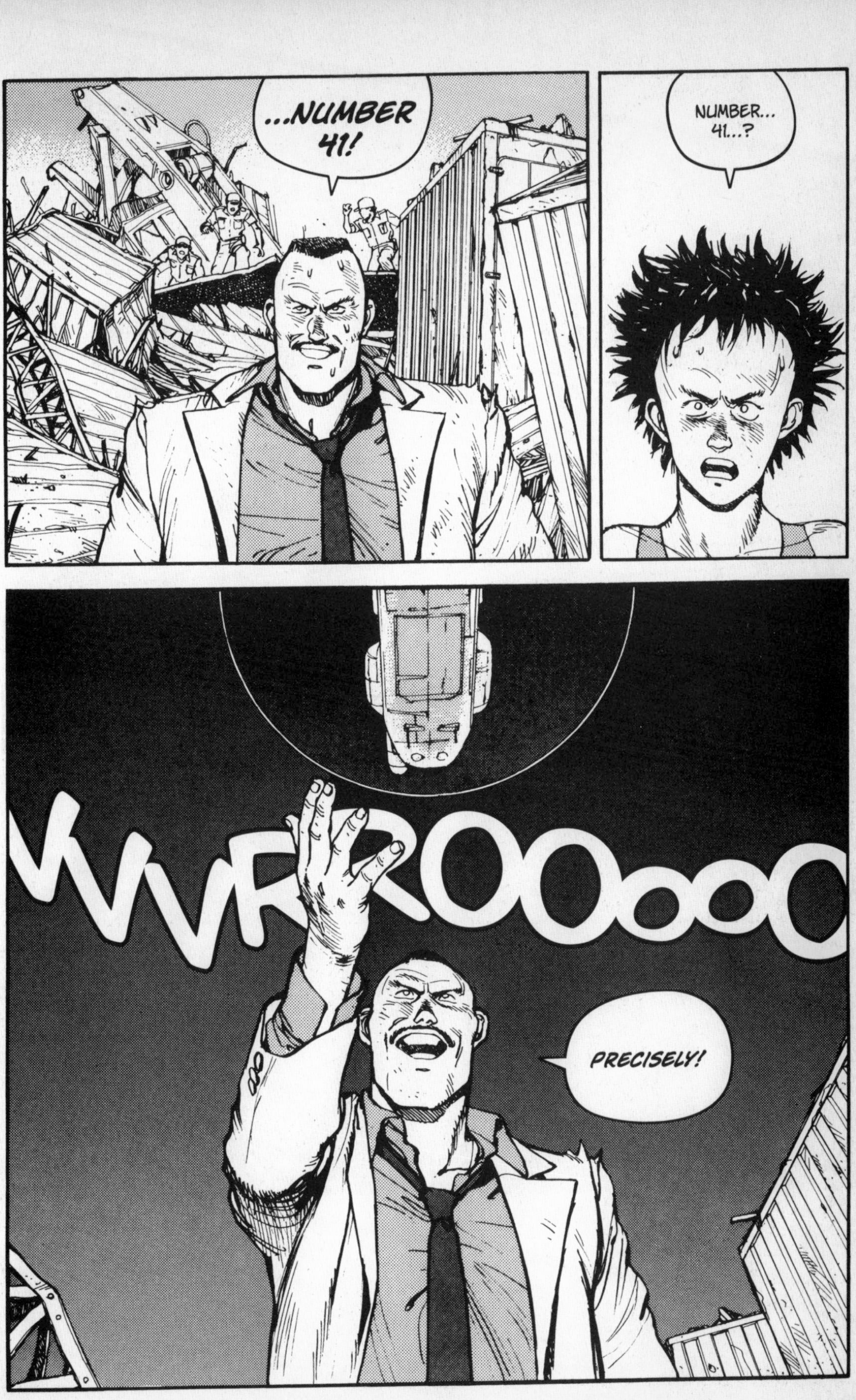
...NUMBER 41!
NUMBER... 41...?
VVROOoooo
PRECISELY!

KATSUHIRO OTOMO

Katsuhiro Otomo was born in 1954 in Japan's Miyago Prefecture, a rural province some 300 miles northeast of Tokyo. While in high school, Otomo became, in his own words, "crazy about the movies." The young artist often travelled three hours by train just to see films, and the influence of cinema is a constant thread that runs through Otomo's work.

Soon after graduating high school, Otomo moved to Tokyo with the goal of becoming a comics artist. His first professional work was *Jyu-sei (A Gun Report)*, an adaptation of the Prosper Mérimée novella *Mateo Falcone*, which appeared in the weekly magazine *Action*. Otomo went on to create a series of short stories, usually twenty to thirty pages, challenging works that captured widespread critical acclaim in Japan. A 1980 review in the *Asahi* newspaper said, "Just as the New Cinema movement had demolished the old style of Hollywood filmmaking to usher in a fresh style of movie production in America, Katsuhiro Otomo...came to Tokyo to create a new comics style and shattered the conventions existing in manga."

In 1979, publication began on Otomo's first serialized work, *Fireball*, a story built around a "man versus computer" theme. Though the series was never completed, *Fireball* marked the beginning of Otomo's interest in science-fiction themes and was the forerunner of future work that would define his comics career and firmly establish him internationally as one of the acknowledged masters of the comics medium. *Domu*, first serialized in 1980 and collected in 1983, became a bestseller and was the first manga to win the coveted Science Fiction Grand Prix Award, Japan's equivalent to America's Nebula Award. The media

attention gained from this landmark achievement made Otomo one of the best-known comics authors in Japan. Critics raved about *Domu*, a story that combined terrifying paranormal genre elements with poignant observation of urban life in modern Japan. From the *Yomiuri* newspaper: "The weirdness that lurks in the seemingly peaceful living environment of a huge housing complex symbolizes the precariousness hidden at the bottom of today's living conditions in Japan."

Upon completion of *Domu*, Otomo began work on *Akira*, a two-thousand-plus-page epic of staggering illustrative virtuosity and gut-wrenching thematic power. Ten years in the making and eventually collected in six volumes, *Akira* went on to win every possible award and spawned video games, an animated feature film directed by Otomo himself — compared favorably by critics to science-fiction masterpieces such as *Blade Runner* and *A Clockwork Orange* — and a blizzard of merchandise. *Akira* has been published in virtually every language and stands not only as one of the crown jewels of manga, but is regarded by many as the finest work of graphic fiction ever created, anywhere. While the completion of *Akira* marked the beginning of Otomo's moving away from comics — his only major comics work since *Akira* has been the writing of *The Legend of Mother Sarah* — it began his odyssey as a filmmaker. After completion of the animated *Akira*, Otomo has gone on to work on a variety of animated films, including *Labyrinth Stories*, *Robot Carnival*, *Roujin Z*, *Spriggan*, and *Memories*, an anthology of adaptations of earlier Otomo comics stories. Otomo also directed the live-action *World Apartment Horror* as well as television commercials for Honda, Suntory, and Canon. Otomo lives and works in Tokyo.

漫画 BACKLIST

A SAMPLING OF 漫画 GRAPHIC NOVELS FROM DARK HORSE COMICS

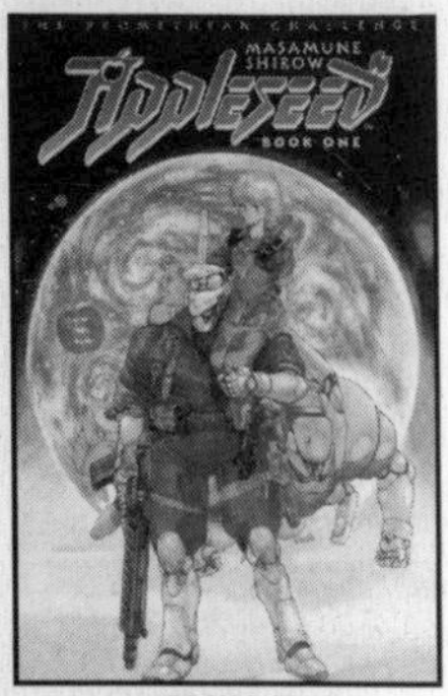
THE PROMETHEAN CHALLENGE
MASAMUNE SHIROW
APPLESEED
BOOK ONE

BOOK ONE
ISBN: 1-56971-070-8 $16.95

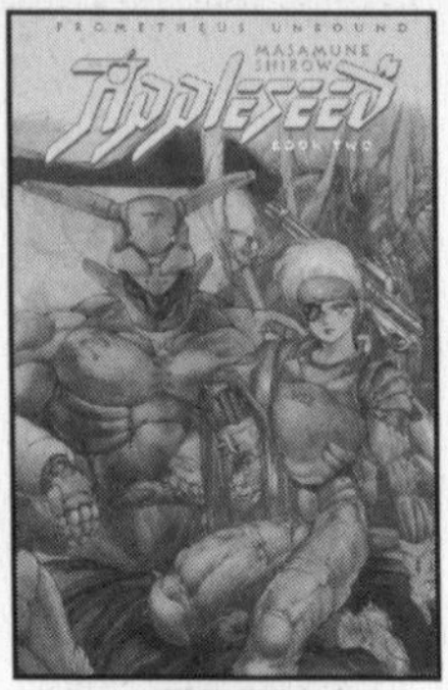
PROMETHEUS UNBOUND
MASAMUNE SHIROW
APPLESEED
BOOK TWO

BOOK TWO
ISBN: 1-56971-071-6 $16.95

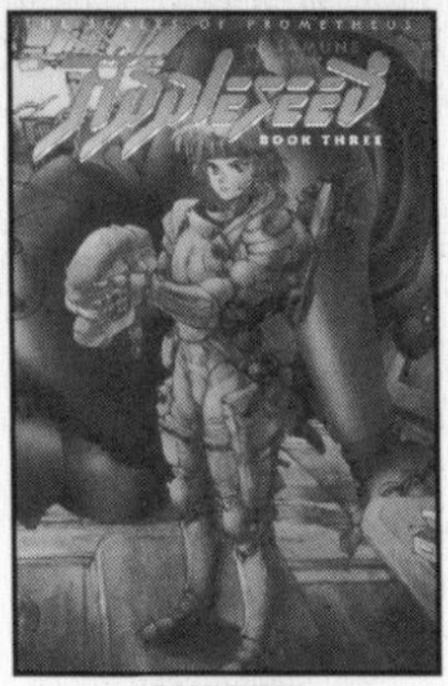
MASAMUNE SHIROW
APPLESEED
BOOK THREE

BOOK THREE
ISBN: 1-56971-072-4 $17.95

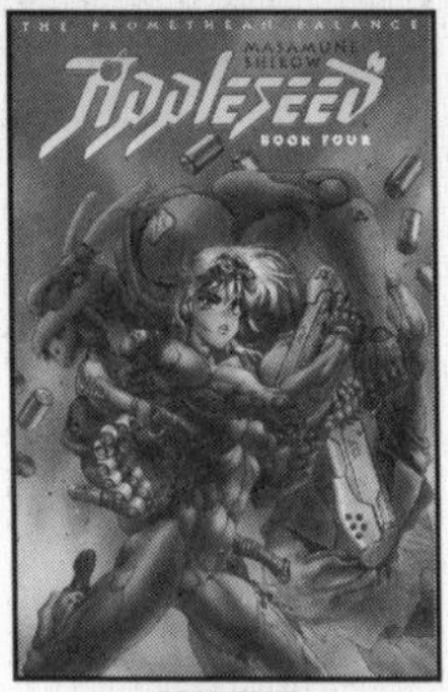
THE PROMETHEAN BALANCE
MASAMUNE SHIROW
APPLESEED
BOOK FOUR

BOOK FOUR
ISBN: 1-56971-074-0 $17.95

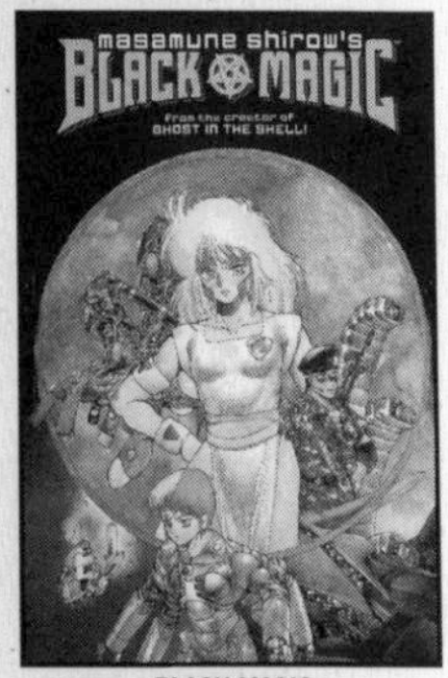
masamune shirow's
BLACK MAGIC
From the creator of
GHOST IN THE SHELL!

BLACK MAGIC
ISBN: 1-56971-360-X $16.95

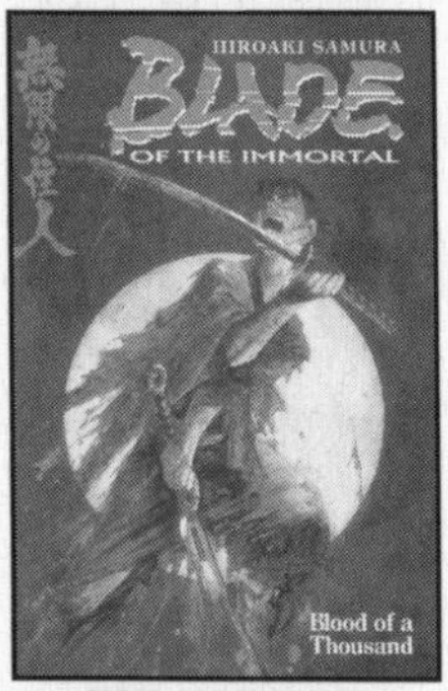
HIROAKI SAMURA
BLADE
OF THE IMMORTAL
無限の住人
Blood of a
Thousand

BLOOD OF A THOUSAND
ISBN: 1-56971-239-5 $14.95

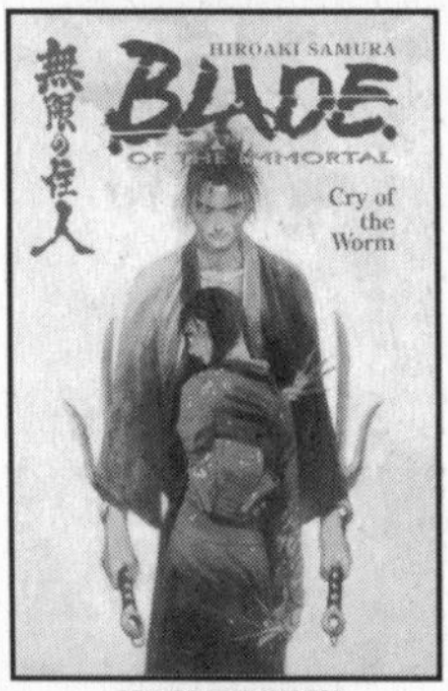
HIROAKI SAMURA
無限の住人
BLADE
OF THE IMMORTAL
Cry of
the
Worm

CRY OF THE WORM
ISBN: 1-56971-300-6 $14.95

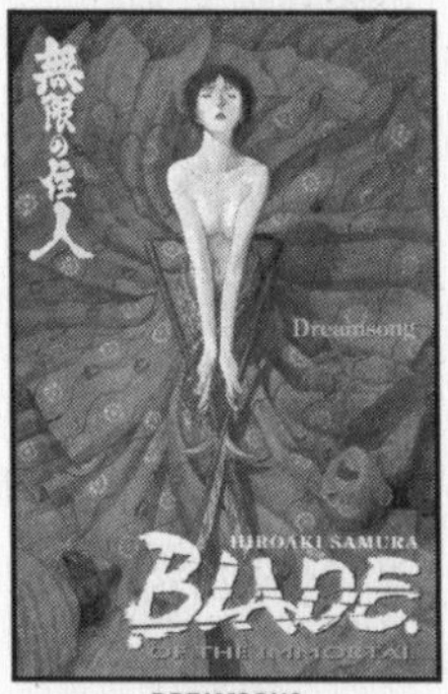
無限の住人
Dreamsong
HIROAKI SAMURA
BLADE
OF THE IMMORTAL

DREAMSONG
ISBN: 1-5-6971-357-X $149.95

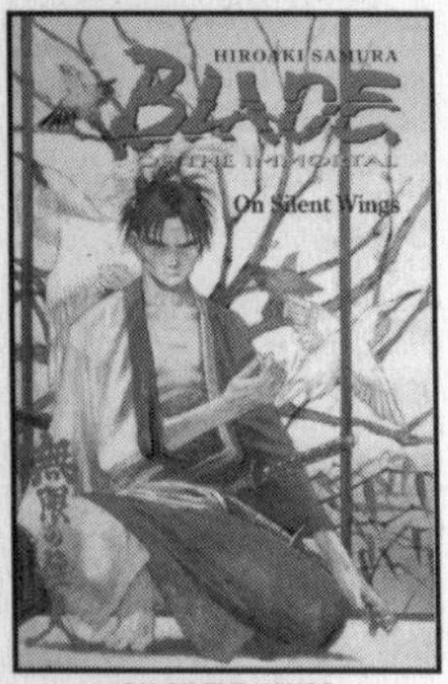
HIROAKI SAMURA
BLADE
OF THE IMMORTAL
On Silent Wings

ON SILENT WINGS
ISBN: 1-56971-412-6 $14.95

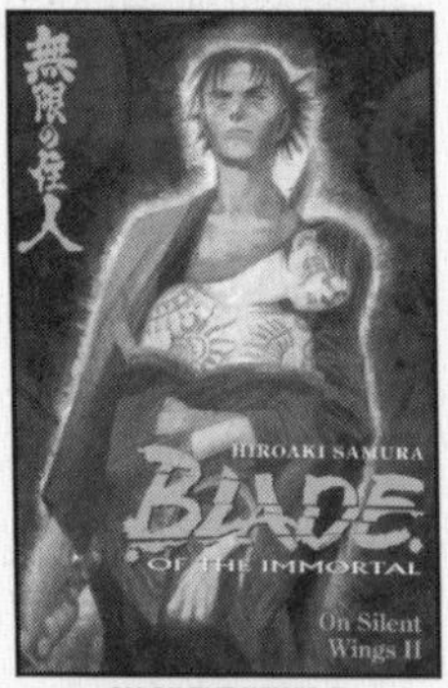
無限の住人
HIROAKI SAMURA
BLADE
OF THE IMMORTAL
On Silent
Wings II

ON SILENT WINGS II
ISBN: 1-56971-444-4 $14.95

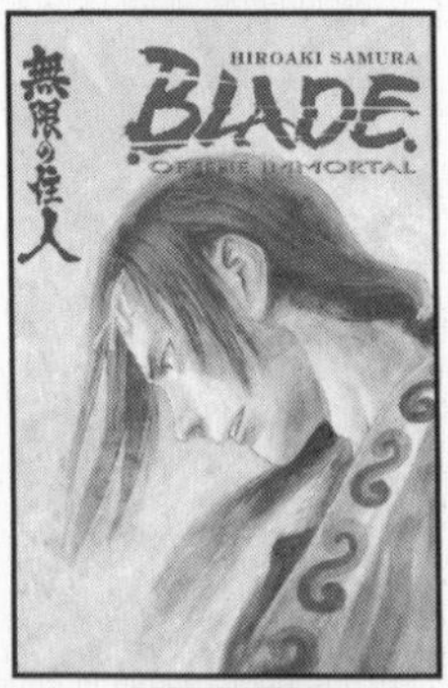
HIROAKI SAMURA
無限の住人
BLADE
OF THE IMMORTAL

DARK SHADOWS
ISBN: 1-56971-469-X $14.95

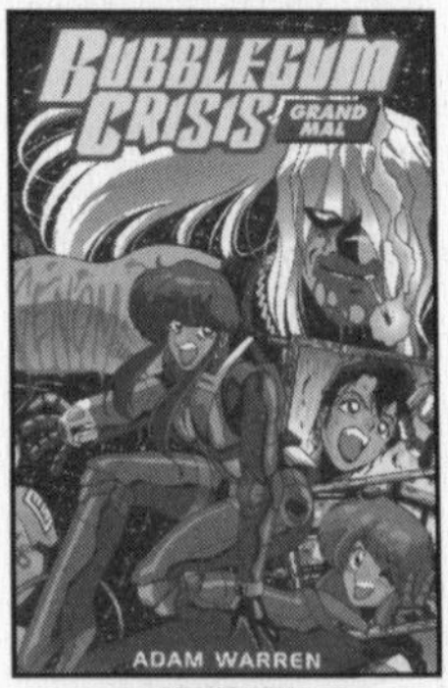
BUBBLEGUM
CRISIS
GRAND MAL
ADAM WARREN

GRAND MAL
ISBN: 1-56971-120-8 $14.95

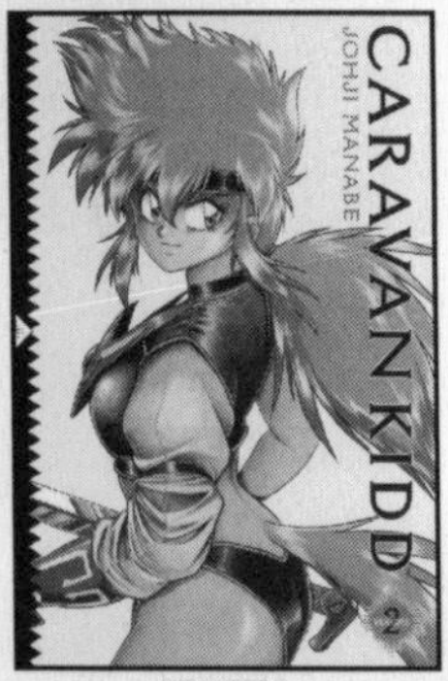
CARAVAN KIDD
JOHJI MANABE
2

VOLUME 2
ISBN: 1-56971-324-3 $19.95

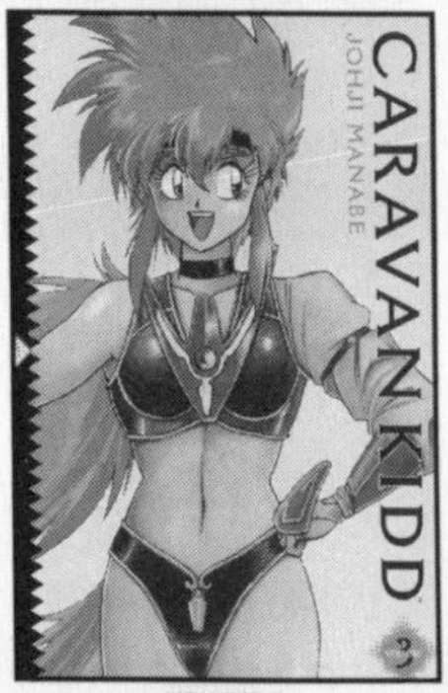
CARAVAN KIDD
JOHJI MANABE
3

VOLUME 3
ISBN: 1-5-6971-338-3 $19.95

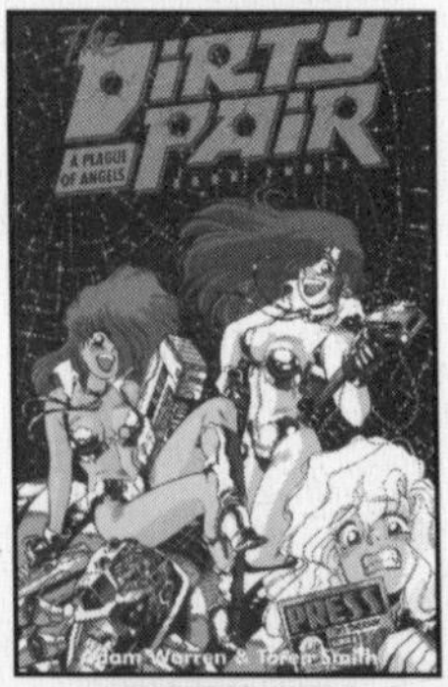
The
DIRTY
PAIR
A PLAGUE
OF ANGELS
Adam Warren & Toren Smith

A PLAGUE OF ANGELS
ISBN: 1-56971-029-5 $12.95

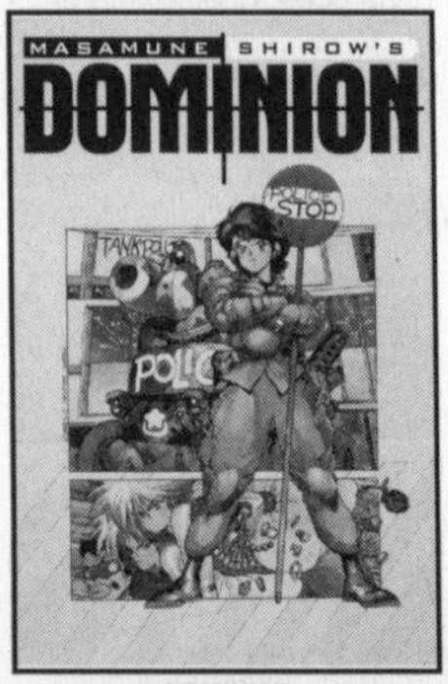
MASAMUNE SHIROW'S
DOMINION
STOP
POLIC

DOMINION
ISBN: 1-56971-488-6 $16.95

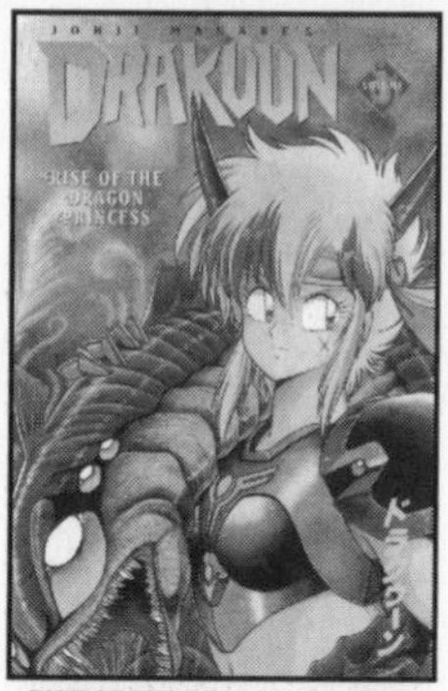
DRAKUUN
RISE OF THE DRAGON PRINCESS

RISE OF THE DRAGON PRINCESS
ISBN: 1-56971-302-2 $12.95

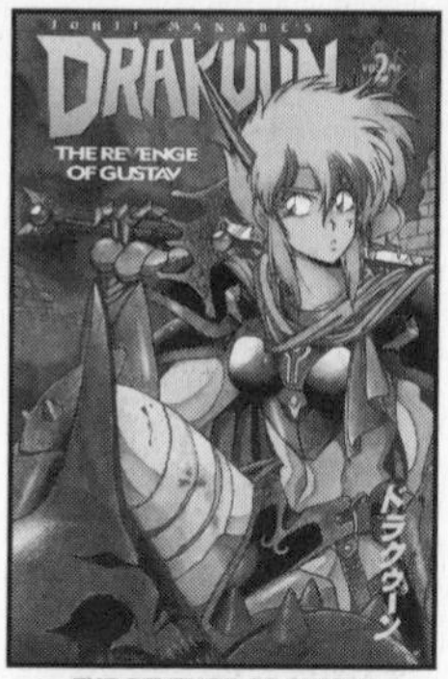
DRAKUUN
2
THE REVENGE OF GUSTAV

THE REVENGE OF GUSTAV
ISBN: 1-56971-368-5 $14.95

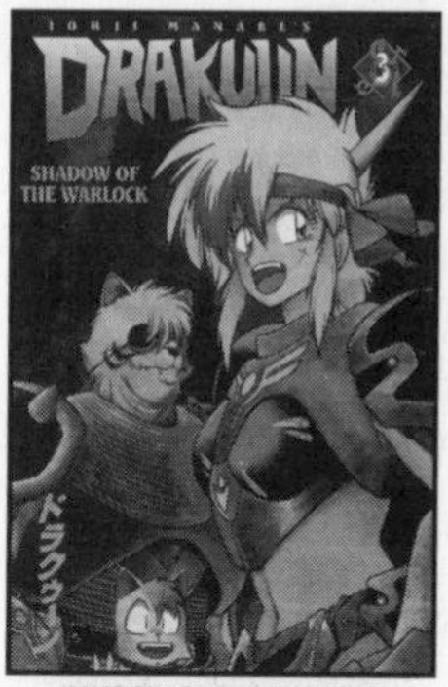
DRAKUUN
3
SHADOW OF THE WARLOCK

SHADOW OF THE WARLOCK
ISBN: 1-56971-406-1 $14.95

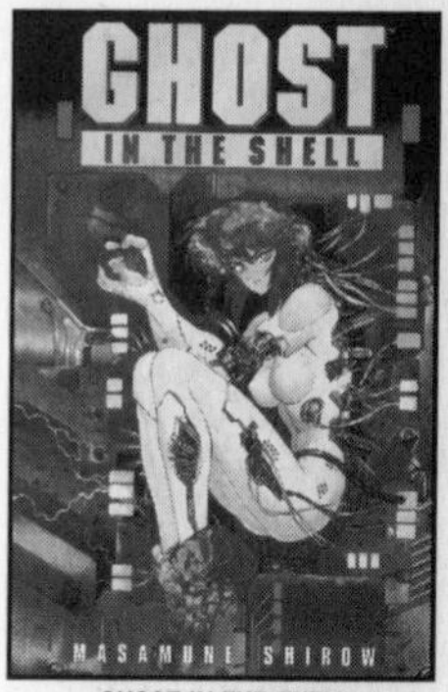
GHOST
IN THE SHELL
MASAMUNE SHIROW

GHOST IN THE SHELL
ISBN: 1-56971-081-3 $24.95

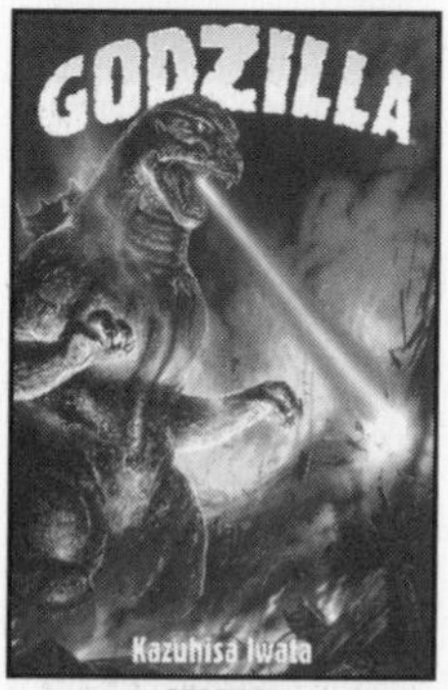
GODZILLA
Kazuhisa Iwata

GODZILLA
ISBN: 1-56971-063-5 $17.95

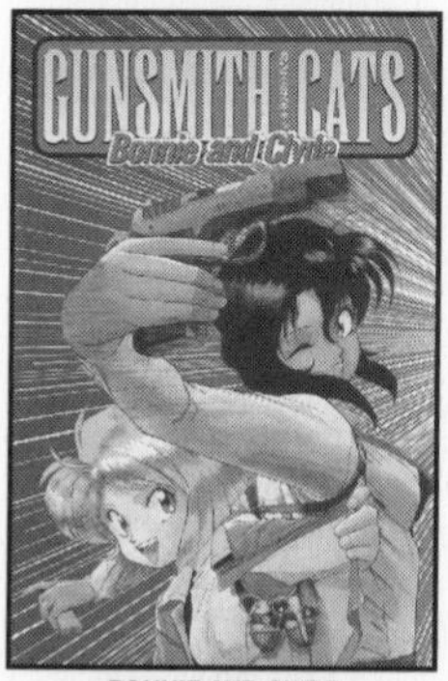
GUNSMITH CATS
Bonnie and Clyde

BONNIE AND CLYDE
ISBN: 1-56971-215-8 $13.95

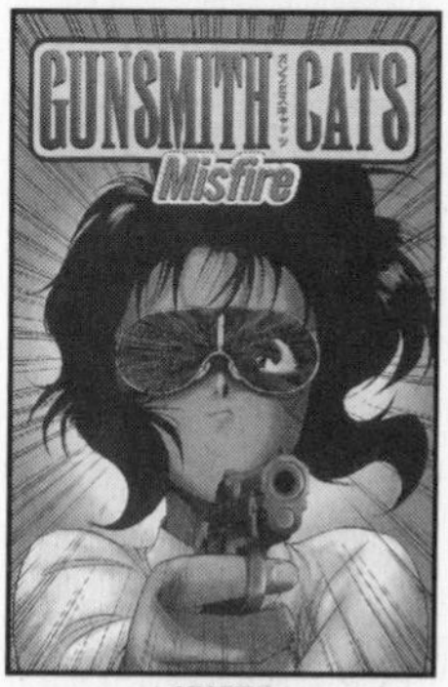
GUNSMITH CATS
Misfire

MISFIRE
ISBN: 1-56971-253-0 $14.95

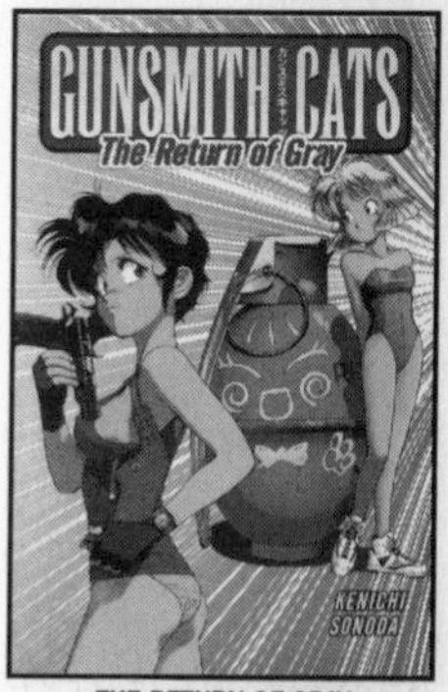
GUNSMITH CATS
The Return of Gray
KENICHI SONODA

THE RETURN OF GRAY
ISBN: 1-56971-299-9 $17.95

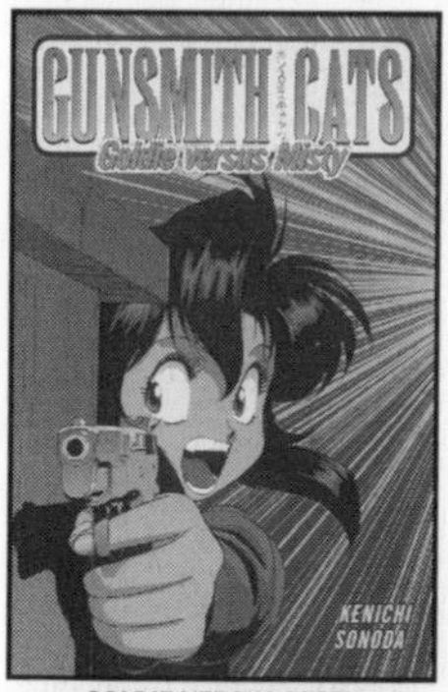
GUNSMITH CATS
Goldie versus Misty
KENICHI SONODA

GOLDIE VERSUS MISTY
ISBN: 1-56971-371-5 $15.95

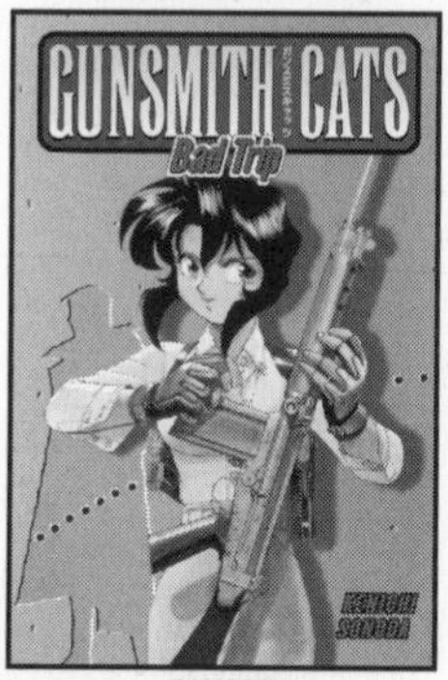
GUNSMITH CATS
Bad Trip
KENICHI SONODA

BAD TRIP
ISBN: 1-56971-442-8 $13.95

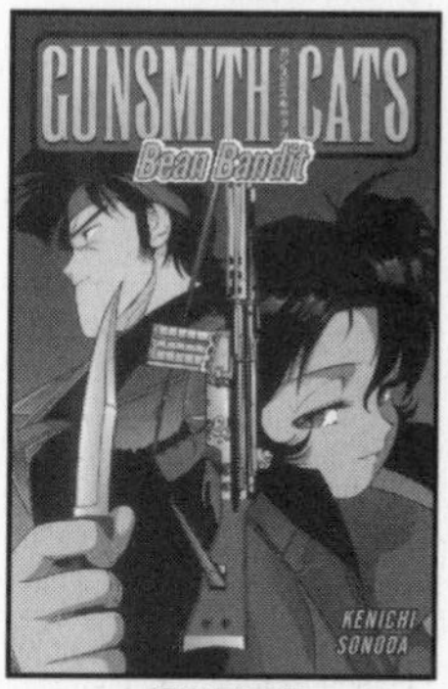
GUNSMITH CATS
Bean Bandit
KENICHI SONODA

BEAN BANDIT
ISBN: 1-56971-453-3 $16.95

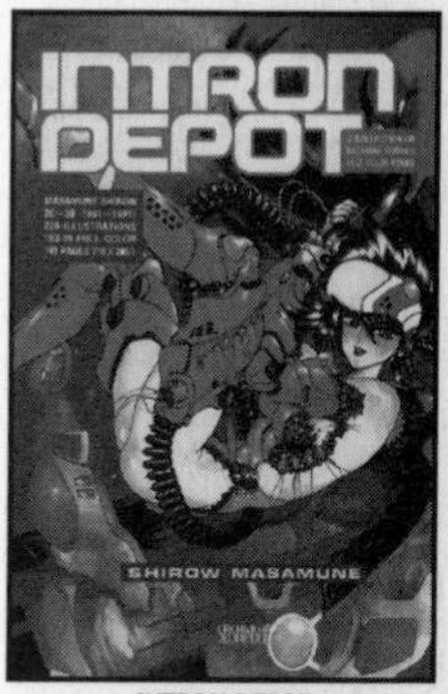
INTRON DEPOT
SHIROW MASAMUNE

INTRON DEPOT
ISBN: 1-56971-085-6 $39.95

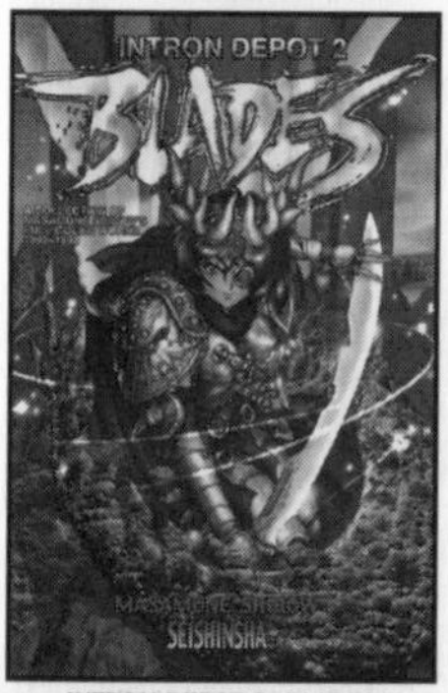
INTRON DEPOT 2
BLADES
SEISHINSHA

INTRON DEPOT 2: BLADES
ISBN: 1-56971-382-0 $39.95

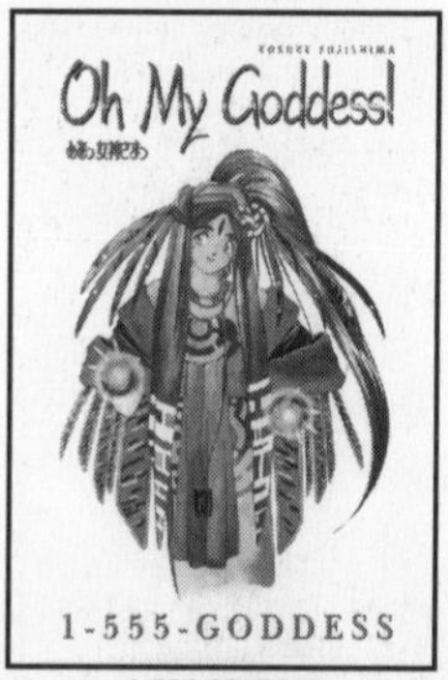
Oh My Goddess!
1-555-GODDESS

1-555-GODDESS
ISBN: 1-56971-207-7 $13.95

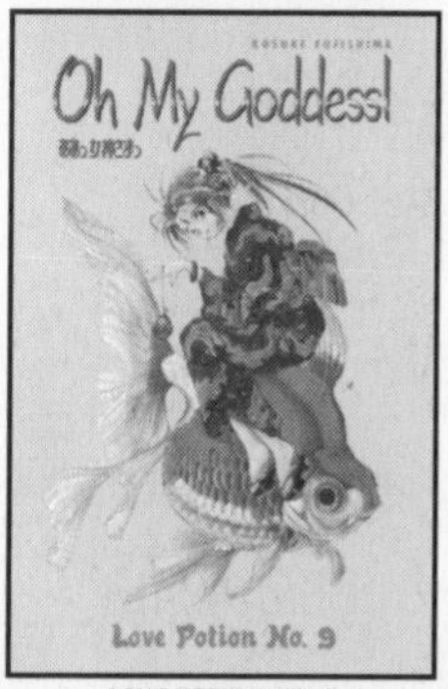
Oh My Goddess!
Love Potion No. 9

LOVE POTION NO. 9
ISBN: 1-56971-252-2 $14.95

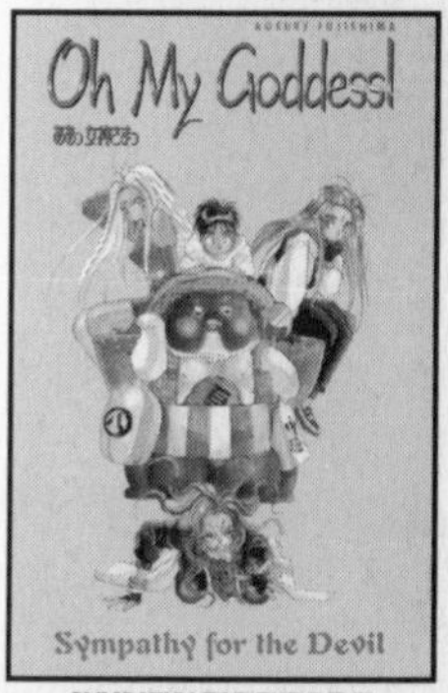
Oh My Goddess!
Sympathy for the Devil

SYMPATHY FOR THE DEVIL
ISBN: 1-56971-329-4 $13.95

AVAILABLE AT YOUR LOCAL COMICS SHOP OR BOOKSTORE

To find a comics shop in your area, call 1-888-266-4226 • For more information or to order direct:
• On the web: www.darkhorse.com • E-mail: mailorder@darkhorse.com
• Phone: 1-800-862-0052 or (503) 652-9701 Mon.-Sat. 9 A.M. to 5 P.M. Pacific Time
**Prices and availability subject to change without notice*

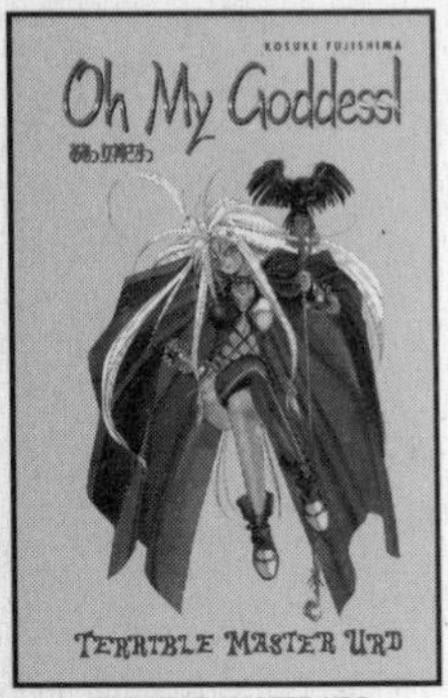
Kosuke Fujishima
Oh My Goddess!
Terrible Master Urd

TERRIBLE MASTER URD
ISBN: 1-56971-369-3 $14.95

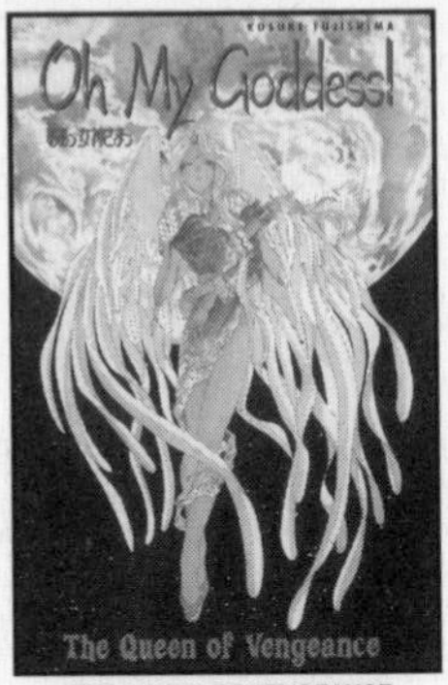
Kosuke Fujishima
Oh My Goddess!
The Queen of Vengeance

THE QUEEN OF VENGEANCE
ISBN: 1-56971-431-2 $13.95

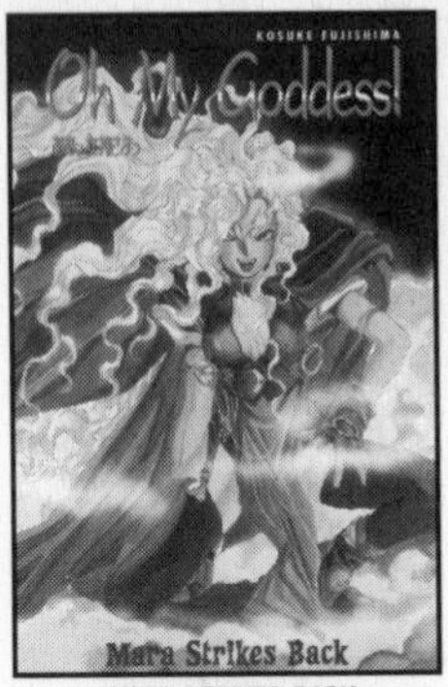
Kosuke Fujishima
Oh My Goddess!
Mara Strikes Back

MARA STRIKES BACK
ISBN: 1-56971-449-5 $14.95

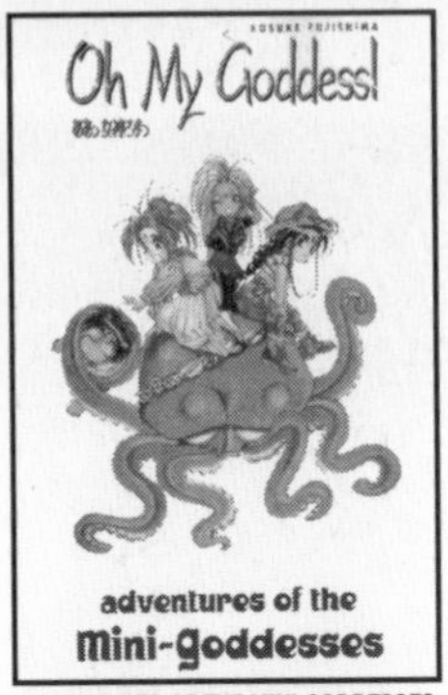
Kosuke Fujishima
Oh My Goddess!
adventures of the
mini-goddesses

ADVENTURES OF THE MINI-GODDESSES
ISBN: 1-56971-421-5 $9.95

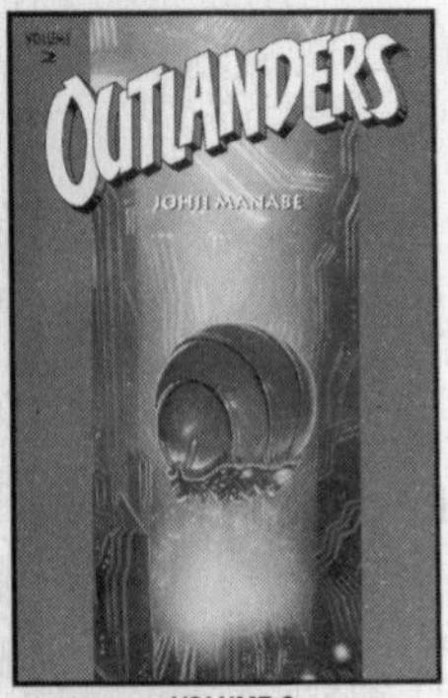
Outlanders
Johji Manabe

VOLUME 2
ISBN: 1-56971-162-3 $13.95

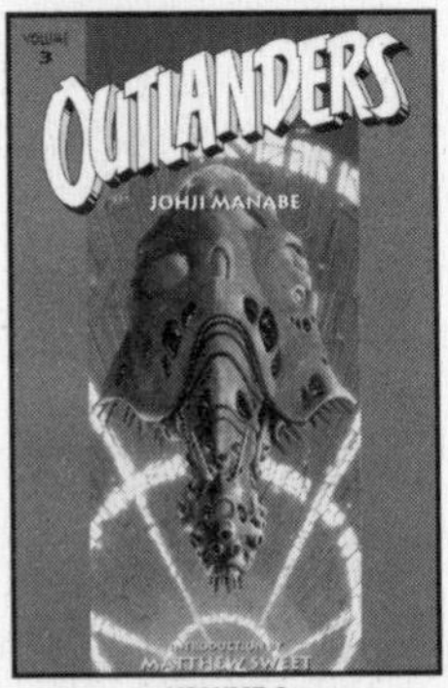
Outlanders
Johji Manabe

VOLUME 3
ISBN: 1-56971-163-1 $13.95

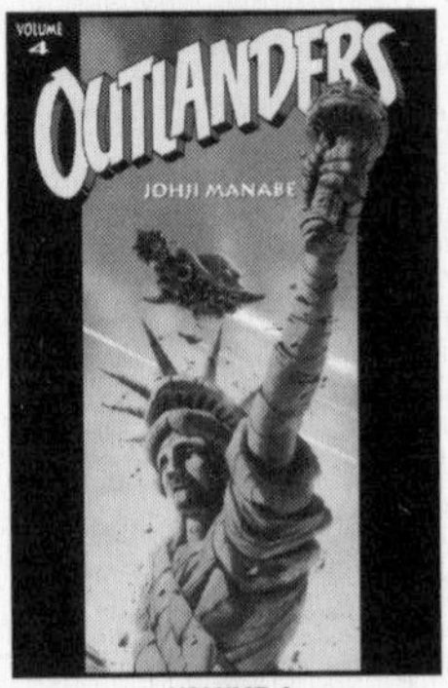
Volume 4
Outlanders
Johji Manabe

VOLUME 4
ISBN: 1-56971-069-4 $12.95

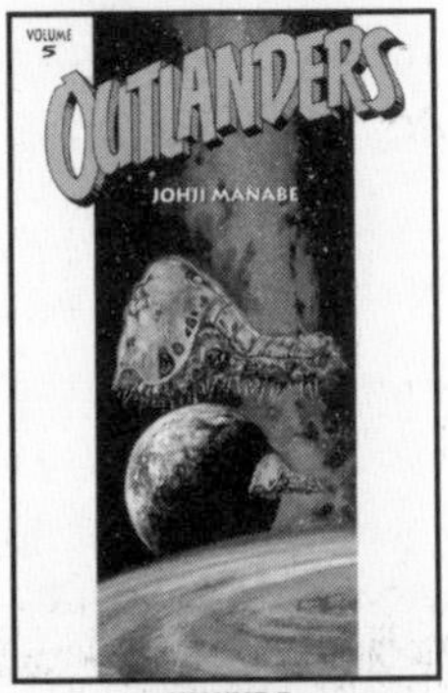
Volume 5
Outlanders
Johji Manabe

VOLUME 5
ISBN: 1-56971-275-1 $14.95

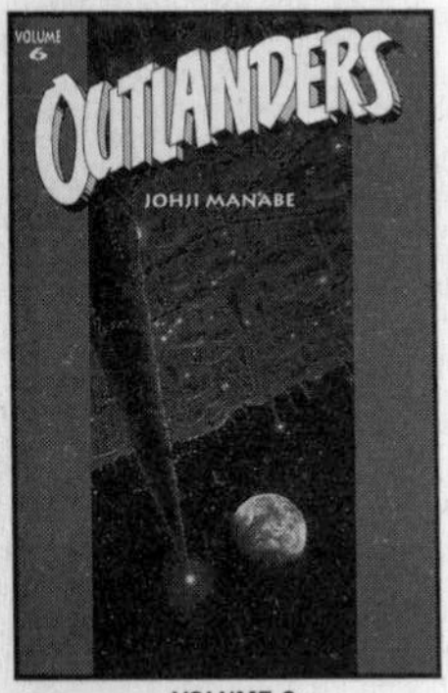
Volume 6
Outlanders
Johji Manabe

VOLUME 6
ISBN: 1-56971-423-1 $14.95

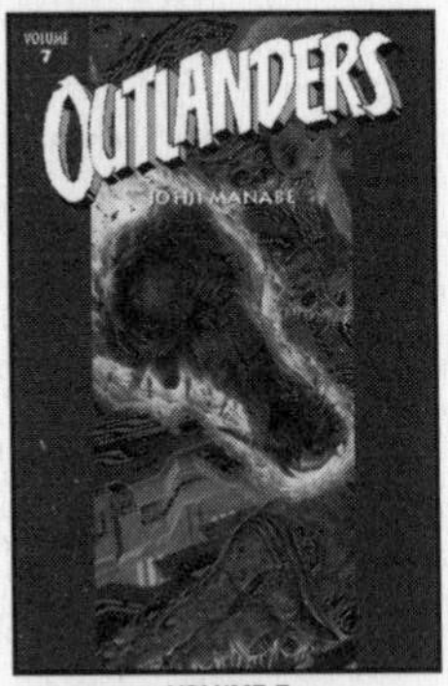
Volume 7
Outlanders
Johji Manabe

VOLUME 7
ISBN: 1-56971-424-X $14.95

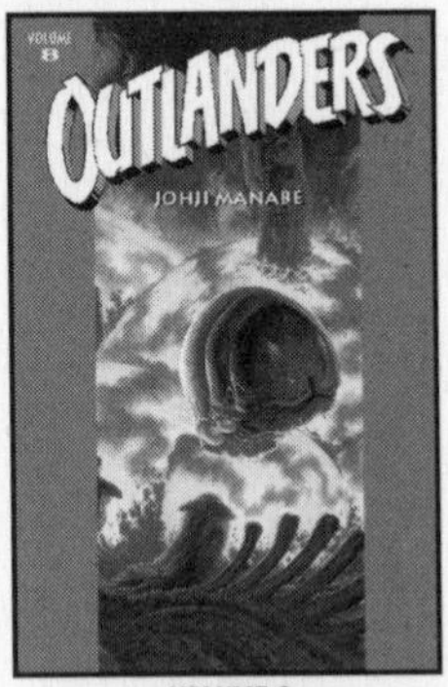
Volume 8
Outlanders
Johji Manabe

VOLUME 8
ISBN: 1-56971-425-8 $14.95

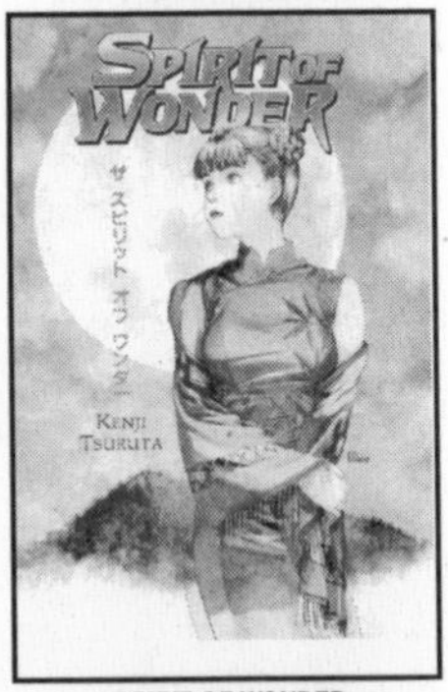
Spirit of Wonder
Kenji Tsuruta

SPIRIT OF WONDER
ISBN: 1-56971-288-3 $12.95

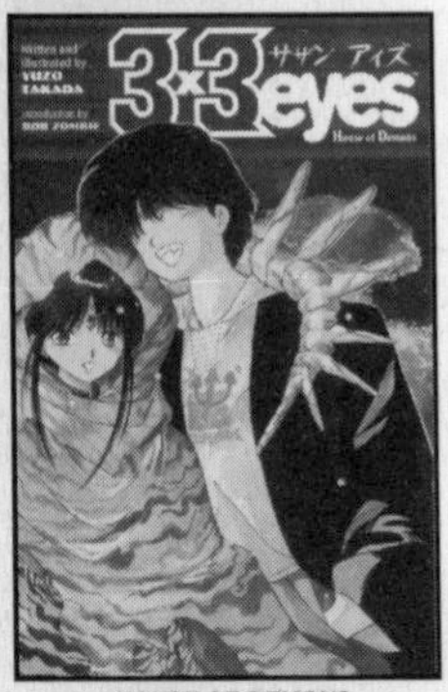
3x3 eyes
House of Demons

HOUSE OF DEMONS
ISBN: 1-56971-059-7 $12.95

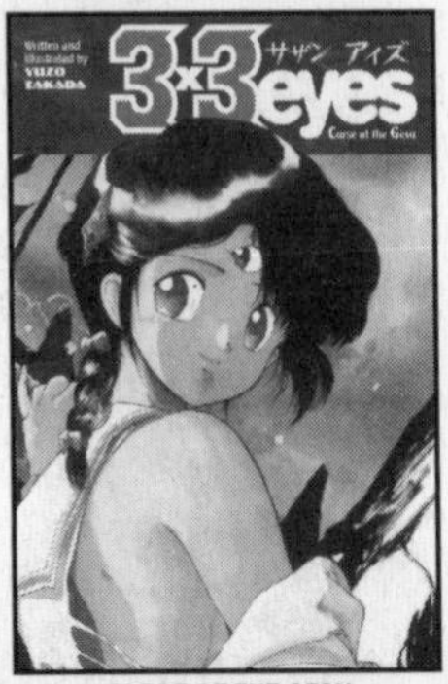
3x3 eyes
Curse of the Gesu

CURSE OF THE GESU
ISBN: 1-56971-175-5 $12.95

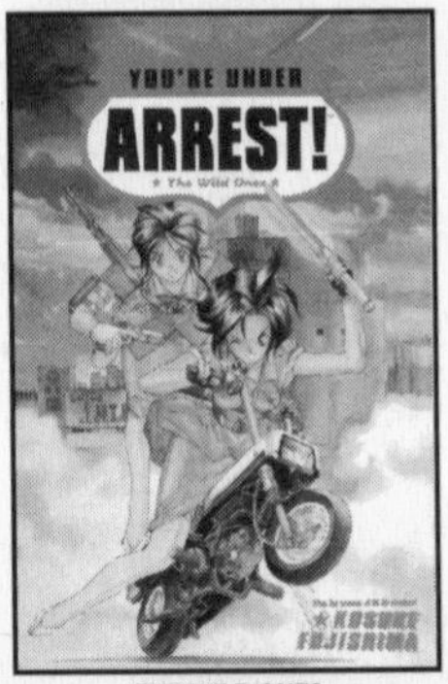
You're Under
Arrest!
Kosuke Fujishima

THE WILD ONES
ISBN: 1-56971-319-7 $12.95

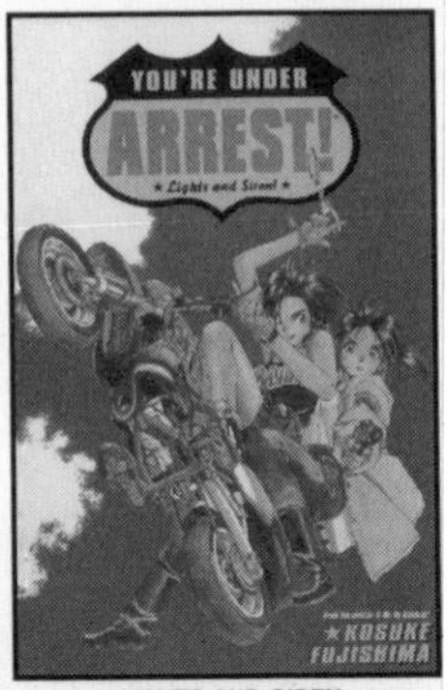
You're Under
Arrest!
Kosuke Fujishima

LIGHTS AND SIREN
ISBN: 1-56971-432-0 $10.95